Encyclopedia of Populism in America

Encyclopedia of Populism in America

A HISTORICAL ENCYCLOPEDIA

VOLUME 1: A–M

Alexandra Kindell and Elizabeth S. Demers, Editors

ABC-CLIO

Santa Barbara, California • Denver, Colorado • Oxford, England

Library of Congress Cataloging-in-Publication Data

Encyclopedia of populism in America : a historical encyclopedia / Alexandra Kindell and Elizabeth S. Demers, editors.
2 volumes ; cm
Includes bibliographical references and index.
ISBN 978–1–59884–567–9 (hard copy : alk. paper) — ISBN 978–1–59884–568–6 (ebook)
1. Populism—United States—Encyclopedias. I. Kindell, Alexandra. II. Demers, Elizabeth S.
JC423.E544 2014
320.56′62097303—dc23 2013012169

ISBN: 978–1–59884–567–9
EISBN: 978–1–59884–568–6

18 17 16 15 14 1 2 3 4 5

This book is also available on the World Wide Web as an eBook.
Visit www.abc-clio.com for details.

ABC-CLIO, LLC
130 Cremona Drive, P.O. Box 1911
Santa Barbara, California 93116-1911

This book is printed on acid-free paper ∞

Manufactured in the United States of America

Contents

VOLUME 2

Preface

The *Encyclopedia of Populism in America* examines the various populist impulses, political movements, organizations, personalities, and legacies that have uniquely marked American history and culture. Many of the entries in these two volumes detail the longest and most sustained populist upwelling that emerged, in the United States, during the late nineteenth century—a movement known as Populism. Anchor articles unpack the thorniest, most complicated elements of Populism itself, while midlength and shorter essays serve to whet students' intellectual appetites by illuminating fascinating events or individuals who played key roles in the movement. Additionally, this work also informs students about the tropes of less-organized populist moments from the colonial period to the present, encouraging readers to see the past through a different lens and thus allowing "the people" to come alive on the page. The *Encyclopedia* provides a broad spectrum of the ways in which both populism, as a generalization, and Populism as a specific political, agrarian movement, have shaped the modern United States.

Organized alphabetically, the encyclopedia covers more than 400 years of American history, from the xenophobia of Bacon's Rebellion in 1676 to the populist rhetoric of Barack Obama in the twenty-first century. The bulk of the work delves deeply into Populism, the late-nineteenth-century political movement that sprang from the agrarian discontent of ordinary farmers and laborers. These men and women were determined to wrest power away from the entrenched economic and political elites and bring it back into the hands of the ordinary people who had created this wealth with their labor. In addition to the experiences of groups and people, the *Encyclopedia of Populism in America* addresses the specific political demands and platforms of the People's Party; the significant events that shaped public opinion and changed laws; and the literature, music, and other cultural components of the era. But despite its influence, the Populist movement failed to create a viable third party and did not displace the traditional power of the two-party system in American politics.

Yet many of the demands of the Populists entered the lexicon of American reform. The Progressives of the early twentieth century; their heirs, the New Dealers; civil rights activists; and others became the legatees of the Populists' concerns, using the very two-party system that had suppressed their political forebears. For this reason, we have included entries dealing with the Progressive Era as well as New Deal and Great Society legislation. Ideas such as the direct election of senators, the graduated income tax, the abandonment of the gold standard, and the enfranchisement of blacks and women became a permanent part of American life. Other ideas that the Populists supported, such as prohibition or cooperative commonwealths, were less successful. To treat the Progressive Era, the Cold War era, or the civil rights era without a thorough grounding in the Populist moment is to do a historical disservice.

Populism touched people of all races, sexes, classes, and religions, but these disparate groups' and individuals' experiences of Populism could differ widely. The *Encyclopedia* highlights the diverse regional aspects of Populism, with essays on the South, Texas, and the Midwest, for example, that show clearly the uniquely regional aspects of Populism in these areas, just as the cultures and political leanings of these regions differed widely from each other as well. Because race played such a key role in politics and the Populist movement, an essay on African Americans and Populism explores this topic in depth. Women raised their voices, published newspapers, and supported various Populist or Progressive ideas. The *Encyclopedia* features articles on Mary Lease, Jane Addams, Frances Willard, and other gendered topics. These entries, like those on labor activism, show how even those who were disadvantaged or disenfranchised were able to fight for their own share of political power and influence and strove to ensure their rights as American citizens. The *Encyclopedia* also examines the experiences of elites, many of whom embraced Populist or Progressive ideas, including Christian Socialism, antipoverty campaigns, temperance, or eugenics.

Moreover, the legacy of Populism is itself diverse. The *Encyclopedia* examines both right-wing and left-wing populist manifestations in American culture, such as the Sagebrush Rebellion, the Tea Party, Barry M. Goldwater, Social Christianity, popular culture, John Steinbeck, and the Ku Klux Klan. These entries are not meant to be exhaustive but are instead thought-provoking and informative. Students and scholars will find new ways of looking at the past, allowing them to use populism as a prism to reinterpret everyday events, to understand the actions of ordinary individuals in extraordinary situations, and to understand the political nature of all organizations from unions, to religious and social utopias, to neighborhood watches, and, finally, to hate groups.

Like the topics themselves, the more than 140 contributors to the *Encyclopedia* are diverse, relying on the knowledge and insight of highly respected academics, librarians, independent scholars, and advanced graduate students—the burgeoning intellectual leaders of the future.

The more than 330 entries are an invaluable resource for students and researchers of American history, from the tenured professional to the buff, from advanced degree programs to high schools. Extensive "See also" cross-references are included in every entry to draw readers deeper into the topics, showing the interconnectedness of populism with everyday life. Accessibly written, diverse in breadth and scope, and rich in subject, the *Encyclopedia of Populism in America* will be an invaluable historical reference for libraries and campuses worldwide.

Alexandra Kindell and Elizabeth S. Demers

Acknowledgments

We would like to thank first all the contributors without whom this book would not exist. We are also grateful to Michael Hermann, Michael Millman, John Wagner and all the staff at ABC-CLIO for helping make this book come to fruition. We would also like to thank our long-suffering friends and families for their support and kindness while our heads were buried in toil.

Working on such a project requires the endurance of the contributors as well as the editors, but it has been a labor of love. This is a topic that changed the nation and may still continue to change the nation if people will listen to the voices of the people. So it seems only fitting to end this with the words of historian John Hope Franklin: "I would only add that when one begins a poem, a hymn, a short story, or even a history, one must be optimistic about its completion and about what it seeks to teach. If one believes in the power of his own words and in the words of others, one must also hope and believe that the world will be a better place by our having spoken or written those words."

Guide to Related Topics

Agriculture and Environment

African Americans and Populism
Agrarianism
Agricultural Issues, Regional
Agricultural Newspapers and Farmer Unrest
Agricultural Wheel
Alliance
Bailey, Liberty Hyde (1858–1954)
Burrows, Jay (1833–1900)
Cleburne Platform (1886)
Colored Farmers' Alliance (CFA)
Cooperative Commonwealth
Country Life Movement
Drought
Environmentalism
Farmers' Alliance
Farmers' and Laborers' Union of America (FLUA)
Farmers' Clubs
Farmers' Mutual Benefit Association (FMBA)
Farmers' Transportation Convention
The Farmer's Wife
Federal Farm Board (FFB)
Federal Intermediate Credit Banks (FICBs)
Granger Movement
Grasshopper Plagues
Illinois Woman's Alliance (IWA)
Jute-bagging Trust
Kansas, Populism in
Kelley, Oliver Hudson (1826–1913)
Macune, Dr. C. W. (1851–1940)
National Alliance Aid Association
National Parks
National Rifle Association (NRA)
National Woman's Alliance
Northern Alliance
Northeast and Industrial Midwest, Populism in the
Olmsted, Frederick Law (1822–1903)
Open Alliance
Overproduction Theory
Pattillo, Walter Alexander (1850–1908)
Peonage
Plains and Midwest, Populism in the
Powers, John H. (1831–1918)
Producerism
Progressive Farmer
Sagebrush Rebellion
Singleton, Benjamin "Pap" (1809–1892)
South, Populism in the
Subtreasury Plan
Sullivan, Louis Henry (1856–1924)
Tenant Farming
Tennessee Valley Authority (TVA)
Texas, Populism in
Timber Culture Act (1873)
West, Populism in the
Western Alliance
Western Rural
Whiskey Rebellion (1791–1794)
Wounded Knee (1890, 1973)
Wright, Frank Lloyd (1867–1959)

Big Ideas

Agrarianism
Antigay Populism
Anti-Imperialism/Colonialism
Boas, Franz (1858–1942)
Cooperative Commonwealth
Darrow, Clarence (1857–1938)
Eight-hour Day
Electricity
"The Elite"
Environmentalism
Eugenics
Film
Freethinkers
Gilded Age
Grant, Madison (1865–1937)
Historians of Populism
Leisure
Mills, C. Wright (1916–1962)
Modernism
Neoconservatives
Neoliberals
Neopopulism
"The People"
Progressivism
Regionalism
Scopes Trial (1925)
Social Christianity
Social Darwinism
Social Gospel
Urbanization

Conflict, Protests, Strikes, and Unrest

Agricultural Newspapers and Farmer Unrest
Anarchism
Bacon's Rebellion (1676)
Bonus Army
Congress of Racial Equality (CORE)
Coxey, Jacob (1854–1951)
Coxey's Army
Cripple Creek War (1894)
Czolgosz, Leon (1873–1901)
Eight-hour Day
Flint Strike (1936–1937)
Freedom Riders
Goldman, Emma (1869–1940)
Gronlund, Laurence (1846–1899)
Haymarket Riot (1886)
Hill, Joe (1879–1915)
Hiss, Alger (1904–1996)
Homestead Strike (1892)
Jones, Mary Harris/Mother Jones (1837–1930)
Pullman Strike (1894)
Red Scare of 1919
Rosenberg, Julius (1918–1953), and Rosenberg, Ethel (1915–1953)
Sagebrush Rebellion
Shays's Rebellion (1786–1787)
Whiskey Rebellion (1791–1794)
Zoot Suit Riots (1943)

Economics, Business, and Banking

Banking System of the Late Nineteenth Century
Clayton Antitrust Act (1914)
Coin's Financial School (1894)
Cooperative Commonwealth
Crédit Mobilier Scandal
Crime of '73
"Cross of Gold" Speech (1896)
Department Stores and Mail Order Catalogs
Depression of 1873
Depression of 1893
Farmers' Mutual Benefit Association (FMBA)
Federal Intermediate Credit Banks (FICBs)
Federal Reserve
Federal Reserve Act (1913)
Federal Trade Commission Act (1914)
Gold Standard/Free Silver
Great Society
Hill, James J. (1838–1916)
International Monetary Conferences
Interstate Commerce Act (ICA) (1887)
Jute-bagging Trust
Long-Haul/Short-Haul Discrimination

National Alliance Aid Association
National Monetary Commission
Northern Securities Case (1904)
Overproduction Theory
Producerism
Quantity Theory of Money
Railroad Regulation
Railroads
Robber Barons
Rochdale Plan
Rural Credits
Sherman Silver Purchase Act (1890)
Silver Republicans
Subtreasury Plan
Tariffs
Technological Unemployment
Union Pacific Railroad
War on Poverty
Wilson-Gorman Tariff (1894)

Education

Addams, Jane (1860–1935)
Charles H. Kerr Publishing Company
Granger Movement
Highlander Folk School
Kelley, Oliver Hudson (1826–1913)
Public Education
Union League
Woman's Christian Temperance Union (WCTU)
Workingman's School
YMCA/YWCA

Labor

American Federation of Labor (AFL)
Chávez, César E. (1927–1993)
Cripple Creek War (1894)
Debs, Eugene (1855–1926)
Eight-hour Day
Goldman, Emma (1869–1940)
Gompers, Samuel (1850–1924)
Gronlund, Laurence (1846–1899)
Hill, Joe (1879–1915)
Industrial Workers of the World (IWW)
Irons, Martin (1827–1911)
Jones, Mary Harris/Mother Jones (1837–1930)
Knights of Labor
Lewis, John L. (1880–1969)
McBride, John (1854–1917)
Overproduction Theory
Powderly, Terence V. (1849–1924)
Producerism
United Auto Workers (UAW)
Valesh, Eva McDonald (1866–1956)
Women's Trade Union League (WTUL)
Workingman's School

Literature, Journalism, Music, and Pop Culture

Alger, Horatio, Jr. (1832–1899)
American Non-Conformist
Anderson, Sherwood (1876–1941)
Barnum, P. T. (1810–1891)
Baseball and Populism
Baum, L. Frank (1856–1919)
Bellamy, Edward (1850–1898)
Boas, Franz (1858–1942)
Capra, Frank (1897–1991)
Cather, Willa (1873–1947)
Charles H. Kerr Publishing Company
Coin's Financial School (1894)
Copland, Aaron (1900–1990)
Department Stores and Mail-Order Catalogs
De Tocqueville, Alexis (1805–1859)
Diggs, Annie L. (1853–1916)
Dixon, Thomas, Jr. (1864–1946)
Dobbs, Louis Carl (1945–)
Donnelly, Ignatius (1831–1901)
The Farmer's Wife
Film
Flower, Benjamin Orange (1858–1918)
Garland, Hamlin (1860–1940)
George, Henry (1839–1897)
George, Milton (1833–unknown)
Gilman, Charlotte Perkins (1860–1935)
"Goodbye, My Party, Goodbye"

Griffith, D. W. (1875–1948) and *The Birth of a Nation* (1915)
Guthrie, Woodrow Wilson "Woody" (1912–1967)
Herron, George Davis (1862–1925)
Hightower, Jim (1943–)
Hill, Joe (1879–1915)
Hollywood Ten
Ivins, Mary Tyler "Molly" (1944–2007)
Kellie, Luna (1857–1940)
Lewis, Sinclair (1885–1951)
Lindsay, Vachel (1879–1931)
Loucks, Henry Langford (1846–1928)
Luhan, Mabel Dodge (1879–1962)
Macune, Dr. C. W. (1851–1940)
Mencken, H. L. (1880–1956)
Merritt, Ada Chase (1852–1933)
Mills, C. Wright (1916–1962)
National Reform Press Association (NRPA)
Pack, Emma (1850–1910)
Pop Music
Popular Culture
The Press and Populism
Progressive Farmer
Punk Music
Rogers, Will (1879–1935)
Sinclair, Upton (1878–1968)
Steinbeck, John (1902–1968)
Sullivan, Louis Henry (1856–1924)
Twain, Mark (1835–1910)
Vaudeville
Veblen, Thorstein (1857–1929)
Western Rural
White, William Allen (1868–1944)
Whitman, Walt (1819–1892)
Wizard of Oz
Wright, Frank Lloyd (1867–1959)

Opposition

Anarchism
Bull Moose Party
Coxey, Jacob (1854–1951)
Czolgosz, Leon (1873–1901)
Dobbs, Louis Carl (1945–)
Flower, Benjamin Orange (1858–1918)
Hightower, Jim (1943–)
Hiss, Alger (1904–1996)
Industrial Workers of the World (IWW)
Jones, Mary Harris/Mother Jones (1837–1930)
Kaweah Colony
King, Martin Luther, Jr. (1929–1968)
Know Nothings
Ku Klux Klan (KKK)
Lease, Mary (1850–1933)
Popular Front
Readjuster Party
Stanton, Elizabeth Cady (1815–1902)
Tea Party
Tillman, Benjamin R. (1847–1918)
Weather Underground
Wounded Knee (1890, 1973)

Party Politics, Politicos, and Legislation

Allen, William Vincent (1847–1923)
Allied Peoples' Party
Altgeld, John P. (1847–1902)
Anarchism
Arnett, Alex Matthews (1888–1945)
Black Panther Party (BPP)
Bland, Richard P. (1835–1899)
Blease, Cole (1868–1942)
Bourbon Democracy
Bryan, William Jennings (1860–1925)
Bull Moose Party
Burrows, Jay (1833–1900)
Bush, George W., Populist Rhetoric of
Butler, Marion (1863–1938)
Carter, James Earl "Jimmy" (1924–)
Clayton Antitrust Act (1914)
Cleburne Platform (1886)
Cleveland, Grover (1837–1908)
Colorado, Populism in
Coxey, Jacob (1854–1951)
Crime of '73
"Cross of Gold" Speech (1896)
Debs, Eugene (1855–1926)

Democratic Party
Donnelly, Ignatius (1831–1901)
Federal Farm Board (FFB)
Federal Intermediate Credit Banks (FICBs)
Federal Reserve
Federal Reserve Act (1913)
Federal Trade Commission Act (1914)
Felton, William Harrell (1823–1909)
Force Bill (1890)
Goldwater, Barry M. (1909–1998)
Great Society
Greenback Party
Hanna, Mark (1837–1904)
Hayes, "Lemonade" Lucy (1831–1889)
Hepburn Act (1906)
Holcomb, Silas Alexander (1858–1920)
Homestead Act (1862)
Ingersoll, Robert (1833–1899)
Interstate Commerce Act (ICA) (1887)
Jefferson, Thomas (1743–1826)
Kansas, Populism in
Kansas City Conference (1901)
Know Nothings
Lewelling, Lorenzo D. (1846–1900)
Long, Huey (1893–1935)
Loucks, Henry Langford (1846–1928)
Maxwell, Samuel (1825–1891)
McCarthy, Joseph (1908–1957)
McKinley, William, Jr. (1843–1901)
Middle-of-the-Road Populists
Nashville Conference (1897)
National Rifle Association (NRA)
Newberry Railroad Rate Bill (1894)
New Deal
Nineteenth Amendment (1920)
Northern Securities Case (1904)
Northwest Ordinance (1787)
Nugent, Thomas (1841–1895)
Obama, Barack, Populist Rhetoric of
Ocala Convention (1890)
Omaha Contract
Omaha Convention of 1892
Palin, Sarah (1964–)
Peffer, William Alfred (1831–1912)
People's Party
Plumb, Preston (1837–1891)
Polk, Leonidas L. (1837–1892)
Populism
Powers, John H. (1831–1918)
Proposition 13 (1978)
Railroad Regulation
Railroads
Reagan, Ronald, Populist Rhetoric of
Roosevelt, Franklin Delano (1882–1945)
Roosevelt, Theodore (1858–1919)
Schilling, Robert (1843–1922)
Sewall, Arthur M. (1835–1900)
Sherman Silver Purchase Act (1890)
Silver Republicans
South, Populism in the
Springfield Convention (1904)
St. Louis Convention of 1896
Streeter, Alson J. (1823–1901)
Sutro, Adolph (1830–1898)
Taubeneck, Herman E. (c. 1855–unknown)
Teller, Henry Moore (1830–1914)
Tennessee Valley Authority (TVA)
Texas, Populism in
Third Parties
Tillman, Benjamin R. (1847–1918)
Timber Culture Act (1873)
Transportation Act of 1920
Tweed, William M. (1823–1879)
Vance, Zebulon (1830–1894)
Vandervoort, Paul (1846–1902)
Van Wyck, Charles Henry (1824–1895)
Waite, Davis (1825–1901)
Wallace, George C. (1919–1998)
Warehouse Act (1916)
War on Poverty
West, Populism in the
White, William Allen (1868–1944)
Williams, Samuel W. (1851–1913)
Willits, John F. (unknown–1910)
Wilson-Gorman Tariff (1894)

Race and Sex

Abolitionism
Addams, Jane (1860–1935)
African Americans and Populism
Black Panther Party (BPP)
Cather, Willa (1873–1947)
Charles, Robert (c. 1865–1900)
Chávez, César E. (1927–1993)
Colored Farmers' Alliance (CFA)
Congress of Racial Equality (CORE)
Diggs, Annie L. (1853–1916)
Dixon, Thomas, Jr. (1864–1946)
Douglass, Frederick (1818–1895)
Eddy, Mary Baker (1821–1910)
Emery, Sarah (1838–1895)
Eugenics
The Farmer's Wife
Feminism
Force Bill (1890)
Freedom Riders
Gilman, Charlotte Perkins (1860–1935)
Griffith, D. W. (1875–1948), and *The Birth of a Nation* (1915)
Haskell, Anna Fader (1858–1942)
Hayes, "Lemonade" Lucy (1831–1889)
Illinois Woman's Alliance (IWA)
Jones, Mary Harris/Mother Jones (1837–1930)
Kellie, Luna (1857–1940)
King, Martin Luther, Jr. (1929–1968)
Ku Klux Klan (KKK)
Lease, Mary (1850–1933)
Merritt, Ada Chase (1852–1933)
National Woman's Alliance
New Woman
Nineteenth Amendment (1920)
Northwest Ordinance (1787)
Obama, Barack, Populist Rhetoric of
Pack, Emma (1850–1910)
Palin, Sarah (1964–)
Pattillo, Walter Alexander (1850–1908)
Peters, Laura Hall (1840–1902)
Piven, Frances Fox (1932–)
Rayner, John (1850–1918)
Sanger, Margaret (1879–1966)
Singleton, Benjamin "Pap" (1809–1892)
Stanton, Elizabeth Cady (1815–1902)
Valesh, Eva McDonald (1866–1956)
Wald, Lillian D. (1867–1940)
Washington, Booker T. (1856–1915)
Wells, Ida B. (1862–1931)
Willard, Frances E. (1839–1898)
Woman's Christian Temperance Union (WCTU)
Women's Trade Union League (WTUL)
Wounded Knee (1890, 1973)
YMCA/YWCA
Zoot Suit Riots (1943)

Reform and Reformers

Abolitionism
Addams, Jane (1860–1935)
Altgeld, John P. (1847–1902)
Bailey, Liberty Hyde (1858–1954)
Bellamy, Edward (1850–1898)
Black Panther Party (BPP)
Chávez, César E. (1927–1993)
Comstock, Anthony (1844–1915)
Congress of Racial Equality (CORE)
Country Life Movement
Diggs, Annie L. (1853–1916)
Douglass, Frederick (1818–1895)
Eddy, Mary Baker (1821–1910)
Eugenics
Feminism
Freedom Riders
Garrison, William Lloyd (1805–1879)
Grant, Madison (1865–1937)
Haskell, Anna Fader (1858–1942)
Haskell, Burnette G. (1857–1907)
Kaweah Colony
National Reform Press Association (NRPA)
Nonpartisan League (NPL)
Peters, Laura Hall (1840–1902)
Piven, Frances Fox (1932–)
Poverty Campaigns
Progressivism
Prohibition (1919–1933)

Rauschenbusch, Walter (1861–1918)
Rochdale Plan
Sanger, Margaret (1879–1966)
Stanton, Elizabeth Cady (1815–1902)
Union League
Wald, Lillian D. (1867–1940)
War on Poverty
Washington, Booker T. (1856–1915)
Wells, Ida B. (1862–1931)
Wheeler, Wayne (1869–1927)
White, William Allen (1868–1944)
Willard, Frances E. (1839–1898)
Woman's Christian Temperance Union (WCTU)
YMCA/YWCA

Religion

Abbott, Lyman (1835–1922)
Abolitionism
Burned-over District
Comstock, Anthony (1844–1915)
Darrow, Clarence (1857–1938)
Diggs, Annie L. (1853–1916)
Eddy, Mary Baker (1821–1910)
Evangelicalism and Populism
Freethinkers
Garrison, William Lloyd (1805–1879)
Hayes, "Lemonade" Lucy (1831–1889)
Modernism
Moody, Dwight (1837–1899)
Rauschenbusch, Walter (1861–1918)
Scopes Trial (1925)
Social Christianity
Social Gospel
Socialism, Christian
Sunday, Billy (1862–1935)
YMCA/YWCA

Rhetoric

Bush, George W., Populist Rhetoric of
Carter, James Earl "Jimmy" (1924–)
"Cross of Gold" Speech (1896)
Goldwater, Barry M. (1909–1998)
Obama, Barack, Populist Rhetoric of
Palin, Sarah (1964–)
Reagan, Ronald, Populist Rhetoric of
Rogers, Will (1879–1935)

Sports and Leisure

Baseball and Populism
Film
Leisure
National Parks
National Rifle Association (NRA)
Olmsted, Frederick Law (1822–1903)
Trans-Mississippi Exposition (1898)
World's Industrial and Cotton Centennial Exposition (1884–1885)

Technology

Automobile
Electricity
Eugenics
Film
Jute-bagging Trust
Railroads
Technological Unemployment
Tennessee Valley Authority (TVA)
Tesla, Nikola (1856–1943)
Union Pacific Railroad

A

Abbott, Lyman (1835–1922)

Lyman Abbott was a Congregational minister who pastored Plymouth Church in Brooklyn after Henry Ward Beecher's death. Abbott also was the editor-in-chief for the *Illustrated Christian Weekly* and the *Christian Union*, later called the *Outlook*. Through his periodical work, Abbott sought to provoke reform among the upper and middle classes.

Lyman Abbott was born on December 18, 1835, in Roxbury, Massachusetts. Abbott studied at New York University and, soon after graduation, began work as a lawyer with two of his brothers. Abbott passed the bar exam in 1856, and his law career was successful but short-lived. On October 14, 1857, Abbott married Abby Frances Hamlin. By 1859, Abbott had abandoned the law to become a minister. Although Abbott received no formal seminary training, he was ordained as a Congregational minister in 1860 and began pastoring in Terre Haute, Indiana.

While in Indiana, Abbott strongly supported the North and opposed slavery. At the end of the Civil War, Abbott left Terre Haute and became the executive secretary of the newly formed American Union Commission, which later became known as the American Freedmen's Union Commission, based in New York City. The Commission sought to further educational efforts in the South but dissolved in 1869. While in New York, Abbott became the pastor of a small Congregational church in the city, but he resigned from the church in 1869 and devoted more time to periodicals.

In 1887, Abbott returned to pastoring by following in Henry Ward Beecher's footsteps and succeeding him as the pastor of Plymouth Church in Brooklyn. Although Abbott did not have Beecher's charisma, Abbott encouraged the church to become more active in the community. Interestingly, Abbott typically refrained from commenting in the pulpit about the political issues that he dealt with as an editor. Abbott continued at Plymouth until 1899.

Early in Abbott's ministry, he held to conservative theology; as Abbott grew older, however, he shifted his emphasis to the emerging liberal theology that had been influenced by the cultural modernism of the late nineteenth century. This viewpoint manifested itself in several key positions. Abbott held to theistic evolution. He also embraced higher critical conclusions on the dating and authorship of various books of the Bible, which denied conservative views. When Abbott moved to liberal theology, he began to popularize his new beliefs among the laity and succeeded in doing so.

Throughout his life, Abbott worked with magazines. While he was executive secretary for the American Freedman's Union Commission, he edited the *American Freedman*. After he left his first church in

Reverend Lyman Abbott was an American Congregationalist minister who worked not only to reform Indian laws but also to change white attitudes toward Native Americans during the late-19th and early-20th centuries. (Library of Congress)

New York, he wrote and edited for *Harper's Magazine* and wrote for other periodicals. Between 1871 and 1876, Abbott took the editorship of the *Illustrated Christian Weekly*, a periodical of the American Tract Society. He left the *Illustrated Christian Weekly* to work for Beecher's *Christian Union*. Abbott became associate editor of the publication and advanced to editor-in-chief in 1881. He transformed the paper from a religious periodical into a magazine on current events. The name changed to the *Outlook* in 1893 to reflect this change.

Through his work at the *Illustrated Christian Weekly* and later at the *Outlook*, Abbott influenced public opinion on almost every major political issue. Abbott attempted to be free from political party divisions throughout his career and actually proposed forming a new party. He used his position as a periodical editor to push for reform throughout the nation. Abbott targeted civil service, tariffs, and currency in particular for reform. He favored low tariffs and international bimetallism. Other issues that found his support included temperance, the international copyright system, and direct primary elections. Reflecting his religious background, he opposed Mormonism. Finally, Abbott opposed the introduction of the income tax and woman suffrage. In the 1880s, Abbott became involved in Indian policy reform. He advocated that the best policy for the Indians was to dissolve the tribe system and assimilate the Indians into citizenship. Abbott thus pushed Congress to break its treaties with the Indians and supported the Dawes Act.

Abbott did not hold to full-fledged socialism, but he maintained that the government should control the natural resources of the country. He also advocated that the government regulate railroads. In his relationship with the working class, Abbott sympathized with their plight but opposed strikes and attempted to find a middle way between management and the workers.

Although Abbott tried to distance himself from both the Republican and Democratic parties, he more often identified himself as a Republican, finding his greatest political ally in Theodore Roosevelt (1858–1919). Abbott and the *Outlook* supported Roosevelt and became a part of his "kitchen cabinet," often being consulted on policy. Abbott's ties to Roosevelt strengthened when the president left office and became a contributing editor to the *Outlook*. When Roosevelt ran for president for the Progressive Party in 1912, however, his ties to the *Outlook* damaged the impartiality of the periodical because it was viewed as a publicity arm of the Roosevelt campaign. In 1914, Roosevelt left the periodical. The *Outlook* never recovered its previous popularity.

Abbott supported the imperial ambitions of the United States. Although he first opposed the Spanish-American War in 1898, he supported intervention in Cuba. He cast American imperialism in a theological light, seeing God as guiding the United States into imperialism. When war clouds broke over Europe in 1914, Abbott supported the Allies. He was against neutrality and isolationism in the Great War, and he popularized a Christian viewpoint for the United States' involvement in the conflict. For his work supporting the Allies during World War I, the French awarded him the *chevalier* of the Legion of Honor in March 1922. Abbott died later that year on October 22, 1922, at his apartment in New York City.

Nathan V. Lentfer

See also: Bull Moose Party; Evangelicalism and Populism; Gilded Age; Modernism; Progressivism; Roosevelt, Theodore (1858–1919); Social Christianity

Reference

Brown, Ira V. *Lyman Abbott: Christian Evolutionist*. Cambridge, MA: Harvard University Press, 1953.

Abolitionism

Abolitionists believed that slavery was morally wrong and should be abolished, and they hoped that their antislavery activism would put an end to racial discrimination, based on the idea of human rights. It stands in contrast to other variants of antislavery sentiments that were less values-based and more economically or socially/culturally based. These movements included colonization, free soil and free labor ideas, gradual emancipation, and compensated emancipation. Abolitionists generally, because of the moral implications of their arguments, expected immediate, uncompensated emancipation for slaves as the end result of their efforts. Abolitionists consisted of roughly 1 percent of northern society, making them the minority among those who believed in antislavery. They also struggled with related issues such as women's rights, but they all strongly agreed on the need for the emancipation of slaves and the devastating consequences of human trafficking and slavery. The significance of these arguments would climax in the years prior to the Civil War, and they seemed to find their first expression in the Emancipation Proclamation and the later postbellum amendments to the U.S. Constitution. In the end, this movement helped free 4 million slaves and helped inspire a new alignment of social relations in the South in the late nineteenth and early twentieth centuries.

While some Western Europeans believed there were inferior social and ethnic groups, some Anglo-Americans found it difficult to justify the enslavement of Africans despite the need for cheap labor in the expansive colonies from New York to the Carolinas. Intellectual currents emanating from the Enlightenment and the Great Awakening emerged to challenge assumption that slavery was part of the natural order, and the members of the Society of Friends (Quakers) added their voices to antislavery prior to the American Revolution. Rejecting the static relationships of subjects and monarchies, Enlightenment thinkers argued that there was no fixed state of being, that is, inferior or superior, and therefore people could improve their conditions through education and other means, allowing them to achieve happiness and form governments to protect their natural rights to live freely and equally within their social-political context. Philosophy turned to religion as the Enlightenment encouraged the need for new religious beliefs and the need for progression. While Christianity did not promote or condemn the need for slavery in the Americas, it did illustrate that God would look over everyone, including slaves, opening the eyes of some Americans to the notion that slaves might have rights; but it would be the Quakers—both English and American—who laid the seeds of the abolitionist movement.

Members of the Society of Friends openly condemned the notion of slavery as an institution beginning in the 1740s. The Quaker community arrived in the early years of the colonies, and some families owned slaves, but they struggled to justify owning another human being with their religious beliefs. Most Quakers lived in the colonies of Pennsylvania and New Jersey, and between 1700 and 1766, slave ownership rose and declined depending on the crops being raised and the availability of indentured servants. By the 1740s, New Jersey Quaker John Woolman journeyed to the southern colonies, preaching about the immoral nature of slavery and advocating the eventual manumission of slaves. Between 1758 and 1774, the Quaker yearly meeting began the process of manumission within the society. Quakers who still owned slaves were expelled from the society after 1774. Quakers then began visiting politicians, as they had their own members, to urge emancipation on a national scale.

Abolitionist sentiment grew during the revolutionary and early national periods as Quakers and some other northerners extended the rhetoric of independence to the idea of freedom to those in bondage. The years during and following the Revolution would prove effective for the Quakers' cause, as their strong opinions about slavery as religiously immoral combined with their new ability to incorporate the revolutionary vocabulary to implicate northerners for their adherence to slavery. The northern states responded with the gradual emancipation of slaves in the states of New Jersey, New York, Pennsylvania, and Rhode Island. Massachusetts residents viewed their new state constitution as an antislavery document. While there were southern sympathizers to the abolitionist cause, most still incorporated racism into their arguments to justify slavery on their plantations, especially since the invention of the cotton gin in 1793 made cotton agriculture on the mainland of North America into a profitable enterprise. The discomfort southerners felt regarding slavery was soon replaced by aggressive defensiveness as the abolitionist movement heated up and the acreage of cotton increased simultaneously.

Non-Quaker antislavery advocates had put their efforts into the American Colonization Society established in 1817, but by the 1830s, the society failed to provide a practical vehicle for eliminating slavery and failed to soothe the consciences of those who believed slavery to be immoral and intolerable. Two important and well-known contributors to the newspapers were Benjamin Lundy, a Quaker who published the newspaper *Genius of Universal Emancipation*, and William Lloyd Garrison, editor of the *Liberator*. Both pushed the need for more active antislavery movements and the need for immediate emancipation. Garrison's demands for uncompensated, immediate emancipation, as well as his moral indignation, activated others who wanted to see the abolition of slavery and ignited a southern backlash prior to the Civil War. Frederick Douglass became another important contributor to the abolitionist movement. Born a slave, Douglass grew up to become a prominent speaker and free man. He not only published his personal narratives; he also established the *North Star*, a newspaper designed to reach out to abolitionists and blacks and encourage equality between blacks and whites. Free blacks and former slaves, including Sojourner Truth and Harriet Jacobs, supported the abolitionist movement through writing in abolitionist newspapers, speaking in public, and publishing their autobiographies.

By 1860, the abolitionist movement reached new heights with numerous contributions of newspapers, abolitionist lectures, and John Brown's zealous pursuit of abolition as seen in his actions in Kansas and at Harper's Ferry. The pitch and tone of the abolitionists put southern slaveholders and their allies on the defensive, leading to a political statement prior to Abraham Lincoln's election to the presidency. Despite Lincoln's commitment to uphold the Constitution, including slavery, southerners expected the end of their "peculiar institution" with the election of a candidate from the Republican Party, an exclusively northern party. Not all abolitionists desired war or slave rebellions, yet the onset of the Civil War brought the abolitionists' cause to the forefront, and Quakers spent much time praying with President Lincoln to pursue the war in a righteous manner, explicitly or implicitly hoping for the emancipation of slaves. While the Emancipation Proclamation of 1863 was a policy shift for the administration, abolitionists also changed their goals to racial equality for freedmen. After the Civil War, abolitionism as a movement dissolved during the Reconstruction era. Its ideals of equality were resurrected during the civil rights era, during which the rights gained by freedmen that were soon trampled upon during Reconstruction were regained through major constitutional victories brought on by the political power of ordinary people.

Matthew Whitlock

See also: Democratic Party; Douglass, Frederick (1818–1895); Emancipation Proclamation; Evangelicalism and Populism

References

"Quakers in Action: Anti-Slavery in North America." Quakers in the World. http://

www.quakersintheworld.org. Accessed January 2, 2013.

Risley, Ford. *Abolition and the Press: The Struggle against Slavery.* Evanston, IL: Northwestern University Press, 2008.

Sorin, Gerald. *Abolitionism: A New Perspective.* New York: Praeger Publishers, 1972.

Addams, Jane (1860–1935)

Jane Addams devoted her adult life to helping the poor, supporting equality for all, and promoting peace. In the late nineteenth century, in response to the needs of people living in overpopulated American cities, Jane Addams cofounded Hull House in the slums of Chicago, Illinois. Addams was among those who established the Women's Trade Union League (WTUL) and was a charter member of the National Association for the Advancement of Colored People (NAACP). Addams participated in the International Women's Peace Conference held in the Netherlands in 1915 and rallied for peace throughout World War I. In 1931 Addams became the first American woman to win the Nobel Peace Prize. She died in 1935.

Jane Addams was born on September 6, 1860, in an upper-middle-class home in Cedarville, Illinois. Her mother, the former Sarah Weber, died when Addams was two, leaving her with four older siblings. While still a child she suffered from Pott's disease, or spinal tuberculosis, which left her with a deformity of the spine. The loss of her mother and the spinal condition she endured increased her sensitivity to the misfortunes of others.

John Huy Addams, Addams's father, was a godfearing, hardworking man whose self-discipline, industriousness, and love of learning influenced his daughter's life. When Addams was three years old she went into her father's study, where she saw a young black man. Signaling for her to leave the room, her father later told her to not talk with anyone about the man who had been at their home. It was not until many years later that Addams learned her father had been helping escaped slaves through the Underground Railroad. He also served on the Illinois state senate and was friends with Abraham Lincoln, whose life and ideals influenced the child as well.

Addams's first glimpse of poverty came when she was almost seven years old. While accompanying her father on a business trip to a nearby town, they passed through an impoverished section where small houses were built close together. When Addams asked her father about the neighborhood, he explained that the people living there were poor, uneducated, and lacked opportunities. Addams decided then and there that when she grew up she would live in a large house among small crowded houses.

Five years after her mother's death, Addams's father married Anna Hostetter Halderman, the widow of John Addams's business competitor. Halderman had two sons.

Cedarville had a one-room schoolhouse that Addams attended from the age of 9 until she turned 17. She wanted to go to college but her father disapproved. Although she was accepted into Smith College in Northampton, Massachusetts,

Addams complied with her father's wishes and went instead to Rockford Female Seminary in Rockford, Illinois. At that time the seminary was undergoing changes to qualify as a college. Determined to earn a college degree, Addams excelled in her studies of philosophy, history, literature, Latin, Greek, French, and higher mathematics.

During her second year Addams was chosen to represent Rockford at the Interstate Oratorical Contest in Jacksonville, Illinois. This was a rare opportunity for women to compete. Addams, considered a good debater, found herself up against peers that included William Jennings Bryan, who later became the presidential nominee for both the Democratic and People's parties in 1896. To the disappointment of her classmates, Addams did not win the contest. Putting the event behind her, she wrote for the Rockford Seminary magazine and in her senior year became its editor. Addams graduated in 1881 with honors and was selected to be valedictorian of her class. It was not until the following year, after Rockford had established itself as a college, that she was awarded the degree she had so long coveted.

That summer Addams accompanied her family on a trip to northern Michigan. While traveling, her father died of appendicitis. In the autumn Addams moved to Philadelphia with her stepmother and attended the Women's Medical College. However, she found it hard to concentrate due to her grieving the loss of her father and her constant back pain. After the first term was over she entered a hospital for treatment of a nervous condition. Later that year she had spinal surgery, from which it took months to recover.

At this time there were not many opportunities for women. Addams did not want to return to medical school but was not sure what to do with her life. An inheritance from her father enabled her to live comfortably, and she decided to take an extended trip to Europe with family and friends. They explored the cities, villages, and countryside of Ireland, Scotland, and England during the first part of the tour.

While in London, Addams witnessed an event that made a lasting impression on her. One Saturday evening she and her party were taken to Mile End Road, where they saw the auction of rotting produce to impoverished, starving people who had gathered to bid on decaying fruits and vegetables. It was then that Addams decided upon her life's work of helping the needy, and she thereafter visited poor sections of London whenever she could.

The European tour continued on through France, Germany, Greece, Italy, Austria, and Holland. Although Addams enjoyed seeing the churches, art galleries, and museums, she took time to explore the impoverished areas of the large cities. During her travels Addams corresponded with her good friend Ellen Starr, whom she had met at Rockford, describing to her the scenes of poverty. After nearly two years of travel, Addams returned to Cedarville.

During the last quarter of the nineteenth century, industry and technology changed the way Americans lived and worked. Products formerly made in people's homes as cottage industries were now produced in cities by machines and manufacturing.

Men and women left rural life behind to seek work in urban factories and businesses. Cities were flooded with millions of immigrants but were ill equipped to handle this influx of people. Provisions for housing, education, health care, and sanitation were inadequate to meet the growing needs of the new city dwellers. Moreover, the Industrial Revolution had widened the gap between the rich and poor, and except for pockets of wealthy neighborhoods, the largest U.S. cities became sprawling slums. Addams, who lived a privileged life, felt guilty knowing that so many people lacked basic comforts and wanted to help them. She just did not know what exactly to do.

In 1887, Addams joined Ellen Starr, who was travelling in Europe. It was during this time that a definite plan of action took shape in Addams's mind. Her idea was to rent a house in an impoverished urban neighborhood. From there she could reach out and help people in practical ways, filling the house with books, art, and ideas that would uplift and enrich their lives. Starr not only understood what Addams was saying, she vowed to help her with this undertaking.

To gain ideas for implementing her plan, Addams attended a missionary conference in London. She visited Toynbee Hall, a settlement house located in a poor section of the city, where male university graduates lived and worked among the poor, helping them in any way they could. Addams also visited the People's Palace, a neighborhood center built in a poor section of London. The Palace contained a library, gymnasium, and swimming pool for the community to enjoy.

Upon their return to the United States, Addams and Starr began to put their plan into action. They decided to settle in Chicago and in 1889 found an empty brick mansion wedged between a saloon and a funeral home. The house had been built by Charles Hull, a businessman, 33 years earlier when the area had been open country. The city had grown around the house, and its first floor was used for offices and warehouses. Behind the mansion a factory had been built.

Addams rented the second floor and a large room on the first floor. She and Starr cleaned and decorated the rooms with beautiful paintings and fine furniture and filled them with books and magazines. The women decided to call their settlement Hull House after its original owner. Word quickly spread about the project, with articles appearing in newspapers and magazines. On September 18, 1889, Addams and Starr moved into this house in the 19th Ward of Chicago.

It was not long before the people in the community turned to the two women for help. Hull House provided something for all ages. There was a nursery and kindergarten for young children, cooking and sewing lessons for young girls, and a club for teenage boys. Addams gave book readings and hosted public lectures featuring speakers such as Susan B. Anthony, John Dewey, and Clarence Darrow. Other educated and idealistic men and women were drawn to Hull House, sharing their unique talents and abilities with the community. Each year Hull House served thousands of people in countless ways.

Seeing children forced to work long days in sweatshops and young people dying of typhoid, the Hull House group became politically active on behalf of children as well as working women. They worked for laws to regulate child labor and improved sanitation practices in the area. In 1903 Addams was among those who established the WTUL, which strove to provide safe working conditions and living wages for factory workers. The WTUL held its meetings at Hull House until it moved its offices in 1908. Addams helped found the National Child Labor Committee in 1904, which sought a federal minimum age law.

In 1894, Addams and Starr incorporated Hull House, and by the 1960s its work spread to locations throughout Chicago's neighborhoods. The Jane Addams Hull House Association provided services to the community until just recently.

Addams worked within a variety of organizations with the hope that she might improve local, state, and national issues. She desired equality for all and was an early member of the NAACP, founded in 1909. Interested in women's rights, Addams attended her first meeting of the National American Woman Suffrage Association in 1906 and was elected its vice president in 1911. Calling herself a pacifist, Addams was a proponent of peace. In 1915 the Women's Peace Party was formed and elected Addams as its head. Soon after, the International Congress of Women was formed to promote peace throughout the world. They met in the Netherlands at The Hague and asked Addams to be their leader. In 1931 Addams received the Nobel Peace Prize but was unable to travel to Norway due to failing health. She donated the $16,480 in prize money to the Women's International League for Peace and Freedom. Addams was a prolific writer and wrote many essays, articles, and books, including *Twenty Years at Hull-House* and *Democracy and Social Ethics.*

Addams' health had never been good, but in the 1920s it began to worsen. She had a tumor removed and suffered a heart attack. Soon after being diagnosed with intestinal cancer, she died on May 21, 1935. Thousands of people attended her funeral at Hull House. She was buried by her mother and father in the Cedarville Cemetery.

Liz Marabeas

See also: Progressivism; Women's Trade Union League (WTUL)

References

Encyclopedia of Chicago. "Women's Trade Union League." http://www.encyclopedia.chicagohistory.org/pages/1373.html. Accessed January 2, 2013.

Henwood, Tom, Ron Meyer, and Mark Reeder. *A History of Women's Achievement in America.* Program Four. New York: Centre Communications for Ambrose Video Publishing, 2006.

Jane Addams Hull-House Museum. http://www.uic.edu/jaddams/hull/. Accessed January 2, 2014.

Knight, Louise W. *Citizen: Jane Addams and the Struggle for Democracy.* Chicago: University of Chicago Press, 2005.

Women in History. "Jane Addams." http://www.lkwdpl.org/wihohio/adda-jan.htm. Accessed January 2, 2013.

African Americans and Populism

African Americans have pursued populist-type reform since the seventeenth century.

Politically conscious blacks articulated their grievances and organized their resources in mass opposition to the systemic injustices they experienced, which intensified during periods of political and economic transformation or power consolidation. They participated as members of the rank and file, and they provided leadership. They did all of this despite laws that deprived them of fundamental rights and full citizenship. Independent politics provided opportunities otherwise unavailable to them as they sought freedom and equality.

People of African descent participated in the populist rebellion that erupted in the Virginia Colony in 1676. Africans, along with people of mixed race, marched with Nathaniel Bacon against the royal governor. These protestors exhibited a range of conditions of servitude from free to slave, evidence of the fluid nature of colonial law, which already linked status to race. They may have believed that they shared grievances with those with whom they marched, given their relatively isolated life on the periphery of the settlement, but they lost more as a consequence of their participation in Bacon's Rebellion than did the gentry. Reactions to this populist rebellion led to stricter regulations for indentured servants and free blacks and harsher punishment for slaves.

Slave revolts during the 1700s and early 1800s conveyed black frustration with ill treatment, often resulted from communication between white laborers (free and unfree) and black slaves, and could represent the radical populist fringe. More often, African Americans, slave and free alike, engaged in less risky collective action. By the American Revolution and throughout the nineteenth-century abolitionist movement, blacks used petitions to convey populist sentiment to elected representatives. Some formed independent black organizations such as the National Negro Convention, which convened in Philadelphia for the first time in 1830. Others, however, resorted to violent resistance or protest, and those incidents, more than petitioning or politicized organizing, captured the public's attention and generated the most backlash.

Diverse antislavery tactics indicated a lack of consensus among black abolitionists over the best activities to pursue. Some resisted the growing interest in political involvement because they believed that politicians reached solutions through compromise rather than problem solving and because securing the vote and campaigning for candidates would distract abolitionists from the moral dilemma at the heart of slavery. Independent political activity slowly gained advocates, however, because, as Omar H. Ali argues, "the balance-of-power voting strategy—that is, supporting individual candidates with antislavery sentiments to sway elections" could effect political change (Ali, *In the Balance of Power*, 32). Yet many remained disenchanted because they believed politics limited, rather than liberated, blacks. They remained committed to independent collective action under the auspices of social and benevolent societies, church organizations, and self-help initiatives.

The few enfranchised black voters prior to the Civil War rallied behind the new Republican Party after 1854. Free blacks and slaves helped make the Civil War a war to end slavery through "disruptive and communal behaviors" as described by Steven Hahn (15). Slaves defied masters, formed organizations, identified spokespersons, and exercised individual choice but engaged in collective action nonetheless, all behaviors that Hahn considers "the very essence of political beings" (15). The slaves' politicized actions, or populism, in concert with national mobilization, ended slavery.

The Republican Party transitioned rapidly from an independent movement involving enfranchised African Americans to the largest party in the nation and the party in which freedmen placed their trust after the war. Freedmen registered to vote and cast ballots for white and black Republican candidates after ratification of the Fifteenth Amendment in 1870. Just as rapidly, however, the Republican Party lost its leverage and will as Democrats regained control of state legislatures and the U.S. Congress, and Republicans became complicit in restricting liberty and denying equality on the basis of race. Thus, African Americans quickly had reason to become disillusioned with the party that had helped them secure their freedom and had involved them in democratic reform.

The failure of Reconstruction prompted many to reinvest in populist action. Conditions for blacks worsened as white southerners refused to extend the agrarian ideal of landownership to the mass of freedmen and banished most freedmen to neoslavery under the crop lien system. Moreover, many Americans experienced financial hardships as the Panic of 1873 deepened into an economic depression. Laissez-faire economic policy allowed corporations to operate with few regulations, and labor unions faced serious restrictions on their right to bargain and protect the interests of their members. Employee or labor relations worsened as a consequence. White and black Populists synchronously mobilized in response to the consolidation of wealth and power that restricted workers, including agricultural laborers' rights and the personal liberty of small-scale landowners.

Numerous special interest groups appeared to ease members' burdens. When black farmers and laborers organized unions, they often met under the auspices of existing organizations such as churches, community-aid organizations, or fraternal or benevolent orders. The unions operated secretly, in keeping with well-honored traditions of other societies; this offered some protection to members who could be perceived as threats to the white Democrats' status quo. Additionally, African American sharecroppers utilized tactics from both agrarian and labor organizations as their status fell within both categories. Black farmer unions appropriated the ideas of cooperative purchasing and marketing from the National Grange of the Order of Patrons of Husbandry. This offered them some protection from the debt spiral associated with the crop lien system. They also engaged in collective action as touted by the Knights of Labor. Thus, they launched strikes to increase laborers' wages when the crops in the fields required tending and landowners were at their most vulnerable. Also in keeping with the Grange model and with earlier abolitionists' commitment to moral suasion, they pledged themselves to nonpartisan activities and focused on self-improvement. They collected funds to provide for ill and disabled members and their families as seen in urban mutual benefit societies. They offered educational programs that ranged from lectures on civics and economic government and scientific agriculture to discussions on how to respond to local challenges. Finally, black farmers published newspapers to facilitate communication.

White Alliances published newspapers, too, and most extant evidence of black Alliance activity comes from these sources. Milton George, proponent of the Northern Alliance and editor of the Chicago-based *Western Rural*, took direct action by organizing a black Alliance in Prairie County, Arkansas, in 1882, even before the Sons of the Agricultural Star formed in neighboring Monroe County. About this time, white farmers in the county organized the Agricultural Wheel, and the Knights of Labor began organizing in the area later. Such appeals from the less overtly racist Northern Alliance could have diverted blacks from membership in the more radical Knights of Labor assemblies.

Nearly a decade later in 1891, the Southern Alliance newspaper, the *National Economist*, sounded self-serving and paternalistic when it called for white farmers to look out for the economic interest of black farmers and protect them from exploitation, an indication of the hardening of racial tension during the Populist movement. White opinion, however, did not reflect black thought or deed. Unjust white landlords exploited black agricultural laborers. African American activism indicated that blacks understood this situation and could make their own decisions about which organizations to join. Further, black political views ranged as broadly as did those held by whites, so conservative blacks sought nonpartisanship, moral suasion, and economic self-help, while others sought radical approaches associated with direct action and party politics.

African Americans organized across the South; they pursued similar goals but were driven by local contexts. For example, the Arkansas Mississippi Delta proved a hotbed of activity for Populist organizing as black farmers in Monroe County, Arkansas, formed a union in 1885 that they called the Sons of the Agricultural Star in the heart of the cotton-poor Delta region. It grew rapidly, and members of the white Arkansas Agricultural Wheel recognized the strength in numbers that the Sons could offer. When the Arkansas Wheel launched a national organization in July 1886, it abandoned the "whites only" membership restriction. At the same time, the Knights of Labor created local assemblies across the rural South and welcomed white and black men and women as members regardless of their occupation. In Arkansas, a rural black Knights assembly near Little Rock launched a cotton pickers' strike during the summer of 1886, demanding a wage increase from 75 cents to $1 per day. The strikers did not win, but the Knights exercised the political philosophy "in the balance of power" by endorsing the Republican opponent to the Democrat sheriff who had put down the strike, nearly defeating him. In 1886, a disgruntled white Knights organizer created a new union for black laborers in the Carolinas, the Cooperative Workers of America. It appealed to workers in the Carolinas and Georgia on the basis of its economic (higher wagers, shorter hours, better working conditions, land reform, inheritance tax), educational (free schools) and political (repeal of the poll tax) goals. Black clubs of the Florida Farmers' Union formed to address farmers' concerns rather than those of wage laborers, and the union acknowledged that black and white farmers shared interests. Yet the union reneged on its support of black farmers' interests when it merged with the all-white Southern Alliance.

The frantic pace of Populist organizing by African Americans in Texas indicated the interest in maintaining separate and independent organizations. The black Alliances emerged in the aftermath of the white alliance state convention in Cleburne, Texas, in August 1886. The Alliance took a controversial political stance at the convention in defiance of Democrats. A committee issued 17 demands known as the Cleburne Demands. Several conservative Alliance men, in defiance, created the Grand State [Farmers'] Alliance in the name of nonpartisanship and civic education. The Texas Alliance mediated the crisis and experienced unprecedented growth as a consequence, claiming 200,000 members in 3,000 suballiances by January 1887.

Any direct correlation between the white momentum and black formation has yet to be documented, but nonetheless, black Alliances formed in the midst of an actively Populist state. One, organized during October 1886 in Caldwell County, Texas, perhaps through the efforts of farm owners in the black settlement of St. John's Colony, carried the moniker Grand State Colored Alliance. Members reputedly invited white Farmers' Alliance members to speak to their group. Another, the Consolidated Alliance, began in Lee County, Texas, during the fall of 1886, likely among freedmen previously enslaved by the family of Andrew J. Carothers, a farmer and son of a Confederate veteran. This Alliance expanded institutionally as the National Colored Alliance, and geographically into all other southern states by 1889. It claimed to have a membership of 250,000. A third Alliance began in December 1886 with the support of farm owners in the freedman community of Vistula in rural Houston County, 150 miles north of the city of Houston in east Texas. Members selected a white farmer, Richard M. Humphrey, a former Confederate with prior political experience in the Union Labor Party in Texas, as superintendent. Milton George's encouragement may have affected formation of this alliance, originally named the Alliance of Colored Farmers of Texas, but the members had experience with community formation and self-help independent of his influence.

Black farmers could use farmers' organizations to facilitate rural development. Railroads passed through Lee and Houston counties during the 1870s, which created market opportunities for some and development opportunities for others including, perhaps, the black farm owners who formed the Alliance. Houston County had a larger black population in proportion to white residents and a less diversified agricultural base, with more blacks involved in cotton farming than in Lee County. Lumbering also began in the eastern portion of Houston County during the 1880s, while ranching and corn and hog production remained important in Lee as well as in Houston County. Historian Charles Postel has made clear the connection between local development and white Alliance activity. This apparently motivated Texas's black farmers. It also helps to explain why independent Alliances continued to develop in east Texas. A fourth organization, the Texas Colored States Alliance, began in Robertson County, midway between Houston and Lee counties, in June 1887. The lines of the Houston and Texas Central Railway passed through the freedman community of Hammond and intersected with the International-Great Northern Railway in Hearne. The increasingly diverse rural economy in postwar Texas held potential for growth rather than entrapment in sharecropping. This could have fostered political activism among laborers, croppers, tenant farmers, and small landowners who turned to alliances as the means to further their goals.

One hundred forty miles separated the counties, but lecturers from both the Lee and Houston county alliances obviously competed for members far beyond the state. Thousands of suballiances, assemblies, and unions with tens of thousands of members existed across the South, partially because of the competitive expansion of the two Texas colored Alliances. By the time they merged into the Colored Farmers National Alliance and Cooperative Union of the United States (Colored Farmers' Alliance) in early 1890, the pressure had exacerbated community tensions in the Texas counties, divided schools and churches, and exhausted members. How much of this reflected differences of opinion about political activism versus business reform remains to be explored. The Alliance membership based in Houston County had emphasized nonpartisanship, but the political stance of the Lee County Alliance has not been documented, nor has the economic philosophy of either Alliance been scrutinized, given the paucity of evidence.

More evidence exists on the Colored Farmers' Alliance than other black Populist organizations because Humphrey, the organization's white superintendent, documented the Alliance's history. He was born in South Carolina, served in an Alabama infantry unit during the war, and then taught school in Texas. He served black Baptist congregations as a lay minister before rising to fame with the Colored Farmers' Alliance. His flair for promotion led him to publish "History of the Colored Farmers' National Alliance and Cooperative Union" in *The Farmers' Alliance and Agricultural Digest* (1891). He positioned himself favorably therein, claiming that formative meetings of the Houston County Alliance occurred on his farm in Lovelady, Texas, and documenting his efforts on behalf of black members. Most believe that Humphrey inflated alliance membership claims of 1.2 million in the aftermath of the merger, including 300,000 women, 150,000 young men and 750,000 adult men. The figures could represent the number of rural blacks in the population in each of 11 southern states that reported membership. They could represent the number of congregants in black churches that hosted suballiances. Some scholars contend that membership might have been closer to 250,000. Whatever the number, rural residents recognized the merits of political organizing.

Yet racial tensions marred Populist experiences despite Humphrey's positive reporting. Terse words captured the animus that existed between white and black Alliance members. "If white organizations shall positively prohibit the [admission] of colored men to its membership, colored organizations shall prohibit the admission of white men to membership"—so reported the Southern Alliance's *National Economist* on March 14, 1889 (Postel 42). As J. W. Carter, a black from Georgia who worked as a legislative spokesman for the Colored Farmers' Alliance, argued, "You white people attend to your business and let us alone.... The politicians and lawyers say you must keep us Negroes down. But that is not right" (Gaither 63). During the fall of 1887 the Southern Alliance merged with the Agricultural Wheel and reimposed its "whites only" membership policy. The Colored State Agricultural Wheel in Arkansas then merged with the Colored Farmers' Alliance in 1888, but as evidence of local determination, Colored Wheels in Tennessee remained independent.

Lack of trust existed among Colored Farmers' Alliance members. Black members of the Georgia Colored Farmers' Alliance considered Humphrey's manipulation of black intent relative to third-party formation at the Ocala meeting in late 1890 demeaning and a violation of the black members' trust. Others grew frustrated with Humphrey's purportedly reprehensible tactics. His major white competitor among black Populists, Andrew Carothers of Texas, along with E. A. Richardson, the black superintendent of the Georgia Colored Alliance, questioned Humphrey's more radical methods, such as calling for a cotton strike, because Carothers and Richardson believed these tactics would create more racial conflict. Richardson went so far as to wonder "why [Humphrey] did not belong to the white people's Alliance instead of the colored Alliance" (Postel 180). Humphrey lost credibility after the 1891 cotton pickers' strike failed.

Scholars have used the term "Black Populists" to identify these African Americans who participated in "democratic and decentralized opposition to the planter and business elite affiliated with the Democratic Party," and one could add that the term also recognizes the willingness of African Americans to risk their security for citizens abandoned by their government and at the mercy of unscrupulous employers, landlords, and even elite members of their own race (Ali, *In the Balance of Power*, 74). Populists faced numerous challenges, so pursuing a common purpose proved daunting. The label Black Populist can imply that a constituency existed and a coherent purpose prevailed, and generally, Black Populists favored publicly funded education, collective purchasing and marketing, local laws that protected personal property from seizure by landlords, and market regulation. They also favored antilynching laws, convict leasing regulation, and voter protection. But the federalist system of local and state authority independent of national oversight resulted in unique local situations that only Civil War–like national mobilization, in combination with Populist support, could have solved, and the national government did not mobilize during the "Populist moment" of the late nineteenth century. This left Black Populists at the mercy of their major opponents, the politically and economically elite.

Scholars have described Black Populists as independent decision makers, pawns of white agrarian organizers, and tokens of interracial cooperation. Without question, independent members made the Colored Farmers' Alliance a formidable organization, but they could not withstand the backlash they endured because of controversial boycotts, labor strikes—specifically a national cotton-pickers strike in 1891—and disfranchisement. Some argue that Black Populists expressed a more communitarian view of landownership, advocating less for private ownership and more for access. Yet black landowners facilitated community development as their financial investment in land theoretically freed them from white oversight. Black tenants controlled more productive resources than sharecroppers, including draft stock, equipment, and family labor, and this gave them some economic leverage in negotiating contracts. Sharecroppers represented the epitome of powerlessness, dependent on landlords and more likely to incur their wrath if caught organizing. Despite the research done to date, some questions remain unanswered. Which class constituted the majority in the ranks of Black Populists—which defined the platform? Did the Colored Alliance's platform address the needs of the propertyless more than the property-owning class? Rural Black Populists who pursued wealth redistribution apparently wanted to break white landowners' monopoly on tillable acreage rather than impose public ownership of land to benefit the propertyless. More research will explicate nuances of class conflict and their effect on Populist goals within the Colored Farmers' Alliance specifically and among Black Populists generally.

Certainly the lessons learned by generations of African Americans sustained Populists through disfranchisement. Without independent decentralized resistance to the elite, often under the auspices of existing church groups and benevolent and fraternal societies, activists could never have sustained the civil rights movement. Individual action took the form of personal resistance, court cases that challenged the constitutionality of discriminatory legislation, and formation of organizations such as the Congress on Racial Equality, the Student Nonviolent Coordinating Council, and other more localized, less visible boycotts and sit-ins. What Steven Hahn has described as slaves' politics mutated into Black Populist politics and then has sustained community organizers and civil rights activists to the present day.

Debra Ann Reid

See also: Agricultural Wheel; Bacon's Rebellion; Cleburne Platform (1886); Colored Farmers' Alliance (CFA); George, Milton (1833–unknown); Granger Movement;

Knights of Labor; Pattillo, Walter Alexander (1850–1908); The Press and Populism; Rayner, John (1850–1918); Texas, Populism in

References

Adams, Anthony J., and Gerald H. Gaither. *Black Populism in the United States: An Annotated Bibliography.* Westport, CT: Praeger, 2004.

Ali, Omar H. *In the Balance of Power: Independent Black Politics and Third-Party Movements*. Athens: Ohio University Press, 2008.

Ali, Omar H. *In the Lion's Mouth: Black Populism in the New South, 1886–1900*. Jackson: University Press of Mississippi, 2010.

Ayers, Edward L. *The Promise of the New South: Life after Reconstruction*. New York: Oxford University Press, 1992.

Cantrell, Gregg. *Kenneth and John B. Rayner and the Limits of Southern Dissent*. Urbana: University of Illinois Press, 1993.

Dickson, Patrick John. "Out of the Lion's Mouth: The Colored Farmers' Alliance in the New South, 1886–1892." M.P.S. Thesis, Cornell University, 2000.

Gaither, Gerald. *Blacks and the Populist Revolt: Ballots and Bigotry in the "New South."* Tuscaloosa: University of Alabama Press, 1977; revised edition issued as *Blacks and the Populist Movement: Ballots and Bigotry in the New South*, 2005. Page numbers for 1977 edition.

Goodwyn, Lawrence. *Democratic Promise: The Populist Moment in America*. New York: Oxford University Press, 1976, abridged ed. published as *The Populist Moment: A Short History of the Agrarian Revolt in America* (1978).

Hahn, Steven. *A Nation Under Our Feet: Black Political Struggles in the Rural South from Slavery to the Great Migration.* Cambridge, MA: The Belknap Press of Harvard University Press, 2003.

McMath, Robert C., Jr. *Populist Vanguard: A History of the Southern Farmers' Alliance*. Chapel Hill: University of North Carolina Press, 1975.

Postel, Charles. *The Populist Vision*. New York: Oxford University Press, 2007.

Sitton, Thad, and James H. Conrad. *Freedom Colonies: Independent Black Texans in the Time of Jim Crow*. Austin: University of Texas Press, 2005.

U.S. Agriculture Census, 1880. http://www.ancestry.com. See especially the categories of tenure, farm size, production, value of land, stock numbers, and products.

U.S. Population Census, 1880. http://www.ancestry.com. See especially the categories of race, occupation, family structure, and literacy. Subscription is required, but manuscript versions are available in many libraries.

Agrarianism

Agrarianism is a social, economic, and political system that promotes the values associated with agriculture and the proximity to the land. Many of the parables within the Bible present spiritual lessons in the language of farmers, thereby providing a moral and ethical basis for agriculture that is absent from other pursuits in commerce or industry. In U.S. history, agrarian values are associated with Thomas Jefferson's veneration of the yeoman farmer and Frederick Jackson Turner's influential frontier thesis.

Many promoters of agrarianism have found inspiration in the Bible. In the 13th chapter of the book of Matthew, Jesus

Christ presents the parable of the sower, in which the soil is blessed when good seed is planted onto good ground. The analogy is to the word of God being received, understood, and propagated. A good agricultural crop is analogous to a good spiritual crop that is blessed by God. In the parable of the weeds, the good seed is compared to the sons of the kingdom, while the bad seed that produces weeds is analogous to the devil. In both of these parables, the cause of righteousness is represented by a farmer with good seed and good soil producing a crop blessed by God, while the devil is represented by poor seed, poor ground, and a useless crop. Americans in the nineteenth century still relied on the Bible and religion for understanding much of their lives, especially in periods of great change. For that reason, agricultural reformers and great thinkers, including Thomas Jefferson, used terminology that resonated with farmers, who were the majority of nation.

After the American Revolution and the establishment of the first federal government, ideas of civic virtue and the survival of the new republic occupied the thoughts of many of the Founders. According to Thomas Jefferson and other Founders interested in establishing a true republican nation, the only way that the American republic could survive was through the promotion of freehold yeoman farmers who, unlike those who labored in commerce or industry, lacked a dependence on others for subsistence. A yeoman farmer was, thus, a true independent citizen and not beholden to others for survival. The civic morality of those who lacked economic dependence preserved the morality of the republic. The conflict between agrarian and commercial interests in the United States was a foundational debate among the Founders. The most eloquent proponent of an American agrarian economy was Thomas Jefferson. According to Jefferson, the only means by which the social and political gains of the American Revolution could be protected was through the establishment of a society of small, independent yeoman farmers. In query XIX of his *Notes on the State of Virginia*, Jefferson cites those that cultivate the earth as "the chosen of God." In Europe, the masses were compelled to work in manufactures only because access to the land was denied to the poor. This lack of access rendered the people dependent on a corrupt aristocratic class that stifled the genius of the people though their control on the land. In Jefferson's vision for the United States, a yeoman farmer's lack of dependency on outside markets or social power structures allowed farmers to act in a moral, upright manner that prevented the spread of political or moral subservience and corruption. Jefferson's theoretical ideals gained political prominence after his election in 1800. In his inaugural address in 1801, Jefferson dedicated his administration to the support of agriculture and cast the world of commerce as the "handmaid" of agriculture. President Jefferson's economic ideals were further expanded in his 1804 letter to economist Jean-Baptiste Say. For Jefferson, the ideal course of economic development in the United States was exclusively agricultural. Any need for manufactured products in the United States could be met by trading surplus agricultural output to Europe, forming a moral economic system in harmony with the laws of nature.

With the founding of the nation, the tenets of agrarianism were set in place, only to be expanded as the population moved west into the nation's expanding hinterland. The course of westward expansion was influenced by the desire to expand the agricultural economy. In the official instructions issued to Meriwether Lewis, the Lewis and Clark expedition was ordered to examine the soils, vegetation, and climate of all unknown territories encountered in their exploration. Lewis and Clark, as well as other explorers over the course of the early nineteenth century, found many opportunities for the expansion of an agricultural economy west of the Mississippi. Subsequent legislation directing the settlement of the public's western domain followed the appearance of Jefferson's yeoman farmer ideal. However, Jefferson's idealism was not universally accepted and in many cases did not reflect economic reality. One version of the Homestead Act was vetoed in 1860 by President Buchanan for the express purpose of preventing the spread of agrarian thought and ideas of public ownership of unsettled territory in the West. Even after the enacting of the Homestead Act in 1862, much of the most agriculturally viable lands in the Great Plains and the West were granted to railroads or sold for cash by the federal government.

The agrarian ideal gained another spokesman in the person of Frederick Jackson Turner. Writing in the 1890s, Turner wrote that the expanding frontier provided a safety valve that allowed the United States to avoid many of the class problems that plagued Europe by providing a forum for the continuous renewal of the United States' democratic institutions. Turner reflected on the contributions of Jefferson, citing Jefferson as the John the Baptist of American democracy for his dedication to promoting the interests of small farmers at the expense of the moneyed classes of society. For Turner, only the presence of free land for farmers in the West reinforced the democratic impulses of the United States. Turner believed that the experience of settlement allowed settlers to recreate American democracy as each wave of settlers in the West was required to recreate the institutions of government isolated from outside influences. The frontier experience encouraged individualism, economic equality, and upward mobility; in short, the frontier promoted the individual characteristics that Turner believed were essential for the survival of democracy. With the closing of the agricultural frontier in the 1890s, the United States suffered from the monopolistic concentration of capital and political influence of corporations that did not promote the growth of the democratic spirit. This concentration of wealth in industry and commerce stifled democracy by denying social and economic mobility to the masses, just as both Jefferson and Turner feared that it would.

Jefferson's social vision and Turner's political theory existed as ideals that were not reflected in reality after the Civil War, although the dire warnings provided in the writings of Jefferson and Turner have not been completely borne out by subsequent events. Unlike Jefferson's theory, the political republic did not collapse as the United States transitioned to an industrial and service-based economy. Unlike Turner's concerns, the American democratic form of government did not disintegrate after the closing of the frontier. Both visions place the center of the American experience with the tillers of the soil, yet to what degree either vision was grounded in reality instead of pious hope is open to debate.

Patrick Callaway

See also: Agricultural Issues, Regional; Homestead Act (1862); Jefferson, Thomas (1743–1826)

References

Koch, Adrienne, and William Peden, eds. *The Life and Selected Writings of Thomas Jefferson.* New York: The Modern Library, 1998.

Jackson, Donald. *Thomas Jefferson and the Rocky Mountains: Exploring West from Monticello.* Norman: University of Oklahoma Press, 2002.

Vogeler, Ingolf. *The Myth of the Family Farm: Agribusiness Dominance of U.S. Agriculture.* Boulder, CO: Westview Press, 1981.

The Holy Bible, King James Version. Nashville: World Publishing, 2004.

Turner, Frederick Jackson. "Contributions of the West to American Democracy." In George Rogers Taylor, ed. *The Turner Thesis Concerning the Role of the Frontier in American History.* Boston: D.C. Heath and Company, 1956.

Agricultural Issues, Regional

The agricultural economy of the United States faced a series of challenges and opportunities in the middle of the nineteenth century that fundamentally reconstructed the experience of farmers in the republic. Some changes, such as the Homestead Act and the expansion of the agricultural frontier to new territory in the Great Plains and the Far West, provided the prospect for the creation of a prosperous agrarian republic. The collapse of the slave-based plantation economy provided the same hope for small farmers in the South. The promise of an agrarian republic, however, did not match the reality. Industrialization and the rise of corporate America created a series of structures that effectively curtailed the development of an agrarian republic and created an agricultural system beholden to the distant markets, capital flows, and the interests of corporate America.

After the Civil War, the national business environment worsened for agricultural interests. The war had been paid for in inflated paper currency that was not pinned to the gold standard. Banking and bondholding interests wanted a deflationary monetary policy that would increase the value of their holdings and create a "hard money" currency backed by and redeemable in gold. The federal government complied. Farmers in both the North and South were hurt by this decision because as the value of each dollar increased, it became more difficult for debtors to pay their loans. The hard money policy coincided with the increased influence of railroads and other technological advances in agriculture that made farmers more dependent on credit, distant markets, and access to capital than their ancestors.

The North

The Homestead Act of 1862 mandated that federal lands in the Great Plains and the West were to be divided into 160-acre holdings that would be virtually given to settlers for establishing family farms on the frontier. The promise of free land did not remove all expenses for farmers. The Department of Agriculture recommended that new farmers possess at least $1,000 to cover the costs of equipment, seed, and other necessities. Despite the promise provided by the act, the ideal of an expanding republic of small freeholders fell prey to other land-distribution systems that granted lands to railroads. Railroad companies used land grants to maintain right-of-ways and earn profits off of settlers who in turn used the railroad for shipping and receiving goods. Corruption also hindered the agrarian republic. Scholars estimate that half of all homesteads were fraudulently held by absentee landowners or corporations.

The presence of the railroad spurred settlement along railroad corridors that promised an easy connection to eastern markets for agricultural goods. The advantage brought by the railroads did not benefit many farmers. Often it cost half of the value of each crop to ship products to the market. One standard railroad practice was to charge "transit fees" that charged each shipper the same rate to transport goods on the railroad regardless of the actual distance from the market. Farmers, especially in the Great Plains, lacked alternatives to railroad transportation, leading many to call for national ownership of the railroad system as a cure for economic exploitation.

The efficiency of the railroad as a means of transporting goods also allowed for the specialization and centralization of markets for agricultural produce. During and after the Civil War, much of the agricultural produce of the Great Plains and Midwest was shipped to Chicago. This concentration of economic influence offended the sensibilities of many farmers who felt that they had no influence upon the market for their products. One example of this alienation was the grain grading system. This legislation permitted a private organization known as the Board of Trade in Chicago to judge the quality, and therefore the value, of all grain shipments into the city's marketplace. The grain grading system was enshrined into Illinois law in 1859. Thus the value of a farmer's crop was dependent upon this judgment from a private organization in which the farmer had no voice and no guarantee of an honest appraisal of the crop.

For many farmers in the Far West and the Great Plains, agriculture became a profession dependent on technology to increase yields, especially for farmers who specialized in a small number of crops or even one crop. Access to technological advances depended on access to capital and credit, but access was subject to distant market pressures. Inventions such as the mechanical reaper increased the productivity of farming; this increase of productivity, however, required the investment of increasing amounts of capital. Unfortunately, interest rates on farm machinery averaged between 16 and 32 percent. Additional economic stress was caused by the decline in prices for agricultural goods. By 1889, Kansas farmers sold their grain for as little as 10 cents per bushel. As the return for crops declined, many farmers found themselves unable to sustain a minimum standard of subsistence. Increased outputs proved to be a mixed blessing. Overproduction of agricultural commodities caused the prices to fall even further as the markets became glutted. Increased production became a trap; each increase in productivity caused a decline in per-unit profit.

The South

The Civil War destroyed the plantation economy based on slave labor, but it did not destroy the plantation. The end of slavery did not create an egalitarian political or economic structure for African Americans or poor southern whites. In theory, freed slaves were to be settled on lands abandoned by plantation owners as yeoman freeholders. This subdivision of land to individual farmers was rare. In practice, African Americans were compelled by economic need, the lack of skills, and even the federal government to labor on plantations as contract laborers with little hope of ever owning land. Under the contract system, agricultural laborers were only paid at the end of each growing season or paid a proportion of the value of the crop after harvest. As the fervor for Reconstruction waned in the 1870s, sharecropping became a primary form of agricultural labor in the South as it combined a disciplined and affordable labor force with the Civil War mandate for abolition.

Much like the farmers of the Far West and the Great Plains, southern farmers faced an exploitive economic structure that favored those with access to outside capital. Merchants with access to northern capital resources established the crop lien system. Unlike plantation slavery, there was not a disciplined system of directly coercive labor; these furnishing agents, however, controlled the only access to seeds, household goods, food, plows, and other resources farmers required to subsist. These goods were furnished on credit at usurious rates of interest, which were repaid with proceeds gained from the sale of the crop. Many farmers were unable to repay their entire debt for the year at the end of the season. In an effort to increase farm profits, many landowners required the planting of cotton to the exclusion of all other crops, including food. Sharecroppers had few options until the two world wars demanded labor in the North and West. In time, the accumulated debt and the inability to gain a profit from agriculture forced many farmers to immigrate west or to remain in the South as landless tenant farmers.

The reforms of Reconstruction were particularly difficult for yeoman farmers. Small landholders lacked the resources to establish a sharecropping-style economy based on scale. In addition, many yeoman farmers in the upland South lacked access to railroads to ship their produce to market. Farmers were also hindered by poor crop yields, a decline in prices for agricultural goods, and an increase in taxes. As a response to this exploitation, many farmers in the South began to organize and demand access to more affordable credit sources, a subtreasury system to inflate the currency, and a more equitable means of transporting their crop to market. Many of these reforms met with little support by the industrial, political, or banking interests of the United States. For many observers, a politically active agrarian Populist party was a threat to private property and the established political and economic order.

After the Civil War, many farmers throughout the United States organized in protest against the abuses of the postwar economy. Deflationary monetary policies, abusive credit terms, and the lack of access to the economic and political system led farmers to demand a new course for the American economy and society that more closely reflected the needs and desires of rural Americans. Many of the ideas proposed by farmers would be incorporated into the Populist and later the Progressive movements, but the agrarian uprising was doomed by the lack of resources.

Patrick Callaway

See also: Colored Farmers' Alliance (CFA); Gold Standard/Free Silver; Homestead Act (1862); Long-Haul/Short-Haul Discrimination; Northern Alliance; Peonage; Populism; Progressivism; Subtreasury Plan; Western Alliance

References

Carlson, Laurie Winn. *William J. Spillman and the Birth of Agricultural Economics*. Columbia: University of Missouri Press, 2005.

Cronon, William. *Nature's Metropolis: Chicago and the Great West*. New York: W. W. Norton and Company, 1991.

Foner, Eric. *A Short History of Reconstruction*. New York: Harper & Row, 1990.

Goodwyn, Lawrence. *The Populist Moment: A Short History of the Agrarian Revolt in America*. New York: Oxford University Press, 1978.

Hine, Robert V., and John Mack Faragher. *The American West: A New Interpretive History*. New Haven, CT: Yale University Press, 2000.

Agricultural Newspapers and Farmer Unrest

Without electronic communication to reach residents in the rural United States, champions of the People's Party movement used agricultural newspapers to spread their messages. It was common to find political rhetoric in weekly farm publications alongside articles about crop prices, community events, births, and obituaries. In addition to newspapers attributed directly to the reform press, articles presenting Populist politics were disseminated through syndicated outlets, agricultural trade journals, and women's periodicals associated with suffrage issues.

The United States has a long history of agrarian journalism, beginning in 1819 with *American Farmer* published by John Stuart Skinner, who sought to educate farmers on state-of-the-art farming practices. A host of similar publications followed, including *Ploughboy* debuting that same year, *New England Farmer* (1822), *New York Farmer* (1827), and *Southern Agriculturalist* (1828). These early publications contained little or no political content, instead featuring articles on developments in horticultural species and animal breeds, reports on successful farming practices, agricultural fairs, and proceedings of society meetings.

Some rural towns had their own local papers, produced by a single editor and a shop assistant. These papers offered farming residents who were distanced by acres of corn and wheat with a sense of community, and isolated farm wives looked forward to hearing news of their neighbors as well as getting homemaking advice. With *American Farmer*, Skinner introduced a tradition of publications specifically for the agricultural community that would gradually transition in content from educational and informative to authoritative and influential, setting the stage for the infusion of political rhetoric during the coming decades.

In February 1839, the Union Agricultural Society incorporated in Chicago, and a year later it introduced its newspaper, the *Union Agriculturalist and Western Prairie Farmer*, later shortening the name to *Prairie Farmer*. In 1849 the publication began urging its readers to join agricultural associations and cooperatives. With its motto, "In Union is Strength," the monthly eight-page publication eventually became the publication of the Illinois State Agricultural Society, a group of farmer-delegates representing Illinois Farmers' Clubs.

In 1873, the *Prairie Farmer* began devoting a page per issue to Grange news and supported the Grange over competing Alliance organizations. A number of small, local newspapers also featured Grange news when the Grange began syndicating boilerplate templates with preprinted inside pages that smaller publishers could then imprint with their own mastheads and local content on the outside pages.

Larger in circulation and more politically motivated than the *Prairie Farmer* was the *Western Rural and Family Farm Paper* (later known as *Western Rural*). In 1880, when Milton George took over the *Western Rural*, his intent was to rouse farmers from their apathy, using the paper to promote the Farmers' Alliance that he organized in Chicago that year. George believed that other farm journals were missing an opportunity for influencing collective thought by featuring only agricultural topics and neglecting calls for reform.

Through his editorial columns he built interest in Alliance causes while continuing to provide mainstream agricultural content. He quickly built support for more than 200 Alliance charters throughout the Midwest, and readers responded with letters to the editor discussing their hardships and praising the Alliance. A shrewd marketer, George then tasked his newspaper agents to serve simultaneously as Alliance lecturers, sending them on speaking engagements in neighboring states. In 1886, George used his subscriber list to mail out a statement of Alliance principles. Farmers who responded with support were made honorary members, reviving enough interest to prompt an Alliance convention that fall.

George was not alone in his use of farm newspapers to foster interest and support in Alliance causes. Included was the *American Non-Conformist*, which was published originally in Kansas beginning in 1879 and later in Indiana from 1892 to

1896 by the Vincent Brothers Publishing Company. In 1895 the paper was taken over by Leroy Templeton, a People's Party candidate for governor. Interspersed among crop news and homemaking features were editorials supporting Alliance causes.

Another successful paper was the *Progressive Farmer*, published in North Carolina and founded in 1886 by Leonidas Polk. Initially Polk used the paper to promote agricultural reform, and he urged readers to organize into Farmers' Clubs. His message was successful. Within a short time there were 400 clubs that eventually became the North Carolina Farmers' Association. In 1887 Polk organized the state's Alliance, one of the largest in the South.

In March 1889, Charles Macune of the Southern Alliance founded what would become the primary newspaper of the Populist Movement. The *National Economist*, published in Washington, DC, reached a circulation of more than 100,000. Macune also distributed political literature across the country through his Alliance publishing company. In 1891 Macune and 1,000 Alliance newspapers formed the National Reform Press Association (NRPA). Similar to the Grange, the NRPA produced and distributed templates to member papers, which then published their own versions, adding local news to the preprinted party rhetoric, In addition to the *National Economist*, the Alliance also published an official journal, *The Advocate*. It was distributed out of Kansas and had a circulation of 8,000.

As the Populist agenda sought to expand its constituency, it looked to women as potential political supporters and aligned itself with the woman suffrage movement. While the editors of the suffrage press typically targeted urban readers, to reach rural women Populist publishers partnered with women's farm newspapers and magazines. One such successful partnership evolved into the *Farmer's Wife*. The newspaper was the collective product of Kansas residents Ira and Emma Pack. Ira was a supporter of the Farmers' Alliance. Emma was a college-educated farm wife who was active in the Grange in Iowa and then the Farmers' Alliance in Kansas.

Before developing the *Farmer's Wife*, Ira was the publisher of a real estate paper, the *City and Farm Record*, and Emma edited *Villa Range: Ladies' Home Journal*, featuring fiction and homemaking articles. In 1891 they abandoned their separate publications to found the *Farmer's Wife* with the intention of disseminating rhetoric on suffrage, prohibition, and the Alliance. The monthly newspaper encouraged readers to become involved in politics through the National Woman's Alliance, founded in part by Emma. While supporting both suffrage and Populist concerns, the paper served to empower to effect social change.

By 1893, circulation of the *Farmer's Wife* was declining, and the publication was printed sporadically as Emma was away much of the time on a suffrage lecture circuit. The last issue was published in October 1894.

The reform press retained popularity until the 1896 presidential elections when the Populist ticket, with *People's Party Paper* editor Tom Watson as a vice presidential candidate, failed to gain support. During the decades leading up to that event, the reform press was being criticized for using the guise of journalism to influence political thought. As the century came to a close, the industry was in another transition as mass publishers such as Joseph Pulitzer and William Hearst were moving away from traditional reporting using competitive and sensationalist techniques to gain circulation.

Carla W. Garner

See also: *American Non-Conformist*; Granger Movement; National Reform Press Association (NRPA); Pack, Emma (1850–1908); People's Party; Plains and Midwest, Populism in the; Polk, Leonidas L. (1937–1892); *Progressive Farmer*; *Western Rural*

References

Endres, Kathleen L., and Therese Lueck. *Women's Periodicals in the United States: Social and Political Issues.* Westport, CT: Greenwood Press, 1996.

Fry, John J. *The Farm Press, Reform, and Rural Change, 1895–1920.* New York: Routledge, 2005.

Garcia, Hazel Dicken. *Journalistic Standards in Nineteenth-Century America.* Madison: University of Wisconsin Press, 1989.

Hicks, John D. *The Populist Revolt: A History of the Farmers' Alliance and the People's Party.* Minneapolis: University of Minnesota Press, 1931.

Mott, Frank Luther. *American Journalism: A History 1690–1960.* New York: MacMillan, 1962.

Scott, Roy V. *The Agrarian Movement in Illinois, 1880–1896.* Urbana: University of Illinois Press, 1962.

Taylor, Carl C. *The Farmers' Movement, 1620–1920.* New York: American Book Company, 1953.

Vaughn, Stephen L., ed. *Encyclopedia of American Journalism.* New York: Routledge, 2008.

Agricultural Wheel

The Agricultural Wheel was a farmers' cooperative alliance founded by William Walker Tedford, William A. Suit, and W. Taylor McBee in Des Arc, Arkansas, in 1882 to improve farming conditions and that existed until 1889 when it merged with the National Farmers' Alliance to form the Farmers' and Laborers' Union of America. It was the precursor to the Populist uprisings of the 1890s that eventually led to the creation of the People's Party.

After the Civil War, the rural South lay in ruins, particularly its banking and credit systems. While the planter class maintained control of a majority of the land, they were unable to afford wage laborers to do the work of cotton agriculture for them. Instead, planters devised a new system, dividing their farms and former plantations into smaller units of 20 to 50 acres on which they allowed former slaves and their families or poor whites to live as either tenants or sharecroppers. In return, the tenants would pay the landlord a fixed rate or a portion of the crops that they harvested.

Because the tenants usually had no income until the crops came in, they were often forced to purchase their tools and daily supplies on credit, at usurious rates, from the local merchant. After harvest, the tenants received a bill that was often greater than the price they received for crops. The tenant then carried that debt into the next year. Southern tenants and farmers referred to these high-interest-rate credit transactions as "anaconda mortgages" because they smothered the debtor, squeezing the life out of their victims like the infamous snake.

This cycle allowed the landlord to dictate which crops were planted. The former planters preferred staple crops, particularly cotton, for which there was always a market. This led to overproduction and low prices. With a majority of the land in the South put into cotton production, prices dropped dramatically throughout the latter half of the nineteenth century, to the point that the cost of production was often more than the price farmers received at market, thus trapping small-scale farmers, tenants, and sharecroppers into a never-ending cycle of poverty.

Forty percent of the farmers in Prairie County in eastern Arkansas were tenants. Even if a farmer owned his own land, state laws and statutes meant to protect landowners made credit difficult to obtain or allowed creditors to maintain a stranglehold on farmers. The new state constitution, passed in 1874, forbade bankers or creditors from foreclosing on a homestead to satisfy a debt. Five years later, another law declared that if a piece of land was seized it must be sold for at least two-thirds its appraised value within one year of the transaction. Thus, the lending of credit to small-scale farmers was seen as a gamble.

The flat terrain of Prairie County, Arkansas, had suffered a severe drought in 1881, ruining almost all of the cotton planted that year. The opening months of the next year were greeted by drenching rains that causes the White River to flood, covering the low lands with water and causing many of farmers and tenants to be unable to get into their fields at the optimal time. With several families mired in debt, the situation reached a crisis point when several local medical doctors met in Lonoke and decided not to provide care and assistance to families that were too indebted to pay them. Unless farmers could provide these doctors with cash or other assets, they would have to turn elsewhere for medical services.

After discussing the plight of their neighbors and their own struggles, W. Taylor McBee and William Suit decided to take matters into their own hands. Inviting friends and neighbors to the McBees' log cabin school house, eight miles southwest of Des Arc, on Saturday, February 12, 1882, the two farmers talked to the nine people who showed up, a group that consisted of seven Prairie County farmers and two from nearby Lonoke County. They explained that local farmers needed to organize and attempt some kind of collective action. There was, as author W. Scott Morgan stated in 1889, no "hope of relief except through united and independent action on the part of the people" (Morgan 237). Twenty-one-year-old William Walker Tedford was elected president, and 30-year-old McBee assumed the role of secretary. W. Taylor's brother, John W. McBee, was asked to join the two gentlemen in drafting the new organization's constitution, by-laws, and secret rituals.

Two nights later, after finishing the drafts, the three farmers agreed that their new organization should be called

Wattensas Farmers' Club. To be a member an individual must "sign the constitution and by-laws" and be "engaged in farming" (Elkins). With meetings twice per month, on the first and third Saturdays, the new society's goal was for the "improvement of its members in the theory and practice of agriculture and the dissemination of knowledge relative to rural and farming affairs" (Blackmar).

Hoping to attract others like themselves, they decided that a name change was in order following their fourth meeting. After narrowing it down to either the Agricultural Wheel or the Poor Man's Friend, they chose the Wheel for its allusions to the prophet Ezekiel and because "no machinery can be run without a great drive wheel, and as that wheel moves and governs the entire machinery, however complex, so agriculture is the great wheel of power that controls the entire machinery of the world's industries." This was a common theme among farmers in the period, as shown in the Granger's song, "The Farmer Feeds Us All" (Elkins).

By early 1883 the group had grown to more than 500 members, and E. R. McPherson was elected Grand President of the State Wheel. Emphasizing progressive farming methods, a move away from cotton, a shift to cooperative buying, and the adoption of new laws to eliminate anaconda mortgages, local Wheels addressed the concerns of their members. Pointing out the lack of availability of credit, declining markets, and the poor harvest of 1881, their first overtly political act was to request Governor Thomas Churchill to call a special session of the state legislature where lawmakers would postpone tax collection on farmers and enact laws that would make money available to them, but Churchill was unwilling to do this.

With the economy in the doldrums, the Wheel found rich soil of discontent in which to grow. On January 9, 1884, at its meeting in Stony Point, Arkansas, the Wheel's ranks had swelled to 114 chapters, representing nearly 5,000 members. By the harvest of 1885, its ranks had grown to 462 local chapters, or subordinates, across the states of Alabama, Tennessee, Mississippi, Texas, and Arkansas.

Pointing to the railroad, banking, other monopolies, and crony rings that these farmers felt had an unfair advantage over them, as well as to the corruption and malpractice by local and state officials, county Wheel organizations decided to run their own candidates for political office, breaking the one-party system that refused to address their needs. Even though it was difficult to get white farmers to leave the Democratic Party, the Wheel achieved some victories in White and Prairie counties.

As in other Populist organizations, Wheel leaders considered combining with other groups. On October 15, 1885, the Arkansas Wheel met with member of the Brothers of Freedom, a northwestern farmers' union, at Greenbrier, Arkansas, to propose a merger. The Brothers were more politically active. Isaac McCracken was elected head of the new combined organization. While depicted in the Democratic press as a mere tool of the Republican Party, this merger allowed the Wheel to become involved in statewide elections. In 1886, they nominated former Greenbacker Charles E. Cunningham as their party's candidate for governor of Arkansas, which ended in failure when Cunningham finished a distant third behind the two major parties.

At the end of July 1886, McCracken sought to create a national organization at a meeting in Litchfield, Arkansas. In a controversial move, the word "white" was dropped from membership requirements, recognizing that blacks shared the same economic problems as whites. Local Wheels could decide whether they wanted African Americans in their ranks, and blacks could form their own subordinates. Soon after, a previously established black farmers' union, the Sons of the Agricultural Star, based in Monroe County, was admitted into the Wheel. In that same year the official newspaper, the *National Agricultural Wheel*, in Litchfield, emerged.

One-half million farmers were members of the Wheel as it expanded into Kentucky, Missouri, Wisconsin, and Indian Territory (now Oklahoma). Among the issues that the growing organization supported were free public education, abolition of national banks, cessation of futures trading, a repeal of any law that favored corporate interests over farmers and the common man, a graduated income tax, national ownership of all communication and transportation venues, a luxury tax, free trade, direct election of all national politicians, and full payment of the national debt. The Wheel also had a strong xenophobic element to it, urging laws that prevented foreign ownership of land and a prohibition of alien labor.

In 1888, at a meeting in Birmingham, Alabama, Wheel members agreed to merge with the National Farmers' Alliance and Cooperative Union of America. Evan Jones became its new leader, with McCracken assuming the vice presidency. While the Agricultural Wheel ceased to exist as an independent organization, the major casualty of this merger was African Americans, who were refused membership in this new Alliance.

Trevor Jason Soderstrum

See also: African Americans and Populism; Colored Farmers' Alliance (CFA); Democratic Party; Farmers' and Laborers' Union of America (FLUA); Farmers' Clubs; Northern Alliance; Peonage; People's Party; South, Populism in the; Tenant Farming

References

Blackmar, Frank W., ed. *Kansas: A Cyclopedia of State History, Embracing Events, Institutions, Industries, Counties, Cities, Towns, Prominent Persons, etc. . . . with a Supplementary Volume Devoted to Selected Personal History and Reminiscence.* Chicago: Standard Publishing Co., 1912. KSGenWeb. http://www.skyways.org/genweb/archives/1912/a/agricultural_wheel.html. Accessed January 2, 2013.

Elkins, F. Clark. "Arkansas Farmers Organize for Action: 1882–1884." http://www.argenweb.net/prairie/History/agwheel.htm. Accessed January 2, 2013.

Morgan, W. Scott. *History of the Wheel and Alliance and the Impending Revolution.* Vol. 3. n.p., 1889.

Alger, Horatio, Jr. (1832–1899)

Horatio Alger Jr., was a prolific and popular writer of juvenile books and serials for boys in the last quarter of the nineteenth century. Alger's works were characterized

Horatio Alger's stories of boys who rose from rags to riches by virtue and hard work made him one of the most popular writers of the late-19th century. (Library of Congress)

by Populist themes, including social mobility and industrial patronage that represented significant departures from the heavy-handed morality works of his predecessors in children's literature and codified the "rags-to-riches" narrative that became so prevalent at that time.

Alger was born on January 13, 1832, in Chelsea, Massachusetts. The son of a Unitarian minister, Alger studied for the ministry early in life. Gaining admission to Harvard College in 1848, Alger sold his first writings, two essays and a poem, while a student there. Graduating in 1852, Alger briefly entered the Harvard Divinity School but left in the next year. He worked as an assistant editor at the *Boston Daily Advertiser* but quit to take up teaching, but he did not give up writing. His first book, *Bertha's Christmas Vision: An Autumn Sheaf*, was published in 1856. He returned to Harvard Divinity School in 1857, this time completing his studies. In 1864 Alger was installed as pastor at the First Unitarian Church and Society in Brewster, Massachusetts. In the same year he also released his first juvenile book, *Frank's Campaign; or, What Boys Can Do on the Farm for the Camp*, published by A. K. Loring, who would go on to publish many of Alger's works.

In 1866, fifteen months after accepting his ministerial post, Alger was forced to resign amid charges of sexual misconduct with some boys in the parish. Alger did not deny the charges and submitted a letter of repentance to Unitarian officials in Boston. Alger left Brewster after promising never to seek any further posting in the church.

Alger arrived in New York City in 1866. All around him were throngs of young males socioeconomically disenfranchised from the larger financial systems of the city. Before arriving in New York, Alger had already penned a juvenile novel, *Charlie Codman's Cruise* (1866), which reflected the typical Alger formula. Moreover, the plight of the "street boy" inspired Alger; he not only became involved in charities designed to help the poor, he also began writing about them in earnest. In 1867 Alger serialized the story that would become his most famous book, *Ragged Dick; or, Street Life in New York with the Boot-Blacks*, in Oliver Optic's influential *Student and Schoolmate* magazine. The book was released by Loring in 1868 and became an instant success for Alger.

Ragged Dick tells the story of the eponymous hero, actually named Richard Hunter, a hardworking boot-black who rises above his station and achieves middle-class respectability. Alger's hero, Ragged Dick, is typical of his novels' protagonists. Dick is a cheerful, industrious lad who is brought to low circumstances by means beyond his control. Still, his pluck, determination, and general good character catch the eye of several possible benefactors around him, and, conversely, these older men often work to aid Dick, sometimes by throwing extra business his way, sometimes by encouraging him or giving him something of use, and, eventually, with one particular individual becoming Dick's mentor and patron.

Alger's importance to the Populist movement in the late-nineteenth-century United States is often directly connected back to *Ragged Dick*. While Alger was not the first writer for juveniles to stress social mobility as a direct outcome for his heroes, he both demarcated and popularized the genre, reaching audiences who had never before considered the possibility of rising above their own stations. Indeed, the essentially American rags-to-riches story can be traced back to Alger and the popularity of his works; the generic formula would go on to inform most of Alger's writing output after 1866. Though the details of his novels would vary, his larger theme remained virtually unchanged, and thus generations of Americans were raised on the notion that economic despondency was not as intractable as popular juvenile culture had previously depicted.

While Alger's rags-to-riches formula is often cited as the natural outcome of his protagonists' own sense of industry and hard work, Alger mostly portrays the hero as a boy aided by a gentleman who is reflective of the larger capitalist structure to which the boy aspires but could never fully reach on his own accord. Alger's populist formula, then, is not an "us-versus-them" or "poor-versus-rich" narrative but rather a depiction of both sides benefiting from interaction with the other. There is no doubt that Alger critiques greedy capitalism that exists only for its own sake, but he also praises those members of the elite who work in charity, aid others, and push for social and political reform, as Alger himself did. Ultimately, Alger creates distinct characterizations for both the lower and upper classes in his populist narratives: the "Alger hero" is hardworking, good-natured, naturally smart, deferential to authority, and willing to help others; the "Alger businessman" is kindly, genteel, successful without lording over others, and always eager to aid those who, in his estimation, "deserve" it.

The success of *Ragged Dick* propelled Alger to write five more books in what is now termed the Ragged Dick series, including two that included Ragged Dick as a recurring character: *Fame and Fortune: or, The Progress of Richard Hunter* (1868) and *Mark, the Match Boy; or, Richard Hunter's Ward* (1869). A prolific writer, Alger published and republished more than 100 books, mostly written for boys and reflecting the same formula established in *Ragged Dick.* Among the most prominent of these are his Luck and Pluck series (four volumes, from 1869 to 1872) and the Tattered Tom series (four volumes, 1871 to 1872), which included one volume featuring a female Alger hero, the only of his works written for juveniles to include a female protagonist.

Alger wrote prolifically throughout his life. When sales of his books began to lag, he moved his heroes away from New York and the Northeast and brought in new themes related to the growing interest in depictions of the American West. Alger wrote about boys adventuring in Colorado, mining in California, and, in one notable volume, searching for gold in Australia. Alger also continued to work with various boys' and moral charities and even acted as a mentor and patron to three street boys, educating them and arranging for positions in particular trades.

After 1880, Alger's works dwindled in popularity, partly because of the repetitious nature of their plots and partly because of changing tastes in literary conventions and social mores. Alger continued to write, however, in part because he needed the money. He often sold his works outright for a flat fee and thus was never made wealthy by his writing. Stricken by ill health in 1896, Alger returned to Massachusetts to live with his sister and her husband, unable to complete his last book, *Out for Business.* Thus he contacted the writer Edward Stratemeyer and requested that he finish it for him. Stratemeyer did, ultimately "completing" 11 books that were published under Alger's name.

Alger died on July 18, 1899. Despite the popularity of his works, his death received little notice in the press of the day. Nonetheless, Alger's legacy has influenced American socioeconomic thought in significant ways. Alger's contribution to populist fiction is built around the mythos he created with his "Alger boy" and "Alger businessman." The popular American notions of social class mobility, the hopeful possibilities of the rags-to-riches transformation, and the beneficence of hard work and business, all key American ideals, were all popularized by Alger and his works.

Michael G. Cornelius

See also: Gilded Age

References

Cawelti, John G. "From Rags to Respectability: Horatio Alger." In *Apostles of the Self-Made Man*. Chicago: University of Chicago Press, 1965.

Karrenbrock, Marilyn H. "Horatio Alger, Jr." In Glenn E. Estes, ed. *American Writers for Children before 1900. The Dictionary of Literary Biography*. Detroit: Bruccoli Clark, 1985.

Scharnhorst, Gary, and Jack Bales. *Horatio Alger, Jr.: An Annotated Bibliography of Comment and Criticism*. Metuchen, NJ: Scarecrow Press, 1981.

Scharnhorst, Gary, and Jack Bales. *The Lost Life of Horatio Alger, Jr.* Bloomington: Indiana University Press, 1985.

Allen, William Vincent (1847–1923)

William Vincent Allen served in the U.S. Senate from 1893 to 1899 and from 1899 to 1901 in separate terms. He was the permanent chairman for the People's Party's 1896 Convention in St. Louis, where he steered the successful nomination of William Jennings Bryan. More conservative than most Populists, he worked to keep the socialists, under Henry Demarest Lloyd, from taking over the party.

Allen was born in Midway City, Madison County, Ohio, on January 28, 1847. His father died during Allen's infancy. His mother remarried an abolitionist Methodist minister when Allen was young. In 1856, the family moved to Iowa. As a child Allen worked with his family transporting runaway slaves for the Underground Railroad. When the Civil War broke out Allen, age 14, tried to enlist. He managed to join the army at age 15 and served with the Iowa Thirty-Second Volunteers, spending some time as a flag-bearer.

After the war, Allen attended Upper Iowa University in Fayette, Iowa. He studied law in West Union Iowa with local attorney L. L. Ainsworth. He practiced law in Iowa before moving to Madison, Nebraska, where he became politically and socially active. He opened a law office as senior partner in the Allen and Robinson Law Firm. He served as senior commander in the Grand Army of Nebraska, attending numerous encampments. Locally, he managed the community baseball team and joined both the Masons and Oddfellows. Eventually he joined the Farmers' Alliance movement, which led to the People's Party.

Prior to becoming a Populist in 1890, Allen was active in the reform wing of the Republican Party, opposing what he deemed the railroads' control of the Nebraska party branch. He regularly attended Nebraska Republican Party conventions as a delegate. He also served as Madison County Republican Party chairman in 1886. Allen believed that reformers needed to defeat the railroads at the polls because the railroads had too much money to be challenged at conventions. Allen frequently corresponded with former senator Charles Van Wyck. The two men discussed forming an antimonopoly party. Van Wyck encouraged Allen to act independently and bring more farmers into the Farmers' Alliance.

As a Populist, Allen was appointed judge of the Nebraska Ninth District Court. He ran for reelection to that post, campaigning against liquor and railroad political power on the People's Independent Party ticket. Allen won with a plurality in that election. In 1892, he was elected state chairman of the People's Party.

In 1893, U.S. senators were elected by the state legislatures. No party commanded a majority in the Nebraska legislature. The election of a U.S. senator required an agreement with two of the parties. Goldbug Democrats, those who favored a single-metal monetary system, acting under orders from President-elect Grover Cleveland, sought to purge Congressman William Jennings Bryan and other Silverites from that party. The goldbugs offered former governor James Boyd and J. Sterling Morton as possible candidates. The Republicans held a caucus to discuss a coalition to elect Morton. Powerful *Omaha Bee* editor and reform Republican Edward Rosewater broke into the caucus to stop the election of the former copperhead. Bryan, with journalist Richard Metcalfe, worked for a Populist-Democrat coalition to elect a Populist. During the election process James Boyd accused Allen of offering him a patronage deal. In a public letter, Allen challenged Boyd to produce evidence of such a meeting. The editors of the *Wealth Makers*, a Lincoln, Nebraska, socialist newspaper, later used the alleged patronage offer when it attempted to gain control of the Nebraska People's Party.

The Populists and Silver Democrats elected Allen to the U.S. Senate as a compromise candidate. He was the only Nebraska Populist and first non-Republican to serve in the Senate. His election automatically made him an enemy of President-elect Cleveland. For his own part, Allen was already on record to organize against Cleveland if Cleveland tried to purge Bryan out of the Democratic Party.

Senators generally refrained from making major speeches in their first year in office. Yet seated next to Kansas Senator William A. Peffer, Allen became a respected Populist speaker in Senate debates. He made major speeches against Cleveland's gold-bond sales. Allen also denounced what he believed was Cleveland's betrayal of a promise to reduce the tariff, and he condemned what he considered a superficial senate investigation of the sugar trust. Allen grew in national stature after a record-setting 15-hour speech against repeal of the Sherman Silver Purchase Act.

Eastern leaders tended to show Allen more respect than other Populists because Allen seemed less outlandish. Allen stood 6 feet 3 inches and weighed about 230 pounds. He possessed an excellent baritone speaking voice. More conservative than most Populists, Allen opposed outright government ownership of major industries, direct elections of senators, and life tenure for civil servants. He believed directly elected senators would eventually destroy the federal system of government. He thought life tenure would create a dictatorial and irresponsible bureaucracy. Allen opposed Coxey's Army but defended their right to march on Washington.

Allen turned down numerous requests to seek the Populist presidential nomination in 1896 because he reported that he did not wish to have the position. Allen predicted that the Democrats would split in 1896, leaving the Republicans unchallenged for 30 years. Allen was later criticized for claiming that the Republicans would spend large sums of money to elect McKinley.

The Populists elected Allen as permanent chairman for the 1896 election. He defeated middle-of-the-road candidate James Campion of Maine. As permanent chairman, he led the move to nominate William Jennings Bryan, arguing it was best to have a unity among currency reform parties. Allen ignored a telegram from Bryan stating that he would turn down the Populist nomination if it meant dropping Democratic vice-presidential candidate Arthur Sewall. After the convention nominated Bryan with Tom Watson of Georgia, Allen, while serving on the interparty coordination committee, worked out details so Bryan could run a fusion campaign with different vice-presidential candidates. Allen officially notified Bryan of the nomination by letter in September 1896. He campaigned for Bryan during the campaign.

In 1899, the Republican-dominated Nebraska legislature voted Allen out of the Senate. Later in 1899 Nebraska Senator Monroe Hayward died while in office. Governor William Poynter appointed Allen, who then served to 1901. *Omaha World-Herald* publisher Gilbert Hitchcock, disgruntled over losing the Senate seat, accused William Jennings Bryan of engineering Allen's appointment. This initiated a Hitchcock-Bryan feud that split the Nebraska Democratic Party. Upon leaving the Senate, Allen returned to Madison County where he operated a successful law practice. He was appointed to the Nebraska Ninth District Court in 1916. He was reelected to that post continually until his death. Allen summarized his political philosophy by claiming all political actions should be governed by Jesus's call to "love thy neighbor as thyself" (*Madison* [NE] *Star-Mail*).

In January 1924, Allen went to Los Angeles to have cancer removed from his tongue. The rapidly spreading cancer required an operation. He died January 12, 1924, due to a reaction to the anesthetics. Nebraska journalist and William Jennings Bryan associate Richard Metcalfe delivered Allen's funeral eulogy.

Randal Craig Fulkerson

See also: Bryan, William Jennings (1860–1925); Coxey's Army; Peffer, William Alfred (1831–1912); Plains and Midwest, Populism in the; Sewall, Arthur M. (1835–1900); St. Louis Convention of 1896; Socialism, Christian; Van Wyck, Charles Henry (1824–1895)

References

Charles Manderson to William V. Allen, 18 February 1893, box 1, Allen Papers, Nebraska Historical Society.

Charles Van Wyck to William V. Allen, 15 November 1889 and 17 December 1889, box 1, Allen Papers, Nebraska Historical Society.

Cherny, Robert. *Populism, Progressivism and the Transformation of Nebraska Politics,*

1885–1915. Lincoln: University of Nebraska Press, 1981.

Coletta, Paolo. "William Jennings Bryan and the Nebraska Senatorial Election of 1893." *Nebraska History* 31 (3): 181–203.

C. W. Phelps to William V. Allen, 21 April 1896, box 1, Allen Papers, Nebraska Historical Society.

Durden, Robert. *The Climax of Populism: The Election of 1896*. Lexington: University of Kentucky Press, 1981.

H. A. Lambert to William V. Allen, 15 July 1896, box 1, William Allen Papers, Nebraska Historical Society.

Hardford [NE] *Telegram,* "William V. Allen," 18 January 1894, scrapbook 1, Allen Papers, Nebraska Historical Society.

London [Ohio] *Times,* "We Raise Senators," 9 February 1893, scrapbook 1, Allen Papers, Nebraska Historical Society.

Madison (NE) *Star-Mail.* "Open Letter to *Wealthmakers.*" May 17, 1895; "Judge Wm. V. Allen Is Back from Coast." August 30, 1923; "Senator William V. Allen Dies Following Operation." January 17, 1924; "Senator William V. Allen Laid to Rest Last Friday." January 24, 1924.

New York World, "A Plea for Coxey," 4 April 1894, scrapbook 2, Allen Papers, Nebraska Historical Society.

Omaha World-Herald. "Allen Is Chairman." July 24, 1896; "Wm. V. Allen Is Senator." December 14, 1899.

Sheldon, Addison E. "William Vincent Allen." *Nebraska History* 19 (3–4): 191–206.

St. Louis Dispatch, "Interview," 30 April 1896, scrapbook 2, Allen Papers, Nebraska Historical Society.

Washington Evening News, untitled article, 19 January 1894, scrapbook 1, Allen Papers, Nebraska Historical Society.

Washington Star, "Forced to Adjourn," 17 October 1893, scrapbook 1, Allen Papers, Nebraska Historical Society.

Alliance

Founded in 1889 by Jay Burrows, the *Alliance* was a publication of the Nebraska Populist movement. Burrows went on to become a major figure in the state's political scenery and used the paper to promote his principles.

The *Alliance* began on June 12, 1889, as a weekly newspaper published out of Lincoln, Nebraska. The earliest issues listed H. G. Armitage as editor, but by September, Burrows had assumed editorship. In December 1889, the name of the publication was changed to *Farmers' Alliance*.

The following year the paper printed a manifesto calling for a convention to nominate Populist candidates for state offices. *Farmers' Alliance* was used to spread the party's platform under Burrows, among them to restore silver as a currency, block land monopolies, create public ownership of railroads and telegraphs, and reduce the work day to eight hours. During the subsequent political campaign, the paper became a vehicle for Burrows's rhetoric while he additionally denounced the opposing opinions of competing newspapers.

Burrows was the newspaper's editor until the spring of 1892 when it merged with another local paper, the *Independent*, to become the *Alliance-Independent* with George Howard Gibson as editor. Under both Burrows and Gibson, the paper maintained a nationalist ideology, inspired by Edward Bellamy's version of socialism in his 1888 novel *Looking Backward*. Gibson additionally added a new Christian slant to the paper's contents, believing not only that money should be distributed equitably but that God's gifts should be shared by all. Following Burrows's lead, Gibson used the paper to promote his viewpoints as a Populist, criticizing the country's unbalanced economic system.

During his tenure as editor, Gibson began looking beyond the economics of Populism, which he ultimately felt promoted individualism over cooperation. His search for a more equitable and generous society was furthered through his growing interest in communal living and farming cooperatives. In response to his shift in personal philosophy, in 1894 Gibson changed the name of his paper to *Wealth Makers of the World.* The publication began to lose readership, however, and in 1896 Gibson sold the paper. He moved to Georgia to found the Christian Commonwealth Colony and edit its newspaper, *Social Gospel.*

Carla W. Garner

See also: Bellamy, Edward (1850–1898); Burrows, Jay (1833–1900); Gilded Age; Kaweah Colony; Plains and Midwest, Populism in the; The Press and Populism; Rochdale Plan; Socialism, Christian

References

Fogarty, Robert S. *All Things New: American Communes and Utopian Movements, 1860–1914.* Chicago: University of Chicago Press, 1990.

Goodwyn, Lawrence. *Democratic Promise: The Populist Moment in America.* New York: Oxford University Press, 1976.

McHugh, Christine. "Midwestern Populist Leadership and Edward Bellamy: 'Looking Backward' into the Future." *American Studies* 19 (2): 57–74.

Pollack, Norman. *The Populist Response to Industrial America: Midwestern Populist Thought.* Cambridge, MA: Harvard University Press, 1962.

Watkins, Albert, ed. *History of Nebraska: From the Earliest Explorations to the Present with Portraits, Maps, and Tables.* Vol. 3. Lincoln, NE: Western Publishing and Engraving, 1913.

Allied Peoples' Party

The Allied People's Party was the last formal national organization that followed the Populists' political teachings. It was the successor of the People's Party, which went down to defeat in the elections of 1896 and 1898. Divided by the issue of fusion with the older Democratic and Republican parties, the People's Party failed to post any notable victories in the election of 1900. As a result, the Allied People's Party, founded in April 1902, tried to offer supporters of almost all reform movements a political home. When the 1904 election cycle rolled around, however, the Allied People's Party failed to attract much notice. It quietly disappeared, and its members departed for other organizations.

In the general elections of 1896, many members of the People's Party reluctantly accepted the idea of fusion with the Democratic Party to support William Jennings Bryan as their candidate for president. Fusion was not seen as a permanent melding of the parties but instead was supposed to be a temporary policy to obtain the goal of issuing more silver coins to increase the money supply. Populists and Democrats usually disagreed on other issues. In the election, Bryan lost to

Republican William McKinley. The failure of fusion strengthened those Populists who believed the party needed to be true to their ideals. Known as the middle-of-the-road Populists, they organized a conference of the People's Party in Nashville, Tennessee, on July 4, 1897, to determine the People's Party's future. Delegates to the Nashville conference organized the National Organization Committee to block further attempts at fusion, if at all possible. Their efforts were not successful in the elections of 1898. The return of some prosperity and improved crop prices led many to abandon the People's Party. Fusionist tickets were formed in the Midwest with the Democrats and in the South with the Republicans. Most of the elections went against the Populists, however, apparently confirming the mid-roaders' opposition to fusion.

In May 1899, the National Organization Committee met in Kansas City, Missouri, to recommend what the People's Party should do in the election of 1900. It called for an end to fusion and threatened to leave the People's Party if the nominating convention in 1900 named a Democrat as the Populist candidate for president. A meeting in Omaha, Nebraska, resulted in a split between fusionists and mid-roaders. The two groups met in separate conventions, in Cincinnati, Ohio, and Sioux Falls, South Dakota, respectively. The fusionists selected Bryan as their presidential nominee again, while the mid-roaders picked Wharton Barker and Ignatius Donnelly as their ticket. Both men were older and lacked the energy for a campaign. The general election was a disaster. Both wings of the People's Party failed to attract significant numbers of votes. Most observers believed the election of 1900 was the end of the People's Party.

A few Populists from the mid-road faction believed their party could be resurrected. They called for a conference of all the reform parties in the United States. The delegates met in Kansas City on September 16, 1901. Representatives of seven parties attended. They included mid-road Populists, fusion Populists, Public Ownership Party members, the Referendum League, the Prohibition Party, Socialists, and the United Christian Party. The platform that the delegates adopted reflected the hopes of many Progressives. It called for public ownership of public utilities, initiative and referendum laws to allow the people to recall elected officials, and "scientific" money issued by the federal government that was not redeemable in gold or silver but was based on the wealth of the nation. The delegates also called for direct election of the president, vice president, federal judges, and U.S. senators by the people. A committee of five was appointed to direct the organization until a national convention was organized, to "unite reform forces against plutocracy" ("Allied People's Party"). The delegates also agreed to call themselves the Allied Party.

The new party met in Louisville, Kentucky, on April 2, 1902. About 200 delegates from eight states attended. The first sessions were noisy and rancorous, but the meeting was dominated from the beginning by members of the People's Party. On April 3, the delegates agreed to form a single party, to be known as the Allied People's Party of the United States. The platform adopted by the convention was virtually identical to the one laid out in Kansas City six months before. Jo A. Parker, a Populist, was named to chair the National Committee and to call future conferences.

On July 5 and 6, 1904, the party met in Springfield, Illinois, to nominate candidates for president and vice president. Thomas E. Watson of Georgia was picked for the top spot, with T. H. Tibbles of Nebraska as his running mate. They attracted few votes in the general election. Four years later, the party again nominated Watson, with as little effect on the general election. By that time, many of the issues that had brought the Allied People's Party together had been adopted by the Republicans and Democrats, helping to end the reason for the party's existence.

Tim J. Watts

See also: Bryan, William Jennings (1860–1925); Democratic Party; Donnelly, Ignatius (1831–1901); Middle of the Road Populists; People's Party; Progressivism; Prohibition (1919–1933); Third Parties; Tibbles, Thomas Henry (1840–1928)

References

"Allied People's Party." *New York Times*, April 4, 1902.

Hicks, John D. *The Populist Revolt: A History of the Farmers' Alliance and the People's Party*. Lincoln: University of Nebraska Press, 1961.

Altgeld, John P. (1847–1902)

John Peter Altgeld served as governor of Illinois during a tumultuous period of labor history. He supported the rights of workers against the large corporations, even while he tried to keep law and order. Altgeld also supported a progressive social agenda, including an increased money supply, more government support for public education, and anti-imperialism.

Altgeld was born on December 30, 1847, in the village of Nieder Selters in Nassau in southern Germany. When he was less than a year old, his parents immigrated to the United States and settled near Mansfield, Ohio. Altgeld received little formal education before working full time on the family farm when he was 12 years old. When Altgeld was 16, he lied about his age and joined the 64th Ohio Infantry Regiment and fought in the Civil War. Like many of his fellow soldiers, Altgeld caught malaria and nearly died. Although

John Peter Altgeld was the outspoken reform governor of Illinois in the 1890s. (Library of Congress)

he survived and fought until the end of the war, the illness affected him the rest of his life. Altgeld returned to the family farm but also studied at a neighbor's private library and at a private school in Lexington, Ohio. He received a teaching certificate and taught school for two years.

In 1869, Altgeld proposed to a fellow teacher, but her father thought he was too poor to marry her. He moved west, literally to seek his fortune. After working on a railroad crew in Arkansas and southern Kansas, Altgeld settled in northwest Missouri. He read law and set up a practice in Savannah, Missouri, in 1871. Three years later, voters recognized his abilities by electing him county prosecutor. In 1875, Altgeld resigned to move to Chicago, where greater opportunities were available. He set up a successful law practice and also made a fortune in buying and selling real estate and investing in street railways. He married his former fellow teacher in 1877 after achieving prosperity. Altgeld considered his most satisfying real estate accomplishment the construction of the Unity Building in 1891. The 16-story building was Chicago's tallest building at the time, located in the heart of the city. Mistakes and cost overruns drained much of Altgeld's personal fortune, but the building became a local landmark for years.

Altgeld's struggles gave him a sympathy for the underdog and for the downtrodden, which influenced the course of his life. His law firm hired talented lawyers with radical views, such as Clarence Darrow. Altgeld was a supporter of institutions that tried to better the conditions of the poor, such as Hull House, founded by Jane Addams. In 1875, he published *Our Penal Machinery and Its Victims*, which argued that the U.S. criminal system favored the rich over the poor. It also claimed that prisons failed to reform inmates but turned them into career criminals instead. Altgeld called for speedier trials and an end to paying prosecutors according to the number of convictions they obtained.

A lifelong Democrat, Altgeld was interested in politics as a way to improve society. In 1884, he ran for the Congress in Illinois's Fourth Congressional District. Although the district was heavily Republican, Altgeld received more than 45 percent of the votes, better than other Democratic candidates. Two years later, he was successfully elected to a Cook County Superior Court judgeship, with backing from both labor and the Democrats. In 1890, Altgeld became the chief judge of the court. He resigned in 1891 to concentrate on his business activities.

In 1892, the Democrats nominated Altgeld for governor at their state convention. He spoke all over the state and narrowly defeated the Republican incumbent, Joseph W. Fifer. Altgeld became the first Democrat to be elected governor of Illinois since 1856, but his health suffered from the strain of the campaign. He suffered a nervous breakdown after the victory, and then his malaria returned. Altgeld was only able to deliver a part of his inauguration speech before being forced to leave.

Despite his rocky start, Altgeld was an active governor and promoted progressive causes and social reform. He managed to get a law enacted for an eight-hour day for women, which was later rejected by the Illinois Supreme Court. Bills for labor arbitration, court reform, and penal reform failed to win legislative approval. A bill to prevent discrimination against members of trade unions failed to pass. Altgeld convinced the legislature to approve a larger appropriation for the University of Illinois. He also expanded state parks and introduced competitive bidding for state contracts. Altgeld appointed a number of women to state offices. One of the most notable was Florence Kelley, who was chief factory inspector for the state.

Altgeld may be best remembered for several incidents involving violence related to labor unrest. In the spring of 1886, a national effort calling for eight-hour days was underway. A strike at the McCormick Harvest Works took place to force the company to accept this measure. On May 4, a demonstration took place in support of the strikers at Haymarket Square in Chicago. As the rally was breaking up, policemen ordered the crowd to disperse. An unknown person threw a bomb at the police, killing one and wounding others. The police fired into the crowd, killing at least four. A round-up of anarchists followed. Eight men were convicted of murder. Four were executed, one committed suicide, and three were sentenced to long prison terms. The trial was widely seen as a miscarriage of justice, with evidence against the men being questionable. When Altgeld became governor, he was approached by those who wanted pardons for the three remaining Haymarket conspirators. After studying the trial transcripts and the evidence, Altgeld issued pardons for all three on June 26, 1893. He stressed the need to preserve law and order, but he condemned the trial as unfair. Officials had manufactured evidence and invented conspiracies to obtain the glory of discovering them, according to Altgeld's pardon. Although conservative and business interests condemned Altgeld's decision, workers were firmly on his side.

A year later, business and conservative leaders again condemned Altgeld for allegedly siding with workers. On May 11, 1894, the workers at the Pullman Corporation went on strike to protest a cut in wages. The company manufactured railroad sleeping cars and related equipment. Altgeld refused to call out the militia to break the strike, as long as it was peaceful. The company turned to the federal government. Attorney General Richard Olney obtained an injunction against the strikers forbidding them from interfering with railroad operations because the railroads carried the U.S. mail. Without Altgeld's permission, President Grover Cleveland ordered several thousand federal soldiers into the Chicago area. Altgeld was incensed at this breach of his authority over his state. He did call out the militia when violence broke out and Chicago's mayor asked for help. The strike collapsed several days later when the leaders were arrested under the terms of Olney's injunction.

Altgeld was determined to break Cleveland's influence over the Democratic Party. He felt that Cleveland had supported the wealthy against the working men. In 1895, Altgeld called for a special convention of the state Democratic Party on the question of money. The meeting came out in favor of issuing silver coins to increase the amount of money in circulation. They believed it would help farmers and workers. Other states followed Altgeld's example.

At the 1896 Democratic National Convention, Altgeld was a leader of the silver forces. The convention passed a free-silver plank, a prolabor plank, an anti-injunction plank, a pro–income tax plank, a plank on personal and civil liberties, and a plank reaffirming the principles of federalism, a direct repudiation of Cleveland's dispatch of troops to the Pullman strike. The party's nominee was William Jennings Bryan, best known for his support of silver currency. Although Bryan was not Altgeld's first choice, he supported the candidate and campaigned for him. Republicans attacked Bryan through Altgeld, calling the governor an anarchist and a murderer. In the general election of 1896, Bryan was defeated. Altgeld himself ran for reelection as governor, but was also defeated.

Altgeld's defeat marked the end of his political success. He ran for mayor of Chicago in 1899. Although an early favorite, he finished a poor third. The defeat was symptomatic of a general decline. He had been in poor health since the Civil War and had suffered from locomotor ataxia from the early 1890s. This condition made it hard for him to walk. Altgeld lost most of his personal fortune in the Panic of 1893 and would have been completely ruined if not for Clarence Darrow. Darrow gave Altgeld a position in his law firm and allowed him to continue to speak out for the underdog. On March 12, 1902, Altgeld traveled to Joliet after a day in court. While speaking to a crowd on behalf of the Boers, then fighting against a British invasion, Altgeld collapsed on stage. He suffered a cerebral hemorrhage and died later that evening. His funeral was held at the Chicago Public Library after thousands had filed past his body. Jane Addams and Clarence Darrow spoke at the services.

Tim J. Watts

See also: Addams, Jane (1860–1935); Bryan, William Jennings (1860–1925); Cleveland, Grover (1837–1908); Darrow, Clarence (1857–1938); Democratic Party; Gold Standard/Free Silver; Haymarket Riot (1886); Pullman Strike (1894)

References

Altgeld, John Peter. *The Mind and Spirit of John Peter Altgeld: Selected Writings and Addresses.* Urbana: University of Illinois Press, 1960.

Barnard, Harry. *Eagle Forgotten: The Life of John Peter Altgeld.* Indianapolis: The Bobbs-Merrill Co., 1938.

Ginger, Ray. *Altgeld's America: The Lincoln Ideal versus Changing Realities.* New York: Funk & Wagnalls, 1958.

American Federation of Labor (AFL)

The American Federation of Labor was one of the first organized federations of labor unions in the United States. Founded in 1886 by Samuel Gompers, an immigrant of Dutch and Jewish ancestry and leader of the Cigarmakers Union, the AFL was a disaffected alliance of craft unions that had previously been members of the Knights of

Labor. Prior to Gompers's founding of the AFL, the Knights of Labor had been the dominant force in union organizing during the 1880s. The Knights actively promoted a type of workers' democracy that included a broad spectrum of reform including free land, income taxes, and public ownership of railroads, equal pay for women, and the abolition of child labor. From its inception, the public did not think much of the AFL's chances for organizational success. However, Gompers believed otherwise. The leader of the Cigarmakers Union argued that labor must conform to the mores of its society rather than attempt to radically alter society. For Gompers, the AFL endured because the federation managed to defend the rights of its members against the values of the industrial age. Gompers's major contribution to the American labor movement was the implementation of an organization structure known as "new unionism" or "business unionism." This meant that the AFL limited its actions to economic and political methods approved by the American capitalist system. As the principal organizer, Gompers drew upon his own understanding of American society, developing distinct labor policies and imposing them upon the organization. His initial interest in the Cigarmakers Union came from its fraternal benefits for workers rather than from its economic function. Gompers specifically developed the AFL because he feared that changing economic conditions threatened his trade. Ultimately, the Cigarmakers Union was ineffective at protecting its members against mechanization and hostile employers. Along with a select group of allies, Gompers formed his new local union and structured the federation much like the British trade unions. This new union employed innovative methods of strikes, boycotts, and negotiations to meet the demands of the American workplace.

In the same manner as the founders of the Knights, the AFL union was initially interested in promoting utopian social reforms. Gompers and the leaders of the AFL even experimented at one point with the idea of forming a workers' political party. However, populist idealism soon gave way to practical concerns, and this led the union to focus on bread-and-butter issues such as higher wages for workers and reduced hours. Gompers's approach was to organize skilled workers with bargaining power and use strikes to achieve their shared objectives. When it was founded in 1886, the union only had 138,000 members, compared to the 730,000 in the Knights of Labor. However, pivotal events such as the Haymarket Riot resulted in the dissolution of the Knights and led Gompers and the AFL to become the dominant force in the labor union movement. As the Knights faded out of existence, the federation gained strength, and AFL unions became important in major industrial cities. In the urban centers, the union opened central labor offices to organize the actions of various AFL-affiliated unions. In the 1890s most strikes were assertions of jurisdiction. Plumbers, for example, used labor strikes to make certain that all construction projects in the city employed union workers. The AFL's political power came from its status as a collective federation. The central union's effectiveness developed from its exceptional ability to unite disparate craft unions under common goals. To achieve their goals, the central federation needed the support of other unions to demonstrate labor solidarity. As such, individual laborers could not exclusively join the AFL; members had to be affiliated with a participating union.

As president of the federation, Gompers actively promoted harmony among the different craft unions that made up the AFL. Primarily focused on higher wages and job security, the AFL was against socialism and the Socialist Party of America. Gompers was no fan of capitalism, yet he vehemently demanded a fair share for labor. The federation lobbied for "a pure and simple unionism . . . better wages, hours and working conditions" (Bailey 539). After 1907 the union formed alliances with the Democratic Party at the local, state, and national levels. The AFL actively supported the United States' war effort in World War I and saw rapid growth in membership and a rise in the wages of its affiliated workers. The AFL was always hostile to communists, primarily because they were a powerful force inside the rival Congress of Industrial Organizations (CIO). The AFL boycotted the World Federation of Trade Unions due to its decision to admit Soviet labor unions. The AFL established a confederation of free trade unions, the International Confederation of Free Trade Unions, which eventually garnered the support of all labor confederations with the exception of those of the Soviet Union and its satellites. The AFL increased and added more members during the very rapid growth period of the late 1930s and the World War II period, yet it avoided the radicalism of the CIO.

The principle method of agitation advocated by the federation was the strike, which was employed to win concessions from employers and to attract recruits. Commenting on the mission of the AFL, Gompers once told a left-wing French politician, "I have my own philosophy and my own dreams, but first and foremost I want to increase the workingman's welfare year by year. . . . The French workers waste their economic force by their political divisions" (Carnes 627). As president of the AFL from 1886 until his death in 1924, Gompers encouraged members to make "intelligent use of the ballot" to further their interests. The AFL's approach to labor issues proved highly successful. Unions with membership of nearly 150,000 workers made up the federation in 1886. In 1892, the federation's membership had risen to 250,000, and by 1901 it had surpassed the 1 million mark.

Christopher Allan Black

See also: Gompers, Samuel (1850–1924); Haymarket Riot (1886); Knights of Labor

References

Bailey, Thomas A., David M. Kennedy, and Elizabeth Cohen. *The American Pageant: A History of the Republic.* Boston: Houghton Mifflin, 1998.

Carnes, Mark C., and John A. Garraty. *American Destiny: Narrative of a Nation.* Vol. 2. New York: Penguin, 2003.

Livesay, Harold C. *Samuel Gompers and Organized Labor in America.* Boston: Little Brown, 1978.

Mandel, Bernard. "Gompers and Business Unionism, 1873–90." *Business History Review* 28 (3): 264–75.

American Non-Conformist

The *American Non-Conformist* was first published in 1879 in Tabor, Iowa, by Leopold and Henry Vincent as a weekly journal devoted to greenback and later union labor causes. In 1886, the Vincent brothers moved the paper to Winfield, Kansas, renamed their journal *The American Non-Conformist and Kansas Industrial Liberator*, and continued to embrace a Union Labor Party outlook. In 1891, the Vincent brothers again moved the paper, this time to Indianapolis, where they hoped the paper would prompt the growth of Indiana's new People's Party. In the mid-1890s, the *Non-Conformist* was estimated to have a weekly circulation of 30,000.

In the paper's inaugural Kansas issue on October 7, 1886, the Vincent brothers asserted that the purpose of the *Non-Conformist* was to educate farmers, workers, and producers in matters important to them, and it would strive to "take the side of the oppressed as against the oppressor." This continued the tone that the paper had taken in Iowa, where the Vincents had described their paper as dedicated to fighting against wage slavery to railroads and to the wealthy and powerful. Over its first few years in Kansas, the *Non-Conformist* became a leading voice of Populism in Kansas and the Midwest, and its editors joined other reform-minded journalists in forming the National Reform Press Association.

The editors consistently railed against attempts to water down the Populist message. In 1888, for example, the *Non-Conformist* argued that it was absurd that reformist Republicans could seriously advocate change through existing GOP structures. In 1891, it maintained that the election of brand-new converts to Populism "would sound to the world as a very mediocre type of reform" (January 15, 1891). And in 1895, the paper strongly argued for upholding the Omaha Platform instead of surrendering to the fusionists who wanted to transform the People's Party into a single-issue silver party.

The Vincents lost control of the *Non-Conformist* in the Panic of 1893. The paper itself did not long survive the disintegration of the People's Party after the election of 1896. The *Non-Conformist* moved to Omaha, Nebraska, in 1898 and was published through 1899.

Kirstin L. Lawson

See also: Greenback Party; Omaha Contract; People's Party; Plains and Midwest, Populism in the; The Press and Populism; Silver Republicans

References

Argersinger, Peter H. *Populism and Politics: William Alfred Peffer and the People's Party.* Lexington: University Press of Kentucky, 1974.

Goldberg, Michael Lewis. *An Army of Women: Gender and Politics in Gilded Age Kansas.* Baltimore, MD: Johns Hopkins University Press, 1997.

Goodwyn, Lawrence. *The Populist Moment: A Short History of the Agrarian Revolt in America.* Oxford, UK: Oxford University Press, 1978.

Anarchism

Anarchists advocate for the replacement of governments with a system of willing cooperation of individuals. Like Populism, anarchism champions common people and seeks to protect them from corrupt rulers and exploitative employers. Anarchism attempts to achieve this goal by reducing or eliminating government—unlike Populism, which typically looks to reform and strengthen government to protect workers and farmers from wealthy elites. Anarchism is a libertarian variant of socialism that dates back at least as far as the seventeenth century, when the term first appeared in the English language. Anarchistic thought influenced the American Revolution, played a role in outbreaks of nineteenth-century labor violence, and led to the political assassinations of Presidents James Garfield and William McKinley. While diminished in popularity since its heyday in the late nineteenth century, anarchism remains an influential philosophy among modern critics of globalization and environmental destruction.

Anarchism's American roots go back to the nation's Founding Fathers, and it gained popularity in the last years of the nineteenth century as a wave of European exiles brought a revitalized anarchism to the United States. A key leader was Johann Most, a Bavarian politician and author, who fled to the United States in 1882 after serving time in a British prison for expressing his gratitude to the killers of Russia's Alexander II. In the United States, European anarchists discovered fertile ground among increasingly radical labor movements attempting to improve the lives of workers. Some anarchists, including Most, advocated violence, but others called for peaceful resistance. The popular urban press often failed to grasp the distinction and argued that all assassins were anarchists.

In 1880, Charles Guiteau turned his attention to politics after failing as a preacher, author, theologian, lawyer, and publisher. He wrote a speech for the presidential campaign of James Garfield and convinced himself that his support tipped the scales in Garfield's favor. After Garfield's inauguration, Guiteau unsuccessfully petitioned the administration for a job, and he consequently felt convinced that God had wanted him to assassinate Garfield. On July 2, 1881 Guiteau pumped two bullets from a Webley revolver into the president at close range, inflicting wounds that led to an infection that killed Garfield on September 19. A jury rejected his plea of insanity and sentenced him to the gallows, where he died on June 30. Although there is no evidence that Guiteau ever espoused anarchism, journalists began to refer to him as an anarchist years later as labor unrest increased. These accounts categorized various figures (including Guiteau and even John Wilkes Booth) who offered violent opposition to the government as anarchists.

During the months of April and May 1886, Americans witnessed a series of strikes as workers demanded an eight-hour work day and increased wages. These conflicts escalated into violence in several locations, with the most famous outbreak in Chicago's Haymarket Square. Following a lethal clash between police and a crowd on May 3, labor leaders held a rally at Haymarket Square on May 4. When police demanded the crowd's dispersal, someone threw a bomb, killing policeman

Matthias Degan almost instantly. The police panicked and opened fire with their revolvers. Seven police officers were killed, and dozens of police and protesters were wounded. A police official confided to the *Chicago Tribune* that most of the wounds, of both civilians and police, resulted from police bullets rather than bomb fragments.

The police quickly arrested several hundred labor leaders and protesters. Authorities were unable to determine who threw the bomb, so they placed eight prominent labor leaders on trial, seven of whom were not present when the bomb exploded, and argued that their rhetoric alone made them guilty of murder. Judge Joseph E. Gary instructed the jury that the prosecutor proved the defendants guilty if he could demonstrate that they were anarchists. The jury found all eight defendants guilty and sentenced seven to death. Before the executions could proceed, one defendant committed suicide and Illinois Governor Richard J. Oglesby reduced two of the death sentences to life in prison. On November 11, 1887, the four remaining men died on the gallows. Labor leader George Engel shouted "Hurray for Anarchy" in his native German moments before his death. In 1893, Governor John Peter Altgeld granted pardons to the surviving three men, citing errors in Judge Gary's rulings and problems with the prosecution's evidence. Incidents of labor violence, such as Haymarket, convinced a young man to strike a blow against the state.

Leon Czolgosz was born to a poor family of Polish immigrants in 1873. After working on a farm and in a wire mill, he suffered a mental breakdown in 1898. Later that year, he became interested in labor movements and anarchism. In May 1901, he attended a lecture by the famed anarchist Emma Goldman. After the lecture he approached her, and she introduced him to some of her anarchist friends. These activists quickly rejected Czologsz for his disturbingly violent fantasies, and some wondered if he was a police informant. On September 5 Czologsz wrapped a revolver in a handkerchief and attended a public speech by President McKinley. Afterwards, he walked up to the president and fired two shots into his chest. The president's bodyguards immediately grabbed the assassin and beat him as McKinley urged them to "Be easy with him, boys." The president died of infection on September 14.

Czologsz told investigators that he was inspired to kill McKinley by Goldman's speeches. Goldman denied any conspiracy but claimed to sympathize with his actions, which she saw as an idealistic attempt to help workers. He was quickly convicted and sentenced to death for the assignation. Czolgosz claimed to feel no remorse for killing McKinley, who Czolgosz saw as an enemy to the working class. He died in the electric chair on October 20, but the violence did not. The American labor movement continued to contain strains of anarchistic thought until at least the 1920s when a series of strikes once again erupted into bloodshed.

Anarchism reemerged in the 1970s as environmentalists such as Edward Abbey encouraged vandalism in defense of nature. In 1999, more than 40,000 protesters, including labor unionists, environmentalists, church activists, and anarchists, descended on Seattle to voice their opposition to the World Trade Organization's meeting. While most protesters, including the anarchists, adhered to a strict policy of nonviolent opposition, others clashed with police and vandalized businesses. Labor leaders told the protesters that if they joined together in a new populist coalition of trade unions, environmentalists, and human rights advocates they could wrestle power from the elites of the World Trade Organization. Anarchists in Greece and Italy recently threw rocks and mailed bombs, but security experts expressed little concern over the violence. One expert, quoted in *Time* magazine, stated that the anarchists occasionally attack in an effort simply to demonstrate their continued existence. Although denounced, imprisoned, ignored, and even executed, anarchists do continue to exist. Ultimately they, and they alone, will write the conclusion to their story.

Christopher Thrasher

See also: Altgeld, John P. (1847–1902); Czolgosz, Leon (1873–1901); Environmentalism; Goldman, Emma (1864–1940); Gilded Age; Haymarket Riot (1886); Knights of Labor; McKinley, William, Jr. (1843–1901); Pullman Strike (1894)

References

Burgan, Michael. *The Haymarket Square Tragedy.* Minneapolis, MN: Compass Point Books, 2006.

Peskin, Allan. *Garfield: A Biography.* Kent, OH: Kent State University Press, 1978.

Tharoor, Ishaan. "A Brief History of Anarchism: The European Tradition." *Time.* http://www.time.com/time/world/article/0,8599,2040304,00.html. Accessed January 2, 2013.

Thompson, Rustin, and Ann Hedreen. *30 Frames a Second: The WTO in Seattle.* DVD, 72 min. Bullfrog Films, Inc., Oley, PA, 2000.

Anderson, Sherwood (1876–1941)

Sherwood Anderson was a fiction writer who chronicled small-town American life and seemed to speak with the voices of the people. He published his first novel at the age of 40, *Windy McPherson's Son*, in 1916. He published eight more novels, three collections of short stories, two notable memoirs, and several other books of nonfiction prior to his death on March 8, 1941. His most famous book is *Winesburg, Ohio: A Group of Tales of Small-Town Life* (1919). Even today, this set of tales set in a fictional midwestern town is considered one of the greatest works of American literature.

Sherwood Anderson was born September 13, 1876, in Camden, Ohio. He was the third of seven children born to Irwin M. and Emma Smith Anderson. When Sherwood was eight, the Anderson family moved to Clyde, Ohio, after his father's business failed. Reportedly, the Anderson family was one of the poorest families in Clyde. It was not long before Sherwood had to share some responsibilities of providing for his family, which caused him to neglect his education.

In 1896, a year after his mother's death, Sherwood Anderson moved in with his brother Karl. He worked as a manual laborer until he enlisted in the army, where he served in Cuba during the Spanish-American War. After his discharge Anderson returned to

Chicago where he worked for Crowell Publishing Company.

In 1900, Anderson moved back to Ohio to attend Wittenberg Academy. He married his first wife, Cornelia Lane, soon after. His desire at this period was to be a professional businessman, but he seemed ill prepared for such a venture despite managing a mail-order business and two different paint manufacturing firms. In 1912, Sherwood suffered psychological problems, causing him to abandon both his family and his business career. Supposedly, he walked out of his office while dictating a letter. Several days later he was found in a hospital in Cleveland, Ohio. Unable to reconcile this aberrant behavior with either his wife or his employer, he moved back to Chicago.

Sherwood Anderson published his first novel, *Windy McPherson's Son*, in 1916. His second novel, *Marching Men*, was published two years later. *Winesburg, Ohio* appeared in 1919, and overnight Anderson became one of the giants of American letters.

Similar to Jean Toomer's *Cane*, *Winesburg, Ohio* is a series of vignettes—sometimes called a composite novel or short-story cycle—that are linked by a predominant theme or themes. Whereas *Cane* evokes the experiences of African Americans in both the North and South during the first decades of the twentieth century, *Winesburg, Ohio* is set in a small town in which everybody calls their neighbors by their first names.

It is widely accepted that his former hometown, Clyde, Ohio, and its residents inspired Anderson. Curiously enough, Anderson and Toomer were correspondents during the time Toomer was writing *Cane*, and Anderson is said to have given literary advice to the younger writer. Both collections are considered early examples of literary modernism.

During this period Anderson was generous toward other writers, including William Faulkner. He helped get Faulkner's first novel, *Soldier's Pay* (1926), published, and he wrote a letter of introduction to Gertrude Stein for Ernest Hemingway. Unfortunately, both Faulkner and Hemingway broke with Anderson after they had established their careers. However, Faulkner never forgot the debt he owed the older writer. In "Sherwood Anderson: An Appreciation," he wrote that Anderson's *Winesburg, Ohio*, his collection of short stories in *The Triumph of the Egg* (1921), and several other short stories in *Horses and Men* (1923), made him realize that at his best Anderson had been a giant in an earth populated by pygmies.

Although Anderson published three successful collections of short stories, *The Triumph of the Egg* (1921), *Horses and Men* (1923), and *Death in the Words and Other Tales* (1933), his novels after the publication of *Poor White* (1920), *Many Marriages* (1923), *Dark Laughter* (1925), *Tar: A Midwest Childhood* (1926), *Alice and the Lost Novel* (1929), *Beyond Desire* (1932), and *Kit Brandon: A Portrait* (1936), never received the critical acclaim that he enjoyed earlier in his career. However, he did write two notable memoirs:*A Story Teller's Story* (1924) and *Sherwood Anderson's Notebooks* (1926).

Anderson also suffered in his personal life. His marriage to his second wife,

Tennessee Mitchel, ended in divorce in 1924. The following year he married his third wife, Elizabeth Prall. They bought farmland beside Ripshin Creek, about four miles outside of Troutdale, Virginia. They called their house Ripshin Farm. 1n 1927, Anderson bought the Marion Publishing Company in Marion, Virginia, and he became editor of two weekly newspapers. The articles he wrote during this period were collected in a book called *Hello Towns!* (1929).

His marriage to Elizabeth Prall ended in 1928, and he married Eleanor Copenhaver in 1933. He and his new wife traveled extensively. They were en route to South America, aboard the cruise liner *Santa Lucia*, when he developed peritonitis from accidentally swallowing a toothpick. He was taken to the hospital in Colon, Panama, where he died March 8, 1941.

Sherwood Anderson was interred at the Round Hill Cemetery in Marion, Virginia. As he had requested, the inscription on his gravestone read: "Life, Not Death, is the Great Adventure."

John G. Hall

See also: Department Stores and Mail Order Catalogs; Gilded Age; Modernism

References

Anderson, Sherwood. *Sherwood Anderson: Collected Stories: Winesburg, Ohio/ Triumph of the Egg/Horses and Men/Death in the Woods/Uncollected Short Stories*. New York: Library of America, 2012.

Anderson, Sherwood. *A Story Teller's Story*. Bel Air, CA: Book Jungle, 2008.

Anderson, Sherwood. *Windy McPherson's Son*. Urbana: University of Illinois Press, 1993.

Anderson, Sherwood. *Winesburg, Ohio*. Edited by Charles E. Modlin and Ray Lewis White. New York: W. W. Norton & Company, 1996.

Esplugas, Celia. "Sherwood Anderson's *Beyond Desire* and the Industrial South." *Mississippi Quarterly: The Journal of Southern Cultures* 63 (3/4): 655–78.

Whalan, Mark. *Race, Manhood, and Modernism in America: The Short Story Cycles of Sherwood Anderson and Jean Toomer*. Knoxville: University of Tennessee Press, 2007.

Antigay Populism

Proposition 6, also known as the Briggs Initiative, appeared on the California ballot in 1978. It was designed to ban any educator "who engages in public homosexual activity and/or public homosexual conduct directed at, or likely to come to the attention of schoolchildren or other school employees." State Senator John Briggs, a Catholic Republican from Orange County with aspirations to run for governor, sponsored the initiative. Through Proposition 6, Briggs and his supporters sought to rescind a 1975 California law prohibiting sexual discrimination against teachers and to assert the "fundamental interests of the State" in "preserving and perpetuating the conjugal family unit" and promoting heterosexuality. The appearance of the homosexual-teacher issue on the California ballot provoked a statewide mobilization of both conservative evangelicals and of gay rights activists and their supporters, and it sparked a widespread debate about the meaning and practice of sexual rights and freedoms. The proposition also signaled the coming of age of "family values politics" for social and religious conservative groups, which used this political campaign to agitate for social change, to sensitize the public to their values, and to create new reactionary and populist coalitions of like-minded citizens.

The proposition, which came on the heels of a nationwide debate over homosexuality, marked the growing importance of gay rights and evangelical activism in U.S. electoral and cultural politics. Briggs and his church-based advocacy group, California's Save Our Children (SOC), emerged directly from a political struggle over gay rights in Dade County, Florida. In 1977, after commissioners in Dade County passed a human-rights ordinance that prohibited discrimination on the basis of "sexual or affectional preference" in the areas of housing, employment, and public accommodations, a coalition of conservatives named Save Our Children emerged (Stanger 18-A). SOC rallied support around the ideas of child protection and parents' rights. It protested the ordinance on the grounds that it would allow gay teachers to corrupt children by acting as "role models" or to molest children. The group's spokesperson was Anita Bryant, a former Miss America runner-up (Miss Oklahoma) renowned at the time as the national spokesperson for Florida Citrus, her Christian literature, and for her best-selling pop albums. Signaling SOC's agenda, Bryant infamously declared that "recruitment of our children is absolutely necessary for the survival and growth of homosexuality—for since homosexuals cannot reproduce, they must recruit, must freshen their ranks" (Bryant 62, "Gay Law" 3-B). After a highly publicized campaign, Dade County voters overwhelmingly rejected the gay-rights ordinance in June 1977.

SOC's campaign, which drew national attention and the support of prominent conservative activists across the country, sharpened a conservative rhetoric of child protection and enshrined a strategy of using referendums to politicize homosexuality. After the Dade County vote, church-based conservative groups in Kansas, Oregon, Washington, and Minnesota sought to repeal municipal gay rights laws through referendums. Dade County served as the blueprint for all of these antigay campaigns, which asserted that gay teachers sought to molest children or convert them into homosexuals. It likewise provided the impetus for Proposition 6 in California. The day after the Dade County vote, California State Senator John Briggs, who had campaigned for SOC in Florida, declared his intention to pass a law in his home state that would prohibit homosexual teachers. Building off a sex education controversy in San Francisco and the state legislature's recent restriction of marriage to heterosexuals, Briggs sponsored a bill in the California legislature to ban gay teachers. Failing to achieve the support in the Senate necessary to pass the law, Briggs decided to advance his cause by placing the question of gay teachers on a statewide referendum. His aspirations were not only based upon the recent municipal backlashes against gay rights but also upon the success of Proposition 13 in California, which was a conservative-sponsored antitax measure that passed in June of 1978.

With the assistance of evangelical churches, Briggs quickly obtained half-a-million signatures, far more than required, to have his antigay measure placed on the November ballot. Anita Bryant and evangelist Jerry Falwell actively supported Brigg's campaign. Early public opinion polling showed that the initiative was heading toward an easy passage with the majority of Californians supporting the measure. However, unlike earlier antigay campaigns that responded to the passage of gay rights laws, Proposition 6 required the state to actively prosecute educators who privately engaged in consenting same-sex sexual behavior. It further mandated firing those educators who in any way supported gay rights regardless of sexual orientation. This difference set the stage for mass mobilization against Proposition 6 that crossed the political spectrum.

Briggs's efforts invigorated activism in the very communities that Proposition 6 threatened. California's gay and lesbian communities and their supporters around the country were galvanized to a heightened level of activism and participation in the political process. Many opponents of the Briggs Initiative emphasized human rights themes to attract supporters who might otherwise be opposed to homosexuality. Yet many of these activists broke new ground when they spoke openly and directly about homophobia and gay liberation, including San Francisco county supervisor and gay activist Harvey Milk, the only openly gay elected official in California. Milk gained increased prominence within the gay community after he debated Briggs over gay rights. Likewise, gay churches, teachers groups, and civil rights organizations raised funds and awareness to challenge the law.

Numerous straight allies including liberal groups and teachers' unions also voiced opposition to the bill, as did religious leaders from mainline Protestant, Jewish, and some Catholic congregations. Likewise, major newspapers in California editorialized against the Briggs Initiative. Further turning the tide against the bill were the voices of prominent conservative politicians such as Ronald Reagan, who described the bill as excessive, costly, and having "the potential of infringing basic rights of privacy and perhaps even constitutional rights" (West A26). Far from affirming same-sex sexuality, these straight opponents of Proposition 6 believed it to be an unconstitutional law and a violation of personal privacy. At stake in the debate were not simply gay rights but whether the state should investigate and police consenting adults' sexual practices. Ultimately, California voters defeated the initiative by a 58–42 percent margin.

Proposition 6 became the stage for one of the most extensive debates on antigay prejudice to that date. It allowed opponents of Proposition 6 to argue coherently and extensively on behalf of gay rights on a wide political stage. Yet, despite its failure, Proposition 6 had far-reaching implications for conservative and reactionary populist movements. It politicized evangelical pastors and churchgoers, who continued their activism, and drew them into closer relationships with socially conservative Republicans. The national implications of Proposition 6 were seen in the institutionalization of evangelicals' antigay rhetoric and strategies within religious conservative coalitions that gained increasing influence at the end of the decade. Louis Sheldon, a key member of California's SOC, founded the Traditional Values Coalition, which by the 1980s became a preeminent anti-gay-rights group. Also inspired by the Briggs Initiative were California ministers Robert Grant and Richard Zone, who in 1979 founded Christian Voice, the first large-scale Christian Right lobbying organization. Christian Voice acted as the lobbying arm of the three-year-old American Christian Cause, which merged preexisting antigay, antipornography, and pro-family groups on the West Coast. Jerry Falwell's Moral Majority, which formed the bedrock of the Christian Right, likewise placed the issue of gay rights at the center of its conservative coalition. The long-term legacies of Proposition 6 are more difficult to evaluate. To date, no similar measure has been passed. Using referendums and the idea that gays and lesbians will threaten children and families, however, to this day remains a powerful tool for right-wing groups to use to stoke populist sentiments against gay marriage.

Gillian Frank

See also: Evangelicalism and Populism; Proposition 13 (1978); Sagebrush Rebellion

References

Bryant, Anita. *The Anita Bryant Story.* Old Tappan, NJ: F.H. Revell, 1977.

D'Emilio, John. *Making Trouble: Essays on Gay History, Politics, and the University.* New York: Routledge, 1992.

Faderman, Lillian. *Gay L.A.: A History of Sexual Outlaws, Power Politics, and Lipstick Lesbians.* New York: Basic Books, 2006.

Frank, Gillian. " 'The Civil Rights of Parents': Race and Conservative Politics in Anita Bryant's Campaign against Gay Rights." *Journal of the History of Sexuality* 22 (1) (2013).

"Gay Law Foes to Plan Vote Drive." *Miami Herald*, January 26, 1977, 3-B.

Hollibaugh, Amber L. *My Dangerous Desires: A Queer Girl Dreaming Her Way Home.* Durham, NC: Duke University Press, 2000.

Howard, Clayton. "The Closet and the Cul de Sac: Sex, Politics, and Suburbanization in Postwar California." Dissertation, University of Michigan, 2010.

Stanger, Theodore. "Dade Approves Ordinance Banning Bias against Gays." *Miami Herald*, January 19, 1977, 18-A.

West, Richard. "Prop. 6 Dangerous, Reagan Believes." *Los Angeles Times*, September 23, 1978, A26.

Anti-Imperialism/Colonialism

Imperialism and colonialism are two sides of a historic situation that peaked in the nineteenth and twentieth centuries when many parts of the globe suffered occupation by powerful Western nations. The basis of colonial occupation is the exploitation of peoples and natural resources without concern for the social, political, and cultural destruction of the occupied populations. While imperialism is the ideological component of the occupation, that is, justifying the exploitation on grounds of intellectual and moral superiority, colonialism is the act of exploitation happening at the structural level. Within the context of imperialism and colonizing various nations, the conquered, that is, the majority of the population—in populist terms, the people—is dominated by the conquerors, who become a self-created elite. In rejecting imperialism, the conquered populace draws on the common backgrounds and shared history of oppression to reject the precepts of those in power over them.

The implications of the term *imperialism* are much more dramatic and global than those of the term *colonialism*, as far as popular usage is concerned. Therefore the polemical use of the term *imperialism* to indicate how powerful nations function is not entirely without basis as it is rooted in an understanding of power relations where weak nations are pitted against stronger ones. While the discourse of colonialism is more situated in terms of a specific time and place, generalizations abound, for instance when we speak of a term such as *colonial mentality*. The difficulty in definition applies both to the terms *imperialism* and *colonialism* as well as to movements and ideologies that oppose imperialism.

The distinction between *anticolonialism* and *postcolonialism* is more subtle: while the former term represents a thesis proposed by the colonized against the colonizer, the latter term indicates an insight into the nature of anticolonialism both as a discourse and as a movement. To be anticolonial is in principle *being* postcolonial because one acts in anticipation of defeating the colonial agenda and imagining a situation in which colonialism becomes a relic of the past. The true meaning of postcolonialism is a complete rejection of all forms of colonial or neocolonial oppression, which prevent individuals or groups from arriving at a sense of autonomy. Therefore the term *postcolonial* can be used as if it meant anticolonial.

From theories of the postcolonial imagination to postcolonial feminism, the word *postcolonial* is attached to various schools of thought. In terms of historical time and geographical space it implies that postcolonial nations have a colonial and a precolonial past, and it refers to the geographical regions often referred to as the Third World: Asia, Africa, and Latin America, which are dominated by poverty, overpopulation, and divisions of class, gender, and ethnicity. Postcolonialism is not just a discourse restricted to the past but a set of ideas that connects a colonial past to a future in which decolonization becomes a reality, allowing subjugated nations and marginal groups an opportunity to express themselves.

What we term Western ways of looking at the world, or westernization, are where the non-Western subject is trapped in a scenario where one ends up creating parameters of judgment that are culturally distant from one's own, local ways of looking at things. This applies to films where light-complexioned heroes and heroines take center stage, as well as to giant malls in cities that dislodge small, local shops. In an article titled "Haiti Can Be Rich Again," Laurent Dubois and Deborah Jenson note that, "In the wake of the earthquake, many have talked about the need to lay foundations for a better future. To do that, Haiti should look to the past, and the system of small farms and the decentralized economy that once provided Haitians with dignity, autonomy and wealth." This need for dignity, autonomy, and wealth defines some of the most important postcolonial concerns surrounding survival-related struggles of vast populations. In other words, despite the fact that colonized nations are no longer legally or technically colonies, their futures are tinged by the metropolitan worldview of the colonizers. "The people" cannot shake the influence, judgment, or advice of "the elite."

Chinweizu Ibekwe, the Nigerian critic and poet, titled his 1975 book *West and the Rest of Us: White Predators, Black Slavers and the African Elite*. The phrase "West and the rest of us" has subsequently entered the postcolonial vocabulary. Its meaning indicates that Western notions of development, or Western lifestyles oriented toward consuming resources without respect toward the environment, are not a solution to the "us" of the Third World. Contrary to westernization, the non-Western world requires that the poor and marginalized acquire power to create a society where individuals can preserve their sense of dignity without having to give up their autonomy.

Prakash Kona

See also: "The Elite"; "The People"

References

Dubois, Laurent, and Deborah Jenson. "Haiti Can Be Rich Again." *New York Times*, January 8, 2012.

Harvey, David. *The New Imperialism.* Oxford, UK: Oxford University Press, 2003.

Jacobs, Jane M. *Edge of Empire: Postcolonialism and the City.* London: Routledge, 1996.

Young, Robert J. C. *Postcolonialism: A Very Short Introduction.* Oxford, UK: Oxford University Press, 2003.

Arnett, Alex Matthews (1888–1945)

Alex Matthews Arnett was a historian and teacher noted as among the first historians to document the Populist movement in a scholarly work. Born near Sylvania, Georgia, to Hamilton and Georgia Arnett, Arnett grew up in a religious family, as his father was a Baptist teacher, educator, and even tax collector. Arnett graduated from Mercer University, a Baptist college in Macon, in 1908 and taught school (English and history) in Georgia from 1908 until 1912. In 1912 he accepted a position teaching history at Shorter College in Rome, Georgia, and earned a master's degree in history from Columbia University in 1913. Arnett married in 1916 and received a Ph.D. in 1922, again from Columbia. After a year teaching at Furman in Greenville, he and his wife settled in Greensboro where he taught at North Carolina College for Women until his death in 1945.

Arnett was a student of Benjamin B. Kendrick, and both were influenced by Charles Beard, even though Beard had left Columbia before Arnett arrived. Beard's progressive interpretation of history left a mark on Arnett, and Arnett's works reflect the progressive view that economic factors shape history as a conflict between the haves and have-nots that would eventually result in a more democratic society. Arnett's dissertation, "The Populist Movement in Georgia: A View of the 'Agrarian Crusade' in Light of Solid-South Politics," was completed in 1922 and published that same year.

Arnett's *Populist Movement in Georgia* continues to have a significant impact on historical studies of Populism. In two reviews, University of Minnesota historian Solon Buck praised Arnett's work as the best history of Populism in print. Arnett drew upon newspapers and manuscripts in his work, combining social, political, and economic history into a concise and clear narrative. With remarkable foresight, he concluded the problems associated with the rise of the Populist movement had not been adequately addressed and change in the nation would be forever associated with liberal causes.

In 1935, Arnett and Kendrick published *The South Looks at Its Past*, a set of historical essays intended as a preface for a broader southern regional study under the direction of Howard Odum of the University Of North Carolina. Arnett provided two essays centering on the South after 1875 and further developed ideas explored in *Populist Movement in Georgia*. His last book, *Claude Kitchen and the Wilson War Policies* (1937) dealt with antiwar sentiment during World War I. In 1933, he coauthored *The Story of North Carolina* as a history for use in the public schools.

Arnett contributed reviews and articles to historical journals throughout his lengthy career, but his *Populist Movement in Georgia* was his most significant and lasting work, still unchallenged as a historical study. He died at an early age in 1945 and is buried in Screven County, Georgia, where his father had been a pastor for over a half a century.

Boyd Childress

See also: Historians of Populism

References

Arnett, Alex Matthews. *Populist Movement in Georgia: A View of the "Agrarian Crusade" in Light of Solid-South Politics.* Studies in History, Economics and Public Law, no. 104. New York: Columbia University, 1922. http://www.archive.org/details/cu31924014468577.

Hirsch, Jerrold M. "Arnett, Alex Matthews." In William S. Powel, ed. *Dictionary of North Carolina Biography.* Vol. 1. Chapel Hill: University of North Carolina Press, 1979, pp. 46–47.

Hofstadter, Richard. *The Age of Reform: From Bryan to F. D. R.* New York: Vintage Books, 1955.

Automobile

The automobile, known colloquially as the car, is an internal-combustion-engine vehicle powered by gasoline. The need for a more effective, cleaner mode of transportation emerged as Americans faced the sordid effects of horse-drawn carriages. At the turn of the twentieth century, it was not uncommon for urbanites to encounter dead horses and excrement, and their resulting foul odors, as they went about their daily obligations. The notion of a carriage moving forward without the aid of animals—whose wastes contaminated city streets and created public health hazards—appealed to Americans of all socioeconomic backgrounds. By the mid-1890s, more than 300 individuals and companies were actively involved in building experimental vehicles that they hoped would improve the transportation situation in the United States. Unfortunately for the public, these experimental automobiles often cost more than the average worker's annual salary. Many city dwellers relied on their feet and trolleys for urban travel until affordable automobiles were available.

Unlike the automobile makers of the late nineteenth century, who were often commissioned only to make one vehicle at a time, Henry Ford of Detroit, Michigan, realized the potential for the national demand for cars and ordered the construction of hundreds of vehicles per day as early as 1906. In 1908 Ford asserted that he would build "a motor car for the great multitude. It will be large enough for the family but small enough for the individual to run and care for. It will be constructed of the best materials by the best men to be hired, after the simplest designs that modern engineering can devise. But it will be so low in price that no man making a good salary will be unable to own one" (Burlingame 62). The result of Ford's promise was the construction of 10,000 vehicles named the Model T. To ensure that he could keep the cost of the automobile as low as possible while maintaining universal appeal, Ford minimized specifications such as exterior color and interior design, two aspects of the automobile that are of the utmost importance to car buyers today. Famously, Ford not only revolutionized the automobile industry but, with the implementation of the moving assembly line, he radically altered the American labor system as well. The effectiveness of the assembly line allowed Ford to stay true to his promise to provide affordable vehicles to the masses. In 1908 the Model T sold for $825; due to the labor system Ford devised, the price fell to $490 by 1914.

Advancements in automobile construction, including the replacement of ineffective, unsafe, two-wheel mechanical brakes with hydraulic brakes, gave way to changes in many other American jobs. For instance, early-twentieth-century department stores relied on high-volume sales to dominate the urban marketplace. Automobiles were able to quickly and efficiently distribute more goods than their horse-drawn predecessors and contributed to the growth of such stores. During the 1920s, the potential uses of the gasoline-powered vehicle seemed infinite and were not at all confined to urban life. Whereas city drivers typically did not rely on their vehicles to withstand heavy loads, rural automobile owners looked to the car for a way to lessen the burdens of agricultural work. The small pickup truck was ideal for farmers because of its expanded space for carrying goods, and it was certain to increase productivity and ease the strains of manual and animal-aided labor. In 1925 Ford introduced a fully assembled pickup truck. Many other companies, including Chevrolet, who would quickly take the lead in this market, followed in Ford's footsteps. Along with the pickup truck, tractors revolutionized farm life. Although tractors had existed in the United States since the first decade of the 1900s, they were often too large and too heavy for use on typical farms; therefore, these early tractors were only suitable for large-farm use such as harvesting wheat in the Great Plains. The Fordson Tractor, which was first produced in 1917, proved to be more versatile than earlier American tractors and permitted laborers to avoid working with animals such as mules and horses. The automobile also decreased the number of laborers necessary; this change provided young men with more free time than ever before imaginable and is considered to be directly responsible for the education boom of the early twentieth century.

With the automobile becoming a staple of American life by the end of the second decade of the 1900s, oil companies such as John D. Rockefeller's Standard Oil opened fueling stations around the country and reveled in this new American industry. These companies brought economic success and power to areas of the nation that had previously not garnered the respect of the American business market, including Louisiana, Oklahoma, and Texas. The reformation of transportation in the United States also led to the development of roads in urban and rural areas alike as well as motor hotels and new interest in seeing national parks.

There of course was a negative side to all of these "advancements" and progress. While cars did not drop manure as they moved, they did create a new health hazard with air pollution. As the middle classes obtained automobiles, they fled the cities and created new suburbs, leaving many of the poorest of the poor in urban slums. Moreover, several oil companies became monopolies, dominating the political and economic life of the nation, corrupting politics in the 1920s and beyond, and edging out public transportation in newly developing areas such as Los Angeles, California. By the late 1920s, the country had become so dependent on the automobile and its industries that when consumer demand went down for cars and homes, the nation succumbed to the worst depression the nation had seen to date. Undeniably, the automobile and its related industries brought some great changes to the nation, but the automobile's adoption also had many unintended consequences.

The automobile remains an important component of modern life and has indelibly altered American life. References to the automobile surfaced in early-twentieth-century commercial jingles, and allusions to the car in literature, film, and television over the course of the last century have ensured its place in American culture.

Brian Hartwig

See also: Environmentalism; Gilded Age; Leisure; National Parks; Popular Culture; Progressivism; United Auto Workers (UAW)

References

Burlingame, Roger. *Henry Ford*. New York: Knopf, 1954.

Kyvig, David E. *Daily Life in the United States, 1920–1940*. Chicago: Ivan R. Dee, 2004.

B

Bacon's Rebellion (1676)

Bacon's Rebellion erupted in Virginia in 1676 as the result of a power struggle between established planters, newer planters, free men (former indentured servants), slaves, and others over tensions about available land and the role of Indians in the colony. Historians, scholars, politicians, and others often point to Bacon's Rebellion as the first "populist moment" in American history. However, they interpret the nature of this populism differently, making Bacon's Rebellion an event that embodies the contradictions inherent in the "usable past."

In the seventeenth century, Virginia's tobacco plantations and settlements were ringed with Native peoples who, through treaty or warfare, had ceded their lands to the English and created new towns on the outskirts of the colony. These local Indians consisted of diverse groups, all of whom had different trading and political relationships with the Chesapeake colonists. Some of these relationships were friendlier than others, causing Indians and whites to live in varying states of tension. Moreover, the internal social structure of the Virginia colony complicated these relationships. Before slavery became widespread, tobacco planters looked to indentured servants to meet their labor needs. A servant signed a contract with a master promising to work for a period of years, perhaps five or seven, depending on the terms of the contract. In return, the master would pay the servant's passage to America and provide all his or her food or clothes for the term of the indenture. Once the period of servitude had ended, the newly freed servant would be able to claim land of his own and take his place as a full member of society, a free man. This meant that while they were indentured, servants were neither technically "free," because their servitude had an end date, nor were they slaves. As time passed, it became harder and harder for newly freed men to find available land. Good lands had already been claimed by the big tobacco planters. Moreover, it became harder to be free. According to historian Edmund S. Morgan, planters did everything in their power to extend servitude contracts through legal means, such as punishment for stealing and running away, which could add years to an existing contract. Morgan asserts that the big planters thus exploited their servants to the fullest extent and made it difficult for them to gain the land and other benefits of free life in Virginia that they had been promised. Thus, the land that was available for free men was often on the fringes of colonial settlement—land that was often already occupied by Indians. This competition for resources among free men and Indians, and between free men and established planters, contributed to Bacon's Rebellion.

The trouble began in 1675 when a party of Doeg Indians helped themselves to some of Thomas Matthew's hogs in exchange for a debt on which they claimed he had reneged. Virginia planters Giles Brent and George Mason, long known as Indian-haters, chased the Doegs down and killed or wounded several of them. They then killed 14 friendly Susquehannahs, who had had nothing to do with the hog theft and were in the neighborhood because they were taking shelter with their allies, the Piscataways, after an attack by Senecas. The English murdered five Susquehannah chiefs after tricking them into a parley. The Susquehannahs then retaliated in several bloody raids against the Virginians. Terror gripped those whites living on the fringes of colonial settlement.

The governor of Virginia, William Berkeley, was reluctant to go to war against the Indians. He had, in fact, authorized a force to chase the Susquehannahs, but he then called it back. Instead, he proposed the building of a series of forts along the frontier. This enraged the English living on the fringe, who felt that the forts would be expensive and ineffectual.

Nathaniel Bacon, age 29, had recently settled in Virginia with his wife, who was a friend of Governor Berkeley's wife. Although young and a fresh arrival, Bacon had money, a seat on the Virginia council, and more than one plantation on the James River. He, like other farmers, had had conflicts with the Indians, and in the spring of 1676 he agreed to head a war party to move against them in defiance of Berkeley's orders. According to Morgan, Bacon was also attempting to diffuse the anger of newly freed men on the frontier by giving them a target for their rage: "The Indians would be the scapegoats. Discontent with upper-class leadership would be vented in racial hatred, in a pattern that statesmen and politicians of a later age would have found familiar" (Morgan 257).

Berkeley still preferred to avoid an Indian war and removed Bacon from the council. Bacon did not seem to care. Instead, he attacked friendly Occaneechees, whom he had tricked into capturing a group of Susquehannahs. He killed the prisoners and then the Occaneechees themselves. Berkeley declared Bacon and his followers to be traitors and rebels. He called for new elections, in which Bacon won his seat back. When he arrived in Jamestown, Berkeley arrested him, "presented him to the House of Burgesses on his knees," then pardoned him after a written confession and apology (Morgan 262). Bacon went home, still without his commission to fight the Indians.

He returned to Jamestown with 500 men and demanded his commission from Berkeley, which he received "at gunpoint" (Morgan 264). Bacon raised even more men and arms and went marching off to kill Indians and loot their wealth. In his absence, Berkeley voided his commission and raised his own army against Bacon's men. Bacon, again an outlaw, marched back into Jamestown on September 19 and burned it down. Then he looted those who were loyal the crown and distributed their possessions. When Bacon died on October 26 from "bloody flux," the rebellion petered out. England had sent warships to Virginia. The rebels pledged anew their allegiance to the governor and the crown, and everyone went home, including the Indians.

Morgan asserts that after Bacon's Rebellion, Virginia returned to a status quo where large planters controlled the colony and newly free white men struggled to gain both land and rights. Yet in the years following, racism in the colony grew as slavery became more profitable and widespread. Whereas Bacon's Rebellion had united whites, blacks, and servants against a common enemy, Indians, its aftermath hardened racial lines against both blacks and Native peoples.

Historian Stephen Saunders Webb takes a somewhat different approach to the meaning of Bacon's Rebellion, which he calls Bacon's Revolution. For Webb, Bacon's Revolution was part of a larger independence movement in colonial America, rooted in ideas of republicanism and local control:

> The institutional expressions of political revolution and American independence in 1676—the association of taxation with representation; the introduction of general elections and popular participation at every level of the extant government; revolutionary rule by committees of associations, bound by oath to resist oligarchy, monarchy, and empire—were 1676's inheritance from the English Revolution and its legacy to the American Revolution of 1776. So too was the public activity of otherwise repressed classes. Women, servants, and slaves organized and fought the revolution, which was excited by Indian attaches and made articulate by educated English emigrants. (Webb 414)

For Webb and Morgan, Bacon's Rebellion—an event that seemingly had little effect on its own society—foreshadowed the spirit of liberty and the populist impulse that culminated in the founding of the American state. Disparate elements of society join together to free themselves from a perceived threat—ostensibly Indians, but also from tyranny and the concentration of power as represented by Berkeley and Virginia's Big Men. Each historian identifies the seeds of racism and repression that followed these events, naming the roots of the some of the primary conflicts in American history.

Yet the racism against Indians inherent in Bacon's Rebellion has caused it to become a standard bearer for "right-wing populism," akin to the Regulator movement in colonial North Carolina, the Ku Klux Klan, the Paxton Boys, the Indian Wars of the nineteenth century, Father Coughlin, the John Birch Society, red-baiting, conspiracy theories, and vigilante-style violence against Mormons, Germans, Chinese, and other suspect Americans. Thus, Bacon's Rebellion stands at the beginning of a thread of bigotry, repression, intolerance, and violence that has shot through American life since the colonial era. In short, it is both the harbinger of liberty and the oracle of hate.

Bacon's Rebellion has much in common with later populist movements in the United States. It was a protest against taxation in that the frontier settlers were unwilling to pay higher taxes on their tobacco crops to fund Berkeley's line of forts. It was the revolt of rural, frontier people against eastern monied interests that were neither responsive nor receptive to their needs: Governor Berkeley continued to deny the frontier settlers' request for adequate protection against Indians. The people on the fringe of the colony felt that they knew best how to handle their problem and took up arms to do so—just as Shays's rebels and the Whiskey rebels did a century later. Yet the failed rebellions all resulted in legislative action that in some cases tightened social controls and in others responded to the demands of the voters. Bacon's Rebellion also united blacks, women, servants, and free whites against the center of colonial power, as the Populist movement sometimes did in the nineteenth century. And, like all of these movements, the immediate effects of Bacon's Rebellion were invisible, yet their reach transformed American culture.

Elizabeth S. Demers

See also: "The Elite"; Ku Klux Klan (KKK); McCarthy, Joseph (1908–1957); Poverty Campaigns; Proposition 13 (1978); Shays's Rebellion (1786–1787); Whiskey Rebellion (1791–1794); Wounded Knee (1890, 1973)

References

Berlet, Chip, and Matthew N. Lyons. *Right-Wing Populism: Too Close for Comfort.* New York: Guilford Press, 2000.

Morgan, Edmund S. *American Slavery, American Freedom: The Ordeal of Colonial Virginia.* New York: W. W. Norton, 1975.

Stock, Catherine McNicol. *Rural Radicals: From Bacon's Rebellion to the Oklahoma City Bombing.* New York: Penguin Books, 1997.

Webb, Stephen Saunders. *1676: The End of American Independence.* New York: Alfred A. Knopf, 1984.

Bailey, Liberty Hyde (1858–1954)

Liberty Hyde Bailey was an influential thinker, writer, and researcher in the areas of horticultural sciences and rural sociology. He taught at, among other institutions, Cornell University. He was a prolific author, writing 65 books and 1,300 articles and editing numerous books and several journals. Renowned for his knowledge of horticultural science, he developed improvements in various plants and has been referred to as the father of modern horticulture. Bailey was instrumental in the Country Life Movement, which in the early twentieth century sought to encourage the development of rural life and agriculture to its fullest potential. Many see Bailey as instrumental in the genesis of the environmental movement. He was a productive author until near the time of his death.

Bailey was born into a family of farmers in 1858 in South Haven, Michigan. He graduated from Michigan Agricultural College (later Michigan State University) with a degree in botany. Bailey assisted a professor of botany at Harvard for one year, making great strides in his understanding of the science of plants. He then taught horticulture and landscape gardening at Michigan Agricultural College for three years.

Bailey was then invited to teach horticulture at Cornell University, where he advocated practical help for farmers. He lobbied the state of New York to establish state-supported agricultural education at Cornell. He became dean of the school and succeeded in establishing the New York State College of Agriculture at Cornell University. He served concurrently as the director of the agricultural experiment station of the university. This new school carried out extensive research beneficial to agriculture. His work at Cornell helped develop the extension system whereby state-supported agricultural schools provided research and guidance in areas related to agriculture. He retired from Cornell in 1913.

While at Cornell, Bailey helped organize a system that would provide New York children with an education related to nature. After years of chaotic post–Civil War urbanization, Americans reevaluated the need for nature in the lives of people, building parks and starting beautification projects to regreen the polluted, poorly planned (usually unplanned) cities. Early urban reformers hoped to use education to instill a knowledge and appreciation of nature into young people who most likely knew little more of the world than their urban confines. Moreover, as so many Americans left the countryside for the city, reformers also hoped to remind people of the value of rural life and its peculiar kind of nature, which might in turn make them more effective in farming. This education would also give provide an understanding of the human role as stewards of nature.

Bailey was greatly concerned with the status of agriculture at the grassroots level, and thus he was an obvious choice for the head of the Country Life Commission established in 1908. Young people had been leaving farms throughout the Gilded Age and the Progressive Era, and this out-migration concerned rural and urban reformers alike. Rural people lacked the social interaction and opportunities for education available in the cities and congested urban areas while forsaking the perceived benefits of the bucolic lives they left. Progressive president and nature lover Theodore Roosevelt called for the creation of the commission to study conditions in the rural United States and to make suggestions for keeping country life attractive to the younger generation. Bailey's commission did extensive research and surveys, producing a report on behalf of the commission as well as Bailey's own uncensored views of the results of the commission's work. In *The Country-life Movement in the United States* (1911), Bailey outlined areas for improvement in rural American life, including conservation of the soil, better education for men and women, and economic justice for farmers in the face of powerful monopolies and middlemen. Overall, he concluded that teaching farmers to be profitable was not enough. Rural life needed to provide both social and economic fulfillment, a balanced life created by the people who lived there instead of by well-meaning but remote urban reformers.

Bailey's prolific writings sold well. The scope of his work was wide, from the philosophical to the highly technical. One of his books was *The Holy Earth*, in which he discussed the value of the earth to humans and their responsibilities toward its well-being. He could dwell on the seasons of work, women's rights, and taxonomy with equal skill and linguistic efficiency. Bailey wedded the more theoretical botany with the more practical horticulture. He achieved great success in both botany and applied plant sciences. He was instrumental in seeing the founding of the first botanical society in the United States and has left his imprint on agricultural leaders such as

Henry A. Wallace, as well as environmental writers like Aldo Leopold. His plant discoveries around the world were legendary, and he received a number of honorary degrees for his long-term efforts in the field. The length and breadth of his work is staggering, especially his impact on generations of scientists, farmers, gardeners, and nature lovers.

Bailey died at his home in Ithaca, New York, on December 25, 1954. The American Horticultural Society instituted an annual award in 1958 named in his honor.

Ken Taylor

See also: Country Life Movement; Environmentalism; Gilded Age; Granger Movement; Olmsted, Frederick Law; Progressivism; Roosevelt, Theodore

References

Bailey, Liberty Hyde. *The Country-life Movement in the United States*. New York: Macmillan Co., 1911. http://archive.org/details/countrylifemove00bailrich.

Banks, Harlan P. "Liberty Hyde Bailey, 1858–1954: A Biographical Memoir." National Academy of Science. http://www.nasonline.org/publications/biographical-memoirs/memoir-pdfs/bailey-liberty-h.pdf. Accessed January 2, 2013.

Jack, Zachary Michael, ed. *Liberty Hyde Bailey: Essential Agrarian and Environmental Writings*. Ithaca, NY: Cornell University Press, 2008.

Banking System of the Late Nineteenth Century

The banking system of the late nineteenth century was plagued by great instability. The Panics of 1873 and 1893 were sparked by banking collapses. As a result, farmers demanded banking reform after blaming the banks for their perilous economic condition in the late nineteenth century.

In 1873, a financial panic was sparked by the collapse of the Jay Cooke and Company banking firm. The firm had been instrumental in selling bonds during the Civil War. Jay Cooke and Company declared bankruptcy due to its overinvestment in the Northern Railroad Company. The collapse of Jay Cooke and Company caused a chain reaction throughout the economy. Credit became scarce. As many as 18,000 businesses and thousands of banks failed throughout the country. By 1876, unemployment reached 14 percent. It took five years for the nation to recover from the Panic of 1873.

Likewise, the banking system proved vulnerable during the Panic of 1893. The panic began when the Philadelphia and Reading Railroad failed. By the time that the Panic of 1893 ended, thousands of businesses and hundreds of banks collapsed. At the height of the panic, more than 3 million Americans were unemployed. The unemployment rate averaged more than 10 percent during the Panic of 1893. The depression was exacerbated by the fact that President Grover Cleveland believed that the federal government should not take any action. According to Cleveland, this was just part of the business cycle and the economy would eventually recover. The economy did not recover from the depression until 1897.

The instability in the banking system aroused anger in many segments of the population—most notably farmers. The late nineteenth century was not a prosperous period for farmers. They faced a number of obstacles including floods, droughts, declining farm prices, and the overproduction of crops. Many farmers went bankrupt and lost their homes. Farmers frequently blamed banks for their problems.

The People's Party was formed in 1890 and gave voice to farmers' anger concerning their economic plight. In 1892, the party nominated James B. Weaver of Iowa as their nominee. Many of their planks were meant to address the economic concerns of farmers. A good example was the Subtreasury Plan, which called for the federal government to create national warehouses where farmers could store their crops. They could then use these warehoused crops as collateral to negotiate favorable loans from bankers. The Populists also wanted to inflate the currency to make it easier for farmers to pay their debts. They proposed printing more paper money as well as the unlimited coinage of silver. The People's Party performed well in 1892, receiving more than 1 million votes and 22 electoral votes. The People's Party died in 1896 when it supported the losing candidacy of Nebraska Congressman William Jennings Bryan.

Lack of government regulation is one main reason for the instability of banking in the late nineteenth century. Politicians such as Grover Cleveland reflected the conventional wisdom of the day, arguing that any government intervention would have a negative impact upon the economy. These men believed that the government that governed least governed best. There did not yet exist a centralized body such as the Federal Reserve System that could influence the lending rates of banks or inject liquidity into the banking system. Unlike today, the deposits of customers were not insured if a bank failed.

While the economy did recover in 1897, there was further banking turmoil into the early twentieth century. In 1907, there occurred another banking panic. It was prompted by a stock market crash, which led to a number of banks and businesses failing. The panic would have been worse but for the intervention of banker and financier J. P. Morgan. Morgan raised millions of dollars from other bankers to help save the nation's banking system.

Public officials realized after the Panic of 1907 that they needed a more stable banking system. Fears of future panics led to the creation of the Federal Reserve System in 1913. The Federal Reserve could inject liquidity into the banking system and could influence the lending rates of banks. Further actions in the twentieth century enhanced the stability of banks. As a part of the New Deal, the Glass-Steagall Act separated commercial and investment banks. The Federal Deposit Insurance Corporation insured customers' deposits in the event of a bank failure. Despite these reforms, banks have not been impervious to collapse in the early twenty-first century.

Jason Roberts

See also: Cleveland, Grover (1837–1908); Depression of 1873; Depression of 1893; Federal Reserve Act (1913); New Deal; Northern Securities Case (1904); People's Party; Progressivism; Railroad Regulation; Subtreasury Plan

References

Chernow, Ron. *The House of Morgan: An American Banking Dynasty and the Rise of Modern Finance*. New York: Atlantic Monthly Press, 1990.

Grant, James. *Money of the Mind: Borrowing and Lending in America, From the Civil War to Michael Milken*. New York: Farrar, Straus, Giroux, 1992.

Hixson, William F. *Triumph of the Bankers: Money and Banking in the Eighteenth and Nineteenth Centuries*. Westport, CT: Praeger, 1993.

Kazin, Michael. *A Godly Hero: The Life of William Jennings Bryan*. New York: Alfred A. Knopf, 2006.

Mackenzie, Kenneth. *The Banking Systems of Great Britain, France, Germany, and the United States of America*. London: Macmillan and Company, 1932.

Wood, John H. *A History of Central Banking in Great Britain and the United States*. Cambridge, UK: Cambridge University Press, 2009.

Barnum, P. T. (1810–1891)

Receiving little schooling, at age six P. T. Barnum adopted his father's drive for marketing and spent many days when he should have been at school working with his father instead. Barnum quickly became educated in the business industry, working with the local lottery under the supervision of his grandfather, Philo Barnum. He later owned a country store following his father's death in 1825. Soon after, Barnum married Charity Hallet and had four children. Following the death of Hallet, Barnum married Nancy Fish. While Barnum is well known for his circus, making him a father of modern popular culture in the United States, Barnum originally focused on politics. He died on April 7, 1891, but his circus remains intact to this day.

Phineas Taylor Barnum was born on July 5, 1810, in Bethel, Connecticut, to Irena Taylor Barnum and Philo F. Barnum. Although his schooling was short, Barnum excelled in arithmetic, far beyond the other students. He argued that his arithmetic skills continued to develop over the years, and by the time he was 12, neighbors waged bets that he could not provide the correct result of math problems without help; he always provided the right answer. At 12 years old, Barnum traveled to New York City by boat. With unfavorable weather, his voyage lasted seven days, during which time his grandfather, Phineas Taylor, entertained the boy, opening young Barnum's eyes to the world of amusement. After investing his funds into a store, Barnum was visited by Hackariah Bailey (no relation to James A. Bailey, Barnum's later partner), who told Barnum about the first elephant imported to the United States. Incorporating his earlier experience with the lottery, Barnum established numerous agents throughout the country to sell tickets, utilizing his entertainment and advertising skills to promote his lottery.

By 1831, Barnum published abolitionist editorials in the Christian newspaper the *Herald of Freedom* and was jailed at one point for libeling an alleged usurer. Being a showman, Barnum rode in an open coach drawn by six horses and accompanied by cannon blasts, making the most of his return from jail. Abolitionist viewpoints aside, Barnum purchased and promoted a supposed 161-year-old slave named Joice Heth, who claimed to be owned by George

Known as America's greatest showman, P. T. Barnum made popular entertainment, promoted through aggressive publicity, was a staple in American life and changed the way Americans viewed leisure time and cultural pursuits. He is best known as the cofounder of the Barnum & Bailey Circus, "The Greatest Show on Earth." (Library of Congress)

Washington, the exhibition of whom brought him $750 weekly. Then Barnum moved into copurchasing a small circus and finally invested in and created Barnum's American Museum, arguably the United States' first public museum.

Perhaps one of his most puzzling efforts was *The Adventures of an Adventurer*, published by Barnum but under the pseudonym Barnaby Diddledum. As the author, Barnum presented the stories of Heth, yet the book appeared to be an opportunity to brag about his personal good deeds; he entertained his audience with jokes and advice and also expressed his feelings about politics. Although Barnum affiliated himself with more northern attitudes about slavery, the book satirizes abolitionists and publicly scorns Heth as an actress who lied about her personal history to receive payment in whiskey.

Realizing that he could capitalize once again on entertainment, Barnum took a different approach to capturing people's fascination. In 1842, Barnum hired a 2-foot-tall, 10-year-old boy known as General Tom Thumb to entertain patrons in the United States and then England. The tour stopped for Queen Victoria and then traveled to Paris after making enormous profits in England. Then, in 1850, Barnum mortgaged everything to bring Swedish soprano Jenny Lind to the United States for 93 highly anticipated concerts, traveling across the country with Tom Thumb and various wild animals as part of his "Great Asiatic Caravan, Museum and Menagerie," which presaged the creation of his great circus. Losing his fortune by 1857, Barnum sold his museum and recuperated his losses with lectures at local universities and more tours with Tom Thumb to purchase another museum. By 1865, his museum burned down, but Barnum rebuilt it nearby.

Following the Civil War, Barnum became a state legislator in Connecticut as a Republican and wrote *The Humbugs of the World*, his autobiography. He also realized that the circus would be the necessary tool to reach immortality. In 1869, Barnum published another autobiography, *Struggles and Triumphs*, which sold 100,000 copies in its first year. Two years later, Barnum completed what he believed to be his ticket to fame, entitled the Great

Traveling World's Fair, soon to be renamed P. T. Barnum's New and Greatest Show on Earth. His circus came into competition with the Great London Circus managed by James Bailey and James Hutchinson, who combined the two circuses into the Barnum and London Circus, diminishing Barnum's role in the circus immensely.

Prior to his death, Barnum helped recreate his circus as the Ringling Brothers and Barnum and Bailey Circus. In 1891, Barnum realized death was imminent. He wrote his own obituary and printed it in the newspaper so he could read it before his death. He died on April 7, 1891, in Bridgeport, Connecticut, having been instrumental in the development of modern popular culture as a means to entertain the masses.

Matthew Whitlock

See also: Abolitionism; Gilded Age; Leisure; Popular Culture

References

Adams, Bluford. *E Pluribus Barnum: The Great Showman and the Making of U.S. Popular Culture*. Minneapolis: University of Minnesota Press, 1997.

HarpWeek. "Phineas Taylor 'P. T.' Barnum." http://elections.harpweek.com/1872/bio-1872-Full.asp?UniqueID=2&Year=1872. Accessed December 1, 2013.

Werner, M. R. *Barnum*. Garden City, NY: Garden City Publishing Company, 1927.

Baseball and Populism

Cultural historian Jacques Barzun's well-known observation, "Whoever wants to know the heart and mind of America had better learn baseball," is a standard fixture of most histories of the United States' pastime. Rural historian David Vaught notes that we hear the rest of the quotation far less often, that we should learn baseball by "watching first some high school or small town teams"(Barzun 159). Despite a founding mythology that places baseball's birth in rural Cooperstown, New York, and frequent references to the pastoral tradition that the game invokes, most historians insist that baseball was an urban game played and enjoyed in vacant lots and green spaces. David Vaught, a historian of both the rural United States and baseball, argues that if we move beyond examinations of professional big-city baseball and turn our gaze toward the countryside it becomes clear that rural people were equally enamored with the game. Baseball became farmers' leisure activity of choice at precisely the same time that the Farmers' Alliance and Populism became farmers' favored political inclinations. Baseball and Populism conquered the countryside simultaneously, and they did so by creating a sense of stability in the increasingly volatile world of agriculture.

Rural Americans had played something similar to baseball for generations. Various stick-and-ball games were familiar sights on colonial New England's commons and southern plantation pastures alike. Early settlers brought the game of rounders with them from England, but over time local variations allowed the game to develop into a uniquely American sport. "Town Ball," "Old Cat," and "Soak Ball," named for the practice of "soaking," or hitting a runner with the ball to get him out, were some of the more popular variations. Town Ball, played on a square infield with anywhere from 8 to 50 players on each side, was the most prevalent version of the game, and rural Americans continued to play it after the Civil War.

By the middle of the nineteenth century, however, a more recognizable form of baseball began to sweep the country. In 1845, the New York City Knickerbocker Base Ball Club established many of the standards of modern baseball, such as a diamond-shaped infield and foul lines. The new rules also outlawed the "soak" and insisted that runners be tagged at the bases rather than hit with the ball. After the Civil War, baseball received an added boost in popularity with the Cincinnati Red Stockings's 1869 barnstorming tour of baseball's traditional heartland. Trouncing local teams in the Northeast, the Midwest, and California, the Red Stockings introduced many Americans in both the city and the countryside to the now familiar flannel uniforms, knee-high socks, and cleats that have become commonplace for the major leagues. Cincinnati's undefeated record was also a testament to the skill and professionalism that could be cultivated among the big-city ball clubs. Professional baseball took hold in the United States' cities, but rural baseball changed very little, and in some cases it actually declined in popularity during the period of the Red Stockings's campaign. In 1867, the *Prairie Farmer*, one of the Midwest's most popular farm journals, reported on the sad state of rural baseball. Several local ball clubs gathered at the Warren County Fair in Illinois for their traditional "grand match," but fewer than a dozen spectators showed up for the game. It was clear to the *Prairie Farmer* observer that "the people around here are satiated with baseball" (*Prairie Farmer*, September 28, 1867, 195).

It seemed like baseball in the countryside was all but dead in the 1870s as the game's popularity soared in the United States' cities. By the mid-1880s, however, baseball rallied in the rural United States as farmers took up the game, not as spectators like their urban brethren but by taking to the field themselves. It is no coincidence that the 1880s and 1890s, the period of baseball's ascendancy on the farms and in the small towns of the rural United States, also played host to the rise of the Farmers' Alliance and the People's Party. Baseball and the push for radical economic and political reform provided by both the Alliance and Populism were born out of the same social, cultural, and economic upheavals in the midst of the greatest transformation American agriculture had ever seen.

By the end of the nineteenth century, American farmers found themselves pawns in an international commodities market controlled by plutocrats in cities around the world. It no longer mattered how hard an individual farmer worked, how much he produced, or what new scientific methods he employed; the success or failure of a farming operation was determined by distant markets over which farmers had no control. This sense of powerlessness drove farmers to challenge corporate ascendancy and inequitable wealth distribution, first through education and economic cooperation in the Farmers'

Alliance and then through national political action in the People's Party. Charles Postel argues that the agrarian movements of the 1880s and 1890s reflected not a backward-looking conservatism but a truly modern vision for a more politically and economically democratic United States. The Alliance and the Populists used modern principles of centralization, organization, and corporatism to bring producers together in marketing cooperatives. These modern institutions allowed farmers to beat the plutocrats at their own game; they would out-monopolize the corporate monopolies, or at least attempt to do so. But at the same time, this corporatism was a tool to maintain a farmer's sense of autonomy. Populism provided a political home for this modern rural ethos, but baseball made it tangible and visible in rural people's everyday lives. On the hometown baseball diamond, farmers played a game where success was clearly governed not only by the prowess of each individual player but also by adherence to Populist principles like cooperation, modern organization, and rational rules of fair play.

Cooperation and Populism offered long-term solutions to a volatile, unregulated, and unfair market for farm commodities. If farmers wanted a more immediate example of what regulation could do and a more reasonable assessment of their successes and failures, they found it on the baseball field. As David Vaught argues, "For young men mystified by the operations of the grain market and wary of what the future held . . . baseball offered excitement, respite, stability, diversion, mutuality, and gratification—all in powerful, albeit short-term, doses" (Vaught, "Our Players Are Mostly Farmers," 19). Farmers latched on to the modern version of baseball precisely because it was so modern. The game's rules were reasonable; they were governed by rhythms of success and failure, runs and outs. Unlike the obtuse and arbitrary rules that governed the price of their harvests, farmer-players quickly naturalized the movements and standards of baseball. Baseball also provided a physical iteration of the Populist ethos of cooperation coupled with individualism. When a team played defense, each player brought a specific set of skills and had a precise role to play in his defensive position on the field, but ultimately he used his individual skills to advance the team's need to get three outs. Likewise, while playing offense, an individual batter did not always hit the ball as hard as he could and hope to score a home run. The batter's ultimate responsibility was to make sure his team chalked up runs, which often meant batting in others without the personal satisfaction of crossing home plate. The lesson of a sacrifice fly or bunt went hand in hand with the dictates of cooperative grain marketing, where the immediate gratification of the individual is deferred for long-term gratification of the many.

In Vaught's study of baseball in rural California, a newspaperman reported on the makeup of his local baseball team, saying "our players are mostly farmers" (Vaught, "Our Players Are Mostly Farmers," 9). In an era of so much upheaval and uncertainty in American agriculture, it is not surprising that farmers found modern baseball so appealing. It fulfilled their desires to experience some measure of success or at least fairly dispensed failure on the baseball field, which they could never find in surveying their own fields. Baseball and Populism addressed the same sense of powerlessness that farmers experienced in the rapidly transforming countryside. In both baseball and Populism, farmers found satisfaction not as spectators but as active participants in the game.

Michael Swinford

See also: Cooperative Commonwealth; Gilded Age; Historians of Populism; Leisure; Long-Haul/Short-Haul Discrimination; People's Party; Populism; Robber Barons

References

Barth, Gunther. City People: The Rise of Modern City Culture in Nineteenth-Century America. New York: Oxford University Press, 1982.

Barzun, Jacques. *God's Country and Mine: A Declaration of Love Spiced with a Few Harsh Words.* Boston: Little, Brown and Co., 1954.

Postel, Charles. *The Populist Vision.* New York: Oxford University Press, 2007.

Prairie Farmer, September 28, 1867.

Seymour, Harold. *Baseball: The People's Game.* New York: Oxford University Press, 1990.

Vaught, David. "Abner Doubleday, Marc Bloch, and the Cultural Significance of Baseball in Rural America." *Agricultural History* 85 (1): 1–20.

Vaught, David. " 'Our Players Are Mostly Farmers': Baseball in Rural California, 1850 to 1890." In Donald G. Kyle and Robert B. Fairbanks, eds. *Baseball in America & America in Baseball.* College Station: Texas A&M University Press, 2008, pp. 8–31.

Baum, L. Frank (1856–1919)

Lyman Frank Baum was the writer of the 1900 children's classic *The Wonderful Wizard of Oz*, as well as many other novels, short stories, and poems.

Baum, commonly referred to as L. Frank Baum, was born in Chittenango, New York, to Benjamin and Cynthia Baum; he was the seventh of nine children. Baum's father amassed his wealth from the Titusville, Pennsylvania, oil fields; this wealth allowed Baum to be home-schooled. At the age of 12 Baum was sent to Peekskill Military Academy in Peekskill, New York, although he only attended the school for two years before returning home. Overall, Baum's cheerful childhood experience is reflected in the tone of his works.

After his experience at Peekskill Military Academy, Baum took a deep interest in writing. Baum's passion for composition led his father to buy a printing press for Baum and his younger brother, who printed amateur newsletters titled "Rose Lawn Home Journal." As Baum's passion developed he became actively involved in drama, eventually managing a theater in Richburg, New York. Baum wrote, directed, and composed music for the plays at the Richburg theater. During mid-1882, one of the plays Baum wrote the words and music for, "The Maid of Arran," became a traveling show with dates from Toronto to Chicago. On November 9, 1882, Baum married Maud Gage, the daughter of the feminist and woman suffrage leader Matilda Joslyn Gage, and moved to what is now Aberdeen, South Dakota, after a fire destroyed Baum's theater.

While in Aberdeen, Baum failed as a shopkeeper and eventually turned to editing *The Aberdeen Saturday Pioneer* newspaper. Baum promoted woman suffrage through the *Aberdeen Saturday Pioneer* and hosted Susan B. Anthony, a friend of Maud's mother, when she came to town. After another failure with the newspaper, Baum moved to Chicago, Illinois, with his wife, four children, and activist mother in-law. While in Chicago, Baum worked as an editor for advertising agencies as well as a traveling salesman. In Chicago, Baum wrote *Mother Goose in Prose* and eventually his most popular book, *The Wonderful Wizard of Oz.* Although many have advanced Populist and free-silver interpretations of *The Wonderful Wizard of Oz,* Baum maintained that the work was written solely as a children's story and nothing more. *The Wonderful Wizard of Oz* preceded many other Oz-related books such as *The Marvelous Land of Oz, Ozma of Oz, Dorothy and the Wizard of Oz, The Road to Oz, The Emerald City of Oz,* and various other works.

After the success of *The Wonderful Wizard of Oz,* the Baum family moved to Hollywood, California, where L. Frank Baum became involved in the film industry. In 1914 Baum started a short-lived film studio called the Oz Film Manufacturing Company. On May 5, 1919, shortly after his failed film-industry venture, Baum suffered a stroke, and he died the following day.

Johnathan Fluitt

See also: Film; Popular Culture; *Wizard of Oz*

References

Baum, Frank Joslyn, and Russell P. Macfall. *To Please a Child.* Chicago: Reilly & Lee, 1961.

Rogers, Katherine M. *L. Frank Baum, Creator of Oz: A Biography.* New York: St. Martin's Press, 2002.

Bellamy, Edward (1850–1898)

Edward Bellamy, an American author and socialist, wrote the influential utopian novel *Looking Backward: 2000–1887.* Bellamy's political and social ideas led to the Nationalist movement, and the members of this movement joined later populist reform movements, including the political manifestation of Populism in the form of the People's Party.

Bellamy was born March 26, 1850, in Chicopee Falls, Massachusetts, a small manufacturing town near Springfield, Massachusetts. He studied literature at Union College in Schenectady, New York, for a year in 1868, but he did not receive a degree. Bellamy then traveled in Europe for about a year. The wretched condition of factory workers in Europe startled him. Bellamy said he had not recognized the poverty present in the United States nor the factories near his home until he was awakened by his overseas experience.

After returning to the United States, Bellamy read law and was admitted to the bar in 1871. He never practiced law and instead became a journalist and worked for newspapers in New York City and Springfield, Massachusetts. In 1879, at his editor's request, Bellamy wrote a serial novel, *The Duke of Stockbridge.* In the story, Bellamy used Shays's Rebellion of 1786 to describe the struggle between debtor farmers and ruthless creditors. He founded the *Springfield Daily News* in 1880 before devoting himself to a literary career. Bellamy wrote romance novels before he returned his attention to social issues.

A series of economic and social calamities forced late-nineteenth-century Americans to consider alternative visions. The Panic of 1873, the Great Railroad Strike of 1877, and the social unrest and threat of anarchy spawned by incidents such as the 1881 assassination of President James Garfield and the Chicago Haymarket Riot of 1886 created an audience receptive to Bellamy's ideas.

In *Looking Backward*, published in 1888, Bellamy offers solutions to the problems caused by economic inequality. The novel tells the story of Julian West, a wealthy young man who falls asleep in Boston one night in 1887 and awakens in the year 2000. His host guides him through a socialist utopia free from the old social problems. Cooperation replaces competition in the new rational and communal society. Nationalism eliminates inefficient and destructive competition among corporations. A single national syndicate controls the nation's wealth with industrial production structured to equally benefit all of society.

The book became a bestseller, with 400,000 copies distributed in the United States within a decade and more elsewhere in the world. *Looking Backward* appealed to the new middle class of white-collar workers and salaried professionals who worried about the corruption of partisan politics, the violence of the lower classes, and the concentration of capital among the wealthy. The social order Bellamy proposed protected the interests of the middle class. Nationalism offered the benefits of industrial progress with bureaucratic control that guaranteed employment and protection from political interference.

Bellamy called for the immediate nationalization of the telegraph, telephone, railroads, and coal mines. Municipalities would acquire gas, water, and electric companies, mass transit lines, and other public services.

The Nationalists claimed to be a conservative party because Bellamy sought to protect republican institutions from the corrupt power of capitalists and monopolists. Nationalism offered economic equality in addition to political equality. Bellamy claimed his ideas belonged to a tradition of American movements seeking a cooperative society.

The first Nationalist club formed in Boston, and Bellamy Nationalist Clubs appeared in 150 cities by 1890. The clubs met weekly to discuss Bellamy's ideas. Clubs appeared in most northern cities, with a concentration of clubs in eastern Massachusetts and California.

Bellamy started a monthly magazine, *The Nationalist*, in May 1889. Bellamy used the journal to further explain his ideas and to promote the clubs. Members of the Boston club formed the Nationalist Education Association to spread their doctrines and named Bellamy as president of the new group.

After suffering from ill health for many years, Bellamy spent several months in the Hawaiian Islands in an effort to regain his strength. A bout with influenza kept him from editing the *Nationalist* in the spring and summer of 1890. Bellamy recovered and launched a weekly newspaper, the *New Nation*, in January 1891.

Many Nationalists and other nonconformists had joined the Populist coalition. In the *New Nation*, Bellamy cheered the spread of the Farmers' Alliance and pledged to support the People's Party. Bellamy applauded the Populist critique of trusts, monopolies, and Wall Street. Nationalists attended the organizational meeting of the People's Party in 1892 in St. Louis.

The Nationalist movement declined during the remainder of the 1890s. The *New Nation* ceased publication in 1894. Bellamy published a sequel to *Looking Backward*, *Equality*, in 1897, but the novel did not gain as much attention as its predecessor. Bellamy died from tuberculosis on May 22, 1898, at his childhood home in Chicopee Falls.

Jeff Wells

See also: *American Non-Conformist*; Co-operative Commonwealth; Depression of 1873; George, Henry (1839–1897); Gilded Age; Northeast and Industrial Midwest, Populism in the; Public Education; Shays's Rebellion (1786–1787)

References

Bowman, Sylvia E. *Edward Bellamy*. Boston: Twayne Publishers, 1986.

Bowman, Sylvia E. *The Year 2000: A Critical Biography of Edward Bellamy*. New York: Bookman Associates, 1958.

Franklin, John Hope. "Edward Bellamy and the Nationalist Movement." *New England Quarterly* 11 (4): 739–72.

Lipow, Arthur. *Authoritarian Socialism in America: Edward Bellamy & the Nationalist Movement*. Berkeley: University of California Press, 1982.

Morgan, Arthur E. *Edward Bellamy*. New York: Columbia University Press, 1944.

Patai, Daphne, ed. *Looking Backward, 1988–1888: Essays on Edward Bellamy*. Amherst: University of Massachusetts Press, 1988.

Thomas, John L. *Alternative America: Henry George, Edward Bellamy, Henry Demarest Lloyd, and the Adversary Tradition*. Cambridge, MA: The Belknap Press, 1983.

The Birth of a Nation. *See* Griffith, D. W. (1875–1948) and *The Birth of a Nation*

Black Panther Party (BPP)

The Black Panther Party (BPP) was founded in Oakland, California, in 1966 by Bobby Seale and Huey P. Newton, who were then students at Merritt Junior College. Originally called the Black Panther Party for Self-Defense, the BPP initially formed in response to accusations of police brutality by Bay Area residents. When the U.S. Supreme Court ruled in *Miranda v. Arizona* that the police had to inform persons of their rights before placing them under arrest, the BPP formed patrols to ensure that the police were following the court's directive. Armed Panthers patrolled neighborhoods and, upon seeing a pedestrian or motorist stopped by the police, the Panthers would pull within 15 feet of the cruiser and observe the interaction to deter the police from employing extralegal force. As the organization grew in scope, it dropped

Huey P. Newton poses in Black Panther poster. (Library of Congress)

the words *Self-Defense* from its title. For the BPP, the name changed also coincided with the group's evolution into a full-fledged revolutionary organization.

The BPP outlined its goals and objectives in a 10-point manifesto. It called for a redistribution of wealth and resources in the United States and for blacks to build and control their own communities and institutions. The group emphasized redress for past and present injustices in the form of employment, decent housing, and an education that reflected the cultural, political, and geographical heritage of people of African descent. They also promoted self-determination. The Panthers' slogan, "All Power to the People," became the battle cry for those who wanted to empower the dispossessed of all races: "Black Power to Black People, Red Power to Red People, and Brown Power to Brown People."

The typical Panther recruit ranged in age from 17 to 22 years. The Panthers attracted people with jail or prison records. They were also noted for their recruitment of gang members. The Southern California Chapter was especially receptive to former gang members, recruiting a fair number of them from the Slausons, one of the city's largest and most feared gangs. In addition to former gang members, there were also a number of ex-servicemen within the party's ranks. While membership was not open to whites, it was open to other activists of color.

The Panthers' uniform, which included a black leather jacket, a powder-blue shirt, and black pants, with impeccably shined black shoes and a black beret, suggested that they were image conscious. Party members also had a flair for the dramatic. In 1967 California state legislator Don Mulford proposed a bill that would make it illegal to carry guns openly in residential and incorporated areas. Panther leaders believed this was a deliberate attempt to disarm the party; hence Newton sent a delegation of 30 Panthers to the Sacramento state house to protest passage of the bill. Newspaper headlines across the state read "Black Militants Invade State Capitol." This stunt garnered national press, which ultimately proved both helpful and harmful to the Panthers' goals.

While many Americans have become infatuated with the more sensational aspects of the BPP, the media often downplays the array of community "survival programs" ranging from the free breakfast program for school kids, to free medical clinics, to the police patrols, to free clothing drives, to escort-service initiatives for senior citizens, to free legal services. This range of services enabled the Panthers to make inroads into communities that other groups could not reach.

The Panthers experienced a turning point in the early 1970s. From late 1970 to 1971, discord between Newton and Eldridge Cleaver forced some party members to take sides. Cleaver believed it was time for the Panthers to wage war against the "pigs." Newton believed that doing so would be counterrevolutionary. He maintained that the Panthers needed to focus on meeting the needs of the community. Toward that end, the Panthers created new initiatives and expanded many of their existing programs. From exile in Algeria (where Cleaver had fled to escape charges that were certain to land him in prison for his role in the botched ambush of Bay Area police officers in April 1968), Cleaver mustered support among the large New York State Chapter of the BPP. When New York Panthers commended the bomb-happy Weathermen for their embrace of armed struggle in an open letter published in February 1971, they also criticized Newton and others for their seemingly reformist approach to alleviating black oppression. Newton responded by expelling the entire New York State Chapter. Weeks later Cleaver aired their differences on a locally televised show. The spat took a turn for the worse as loyal factions for both men implicitly declared war on the opposing camp, culminating in the deaths of at least two Panthers.

Given the organization's efforts at political mobilization, it is not surprising that the Panthers faced heavy institutional repression. One of the government's most commonly used methods was red-baiting. With the Panthers' founding coming on the heels of Senator Joe McCarthy's Red Scare, this tactic was highly effective. It is also important to recognize that the BPP was founded during the height of the Cold War and the United States' escalation in the Vietnam War. Consequently, the U.S. government targeted anyone who expressed sympathy or demonstrated support for communist regimes.

Using red-baiting, the government tried to create an atmosphere in which it would be difficult for the Panthers to gain support. Moreover, because the United States was fighting communism abroad, red-baiting provided domestic law enforcement with a convenient excuse to engage in tactics that were usually reserved for enemies of war, not U.S. citizens. In the minds of some government officials, if these subversive organizations were allowed to gain a foothold in U.S. cities they would threaten the country's way of life, its mores, and its values. Law enforcement officials targeted the Panthers in ways that they did not pursue other activists, especially in the case of the Federal Bureau of Investigation (FBI). Of the 295 counterinsurgency tactics employed by the FBI's Counter-Intelligence Program (COINTELPRO), 233 were directed at the Panthers. Not only were other groups not subjected to the volume of repression heaped upon the Panthers, but also the nature of the repression that other groups encountered was less ferocious. It is possible that, because the Panthers, more so than any other group of its era, spent a lot of time traveling abroad, meeting with dignitaries, and making public statements in support of leaders and nations with whom the United States was not friendly, some in government may have feared that the Panthers were attempting to muster support for socialist and communist regimes on U.S. soil.

It is also possible that FBI Director J. Edgar Hoover did not harbor the same level of antipathy toward white activists or even other activists of color. Hoover believed that blacks were inferior, intellectually and otherwise. Blacks were also the largest minority group in the country at that time, and some public opinion polls revealed that a sector of the black population admired the Panthers. Hence, Hoover believed that the Panthers had the potential to win over recruits. Furthermore, Hoover believed that the breakfast program was a subterfuge for indoctrinating children with antiestablishment teachings, thus creating a generation of nonconformist blacks.

At its apex the Party claimed to have nearly 40 chapters and branches in cities across the United States. The Panthers also boasted an international chapter in Algiers, Algeria. Moreover, the Panthers were the only group that carried guns in plain sight and thus monitored police behavior with the threat of armed resistance. Law enforcement officials found the Panthers' militant posture and inflammatory rhetoric particularly insubordinate, especially for blacks. Consequently, local police departments in conjunction with other law enforcement agencies such as the Internal Revenue Service (IRS), Bureau of Alcohol, Tobacco, Firearms and Explosives (ATF), Army Intelligence, Central Intelligence Agency (CIA), and state police worked to neutralize the Panthers by jailing and murdering some of their most important leaders.

The Panthers enjoyed enormous success, considering the barriers against which they fought. Their impact was far-reaching. Students of 1960s social movements understand that some of the radical groups founded after 1966 inside and outside of the United States were modeled after the BPP, such as the Young Lords, the American Indian movement in the United States, and the Black Beret Cadre in the Bahamas, as well as the Untouchables in India. But the BPP was not without its problems.

From 1967 to 1968, the BPP grew from a regional outfit that was once limited to the West Coast to an international organization with outposts in Africa. Unfortunately, the Panthers did not have the people power or resources to accommodate such rapid expansion. The proliferation of Panther branches across the country, in particular, presented a number of challenges with which the Panthers were not equipped to deal.

By the late 1970s, the Panthers were decimated by a host of factors that were not limited to governmental repression, but the BPP left behind a rich legacy of bold activism that transformed American history and culture and that resonates worldwide in social movements today.

Judson L. Jeffries

See also: African Americans and Populism; McCarthy, Joseph (1908–1957); Weather Underground

References

Churchill, Ward, and Jim Vander Wall. *Agents of Repression: The FBI's Secret Wars against the Black Panther Party and the American Indian Movement*. Boston: South End Press, 1990.

DuBois, W. E. B. *The Philadelphia Negro*. 1899. Reprint, New York: Schocken Books, Inc., 1967.

Feagin, Joe, and Harlan Hahn. *Ghetto Revolts*. New York: Macmillan, 1973.

Harris, Louis, et al. *The Harris Survey Yearbook of Public Opinion 1970: A Compendium of Current American Attitudes*. New York: Louis Harris and Associates, 1971.

Jeffries, Judson L., ed. *Comrades: A Local History of the Black Panther Party*. Bloomington: Indiana University Press, 2007.

Jeffries, Judson L. *Huey P. Newton, The Radical Theorist*. Jackson: University Press of Mississippi, 2002.

Woodson, Carter G. *Mis-education of the Negro*. 1933. Reprint, Washington, DC: African World Press, Inc., 1990.

Zane, Jeffrey, and Judson L. Jeffries. "A Panther Sighting in the Pacific Northwest: The Seattle Chapter of the Black Panther Party." In Judson L. Jeffries, ed. *On the Ground: The Black Panther Party in Communities across America*. Jackson: University Press of Mississippi, 2010.

Bland, Richard P. (1835–1899)

A Democratic politician from Missouri, Richard P. Bland was nicknamed "Silver Dick" and then "The Great Commoner"—the first sobriquet came from his campaigning for the use of silver in the coinage, which made him very popular with many miners. He later cosponsored the Bland-Allison Act in 1878.

Richard Parks Bland was born on August 19, 1835, on the family property near Hartford, Kentucky, the son of Stoughton Edward Bland and Margaret Parks (née Nall). Both his father's and his mother's families were originally from Virginia, although both of them had been born in Kentucky.

When Bland was two months short of his seventh birthday, his father died, and he was brought up by his mother, who died when he was 14. Bland had been educated at Hartford Academy, and after being orphaned, he left the school as a student and then returned there to teach, moving to Wayne County, Missouri, in 1855 when he was 20. However, in 1856 he moved to California and was involved in mining camps there and in Colorado and Nevada. He also taught in some local schools and ended up studying law and being admitted to the bar, serving as the treasurer of Carson County, then in the Utah Territory.

It was not until 1866 that he returned to Missouri and started practicing law in Rolla, working with his brother Charles C. Bland. In 1869, he moved to the nearby town of Lebanon, which was growing in prosperity due to the presence of the St. Louis and San Francisco Railroad.

In 1872, Richard Bland was elected to the U.S. House of Representatives as a Democrat, serving in the 43rd Congress. He remained in the House until 1894 when he was narrowly defeated. He regained his seat in 1896 and was reelected in 1898, one year before his death. Although the boundaries of his congressional district did change, he always represented the

Ozark country, the highland region in southern Missouri. This area was heavily involved in silver mining, and Bland, having also been involved in mining himself, championed their cause as the chairman of the Committee on Mines and Mining in the 44th Congress. He was later chairman of the Committee on Coinage, Weights, and Measures in the 48th Congress, the 49th Congress, the 50th Congress, the 52nd Congress, and the 53rd Congress, where he also dealt with issues related to gold and silver.

The major political move by R. P. Bland was his cosponsoring of the Bland-Allison Act in 1878 with Republican William Allison of Iowa. The authors of this bill wanted to end the five-year depression that been sparked by the Panic of 1873. The Coinage Act of 1873 had ensured that U.S. currency adhered to the gold standard. Bland wanted a return to silver coinage and particularly bimetallism, which would embrace the use of both gold and silver.

President Rutherford B. Hayes vetoed the bill, but the U.S. Congress voted to override the veto, and the bill became law. It was eventually replaced by the Sherman Silver Purchase Act in 1890, which was repealed by Congress three years later.

The use of silver was something that was much wanted by the miners as it would not only create a much larger demand for silver but would also stabilize the price of silver, which fluctuated far more than that of gold. The Bland-Allison Act, however, did not shore up the price of gold, which declined from a ratio of the gold price to that of silver of 16:1 in 1873 to 30:1 twenty years later. This was largely because of the major discovery of silver deposits in Nevada and nearby states.

R. P. Bland contested the 1896 Democratic presidential nomination. He lost to William Jennings Bryan and then loyally supported Bryan, who in turn lost to William McKinley. Bland died on June 15, 1899.

Justin Corfield

See also: Bryan, William Jennings (1860–1925); Depression of 1873; Gold Standard/Free Silver; McKinley, William, Jr. (1843–1901); Sherman Silver Purchase Act (1890); Silver Republicans

References

Schlesinger, Arthur M., ed. *The Election of 1876 and the Administration of Rutherford B. Hayes*. Philadelphia: Mason Crest Publishers, 2003.

Unger, Irwin. *The Greenback Era: A Social and Political History of American Finance, 1865–1879*. Princeton, NJ: Princeton University Press, 1964.

Blease, Cole (1868–1942)

A politician from South Carolina, Coleman Livingston Blease was a member of the state legislature and from 1911 until 1915 was the governor of South Carolina. He was also a U.S. senator from 1925 until 1931. His political career was one of a populist who used racism and demagoguery to gain the support of the poor whites.

"Cole" Blease was born on October 8, 1868, near Newberry, South Carolina, the second son of Henry Horatio Blease and his wife Mary Ann (née Livingston). His father had migrated to the United States from Liverpool, England, and established a hotel and stabling business that flourished. His mother died when he was five, and his father died in 1892.

Educated at Newberry College and South Carolina College (later the University of South Carolina), Blease was expelled for plagiarism in 1887 and always held a grudge against the university. In the following year he went to Georgetown University, graduated, and then started practicing law at Newberry. In 1890, he helped Benjamin Ryan Tillman, who was standing for elections to the state house of representatives. Tillman managed to get support from the wealthy farmers, but Blease saw that his own appeal was to the tenant farmers and textile mill workers, who were becoming increasingly more numerous. This emergence in state politics in South Carolina coincided with an agrarian upheaval that saw many people lose their lands.

Blease gained much support from within the Democrat Party and in 1911 was elected as governor of South Carolina. His period as governor—from January 1911 until January 1915—was extremely controversial. Race had remained a major issue in South Carolina politics, and Blease maintained hard-line policies against the aspirations of African Americans, with their education system remaining massively underfunded. Blease also turned a blind eye to lynching, to the point that some argue that he actually encouraged the practice. He openly referred to African Americans as "baboons and apes."

These attacks on African Americans won him support from many of the poor white mill workers and sharecroppers who otherwise would have been critical of his opposition to child labor laws, his criticisms of factory inspections, and his attacks on compulsory school attendance. His supporters also delighted in his attacks on the wealthy. Blease did manage to establish a state tuberculosis sanatorium and closed down a badly run textile mill in the state penitentiary. His populist appeal became known as "Bleaseism." In his doctoral thesis, Ronald D. Burnside noted that Bleaseism was an incoherent protest that was wracked by partisan politics.

Just as controversial as his racial policies, Blease was also active in pardoning convicted criminals. These included his chauffeur, who was twice fined for speeding, and also some 1,500 to 1,700 prisoners, with allegations made that he accepted payments for including people in the lists.

The main political opponent of Blease was Tillman, who had earlier been an ally. Tillman felt that Blease was running an openly corrupt administration. The two fought a bitter series of battles for control of the Democratic Party in South Carolina. Blease was reelected governor in 1912, but two years later he narrowly failed in his bid for election to the U.S. Senate, defeated by Ellison D. Smith. He then lost the gubernatorial election by less than 5,000 votes, but many of his supporters were elected to important positions in the state.

Coleman Blease was eventually elected in 1924, defeating James F. Byrnes, who Blease had portrayed as conniving. Blease was also keen to point out that Byrnes had been raised as a Roman Catholic. The election was closely fought, and Byrnes only narrowly lost it. Blease took up his seat in 1925 and served one term of six years. In 1930 Byrnes finally defeated Blease, who then retired from politics. He died on January 19, 1942. He had married twice. After the death of his first wife, he eventually separated from his second wife.

Justin Corfield

See also: Democratic Party; Tillman, Benjamin R. (1847–1918)

References

Burnside, Ronald Dantan. *The Governorship of Coleman Livingston Blease of South Carolina, 1911–1915.* Ph.D. dissertation, Indiana University, 1963.

Hollis, Daniel W. "Cole Blease: The Years between the Governorship and the Senate, 1915–1924," *South Carolina Historical Magazine* 80 (1): 1–17.

Lander, Ernest McPherson. *A History of South Carolina.* Chapel Hill: University of South Carolina Press, 1970.

Logue, Cal M., and Howard Dorgan. *The Oratory of Southern Demagogues.* Baton Rouge: Louisiana State University Press, 1981.

Miller, Anthony Barry. *Coleman Livingston Blease: South Carolina Politician.* Master's thesis, University of North Carolina, 1971.

Boas, Franz (1858–1942)

Franz Boas was born in Germany, where he earned a doctorate degree in physics from the University of Kiel. Even though his background was in the natural sciences, Boas developed a deep interest in the history of culture, which prompted him to take part in a scientific expedition to Baffin Island in the Canadian arctic. This journey eventually solidified his reputation as an influential anthropologist in the United States. A generation of Boas's students included Alfred Luis Kroeber (1876–1960), Edward Sapir (1884–1939), and Ruth Fulton Benedict (1887–1948). Boas and his students used the anthropological method to explore the intellectual challenges of the day, most notably racial differences in terms of differing cultural traditions—which was an opposing view to the march of evolutionary progress—as well as patterns of culture, which called into the question the idea of the superiority of civilization over primitivism. These ideas valued "the people" over "the elite."

After his trip to Baffin Island, Boas became fascinated by Inuit culture and dedicated his life to the study of anthropology. He was engaged at the Royal Ethnological Museum in Berlin (Museum für Völkerkunde) and at the University of Berlin. Boas was at first an outsider, however, within the evolutionarily oriented discipline of American anthropology, because of his broad view on the complexity of culture. Boas eventually played a crucial role in developing the frameworks used in modern American anthropology and has received both credit and criticism as a result.

Boas's contributions to the concept of culture in anthropology made him a public figure and an outstanding but controversial scholar in the field. Before Boas provided much of the basis of its modern anthropological meaning, the idea of culture fit neatly into the discourse of progressive social evolutionism. According to social evolutionism, culture created a platform for the perception of human groups in hierarchical terms, differing widely in the degree to which they compared against the gold standard of the era—civilized white man. According to Boas, such an assumption of culture was too schematic, and he called instead for empirical evidence. In an attempt to account for the critique of evolutionism, he wrote "the grand system of evolution of culture, that is valid for humanity, is losing much of its plausibility. In place of a single line of evolution there appears a multiplicity of converging and diverging lines which it is difficult to bring under one system" (Boas 1940, 522). Boas himself was a skillful field researcher who expounded a more empirically oriented anthropology. Yet Boas was unable to create any general theory because of his fears that such an abstract theory would show little understanding of the complex realities of human life. Thus, he focused on the individual cultural phenomenon in its historical context rather than collective elements in an evolutionary sequence.

Boas moved anthropology beyond the comparative method of evolutionism and racial typology. His famous work, *The Mind of Primitive Man* (1911), underscored the need for a better understanding of racial differences in terms of differing cultural traditions. Boas proved that thought, choice, and action, whether primitive or civilized, were largely determined by the body of custom and traditional material that arose through the enculturative process. For this reason, primitive men had all the characteristic human mental powers. In other words, Boas rejected traditional racial assumptions, widely held in American society, about racial achievement. He posited that no racial group was inherently inferior or superior. Boas's views on race and culture went beyond mere academic debate because the discourse of civilization enforced color-line politics in American society by asserting control over different, supposedly inferior, races. Boas's book was referred as the "Magna Charta of self-respect for lower races" (Baker 42).

According to Boas, scientific approaches completely disproved notions of race and culture that were based on ideological investments in the superiority of one's own race. Thus, Boas conceived the relativity of standards of valuation to validate a new method of inquiry whereby physical, environmental, and historical factors could be utilized to investigate human behavior. Boas negated traditional generalizations on primitive mentality on the basis of his own experiences in field work, thereby facilitating the role of research in anthropology. Boas perceived his work as presenting a more plausible view of primitive cultures because they involved the rejection of ethnocentric standards of culture.

In his book *Race and Democratic Society*, Boas underscored the "task of weaning the people from a complacent yielding to prejudice," which helped them to get a better understanding of the problems that confronted them (1945, 2). These words reflected Boas's influence on public thought. Boas appeared fully aware of the importance of race and culture in public discourse. He maintained a steadily scientific view on racial issues beyond the world of politics. On the other hand, admittedly, he crossed the boundaries of academic and public spheres to play the role of scientific expert in tracing down scientifically implausible concepts. Boas contradicted court rulings that allowed the legal sterilization of individuals and these courts' notoriously vague ideas on race. When the Nazis' program of race betterment provoked a sharp reaction against eugenics everywhere in the Western world, Boas was widely recognized as an intellectual who had attacked such scientific fraud years before Hitler's diatribes against Jews. Due to his authority, Boas led a successful campaign to unite scientists against the pseudoscientific dictum of race.

Currently, Franz Boas's ideas are still inspiring public discourse. Anthropologist Lee D. Baker notices that "as we move into 21st century, Franz Boas remains the scholar hard-core nativists and white supremacists love to hate" (46). According to Baker, there is a striking parallel between attacks on Boas in the nineteenth and twenty-first centuries because Boas's legacy remains "a threatening body of work for those vested in white supremacy" (Baker 46). Due to Boas's influence, social scientists have begun to perceive race as a cultural construct. What made Boas's theories revolutionary is that currently one sees differences among cultures as a result of historical events and circumstances and not from physically determined factors. Boas died in New York City, New York, on December 21, 1942.

Łukasz Albański

See also: "The Elites"; Gilded Age; "The People"; Social Darwinism

References

Baker, Lee D. "Franz Boas Out of the Ivory Tower." *Anthropological Theory* 4 (1): 29–51.

Barkan, Elazar. "Mobilizing Scientists against Nazi Racism, 1933–1939." In George W. Stocking, ed. *Bones, Bodies, Behavior: Essays on Biological Anthropology.* Madison: University of Wisconsin Press, 1988, pp. 180–205.

Boas, Franz. *Anthropology and Modern Life.* 1928. Reprint, New York: W. W. Norton, 1962.

Boas, Franz. *The Mind of Primitive Man.* New York: Macmillan Co., 1911.

Boas, Franz. *Race and Democratic Society.* New York: J. J. Austin, 1945.

Boas, Franz. *Race, Language and Culture.* New York: Macmillan Co., 1940.

Darnell, Regna. "Re-envisioning Boas and Boasian Anthropology." *American Anthropologist* 102 (4): 896–900.

Stocking, George W. "Franz Boas and the Culture Concept in Historical Perspective." *American Anthropologist* 68 (4): 867–82.

Bonus Army

The Bonus Expeditionary Force, better known as the Bonus Army, was a group of World War I veterans who descended on Washington, DC, in 1932 to demand early payment of the bonuses promised for their service in the Great War. Led by Sergeant Walter S. Waters, the group combined the term spurring their movement with the name of their former service under the American Expeditionary Force.

In the face of the worst depression the nation had yet seen, unemployed veterans voiced their needs in an increasing chorus of the desperate, only to be met with disappointment and violence. These men created a small community outside of the capital so that their plight would be visible to lawmakers and to make their demands known to the Congress and president. In the end, the government's representatives chose fiscal responsibility in the form of a balanced budget. In this era before the New Deal, neither the legislative nor executive branch saw social welfare as a responsibility of the federal government and turned the Bonus Marchers away to fend for themselves.

In 1925, despite President Calvin Coolidge's parsimony, Congress had passed a bill to provide World War I veterans with "adjusted compensation certificates," or bonuses. The 1920s had been an era of prosperity because of business-oriented politics and tight federal budgets, but the war loomed large in American minds, so congressmen were able to pass the bill over Coolidge's veto. Soldiers in previous wars had gained compensation, such as the Revolutionary War soldiers who received land scrip after the peace. As passed, each World War I veteran would receive a Treasury-paid endowment based on years of service during the war. Set to be paid in 1945, Bonus Marchers went to Washington and camped on Anacostia Flats in the southeastern part of Washington and in tents on the Mall to encourage the federal government to give them their bonuses early, which to the protesters seemed more like common sense than charity. They developed a "sophisticated social organization" with committees to manage the mass of protesters, estimated between 15,000 and 29,000 (Parrish 259). The infamous "Hoovervilles" had popped up around the nation to expose the severity of the economic downturn and blame Hoover for people's loss of jobs and homes. Now veterans also mocked Hoover's handling of the depression. One Bonus Army newspaper article reminded readers these men were "Heroes in 1917; They Call Us 'Criminals' Now" (Library of Congress).

Congress had attempted to pass some limited legislation only to be vetoed by President Herbert Hoover. Hoover ignored the demands of the veterans who stood behind Republican economic policies and old American ideals about the poor. For Hoover, the veterans could "care for themselves" (quoted in Parrish 259). Prior to the Great Depression, Americans accepted that were some "worthy poor," mostly women, children, and the disabled, who deserved some consideration, from private charities to pensions for soldiers' widows. But able-bodied men who could not provide for themselves for themselves or their families fell within the category of the unworthy poor. Their characters were deemed suspect because able-bodied men had no excuse not to work hard and succeed. Yet the Market Revolution (1815–1860) had transformed the economy from one of use and barter to a capitalist, competitive, and increasingly nationally interconnected one that created opportunities but simultaneously created conditions for failure by even the most hard-working people. The veterans thus fell into this category of the unworthy poor. Moreover, they did not demand charity but merely the early payment of their bonuses. Because some congressmen and the president rejected their pleas from a distance, veterans marched into Washington to provoke legislation, not riots. Hoover remained cold and aloof to the needs of these men when he refused to meet with them, although he did meet with other Americans and was filmed feeding his dog for newsreels.

By the summer of 1932, Hoover made matters worse by forcing the removal of the Bonus Marchers. Approximately one-quarter of the veterans left after Secretary of War Patrick Hurley and Secretary of Treasury Ogden Mills announced that they would be clearing out the protesters at Anacostia Flats to repurpose the abandoned federal buildings on that site. With thousands still in Washington, Hoover encouraged Congress to appropriate $100,000 to remove the remaining men who would not leave, money to be subtracted from their eventual bonus payments. In the attempt to clear marchers out, a scuffle ensued, and Hoover ordered General MacArthur to restore order. MacArthur had been convinced that this protest movement was a communist conspiracy to take over the government and took his cavalry, along with machine guns, bayonets, and tear-gas, to clear out the last of the veterans and their families camping on the Anacostia River. Instead of chastising MacArthur for disobeying orders, Hoover blamed the protesters. There is no evidence of a conspiracy or that the Bonus Army was more than a populist uprising during hard times.

Americans were appalled that poor, homeless men, women, and children were manhandled by the military. Hoover's treatment of the Bonus Army only added to perception that Hoover did not care about the people suffering during the Great Depression. Americans blamed President Hoover for the depression and for the government's lack of response to the people's suffering. In addition to Hoovervilles, turned-out empty pockets were called "Hoover flags," while "Hoover blankets" were in reality old newspapers.

Hoover rode into office on the prosperity of the 1920s, which Republicans claimed came from years of laissez-faire policies that had seemingly made the 1920 roar. By 1932, the Depression had raged for several years, and Americans became increasingly angry about his hands-off approach to the economy. As people struggled to feed their families and make homes, others drummed up support to rattle Washington into action. Farmers protested with the Farmers' Holiday movement, Hoover mishandled the Bonus Army, and 1932 was an election year. While Hoover ignored the voices of the people, New York Governor Franklin Delano Roosevelt was listening. In November 1932, the warm and amiable Roosevelt, who promised to help the "forgotten man," beat Hoover in a landslide election. Because Roosevelt had never explained what his "new deal" would look like, it is arguable from the events of 1932, such as the government's indifference to the Bonus Army, that many Americans voted for the man who was not Herbert Hoover.

Alexandra Kindell

See also: Coxey's Army; New Deal; Roosevelt, Franklin Delano (1882–1945); Shays's Rebellion (1786–1787)

References

American Experience. "The Bonus March (May–July, 1932)." http://www.pbs.org/wgbh/amex/macarthur/peopleevents/pandeAMEX89.html. Accessed January 2, 2013.

Hofstadter, Richard. *The American Political Tradition and the Men Who Made It.* New York: Vintage Books, 1989.

Library of Congress. "The Bonus Army March." http://www.loc.gov/exhibits/treasures/trm203.html. Accessed January 2, 2013.

Parrish, Michael E. *Anxious Decades: America in Prosperity and Depression, 1920–1941.* New York: W. W. Norton and Co., 1992.

Bourbon Democracy

The Bourbon Democrats were an important faction within the Democratic Party from the Reconstruction era until 1904. For much of that period they were the dominant force within the Democratic Party and played an influential role in party and national politics, including selection of the party's presidential nominee. "Bourbon Democrat" originated as a largely pejorative term used by critics who sought to equate many of the group's policy stances to the elitist, traditionalist views of Bourbon France, before the Revolution of 1789. It also referred to the influence of conservative southern Democrats (i.e., bourbon whisky) in general and specifically to those southern Democrats who opposed Reconstruction.

Bourbon Democrats were a combination of several constituencies including southerners, political and fiscal conservatives, and classical liberals. Bourbons supported the gold standard, seeing the policy as a means of stabilizing currency and the economy. They generally supported the U.S. business establishment and the ideas of limited government and laissez-faire economics, and they opposed commercial or agricultural subsidies and protectionist trade policies. They also opposed the expansion of U.S. territorial ambitions and military interventions abroad, stressing the need to focus attention upon critical domestic issues instead.

Although the faction and some of its candidates could espouse campaign rhetoric claiming to support the interests and rights of the common man, Bourbon attitudes were in general not favorable to the working classes of the era. The faction was opposed to organized labor, regarding stronger unions as both unhealthy for economic growth and as a threat to the continued political hegemony of traditionally influential elements within American society. Many leaders among the Bourbon Democrats were also averse to increased political participation on the part of small-scale farmers, the landless poor, and blue-collar urban workers, fearing that the working classes could upset the traditional balance of power and thus control the direction of the Democratic party.

The era of the Bourbon Democrats partially overlapped with the time period of Republican ascendency in U.S. national politics between 1860 and 1914. Due to Republican dominance and also to factionalization within Democratic ranks throughout much of the era, Bourbons were only able to win two presidential elections, but they did succeed in electing many members of Congress and in maintaining control of the Democratic Party for decades. Critics of the Bourbons and their motives have argued that taking the White House and winning elections in general may have been a less critical goal for the Bourbon leadership than maintaining the political and socioeconomic status quo within the party and nation.

The faction began to coalesce after the U.S. Civil War and was initially concentrated primarily in the South and Midwest prior to becoming influential in other parts of the country. In the presidential election of 1872, Bourbons supported the candidacy of Charles O'Conor, who declined the nomination in deference to Horace Greeley, who in turn lost to Republican Ulysses S. Grant. Four years later, the Bourbons succeeded in awarding the Democratic nomination to Samuel Tilden, who won the popular vote but narrowly lost the election to Republican Rutherford Hayes because of a highly controversial and contested Electoral College vote and what was known as the Compromise of 1877.

Bourbon Democrats frequently ran on anticorruption platforms, publicly denouncing graft at all levels of government. They were famously among the first influential groups to expose and condemn the malfeasance of the Tammany Hall political machine of New York, ultimately leading to its demise. The role played by the Bourbons in ending the Tammany Hall graft and in calling for other political change, such as civil service reform, which replaced the traditional system of political patronage, garnered them significant public support in the 1880s including the votes of Republican defectors disillusioned by scandals affecting their own party and its candidates.

Bourbon Democrats won their first presidential election in 1884 when their leader Grover Cleveland succeeded in portraying himself to voters as a reformer in contrast with Republican candidate James Blaine, who had been negatively affected by allegations of improper past business dealings. During his first term in office Cleveland exemplified Bourbon ideals, vetoing many bills that would have expanded federal spending or authority, reducing tariffs, condemning corruption, and supporting the gold standard and an isolationist U.S. foreign policy. In the 1888 election, Republican Benjamin Harrison championed the position of industrialists and labor unions in maintaining high tariffs, and although Cleveland won the popular vote, Harrison won the Electoral College and the presidency.

Four years later, the 1892 election centered primarily on the currency issue, specifically whether U.S. currency should be on the gold standard as most Bourbon Democrats advocated. The Democratic vote and Bourbon influence were weakened somewhat by the formation of a third party, the People's Party, or Populists, who fielded their own presidential candidate, Congressman James Weaver. The Populists drew support primarily from farmers and organized labor who increasingly felt alienated by the policies of both major parties of the era. Cleveland won both the popular and electoral votes, becoming the only president in U.S. history to serve two nonconsecutive terms and continuing to promote Bourbon policies.

The influence of Bourbon Democrats arguably reached its zenith with Cleveland's second term. In the 1896 elections, the probusiness, antilabor Bourbons were unsuccessful in securing the Democratic nomination. Instead, the Democratic and People's Parties both supported the candidacy of William Jennings Bryan, who lost the general election to Republican William McKinley. Bryan, known for his opposition to many Bourbon policies, again ran unsuccessfully against McKinley in 1900. The last candidate for the U.S. presidency fielded by the Bourbon Democrats was Alton Parker, who was handily defeated by Republican Theodore Roosevelt. This was to be the final national repudiation of a Bourbon candidate, and most of what remained of the faction's leaders and supporters faded from politics or transitioned to other political affiliations.

Barry Mowell

See also: Bryan, William Jennings (1860–1925); Cleveland, Grover (1837–1908); Democratic Party; Gilded Age; Gold Standard/Free Silver; McKinley, William, Jr. (1843–1901)

References

Going, Allen J. *Bourbon Democracy in Alabama 1874–1890*. Westport, CT: Greenwood Press, 1972.

Kent, Frank R. *The Democratic Party: A History*. New York: Century Co., 1928.

Merrill, Horace S. *Bourbon Democracy of the Middle West 1865–1896*. Seattle: University of Washington Press, 1967.

Perman, Michael. *The Road to Redemption: Southern Politics, 1869–1879*. Chapel Hill: University of North Carolina Press, 1985.

Bryan, William Jennings (1860–1925)

William Jennings Bryan, political leader, secretary of state, and Populist icon, was born to Silas L. Bryan and Mariah Elizabeth Bryan on March 19, 1860. Silas Bryan was a reputable lawyer and a state senator. His son William then studied at Union Law College in Chicago and afterwards practiced law in Jacksonville from 1883 to 1887. After shifting to Lincoln, Nebraska, he was attracted to politics. In 1890, Bryan was elected to Congress as part of a Democratic tidal wave. He was reelected two years afterwards and began to make his presence felt in national politics, especially after the repeal of the Sherman Silver Purchase Act in 1893 had caused a collapse of the silver market. Bryan advocated for Populist causes such as free silver and the removal of high tariffs. From 1894 to 1896, he was editor in chief of the *Omaha World-Herald*. Bryan traveled a lot in the United States, becoming popular as a politician who understood the needs of the countryside while most politicians were focusing on those of urban areas.

The Democratic National Convention at Chicago in 1896 catapulted him to national prominence. At the age of 36, he became the presidential candidate after the famous "Cross of Gold" speech of July 9, 1896. The People's Party also

William Jennings Bryan, Democratic party presidential candidate, 1896. (Library of Congress)

nominated him. He espoused the free and unlimited coinage of silver as a panacea for the economic woes affecting farmers and industrial workers. Bryan vehemently criticized supporters of the gold standard. The speech won him the Democratic nomination for president in 1896. However, he lost the tough contest to the Republican candidate, William McKinley. The Republican Party controlled the presidency for 28 of 36 years from 1896 to 1932. Although Bryan was defeated, he had a solid base in the South and Plains states.

During the Spanish-American War of 1898, Bryan became a colonel in the Nebraska regiment but did not go to the front because of contracting typhoid fever. Afterward, he became vocal as an anti-imperialist crusader. He strongly opposed the annexation of the Philippines, arguing that the United States did not have any moral authority to incorporate another country. Bryan received the Democratic Party nomination in 1900, and his adversary was again McKinley. The agenda of the Democrats was anti-imperialism and the silver issue. The former did not appeal to the electorate. The latter had lost its luster after the passing of the Gold Standard Act of 1900. Bryan criticized potential U.S. foreign domination, like that of the European empires, in a speech, "The Paralyzing Influence of Imperialism," at the Democratic National Convention held in Kansas City. In spite of hectic campaigning, he lost the election for the second time, receiving 155 Electoral College votes compared to the 292 that McKinley received. Even after losing two presidential elections, Bryan was undaunted, keeping up his lecture program and reiterating his opinion regarding popular issues. In 1901, Bryan founded a weekly newspaper, *The Commoner*. It harped on various topics such as consumer protection, regulation of trusts, and anti-imperialism.

Bryan made a third attempt at the presidency as the Democratic Party candidate in the 1908 election. William Howard Taft was the Republican nominee, while Bryan's slogan was, "Shall the People Rule?" He lost to Taft by 321 to 162 electoral votes. Subsequently, he became involved in the adult education movement, Chautauqua, which had spread throughout the American countryside. He informed attendees about the value of public service, religion, and morality. Due to his

Populist activities and his work with Chautauqua, Bryan became one of the prominent public speakers of the nation. He was secretary of state during the administration of President Woodrow Wilson. Bryan was not a hawk in foreign affairs and negotiated arbitration treaties with 28 nations, which stipulated arbitration of disputes to avoid war. Yet he was not able to sign a treaty with Germany. When World War I broke out, Bryan was an avid supporter of American neutrality. He had policy differences with Wilson and resigned in June 1915 following the sinking of the *Lusitania.*

Bryan remained active in the public arena. During the Progressive Era, Bryan espoused reform issues such as woman suffrage, prohibition, graduated federal income tax, popular election of American senators, peace, and Christian fundamentalism. Although he failed to achieve many of these objectives during his lifetime, some of these were enacted into law. A dedicated public servant and a guardian of the interest of workers, farmers, and religious Americans as well as ethnic minorities, Bryan died on July 26, 1925.

Patit Paban Mishra

See also: "Cross of Gold" Speech (1896); Democratic Party; Gold Standard/Free Silver; McKinley, William, Jr. (1843–1901); Progressivism

References

Anderson, David D. *William Jennings Bryan.* Boston: Twayne Publishers, 1981.

Boller, Paul F. *Presidential Campaigns from George Washington to George W. Bush.* Oxford, UK: Oxford University Press, 2004.

Brands, H. W. *The Reckless Decade: America in the 1890s.* New York: St. Martin's Press, 1995.

Cherny, Robert W., and Oscar Handlin. *A Righteous Cause: The Life of William Jennings Bryan.* Boston: Little, Brown, 1985.

Clements, Kendrick A. *William Jennings Bryan, Missionary Isolationist.* Knoxville: University of Tennessee Press, 1982.

Coletta, Paolo E. *William Jennings Bryan.* Lincoln: University of Nebraska Press, 1969.

Kazin, Michael. *A Godly Hero: The Life of William Jennings Bryan.* New York: Knopf, 2006.

Leinwand, Gerald. *William Jennings Bryan: An Uncertain Trumpet.* Lanham, MD: Rowman & Littlefield Publishers, 2007.

Rieser, Andrew. *The Chautauqua Moment: Protestants, Progressives, and the Culture of Modern Liberalism.* New York: Columbia University Press, 2003.

Whicher, George F. *William Jennings Bryan and the Campaign of 1896.* Boston: Heath, 1953.

Williams, Wayne C. *William Jennings Bryan: A Study in Political Vindication.* Eastbourne, UK: Gardners Books, 2007.

Bryce, James (1838–1922)

James Bryce was a prominent British historian, political scientist, politician, and diplomat. He was best known for his work *The American Commonwealth*, his two-volume study of the U.S. political system in the late nineteenth century. Bryce was born in Belfast, Ireland, on May 10, 1838. He received his education from Oxford College and the University of Glasgow. Bryce was admitted to the bar in 1867. He was a professor of law at Oxford University from 1870 to 1893 and at the University of Manchester from 1870 to 1875.

Bryce established himself early on as a distinguished scholar with the well-received work *The Holy Roman Empire* in 1864. He also wrote about his observations of South Africa in his book *Impressions of South Africa*, written after an 1897 visit. Bryce later became a critic of the harsh British tactics towards Boer civilians during the Boer War between Great Britain and South Africa. His most famous work was *The American Commonwealth* (1888), which was a comprehensive study of the U.S political system covering the workings of Congress, the presidency, the Supreme Court, state governments, and municipal governments. *The American Commonwealth* is still highly regarded by American historians and political scientists for its thorough and perceptive examination of the U.S. political system in the late nineteenth century.

Bryce represented the British tradition of engaging in both scholarship and politics. In British politics, Bryce was a member of the Liberal Party. From 1880 to 1906, he served in the House of Commons. From time to time, Bryce held a number of offices in Liberal governments (usually under Prime Minister William Gladstone). These included chairman of the Royal Board of Secondary Education, undersecretary of state for foreign affairs, president of the Board of Trade, and chief secretary for Ireland.

From 1907 to 1913, Bryce served as an ambassador to the United States. Bryce helped to solidify the already intimate ties between the United States and Great Britain. He established close relationships with a number of American political figures including Presidents Theodore Roosevelt and Woodrow Wilson.

After returning to England, Bryce became a member of the House of Lords and was given the title Viscount Bryce. At the beginning of World War I, Bryce was selected to write a report concerning allegations of German atrocities in Belgium. Known as the Bryce Report, this document, published in 1915, offered compelling evidence of German atrocities in Belgium. Bryce was also outspoken during World War I, criticizing the Ottoman Empire's treatment of Armenians. He condemned the treatment of Armenians by the Ottoman Empire as genocide in both his speeches and writings.

After World War I, Bryce served as a member of the International Court at The Hague and campaigned for the creation of the League of Nations. Bryce died in 1922 at the age of 83.

Jason Roberts

See also: Gilded Age; Historians of Populism; Progressivism; Roosevelt, Theodore (1858–1919)

References

Bryce, James. *The American Commonwealth.* New York: Macmillan and Company, 1888.

Bryce, James. *Modern Democracies.* New York: The Macmillan Company, 1921.

Fisher, H. A. L. *James Bryce.* New York: The Macmillan Company, 1927.

Ions, Edmund. *James Bryce and the American Democracy.* London: Macmillan, 1968.

Seaman, John T. *James Bryce: A Citizen of the World.* New York: Palgrave Macmillan, 2006.

Tulloch, Hugh. *James Bryce's American Commonwealth: The Anglo-American Background.* Wolfeboro, NH: Boydell Press, 1988.

Bull Moose Party

The National Progressive Party, popularly known as the "Bull Moose Party," was founded in 1912 by disaffected Republicans and was one of the most successful third parties in U.S. history. The establishment of this new political party was part of a much larger Progressive movement, an attempt to solve large social problems brought about by rapid urbanization and industrialization in the United States during the late nineteenth and early twentieth centuries. The Bull Moose Party was closely linked to former president Theodore Roosevelt, who was its standard bearer in 1912. The election of 1912 was, in fact, the party's high-water mark, and by 1916 it had largely faded. Though short lived, the group was highly influential, and within a few decades most of the positions advocated by the Bull Moose Party had become law.

The origin of the National Progressive Party had its roots in both the personal and the political. Roosevelt left the presidency in 1909 with his handpicked successor, Republican William Howard Taft, in office. The two men were friends, but a thank-you letter sent by Taft to the former president in which Roosevelt felt he was slighted began to erode the friendship. Roosevelt also missed the political limelight. Taft was more conservative politically, and a rift soon developed between progressive and conservative Republicans. While both men called themselves Progressives, Roosevelt believed much more strongly in social action through direct government intervention, while Taft believed the Constitution did not permit this. By 1910, Roosevelt was criticizing Taft and his policies publicly in speaking tours across the nation, and in early 1912 he decided to challenge his former friend. This was the first election in which primaries played a significant role in the nominating process, and though Roosevelt won a majority of these state contests (and more popular votes) by a large margin, the more conservative Taft forces controlled the party apparatus. Taft was nominated as the Republican presidential nominee on June 22; Roosevelt delegates then bolted the convention.

By August 1912, Roosevelt and his supporters had decided to form a third-party challenge to the president and held a convention to nominate their candidate and adopt a platform. When queried by reporters upon his arrival in Chicago for the gathering, Roosevelt said he felt like a "bull moose." The image soon gained popularity. The new party nominated Roosevelt to lead the ticket, with California Governor Hiram W. Johnson as its vice-presidential candidate. Though the Bull Moose Party had only a few short months in which to build a political party and mount a presidential bid, it succeeded in fielding candidates for state and national offices across much of the nation, in addition to the presidential ticket. The program advocated by these Progressives became known as "New Nationalism." The New Nationalism platform consisted of a host of Progressive policies including the direct election of U.S. senators, graduated income and inheritance taxes, closer regulation of business, woman suffrage, health coverage for all, workers compensation, and social insurance to provide for the disabled, unemployed, and aged.

Though the Bull Moose Party would have some success, the biggest winners in the Republican split were the Democrats and their nominee, New Jersey Governor Woodrow Wilson. By late in the evening on election day, a Wilson landslide was evident. He won 40 states with 433 electoral votes, but the third-party Progressives finished a strong second, winning 6 states and 88 electoral votes. The incumbent Republican won only 2 states. The Bull Moose Party won the popular votes of more than 4 million, compared to Wilson's total of slightly more than 6 million. The Progressives succeeded in winning one senate seat and 17 seats in the U.S. House of Representatives, and elected 260 members to state legislatures, though winning no governorships. It was a strong start for a party not even four months old, and Progressives came out of 1912 with high hopes for the future.

This optimism, however did not last. Despite some success on the local level in 1913, fissures within the party were already developing. There were disagreements over leadership, and some advocated reuniting with the Republicans. In 1914 a schism developed between those party members who advocated for educating the public on Progressive ideas and those wanting to emphasize political organization. Members arguing for a focus on the political won out, and many left the party in frustration. The 1914 mid-term elections were a disaster for the Bull Moose Party. They won in only one state, California, and in several states finished in fourth place, behind even the socialists. Party leaders and members began drifting back into the Republican fold at an accelerating pace. By 1915, a further rift developed in the already weakened party. On one side, led by Roosevelt, were those advocating preparedness for possible involvement in the war in Europe. Others, notably Jane Addams of Chicago, opposed preparedness and any American involvement in a European war. In 1916 Roosevelt declined the presidential nomination of the Bull Moose Party and announced his support for the Republican ticket. Unable to agree on another nominee, the few remaining party leaders disbanded, most returning to the Republican Party, though several moved on to support Wilson and the Democrats.

Despite the Bull Moose Party's short lifespan, its Progressive ideas flourished. President Wilson came to support much of its platform including woman suffrage and prolabor legislation. Shortly after the 1912 election, a progressive income tax and direct election of senators became law. Attempts at resurrecting the Progressive movement were led by Robert La Follette of Wisconsin in 1924 and Henry Wallace in 1948 but did not have the success of 1912. Many leaders of the Bull Moose Party played an active role in developing and administering Democrat Franklin Roosevelt's New Deal, most notable for the establishment of Social Security in the 1930s. Other progressive programs such as Medicare and Medicaid would be signed into law by President Lyndon Johnson in 1965, while health coverage for nearly all Americans would be enacted in 2010 under President Barack Obama.

Rick Primuth

See also: Addams, Jane (1860–1935); Great Society; New Deal; Obama, Barack, Populist Rhetoric of; Progressivism; Roosevelt, Franklin Delano (1882–1945); Roosevelt, Theodore (1858–1919)

References

Broderick, Francis L. *Progressivism at Risk: Electing a President in 1912.* New York: Greenwood Press, 1989.

Gable, John A. *The Bull Moose Years: Theodore Roosevelt and the Progressive Party.* Port Washington, NY: Kennikat Press, 1978.

Gould, Lewis L. *Four Hats in the Ring: The 1912 Election and the Birth of Modern American Politics.* Lawrence: University Press of Kansas, 2008.

Milkis, Sidney M. *Theodore Roosevelt, the Progressive Party, and the Transformation of American Democracy.* Lawrence: University Press of Kansas, 2009.

Burned-over District

The Burned-over District was both a place and a phenomenon. First of all, the district comprised a region of western New York State, which in the nineteenth century experienced a boom in both industry and population as many migrants sought opportunity west of the already populous eastern seaboard. The Burned-over District also describes the effect of a religious revival. Charles Grandison Finney gave the district its name, describing the region as "burned-over," in which he meant that the fires of the holy spirit had spread rapidly and totally, leaving few unscathed or unaffected, as would have any real forest fire. The sheer scope of the revival in terms of intensity and length of time (1800–1850) reinforced the idea that this region of New York, above any other in the country, had borne particular witness to the saving works of God. The place and the phenomenon were intimately related, for it was the particular geographic and demographic makeup of this region of the country that enabled the growth and maintenance of one of the most fervent and long-lived periods of revival in American history. Further, it was in this part of the country during this time that many of the most radical and innovative religious movements in the United States found root. The Burned-over District was the eye of the storm in a country and a time when revival was rampant and religious experimentation was at a high.

Historians have speculated as to why the Burned-over District experienced such an overwhelming and lengthy period of revival in contrast to nearly every other part of the United States during this time. One of the most probable causes was the physical landscape. Rife with rivers and canals (most important of which was the Erie Canal), western New York was made up of a series of "port" cities. The rivers made it possible to travel and communicate across long distances, a factor that allowed news to travel swiftly from town to town. Second, no one religious group dominated the area. Competition among various Christian denominations and movements meant that the inhabitants of western New York were primed to hear the word from various people. Finally, many people were migrating to western New York from New England during this time, hoping to benefit from the booming economy of the district. Most of these bore an intense morality and religious sensibility, instilled in them by the religious tradition of their New England homeland. Many were still feeling the after-effects of the Great Awakening, a period of revival in New England that began in the 1740s, and thus were accustomed to enthusiastic religion. The booming port culture along with the heightened sense of religious competition and the spiritual readiness of new settlers from the East set the stage for the unprecedented season of revivals to come.

Beginning in the winter of 1799–1800, western New York experienced what came to be called the Great Revival. These first few months marked the beginning of a series of revivals that would occur over the next 50 years. After this first winter, revivals occurred across the region almost simultaneously. Swift communication of revival news was aided by the river trade routes and the great amount of traffic between towns during that time. Also facilitating the great speed and symmetry with which these revivals occurred were the many societies that arose out of this first period of revival. Every denomination and religious group formed a society whose duties were to seek converts, at least at first. The greater goal ultimately became broad-scale revival across religious lines—a fact reflected in the Plan of Union in 1801 and the American Home Missionary Society (AHMS) in 1826. The latter grew out of the many local societies that had been sustaining revivals for more than two decades. The AHMS effectively centralized missionary efforts in the region, ensuring that revivals spread and persisted across the region. Though revival occurred consistently throughout the first half of the nineteenth century, revival was at its highest pitch prior to 1825. The various organizations and mechanisms put in place, as well the momentum built by the many successful revivals in the region and what one historian calls "the growing appetite of the region for exhibitions of zeal," combined to make the next 25 years a time of unprecedented conversion and religious spirit (Cross 30).

One of the effects of such a broad-scale, cross-denominational revival was a shock of new religious movements. Though most of the converts remained Protestant and generally affiliated with one Protestant denomination or another, there were quite a few for whom the religious fervor of the district led down a less conventional route. The Burned-over District was home to Joseph Smith, whose own experience of confusion during the revival led to his founding of the Church of Jesus Christ of Latter-day Saints (Mormons). As Smith told the story, his confusion over the multiplicity of religious choices caused a spiritual crisis during which he experienced a series of visions that ultimately led him to his calling as a prophet. In spite of the seeming eccentricity of some of Smith's claims (that an angel led him to find a set of golden, scriptural plates), the general tenor of religious zeal during that time meant that his message was more likely to be heard. He eventually gathered a strong group of followers who would leave the state for Ohio in the 1830s. In addition to the Latter-day Saints, William Miller and his "Millerites" found a home in the Burned-over District. Miller was a millenarian who predicted the precise date on which Christ's Second Coming would occur (first on March 21, 1844, and then on October 22, 1844). In spite of the fact that Miller's predictions did not come true, he retained a great following in Upstate New York, some of whom would become Seventh-day Adventists, the offshoot of Millerism. The Burned-over District was also home to many utopian religious experiments, most famously John Humphrey Noyes's Oneida Community. The community was best known for its communal living and working arrangements (and array of products it produced), but mostly for its practice of plural or shared marriage. The Burned-over District also played host to social reform. Both the women's rights and temperance movements received a great deal of support in the region during this time, as did the antislavery movement during the Civil War.

The effects of religious enthusiasm in the Burned-over District would last long after the last revival tent was dismantled. The converts and religious movements it produced, as well as the commerce it helped support and the social reform it spawned, were proof of the overarching effects of the Great Revival. Further, in the annals of American religious history, western New York will forever be viewed as a place so saturated with the spirit and popular zeal that it was literally "burned over."

Lydia Eeva Natti Willsky

See also: Eddy, Mary Baker (1821–1910)

References

Barkun, Michael. *Crucible of the Millennium: The Burned-over District of New York in the 1840s.* Syracuse, NY: Syracuse University Press, 1986.

Cross, Whitney. *The Burned-over District: The Social and Intellectual History of Enthusiastic Religion in Western New York, 1800–1850.* Ithaca, NY: Cornell University Press, 1950.

Evans, Robert. *Fire from Heaven: A Description and Analysis of the Revivals of the "Burned-over District" of New York 1800 to 1840 and Spiritual Deceptions.* Hazelbrook, Australia: Research in Evangelical Revivals, 2005.

Smith, Timothy L. *Revivalism and Social Reform: American Protestantism on the Eve of the Civil War.* Baltimore, MD: Johns Hopkins University Press, 1980.

Wellman, Judith. *Grass Roots Reform in the Burned-over District of Upstate New York: Religion, Abolitionism, and Democracy.* New York: Garland Publishing, 2000.

Burrows, Jay (1833–1900)

Jay Burrows of Gage County, Nebraska, served as a prominent member of the National Farmers' Alliance during the late nineteenth century. In the early 1880s, Burrows became the Alliance's secretary of state. In November 1887, he was elected as president of the National Farmers' Alliance. Burrows also served as the editor of the *Alliance*, which was a weekly newspaper published in Lincoln, Nebraska.

Later renamed the *Farmers' Alliance*, the newspaper examined the hardships faced by western farmers as well as potential solutions to the nation's social and economic problems. Additionally, Burrows was one of the principal organizers of the People's Party in Nebraska. During the 1890s, the newly established party represented a political threat to the Republicans and Democrats in Nebraska.

On March 4, 1833, Jay Burrows was born in Mayville, New York. While growing up in western New York, he worked as a printer for several local newspapers. Following the outbreak of the Civil War, Burrows supported the use of coercive action by the federal government to preserve the Union. In 1862, Burrows enlisted in the military service, where he served in the Ninth New York Cavalry during the Civil War. Under the command of Major General Philip H. Sheridan and Lieutenant Colonel George A. Custer, Burrows participated in several military campaigns in the Shenandoah Valley. At the conclusion of the Civil War, Burrows and his family moved to Iowa to pursue agricultural interests. By 1880, Burrows relocated his family to Nebraska, where they purchased a homestead in Gage County. During the next 10 years, Burrows and his family built a comfortable life for themselves as they cultivated their land and sold agricultural products at nearby markets.

During the late 1880s, Nebraska farmers suffered economic hardships as agricultural prices declined rapidly while the price of consumer goods and railroad freight rates continued to rise. The lack of currency and credit as well as burdensome mortgages added to the farmers' grievances during the late nineteenth century. Accordingly, the depressed economy created an agrarian revolt throughout the United States. In October 1887, members of the National Farmers' Alliance held a convention in Minneapolis, Minnesota, where they adopted a series of demands to solve the farmers' social and economic problems. These demands called for federal ownership of the railroads as well as the unlimited coinage of silver money. The following month, Alliance members elected Burrows as president of the National Farmers' Alliance. During the late 1880s, Burrows endorsed Alliance demands, and he promised to improve western farmers' lives.

With the growing discontent among western farmers, the Nebraska Farmers' Alliance established several cooperatives stores, which offered farmers economic relief by marketing their agricultural products and selling consumer goods at wholesale prices. Aside from the Alliance's cooperative programs, the organization also relied on traveling lecturers and newspapers to advance its goals. In 1889, Burrows moved to Lincoln, Nebraska, where he founded the *Alliance*. Serving as the official newspaper for the Nebraska Farmers' Alliance, the *Alliance* addressed the concerns of local farmers who were at risk of losing their homes and landholdings.

Initially, Burrows urged members of the Nebraska Farmers' Alliance to remain nonpartisan, but the growing influence of the railroad industry within the Republican Party led him to support the establishment of an independent political party. On April 22, 1890, Alliance county presidents and local representatives met in Lincoln, Nebraska, to discuss the creation of the People's Party. The delegates agreed that independent political action was necessary to improve their economic conditions, and they circulated petitions calling for a People's Party state nominating convention. After obtaining nearly 15 thousand signatures from across the state, Alliance leaders issued a call for a convention, which was held in Lincoln, Nebraska. On July 29, 1890, Nebraska Farmers' Alliance members met with Union Laborites, the Knights of Labor, and Grangers to select Populist candidates for statewide offices. The delegates at the convention also adopted a party platform, which advocated land reform and economic democracy.

During the early 1890s, Burrows continued to serve as the editor of the *Farmers' Alliance*, which promoted cooperative programs among western farmers. In the summer of 1892, Burrows sold his interest in the *Farmers' Alliance* after he became disillusioned with the agrarian movement in Nebraska. While Burrows had recommended that the National Farmers' Alliance and the National Famers' Alliance and Industrial Union work together to solve farmers' problems, he opposed a consolidation of the two groups. Burrows maintained that the sheer size of the National Farmers' Alliance and Industrial Union would subordinate western farmers' interests to the demands of the southern organization. Accordingly, Burrows's argument influenced Alliance members to block the merger between the National Farmers' Alliance and the National Farmers' Alliance and Industrial Union during the late nineteenth century.

Despite the failure of the National Farmers' Alliance and the National Farmers' Alliance and Industrial Union to merge as a national coalition, Alliance members in Nebraska endorsed a fusion among the Populists and Democrats during the mid-1890s. Burrows asserted that the political alliance would enable the Populists to win state and national elections. Nevertheless, the fusion strategy led to the downfall of the People's Party as Democratic candidates ignored the Populists' political demands. By the late 1890s, Nebraska Populists struggled to reorganize the third-party movement because the People's Party had lost its political identity.

Following the demise of the People's Party in Nebraska, Burrows travelled throughout the Lincoln area, where he lectured on various issues including prohibition and the nationalist movement. On January 16, 1900, Burrows died in Lincoln, Nebraska.

Kevin M. Brady

See also: Agricultural Newspapers and Farmer Unrest; *Alliance*; Granger Movement; Knights of Labor; Plains and Midwest, Populism in the; People's Party; Powers, John H. (1831–1918); Willits, John F. (unknown–1910)

References

Goodwyn, Lawrence. *The Populist Moment: A Short History of the Agrarian Revolt in America.* New York: Oxford University Press, 1978.

Hicks, John D. *The Populist Revolt: A History of the Farmers' Alliance and the People's Party.* Minneapolis: University of Minnesota Press, 1931.

Kazin, Michael. *The Populist Persuasion: An American History.* New York: Basic Books, 1995.

McMath, Robert C., Jr. *Populist Vanguard: A History of the Southern Farmers' Alliance.* Chapel Hill: University of North Carolina Press, 1975.

Bush, George W., Populist Rhetoric of

Two-term Republican president George W. Bush (2001–2009) used populist appeals to redefine his privileged upbringing and position himself as the leader of a moral and democratic global majority standing against a powerful minority of violent extremists. As a presidential candidate, Bush sought to transform his image from a Connecticut-born, oil-wealthy son of a former president into that of a humble Texas rancher who found God, quit drinking, and became a family man. Bush used his middle initial, W. (or "Dubya," according to pundits) to avoid the moniker "George Bush Jr." In 1999 the Bushes bought their ranch in Crawford, Texas, where Bush spent significant time during his presidency, and which he sold shortly after leaving office. At the 2000 Republican National Convention, Bush spoke about his childhood in Midland, Texas, where people worked hard for better lives and embraced the town's motto, the "sky was the limit." Each person, regardless of individual differences, believed he or she had an equal claim to the United States' promise because all people are equal before God.

Al Gore, the Democratic challenger in 2000, also utilized populist appeals, leading some observers to frame the election as a battle of rival populisms. Gore pledged to defend working families against "big" enemies, such as big oil and big polluters. He presented Bush, and his running mate Dick Cheney, as wealthy Republicans who would spend billions on tax relief for top investors, income earners, and inheritors of large estates. Yet Bush himself fostered an identity as a simple man who shared the values and perspectives of the common people rather than those of Washington. Gore's strategy received criticism from the political right, who claimed the candidate was engaged in class warfare, and from the political left, who questioned his reliance on economic populism after a substantial period of economic growth.

Though Bush ultimately won the Electoral College vote, the popular vote went to Gore; thus the Bush presidency began with a disputed victory that was ultimately settled by the Supreme Court. As a result, Bush did not receive the "honeymoon period" afforded most presidents. This produced a dubious political mandate that, coupled with criticisms of Bush's perceived lack of intellectual abilities and tendency to malaprop, created an unfavorable image for the new president.

Bush campaigned on a small number of issues, including lower taxes; educational, health, and social security reform; and the creation of a ballistic missile system. His practice, as governor of Texas and as president, was to campaign and govern around a clear set of goals. Bush spent several weeks after the inauguration courting Democrats in what the press labeled a "charm offensive" before mobilizing congressional Republicans in the hopes of passing a $1.6 billion tax cut. The cut was passed in a reduced form, but Bush declared victory, and the tax cuts became a major component of Bush's domestic policy agenda.

Since Dwight Eisenhower, a war hero turned chief executive, presidents have sought to develop the image of the president as a hero. For John F. Kennedy and his supporters, for example, "the White House was an historic theater in which the hero should seek the center stage" (Roper). For Bush, the War on Terror following the September 11, 2001, attacks provided him with his moment. The president's public approval ratings on September 10, 2001, were the lowest of his presidency to that date. "Majority opinion was against him on a range of policy issues" (Roper). He was in danger of mirroring John Quincy Adams, who, like his father, was a one-term president. After September 11, Bush received the longest stretch of approval ratings over 60 percent for any president in the last 40 years. The remarkable transformation was "a roller coaster of political reinvention" (Roper). On the day of the attack, Bush appeared less than fully confident. From then on, however, he "radiated a sense of self-assurance and calm determination" (Greenstein). Bush assumed a mantle of heroic presidential leadership and "appeared as a president tested and tempered by the crisis" (Roper).

In the first year of the War on Terror, Bush articulated fundamental differences between the United States and its enemies, invoking American ideas of exceptionalism and moral rectitude. Bush appealed to the notion of faith in proclaiming the United States' strength as a compassionate and loving nation in contrast to those who opposed American values, such as freedom and democracy. Bush explained:

> I see things this way: The people who did this act on America and who may be planning further acts are evil people. They don't represent an ideology. They don't represent a legitimate political group made of people. They're flat evil. That's all they can think about, is evil. And as a nation of good folks, we're going to hunt them down and we're going to find them and we will bring them to justice. (September 25, 2001)

The president chose to depict terrorists as "evildoers" who valued the accumulation of power and the sacrifice of human life, in response to those who questioned whether the United States was in some way deserving of the 9/11 attacks. Bush "wanted to make it clear that he saw absolutely no moral equivalence," as his speechwriter David Frum explained, "so he reached right into the Psalms for that word" (Fineman). Presidents at war traditionally avoided fault by constructing "narratives that depict enemies as coercive antagonists that impel action" (Winkler). This legitimizes presidential initiatives as defensive actions in the name of national security.

In the weeks after 9/11, the president claimed that the United States was awakened to danger, and he encouraged citizens not to lose sight of the core mission: fighting terrorism on all fronts. He framed this mission as timeless and all-encompassing, complete only when "every terrorist group of global reach has been found, stopped, and defeated." God was on the United States' side. According to the president, "the course of this conflict is not known, yet its outcome is certain. Freedom and fear, justice and cruelty, have always been at war, and we know that God is not neutral between them" (September 20, 2001). Within his anger he presented a clear vision of what the United States needed to do: defend its freedom and way of life. By framing the attack in terms of Western values, the War on Terror was positioned as a blessed fight to defend U.S. civilization and the world.

The message Bush delivered after 9/11 was unique in that "war messages are typically thoughtful rather than angry; they explain the origins of the immediate problem and the necessity for war; normally arguing that military force is being used as a last resort." The president and nation "were angry rather than thoughtful, the origins of the immediate problem and the enemy were unknown, and the military force seemed a necessary first resort" because "the national trauma demanded retribution" (Smith). This led to the development of "crisis rhetoric" where policies were questioned on the basis of support for the mission rather than their plausibility and perceived effectiveness. Achievement became a matter of faith and determination rather than a matter of proof and rational calculation.

Bush's early war rhetoric was full of evangelical language. He identified two awakenings experienced by the American people. The nation first awoke to danger after the attacks on the World Trade Center and recognized that American values and culture were not safe in the post–Cold War world. The second awakening came in determining how to respond to the attacks. Militarily, Americans realized that they must support an all-encompassing mission of eradicating terror. Americans also drew comfort from being a loving nation, and they responded through service. This latter point laid the foundation for the domestic component of the War on Terror, an often overlooked portion of Bush's war rhetoric.

In the 2002 State of the Union Address, the president stated his hope "that all nations will heed our call, and eliminate the terrorist parasites who threaten their countries and our own." If governments were timid in the face of terror, the United States would act. "Every nation should know," Bush explained "that for America, the War on Terror is not just a policy, it's a pledge. I will not relent in this struggle for the freedom and security of my country and the civilized world" (March 11, 2002). Moreover, other countries were either "for us" or "against us." He defined Western values as universal desires. Bush explained that "prosperity and freedom and dignity are not just American hopes or Western hopes. They are universal, human hopes . . . even in the violence and turmoil of the Middle East, America believes these hopes have the power to transform lives and nations" (June 24, 2002).

Bush's concept of moral truth, drawn from his personal devotion to evangelical Protestantism, emerged when the president discussed what average American citizens could do to assist the War on Terror. Bush believed that the United States was born again with love, compassion, and kindness, saving the nation's collective soul. The president stated that people could fight terror and evil with millions of acts of kindness. In essence, Bush's evangelical rhetoric subsumed his populism by calling to the most basic good of every American. Bush's emphasis on faith and love colored his public statements far more frequently than those of other recent presidents. He understood unconditional love as the greatest gift from God, particularly as articulated in the Christian gospel, because Christ's death "stands out in history as the perfect example of unconditional love" (Kengor).

The terrorist attacks caused Americans to reassess what was important. Bush viewed part of his job as capturing this "new spirit." He believed that "for too long our culture has said 'if it feels good, do it.' " The sacrifice of soldiers, the brotherhood of firefighters, and the bravery and generosity of citizens revealed a glimpse of a "new culture of responsibility" (State of the Union, 2002). This responsible society was part corporate, part personal, and part social. Businesses had to be more forthcoming in their accounting practices. Individuals should love their neighbors. American society had to pursue greater peace and compassion at home and abroad. Serving something larger than one's self became the new definition of patriotism. Bush frequently spoke about his "soldiers" in the "armies of compassion" and recognized dozens by name in campaign speeches.

After dehumanizing Al-Qaeda and mobilizing the armies of compassion, Bush turned his attention toward Iraq. The notion of fighting terrorists abroad in the pursuit of national security was not on its face extraordinarily controversial. Launching a preemptive strike in Iraq, however, became a highly disputed expansion of the War on Terror. Iraq did not have the clear connection to the war that Afghanistan did. Afghanistan's ruling Taliban regime refused to give up Bin Laden, the founder of Al-Qaeda, the terrorist organization responsible for the 9/11 attacks. In contrast, Bush feared that if weapons of mass destruction (WMDs) came into possession of rogue dictators, such as Saddam Hussein in Iraq, the United States would be in great danger. In 2003 the Bush administration asserted that Iraq possessed WMDs that posed a direct and immediate threat to the United States. In fact, however, the 9/11 Commission later concluded that Iraq and Al-Qaeda did not have a collaborative relationship prior to September 11 and that Iraq did not give refuge to top Al-Qaeda leaders, as the Taliban had with Bin Laden. Bush eventually acknowledged that Iraq did not have WMDs and that Saddam Hussein had no direct connection with 9/11, despite intimations in the 2004 campaign that he did. During the campaign Bush framed his Democratic opposition as questioning whether the United States was really at war and as viewing terrorism as a crime that should be dealt with as a law enforcement issue. Bush presented himself as a tested leader who understood the necessity of a proactive military approach during a time of great danger, the hopeful hero seeking center stage of the debate.

In his second term Bush went from being among the most popular presidents in U.S. history to among the most unpopular. As a result, Republicans lost control of Congress in 2006. Establishing democratic governments in Afghanistan and Iraq proved to be much more difficult than originally anticipated. Tactics adopted by the administration, such as secret CIA prisons, torture, and extraordinary rendition, received heavy scrutiny. Domestically, Bush unsuccessfully sought to privatize social security and reform immigration policy, two political priorities of his second term. Meanwhile, the federal government faced widespread criticism for its response to the devastation caused by hurricanes that devastated the Gulf Coast, including the city of New Orleans, and the economy experienced the greatest downturn since the Great Depression. These factors, and more, contributed to Bush leaving office as the most unpopular president since Richard Nixon. Consequently, John McCain, the Republican candidate in 2008, distanced himself from Bush in the campaign, and Republicans experienced resounding defeats in the House, Senate, and Executive Office. Bush had betrayed his populist rhetoric with actions that offended a large enough number of Americans, resulting in a Democratic turnover in 2008.

Bush effectively used populist appeals to present himself as small-town Texas rancher to whom the masses could relate, irrespective of his wealthy upbringing in a powerful political family. He overcame the disputed 2000 election, the lack of a popular mandate, and doubts surrounding his governing ability to become an effective and popular leader in the aftermath of 9/11. As a wartime president, Bush used populist appeals to build support for the war efforts and subsequent policy decisions made by his administration. The defense of freedom was the centerpiece of these efforts. Bush developed a rhetorical framework premised on a sharp contrast between the global majority of freedom-loving people and the terrorist elite, who aggressively threatened the safety of democratic citizens, embodied in the "for us" or "against us" dichotomy he employed.

Similar to other politically conservative populists, Bush's populism exhibited a strong religious component, which for him was inspired by his evangelical Christian faith and his struggle to overcome alcoholism. These contributed to his views of compassionate conservatism at home and to his foreign policy ambitions of ending tyranny abroad and spreading democracy throughout the world. The human and financial cost of a two-front war and related nation-building efforts strained Bush's image and popularity during his second term. The 2007 economic collapse eliminated any domestic credibility Bush had maintained. When accepting his party's nomination for president in 2000, Bush joked that the United States' first president, and arguably one of the greatest, referred to himself as "George W." Upon leaving office in 2008, the George W. of the twenty-first century hoped that his legacy would grow to resemble that of Abraham Lincoln or Harry Truman, both of whom faced great challenges and widespread unpopularity only to become great U.S. presidents in posterity.

Luke Perry

See also: Evangelicalism and Populism; Obama, Barack, Populist Rhetoric of

References

Bush, George W. Speeches. http://www.votesmart.org. Accessed January 2, 2013.

Bush, George W. "Text of the President Bush's 2002 State of the Union Address." *Washington Post*, January 29, 2002. http://www.washingtonpost.com. Accessed January 2, 2013.

Cooperman, Alan. "Bush's References to God Defended by Speechwriter." *The Washington Post*, December 12, 2004.

Fineman, Howard. "Bush and God." *Newsweek*, October 23, 2007.

Formisano, Ron. "Populist Currents in the 2008 Presidential Campaign." *Journal of Policy History* 22 (2): 237–255.

Greenstein, Fred. "The Changing Leadership of George W. Bush: A Pre- and Post-9/11 Comparison." *Presidential Studies Quarterly* 32 (2): 387–396.

Ivie, Robert. "Fighting Terror by Rite of Redemption and Reconciliation." *Rhetoric and Public Affairs* 10 (2): 221–248.

Jacobson, Gary. "The Bush Presidency and the American Electorate." *Presidential Studies Quarterly* 33 (4): 701–729.

John, Sue Lockett, David Domke, Kevin Coe, and Erica Graham. "Going Public, Crisis after Crisis: The Bush Administration and the Press from September 11 to Saddam." *Rhetoric and Public Affairs* 10 (2): 195–220.

Kazin, Michael. *The Populist Persuasion: An American History.* New York: Basic Books, 1995.

Kengor, Paul. *God and George W. Bush.* New York: Regan Books, 2004.

Roper, Jon. "George W. Bush and the Myth of Heroic Presidential Leadership." *Presidential Studies Quarterly* 34 (1): 132–142.

Smith, Craig Allen. "President Bush's Enthymeme of Evil." *American Behavioral Scientist* 49 (1): 32–47.

Tenpas, Katherine Dunn, and Stephen Hess. "The Bush White House: First Appraisals." *Presidential Studies Quarterly* 32 (3): 577–585.

Winkler, Carol. "Parallels in Preemptive War Rhetoric: Reagan on Libya; Bush 43 on Iraq." *Rhetoric and Public Affairs* 10 (2): 303–334.

Woodward, Bob. *Bush at War.* New York: Simon & Schuster, 2003.

Yates, Joshua. "The Resurgence of Jihad and the Specter of Religious Populism." *SAIS Review* 27 (1): 127–144.

Butler, Marion (1863–1938)

Marion Butler was a Populist leader and politician from North Carolina who was most active during the last decade of the nineteenth century. Butler supported certain reforms, including a national currency based on silver and federal ownership of railroads and telegraphs, which would benefit his rural followers. He also recognized the need for Populists to cooperate with other parties to achieve the political power necessary for reforms. After one term in the U.S. Senate, Butler spent the remainder of his life as a businessman and supporter of the farming community.

Marion Butler was born on May 20, 1863, in Sampson County, North Carolina, near Clinton. His father was a Confederate veteran and farmer. Although the family was not wealthy, Butler was able to attend the University of North Carolina. He graduated in 1885 and began to study law, but his studies were cut short by his father's early death. As the eldest of six children, Butler shouldered the responsibility of managing the family farm. He also organized schooling for his siblings and for the children of neighbors.

In the late 1880s, the Farmers' Alliance movement spread from Texas to North Carolina, working for the economic improvement of farmers. Butler was attracted to the movement, and it quickly proved to be a path for his professional advancement. Unlike most other farmers, he possessed the educational background and articulateness needed to spread the Farmers' Alliance message. Butler rose through the ranks rapidly and was elected president of the Sampson County Farmers' Alliance when he was 25. Butler bought into a newspaper in Clinton, the *Caucasian*, and used it to spread the Farmers' Alliance movement's message. He later moved the paper to Goldsboro and Raleigh as his political fortunes advanced. The *Caucasian* became a leading agrarian publication with a regional following.

As Butler's standing as a leader of the Farmers' Alliance grew, he turned to politics. In 1890, his fellow farmers elected Butler to the North Carolina state senate as an "Alliance Democrat." While in the state legislature, Butler helped to create a state college for women at Greensboro and a state railway commission. His political affiliation remained with the Democratic Party, but Butler was viewed as a champion of the farmers and a leader of the movement. In 1891, even though he was still young at only 28 years old, members of the Farmers' Alliance elected Butler president of the North Carolina Farmers' Alliance. The next year, Leonidas L. Polk, another North Carolinian and leader of the farmers' movement, died unexpectedly. His death raised leadership opportunities for Butler on the national stage. In 1893, Butler was elected president of the National Farmers' Alliance.

By that time, Butler had largely broken with the state Democratic Party. The party's candidate for president in 1892 was Grover Cleveland. Cleveland favored currency based on gold and other measures friendly towards businesses. Although farmers did not want to support Cleveland, the North Carolina Democratic Party would not let members split their support. Butler led a mass exodus of farmers and agrarian interests from the Democrats, therefore, to join the People's Party in 1892. The Populists entered the 1892 campaign in North Carolina too late to hope for victories, but they and the Republicans received a majority of the ballots cast.

The Democrats labeled Butler the "sly fox of Sampson County," and he became the party's chief nemesis for the rest of the decade. While remaining the national leader of the Farmers' Alliance, he took over the position of state chairman of the People's Party. Butler advocated fusion between the Populists and Republicans. This was less than a merger of the party, but represented a cooperative effort to enact reforms to reach joint goals. In 1894, the Populists and Republicans swept the state elections and gained control over the state legislature. The state senate elected Butler to the U.S. Senate, where he took office in 1895.

As a U.S. senator, Butler spoke out in favor of reforms favored by farmers. He got legislation passed that funded experiments in free rural delivery of mail, leading to the national program that provided postal deliveries to farmers. He also helped establish postal savings banks that served small depositors. Butler had less success with his other issues, including a national currency based on silver. He and others believed that financial reform would make more money available, reducing interest rates and making loans more available for farmers and working men. Butler also tried to introduce legislation for governmental control or ownership of the railroads and the telegraph. He hoped that by eliminating monopolies, the cost of transporting goods to market would be reduced, allowing farmers to earn more of a profit. These reforms failed to pass. Butler's influence in the Senate was limited because he was one of only a small number of Populists in office, and members of other parties were not willing to work with him.

In 1896, Butler reached the peak of his national political importance by carrying his policy of fusion to its greatest extreme. He convinced his fellow Populists to nominate William Jennings Bryan as their candidate for president at their convention in St. Louis. Bryan had already been nominated by the Democratic Party and supported many of the same goals as the Populists, including silver-based money. The party showed its independence, however, by nominating Populist Thomas E. Watson as vice president to run with Bryan, while the Democrats had a different vice-presidential candidate. During the election campaign, Butler worked closely with the Democratic leaders to develop joint lists of presidential electors in each state. Ironically, even while Butler was working for fusion with Democrats on a national level, he remained committed to joint campaigns with Republicans at the state level in North Carolina.

Before the elections of 1898 and 1900, the North Carolina Democratic Party refused to cooperate with the Populists. Instead, they campaigned to win voters away from the fusion Populist and Republicans. Democratic leaders used race as an issue, presenting themselves as the "white man's party." Butler made many campaign appearances in the state, debating Democratic leaders and pushing his program of reforms. As election day in 1898 drew near, Butler's paper, the *Caucasian*, resorted to accusing Democrats of appointing many African Americans to offices and presenting the Populists as the true white man's party. Nonetheless, the Populist control over the state government was broken by the two elections.

When Butler ran for reelection to the U.S. Senate in 1900, his foes in the state senate were able to defeat him. While still a senator, Butler had finished his law degree at the University of North Carolina. After he reentered private life in 1901, Butler practiced law in Washington, DC. He remained chair of the Populist Party in 1904. That year, Butler left the party and became a Republican. He favored the progressive wing of the Republican Party and supported Theodore Roosevelt in 1912. Butler died on June 3, 1938.

Tim J. Watts

See also: Bryan, William Jennings (1860–1925); Cleveland, Grover (1837–1908); Gold Standard/Free Silver; Polk, Leonidas L. (1937–1892); The Press and Populism; Roosevelt, Theodore (1858–1919); South, Populism in the

References

Beeby, James M. *Revolt of the Tar Heels: The North Carolina Populist Movement, 1890–1901*. Jackson: University Press of Mississippi, 2008.

Durden, Robert F. "Marion Butler." *Dictionary of North Carolina Biography*. Vol. 1. Chapel Hill: University of North Carolina Press, 1979–1996.

Hunt, James L. *Marion Butler and American Populism*. Chapel Hill: University of North Carolina Press, 2003.

C

Capra, Frank (1897–1991)

During his presidency, Ronald Reagan criticized Congress for its opposition to his Supreme Court nominee, the right-wing Robert Bork, by citing one of the most iconic scenes from Frank Capra's oeuvre: Jefferson Smith's stand against the corrupt machinations of Washington in *Mr. Smith Goes to Washington* (1939). "Jimmy Stewart stands in the well of the Senate," Reagan summarized for the representatives, "and says that the lost causes are the only ones worth fighting for . . . I'm going to stay right here and fight for this lost cause even if this room . . . is filled with lies. So will I" (Rogin and Moran 215). Reagan's alignment of himself with Jefferson Smith, the naïve Washington outsider who recalls the Senate to its lost ideals, was later repeated in Sarah Palin's 2010 autobiography, *America by Heart: Family, Flag, and Freedom.* Palin explains the enduring popularity of *Mr. Smith* by stating, "It's about an ordinary man who stands up and says, 'We're taking our country back.' " Reagan's and Palin's respective references to Capra's film attest to the influence of Frank Capra's cinematic populism on U.S. politics and how politicians have appropriated his narratives and imagery.

Director Frank Capra was a first-generation Italian immigrant whose family moved to the United States in 1903 and settled in Southern California. Hailed as one of the most notable progressive directors of the 1930s by the proletariat newspaper *Daily Worker*, Capra's career ranged from his production of canonical romantic comedies of the 1920s and 1930s such as *Lady for a Day* (1933) and *It Happened One Night* (1934) to his seven-film propaganda series *Why We Fight* (1945), chronicling the United States' involvement in World War II. Arguably, he is most well known for *It's a Wonderful Life* (1946) and his "little man" trilogy of the 1930s, including *Mr. Deeds Goes to Town* (1936), *Mr. Smith Goes to Washington* (1939), and *Meet John Doe* (1941). Capra himself made a distinction between the screwball comedies of his early career and his political films of this trilogy and his *Why We Fight* series. In his autobiography, *The Name Above the Title* (1971), he claimed that the "little man" of his conscience recalled him to his responsibility to produce movies that would promote American democracy and combat the influence that Hitler wielded. Indeed, the "little man" of Capra's conscience is represented in the embattled idealists—Longfellow Deeds, Jefferson Smith, and Long John Willoughby—who, in each of the films, attempt to reform the government or protect their communities from corrupt establishments (alternately the government, the news media, banking monopolies, or a combination of the three). The reform that they affect, however, is curbed by conservative circumscriptions; the "people" whom the hero represents are almost exclusively white, middle- to lower-middle-class citizens; and Deeds, Smith, and Willoughby do not advocate for the organization of unions or wage equity. Rather, Capra's films celebrate the moral citizen who is guided by the Christian edict of "love thy neighbor" and, by extension, love thy nation.

Released during the same year that Mount Rushmore was unveiled, *Mr. Smith* foregrounds national monuments and seeks to repair the divide between the nation's ideals and its governmental practices. Jefferson Smith, the leader of the Boy Rangers (an organization inspired both by the Boy Scouts and the New Deal–era Civilian Conservative Corps), is appointed to an open Senate seat by corrupt politicians who hope to capitalize on his ignorance of politics and the mainstream appeal of his patriotism. "He knows Washington by heart," an earnest Boy Ranger advertises. This statement is later reiterated to ironic effect by the compromised Governor Hubert Hopper, who assures his boss, Jim Taylor, that Jefferson Smith does not, in fact, know the operations of Washington by heart and will therefore be compliant. While Smith is dismissed by his colleagues and the news media as a "Daniel Boone" who needs to return to the backwoods of his western American hometown, Smith's proposal of a bill that would establish a camp for boys and his commitment to the nation's ideals results in the exposure of his corrupt colleagues. In the penultimate scene that President Reagan later cited, an exhausted Smith embarks upon an extended filibuster consisting of passages from the Constitution, the Declaration of Independence, and the Bible. After he is shown telegrams demanding his resignation as a result of Jim Taylor's smear campaign against him, Smith insists that he will continue to fight for the lost causes and faints onto the floor. His collapse prompts his fellow representative to confess to the plot against Smith and predicts the recuperation of the nation's integrity and innocence.

At the time of its release, *Mr. Smith* was denounced by politicians for what they charged was its cynical portrayal of U.S. democracy. As Eric Smoodin and Michael Rogin and Kathleen Moran have documented, Ambassador to England Joseph P. Kennedy tried to prevent the film's distribution in Europe, and House Majority Leader Alben Barkley averred that it was " 'as grotesque as anything I've ever seen!' " (Rogin and Moran 214). Yet the film was commercially successful and subsequently canonized as a model of how government should work. Photoplay Guides, a publishing firm that produced educational guides for junior high and high school curricula, produced editions that focused on the film and provided discussion questions for instructors who wished to use it in their classrooms. Although *Mr. Smith*'s successor, *Meet John Doe*, explored darker concerns with the manipulation of the people through news media, it, too, provided a similar lesson in the power of the people to ultimately triumph over moneyed interests.

Frank Capra died in 1991. While he was not able to sustain the success he enjoyed during the 1930s and early 1940s, his films continue to influence both directors and politicians. As cultural studies theorist Lauren Berlant has argued, *Mr. Smith* forwarded the plot of the idealistic Washington outsider who, through his or her commitment to family values (particularly children) and national ideals, affects change in government that so informed Reagan-era (and post–Reagan era) politics. Indeed, Capra's cinematic brand of patriotism and populism are present in Sarah Palin's "Mama Grizzlies" video in which she claims that mothers intuitively know when something is wrong with their children and, by extension, their nation, and the January 2011 reading of the Constitution by the 112nd congressional class recalls Jefferson Smith's filibuster reading of both the Constitution and the Declaration of the Independence. Finally, in *It's a Wonderful Life*, George Bailey's impassioned defense of his father's small loan and bank company against a slum lord and banking magnate, Henry Potter, articulates both the unifying refrain of Capra's films and a relevant response to the conjoined 2007–2008 subprime mortgage and financial crises: "This rabble that you're talking about—they do most of the working and the paying and the living and the dying in this town . . . is it too much to ask that they work and pay and live and die in a couple of decent rooms and bath?"

Rachel Ann Walsh

See also: Film; New Deal; Palin, Sarah (1964–); Reagan, Ronald, Populist Rhetoric of; Socialism, Christian; Tea Party

References

Berlant, Lauren. *The Queen of America Goes to Washington City: Essays on Sex and Citizenship*. Durham, NC: Duke University Press, 1997.

Gehring, Wes D. *Populism and the Capra Legacy*. Westport, CT: Greenwood Press, 1995.

It's a Wonderful Life! Dir., Frank Capra. RKO Radio Pictures, 1946.

Meet John Doe. Dir., Frank Capra. Warner Bros, 1941.

Mr. Deeds Goes to Town. Dir., Frank Capra. Columbia Pictures Incorporated, 1936.

Mr. Smith Goes to Washington. Dir., Frank Capra. Columbia Pictures Incorporated, 1939.

Palin, Sarah. *America by Heart: Reflections on Faith, Flag, and Freedom*. New York: HarperCollins Publishers, 2010.

Rogin, Michael P., and Kathleen Moran. "Mr. Capra Goes to Washington." *Representations* 84 (1): 213–248.

Smoodin, Eric. " 'Compulsory' Viewing for Every Citizen: *Mr. Smith* and the Rhetoric of Reception." *Cinema Journal* 35 (2): 3–23.

Carter, James Earl "Jimmy" (1924–)

By the 1970s, every serious political candidate and quite a few wannabes, it seemed, had to have a populist credential. Carter's inaugural address set the tone—he and his wife got out of their limousine to walk to the ceremony. Even the decorations were frugal, limiting the number of flowers. Carter also eschewed "Hail to the Chief" for himself and limousine service for his staff. He invited plain folk to state dinners and stopped often to meet with the common people. His image was that of homey, casual sweaters rather than coats and ties. But as a populist, he was the embodiment of the common man rather than a charismatic Tom Watson or an electrifying William Jennings Bryan.

Carter was first on his father's side to finish high school. His home was in Populism's stronghold, rural red-dirt Georgia. He shared the moral values of religion and southern culture. He was a southern populist, progressive, and Baptist. He claimed that the people were his strength and that his decisions had to have the backing of the people. He wanted to deserve their support, to be seen as worthy in their eyes. He attempted whenever possible to be close to the people—physically, emotionally, and culturally.

Rhetorically, he was grounded in populism. When he ran for governor in 1971 he attacked privilege and power and called for justice for the poor, weak, black, or rural. Running for president in 1974, he attacked ivory-tower government and business tax breaks. At the Democratic convention in 1976 he attacked elite domination of the economy and the political system and called for national health care. He even self-identified as a populist.

At the same time, he was a technocrat. In his first office, state senator, he was a cost-conscious liberal. His bywords were competence and compassion. As governor, he pleased business with government reforms and moderate taxes. When he chose the strongly liberal Walter Mondale as his vice-presidential running mate, Republican Bob Dole described Carter as a liberal in conservative attire, a southern-fried George McGovern or Hubert Humphrey.

Carter's technocratic side fought with his populist ideals. He believed that the people would make the right decision, or follow it, if the decision was reached openly. Carter did not understand that sometimes people cannot make the right decision because of socioeconomic or other compelling situations.

He ran on the anti-Washington mood that was prevalent after the Watergate scandal, calling for a Jacksonian return of government to the people. Yet Carter was more talk than action, and his administration enacted little in the way of reform. The pious Sunday school teacher who wanted to restore faith in government instead began to roll back the welfare state, began the defense buildup carried on by Ronald Reagan, gave corporations tax breaks and lighter regulation, and weakened unions. During his term, wealth began concentrating in the hands of a few, average living standards stagnated, and the United States began arming and backing tyrants in Indonesia, Iran, and elsewhere.

Carter pandered to elites, according to his critics. They argued that populism is antielitist and determined to upset the status quo. Carter's rhetoric of populism thus did not match his actual policies, which upheld the status quo and benefited the privileged. Populism reflects the interests of the workers and middle class. The populist shares this working- or middle-class background but cannot fundamentally be an elitist or a graduate of Harvard, a billionaire, or a child of power or wealth. The middle-class Carter, conversely, espoused populism but promulgated elitism.

Throughout his presidency (1976–1980), Carter was the outsider, the populist everyman, the representative citizen. His populism was in his technique and rhetoric rather than in his ideology or platform. He never articulated any specific goals but merely assumed that the right process—the open and moral approach—would inevitably lead to the right outcome. He preached a messianic message of lowered expectations and postimperial humility.

Leaders without vision lack followers. Carter lost to conservative populist Ronald Reagan in 1980. Since his retirement from public office, Carter's populist vision has flowered in his work with Habitat for Humanity, a nonprofit organization that builds houses for the poor. He has also become a writer and a statesman-errant, helping to broker international peace deals beyond the scope of government agency.

John H. Barnhill

See also: Bryan, William Jennings (1860–1925); Democratic Party; Reagan, Ronald, Populist Rhetoric of

References

Bjerre-Poulsen, Niels. "Populism—A Brief Introduction to a Baffling Notion." *American Studies in Scandinavia* 18 (1): 27–36. http://rauli.cbs.dk/index.php/assc/article/viewFile/1190/1191.

"Democrats: How Populist Is Carter?" *Time*, August 2, 1976. http://www.time.com/time/magazine/article/0,9171,914428,00.html. Accessed January 3, 2013.

Domin, Gregory Paul. *Jimmy Carter, Public Opinion, and the Search for Values, 1977–1981*. Macon, GA: Mercer University Press, 2003.

Dumbrell, John. *The Carter Presidency: A Re-evaluation*. Manchester, UK: Manchester University Press, 1995.

Hirschhorn, Joel S. "Would You Like to Be a Populist?" *The Progress Report*. http://www.progress.org/2006/joel02.htm. Accessed January 3, 2013.

Morris, Kenneth Earl. *Jimmy Carter, American Moralist*. Athens: University of Georgia Press, 1996.

Smith, Michael. "False Saviors—Jimmy Carter." *legalienate*, July 3, 2009. http://legalienate.blogspot.com/2009/07/false-savios-jimmy-carter.html. Accessed January 3, 2013.

Cather, Willa (1873–1947)

American author Wilella Seibert Cather, more commonly known as Willa, was one of the nation's best-known early-twentieth-century authors. Although her writing covered many states and topics, she is best known for her works about the Great Plains in general, and Nebraska in particular. Cather's work, while not overtly political, celebrated and explored the lives of the farmers and westerners who formed the backbone of nineteenth-century American Populism.

Although born in 1873 on her grandmother's Virginia farm, Cather identified herself as a westerner. In 1883, her family moved to Nebraska in an abortive attempt at farming. Eighteen months later, her father moved the family again, this time to the town of Red Cloud, where he began a career in real estate and insurance. On the south-central border of the state, Red

Set variously in Nebraska, the American Southwest, and her native Virginia, the novels and stories of Willa Cather reflect a keen sense of place and the values of the American pioneers. Her best-known books include *My Antonia* and *Death Comes for the Archbishop.* (Library of Congress)

Cloud was barely beyond its first decade of settlement when the Cather family arrived. As a young adult, Cather left Red Cloud for the University of Nebraska with the intention of becoming a physician. She quickly became interested in writing, however, and graduated in 1894 with a bachelor's degree in English. Her work took her to Pittsburgh and then on to New York City, where she took a job on the editorial staff of *McClure's* magazine. In 1912, *McClure's* serialized her first novel, *Alexander's Bridge*. Upon the advice of her mentor, author Sarah Orne Jewett, she turned to writing about what she knew best, rural Nebraska.

Although the author of 12 books and numerous other works, Cather is perhaps best known for two of her Nebraska novels, *O Pioneers!* (1913) and *My Antonia* (1918). In each of these works she examined topics near and dear to the souls of westerners: the beauty of the land, the hard work required to master it, and the fortitude required of settlers. Loving descriptions of Great Plains landscapes abound in Cather's work. In her writings, the land came alive as a sea of grasses, vibrant with color and life. While the landscape had the power to destroy, and such destructions were not uncommon in her work, it also had the power to nurture those who would work with it instead of against it. Cather described as beautiful a place that many characterized as empty and harsh.

While the land was beautiful, Cather's people were a tough and determined lot. The hard work and fortitude described in Cather's novels generally came in the form of capable women. Although *My Antonia* is ostensibly about a young Jim Burden, sent to Nebraska to live with his grandparents, the more important story is that of Antonia Shimerda, the daughter of Bohemian immigrants and Jim's neighbor. The tough Nebraska sod, and his general inability to adapt to it, drove Antonia's father to suicide, leaving her to manage her family's business. Although she stumbled at times, she succeeded. Likewise, *O Pioneers!* is the story of a hard-working immigrant woman, the Swedish

Alexandra Bergson, who took over the management of her family's farm after her father's untimely death from cancer. She pushed forward against hard times and difficult conditions, making a prosperous farm in a place where many men failed. Both women took over for fathers whom the land had defeated. Both women, driven to succeed, did the hard work of making Nebraska farms livable and made profitable homes for themselves and for their families. Antonia Shimerda and Alexandra Bergson are the best known of all of Cather's literary creations.

Cather died in New York City in 1947. She produced three works of nonfiction, 12 novels, and six collections. Her career as a professional writer extended from 1909 until 1956, when her estate published a final work nine years after her death. Although her books had great critical and popular success, her working life ended on a discouraging note. During the 1930s, critics panned her writing for being idealized, romantic, and essentially backward-looking. This may explain why she destroyed the vast majority of her correspondence and forbade the publication of what was left after her death. The lack of material has made it difficult for scholars to explore other facets of her life, such as her sexual orientation. She cross-dressed and called herself William for a time during her college years and had a female, life-long companion named Edith Lewis. The nature of that relationship, however, remains somewhat of a mystery and a subject of much scholarly debate. Despite her contemporary critics, the majority of her titles remain in print, and *O Pioneers!* and *My Antonia* are firmly ensconced in American literature, western history, and U.S. history survey courses a century after their publication.

Pamela Riney-Kehrberg

See also: Anderson, Sherwood (1876–1941); Baum, L. Frank (1856–1919); Garland, Hamlin (1860–1940); Rogers, Will (1879–1935); Plains and Midwest, Populism in the; Steinbeck, John (1902–1968)

References

Ahearn, Amy. "Biographical Sketch." The Willa Cather Archive, University of Nebraska, Lincoln. http://cather.unl.edu/life.longbio.html. Accessed January 3, 2013.

Cather, Willa. *My Antonia.* Boston: Houghton Mifflin Company, 1918.

Cather, Willa. *O, Pioneers!* Boston: Houghton Mifflin Company, 1913.

Robinson, Phyllis C. *Willa: The Life of Willa Cather.* Garden City, NY: Doubleday, 1983.

Charles, Robert (c. 1865–1900)

Robert Charles was born in Copiah County, Mississippi, in 1865 or 1866. His precise date of birth is unknown, though it is evident that he was born to sharecropper parents who farmed in the lowlands of Bayou Pierre, the same site where they had been enslaved. Collectively, his family embodies all of the "four migrations" that have, in the telling of historian Ira Berlin, shaped "African America" (Berlin 8). Ancestors were kidnapped from Africa to America and shifted from Virginia to Mississippi with the contraction and expansion of cotton cultivation. Charles then left rural Copiah to move to two urban centers—first Vicksburg, then New Orleans; millions of African Americans would follow this urbanizing trajectory in subsequent decades. Once he reached the city, Charles yearned for Africa and recruited for the International Migration Society across the Gulf South. On July 23, 1900, he shot a police officer who harassed him while he sat on the steps of a white family's house waiting for a woman. "If you shoot one officer, it's more than right that another officer will come to take his place," Jelly Roll Morton explained to folk-music collector Alan Lomax after he refused to sing the ballad of Robert Charles at Lomax's request, citing personal safety (Morton 2005). Indeed, in the four-day manhunt that followed his chance encounter with Patrolman August T. Mora, Charles killed 7 people and wounded 20 more before being shot and mutilated in a spectacle of mob violence.

Despite pathologizing accounts of his "bad" nature, Charles was not simply a troublemaker but a political agent informed by migration movements and emergent southern Populism. Responding to the racialist rhetoric of the 1896 election—during which rural, plantation-dominated Democratic counties stole the election from the Populist-Republican ticket that had won the majority of votes—he seems to have joined the International Migration Society in hopes of shifting beleaguered African American populations to Liberia. In the days before his shooting spree, he might have told William Butts, a fellow levee worker, that "it was the duty of every Negro to buy a rifle and keep it ready against the time they might be called upon to act in unison" in the event of a lynching like that of Sam Hose, murdered outside of Atlanta 15 months earlier by a mob of thousands (Hair 108). Upon Charles's death—which included the pro forma postlynching ransacking of his person and possessions—a fiery speech by Dennis Sholars, former Populist candidate for the Louisiana lieutenant governorship, was found in his pocket. Conservative Louisiana media routinely portrayed Sholars as a radical who had proposed to "exterminate" the state's Democratic Party and Charles as a lunatic bent on instigating a race war but influenced more by cocaine than politics ("Local News Item" 2). Ida B. Wells, who conducted an investigation of the Charles case, asked that he be remembered as a "student who faithfully investigated all the phases of oppression from which his race has suffered" (Wells 198).

The immediate aftermath in New Orleans allowed for no nuance in representations of Charles. On the night he shot Mora, Charles caught a bullet in the leg, went home to his cottage to clean his wound, and shot two more policemen who came to his house to arrest him. The next morning, bloodhounds in the service of the New Orleans Police Department began the search but found that Charles had baited them by leaving his clothes in a neighbor's shed. Interrogations of friends and even his girlfriend Virginia Banks painted a picture of a violent man: "a low Negro and a free lover" with many mistresses ("Two Police Victims of an Assassin's Weapon" 1). Historian William Ivy Hair has suggested that Banks's testimony might have been designed to protect her from recriminations that later befell his so-called conspirators; each member of the Jackson family, which gave Charles shelter during the manhunt, spent more than one year in Orleans Parish Prison. Several of the Jacksons were later indicted for murder; Silas Jackson was convicted of manslaughter but had his conviction overturned. In light of this treatment by the police and courts, it became useful for respectable African Americans like local minister J. Madison Young to denounce Charles as a "lawless brute" and promise to "aid . . . in bringing the lawless ones of our race to order and law" ("Vox Populi: Correspondence Which Speaks for Itself" 9).

In the days between the initiating incident and his death, Robert Charles sought shelter in New Orleans's Central City, a neighborhood that was and remains a crossroads of the black community. White populations within the city, meanwhile, exploded with rage. Police arrested African Americans rumored to approve of Charles's actions. A white man who noted that Charles acted in his own defense and deserved a fair trial was nearly lynched and ultimately arrested for being too "broad-minded on racial matters" (Hair 143). A mob gathered at Lee Circle—a roundabout surveyed from above by a statue of Robert E. Lee—threatening to overtake the prison and lynch the alleged conspirators. At the urging of police officers, the mob instead spent its energy in Storyville, New Orleans's red-light district, where "houses that specialized in black or mixed-blood prostitutes were shut and unlighted" in fear of racial violence (Hair 152). A school for children of color was burned, and an elderly man was shot in the French Market, a locus of tourist traffic in the Vieux Carre. Suburban parishes became zones of distress because of rampaging mobs.

On July 27, a Central City man named Fred Clark informed the police of Charles's whereabouts. The police came to find him, and a mob formed. Wielding the Winchester that shot Mora and his own homemade bullets, Charles fired 50 shots and made contact 24 times. One thousand guns were aimed on Charles; 500 bullet holes were subsequently found in the house that provided him with shelter. It would take the courts almost a year to adjudicate the question of whose gun provided the mortal wound and, thus, disburse the bounty levied by the city government. His body was horribly mutilated, and his house in Uptown New Orleans was ransacked; his voluminous essays, handwritten in composition books, were destroyed, thereby silencing his insurrectionary voice. Within days, *The Daily Picayune* would remark on New Orleans's restored tranquility, noting that "the city's troubles [were] seemingly buried [with] Charles' disfigured carcass" ("New Orleans Is Peaceful Once Again" 1).

Jennie Lightweis-Goff

See also: African Americans and Populism; Pop Music; South, Populism in the; Wells, Ida B. (1862–1931)

References

Banner Democrat. "Local News Item." April 6, 1901, p. 2.

Berlin, Ira. *The Making of African America: The Four Great Migrations.* New York: Viking Adult, 2010.

Daily Picayune. "New Orleans Is Peaceful Once Again." July 30, 1900, p. 1.

Daily Picayune. "Two Police Victims Of An Assassin's Weapon." July 25, 1900, p. 1.

Daily Picayune. "Vox Populi: Correspondence Which Speaks for Itself." July 29, 1900, p. 9.

Gussow, Adam. " 'Shoot Myself a Cop': Mamie Smith's 'Crazy Blues' as Social Text." *Callaloo* 25 (1): 8–44.

Hair, William Ivy. *Carnival of Fury: Robert Charles and the New Orleans Race Riot of 1900.* Baton Rouge: Louisiana State University Press, 1976.

Morton, Jelly Roll. *The Complete Library of Congress Recordings.* 2005. MP3.

Wells, Ida B. *Southern Horrors and Other Writings: The Anti-Lynching Campaign of Ida B. Wells, 1892–1900.* Edited by Jacqueline Jones Royster. New York: Bedford/St. Martin's, 1996.

Charles H. Kerr Publishing Company

Throughout the first three decades of the twentieth century, the Charles H. Kerr Publishing Company was the preeminent socialist press in the English-speaking world. From its headquarters in Chicago it disseminated the classic texts of the European socialist tradition and published a variety of original books and periodicals promoting radicalism on both sides of the Atlantic. The company's influence waned considerably in the decades after 1928, when its founder retired, though it remains active to this day.

Charles H. Kerr founded his press in 1886, and for most of the following four decades its evolution closely paralleled his own as a reformer. Kerr was born in LaGrange, Georgia, in the spring of 1860 as secessionism was on the rise. He soon moved with his abolitionist parents to the North. The family eventually settled in Madison, Wisconsin, where Kerr spent his teenage and college years before graduating from the University of Wisconsin in 1881. Shortly thereafter he moved to Chicago, where he befriended Unitarian minister Jenkin Lloyd Jones. Jones was the pastor of All Souls Church and the editor of *Unity*, the Midwestern beacon of liberal Unitarianism. Kerr became *Unity*'s business manager and editorial assistant in 1883 and served in that capacity until 1886, when he assumed full responsibility for the paper's publication under the auspices of the newly launched Charles H. Kerr & Company.

Over the course of its first seven years the company developed into the most prominent Unitarian publisher in the Midwest. Kerr devoted much of his energy to *Unity* while he also expanded the business. Initially he did so by printing a variety of books and pamphlets, most written by Jones and others in his liberal Unitarian circles. In the early 1890s, however, Kerr became enamored with the Populist movement then sweeping the nation. Gradually he began to drift away from his Unitarian moorings. This ideological shift generated tension between him and Jones, who remained the editorial force behind *Unity*; in 1893 the two men elected to part ways.

The separation from Jones and *Unity* also brought an end to the company's Unitarian phase, as Kerr steered it in a new, reformist direction. In 1893 he began to publish *New Occasions*, a weekly that offered reformers of all different stripes a space to exchange and debate ideas. In the course of a few short years the journal morphed from an open forum into a bully pulpit, which Kerr used to broadcast his own hardening political views. He had been deeply affected by a decade of proximity to the harsh realities of life in Chicago, where intractable poverty and degrading work were often the norm, especially for the masses of unskilled, foreign-born wage earners who flocked to the city in the late nineteenth century. These conditions bred periodic spasms of working-class unrest. Kerr had been mostly quiescent throughout the Great Upheaval of the mid-1880s, which culminated in the notorious Haymarket Affair in 1886. But when the Panic of 1893 catalyzed a new series of labor disruptions, including most notably the Pullman strike and boycott, he plunged into the fray. In August 1894 the company published the Reverend William H. Carwardine's *The Pullman Strike*, which was deeply sympathetic to the workers' cause. Kerr donated all proceeds from its sale to the strikers and their families. His concern for the plight of the poor in the industrializing United States would only mount as the crisis of the 1890s faded into a new century.

In 1899, Kerr announced that the company's publications would henceforth reflect his new commitment to socialism. His adoption of the socialist cause was facilitated by his friendship with Algie M. Simons, the editor of the Socialistic Labor Party's *The Worker's Call*. Conversations with Simons cemented Kerr's developing commitment to radical politics, and the two men soon became co-collaborators. In 1900 they founded the *International Socialist Review* (*ISR*), a monthly paper that would prove a touchstone of American socialism for the better part of two decades. Throughout its first eight years the paper functioned as a sounding board for different strains of socialist thought. ISR was thoroughly internationalist in its orientation, reporting on developments in every corner of the world. Yet it also undertook a mission to familiarize workers in the United States with the basic teachings of socialism. Kerr augmented ISR's efforts in this regard by producing and distributing English editions of radical classics such as Marx's *Capital*. Moreover, the company printed a variety of original books and pamphlets with titles such as *What Socialism Is* and *What Socialists Think*. Kerr hoped that by answering the criticisms of socialism's American detractors, these publications would extend the movement's reach into working-class communities.

By 1908, Kerr's ongoing political evolution had led him into the revolutionary socialists' camp. Whereas many gradual socialists were willing to abide the American Federation of Labor's quest for incremental gains, Kerr increasingly preferred the more radical calls for change issued by the Industrial Workers of the World. This shift prompted him to dissolve his partnership with Simons, a gradualist, and to guide the company even further to the Left. In the years that followed, ISR evinced less of an interest in theoretical debates. Aiming to speak directly to workers about matters of immediate concern to them, the publication focused more and more on the realities of life for the working class. During these same years Kerr expended much energy upon socialist infighting, but the build-up to World War I offered a moment of moral clarity. Throughout the United States' mobilization for and prosecution of the conflict the company stood as a stalwart of the antiwar movement. The federal government eventually cracked down, revoking the company's access to the mail via the Espionage Act. In contrast with many other socialist presses, however, the company weathered the fierce antiradicalism of the period, emerging weakened but no less resolved.

Kerr retired from the company in 1928, and in the decades that followed it faded from prominence. Now a nonprofit cooperative, the Charles H. Kerr Publishing Company continues to print works of radical history, criticism, and theory.

Heath W. Carter

See also: American Federation of Labor (AFL); Depression of 1893; Gilded Age; Haymarket Riot; Industrial Workers of the World; Pullman Strike (1894); Socialism, Christian

References

Garon, Paul, ed. *The Charles H. Kerr Company Archives, 1885–1985: A Century of Socialist and Labor Publishing.* Chicago: Charles H. Kerr Publishing Co., 1985.

Roediger, Dave, and Franklin Rosemont, eds. *Haymarket Scrapbook.* Chicago: Charles H. Kerr & Company, 1986.

Ruff, Allen. *"We Called Each Other Comrade": Charles H. Kerr & Company, Radical Publishers.* Urbana: University of Illinois Press, 1997.

Chávez, César E. (1927–1993)

César E. Chávez was a central figure in the drive towards greater equality for Mexican Americans. Propelled to national prominence in the early 1960s, Chávez illuminated *La Causa* ("the cause"), the fight against the socioeconomic inequalities endured by those of Mexican heritage. Until his death in 1993, Chávez tirelessly advocated the plight of farm laborers and the socially marginalized. Fundamentally, he fought against the elite California growers who wielded far more power than most groups in the state.

Césario E. Chávez was born March 31, 1927, in Gila, Arizona, to Librado and Juana Chávez. Librado was a modestly successful businessman, owning a grocery store, auto repair shop, and pool hall. Librado also maintained a farm. Chávez often worked beside his father, learning practical organizing skills and the values of hard work. Juana was a deeply pious Catholic who ingrained in her son both strong moral fiber and the importance of nonviolent means to resolve disputes. His parents regaled him with stories of Father Hidalgo, the revolutionary priest who challenged Spanish rule in Mexico using the Virgin of Guadalupe as his symbol. Through these teachings, Chávez gained sympathy for the poor.

When the Great Depression began, Chávez's family was initially prepared; their farm contained livestock and produce for sustenance while Librado's businesses generated income. Yet Librado had extended credit to several family members and deferred his annual property tax

César Chávez organized the first effective migrant worker union in the United States. His political skill and his unswerving dedication to one of society's most unprotected sectors made him a popular hero. (Library of Congress)

payments. By 1937, Chávez's father owed the state of Arizona more than $4,000. After Librado was denied a bank loan, the state took possession of his farm. At the age of 12, Chávez, along with his parents and siblings, moved to California to become a migrant farm worker.

In Depression-era California, witnessing an influx of Dust Bowl refugees, competition for jobs was fierce. The Chávez family settled in Oxnard where they picked beans and walnuts. To help support his family, Chávez spent half of his days in school while the rest of the time he worked the fields. He attended dozens of schools during his youth due to the migratory nature of farm work. In the late 1930s, the Chávez family moved to Sal Si Puedes, an impoverished *colonia* near San Jose. Farm work was grueling, and laborers were often cheated out of their wages. Being of Mexican heritage, the Chávez family feared immigration authorities, for the Immigration and Naturalization Service (INS) used deportation to loosen the state's occupational gridlock, deporting even U.S. citizens of Mexican descent. Though the Border Patrol once detained the Chávez family for questioning, they were released without incident.

Due to financial necessity, Chávez eventually quit school. He noticed attempts by the state to minimize Mexican heritage and force those of his background to adopt Anglicized ways. During World War II, Chávez served in the U.S. Navy as a deckhand but never saw combat. Returning to California after the war, his employment prospects, save for farm work, looked dim. In 1948, he married Helena Fabela. In that same year, he experienced his first labor strike, which failed due to the workers' lack of solid organization. With defeat regularly surrounding the union movements in California, Chávez developed awareness for the plight of workers. This awareness grew after Father Donald McDonnell arrived in Sal Si Puedes. McDonnell, who had come to establish a Catholic congregation, mentored Chávez and instructed him on how to rally people together.

To illustrate the divide between produce growers and the powerless workers, McDonnell showed Chávez pictures of mansions and shanties. He also introduced

Louis Fischer's biography of Mohandas Gandhi to Chávez. In the book, Chávez found parallels between Indians under British colonial rule and farm workers at the mercy of powerful growers. Already steeped in doctrines of nonviolence, Chávez found Gandhi's model of social activism appealing. When Chávez met Fred Ross, who had assisted farm laborers in the Coachella Valley, he learned vital organizing skills. Saul Alinsky, a national organizer who worked for the Industrial Areas Foundation, also had an impact on Chávez. In 1952, Ross hired him to organize voter registration drives in California's barrios. Conducting small meetings house to house, Chávez also fought for neighborhood improvements and against police brutality. Eventually, his work with Ross captured the attention of the Democratic Party, which had been in retreat since the early 1950s. The Republican Party in California, aligned with the interests of powerful growers, also noticed Chávez's organizing skills. As he continued, with Ross's organization, to champion La Causa, Republicans in the state alerted the FBI to his activities, portraying Chávez as a communist threat.

Chávez faced his greatest test in the 1960s. Between 1962 and 1964, he struggled to unite California's farm workers. Through patience, persistence, and charisma, Chávez had by 1964 laid the groundwork for the National Farm Workers Association (NFWA) with nearly 1,000 members and a credit union with $25,000 in assets. Chávez worked tirelessly in and near the town of Delano, California. With some 5,000 workers laboring for growers such as Di Giorgio and Schenley, this was one of the richest grape-growing regions in the state. For Chávez, the link between the Catholic Church and the NFWA was critical, as both espoused a genuine sympathy for uplifting the poor. Chávez stood at the center of a loose coalition of other activists, priests, and organizing agencies. National events, such as the civil rights movement, lent La Causa greater visibility.

Taking only $50 per week for his organizing activities, Chávez still toiled beside his family in Delano's fields. By the summer of 1965, worker discontent and rumors of a strike circulated throughout the town. At first, Chávez was unsure if the NFWA could weather a long and costly strike. When the Agricultural Workers' Organizing Committee (AWOC) called for a strike and enlisted Chávez's support, rather than risk splintering La Causa, Chávez brought the matter to a vote in September. The vote in favor of a strike was unanimous.

The Delano grape strike garnered national attention; Walter Reuther, head of the United Auto Workers (UAW), pledged $5,000 a month while the Migrant Ministry solicited support from around the country. To achieve greater solidarity, in 1966 the NFWA and the AWOC merged into the United Farm Workers Organizing Committee (UFWOC). At first, the large growers were not dissuaded, painting the strikers as communists and hiring scab labor from California and Mexico. Chávez was convinced that a strike alone would not suffice. Emulating Gandhi, Chávez employed the nonviolent tactic of boycotting. Across the country, grocery stores, restaurants, and other unions boycotted the products of Di Giorgio, Tree Sweet, Schenley, and S&W Fine Foods, all of which had interests in Delano. He utilized the power of the people and their consumer voice to battle the economically powerful growers and the politicians who supported them.

In August 1966, California Governor Pat Brown ordered the Schenley and Di Giorgio companies to sign a contract with UFWOC. Though Chávez received praise from Martin Luther King Jr. and elsewhere throughout the nation, he felt the battle was not yet won. He routinely faced intimidation from other growers and death threats. Moving beyond strikes and boycotts, in February 1968 Chávez began a fast at Forty Acres, the Delano headquarters of UFWOC. Some supporters did not appreciate the religious aura of the fast, yet the act itself became a media sensation. Chávez maintained his fast for 25 days. On March 11, 1968, Robert F. Kennedy, on the campaign trail for president, arrived to break bread with Chávez, who ended his fast that day. The strike, however, continued through 1969.

In the spring of 1970, 23 more growers signed contracts with UFWOC, with some printing the UFWOC black eagle insignia on their produce boxes. The Delano strike officially ended July 29, 1970. Despite a victory for Chávez and the elevated position he held, the next two decades were difficult. As the spirit of the 1960s gave way to division, radicalization, and defeat in the early 1970s, crusades such as the one led by UFWOC held less appeal for many Americans. The twin crises of Vietnam and Watergate had caused much of the previous decade's hope to wither. In 1970, Chávez was arrested for disobeying an injunction against boycotting a lettuce grower. Some of his strongest supporters questioned his leadership and felt he did not delegate authority. In addition, UFWOC membership dropped precipitously, from 50,000 in 1971 to just 10,000 by 1973.

In the mid-1980s, Chávez lobbied California Governor George Deukmejian against pesticide use in the fields. As undocumented workers streamed into the state, Chávez found this to be an obstacle in organizing and fighting scab laborers. In 1991, a California court upheld an earlier ruling against UFWOC, citing it for $2 million in damages and the death of a worker during a 1979 strike. By the 1990s, many Americans no longer were sympathetic to unions and Chávez's message seemed drowned out by the changing times. In April 1993, Chávez traveled to Arizona to assist farm workers who were being sued by a lettuce grower. Hoping to inspire them, he began fasting. When friends noticed his failing strength, they begged him to stop. On April 23, 1993, Chávez ended his fast, went to bed, and died in his sleep.

Stephen E. Nepa

See also: King, Martin Luther, Jr. (1929–1968)

References

Acuna, Rodolfo. *Occupied America: A History of Chicanos.* New York: Harper and Row, 1988.

Etulain, Richard, ed. *César Chávez: A Brief Biography with Documents.* New York: Palgrave Macmillan, 2002.

Ferriss, Susan, and Ricardo Sandoval. *The Fight in the Fields: Cesar Chavez and the Farm Workers Movement.* New York: Harcourt Brace, 1997.

Griswold de Castillo, Richard, and Richard A. Garcia. *César Chávez: A Triumph of Spirit.* Norman: University of Oklahoma Press, 1995.

La Botz, Dan. *César Chávez and La Causa.* New York: Pearson Longman, 2006.

Levy, Jacques. *César Chávez: Autobiography of La Causa.* Minneapolis: University of Minnesota Press, 2007.

Matthiessen, Peter. *Sal Si Puedes: Cesar Chavez and the New American Revolution.* New York: Random House, 1969.

Clayton Antitrust Act (1914)

The Clayton Antitrust Act of 1914 (38 Stat. 730), enacted during the first term of the Woodrow Wilson administration, operated as a supplement to the Sherman Antitrust Act of 1890 (26 Stat. 209) clarifying federal anticompetitive legislation through a heightened regime of proscribed business practices. The Clayton act targeted both organizational and substantive business reforms. Major substantive provisions of the act eliminated price fixing, exclusivity agreements, and owning stocks in competing corporations. The act also sought to control structural elements of businesses through the elimination of interlocking directorates and mergers and acquisitions. Portions of the act were designed to dissuade the predatory and abusive practices of businesses, thereby encouraging competition, consumer choice, lower prices, and innovation in the marketplace. Unlike the trailblazing legislation embodied in the Sherman Antitrust Act, the Clayton Antitrust Act signified the continuing efforts of the federal government to spell out appropriate business practices. The act sought to discourage more generally the consolidation of businesses and economic power into too few hands.

The Sherman Antitrust Act was the first foray by the federal government into the realm of business regulation. The act was designed to deter restraints on trade and the formation of business, sapping trusts and monopolies. The Sherman act grew out of state anticompetitive laws, such as those in place in Ohio and Wisconsin, which had a mixed record of success. Businesses were able to fashion novel legal devices enabling corporations to own other business entities, thus effectively circumventing the letter of state law. This led to the passage of the Sherman Antitrust Act. Unfortunately, the act was seldom used in its infancy until the administration of Theodore Roosevelt, who assumed the mantle of progressive reform and the mixed record of William Howard Taft. Early "trust busting" efforts against John D. Rockefeller's Standard Oil and J. P. Morgan's Northern Securities Trust are noteworthy. Due to a lack of legislative specificity and an inadequate enforcement regime, legal ambiguities became obvious, hindering the intent of the Sherman Antitrust Act.

The agenda of Woodrow Wilson was bold in vision and reach. Part of his program of reform included a radical overhaul of Sherman and contemporary antitrust legislation. The Clayton Antitrust Act was calculated to close legislative loopholes and enhance the functioning of the Sherman act. It was part of a comprehensive regulatory regime overseeing anticompetitive business practices and not merely the elimination of monopolies. Section 2 of the Clayton Antitrust Act targets discriminatory prices, services, and facilities used by businesses in the stream of commerce. Section 3 makes it unlawful to contract with a party not to engage in legitimate business with another. Section 4 sets amounts of damages, costs, and interest to be recovered in suits arising under the act. Section 6 excludes the activities of labor unions and agricultural cooperatives from scrutiny even though such organizations were regarded as anticompetitive. It also carved out protected labor activities such as boycotts and strikes. Section 7 forbids the acquisition of stock in companies that diminish competition or possibly lead to the creation of a monopoly. Sections 15 and 16 provide for injunctive relief, punishments, and temporary restraining orders. The Federal Trade Commission (FTC) was formed in 1914 to enforce the terms of the Clayton act and ensure the public was protected from anticompetitive and monopolistic practices. As an independent agency, the FTC is composed of five commissioners selected by the president. It investigates charges arising under Sherman, Clayton, and their progeny, protecting consumer interests, merger oversight, and reporting requirements.

The Clayton Antitrust Act was further updated by the Robinson-Patman Act of 1936 (49 Stat. 1526) forbidding price discrimination by producers. Robinson-Patman specifically aimed at the removal of tiered pricing schemes benefiting business-to-business transactions at the expense of sales to individual purchasers. The object of the act was industry-wide fairness in pricing and sales schemes. The Celler-Kefauver Act of 1950 (64 Stat. 1125) further amended the Clayton act through the exclusion of anticompetitive mergers. Businessmen were able to exploit loopholes in Clayton language enabling stock purchases of firms in varied industries, referred to as conglomerate mergers. Additionally, Celler-Kefauver outlawed the formation of vertical mergers, augmenting earlier proscriptions against horizontal ones. The Hart-Scott-Rodino Antitrust Improvements Act of 1976 (90 Stat. 1390) mandated reporting requirements for mergers, acquisitions, and tenders.

The Clayton Antitrust Act represents an evolution in federal anticompetitive legislation, standing behind Sherman and in front of Robinson-Patman, Celler-Kefauver, and others. It brought clarity to regulations and teeth to enforcement, and sought to level the economic playing field toward consumers and small businesses.

Jonathan C. Bergman

See also: Federal Trade Commission Act (1914), Gilded Age; Hepburn Act (1906); Interstate Commerce Act (ICA) (1887); Northern Securities Case (1904); Progressivism

References

Banerji, Sanjay. "End of a Dream." *Businessworld*, November 27, 2010.

Buttigieg, Eugene. *Competition Law: Safeguarding the Consumer Interest. A Comparative Analysis of U.S. Antitrust Law and EC Competition Law*. Alphen aan den Rijn, Netherlands: Kluwer Law International, 2009.

Davis, Mark. "History of the U.S. Federal Trade Commission." *San Francisco Chronicle*, December 2, 2010.

Federal Trade Commission. http://www.ftc.gov/. Accessed January 3, 2013.

Freyer, Tony A. *Regulating Big Business: Antitrust in Great Britain and America, 1880–1990*. New York: Cambridge University Press, 1992.

Hylton, Keith N. *Antitrust Law: Economic Theory and Common Law Evolution*. New York: Cambridge University Press, 2003.

Kokkoris, Ioannis, and Rodrigo Olivares-Caminal. *Antitrust Law amidst Financial Crises*. New York: Cambridge University Press, 2010.

Letwin, William. *Law and Economic Policy in America: The Evolution of the Sherman Antitrust Act*. Chicago: University of Chicago Press, 1981.

Rockefeller, Edwin S. *The Antitrust Religion*. Washington, DC: CATO Institute, 2007.

Sanders, Elizabeth. *Roots of Reform: Farmers, Workers, and the American State, 1877–1917*. Chicago: University of Chicago Press, 1999.

Sullivan, E. Thomas. *The Political Economy of the Sherman Act: The First One Hundred Years*. New York: Oxford University Press, 1991.

Cleburne Platform (1886)

During a meeting in August 1886, delegates of the Grand State Farmers' Alliance of Texas developed 16 political planks, later known as the "Cleburne Demands" or the "Cleburne Platform." In these demands, the Texans requested that the government nationalize the railroads, eradicate public debt, regulate banking, and enact legislation more favorable to farmers and labor.

Cleburne, Texas, a small community about 29 miles south of Fort Worth, has been a center for agricultural commerce, including stockyards, since the mid-nineteenth century. Cleburne's population grew from 683 in 1870 to 3,727 in 1890. By 1886, both cattle syndicates and the railroads had decreased the land available for settlement. The federal and state governments had granted the railroads ownership of more than 179 million acres. During meetings on August 3–7, 1886, at Lee's Academy in Cleburne, 240 delegates of the Grand State Farmers' Alliance of Texas chose as their official journal the weekly *Dallas Mercury*, known for its antimonopoly stance. This later became the *Southern Mercury*. These delegates then developed 16 political planks resulting in the Cleburne Platform. These demands resembled earlier reform philosophies dating back to informal coalitions in 1872. Five pertained to labor, three sought to remedy the monopolies of the railroads, two referred to monetary issues, and six were agricultural in nature. These were followed by a resolution for action. The delegates at Cleburne also demanded that land held for speculation be taxed or, in the case of railroad land, be surrendered to the government for sale to settlers.

The *Dallas Morning News* reported that the sessions of August 4 were all held behind closed doors. The next day it reported that a guest speaker at the convention, former Congressman Olin Wellborn, spoke at length about the tariff question. The *Dallas Morning News* was the first newspaper in region to publish the Cleburne Demands, on August 8, 1886:

> We, the delegates to the Grand State Farmers' Alliance of Texas, in convention assembled at Cleburne, Johnson County, Texas, A. D. 1886, do hereby recommend and demand of our State and National governments, according as the same shall come under the jurisdiction of the one or the other, such legislation as shall secure to our people freedom from the onerous and shameful abuses that the industrial classes are now suffering at the hands of arrogant capitalists and powerful corporations. We demand:
>
> 1. The recognition by incorporation of trade unions, co-operative stores, and such other associations as may be organized by the industrial classes to improve their financial condition, or to promote their general welfare.
> 2. That all public school land be held in small bodies, not exceeding three hundred and twenty acres to each purchaser, for actual settlement, on easy terms of payment.
> 3. That large bodies of land held by private individuals or corporations, for speculative purposes, shall be rendered for taxation at such rates as they are offered to purchasers, on credit of one, two, or three years, in bodies of one hundred and sixty acres or less.
> 4. That measures be taken to prevent aliens from acquiring title to land in the United States of America, and to force titles already acquired by aliens to be relinquished by sale to actual settlers and citizens of the United States.
> 5. That the lawmaking powers take early action upon such measures as shall effectually prevent the dealing in futures of all agricultural products, prescribing such procedure in trial as shall secure prompt conviction, and imposing such penalties as shall secure the most perfect compliance with the law.
> 6. That all lands, forfeited by railroads or other corporations, immediately revert to the government and be declared open for purchase by actual settlers, on the same terms as other public or school lands.
> 7. That fences be removed, by force if necessary, from public or school lands unlawfully fenced by cattle companies, syndicates, or any other form or name of corporation.
> 8. That the statutes of the State of Texas be rigidly enforced by the attorney-general, to compel corporations to pay the taxes due the State and counties.
> 9. That railroad property shall be assessed at the full nominal value of the stock on which the railroad seeks to declare a dividend.
> 10. We demand the rapid extinguishment of the public debt of the United States, by operating the mints to their fullest capacity in coining silver and gold, and the tendering of the same without discrimination to the public creditors of the Nation, according to contract.
> 11. We demand the substitution of legal tender treasury notes for the issue of the National banks; that the Congress of the United States regulate the amount of such issue by giving to the

country a per capita circulation that shall increase as the population and business interests of the country expand.

12. We demand the establishment of a National bureau of labor statistics, that we may arrive at a correct knowledge of the educational, moral, and financial condition of the laboring masses of our citizens; and further, that the commissioner of the bureau be a cabinet officer of the United States.
13. We demand the enactment of laws to compel corporations to pay their employees according to contract, in lawful money, for their services, and the giving to mechanics and laborers a first lien upon the product of their labor to the full extent of their wages.
14. We demand the passage of an interstate commerce law, that shall secure the same rates of freight to all persons for the same kind of commodities, according to distance of haul, without regard to amount of shipment; to prevent the granting of rebates; to prevent pooling freights to shut off competition; and to secure to the people the benefit of railroad transportation at reasonable cost.
15. We demand that all convicts shall be confined within the prison walls, and the contract system be abolished.
16. We recommend a call for a National labor conference, to which all labor organizations shall be invited to send representative men, to discuss such measures as may be of interest to the laboring classes.

Resolved, [17] That the president of the Grand State Alliance be, and he is hereby, directed to appoint a committee of three to press these demands upon the attention of the legislators of the State and Nation, and report progress at the next meeting of the Grand State Alliance. That newspapers be furnished copies of these demands for publication. That the president of the Grand State Alliance have fifty thousand copies of these demands and resolutions printed and distributed to the Sub-Alliances, through the respective county secretaries. That each delegate to this State Alliance present a copy of these demands and resolutions as early as possible to each candidate for a legislative office, State or National, and endeavor to secure his endorsement and assistance in carrying them to a successful issue (Winkler 1916).

This document was signed by members of the Committee on Demands and Good of the Order of Farmers' Grand State Alliance: W. M. Mathes, J. M. Pardue, H. T. Clark, B. F. Rogers, E. B. Warren, J. H. Morrow, and Geo. H. Stovall. The document was submitted by Andrew Dunlap, president.

Two factions emerged from the Cleburne convention; one faction advocated both economic and political actions, while the other desired a "purely business organization" (Barnes 1984). The final vote showed 92 in favor and 75 against the 16 demands. A minority protest, signed by B. M. Camp and others, issued a statement of "dissociation" and led to the organization of a rival Farmers' Alliance of Texas.

A rising leader, lawyer-physician C. W. Macune, was elected chairman of the state executive committee during the Cleburne convention. Andrew Dunlap, who stood with a "strictly business" attitude for the Farmers' Alliance, resigned as president.

Macune, who succeeded him to the presidency, called a special convention, held in Waco, Texas, on January 18, 1887; here, he proposed a centralized state alliance to wield greater power and coordination for the cotton crop and to serve as a central publishing house. Instead of discord, Macune urged interstate cooperation, and the Texas Farmers' Alliance and the Louisiana Farmers' Union merged to become the National Farmers' Alliance and Co-operative Union. This eventually became the National Farmers' Alliance and Industrial Union.

The Cleburne Demands were modified at the St. Louis Meeting of Alliances (1889) and subsequently at meetings in Ocala, Florida (1890), and Indianapolis, Indiana (1891).

Ralph M. Hartsock

See also: Bourbon Democracy; Greenback Party; Interstate Commerce Act (ICA) (1887); Macune, Dr. C. W. (1851–1940); Ocala Convention (1890); The Press and Populism; Railroad Regulation; Texas, Populism in

References

Barnes, Donna A. "Farmers' Alliance." *Handbook of Texas Online*. http://www.tshaonline.org/handbook/online/articles/aaf02. Accessed January 3, 2013.

Barnes, Donna A. *Farmers in Rebellion: The Rise and Fall of the Southern Farmers Alliance and People's Party in Texas.* Austin: University of Texas Press, 1984.

Clanton, Gene O. *Populism: The Humane Preference in America, 1890–1900.* Boston: Twayne, 1991.

"Cleburne Local Cullings." *Dallas Morning News*, August 5, 1886.

Goodwyn, Lawrence. *The Populist Movement: A Short History of the Agrarian Revolt in America.* New York: Oxford University Press, 1978.

"The Minority Protest." *Dallas Morning News*, August 8, 1886.

"Mr. Wellborn at Cleburne." *Dallas Morning News*, August 6, 1886.

"Rebuttal to Minority Report." *Dallas Morning News*, August 9, 1886.

Smith, Ralph A. "The Farmers' Alliance in Texas, 1875–1900: A Revolt against Bourbon and Bourgeois Democracy." *Southwestern Historical Quarterly* 48 (3): 346–369.

Smith, Ralph A. " 'Macuneism,' or the Farmers of Texas in Business." *Journal of Southern History* 13 (2): 220–244.

"What the Farmers Demand." *Dallas Morning News*, August 8, 1886.

Winkler, Ernest William. "Platforms of Political Parties in Texas." *Bulletin of the University of Texas,* no. 53 (Sept. 20, 1916). http://www.archive.org/stream/platformsofpolit00winkrich#page/n5/mode/2up.

Cleveland, Grover (1837–1908)

Stephen Grover Cleveland was the 22nd (1885–1889) and 24th (1893–1897) president of the United States. He was born in Caldwell, New Jersey, on March 18, 1837. He died on June 24, 1908. His presidencies were known for advocating civil service, tariff reform, and the gold standard amid an era of cronyism, protectionist politics, and strong silver agitation.

Cleveland entered Democratic politics while a successful attorney in Buffalo, New York. In 1881, he was elected mayor of Buffalo, where he quickly acquired a reputation for principled stewardship and for avoiding political partisanship and

Grover Cleveland held office through partisan battles over civil service reform, the beginnings of the free silver controversy, and a devastating nationwide financial depression. (Library of Congress)

cronyism. The next year, he won the New York gubernatorial contest. Under his leadership, the state of New York instituted various civil service and regulatory reforms that earned him positive national attention. As a result, in 1884 he received the Democratic nomination for president as well as the backing of the influential Republican independents known as Mugwumps. Cleveland narrowly defeated the corruption-laden Republican presidential candidate, James G. Blaine, thereby becoming the first Democratic president since before the Civil War.

During Cleveland's first term, various regulatory reforms were enacted. The Interstate Commerce Commission was created in 1887, which is considered the first significant federal attempt to regulate industry. Cleveland also showed his modest support for American agrarians through his approval of the Hatch Act (1887) and by approving the raising of the Department of Agriculture to cabinet status (1889). Cleveland's regulatory and civil service reforms were perhaps only superseded by his willingness to veto what he considered excessive legislation, which even included pension bills for Civil War veterans and purchasing seed grain to help drought-ridden Texas farmers. He issued a total of a record 414 vetoes in his first term.

Cleveland had entered presidential office with the support of various reformers seeking an end to political cronyism, partisanship, and economic protectionism. Cleveland himself admitted to knowing little of economic matters upon entering office. He turned to Mugwump reformers such as David Ames Wells, Edward Atkinson, and R. R. Bowker for economic advice. By the end of his first term, Cleveland had become a staunch defender of the gold standard and an avowed advocate for tariff reform. His famous 1887 annual address focused upon the sole issue of reducing the tariff. His speech reverberated throughout the country as, along with the silver issue, the tariff issue dominated the national political scene in the Gilded Age.

One result of Cleveland's message was a proposed Democratic tariff bill named after the chair of the Committee on Ways and Means, Roger Q. Mills. The 1888 Mills Bill incorporated Cleveland's call for moderate reductions. The Mills Bill was nevertheless defeated by the protectionist elements in the Senate, and its failure was a severe setback to Cleveland's reelection. His 1888 campaign was also hurt owing to his administration's amicable settlement of an 1887 Canadian fisheries dispute—which incurred anglophobic ire—and because of the strong opposition to tariff reform stemming from powerful American protectionist circles. Cleveland's annual message and subsequent failed Mills Bill also effectively turned the approaching presidential elections into a national referendum over the tariff, in what became known as "The Great Debate" of 1888.

Cleveland's Republican opponent in the 1888 presidential contest was Benjamin Harrison of Indiana, an avowed supporter of the Republican Party's protectionist plank. Cleveland chose as his vice presidential running mate Allen G. Thurman, a moderate on both the silver and tariff issues. When the final votes were counted, Cleveland had won a narrow plurality, but Harrison received the electoral majority. Despite Harrison's minority victory, Republicans nevertheless viewed Harrison's election as a referendum for the party's policy of protectionism. In 1890, the Harrison administration pushed for the passage of the high McKinley Tariff, as well as the Sherman Silver Purchase Act, to ensure the support of the Silver Republicans. Cleveland strongly condemned both acts of legislation as he geared up for the 1892 presidential elections. Having secured the Democratic presidential nomination, Cleveland's 1892 vice presidential running mate was Illinois's Adlai Stevenson, whose western sympathies earned Cleveland much-needed support from the Democratic Party's silver faction. The election, however, focused primarily on the tariff issue. Cleveland blamed Republican legislation, particularly the Sherman Silver Purchase Act and the McKinley Tariff, for the country's burgeoning economic ills.

His campaign was a success, but the troubling economic rumblings of the early 1890s erupted in the Panic of 1893 soon after Cleveland took office. Cleveland encouraged sound money and tariff reductions as the solution to the country's economic woes and turned his attention to first overturning the Sherman Silver Purchase Act, which had increased the outflow of the treasury's already dwindling gold supply. Democratic congressmen followed up this repeal measure with one of tariff reduction by replacing the McKinley Tariff with the more moderate Wilson-Gorman Tariff in 1894. Cleveland also resorted to floating bonds to further halt the run on treasury gold, which had the adverse effect of seemingly putting Cleveland in close alliance with J. P. Morgan and other eastern financiers who purchased the bonds.

The timing of the Panic of 1893 made Cleveland an easy political scapegoat. Nor did Cleveland's prescriptive legislation immediately cure the ailing American economy as the depression stretched into the remaining years of his second term. His classical liberal belief in letting the market sort itself out kept him from attempting any aggressive federal intervention in the economy. Joblessness, debt, and deflation hit new highs. Jacob Coxey's 1894 Populist march on Washington to demand government-funded public works programs gave a national voice to the country's jobless and hungry and undercut the president's flagging popular support. Attorney General Olney's use of federal troops to break up the Pullman Strike in 1894 further alienated American laborers, especially union members and leaders.

Cleveland's popularity within his own party plummeted to new lows. Many western Democrats, along with Populists and Silver Republicans, believed Cleveland, through his unswerving support of the gold standard and dealings with eastern financiers, was involved in a conspiratorial plot concocted by Wall Street and the city of London. Furthermore, the Wilson-Gorman Tariff's income tax provision, which had earned the favor of the Populists, was ruled unconstitutional by the Supreme Court in *Pollock v. Farmers' Loan and Trust Co.* in 1895, undermining whatever remained of Cleveland's Populist support. With the backing of Silver Republicans, Populists, and the silver wing of the Democratic Party, William Jennings Bryan thereafter easily defeated Cleveland for the Democratic presidential nomination in 1896. Cleveland retired from political office but remained active in American affairs. Following the Spanish-American War and American acquisition of the Philippines, Cleveland spent many of his remaining years as an outspoken critic of American imperialism until his death in 1908.

Marc-William Palen

See also: Bourbon Democracy; Bryan, William Jennings (1860–1925); Coxey's Army; Democratic Party; Depression of 1893; Interstate Commerce Act (ICA) (1887); People's Party; Sherman Silver Purchase Act (1890); Silver Republicans; Wilson-Gorman Tariff (1894)

References

Calhoun, Charles W. *Minority Victory: Gilded Age Politics and the Front Porch Campaign of 1888*. Lawrence: University Press of Kansas, 2008.

Merrill, Samuel. *Bourbon Leader: Grover Cleveland and the Democratic Party*. Boston: Little, Brown, and Co., 1957.

Nevins, Allan. *Grover Cleveland: A Study in Courage*. New York: Dodd, Mead & Company, 1933.

Welch, Richard E., Jr. *The Presidencies of Grover Cleveland*. Lawrence: University Press of Kansas, 1988.

Coin's Financial School (1894)

Coin's Financial School is a short fictional book that was self-published by William Hope Harvey in 1894 to promote the free coinage of silver. Approximately 1 million copies of the book were sold. William Jennings Bryan, the bimetallist Democratic candidate for president in 1896, suggested that it was "the most potent of educational forces at work in behalf of bimetallism" (Harvey 5). *Coin's Financial School* opens with "a young financier" named Coin who opens a school of finance in the Art Institute of Chicago. Coin's goal is to "instruct the youths of the nation, with a view to their having a clear understanding of what has been considered an abstruse subject," namely, the question of the monetary role of silver (Harvey 94). Coin himself is depicted as a small man with a boyish face. Coin's youth provides a stark contrast with the older figures in the course who challenge his ideas, suggesting both that bimetallism is easy for even the uninitiated to understand and a rejection of the old monetary system. The book follows Coin through a series of six lectures.

Coin's Financial School garnered significant public acclaim in large part because it was so accessible. Cheap versions of the book were printed so that they could be easily acquired by anyone interested, and the text was accompanied by many illustrations and diagrams. The book also incorporated well-known public figures, such as the prominent banker Lyman Gage and the economist J. Laurence Laughlin, who engaged in dialogue with the fictitious character of Coin. Many readers, not realizing the *Coin's Financial School* was a fictional work, wrote letters to Gage, Laughlin, and others inquiring about the lectures.

The first lecture introduces the Coinage Act of 1873, also known as the "Crime of 1873." Coin's critique of the act is twofold; first, that it changed the unit of account from silver to gold, and second, that it demonetized silver. He suggests that the effects of demonetization would become particularly burdensome when the federal government began resuming specie payments (expected within the next several years) on a gold standard. The second lecture addresses the question of how a government-mandated ratio of the value of monetary gold to monetary silver could remain stable when the demand for gold and silver constantly fluctuated. Coin argues that the unlimited demand for silver and gold at the established ratio ensured that fluctuations in demand for nonmonetary silver and gold would be reflected in adjustments in the quantity of monetary silver and the quantity of monetary gold but not in the of the value of the two metals. Bimetallism is therefore stabilized by the unlimited demand for silver at the established price. The third and fourth lectures cover the history of bimetallism in the United States and the emergence of the Latin Monetary Union in Europe. The fifth lecture reviews the quantity theory of money, which establishes a proportional relationship between the amount of money in an economy and the price level. In this lecture, Coin emphasizes the impact that the demonetization of silver has on real debt burdens. Because the values of debt burdens are fixed in nominal terms, Coin argues that an increase in the value of money precipitated by a reduction in the money supply increases the burden of a given level of debt. The sixth and final lecture outlines Coin's plan for the independent free coinage of silver.

Daniel Kuehn

See also: Crime of '73; International Monetary Conferences; Quantity Theory of Money

References

Fisher, Willard. " 'Coin' and His Critics." *Quarterly Journal of Economics* 10 (2): 187–208.

Harvey, William H. *Coin's Financial School.* Edited by Richard Hofstadter. Cambridge, MA: The Belknap Press of Harvard University, 1963.

Colonialism.

See Anti-Imperialism/ Colonialism

Colorado, Populism in

The Populist movement in the state of Colorado coalesced most significantly in the form of the state's People's Party, the leader of which, Davis H. Waite, successfully ran for governor in the election of 1892. Populism in Colorado was remarkable for its wide-ranging platform. Alongside the traditional call for monetary, agrarian, land, and transportation reform were planks for woman suffrage and comprehensive labor reform. Although Waite was defeated after only one two-year term, the reforms he attempted to introduce made his gubernatorial administration one of the most progressive in the state's history, and indeed of the entire Populist movement.

The formation of the Colorado's People's Party in 1892 marked the culmination of more than a decade of disaffection with the traditional two-party system and the belief that the "Eastern Establishment" did not sufficiently meet the needs of Coloradans. The Greenback Party, Knights of Labor, and the Farmers' Alliance were all active in the state throughout the 1870s and 1880s. However, the advent of Populism as a national political movement by 1892 afforded these reformist organizations the first real opportunity to operate under the auspices of a united movement. In July 1892, the Colorado People's Party nominated Davis H. Waite as its candidate for governor. A prospector and lawyer, Waite achieved prominence across the state as coeditor of the *Aspen Union Era*, a highly influential proreform and Populist weekly. He based his campaign upon the promises of the Omaha Platform adopted by the national People's Party at its convention in 1892.

Silver played the key role in Waite's campaign as the precious metal's preeminent position in Colorado's economy made it an issue supported by mine owners and miners alike. The three state parties supporting bimetallism did so to varying degrees. The Republicans adopted a moderate platform, hoping to attract voters on both sides of the issue, while the Democratic slate became dominated by hard-line Silverites. Waite and the Populists espoused the most radical view and ultimately attracted votes from Silver Republicans and Democrats dissatisfied with the conservatism of their respective parties. Waite decisively won the governorship primarily upon the strength of silver, becoming one of only two Populist governors elected nationwide. The Republican Party maintained control of Colorado's House and Senate.

The struggle to implement Populist reforms dominated the first half of Waite's administration. In his inaugural speech the newly elected governor articulated his vision for change in Colorado: less discriminatory operation of the railroads, the ceding of federal arid lands to the state, wide-ranging labor reforms, and the free coinage of silver. However, the Republican majority in the Ninth General Assembly of Colorado voted down the majority of Waite's proposed bills, although the reformists made some modest gains in such areas as agricultural and food inspection and regulation, and in establishing an eight-hour day for state employees. Waite struck back actively against his opponents, vetoing 40 bills in the first session of the Assembly alone, but without a larger Populist contingent in the state congressional assembly passing of comprehensive reforms was virtually impossible.

The Populists did enjoy one of their most noteworthy successes when on November 7, 1893, Colorado's citizens voted for woman suffrage in a general election. The woman suffrage movement in the state had a long history and found support, much like Populism itself, from a diverse number of sources including labor unions, leaders of the business community, the Women's Christian Temperance Union, and religious organizations. Waite himself had called for woman suffrage as editor of the *Aspen Union Era* and made an election to determine the extension of the vote to the women of the state an explicit plank of his gubernatorial platform. The victory of the November 1893 general election made Colorado the first state to adopt woman suffrage by popular vote, predating the Nineteenth Amendment to the Constitution by 27 years.

Despite such victories as the establishment of woman suffrage, the national economic depression of 1893 further polarized Populists and Republicans and compounded Waite's difficulties in further promoting his reformist agenda. The economic slowdown coupled with the repeal of the Sherman Silver Purchase Act resulted in widespread unemployment throughout Colorado. In response Waite called a special session of the State Assembly wherein he introduced an extensive program of bills designed to ease the plight of Colorado's working classes. The conservatives in the Assembly viewed most of these bills as too radical, a view not helped by Waite, who earned the nickname "Bloody Bridles" after a militant speech in which he railed against the domination of the common man by the "money power" and warned it would be "infinitely better that blood should flow to the horses' bridles than our national liberties should be destroyed." As a result of Republican ideological opposition and growing fragmentation of the Populists between labor, agriculture, and Silverites brought on by the economic panic, the special session passed only 11 of Waite's 78 proposed bills into law. Although Waite's proposed special session reforms were largely unsuccessful, his attempts to implement a comprehensive legislative program to palliate the effects of the economic crisis were mirrored by Franklin D. Roosevelt's New Deal almost 40 years later.

Controversy continued to dog Waite into 1894. In February a bitter strike erupted at Cripple Creek, one of the few lucrative mines operating in economically ravaged Colorado, when the mine's owners attempted to increase arbitrarily the laborers' work day. When the county sheriff amassed a sizeable armed force with which to break the strike, Waite intervened and ordered the state militia to protect the protesting miners. The confrontation ended in favor of the strikers and won the enduring support of labor in the state for Waite, but the governor's actions alarmed mine owners and other members of Colorado's financial elite.

In the gubernatorial campaign of 1894 Waite's detractors used his actions at Cripple Creek, the "Bloody Bridles" speech, and his attempts to legislate Populist reforms as evidence of the incumbent governor's radicalism. In addition, by this time the diversity of the Populist coalition, which had proved crucial to Waite's election in 1892, now proved a significant weakness as the unity of the party's constituent components broke down under the worsening economic depression. As a result of these factors, Davis lost the state election of 1894 to Republican candidate Albert McIntire.

Davis's loss to McIntire did not signal the end of Populist agitation in Colorado. The now ex-governor continued to promote his reformist agenda for many years after his gubernatorial term even as Populism's influence as an overt political force began to wane as the new century approached. Indeed, even after the movement's decline, Populist tenets lived on as part of the Progressive movement of the early twentieth century. Waite's administration left an indelible legacy upon Colorado state politics and demonstrated the power and appeal of the Populist movement at its zenith.

Brendan Dominick

See also: Cripple Creek War (1894); Gold Standard/Free Silver; People's Party; Plains and Midwest, Populism in the; Sherman Silver Purchase Act (1890); Waite, Davis (1825–1901); West, Populism in the

References

Morris, John R. *Davis H. Waite: The Ideology of a Western Populist.* Washington, DC: University Press of America, 1982.

Morris, John R. "The Women and Governor Waite," *Colorado Magazine* 44 (1): 11–19.

Wright, James Edward. *The Politics of Populism: Dissent in Colorado.* New Haven, CT: Yale University Press, 1974.

Colored Farmers' Alliance (CFA)

Precursors to the Colored Farmers' Alliance (CFA) were forming as early as 1886, many of them based on older secret agrarian societies. Known originally as Colored Farmers' National Alliance and the Cooperative Union, the CFA grew out of black and white radical reaction to the exclusion of black farmers in the Southern Alliance.

In Lovelady, Texas, more than a dozen black farmers met on the farm of the white minister, farmer, and ex-Confederate officer R. M. Humphrey. They established the CFA on December 11, 1886, and elected J. J. Shuffer, a black farmer, president, though Humphrey was made general superintendent for the organization and remained its national spokesperson for the next two years. In short, the CFA, along with black churches, schools, and fraternal organizations, was at the very center of late-nineteenth-century self-help ideology and reform in the black community.

After the Civil War, African Americans set out to gain the economic independence and political rights that had been denied them under slavery. The questions surrounding freedwomen's and freedmen's access to property and their control over their own labor remained contentious and unresolved during the first generation of freedom.

Motivated by land ownership, black farmers mobilized through the Republican

Party, and later through the Populist movement, to form interracial partnerships. Having been denied the promises of "forty acres and a mule" pledged by the U.S. government and military following the Civil War, blacks resisted falling into tenant farming and sharecropping. The significance of Reconstruction in the South, and its eventual demise, turned largely on the issues of landownership among African Americans and previously landless whites. The crop lien system, which emerged in the 1870s, precipitated greater indebtedness for black and white tenant farmers and sharecroppers, denying them choice of crops, marketplace, and terms of payment.

For a few independent African American farmers in the South, economic and political organizing faced challenges from the growing inflexibility of segregation. Disfranchisement of southern African Americans, orchestrated through measures including literacy tests and grandfather clauses, chipped away at black voting power over the next decade. In addition, southern Democrats stripped black and some white voters of their rights to forestall collaboration between the People's and Republican parties. The formation of Alliances of farmers and farm workers put into motion a series of strategies designed to resist plummeting agricultural prices, higher railroad rates, and inaccessible credit. Black farmers' and workers' organizations developed alongside other key community institutions to protect civil and economic rights during the late nineteenth century. Despite dwindling support for black farmers, African American elected officials were still overwhelmingly drawn from black farming more than any other occupation. Ultimately, African Americans were abandoned in their efforts but not before they had created an impressive network of grassroots organizations.

Within in a short period of time the CFA had spread from Texas to nearly every other state in the South. Drawing on the energies of more than 1 million members, both women and men, the CFA took on the outlines of something even more transformative than an agrarian collective. Actual membership numbers are difficult to ascertain because black Alliance lecturers circulated in the South covertly, not wanting to draw unwelcome attention to black and interracial agrarian organizing. Several prominent African American Alliance leaders emerged in several states: in Alabama, Frank Davis, J. S. Jackson, and J. F. Washington; in Georgia, J. W. Carter and E. S. Richardson; in Florida, J. L. Moore; in North Carolina, W. A. Patillo; in Virginia, William Warwick; in Texas, H. J. Spenser; in Mississippi, Joseph H. Powell; and in Louisiana, L. D. Laurent.

CFA members both acquiesced to and rejected the demands of the Jim Crow South. It was very common, though not uniformly practiced throughout the South, to have white superintendents in the CFA; blacks saw this as a necessary but temporary concession to the racial status quo. For African Americans within the CFA itself, the pursuit and preservation of black property rights and civil rights were seen in the larger campaign of uplifting the race through hard work, thrift, and moral rectitude. The CFA also represented a challenge to the racial status quo. The political education gained through the

CFA enabled many black men to challenge disenfranchisement. Facing white Democratic opposition on one side and Republican hostility, black and white, to rural radicalism on the other, CFA members maintained a delicate balance between spreading the messages of Populism and the realities of Jim Crow.

Black voting power in the South was effectively eliminated by the 1880s; however, white voters began to divide along class lines as the rise of the New South further depressed the economic conditions for poor farmers, black and white. The People's Party attempted to protect black voters in the South in an ill-fated coalition of black and white farmers. In retaliation the Democratic Party allied temporarily with the People's Party, attempting to push African Americans out of the southern Populist movement or to force them to vote the Democratic ticket. Occasionally the interracial efforts of black and white farmers bore political fruit, but they were always met with a violent backlash.

Against the backdrop of regional change for African Americans, violence and other forms of oppression continued to curtail the progress of black farmers. In 1892, a record 226 lynchings in the South and Southwest claimed mostly African American lives. The period that would become known as the nadir in African American history was marked by lynchings, disfranchisement, and economic displacement of poor blacks.

The year 1892 was also the year the Democratic Party in the South mobilized to corner the black vote by any means at its disposal. Alarmed by the growth of the CFA, white southern Democrats used various forms of persuasion, promises, and violence to gain votes among African Americans. Jim Crow legislation negated the citizenship rights of African Americans as well as their ability to cooperate and organize with other poor farmers and workers. However, the People's Party, with the leadership of John B. Rayner and other black Populists, persuaded many black farmers that a third political party offered the best hope for farmers' aspirations. In the end the ballot was withheld from the majority of black citizenry, while the CFA continued to provide some means of political organizing, however cloaked in self-protective secrecy.

Notwithstanding the considerable external pressures, internal divisions were equally to blame for the CFA's demise. Conflicts of interest arose as it became apparent that landowning blacks and landless blacks disagreed on the most pertinent issues facing black farming life. Saddled with debt and no property left black sharecroppers at odds with black landowners. As cotton pickers' strikes rippled through the Belt in the 1880s and 1890s, struggles over wages and working conditions dominated the lives of black sharecroppers living at subsistence levels. By 1892, the CFA was sufficiently weakened by numerous internal and external factors to the point that white contingents in the Alliance and both major political parties had effectively silenced the organization.

Despite the defeat of the CFA, African American farmers and workers continued organizing into the twentieth century. Black farmers in poultry, cotton, and wheat formed cooperatives to purchase supplies and manage resources collectively in Georgia, Tennessee, and elsewhere in the South. Meanwhile, African American dockworkers and steamboat workers in the North and South formed nascent interracial labor coalitions to organize for better wages and working conditions. The CFA wove together self-help ideology and a third-party movement. In doing so, it became one of the largest African American institutions of its time, laying the groundwork for the economic and political uplift of the black community at large.

Robin Dearmon Muhammad

See also: African Americans and Populism; Democratic Party; Pattillo, Walter Alexander (1850–1908); People's Party; Railroads; Rayner, John (1850–1918); Wells, Ida B. (1862–1931)

References

Beeby, James M. *Revolt of the Tar Heels: The North Carolina Populist Movement, 1890–1901*. Jackson: University Press of Mississippi, 2008.

Berry, Mary Frances. *My Face Is Black Is True: Callie House and the Struggle for Ex-Slave Reparations*. New York: Alfred A. Knopf, 2005.

Dawson, Michael C. *Behind the Mule: Race and Class in African-American Politics*. Princeton, NJ: Princeton University Press, 1994.

Diner, Steven J. *A Very Different Age: Americans of the Progressive Era*. New York: Hill and Wang, 1998.

Franklin, John Hope. *From Slavery to Freedom: A History of Negro Americans*. New York: Alfred A. Knopf, 1967.

Gaither, Gerald H. *Blacks and the Populist Movement: Ballots and Bigotry in the New South*. Tuscaloosa: University of Alabama Press, 2005.

Goodwyn, Lawrence. *The Populist Moment: A Short History of the Agrarian Revolt in America*. Oxford, UK: Oxford University Press, 1978.

Holmes, William F. "The Arkansas Cotton Pickers Strike of 1891 and the Demise of the Colored Farmers' Alliance." *Arkansas Historical Quarterly* 32 (2): 107–119. Republished in Donald G. Nieman, ed. *From Slavery to Sharecropping: White Land and Black Labor in the Rural South, 1865–1900*. New York: Garland Publishing, 1994.

Jones, William P. *The Tribe of Black Ulysses: African American Lumber Workers in the Jim Crow South*. Urbana: Illinois University Press, 2005.

Kazin, Michael. *The Populist Persuasion: An American History*. Ithaca, NY: Cornell University Press, 1995.

McMath, Robert C., Jr. *American Populism: A Social History, 1877–1898*. New York: Hill and Wang, 1993.

Comstock, Anthony (1844–1915)

Anthony Comstock emerged in the 1870s as a reformer seeking to restrict materials and information about human sexuality. The legislation that he influenced, often referred to as the "Comstock Laws," limited the availability of erotica, birth control devices, sexualized literature, and abortion at the state and federal levels. Comstock combined a middle-class, evangelical sensibility with a desire for fame and prestige into a life-long career of vice suppression. Although he worked primarily in urban areas such as New York City, his ideas about limiting birth control information and abortion later appealed to those worried about "race suicide"

Anthony Comstock was such a well-known defender of public morality in the United States around the turn of the 19th century that his name became synonymous with moralistic censorship. (Library of Congress)

among white, Anglo-Saxon Protestants. Comstock's ability to consolidate power from federal, state, and private interests helped make him one of the most outspoken advocates for Victorian morality.

Born in 1844 in New Canaan, Connecticut, to Thomas and Polly Comstock, Anthony Comstock received an education limited by his family's means and his need to work as a clerk when he was a teenager. His interest in suppressing materials he deemed sinful began in earnest during his career as a member of the 17th Connecticut, stationed in Florida during the Civil War. His fellow soldiers behaved in ways that Comstock found distasteful; they swore, drank, used tobacco, and viewed lewd images. After picking up assorted jobs at the end of the war, Comstock eventually secured a job as a clerk in New York City, where he again found himself surrounded by materials he believed to be immoral. At the same time that Comstock discovered the highly sexualized surroundings of New York City, the Young Men's Christian Association (YMCA) actively campaigned to purify the lives of young, middle-class men living in the city.

His disgust with obscene materials connected him with the mission of the YMCA, and he became a member.

In Brooklyn, New York, Comstock became the neighborhood enforcer of rules about prohibiting saloons from opening on Sunday, and he reported shops selling materials he deemed inappropriate. Repeatedly he investigated and reported such happenings to officials and became involved with the prosecutions of cases. Thanks to his relationship to the YMCA and his desire to involve himself in neighborhood business, Comstock ultimately found himself working on behalf of the YMCA to shut down stores and publishers of erotic material.

His partnership with the YMCA came in the first years of the 1870s when he requested funds to purchase and eliminate from the marketplace erotic photograph plates from a well-known purveyor of adult materials. After this successful effort he received a salary from the YMCA to remove obscene material from the marketplace in New York City. The evangelical zeal with which the YMCA pursued this course reflects, in part, the large numbers of young men who poured into the city looking for new opportunities. Surrounded by brothels, saloons, and the sporting culture, members of the YMCA did not want middle-class men to fall victim to the ills of pornography and vice. Comstock and other members of the YMCA believed that long-term health problems could be caused by using or viewing sexualized materials. In addition to written and printed materials Comstock's campaign also sought to destroy rubber devices used for birth control and masturbation. They intended for their efforts to help women, men, and children maintain their traditional family roles in the face of the temptations of modern American life.

In 1872, Comstock led efforts to prosecute publishers Victoria Woodhull and her sister Tennessee Claflin, who printed a newspaper that he believed to be circulating obscene information about free love and gossipy indiscretions. When the court acquitted the sisters because the federal law used for prosecution did not include newspapers, Comstock began working on stronger federal legislation. His backers, not only at the YMCA but also independently wealthy New Yorkers concerned about the spread of vice, sent him to Congress to lobby for an improved bill regarding obscenity law.

His efforts in Congress found support with Supreme Court Justice William Strong, who worked unsuccessfully to include the word "God" into the Constitution. In the successful legislation that followed Comstock's efforts, a new position was created: special agent of the U.S. Postal Office, which he held until his death in 1915. The 1873 law to suppress the trade of obscene materials influenced state laws that made it a misdemeanor punishable by fine and prison to sell, print, distribute, give away, or offer any image, paper, printed and written material, or device of any kind that was considered obscene at the time or that dealt with conception, blocking conception, or abortion. Comstock used his position as special agent alongside these laws to limit the information available to people about their own physiology. He justified these restrictions by appealing to fears that children could easily access and be influenced by sexual materials. Although most of his confiscations and prosecutions took place in New York City, by securing legislation at the federal and state level for something once considered private, Comstock paved the way for other reformers to use legislation to influence morality.

Comstock soon discovered that arresting and confiscating offenders proved easier than getting a conviction. In some New York courts, cases did not reach the punishment phase because prosecutors and judges were not receptive to Comstock, his methods, and his ideas. In New York City Comstock possessed powerful upper-class patrons who aided his efforts, but away from those backers, he struggled to implement the laws. Opposition formed, using the First Amendment to argue that such stringent limitations destroyed the right to free speech and freedom of the press. Comstock could not keep up with the massive flow of information despite destroying tens of thousands of pieces of "obscenity." During the late 1800s, Comstock continued his work in the face of increasing immigration. These new Americans heightened reformers' concerns about lewd behavior, loose morals, and corruption. Comstock and his supporters believed that eradicating sexualized material could save young men from frequenting brothels, young women from premarital relations, and children from harmful sexual influence.

The Comstock Laws of the 1870s reflected a larger concern among Americans about the influences of modernization on young people. Using these concerns Comstock tried to ban certain books, such as Walt Whitman's *Leaves of Grass*, and art displays at various museums. Other reform campaigns—directed toward familial behaviors such as the campaign to prohibit alcohol and efforts to intercede in families on behalf of women and children through social workers and charity agencies—took hold in the decades following the Comstock Laws. Helen Leftkowitz Horowitz referred to Comstock's message as "evangelical rhetoric," which can be seen in populist uprisings of the nineteenth, twentieth, and twenty-first centuries. Notions about appropriate middle- and upper-class influences in government can be seen in Comstock's antivice crusade and social movements demanding government intervention in regards to women and children. Comstock's influence on the U.S. legal system lasted well into the twentieth century, when the Supreme Court ruled that refusing access to birth control (*Connecticut v. Griswold*, 1965) and abortion (*Roe v. Wade*, 1973) violated privacy rights.

Comstock's work also had unintended consequences; the eugenics movement, concerned with preserving white Anglo-Saxon dominance during the late 1800s and early 1900s, began as a cry for help against the expansion of immigrant births. Birth control advocates such as Margaret Sanger, who battled Comstock for two decades, believed that limiting the number of immigrant births would ultimately lead to better maternal survival, less poverty, and by extension fewer immigrant children. However, Comstock believed strongly that the ability to limit births would negatively affect middle- and upper-class families and would allow women to be sexually permissive outside of marriage. He expressed these concerns by actively initiating prosecutions of abortion providers in the New York City area.

When Comstock began his work in the 1870s, his ideas about appropriate sex and class roles aligned with dominant white, middle- and upper-class interests. Comstock, a vigilant social conservative, understood the power of preserving the assumed moral vigilance of white middle-class Americans, and he did so with the aid of powerful patrons and politicians. His rejection of progressives such as Sanger and radical ideas such as the free love movement foreshadow the social conservatism and family-values emphasis of later periods. Comstock's success came from his ability both to shape the laws and to enforce them himself, becoming in many ways a one-man army against information he believed to be damaging to prevailing American values. Although perhaps not justly deserved, the late 1800s hold a reputation for sexual prudery that stems, in part, from the campaigns of Anthony Comstock.

Megan Birk

See also: Progressivism; Sanger, Margaret (1879–1966); Whitman, Walt (1819–1892); YMCA/YWCA

References

Abrams, Richard M. *America Transformed: Sixty Years of Revolutionary Change, 1941–2001*. Cambridge, UK: Cambridge University Press, 2006.

Beisel, Nicola. *Imperiled Innocents: Anthony Comstock and Family Reproduction in Victorian America*. Princeton, NJ: Princeton University Press, 1997.

Grossberg, Michael, *Governing the Hearth: Law and the Family in Nineteenth-Century America*. Chapel Hill: University of North Carolina Press, 1985.

Leftkowitz Horowitz, Helen. *Rereading Sex: Battles over Sexual Knowledge and Suppression in Nineteenth-Century America*. New York: Vintage Books, 2002.

Congress of Racial Equality (CORE)

The Congress of Racial Equality (CORE) was founded in 1942 at the University of Chicago by a group of interracial students who followed the teachings of Mahatma Gandhi, the leader who resisted British rule in India. CORE began a nonviolent campaign of civil disobedience, fighting against racial discrimination in the United States. By 1961, CORE had 53 chapters throughout the United States. By 1963, CORE chapters existed in most urban centers of the Northeast, Midwest, and West Coast and on some college campuses. CORE brought together people—despite their outward differences—to fight for the rights of those who had lost their civil rights gained in the Civil War but lost soon after, especially in the southern states.

Long before the Freedom Rides, CORE members challenged segregation in transportation in the South, as sanctioned by the Supreme Court in *Plessy v. Ferguson* (1896). CORE sent a group of eight white men and eight black men through Virginia, North Carolina, Tennessee, and

Kentucky in 1947, challenging the status quo of segregation in interstate travel. The men were arrested several times, but they received a lot of publicity; this was the beginning of campaigns to end segregation on buses. In the 1950s, public transit in the South was finally desegregated due to several events, most commonly marked by Rosa Parks's refusal to give up her seat on the bus for a white passenger in Montgomery, Alabama. CORE helped organize the Montgomery Bus Boycott. Later Freedom Riders, women as well as men, rode interstate buses in the early 1960s into the Deep South to force desegregation of interstate transportation and bus terminals, which was no longer sanctioned by the Interstate Commerce Commission. The riders encountered violent opposition and attracted national attention, including that of the Kennedy administration and Martin Luther King Jr.

These efforts toward gaining fair treatment in transportation did not distract CORE members away from key issues such as education and political participation. In 1954, CORE members played a crucial role in the Supreme Court case *Brown v. Board of Education*, which ended racial segregation in public schools. While implementation was slow, *Brown* was an important legal victory. In 1960, the Chicago chapter of CORE began to challenge segregation in the Chicago public schools. Overcrowding, high drop-out rates, and low educational standards were common in Chicago's African American schools. This chapter's members brought attention to the problems of Chicago's black youth but also highlighted the difficulties of dismantling the de facto segregation found in the North that contrasted with the legally mandated southern version of segregation that was easier to attack.

CORE was one of five organizations that helped organize the March on Washington on August 28, 1963. More than 250,000 people marched peacefully to the Lincoln Memorial to demand equal justice for all citizens under the law. At the end of the march, Dr. Martin Luther King Jr. delivered his famous "I Have a Dream" speech.

In 1964, CORE members joined activists involved in other civil rights organizations, including the Student Nonviolent Coordinating Committee (SNCC), in the Freedom Summer project that attempted to end political disenfranchisement of African Americans in the Deep South. They set up schools that later served as the model for Head Start programs and ran voter registration drives. Black volunteers involved in the Freedom Summer projects faced increased violence, and Ku Klux Klan members specifically targeted leaders in the movement, such as Anne Moody, who survived, while three members of CORE did not. James Chaney, Andrew Goodman, and Michael Schwerner were murdered by the Ku Klux Klan on June 21, 1964. Their deaths created nation-wide awareness for the campaign.

CORE members were the pioneers of civil resistance in the United States, playing leadership roles in boycotts, sit-ins, and freedom rides in the South and throughout the United States. Like other black civil rights organizations, its members moved away from an early emphasis on nonviolent civil disobedience and became associated with black nationalism during the 1960s. Today, the group fights against discrimination because of immigration status, sexual orientation, disabilities, and gender, as well as race. The CORE goal is that "All men will be judged by the content of their character, not the color of their skin" (CORE).

Sandra Leland Price

See also: Democratic Party; Freedom Riders; Interstate Commerce Act (ICA) (1887); King, Martin Luther, Jr. (1929–1968); Ku Klux Klan (KKK)

References

CORE. CORE Homepage. http://www.core-online.org. Accessed January 3, 2013.

Franklin, John Hope. *From Slavery to Freedom: A History of Negro Americans* (4th ed.). New York: Alfred A. Knopf, 1974.

Moody, Anne. *Coming of Age in Mississippi.* New York: Dell, 1992.

Sitkoff, Harvard. *The Struggle for Black Equality, 1954–1980.* New York: Hill and Wang, 1981.

Van Deburg, William L. *New Day In Babylon: The Black Power Movement and American Culture, 1965–1975.* Chicago: University of Chicago Press, 1992.

Weisbrot, Robert. *Freedom Bound: A History of America's Civil Rights Movement.* New York: Norton, 1990.

Cooperative Commonwealth

The cooperative commonwealth, one of the oldest ideas in American Populist thought, was also one that proved harder to translate into widespread and sustainable action in the United States. In fact, the cooperative commonwealth was brought closer to full realization in other parts of the English-speaking world, most notably in Canada. Nonetheless, the cooperative commonwealth ideal would both illuminate and inspire rural and urban labor Populist activists throughout the United States during the nineteenth and early twentieth centuries.

As the nineteenth century progressed, modern capitalism and wage labor became the increasing economic norm in the United States and displaced the traditional small-scale craft manufacturing that had been integral previously to the U.S. economy. As a result, manufacturing workers increasingly lost independence, and economic inequality grew. At the same time, farmers lost much of their traditional independence as the market revolution transferred profits from the trade of farm products increasingly out their hands. As a result, first labor and then agricultural activists were inspired by the philosophy of producerism. Producerism was the idea that workers and farmers, the "producers" of the nation's wealth, should enjoy the economic fruits of their own labors. These early populist activists also promoted the idea of the cooperative commonwealth, in which industrial capitalism and wage work would be replaced by worker-owned cooperatives, where workers would collectively own and profit from their industries. The period immediately following the Civil War saw the height of producerism in the United States, and with it the heyday of union-sponsored cooperatives in several industries. By contrast, the farmers' cooperative movement did not emerge until the closing decades of the nineteenth century.

One of the most important proponents of the cooperative commonwealth idea in the United States was the Noble and Holy Order of the Knights of Labor (KOL). The Knights of Labor, the first successful post–Civil War labor federation, began in 1869 as a secret society due to severe anti-labor hostility, but by the 1880s it organized openly under the leadership of Terrence V. Powderly. The KOL, in contrast to the American Federation of Labor that succeeded it, was noted for its openness to nearly all workers, excluding only lawyers, liquor distributors, and other groups deemed "parasites." The KOL was also noted for its opposition to strikes and similar labor actions in favor of binding arbitration and, more significantly, for its goal of ending the wage system and replacing it with worker cooperatives. Notably, Powderly favored neither socialism nor government ownership of industry but instead urged workers to collectively save enough to purchase the industries that were their "means of production" and run them on a cooperative basis. According to this incarnation of the cooperative commonwealth, when workers became owner-producers, the labor-management divide would be eliminated and industry-generated wealth would be more justly distributed than was possible under the traditional capitalist system. The cooperative commonwealth movement promoted by the KOL, therefore, effectively rejected the prospect of a permanent wage-earning class and appealed to the producerist ideals of many labor activists in the first decades following the Civil War. In the end, however, the collapse of the KOL and its replacement by the craft-oriented AFL largely ended the cooperative commonwealth ideal in the American labor movement. Although the AFL mildly supported consumer cooperatives, never again would the mainstream American labor movement be a promoter of producer cooperatives.

Although there were some farm cooperatives prior to the Civil War, the height of the agricultural cooperative commonwealth movement took place in the late nineteenth century and continued well into the twentieth century. It began with the founding of the Patrons of Husbandry, which became popularly known as the Grange. The Grange, which began as a farmer-self-help organization, soon turned to political activism and promoted the idea of farmer-owned transport and storage cooperatives as a way of retaking control of the storage, transportation, and distribution of agricultural products. The Grange and its political successor, the Farmers' Alliance, however, would be more successful in promoting the regulation of freight rail and grain distribution than in creating alternative ownership of railroads, grain elevators, and other means of distribution. The Farmers' Alliance, which was formally organized in 1890, took even more action in promoting a farmers' cooperative movement. Beginning with a nationwide series of lectures, followed by a journalistic campaign to promote the movement, the Farmers' Alliance supported the foundation of a number of production and retail cooperatives. The cooperative movement, in turn, helped increase the national prominence of the Alliance. The cooperatives that developed, however, suffered from lack of credit and from other prohibitive financial practices that left the rural economy essentially unchanged. And the eventual collapse of the Farmers' Alliance would largely shrink the idea of a rural cooperative commonwealth to a more limited (yet uniquely successful) system of farm cooperatives.

Although the dream of the cooperative commonwealth was never able to displace the dominance of American capitalism, the Populist ideal of worker (or consumer) ownership of the means of production has never entirely disappeared. Farm and natural food co-ops remain a familiar part of the American economic landscape, and although somewhat different from the ideal of worker-owned cooperatives, employee ownership or majority ownership has become a feature of many American corporations, and in the early twenty-first century there has been a growing interest in cooperative enterprises that also emphasize environmental sustainability. Most significantly, the cooperative commonwealth ideal remains a relevant example of the long history of populist challenges to the economic and cultural norms of American capitalism.

Susan Roth Breitzer

See also: American Federation of Labor (AFL); Farmers' Mutual Benefit Association (FMBA); Farmers' Transportation Convention; Granger Movement; Knights of Labor; Producerism; Railroad Regulation; Rochdale Plan; Rural Credits; Subtreasury Plan; Warehouse Act (1916)

References

Hild, Matthew. *Greenbackers, Knights of Labor, and Populists: Farmer-Labor Insurgency in the Nineteenth-Century South*. Athens: University of Georgia Press, 2007.

Ware, Norman J. *The Labor Movement in the United States, 1860–1895*. New York: D. Appleton and Company, 1929.

Weir, Robert. *Knights Unhorsed: Internal Conflict in a Gilded Age Social Movement*. Detroit, MI: Wayne State University Press, 2000.

Copland, Aaron (1900–1990)

Aaron Copland was an American composer who created a distinctive American sound in classical music, often referred to as a populist style. Copland was born in Brooklyn, New York, and trained as a composer in New York and Paris. He used folk music, jazz, and other American styles to create new compositions for symphonies, movies, and the ballet. His first major orchestral piece, commissioned for the Boston Symphony Orchestra, was entitled *Symphony for Organ and Orchestra* (1925). Much of his music evokes the sense of wide-open spaces and combines European classical form with a twentieth-century feeling. Considered to be too radical for American classical music, his early works were hissed at by audiences and criticized heavily by music writers.

As his career continued, he enjoyed much success. His *Fanfare for the Common Man* (1942) was composed in response to the entrance of the United States into World War II and was widely popular. Copland won a Pulitzer Prize for Music for composing the ballet *Appalachian Spring* (1945). His ballets *Rodeo*,

Billy the Kid, and *Appalachian Spring* all dealt with western themes and had an exuberant and lively sound that fused American western folk music and classical music. Copland also won several other awards including an Academy Award for his music in the film *The Heiress* (1949), the Presidential Medal of Freedom (1964), a Kennedy Center Honor (1979), and the Congressional Gold Medal (1986).

Active in helping young composers, he was a director of the League of Composers and taught at Harvard, Tanglewood, and the New School for Social Research. He wrote many articles, essays, and books about music and his life. Copland conducted in the last few decades of his working life, making his debut at the New York Philharmonic in 1958, and acted as guest conductor with many symphonies. He left his estate to music, and his home in Cortlandt Manor, New York, is now known as Copland House and is a retreat for composers.

Lynn Elizabeth Marlowe

See also: Guthrie, Woodrow Wilson "Woody" (1912–1967); Highlander Folk School; Pop Music

References

Perlis, Vivian, and Libby Van Cleve. *Composers' Voices from Ives to Ellington: An Oral History of American Music*. New Haven, CT: Yale University Press, 2005.

Pollack, Howard. *Aaron Copland: The Life and Work of an Uncommon Man.* New York: Henry Holt and Company, 1999.

"Timeline: Aaron Copland," Copland House website, accessed November 17, 2011. http://www.coplandhouse.org/aaron-copland/timeline/. Accessed December 1, 2013.

Country Life Movement

The Country Life Movement was a sometimes loosely organized reaction to the challenges faced by those who lived on farms and in rural societies during the early twentieth century. These difficulties included a mass movement of people from the country to the city. Urbanites and sociologists thought that rural residents were demoralized because they faced an inability to succeed at agricultural production. These reformers pushed for reforms that would preserve the countryside as the embodiment of American values and as the agricultural wellspring of the nation. The reforms they proposed were not merely agricultural but affected broader rural social structures as well. As the Progressive movement began to look at reforming the cities, some also turned their attention to reforming these rural communities.

Industrialization concentrated new job opportunities in the cities. Simultaneously, small-scale farmers and farm laborers faced difficult economic conditions, which made the better paying work in the urban centers a powerful magnet. Black Americans were also migrating out of the rural South, heading north to take advantage of these bountiful industrial jobs. Rural school systems were falling behind their urban counterparts. As land prices rose, more farmers were forced into tenancy, creating a vicious cycle of debt. Some also feared the increasing number of immigrant farmers who flooded the Great Plains and other open areas, feeling that the newcomers' farming practices were not up to par.

Just before he left office, President Theodore Roosevelt in 1908 instituted a Country Life Commission to address these concerns. He appointed Liberty Hyde Bailey of Cornell University as the chairman of the commission, which sent out hundreds of thousands of surveys across the nation and conducted hearings across the country. Bailey submitted a report to the president that made a number of proposals to improve country life, including the reform of country churches and schools. These institutions could be strategic in providing skills training that would keep people on the land. President Roosevelt did not have the time to push the commission's initiatives through Congress, and the recommendations were not acted upon by the next president or congress.

Even though its recommendations were not immediately adopted, the commission's impact led to a number of advancements. One result was the founding of the American Country Life Association in 1918, an organization that had many of the same concerns as the Country Life Commission. The efforts of this movement eventually resulted in the formation of the American Farm Bureau. The Cooperative Extension Service also arose out of the Country Life Movement. The Extension Service was, and is, an invaluable liaison between farmers and agricultural research. Country Life played an important part in the budding conservation movement.

The response of local churches to rural renewal efforts was less successful. Some country lifers criticized the lack of unity of churches. Others insisted that churches should offer nonreligious outlets for area residents. Some churches did create humanistic missions to help local people via educational outreach and other programs. Yet many churches rejected these as an interference with their autonomy. Some churches viewed the Country Life Movement as promoting the social gospel, which had been more popular in cities. The social gospel emphasized changing society as a whole rather than bettering the world through individual conversion.

The American Country Life Association continued to hold annual meetings well into the 1970s. However, World War II drained resources away from the association, and it never had the same influence again after the 1940s. In addition to the Extension networks, the Country Life Movement succeeded in making better roads in rural areas and instituted a parcel-post delivery system that eliminated the need to go to town for every supply.

Ken Taylor

See also: Bailey, Liberty Hyde (1858–1954); Peonage; Public Education; Roosevelt, Theodore (1858–1919); Social Gospel

References

Bowers, William L. *The Country Life Movement in America, 1900–1920.* Port Washington, NY: Kennikat Press, 1974.

Roth, Dennis. "The Country Life Movement." In *Federal Rural Development Policy in the Twentieth Century.* United States Department of Agriculture, Economic Research Service. http://www.nal.usda.gov/ric/ricpubs/rural_development_chap1.pdf. Accessed January 3, 2013.

Wunderlich, Gene. "Theodore Roosevelt's Country Life Commission and the

American Country Life Association." Paper presented at the meeting of the American Agricultural Economics Association, Denver, August 1–4, 2004. http://ageconsearch.umn.edu/bitstream/20178/1/os04wu01.pdf. Accessed January 3, 2013.

Coxey, Jacob (1854–1951)

Jacob Coxey was a businessman in the early 1890s who noticed an opportunity for the government to assist common folk during the Depression of 1893. Coxey organized the first, albeit unsuccessful, march to the Capitol to promote changes in the ways that the federal government dealt with the poor. Coxey was significant because of his ideas rather than his political career. His notions of reform came from his affiliation with the Greenback Party in the late 1880s.

Jacob Sechler Coxey was born on April 16, 1854, in Selinsgrove, Pennsylvania. He dropped out of school early and found temporary work. At the age of 27, Coxey moved to Massillon, Ohio, where he made a name for himself as a businessman near the end of the Gilded Age. While he was far from a robber baron, Coxey realized that hardworking middle- and lower-class people were not being adequately compensated for their labor. Those who were out of work caught his attention most.

During the early 1880s, Coxey noticed the effects the economic downturn had on those around him. Coxey believed that the government should offer public works projects to offer jobs to the unemployed in an attempt to counteract the negative aspects of the economy. In the effort to reach this goal Coxey modeled his ideas after those of the People's Party. Predating the New Deal, Coxey had formulated a legislative bill that would have provided funds for the improvement of roads across the United States. The bill called for appropriations of $500 million to run the project known as the General County Road Fund System. Workers would have received at least $1.50 per day for an eight-hour work day.

In 1893, the economy again gave way to depression, but this time on a much larger scale. Coxey began laying plans for a movement of the poor to petition for assistance. "Coxey's Army" left for Washington, DC, in March 1894. This group of poor and unemployed workers attracted the attention of the country because of extensive media coverage, which was, unfortunately, mostly negative. Newspapers portrayed Coxey as a radical, and most Americans thus ignored his ideas. Upon arrival in the capital, Coxey received a 20-day jail sentence after being arrested for trespassing on the grounds of the Capitol.

Despite the failure of the march, Coxey continued his political career. He lost multiple elections on different party ballots. He laid out his intentions for a second march in 1914 in his book, *The Coxey Plan*. Coxey wanted the government to provide guaranteed employment and regulated wages for the poor. This time he addressed a crowd in Washington, DC, but with little result.

The assistance for which Coxey pleaded was realized during the Great Depression by Franklin D. Roosevelt, whose New Deal included a number of the "radical causes" that Coxey's Army had espoused. Coxey was a candidate for president in the election of 1932, under the Farmer Labor Party, which focused on economic issues.

Coxey was invited to Washington, DC, in 1944, to deliver the speech he had planned to give at the end of his first march on Washington. At the age of 90 years old, Coxey read the speech commemorating the 50th anniversary of Coxey's Army's failed march. While Coxey never had the opportunity to implement change himself, he proved that one person can make a difference, albeit sometimes through the actions of others who were influenced by his ideas. Coxey died in his hometown of Massillon, Ohio, on May 18, 1951. He was 97 years old.

Joshua Butler

See also: Cleveland, Grover (1837–1908); Coxey's Army; Depression of 1893; Gilded Age; Greenback Party; New Deal

References

Brands, H. W. *The Reckless Decades: America in the 1890s*. Chicago: University of Chicago Press, 2002.

Schwantes, Carlos A. *Coxey's Army: An American Odyssey*. Moscow: University of Idaho Press, 1994.

Coxey's Army

On Tuesday, May 1, 1894, four years before the Spanish-American War, a group of unemployed men and women, many of them joined by their spouses and children, marched on Pennsylvania Avenue in Washington, DC, In the midst of a depression year, many faced financial hardships and struggled to feed their families, and some of those who were out of work and afflicted decided to take a stand to promote progress. Led by businessman Jacob Sechler Coxey, the crowd of more than 500 hoped that the march would get President Grover Cleveland's attention so that Cleveland would create public works jobs to help improve the U.S. economy.

Coxey, born April 16, 1854, in Selinsgrove, Pennsylvania, was the owner of a crushing mill in Massillon, Ohio, in addition to several ranches in other states. He was a member of the Greenback Party, founded in 1874 in support of currency expansion. The march, which began in Massillon, lasted six to seven weeks and faced many obstacles along the way: a snow storm, arrests, and internal disagreements. The army arrived in Washington, DC, on the last day of April, and government authorities feared the worst, taking special precautions to prevent any violent outbreaks.

On May 1, after reaching the capital, Coxey and Carl Browne, the man who is said to have been the one to conceive the march, were arrested for a period of 20 days for trespassing, reportedly for having walked on the grass. Fellow marchers gradually disbanded, and the march proved unsuccessful, failing to bring about any legislation. It was, however, part of the inspiration to create unemployment insurance, the Social Security Act, and other New Deal programs later passed by President Franklin Delano Roosevelt as a response to the Great Depression.

Gustavo Adolfo Aybar

See also: Bonus Army; Cleveland, Grover (1837–1908); Coxey, Jacob (1854–1951); New Deal; Panic of 1893

References

McMurry, Donald L. *Coxey's Army: A Study of the Industrial Army Movement of 1894.* Seattle: University of Washington Press, 1968.

Schwantes, Carlos A. *Coxey's Army: An American Odyssey.* Lincoln: University of Nebraska Press, 1985.

Crédit Mobilier Scandal

Among the numerous public scandals that occurred during President Ulysses Grant's second term, the Crédit Mobilier affair drew the most attention. In 1864, the federal government issued a cash payment of $100 million dollars to the Union Pacific Railroad to complete the transcontinental railroad west from the Missouri River. The government also provided a $60 million loan and a generous 20 million acre land grant with a cash value between $50 to $100 million. Due to the rough terrain, high freight costs, and fear of Indian attacks, no companies accepted this offer. A House committee led by Oakes Ames devised a plan in which the government assumed all the financial risk and backed all the stock. Ames and associates realized that the cost would be less than what the government had invested. To acquire the total capital needed to build the Union Pacific, stockholders formed a second corporation that they dubbed a "construction company," known as Crédit Mobilier of America, which required the railroad to turn over its bonds and stocks. As a result, the Union Pacific lost control of everything except its road and equipment while the so-called construction company paid the rates and kept the profits.

People involved in the scandal included Thomas Durant, vice president of Union Pacific; Cornelius Bushnell, a Union Pacific financier; and John Alley, a representative from Massachusetts who became connected with the Union Pacific Railroad. They and their associates formed the Crédit Mobilier of America and obtained a majority of the stock. In 1866, the federal government also extended contracts to the Central Pacific Railroad to build transcontinental lines east from California, which began a race with the Union Pacific to see which railroad could lay the most track. By December 1868, Crédit Mobilier collected $43,929,328.34 in net profits, and as its stock prices increased, jealousy grew among the stockholders. They quarreled over the division of profits to the point that the stockholders almost exposed their scandalous operation. In 1867, H. S. McComb filed a lawsuit for alleged stock-ownership in Crédit Mobilier that sparked scrutiny of the company. When Representative Elihu Washburne of Illinois began an investigation, Ames paid congressmen in stock shares to stay quiet, and to appease McComb, he provided the names of the congressmen who had purchased Crédit Mobilier shares.

McComb kept his information about these shares under wraps until the presidential election of 1872. He published the list of names and added others, including Schuyler Colfax, vice president of the

United States; Henry Wilson, vice president elect; and James Blaine, speaker of the House. In 1873, after a congressional investigation had been held, it confirmed that illegal transactions had been made and recommended Ames be expelled for using his position to influence votes in Congress. The investigation also censored James Brooks, the government director of the Union Pacific, for using his title to obtain stocks.

The impact of the Crédit Mobilier scandal is difficult to decipher. The investigation showed that the company had provided shares to 30 representatives in Congress, one of whom was James Garfield. He denied involvement in the scandal when he became president. Colfax lost his renomination bid on the Republican Party ticket for vice president as a result of his involvement. The Crédit Mobilier scandal serves as one of the best examples of railroad corruption during the Gilded Age.

Joshua A. Camper

See also: Railroad Regulation; Railroads; Union Pacific Railroad

References

Ambrose, Stephen. *Nothing Like It in the World: The Men Who Built the Transcontinental Railroad, 1863–1869.* New York: Touchstone, 2000.

Foner, Eric. *Reconstruction: America's Unfinished Revolution, 1863–1877.* New York: HarperCollins Publishers, 1988.

Morison, Samuel Eliot. *The Encyclopedia Americana: A Library of Universal Knowledge.* New York: Encyclopedia Americana Corporation, 1918.

Morison, Samuel Eliot. *The Oxford History of the American People.* New York: Oxford University Press, 1965.

Crime of '73

"The Crime of '73" is a nickname for the Fourth Coinage Act of 1873, given by opponents who saw the planned restriction of specie as an attack against farmers and debtors. The fiscal panic that occurred in that year was seen by critics of the law as the result of a "gold conspiracy" of creditors and gold mining operations to control the economy at the expense of average Americans. The law combined with other financial issues of the time, such as the Crédit Mobilier scandal, in convincing many that the government was corrupt. A grassroots campaign to change the system developed into the Populist movement of the late nineteenth century. The phrase "Crime of '73" became popular during the three decades following the passage of the act when silver mining operators cooperated with farmers in creating new national political parties whose goals included reversing the deflationary trend by returning to bimetallism (gold and silver) and including paper money.

The Coinage Act of 1873 demonetized silver, making gold the only acceptable specie for currency. Before the law, U.S. currency consisted of both silver and gold currency. Miners could submit gold or silver to a U.S. mint and receive coins in equal value in return, minus fees. Most silver coins were in denominations under a dollar (dimes, quarters, half-dollars) while most gold currency was coined in various amounts equal to or above one dollar. Concerns about rapid inflation combined with the discovery of large deposits of silver in the American West in the mid-nineteenth century led investors and creditors to demand that gold alone become the standard for U.S. currency. Known pejoratively as "gold bugs" by their opponents, these individuals became highly influential in the Republican Party and were instrumental in the passage of the act. Also, many other nations were adopting gold as the only standard for currency at the time, increasing the amount of silver floating on the market and driving down its value. "Gold bugs" argued that the United States must follow the lead of other nations to maintain a stable economy. The Coinage Act of 1873 met their demands and placed the nation on the gold standard, leading to deflation in the nation's money supply.

The Panic of 1873, which led to widespread layoffs and foreclosures in the United States, was blamed by many on the Coinage Act of 1873. During the panic, the major banking firm of Jay Cooke failed, almost one-quarter of the nation's 364 railroads went bankrupt along with almost 20,000 other businesses, and unemployment ran close to 15 percent. The depression cost the Republicans votes in Congress and was one of the contributing causes of the railroad strike of 1877.

Initially silver miners became the most outspoken opponents of the Coinage Act of 1873. Demanding "free silver," these "Silverites" attacked the Coinage Act of 1873 and called for bimetallism., Through their efforts they managed to get Richard Bland and William Allison to sponsor the Bland-Allison Act in 1878, which established the coinage of silver to gold at a ratio of 16 to 1. Bland's ties to silver mining earned him the nicknames "Silver Dick" and "the Great Commoner." In 1896 he competed with William Jennings Bryan for the Democratic nomination before supporting Bryan's candidacy against the Republicans.

At the same time, farmers seeking easier credit and cheaper money joined together to form the Independent (National) Party. Meeting in Indianapolis, Indiana, in 1874, the party's strong interest in currency reform and paper currency led to it being known as the Greenback Party. The Party had a strong following in the Midwest among farmers who feared foreclosure. Greenbackers had close connections with the Grange movement, which already organized farmers on the issue of railroad regulation. With this base the party nominated Peter Cooper, a wealthy American businessman who had become a champion of civil rights for African and Native Americans. As early as 1873 Cooper spoke out against the deflationary policies of the Republican Party and supported paper money. The Greenback Party tried to nominate Newton Booth, a senator from California, as vice president, but Booth, preferring to stay in the Senate, declined the nomination and was replaced by prohibitionist lecturer Samuel F. Cary. The party did not perform well in the election, garnering only clusters of votes, mainly in the West, with a popular vote tally of 75,937. At its height in 1878, the Greenback Party had elected 13 congressmen. By 1882, they were only able to elect 3 congressmen and worked toward merging with the Democrats.

Weaver, feeling that merging with the Democrats meant losing the Greenback focus on supporting paper money, left the party and began working with farmers to create the People's Party in 1891. The new party appealed to farmers who were suffering due to declining cotton prices and a drought that forced Plains farmers deeper into debt. Besides the currency reform, the People's Party platform called for direct election of senators, a graduated income tax, civil service reform, the eight-hour workday, and federal control of public utilities and transportation. Its platform, called the Omaha Platform, was written in Nebraska by Ignatius Donnelly at the party's first convention. The party nominated James Weaver for president and James Field, a southerner, for vice president. The party tried unsuccessfully to merge northern and southern farmers of both races but met with violent resistance, especially in the South. Despite these problems, the party did well in national and local elections in 1892 with Weaver carrying Kansas, Colorado, Idaho, and Nevada, while also receiving one electoral vote each from Oregon and North Dakota for a total of 22 electoral votes and 285,297 popular votes. The Populists also elected governors in Kansas and Colorado and made gains in Congress, adding one more senator to the two already elected in 1890 and three more members to the House of Representatives to join the eight already sitting. Some bimetallists from western mining states also joined together in the election of 1892 in support of Silver Party candidates and managed to get a member elected to Congress. They felt the People's Party was distracted by issues other than monetary policy but cooperated with them on the goal of reversing the Crime of '73.

Racial divisions encouraged some Populists to consider merging with the Republicans or Democrats. This discussion led the Populists to nominate William Jennings Bryan, the Democrats' nominee for president in 1896. Bryan had been an outspoken supporter of bimetallism and at the Democratic Convention gave his famous "Cross of Gold" speech that attacked the Crime of '73. Many Populists felt Bryan gave them their best chance of winning the White House, but they did not want to become a part of the Democratic Party. At the People's Party Convention in St. Louis, they nominated one of their own for vice president, Thomas Watson, and supported a large slate of congressional candidates. The silver issue played a large role in the 1896 election partially because of Grover Cleveland's successful efforts to repeal the Bland-Allison and Sherman Silver Purchase Act in 1893, even causing some Republicans to split from their own party on the issue, forming a "Silver" Republican Party. Bryan lost the election to William McKinley, but Populists held 5 senate seats and won 22 seats in the House. Other "Silver" and "Republican Silver" candidates also won.

The year 1896 was the high-water mark for the People's Party. Internal dissention and disagreements over combining with the Democrats weakened the support for the party. In 1900 the party nominated Wharton Barker for president with Ignatius Donnelly as his running mate. They were unable to capture many votes, and the party also lost ground in Congress. Attempts to maintain the party caused it to reform and struggle through the 1904 and 1908 elections, but it was no longer a national force.

Michael L. Faubion

See also: Banking System of the Late Nineteenth Century; Bland, Richard P. (1835–1899); Bryan, William Jennings (1860–1925); Crédit Mobilier Scandal; "Cross of Gold" Speech (1896); Depression of 1873; Donnelly, Ignatius (1831–1901); Drought; Gold Standard/Free Silver; Greenback Party; People's Party; Prohibition (1919–1933); Sherman Silver Purchase Act (1890); Silver Republicans

References

Friedman, Milton, and Anna J. Schwartz. *A Monetary History of the United States, 1867–1960.* Princeton, NJ: Princeton University Press, 1963.

Goodwyn, Lawrence. *Democratic Promise: The Populist Moment in America.* New York: Oxford University Press, 1976.

Hicks, John D. "The Sub-Treasury: A Forgotten Plan for the Relief of Agriculture." *Mississippi Valley Historical Review* 15 (3): 355–373

Hild, Matthew. *Greenbackers, Knights of Labor, and Populists: Farmer-Labor Insurgency in the Late-Nineteenth-Century South.* Athens: University of Georgia Press, 2007.

Hofstadter, Richard. "Free Silver and the Mind of 'Coin' Harvey." In *The Paranoid Style in American Politics and Other Essays.* Cambridge, MA: Harvard University Press, 1996.

Palmer, Bruce. *Man over Money: The Southern Populist Critique of American Capitalism.* Chapel Hill: University of North Carolina Press, 1980.

Stock, Catherine McNicol. *Rural Radicals: Righteous Rage in the American Grain.* Ithaca, NY: Cornell University Press, 1996.

Cripple Creek War (1894)

The Cripple Creek War, also known as the Cripple Creek miners' strike of 1894, was a five-month strike instigated by the Western Federation of Miners (WFM) in Cripple Creek, Colorado. The miners' strike resulted in a significant victory for the WFM and was followed in 1903 by the Colorado labor wars. The Cripple Creek strike was a significant event in the development of Populist labor movements in the Far West because it was the only time in U.S. history when a state militia was enlisted in support of striking workers. The strike at Cripple Creek, Colorado, was characterized by violent firefights, involved the use of dynamite, and was brought under control after a confrontation between the Colorado state militia and a private army working for the owners of the local mines. The Cripple Creek strike greatly contributed to the WFM's increasing political presence and popularity among miners in Colorado and the western region.

At the close of the nineteenth century, the mining community of Cripple Creek was the second largest town in Colorado with a population of nearly 15,000. Located just to the southwest of Pikes Peak, surface gold was discovered in the region in 1891, and within a three-year period more than 150 mines operated in the area. Until this time, the Colorado mining economy had been heavily invested in silver extraction. However, the panic of 1893 caused the price of silver to plummet. Yet the price of gold remained high. In the 1890s, gold was desperately sought after to replenish the banks holding federal deposits. The discovery of gold in Colorado resulted in an increase of silver miners seeking work in the newly opened gold mines. This infusion of former silver miners into the gold-producing facilities contributed to a lowering of wages. Mine owners at Cripple Creek forced their employees to work longer hours and endure extremely hazardous conditions for less pay.

In 1894, the owners of the Cripple Creek Mine, J. J. Hagerman, David Moffat, and Eben Smith, instituted a lengthening of the work day to 10 hours from 8 hours per day. These three men controlled the salaries of nearly one-third of the miners, yet they were unwilling to raise the daily wage from $3 per day. The former silver miners protested, and the mine operators agreed to the 8-hour work day, but they would only pay the workers $2.50 a day. Shortly before this incident, miners at Cripple Creek, along with the Knights of Labor, had created the Free Coinage Union. With the new changes in pay and working conditions, the Free Coinage members merged with the WFM, becoming Local Chapter 19. In February 1894, the mine owners at Cripple Creek began enforcing the 10-hour work day. The president of the WFM, John Calderwood, delivered a notice to the mine owners demanding that they reinstate the 8-hour work day at the $3 per day pay rate. When Hagerman, Moffat, and Smith did not comply with the WFM's demands, the union officially struck on February 7. Portland, Pikes Peak, and Gold Dollar, along with some of the smaller mines, quickly agreed to the 8-hour work day and maintained daily operations. However, owners of larger facilities such as the Cripple Creek Mine held out, refusing to give into workers' demands.

The Cripple Creek strike had an instant impact. At the end of February 1894, almost every smelter and ore processing facility was either shut down or operating part time. In March, the Gold King and Granite mines capitulated and resumed operations under the 8-hour day. However, many mine owners held out for the 10-hour day, and they attempted to reopen their mines; several owners brought in strikebreakers. The WFM attempted to convince the strikebreakers to join the union and strike, but they were ultimately unsuccessful. The violent and lawless WFM threatened nonstriking miners, and their predatory tactics were successful in preventing the nonunion miners from continuing work.

The Cripple Creek Miner's Strike was a pivotal event in the history of the Populist labor movement in the latter half of the nineteenth century because it represented the first attempt by western miners to organize a successful labor union. Colorado miners and railroad workers supported Populist labor organizations such as the Knights of Labor. The Southern (Farmers') Alliance entered the state in 1888 promoting aggressive economic cooperation and antimonopolism. Western miners, farmers, and laborers viewed themselves as victims of a colonial economy primarily dictated by the banks in London and New York. Prior to the 1894 strike, miners in the Colorado territory had been largely powerless to advocate for their economic and civil rights. The Cripple Creek strike was the first victory for the fledgling WFM. The Colorado miners' victory over the hostile mine operators established the union as a major political force to be reckoned with in the western United States.

Christopher Allan Black

See also: Colorado, Populism in; Depression of 1893; Knights of Labor; Waite, Davis (1825–1901)

References

Carnes, Mark C., and Garraty, John A. *American Destiny: Narrative of a Nation.* Vol. 2. New York: Penguin, 2003.

Clements, Eric L. "Pragmatic Revolutionaries?: Tactics, Ideologies, and the Western Federation of Miners in the Progressive Era." *Western Historical Quarterly* 40 (4): 445–467.

Foner, Phillip S. *History of the Labor Movement in the United States: From the Founding of the A.F. of L. to the Emergence of American Imperialism.* 2nd ed. New York: International Publishers, 1975.

Jameson, Elizabeth. *All that Glitters: Class Conflict and Community in Cripple Creek.* Urbana: University of Illinois Press, 1998.

McMath, Robert C., Jr. *American Populism: A Social History 1877–1898.* New York: Hill and Wang, 1993.

Strangeland, Charles Emil. "The Preliminaries to the Labor War in Colorado." *Political Science Quarterly* 23 (1): 1–17.

"Cross of Gold" Speech (1896)

The "Cross of Gold" speech of William Jennings Bryan has become one of the seminal documents of American history. Given at the Democratic convention of July 9, 1896, the speech, with its simple, moral appeal, transformed an ordinary American politician into a crusading orator. Born in Illinois, Bryan attended Union Law College in Chicago and practiced law in Jacksonville, Illinois, between 1883 and 1887. As a young lawyer, he moved to Lincoln, Nebraska, in 1887 and joined the Democratic Party. He rose rapidly in the party echelon and was elected to the U.S. Congress in 1890. He was reelected two years later but lost the Senate race in 1894. Bryan, who became editor of the *Omaha World-Herald,* traveled the countryside as a proponent of free silver, due to the collapse of the silver market, and silver became the issue that would bring him to prominence.

At the Democratic National Convention in 1896, Bryan delivered the famous "Cross of Gold" speech. President Grover Cleveland was the leader of probusiness Democrats, or Bourbon Democrats, which became a derogatory term meaning "old-fashioned." Cleveland's supporters were also known as the Gold Democrats or Gold Bugs. The silverite-agrarian faction stood for the free minting of silver coins, which they believed would end the depression of the 1890s. As one of these Silverites, Bryan had launched a crusade against the supporters of the gold standard. His "Cross of Gold" speech influenced the delegates because of its popular appeal, dramatic rhetorical style, biblical overtones, and solid argument. The issue at the convention was the endorsement of the free coinage of silver with a ratio to gold of 16 to 1. Money in circulation would help the farmers, who were burdened with debt. They believed that paper money backed primarily with gold should end, and instead currency should be backed with silver also. This would increase the value of the paper money in circulation and improve buying power for farmers and workers.

Bryan was an excellent orator, and his powerful and booming voice reverberated to all corners of the convention hall in the days before microphones. He rose to speak and began humbly, saying, "I would be presumptuous, indeed, to present myself against the distinguished gentlemen to whom you have listened if this were but a measuring of ability; but this is not a contest among persons" (Bryan). Bryan told the gathering that all Americans were equals: a merchant in a store at a crossroads and a merchant in New York, an attorney in a small town and a corporate lawyer, a miner and a financial magnate, and a farmer and a member of the Board of Trade all had the same rights to prosperity. Bryan opined that he was against accumulation of wealth. He criticized vehemently the followers of the gold standard as persons willing to sacrifice the right of American self-government to place power in the hands of wealthier foreign powers. The votaries of free silver were, instead, on the side of the struggling masses. Bryan ended his speech to thundering applause by saying, "Having behind us the commercial interests and the laboring interests and all the toiling masses, we shall answer their demands for a gold standard by saying to them, you shall not press down upon the brow of labor this crown of thorns. You shall not crucify mankind upon a cross of gold" (Bryan). After the speech, the crowd went into frenzy. The next day, Bryan was nominated as the presidential candidate on the fifth ballot. The 36-year-old Bryan also was nominated by the People's Party.

Bryan became an overnight sensation after the "Cross of Gold" speech. He traveled throughout the United States. He reiterated the cause of free silver during his 18,000-mile trek. The rural population of the South and Midwest generally supported Bryan. However, he lost the election by 271–176 in electoral votes and paved the way for Republican dominance. After the passing of Gold Standard Act of 1900, the silver lobby became redundant. But the irrepressible Bryan did not fade into oblivion. He made his presence felt as secretary of state and remained publicly active. As a Chautauqua speaker, he repeated the "Cross of Gold" speech many times. In 1921, Gennett Records made a recording of Bryan giving the speech. The "Cross of Gold" speech has remained one of the most famous and influential speeches in U.S. political history.

Patit Paban Mishra

See also: Cleveland, Grover (1837–1908); Depression of 1893; Gold Standard/Free Silver; People's Party; Silver Republicans

References

Bensel, Richard F. *Passion and Preferences: William Jennings Bryan and the 1896 Democratic National Convention.* New York: Cambridge University Press, 2008.

Boller, Paul F. *Presidential Campaigns from George Washington to George W. Bush.* Oxford, UK: Oxford University Press. 2004.

Bryan, William Jennings, "Cross of Gold," *Official Proceedings of the Democratic National Convention held in Chicago, Illinois, July 7, 8, 9, 10, and 11, 1896.* Logansport, Indiana, 1896, pp. 226–234.

Also available on History Matters, http://historymatters.gmu.edu/d/5354/.

Finkelman, Paul, and Bruce A. Lesh. *Milestone Documents in American History: Exploring the Primary Sources that Shaped America.* Dallas, TX: Schlager Group, 2008.

Kazin, Michael. *A Godly Hero: The Life of William Jennings Bryan.* New York: Knopf, 2006.

Leinwand, Gerald. *William Jennings Bryan: An Uncertain Trumpet.* Lanham, MD: Rowman & Littlefield, 2007.

Suriano, Gregory R. *Great American Speeches.* New York: Gramercy Books, 1993.

Williams, Wayne C. *William Jennings Bryan: A Study in Political Vindication.* Eastbourne, UK: Gardners Books, 2007.

Czolgosz, Leon (1873–1901)

Leon Czolgosz was an American anarchist and assassin who gained notoriety for shooting U.S. President William McKinley at the Pan-American Exposition in Buffalo, New York, on September 6, 1901. Czolgosz contended that anarchists, particularly Emma Goldman and Alexander Berkman, heavily influenced him, but the precise motivation behind the assassination remains unknown. After a quick trial, Czolgosz was convicted and executed by electrocution. Following Czolgosz's murder of McKinley, the anarchist movement suffered legal and public recriminations, but anarchists still assumed Czolgosz as a martyr figure for their cause. McKinley's death also ushered in the presidency of Theodore Roosevelt, thus instigating Progressivism on the federal level.

Czolgosz was born in May 1873 in Detroit, Michigan, to Polish-Russian immigrants and had six other siblings. In 1881 his parents moved the family to a small farm near Cleveland to pursue the agrarian dream of independent farming. The farm did not provide Czolgosz's family adequate income, however, and Leon was sent to work in a wire mill at age 10 with his brothers. Two years later, all the boys were fired when mill workers went on strike. At age 16 Czolgosz then worked in a glass factory in Pennsylvania before suffering a mental breakdown in 1898. With no other support network, Czolgosz begrudgingly returned to the family farm, but he rejected his family's Roman Catholicism and became increasingly interested in anarchistic ideology. Czolgosz began insulating himself against outside society, and he spent a great deal of his time reading socialist and anarchist newspapers in his mother's basement. In July 1900, American newspapers reported that Italian-American Gaetano Bresci had returned to Italy and assassinated King Umberto. Bresci contended he had shot Umberto because the king had celebrated the killing of unarmed demonstrators who had marched on the palace demanding a reprieve from high bread prices. Bresci's actions appealed to Czolgosz and other anarchists because Bresci represented the struggle against an unsympathetic monarchy. Reading accounts of the assassination inspired Czolgosz to leave the family farm and attend anarchist meetings.

Arriving in Cleveland on May 6, 1901, Czolgosz heard a speech at the Federal Liberal Club by famed anarchist Emma Goldman. He appears to have become enamored with Goldman, and he spoke with her after the Cleveland meeting and

Anarchist Leon Czolgosz shoots U.S. president William McKinley with a concealed revolver at the Pan-American Exposition reception on September 6, 1901. McKinley died a week later and Czolgosz was executed for his crime. (Library of Congress)

followed her to Chicago and other cities where she gave lectures. Despite (or because of) his apparent enthusiasm for both anarchism and Goldman, Czolgosz fell under suspicion by other anarchists, particularly Abraham Isaak. Isaak was the publisher of the *Free Society*, an American anarchist weekly, and he suspected that Czolgosz's repeated call to violence in anarchist meetings meant that Czolgosz was a spy for the U.S. government. Isaak believed Czolgosz was trying to infiltrate the anarchists and pass incriminating evidence to the government, a warning Isaak reiterated publicly in *Free Society*. As a result, many anarchists shunned Czolgosz.

On a trip to Chicago, Czolgosz learned from newspapers that President William McKinley planned to visit the upcoming 1901 Pan-American Exposition in Buffalo, New York. Czolgosz purchased a pistol on September 3, and two days later he was in the audience when McKinley gave a speech at the Exposition's Temple of Music. Czolgosz managed to approach McKinley, despite McKinley's large coterie of bodyguards, and he fired two shots at the president, hitting him in the chest and abdomen. Secret Service agents immediately captured Czolgosz. McKinley was taken to a nearby hospital, where doctors discovered his chest wound was superficial but the bullet in his abdomen had torn through his stomach wall and his kidney. Initially, doctors predicted McKinley would recover, but the wound became gangrenous, and the president died on September 14.

Czolgosz was indicted for first-degree murder by a grand jury on September 16. Attorneys Robert C. Titus and Lorin L. Lewis were assigned to defend Czolgosz, but Czolgosz refused to interact with them or the psychiatrist sent to determine his sanity. Lewis argued Czolgosz could not be found criminally responsible because he was insane at the time of the shooting, but he could not mount a substantial insanity defense due to Czolgosz's disinterest. During Czolgosz's trial Lewis did not call any defense witnesses. District Attorney Thomas Penney repeatedly referenced Czolgosz's anarchist affiliations and the public desire to see McKinley's assassin quickly tried and executed. The judge presiding over the case, Truman C. White, closed the final minutes of the trial by telling the jury Czolgosz was not insane and he understood his actions in assassinating the president. The inability of Czolgosz's attorneys to mount a defense because of Czolgosz's lack of cooperation, the expert work of District Attorney Thomas Penney, and Judge Truman C. White's failure to preside impartially led the jury to deliberate for only one hour. On September 24, 1901, the jury found Czolgosz guilty, and two days later they unanimously recommended the death penalty. Czolgosz gave no visible or audible reaction to either the conviction or sentencing, and he was electrocuted on October 29, 1901.

Czolgosz's motivation for murdering McKinley remains a mystery. Czolgosz last words before his execution were "I killed the President because he was the enemy of the good people—the good working people. I am not sorry for my crime" (Rauchway 53). His association with anarchists and his last words suggests Czolgosz killed McKinley to dislodge the symbol of U.S. democracy and upset the structure of government that widened the gap between the poor and the wealthy. However, Czolgosz was a Republican with a history of voting in Republican primaries, and McKinley was a GOP president. At the time of the assassination, Czolgosz had been alienated from the anarchists due to their suspicions about his motives. While some anarchists, notably Emma Goldman, exploited Czolgosz's image after McKinley's assassination, many disavowed any knowledge of the assassin and claimed he had damaged their movement. In *Murdering McKinley* Eric Rauchway raised a strong argument for Czolgosz's long-term depression and alienation. According to Rauchway, Czolgosz experienced much disappointment in his 24 years with his inability to find employment or purpose. On one job application, Czolgosz used the alias Leon Nieman ("no one" or "no man"), an indication he felt profoundly divorced from society. The rejection by anarchists and Goldman only aggravated Czolgosz's sense of alienation, and Czolgosz may have sought to realize his potential and celebrity by murdering McKinley.

By assassinating McKinley, Czolgosz unwittingly changed the office of president. Theodore Roosevelt, McKinley's vice president, entered the presidency promising to continue his predecessor's policies and retaining the late president's cabinet. Roosevelt largely lived up to these vows, but he also launched aggressive attacks on trusts, helped launch Progressive reforms, and, through the force of his personality, made character an important component of the presidency. McKinley's assassination also made anarchism, already a fringe movement, increasingly unattractive. Emma Goldman was arrested in the wake of the assassination under suspicion of aiding Czolgosz but was later released. She went on to publish "The Tragedy at Buffalo," an article that suggested Czolgosz had freed the United States from a potential tyrant. The article and Goldman's continued belief that the anarchists should aid Czolgosz led to a split within the anarchist movement. Within the larger public arena, anarchism came under increasingly heated scrutiny; antianarchist laws were passed in some areas, and vigilantes attacked anarchists and anarchist colonies.

Emily Meyer

See also: Anarchism; Depression of 1893; Goldman, Emma (1869–1940); McKinley, William, Jr. (1843–1901); Progressivism; Roosevelt, Theodore (1858–1919)

References

Faulk, Candace. *Love, Anarchy, and Emma Goldman: A Biography.* New York: Rutgers University Press, 1990.

Fine, Sidney. "Anarchism and the Assassination of McKinley." *American Historical Review* 60 (4): 777–799.

Goldman, Emma. *Living My Life*. New York: Alfred A. Knopf, 1931.

Miller, Scott. *The President and the Assassin: McKinley, Terror, and Empire at the Dawn of the American Century.* New York: Random House, 2011.

Rauchway, Eric. *Murdering McKinley: The Making of Theodore Roosevelt's America.* New York: Hill and Wang, 2003.

Rauchway, Eric. "William McKinley and Us." *Journal of the Gilded Age and Progressive Reform* 4 (3): 235–253.

D

Darrow, Clarence (1857–1938)

Clarence Darrow was born in Kinsman, Ohio, on April 18, 1857, the son of Amirus and Emily (Eddy) Darrow. His father was a former Unitarian minister who abandoned his faith to become an agnostic. Both parents were supporters of abolitionism and women's rights, and it was in such a free-thinking and reformist household that Clarence Darrow was raised. Darrow attended Allegheny College and the University of Michigan Law School, gaining admission to the Ohio bar in 1878. Over the next nine years he practiced law in Ohio; married Jessie Ohl in 1880; fathered a son, Paul, in 1883; and, looking for wider legal horizons, moved his family to Chicago in 1887.

In Chicago he became involved in Democratic Party politics, becoming a friend of Governor John Altgeld as well as an advocate of prison reform, which included ending capital punishment. Through his friendship with Altgeld, Darrow supported the drive to pardon the surviving defendants convicted of participation in Chicago's 1886 Haymarket bombing. In 1890, he took up corporate law, becoming an attorney for the Chicago and Northwestern Railroad. His corporate career, however, was short, for Darrow became alarmed over the treatment of workers during the 1894 Pullman strike, and his natural sympathies drew him to support the period's organized labor struggles. He befriended the socialist president of the American Railway Union, Eugene Debs, and later unsuccessfully defended Debs when he was repeatedly prosecuted for contempt in regard to his union agitation. In 1894, Darrow also became involved in his first significant murder trial, that of Patrick E. Prendergast, the assassin of Chicago mayor Carter H. Harrison Sr. (1825–1893). Although unsuccessful in his defense, this trial was a key first step in Darrow's long career defending numerous defendants charged with capital crimes.

During the 1890s, Darrow joined forces with the emerging Illinois Populists, whose grievances overlapped with his own antimonopoly and prolabor viewpoints. The depression of the 1890s fueled a drive for change, and Darrow in 1894 was keen to open Chicago to Populism. He helped to organize rallies in support of the Chicago People's Party and employed his oratorical skills to garner support for the movement. Ultimately internal divisions between agrarians and urban socialists unraveled any possibility of a successful working coalition. This situation contributed to the Populists finishing third in Chicago's 1894 elections. The experience did whet Darrow's appetite for politics, leading him to become a Democratic or "Popocrat" candidate for Congress in 1896, an election he lost to Republican Hugh R. Belknap (1860–1901). In 1903 he contemplated running for mayor of Chicago but soon abandoned the idea.

During the early years of the twentieth century, Darrow increasingly participated in radical causes, promoting organizations such as the Intercollegiate Socialist Society and defending high-profile radical labor activists. In 1906 he represented Industrial Workers of the World leader William D. "Big Bill" Heywood and associates who were accused of the 1905 murder of Idaho Governor Frank Steunenberg (1861–1905). Through a series of trials, Darrow demonstrated his commitment to these causes even when a true victory was not achievable. He also defended the trade unionists John and James McNamara who were accused of the bombing of the *Los Angeles Times* building in 1910 that resulted in the deaths of 21 people. Darrow persuaded the brothers to change their not guilty plea to guilty in light of the convincing evidence against them, a move that saved the McNamaras from the death penalty. The 1911 McNamara trial also proved highly contentious, and Darrow was subsequently charged, but later acquitted, with bribing jurors.

Darrow continued his support of labor causes during World War I when many labor, anarchist, and socialist agitators ran afoul of the Espionage Act, which he viewed—although himself a supporter of the Allied war effort—as an attempt to silence criticism of the war. Moreover, Darrow's understanding of the root causes of illegality and antisocial behavior was evolving. He increasingly believed that unsatisfactory environmental and social factors, as well as psychological disorders, shaped wrongdoing. In this way his defendants were not simply criminals but also victims whose acts were precipitated by a variety of negative societal experiences that led them to actions beyond their immediate control. His defense in the sensational 1924 Leopold-Loeb murder case rested upon his clients' inability to distinguish right from wrong due to their prevailing psychological and philosophical orientations.

Clarence Darrow is best remembered for his 1925 defense of the Tennessee biology teacher John T. Scopes, who was accused of teaching evolution in violation of Tennessee's Butler Act. The case became a national sensation as the prosecution team included as an expert witness former presidential candidate and Democratic-Populist William Jennings Bryan, who supported the literal interpretation of scripture. Although Scopes was convicted and fined $100, his case was eventually overturned on a technicality.

Throughout his distinguished life, Darrow was a defender of civil liberties. His commitment to fairness extended to battles against racial prejudice, as seen in his defense during the 1925–1926 Sweet case in which a black Detroit family faced charges after using force to resist white mob violence. In addition, he made legal contributions to defense counsel in the famous 1931 Scottsboro Boys case, when nine young black men were accused of rape in Alabama. Although during the 1930s his activism slowed with age, Darrow did serve the Roosevelt administration as a commission chairman overseeing National Recovery Act operations. Clarence Darrow, one of the United States' most illustrious and influential twentieth-century lawyers, died on March 13, 1938.

Theodore W. Eversole

See also: Altgeld, John P. (1847–1902); Bryan, William Jennings (1860–1925); Debs, Eugene (1855–1926); Haymarket Riot (1886); Industrial Workers of the World; Progressivism; Pullman Strike (1894); Scopes Trial (1925)

References

Darrow, Clarence. *The Story of My Life*. Cambridge, MA: Da Capo Press, 1996.

Jensen, Richard J. *Clarence Darrow: The Creation of an American Myth*. Westport, CT: Greenwood Press, 1992.

Postel, Charles. *The Populist Vision*. New York: Oxford University Press, 2007.

Ravitz, Abe C. *Clarence Darrow and the American Literary Tradition*. Cleveland, OH: Western Reserve University Press, 1962.

Stone, Irving. *Clarence Darrow*. New York: Doubleday, 1989.

Debs, Eugene (1855–1926)

The life of Eugene Victor Debs is so intertwined with the history of American socialism that to associate him with the rural preoccupations of Populism might seem incongruous. For Debs, however, Populism was one of the first political movements that he encountered and one that arguably shaped his understanding of the socialist program he ultimately promoted. Frequently forgotten is that in the climactic presidential campaign of 1912, Debs secured his best result in Oklahoma, a state hardly renowned for its industrial workforce. Socialism as expounded by Debs was an intensely American creed that rejected much of the harsh language of class struggle evident in its European counterpart in favor of appeals to a common humanity that transcended divisions between middle-class and working-class Americans and was more characteristic of the language employed by Populists during the 1890s.

Born into the rapidly industrializing community of Terre Haute, Indiana, Debs's sense of community was heightened by participation in the Brotherhood of Locomotive Engineers, where the virtues of benevolence, sobriety, and hard work were celebrated and industrial action was viewed with considerable reserve. In his first foray into politics in 1879, he secured election as city clerk on a Democratic ticket, with support from the business community and the backing of both affluent and working-class wards. Elected to the state legislature in 1884, Debs endeavored to articulate the idea of the state as a neutral meeting ground for the resolution of the differences of competing sectional interests in favor of the common good, and he continued to stand aloof from union organizations like the Knights of Labor, who were actively engaged in politics.

In 1885, a successful strike against Jay Gould's Wabash Railroad coupled with sympathy strikes against his Missouri, Kansas, and Texas and Missouri Pacific lines shut down the entire Gould network and forced the railroad magnate to rescind a reduction in wages for the Wabash shopmen. Senior figures within the Brotherhood, however, continued to express reservations about strike action, polarizing the union and driving Debs toward the view that existing unjust legislation impeded the ability of the working man to live a comfortable existence, and political action might be necessary to improve his lot. Even then, the language that Debs chose to employ spoke not of a new order but of the resurrection of the principles on which he believed the republic had been founded, including equality of opportunity, individual responsibility, personal liberty, and a prevailing sense of "fair play." As a result, he tended to emphasize not the rights of the working class as such but the rights of man.

Despite his lack of denominational affiliation, religious rhetoric permeated much of Debs's discourse, and he frequently echoed the Populist lament on the declining availability of free land. Also like the Populists, he initially expressed little concern about the plight of racial and ethnic minorities and could, on occasion, even sound a reactionary note.

Debs's epiphany came with the 1888 strike on the Chicago, Burlington, and Quincy Railroad, when he endorsed the right to strike and for the first time saw the importance of labor solidarity, arguing that corporate power threatened the stability of the nineteenth-century United States. He articulated a new vision of citizenship, though one still contained within the American tradition, and he continued to express a belief in craft unionism, rejecting the notion that the worker was either a simple commodity to be purchased or a mere political animal. Toward Populism as a political movement, however, he remained guarded, unconvinced of its solidarity with the working class.

Several events projected Debs to the forefront of the union movement. Debs became a leading figure of the newly organized American Railway Union (ARU) in 1893, which conducted a series of successful strikes thereafter on the Great Northern Railroad. These actions won the support of Ignatius Donnelly and the People's Party of Minnesota. Debs still hoped that this would presage a greater degree of cooperation between management and unions, but when the battle spread to the Pullman Car Works in Chicago in 1894 matters proved very different. The ultimate failure of that strike led Debs to break with Samuel Gompers of the American Federation of Labor, particularly after Gompers described the ARU-inspired strike as "impulsive" and condemned sympathy strikes by members of other AFL unions. While Gompers continued to focus on industrial stability and the needs of a relatively small cadre of skilled workers, Debs emerged from the struggle committed to a broader undertaking.

After the Pullman strike, the politically emergent Debs was committed to a vision of the rights of the working man that extended beyond the industrial working class. Boosted as a candidate for governor of Indiana on the Populist ticket in 1894, he ultimately declared himself a "People's party man." At the June convention of the ARU, he was successful in his attempt to endorse the party, and many members in Minnesota and Illinois declared their active allegiance. As a Populist, therefore, Debs proved to be one of the few working-class leaders able to bridge the divide between farmer and industrial worker, something many of the former would remember in later years.

For Debs, the model of future society was always at least as much the co-operative commonwealth as industrial socialism, and he persisted in drawing parallels between socialism and the American revolutionary tradition, as revealed in the writings of Jefferson and Lincoln. He declined to be drafted as the People's Party presidential nominee in 1896, despite the backing of delegates from 16 states, not least because of his admiration for the Democratic nominee William Jennings Bryan (he was the only significant union leader to give Bryan an endorsement), but he undertook a nationwide speaking tour that won him wide acclaim. With the eclipse of Populism, however, Debs was ready to make the transition, accepting election to the executive committee of the Social Democratic Party in 1898 (renamed the Socialist Party of America in 1901). For the next 20 years he would be the perennial Socialist Party candidate for president (Salvatore 1982).

Despite his conversion, Debs's early relations with more conventional socialists such as Victor Berger were frequently tense. He was an early advocate of the formation in a sparsely populated western state of socialist "colonies" that could in time attain power through the ballot box and then build a cooperative utopia that would provide the model for wider society. Dismissed as utopian by practical socialists, it reflected Deb's continued fascination with the building of an ideal community. He continued to be critical of those who emphasized class consciousness at the expense of the American moral tradition and the importance of individual freedom of action. He was, moreover, suspicious of how much even labor unions could accomplish.

Debs's political career from 1900 to 1919 marked the maturation of a man who had begun his career steeped in the ideals of Populism. A recurrent socialist presidential candidate, he brought the language of the cooperative commonwealth to a national audience while reminding his listeners that the forbears of this practice included such American literary giants as Ralph Waldo Emerson and Henry David Thoreau. His message had particular resonance in the Southwest where many former Populists took their cue from the Girard, Kansas-based *Appeal to Reason*, published by Julius Wayland, which emphasized the compatibility of socialist ideas with American individualism and Christian beliefs.

During the 1912 presidential campaign, Debs faced a charismatic cast of major-party candidates but still secured almost 900,000 votes (or 6 percent of the total), running proportionately better in the western and southwestern states that formed part of the old Populist heartland, but he continued to face the reality that socialism was a marginal force in the United States. For all his rhetorical skill, even Debs could not shake the "un-American" stigma that clung to his party, and his subsequent record of active opposition to World War I served only to confirm this impression, though many populists were inclined to be isolationists. At his trial for violations of the Espionage

Act, Debs invoked the legacy of such figures as Thomas Paine and John Adams, once again affirming the tradition in which he believed himself to stand. While he might have moved somewhat beyond Populism, it was a populist vision of socialism that he, ultimately unsuccessfully, endeavored to present to the United States.

Jeremy Bonner

See also: Cooperative Commonwealth; Gompers, Samuel (1850–1924); Knights of Labor; Progressivism; Pullman Strike (1894); Railroads; Socialism, Christian

References

Graham, John, ed. *"Yours for the Revolution": The* Appeal to Reason, *1895–1922.* Lincoln: University of Nebraska Press, 1990.

Green, James R. *Grass-Roots Socialism: Radical Movements in the Southwest, 1895–1943.* Baton Rouge: Louisiana State University Press, 1978.

Salvatore, Nick. *Eugene V. Debs: Citizen and Socialist.* Urbana: University of Illinois Press, 1982.

Weinstein, James. *The Long Detour: The History and Future of the American Left.* Boulder, CO: Westview Press, 2003.

Democratic Party

When the Democratic Party first encountered Populism, it was resting upon past laurels. Though still tarnished by its association with the Civil War, the Democratic Party had restored the political equilibrium through divided control of Congress and even succeeded in sending a Democrat to the White House in 1884 and 1892. A new spirit of economic development was at work in the states of the old Confederacy, in which the Democratic majority took considerable satisfaction. The party's leaders advocated low tariffs, conservative fiscal policy, and a minimum of government intervention.

Despite its success, a serious challenge was brewing that threatened to undermine the Democratic Party in its southern bastion. The growth of the New South brought little benefit to the many small-scale farmers—white and black—who operated under the constraints of the crop lien system that subjected them to the whims of large-scale landowners and merchants. With the demonetization of silver in 1873 and the subsequent sharp decline in commodity prices, many such farmers, particularly in Texas, were spurred into organizing a cooperative movement, the Farmers' Alliance, in 1877.

While the Alliance's reach ultimately extended across the nation—especially in the agricultural Midwest—it was in the Democratic South where Lawrence Goodwyn identified a "movement culture" that it proved most enduring. The Alliance promoted numerous cooperative marketing and purchasing initiatives at the state level, but its theorists also developed what came to be known as the subtreasury plan, which proposed the erection of federal warehouses in which farmers could stockpile crops until the market price rose to an acceptable level, and from which they could borrow up to 80 percent of the market price of crops so deposited. The subtreasury plan was the cornerstone of the Populist movement, but it was entirely unacceptable to many financial interests across the South.

Alliance members were Democrats before they joined the People's Party and generally returned to their former party allegiance following the collapse of the Populist movement. Indeed, the Alliance's first foray into electoral politics in 1890 involved not the creation of a new party but the election of pro-Alliance Democrats to state offices, most notably in Tennessee and Georgia.

The Populists soon found themselves outmaneuvered by Democratic Party leaders, some of whom, most notoriously Ben Tillman of South Carolina and James Hogg of Texas, exploited Populist discontent to secure their own political ambitions, without embracing the Populist program. Furthermore, the Populists' decision to nominate a former Union general as their presidential candidate in 1892 allowed southern Democrats to appeal to traditional voting loyalties, even as they manipulated the returns in black-majority areas, to ensure Populist defeat. Within a decade, Populism as a political force in the South had largely dissipated.

If the Democratic Party contributed materially to the destruction of southern Populism, an equally vital factor was the role played by William Jennings Bryan. A former Nebraska congressman, Bryan had witnessed firsthand the rise of Populism in neighboring Kansas. Popularly dubbed the Great Commoner, he enjoyed a personal affinity with the common people, which set him apart from many in his own party. Bryan, however, laid greater stress upon the necessity of individual equality of opportunity and moral reform—for example, universal education—than he did upon wholesale economic restructuring.

Nominated by his party in 1896, Bryan delivered his famous "Cross of Gold" speech to the Democratic National Convention in Chicago, the meeting point of urban East and rural West, in which he formally articulated the cultural and economic sectionalism that would come to define the United States until the Great Depression (and indeed after), the cosmopolitan cities against the pietistic countryside. It was a set of attitudes and prejudices that served to define the populist spirit within the Democratic Party for more than a century.

Historically, the language of Populism predisposed Democrats in its favor. Its icons included Thomas Jefferson (for his resistance to the centralization of government functions) and Andrew Jackson (for his assaults on the "money power" and resistance to special privilege). The Republican Party's post–Civil War commitment to state-building, meanwhile, sat uneasily with Populists, and later with former Populists, who sought to extricate the "common man" from the toils of industrial society. They called for a "counterrevolution" to restore the "moral community" and the defeat of monopoly power, sentiments that many Democrats were happy to embrace.

Key Populist themes of the late nineteenth and early twentieth centuries included a commitment to the agricultural periphery, distrust of government "experts," suspicion of banking interests, and hostility to urban and cosmopolitan culture. These were staple prescriptions of many rural Democratic political leaders, who also were the dominant force in the party's congressional wing. With the return of former Populists such as Tom Watson to the party ranks, the movement's cultural concerns, at least, were assured of consideration.

From 1896 until the election of Woodrow Wilson as president in 1912, Bryan and his wing of the party actively resisted the post-1898 imperialist policies and the protective tariffs that were the cornerstone of Republican policy but that offered little to the agricultural South and West. A vocal proponent of antimonopoly legislation, Bryan maintained that the destruction of monopolies before they became all-powerful was preferable to regulation by the state (a point later adopted by Woodrow Wilson). In his quest to give "the people" a voice, Bryan also championed the direct election of senators and ensured its inclusion in successive Democratic Party platforms.

Such residual Populism could hardly be denied a seat at the table when the Democrats regained control of all three branches of government in 1912, and Bryan succeeded to the office of secretary of state. Much of the early agenda of the Wilson administration, from cutting tariffs and passing antitrust legislation to the establishment of the Federal Reserve as a combination of decentralized regional reserve banks and a central supervisory board, sought to address the concerns of the rural periphery and make access to credit in those regions more achievable.

Faced with the outbreak of war in Europe in 1914, however, the Wilson administration shifted to a more statist model of intervention that reached its apogee in 1917–1918. While Democratic populists rejoiced at the final victory of national prohibition and the achievement of woman suffrage they took less satisfaction in wartime mobilization and the attendant suppression of dissent. The Republican victories of 1920 paved the way for a decade of bitter internal conflict within the Democratic Party in which populist language served to defend a rural community increasingly seen as under threat.

The growing importance of an urban, and heavily Catholic, vote to the Democratic coalition presented a severe crisis of confidence for many populist Democrats, reflected in the dramatic rise of the Ku Klux Klan in the 1920s and its impact on the politics of the South (not to mention the famous deadlocked national convention of 1924). Populism and nativism came to be increasingly synonymous within the Democratic Party, as was a commitment to the maintenance of Prohibition. The economic elements of the older Populist agenda were either abandoned or modified by an emerging cadre of urban Democrats who championed a pluralistic form of Americanism.

With the coming of the Great Depression in 1929, there arose a challenge to the social order that had not been witnessed since the 1890s. Democrats reveled in the ability of their patrician presidential candidate, Franklin Roosevelt, to employ populist idioms, whether in his 1932 "Forgotten Man" speech or later in his "fireside chats," but his administration's policies soon demonstrated that the New Deal could be termed populist only by a significant redefinition of that word. For all its pattern of cooperative federalism, the New Deal's reliance on experts and general ambivalence to the idea of the moral community emphasized its separation from populist culture.

In the South, however, populist Democrats did find a champion with a national agenda who spoke their language, Huey Long of Louisiana. A charismatic son of Louisiana's Winn Parish (where the state's People's Party was born), Long entered politics in 1916 and soon acquired a reputation as a scourge of corporate interests, particularly the Standard Oil Company. In 1928 he won election as governor with solid backing from the small-scale farmers of the state, pushing through a reform program that included free textbooks for school students and revision of the tax code to impose greater burdens on oil and gas interests. Moving on to the U.S. Senate in 1930, he continued to exercise control of Louisiana politics through his supporters.

In one sense, Long's methods were, at times, ruthless and would seem to have placed him outside the populist mainstream, yet Long argued that his regime enjoyed widespread popular support. His achievements included a major highway construction program and the improvement of the state's public health facilities, and he avoided the southern populist tendency to exploit racial prejudice. By 1931, he had set his sights on achieving a more pronounced national profile and quickly broke with the southern Democrats who controlled the Senate committee system.

Although he backed Roosevelt for president in 1932 and campaigned in the agricultural Midwest where he was warmly received, Long soured quickly on the new president, castigating the New Deal for its early economic conservatism. As an alternative he began to publicize what came to be known as the Share Our Wealth Plan, which proposed punitive taxes on income and inheritances above $1 million used to guarantee a minimum household income to every American. Although economically unsustainable, the simplicity of Long's plans for redistribution and its emphasis on increasing the purchasing power of ordinary Americans caught the popular imagination. The subsequent development of a national network of Share Our Wealth clubs—echoing to some degree the earlier modus operandi of the Farmers' Alliance—signaled an intention to become a national movement, only aborted by Long's murder in 1935.

Long was unquestionably in a class by himself among populist Democrats, not least in his ability to transcend the racial issue. His passing marked the final phase of insurgent Democratic populism with a broad economic appeal and its replacement by a populism that stressed its cultural conservatism in the face of the perceived threat, now posed less by corporations than by the federal government. During the 1940s and 1950s, populist rhetoric against, for example, communist infiltration of the federal government came mostly from Republicans, but by the early 1960s, southern populists had found a new champion, this time from Alabama.

The rise to prominence of George C. Wallace remains one of the more fascinating stories of the 1960s. Often crudely depicted simply as a racist, Wallace embodied the fears of many for whom modern liberalism failed to speak. Very much a political opportunist, he invoked the cause of segregation knowing that it resonated with southern resentment at federal involvement in general. Yet Wallace contrived to articulate the voice of ordinary blue-collar Americans even beyond his own region. Nor did he entirely reject the involvement of government, so long as it excluded schools, unions, and family life from its agenda. His focus on law and order—a popular refrain in the late 1960s—had as much appeal in Michigan as in Georgia.

The Wallace voters who backed his independent candidacy in 1968 and voted for him in Democratic primaries that year and in 1972, in a sense, represented a culmination of the Populist experiment. Like Bryan, Wallace appealed to the middling white producers and against eastern elites, and like Bryan his success owed much to his own unique style. Unlike Bryan, however, he worked without even partial support from the party of which he was nominally a member and faced the same hurdles that confronted his populist forbearers in 1892.

Since Wallace, the Democratic Party has largely failed to produce a leader with the capacity of mobilizing that particular constituency. The increasing power of liberal activists in positions of leadership has tended to work against any Democratic politician who professes more than moderately culturally conservative credentials, a very necessary ingredient in building populist support. While it has been argued that the efforts of politicians such as Jesse Jackson to build a biracial coalition might be dubbed populist, this requires a complete redefinition of the meaning and the history of the term.

Populism as a political movement at one time challenged the very existence of the Democratic Party, which responded with ruthless efficiency to suppress it. This did not prevent the incorporation of populist ideas into the very fabric of the party and—for a while—even bringing them to the seat of power. The reconstruction of the American state after 1933, as well as the shift in the electoral coalition that sustained the Democratic Party, led to the association of populist ideas with that section of the Democratic Party that felt peculiar reservations about rule from the center, particularly when that rule threatened to impinge upon that central institution of the South—segregation. The earlier populist economic critiques of society gave way to a cultural critique more easily accommodated by post—New Deal Republicanism, embodied in the person of Ronald Reagan. Reagan's election as president in 1980 marked the defeat of the last southern Democrat who even attempted to assert his populist credentials, namely Jimmy Carter.

Jeremy Bonner

See also: Bryan, William Jennings (1860–1925); Carter, James Earl "Jimmy" (1924–); "Cross of Gold" Speech (1896); Federal Reserve Act (1913); Gold Standard/Free Silver; Jefferson, Thomas (1743–1826); Ku Klux Klan (KKK); Long, Huey (1893–1935); New Deal; Obama, Barack, Populist Rhetoric of; Progressivism; Roosevelt, Franklin Delano (1882–1945); South, Populism in the; Silver Republicans; Subtreasury Plan; Tillman, Benjamin R. (1847–1918)

References

Bensel, Richard F. *Sectionalism and American Political Development, 1880–1980.* Madison: University of Wisconsin Press, 1984.

Brinkley, Alan. *Voices of Protest: Huey Long, Father Coughlin and the Great Depression.* New York: Alfred A. Knopf, 1982.

Burner, David. *The Politics of Provincialism: The Democratic Party in Transition, 1918–1932.* New York: Alfred A. Knopf, 1968.

Carter, Dan T. *The Politics of Rage: George Wallace, the Origins of the New Conservatism, and the Transformation of American Politics.* New York: Simon and Schuster, 1995.

Goodwyn, Lawrence. *Democratic Promise: The Populist Movement in America.* New York: Oxford University Press, 1976.

Kazin, Michael. *The Populist Persuasion: An American History.* Ithaca, NY: Cornell University Press, 1998.

Department Stores and Mail-Order Catalogs

The availability of mass-produced consumer goods to the working and middle classes grew in two forms during the late nineteenth and early twentieth centuries, with mail-order catalogs meeting the needs of rural Americans and department stores serving metropolitan areas. Crucial to the success of both were concepts of customer service and standard pricing, as well as infrastructure such as railroads and postal service. As the types of merchandise expanded and inventories swelled beyond the service capacities of general stores and dry-goods merchants, several individual entrepreneurs built enterprises that generated iconic brands and shaped the shopping patterns and tastes of the American public.

Montgomery Ward produced the first mail-order catalog in 1872. The Montgomery Ward catalog expanded rapidly, with a listing of 10,000 items by 1883. In 1888, the initial offering of Sears appeared as the R. W. Sears Watch Company. Founder Richard Sears added a partner, Alvah Roebuck, and their first catalog under the name Sears, Roebuck and Co. was distributed in 1892. Both Ward and Sears targeted farmers as their main customers, and both benefited from federal legislation that supported mail delivery to this audience, the rural free delivery implemented in 1896 and the Parcel Post Service in 1913. As both companies were headquartered in Chicago, the proximity to a major hub of nationwide rail lines combined with demand for rural delivery supported the growth of mail order. Besides serving as a tool for ordering items, customers in areas without opportunities for shopping could learn about new products and fashion trends. While Ward's and Sears remained the top companies, smaller specialized mail-order companies such as Burpee Seeds, Caswell-Massey, and L. L. Bean also profited. The J. C. Penney Company was originally established as a department store but released a catalog in 1963 that drove millions in sales. The mail-order companies such as Ward's and Sears ultimately opened department stores of their own. Sears opened its first store in 1925. Montgomery Ward began to open stores in 1926. The Sears catalog was discontinued in 1993 as one large book and was split into specialized interests.

One of the earliest founders of a department store in the United States was Roland H. Macy, who had attempted stores in various locations but found his fifth attempt in 1858, a retail store in Manhattan, to be the foundation of his future success. Macy strictly adhered to his policy of selling at one low fixed price to all customers for cash only. Macy's policy of stated prices for merchandise eliminated the need for price negotiation between shopper and shopkeeper and encouraged shoppers to browse the merchandise. By 1870 Macy's had more than $1 million in sales and a diversified inventory of dry goods, clothing, and decorative items. Searching for a partner to ensure the long term success of the store, Macy created a partnership with L. Straus and Sons, a successful china-importing company. The Straus family operated Macy's for many years and was responsible for building the landmark Macy's building in Herald Square at 24th and Broadway in 1902.

Other major department stores in American cities in the early twentieth century included Marshall Field's of Chicago; Belk's of Charlotte, North Carolina; Wanamaker's of Philadelphia; and the Broadway Department Store in Los Angeles, which was operated by Carter Hawley Hale Stores, Inc. Beyond the offerings of reasonably priced desirable goods, the department store as destination became part of the consumer experience. The 1902 Macy's building featured new technologies such as escalators and customer-friendly lounges and restrooms. Marshall Field's incorporated a tea room and later a restaurant, setting a precedent for department stores to serve food.

In 1877, the Middle West saw the development of the future department store giant the May Company with the firm of May, Holcomb and Dean that formed in Colorado to sell clothing and supplies to miners. When that partnership dissolved, company founder David May joined with Moses Shoenberg. By 1885, May bought out Shoenberg and opened two additional locations in Colorado. David May's approach of marketing merchandise to middle-class buyers combined advertising and fast stock turnover. He later leveraged his approach of gathering large inventories and selling them quickly to buying entire stores. May shrewdly purchased existing department stores in urban areas and merged them, using the buying power of his company to increase inventories. The May Company merged two Missouri stores, Famous Department Store, which it had acquired in 1892, and William Barr Dry Goods, which it bought in 1911, and created Famous-Barr. The May Company continued to purchase existing chains well into the twentieth century, including major stores such as Lord and Taylor, Filene's, and Kaufmann's.

Another significant department-store holding company was Federated Department Stores, Inc., which incorporated in Ohio in 1929. Bloomingdale's joined the Federated group in 1930. Federated added major department stores through the 1950s, 1960s, and 1970s. Heavy expansion into additional retail areas such as supermarkets ultimately brought down Federated, and in 1988 it was acquired by Campeau Corporation. Resurfacing in 1992 after an elaborate bankruptcy restructuring involving a merger with

Allied Stores Corporation and a separation from Campeau, Federated Department Stores purchased Macy's in 1994 and May Department Stores in 2005. Many stores that had previously been known under other names were rebranded as Macy's, even Marshall Field's iconic State Street flagship store.

The landscape of rural and urban shopping was changed by the American highway system and the development of suburban shopping centers in the 1950s and 1960s. As the economy of major urban centers declined, many landmark department stores gave way to mall-based presences in suburban areas. In the twenty-first century, print-based catalogs have been diminished by the availability of company websites as well as online mail-order houses such as Amazon.com, a company formed in 1995 as an Internet-based bookseller that now offers an inventory it describes as "Earth's Biggest Selection."

Rebecca Feind

See also: Leisure; New Woman; Railroads; Women's Trade Union League (WTUL)

References

Cherry, R. *Catalog: The Illustrated History of Mail-order Shopping*. New York: Princeton Architectural Press, 2008.

Paquet, L. *Urge to Splurge: A Social History of Shopping*. Toronto, Canada: ECW Press, 2003.

Depression of 1873

The depression of the 1870s was part of an economic downturn that began in 1873. The primary cause was the temporary collapse of the railroad industry. Prior to 1873, robust railroad expansion had helped fuel economic growth; however, the expansion of railroad track had primarily taken place west of the Mississippi River. Because of long distances and sparse population, those railroads that had invested in western expansion were often unprofitable. By 1872, nearly two-thirds of the nation's railroad companies were not paying dividends to their investors.

The precipitating event of the 1873 panic was the September 18 bankruptcy of Jay Cooke and Company, which was financing the construction of the Northern Pacific railroad. The failure of Cooke's bank set off a wave of selling on Wall Street, eventually forcing the stock exchange to suspend trading for 10 days. Additional railroad companies were unable to make bond payments. Consequently, the construction of railroad track, a major driver of economic activity, came to an abrupt halt. The impact of constrained railroad construction reverberated throughout the U.S. economy. By the end of 1873, approximately 5,000 businesses had failed, with a total of $775 million in capital lost.

The human toll of the depression, however, was the most devastating. In 1873 alone, nearly 500,000 workers lost their jobs. During the last half of the nineteenth century, many social commentators spoke of the growing economic inequality in the country. Although figures on unemployment vary, some scholars estimate that by 1877 nearly 20 percent of Americans were out or work with another 40 percent underemployed. Without a social safety net or regular governmental relief, many unemployed were forced to live in ramshackle shanty-towns. Depression also made things difficult for organized labor as union membership fell from almost 300,000 to 50,000.

One of the most visible outcomes of the depression was an increase in worker violence. The most harrowing example of labor unrest came in 1877 when disgruntled workers struck back at the Pennsylvania Railroad for wage cuts and poor working conditions. As the economic downturn continued into 1877, railroad workers, who typically worked 15–18 hours shifts, had experienced pay cuts amounting to 35 percent. When the Pennsylvania Railroad initiated an additional 10 percent cut, workers began a series of strikes at Camden Junction, Maryland; Martinsburg, West Virginia; and, most prominently, Pittsburgh, Pennsylvania, on July 19, 1877. The riots were eventually quelled by federal troops but only after the loss of 25 lives and the destruction of some $10 million of railroad property.

For the nation's farmers, the depression had a significant impact. First, the decline of business activity meant less demand for agricultural commodities, something that exacerbated overproduction and price erosion. Since the end of the Civil War, the federal government had pursued a policy of currency contraction, retiring greenbacks that had been generated during the war. This policy was based on the belief that all currency must ultimately be based on the amount of gold bullion that the U.S. Treasury has in reserves. In 1873, Congress passed the Coinage Act, which prohibited the additional monetizing of silver (the so-called Crime of 1873). In 1875, the Resumption of Specie Payment Act was passed that stipulated the retirement of all greenbacks and the resumption of hard-currency payments on January 1, 1879. This policy of currency contraction was disastrous for farmers who, throughout the depression, saw the value of their crops decline while their debts stayed the same.

The depression of 1873 revealed that the power of government was often aligned against workers and small farmers. When angry workers struck to protest their plight, the power of government was turned against them. While farmers lobbied for an expanded money supply, the government pursued a policy that contracted the money supply. Indeed, the federal and state governments seemed allied with large business and commercial interests; the rules seemed to be written to ensure that the wealthy were protected while the interests of average workers and farmers were ignored.

Bruce Tap

See also: Banking System of the Late Nineteenth Century, Crime of '73, Depression of 1893, Gold Standard/Free Silver, Granger Movement, Railroads

References

Calhoun, Charles W., ed. *The Gilded Age: Essays on the Origins of Modern America.* Wilmington, DE: Scholarly Resources, 1996.

Cashman, Sean Dennis. *America in the Gilded Age: From the Death of Lincoln to the Rise of Theodore Roosevelt.* New York: New York University Press, 1984.

Edwards, Rebecca. *New Spirits: Americans in the Gilded Age, 1865–1895.* New York: Oxford University Press, 2006.

Goodwyn, Lawrence. *The Populist Moment: A Short History of Agrarian Revolt in America*. New York: Oxford University Press, 1978.

Trachtenberg, Alan. *The Incorporation of America: Culture and Society in the Gilded Age*. New York: Hill & Wang, 1982.

Depression of 1893

Like the panic of 1873, the depression of 1893 was a major economic downturn that had significant impact on the Populist movement. While related to an economic slowdown in Europe which began in 1890, the downturn in the United States was facilitated by the failures of major railroads. Just after the inauguration of President Grover Cleveland in March 1893, the Philadelphia and Reading railroad went under. By the end of the summer of 1893, four additional railroads had failed: the Erie, Northern Pacific, Union Pacific, and Santa Fe. Additionally, the U.S. banking system was tottering. The collapse of a major Philadelphia firm, the National Cordage Company, caused two Chicago banks to fail. This, in turn, caused a run on New York bank deposits as panicked customers withdrew cash because of uncertainty about bank stability. By the end of 1893, 15,000 banks had failed in the United States with the largest portion of bankruptcies in the South and the West.

As banks and railroads failed, many businesses were forced to contract their operations, leading to job loss and an estimated national unemployment rate between 20 and 25 percent. In the nation's cities, misery was apparent, particularly in the winters when many starved to death or died of exposure. In the farming areas of the West and South, impoverished farmers and unemployed agricultural workers were often visible traveling as tramps, hoping to scrape together a living as best they could. Responding to reduced wages and layoffs, angry workers vented their frustration by staging a number of strikes in different industries and different regions of the country. There were strikes in Pennsylvania steel mills, the mines of West Virginia and Idaho, and the cities of Buffalo, New York, and New Orleans. The most significant was the strike on the Pullman Car Company in 1894, led by Eugene V. Debs and the newly formed American Railway Union (ARU). Precipitated by a drastic 25 to 40 percent reduction in wages, the ARU practically halted railway traffic in the United States, forcing President Cleveland to send troops to Chicago to break the strike and restore railroad transportation.

The federal response to the depression was passive and anti-interventionist, the prevailing wisdom being that economic downturns had to be allowed to run their course. Nineteenth-century presidents believed in the motto "the government that governs least, governs best." Besides quelling labor violence, the only action undertaken by President Cleveland was currency reform, a series of measures that would alienate workers and farmers still smarting from the era's deflationary trends. In particular, Cleveland used the depression to return the United States to the gold standard. In 1890, as a response to western mining interests and inflationist, Congress had passed the Sherman

Silver Purchase Act, which authorized the treasury department to purchase a fixed amount of silver each month. The principal point of the measure was to allow the nation's money supply to expand. Utilizing Republican votes in Congress, Cleveland was able to secure repeal of the Silver Purchase Act. While Cleveland's measures were ineffective in solving the problems of recession, many accused him of pursuing policies that benefited financial interests that advocated a return to the gold standard.

Critics of Cleveland's financial policies wanted to expand the money supply. Some critics, such as Jacob Coxey, a Massillon, Ohio, resident, wanted the federal government to attack the depression by massive public works projects that would hire the nation's unemployed workers and pay them through interest-free bonds that could also be circulated as legal tender. To emphasize his point, Coxey organized an 1894 march on Washington, DC, with supporters known as "Coxey's Army."

For the nation's farmers and members of the People's Party, the depression of 1893 underscored the inadequacy of the nation's money supply. Faced with high credit costs, onerous railroad rates, and fixed mortgage payments, farm groups believed that Cleveland's policy of currency contractions made agricultural problems worse. Contracting the money supply meant that it took more and more crops to generate the same amount of cash to meet financial obligations; however, the more farmers produced, the lower commodity prices fell. It was a vicious cycle that most farm advocates believed could only be overcome by pursuing inflationist monetary policies. Where in prior years Populist advocates had attached themselves to greenback ideas of fiat currency, during the middle 1890s, influenced by western silver-mining interests and ambitious Democratic politicians eager to coopt the Populist vote, much of the agrarian agenda was reduced to the free coinage of silver.

Bruce Tap

See also: Cleveland, Grover (1837–1908); Coxey, Jacob (1854–1951); Coxey's Army; Debs, Eugene (1855–1926); Depression of 1873; Gold Standard/Free Silver; Greenback Party; People's Party; Sherman Silver Purchase Act (1890); Union Pacific Railroad

References

Calhoun, Charles W., ed. *The Gilded Age: Essays on the Origins of Modern America.* Wilmington, DE: Scholarly Resources, 1996.

Cashman, Sean Dennis. *America in the Gilded Age: From the Death of Lincoln to the Rise of Theodore Roosevelt.* New York: New York University Press, 1984.

Edwards, Rebecca. *New Spirits: Americans in the Gilded Age, 1865–1895.* New York: Oxford University Press, 2006.

Goodwyn, Lawrence. *The Populist Moment: A Short History of Agrarian Revolt in America.* New York: Oxford University Press, 1978.

Trachtenberg, Alan. *The Incorporation of America: Culture and Society in the Gilded Age.* New York: Hill & Wang, 1982.

De Tocqueville, Alexis (1805–1859)

Alexis de Tocqueville was born in Paris, France, on July 29, 1805, to an aristocratic French family that was loyal to the exiled

House of Bourbon and to the Roman Catholic Church. He could trace his lineage back to the Normans who fought at the Battle of Hastings.

De Tocqueville's family connections and his impressive academic achievements opened up to him a legal career in government service in 1827. In 1830 the July Monarchy (*la monarchie de Juillet*) came to power. It was a liberal constitutional monarchy that remained in power until the revolution of 1848. While studying French and English history, he acquired a liberal political outlook, and in turn he became disgusted by the folly of the restored Bourbon monarchy. As a result he took liberty as his central political idea.

While serving as a junior magistrate at Versailles, de Tocqueville met Gustave de Beaumont, who became his lifelong friend. In 1831, the July Monarchy sent him to examine prisons and penitentiaries in the United States. He and Beaumont sailed for the United States, where they did visit some prisons, but overall it was their wide travels in the United States that bore the most fruit. Throughout these travels, de Tocqueville took extensive notes and observations that he would use later in his writing.

In the years before de Tocqueville visited the United States, the old Federalist conservatism had crumbled. The Jeffersonians promoted the yeoman farmer as the source of the nation's power at the expense of industry, capital, and a strong federal government. The Frenchman thus arrived in the bloom of the Age of Jackson, during a resurgence of democratic rhetoric. His experiences on the frontier and his interactions with intellectual individualists, members of utopian communities, and independent workers impressed him. He saw the aristocratic order fading and a new democratic order beginning to emerge. (What he missed, however, was the impact of Scottish Realism upon the United States, which promoted a laissez-faire independence.)

Beaumont and de Tocqueville returned to France where they prepared their joint report on U.S. prisons. Next de Tocqueville wrote a two-volume work, *Democracy in America*. The first volume was published in 1835, in the same year that he married Mary Mottley, an Englishwoman. The second volume was published in 1840. Its success won him election to the Académie Française in 1841.

Alexis de Tocqueville was greatly impressed by the egalitarianism of American society in the 1830s. His aristocratic training gave him a cool detachment for observing American democracy and both its virtues and its failings. He saw that the impact of equality, an aspiration of the French Revolution, was strong on the American people. However, he came to believe that equality was a double-edged sword. For him equality's great danger for liberty was the tyranny of the majority. It could evoke a political correctness that would suffocate unpopular opinions. He observed the centralizing tendencies of the uniformity of thought that the emerging industrialism could produce. This egalitarian conformity was a threat to liberty. He felt that populist impulses could be beneficial as well as dangerous. He observed that inequality could serve as motivation for improvement.

The open-mindedness that de Tocqueville possessed enabled him to see that American life was fluid and contained the possibility of overcoming excessive egalitarianism. In contrast to France, in Americans he saw political equality leading to social equality.

De Tocqueville was elected to the French Assembly in 1839 and remained an elected member until 1851. He served as a foreign minister under Louis Napoleon Bonaparte for five months in 1849. From 1850 to 1851 he wrote *Reflections of the Revolution of 1848*. The last work produced by de Tocqueville was *The Ancien Regime and the French Revolution*, which was published in 1856. It was intended as the first part of a grand study of the French Revolution; however, he died in April 16, 1859, at Cannes, unable to finish it.

Andrew J. Waskey

See also: Jefferson, Thomas (1743–1826); Shays's Rebellion (1786–1787)

References

Brogan, Hugh. *Alexis de Tocqueville: A Biography*. London: Profile Books Limited, 2006.

De Tocqueville, Alexis. *Democracy in America*. New York: Penguin, 2003.

Epstein, Joseph. *Alexis de Tocqueville: Democracy's Guide*. New York: HarperCollins, 2009.

Welch, Cheryl. *De Tocqueville*. New York: Oxford University Press, 2001.

Diggs, Annie L. (1853–1916)

Annie L. Diggs was a Kansas author, speaker, and publisher who backed Alliance and People's Party goals both locally and nationally. Diggs's work represents a synthesis of causes evident throughout Populism: advocacy for the farmer, the worker, and the small producer; a defense of women's rights as well as unqualified support for woman suffrage and temperance; a critique of unrestrained capitalism; and, as a foundation for all of these causes, religious liberalism.

Born on February 22, 1853, in Ontario, Canada, Annie LaPorte moved to New Jersey as a young child. When she was 19, she moved to Lawrence, Kansas, where within a year she met and married local postal worker A. S. Diggs and settled into a middle-class life. She became active in the Unitarian Church, eventually serving in the pulpit there for about a year. She became known as a prominent silkworm aficionado as well as a supporter of religious liberalism.

In 1877, Diggs became politically active when she noted that University of Kansas students were being corrupted by alcohol consumption. She joined local women's clubs, where she began publically speaking for temperance. Expounding on the standard temperance argument that alcohol use led to poverty, she argued that intemperance was a symptom of a larger disease. She asserted that poverty, as well as shame and helplessness, resulted from money and power being controlled by a monopoly of the elite. It was this poverty that was the real threat to American liberty and thus drove people to drink. Recognizing the connections between temperance, other social ills, and woman suffrage Diggs joined the Woman's Christian Temperance Union, the Social Science Federation, and the Kansas Equal Suffrage Association.

A committed religious liberal, Diggs established the Kansas Liberal Union in 1881. This organization included Unitarians, like herself, as well as Universalists, socialists, spiritualists, and agnostics. Over the following year, Diggs lived in Boston, where she continued making connections with other religious liberals who elected her vice president of the Free Religious Association. She also began to write newspaper columns for local as well as national papers. Finally, she and her husband began publishing the *Kansas Liberal*, a paper that asserted that the U.S. economic system should be reformed to allow farmers and the working class to have access to the money and power that had been monopolized to this point.

On her return to Kansas, Diggs became involved in the early Farmers' Alliance movement there. Despite never having lived on a farm, Diggs embraced Alliance causes, and in the late 1880s she was able to convince the *Lawrence Journal* to publish articles she wrote in support for Kansas farmers. She argued that farmers should recognize their connections with the merchant class as both of these groups were subjected to the whims of those who had great wealth and power. Her reputation as a strong and respectful Alliance advocate having been established, she was hired as an associate editor of the Topeka *Advocate*. Noting the fact that real political change could only happen if voters could influence elections, Diggs led the Farmers' Alliance legislative committee in 1890 in a campaign to secure woman suffrage. As part of that campaign, she began writing prosuffrage and women's rights columns for the *Farmer's Wife* newspaper.

Given her middle-class urban background, her commitment to economic reorganization, and her support for woman suffrage it was only natural that she adjusted her activism seamlessly from Alliance advocacy to Populism. In 1891, Diggs began working to establish People's Party organizations in Kansas and in other areas of the country. She traveled through Alabama and Georgia with other nationally known figures, such as Kansas Populists Jerry Simpson and Mary Elizabeth Lease, and she helped organize the Ohio People's Party. Continuing her early suffrage activism, Diggs succeeded in getting suffrage on the Populist plank at the state convention in Topeka in 1894. And, recognizing the realities of political maneuvering, she argued for fusion in 1897.

Reflecting on her work in the Alliance and as a Populist, Diggs maintained that Populism's importance came from its ability to reveal that the major political parties served those who were already rich and powerful; its decline came when Populists themselves began to seek traditional political compensation. Diggs served as Kansas State librarian from 1898 to 1902 and as president of Kansas Press Women in 1905. She published *The Story of Jerry Simpson* in 1908 and *Bedrock Education and Employment: The Foundation of the Republic* in 1912. She moved to Detroit, Michigan, in 1912 and died there on September 7, 1916.

Kirstin L. Lawson

See also: Kansas, Populism in; Lease, Mary (1850–1933); Plains and Midwest, Populism in the; The Press and Populism; Prohibition (1919–1933); Woman's Christian Temperance Union (WCTU)

References

Argersinger, Peter H. *Populism and Politics: William Alfred Peffer and the People's Party.* Lexington: University Press of Kentucky, 1974.

Goldberg, Michael Lewis. *An Army of Women: Gender and Politics in Gilded Age Kansas.* Baltimore, MD: Johns Hopkins University Press, 1997.

Hicks, John D. *The Populist Revolt: A History of the Farmers' Alliance and the People's Party.* Minneapolis: University of Minnesota Press, 1931.

Dixon, Thomas, Jr. (1864–1946)

Thomas Dixon was born on January 11, 1864, in the rural highlands of Shelby, North Carolina, the son of a farmer and Baptist minister. His early years were shaped by Reconstruction and the military occupation of the South, which he later viewed as a crime against southern life and culture. Dixon established an early academic reputation in history and political science at Wake Forest, where he earned a master's degree in 1883. After winning a scholarship, Dixon began his studies at John Hopkins University, where he became a friend of Woodrow Wilson; however, in 1884 he left his political science course to become an actor in New York City.

Failing on the stage, Dixon returned to North Carolina to attend Greensboro Law School, where he received his degree in 1885. Dixon would at various times pursue careers embracing law, the ministry, and state politics and, most significantly, as a lecturer and writer. From 1902 until 1939, Dixon wrote 22 novels, mostly in a nineteenth-century romantic vein that often glorified southern womanhood. He also wrote numerous plays, sermons, and works of nonfiction. In later years his reputation blossomed as a national lecturer. His themes describing the pains of Reconstruction in the South, the travails of hardworking families, and the threat of socialism found a ready and receptive audience.

During the early years of the twentieth century, Dixon achieved his most noted fame through bestselling novels set during the Reconstruction era. *The Leopard's Spots* (1902), *The Clansman* (1905), and *The Traitor* (1907) formed his highly successful Clan trilogy. Dixon used historical fiction, in these and in other books, to examine racial conflict in a light that demeaned blacks and portrayed the South as a misunderstood victim of northern oppression. Although neither Dixon nor his family was supporters of slavery, his writings were segregationist and reflected much of American opinion at the time. Dixon also exploited race as a common American social dynamic whose constancy ultimately proved divisive to the development of a unified southern Populism. In addition, Dixon's popularity gave vigor to his negative racial viewpoints and helped his ideas circulate more widely across the country. The dissemination of his particular historical worldview became even more persuasive when *The Clansman* became the source for D. W. Griffith's classic motion picture *Birth of a Nation* (1915). Griffith's film would have a lasting impact on American attitudes toward both Reconstruction and African Americans.

Some writers argue that the success of *Birth of a Nation* contributed to the revival of the Ku Klux Klan in the 1920s.

Thomas Dixon also employed inflammatory themes such as incest and interracial sex in his play and later novel, *Sins of the Father* (1910–1912). In *Comrades* (1909), later made into a film, and *Bolshevism on Trial* (1919), Dixon directed his attention to the threat of socialism. He was especially critical of socialist themes as espoused in works such as Edward Bellamy's highly popular novel *Looking Backward* (1887). In Dixon's last work, *Flaming Sword* (1939), he critiqued both the prospects of racial equality and communism. Thomas Dixon died in Raleigh, North Carolina, on April 3, 1946, and is buried in Shelby, North Carolina.

Theodore W. Eversole

See also: Bellamy, Edward (1850–1898); Griffith, D. W. (1875–1948), and *The Birth of a Nation*; South, Populism in the

References

Gillespie, Michele K., and Randall Hall, eds. *Thomas Dixon Jr. and the Birth of Modern America*. Baton Rouge: Louisiana State University, 2009.

Gilmore, Glenda Elizabeth. *Gender and Jim Crow: Women and the Politics of White Supremacy in North Carolina, 1896–1920.* Chapel Hill: University of North Carolina Press, 1996.

Ruiz-Velasco, Chris. "Order Out of Chaos: Whiteness, White Supremacy and Thomas Dixon, Jr." *College Literature* 34 (4): 148–165.

Slide, Anthony. *The Life and Times of Thomas Dixon*. Lexington: University Press of Kentucky, 2004.

Williamson, Joel R. *The Crucible of Race: Black White Relations in the American South since Emancipation.* New York: Oxford University Press, 1984.

Dobbs, Louis Carl (1945–)

Louis Carl Dobbs is a political commentator, author, and television personality. Throughout the first decade of the twenty-first century, Lou Dobbs established himself as one of the most influential populist voices in the United States. As the host of CNN's *Lou Dobbs Tonight*, which aired from 2003 through 2009, Dobbs expressed his generally libertarian, albeit passionate, political viewpoints to nightly audiences of more than 800,000 viewers. Dobbs is best known for his outspoken opposition toward illegal immigration, as well as his criticism of globalization and free-trade economic policies. He indicates that through the federal government's alleged failure to properly address these two issues, the power elites within both major political parties have initiated a de facto "war on the middle class" in the United States. Dobbs hosted *Moneyline* on CNN from the cable news channel's inception in 1980 until his departure from the network in 1999; he returned to CNN in 2001 and eventually renamed the program *Lou Dobbs Tonight*. Dobbs left CNN in November 2009. He has also hosted the daily *Lou Dobbs Radio* program since 2009 and returned to television in late 2010 when he resumed *Lou Dobbs Tonight* on the Fox Business Network channel.

During his first stint with CNN, Dobbs, whose background was in business and government, served primarily as an analyst for economic and financial issues, expressing support for free trade and economic liberalism, that is, free-market capitalism. Following his return, however, Dobbs began railing against free-trade policies, such as NAFTA, for negatively impacting American workers by undercutting wages. He has also condemned free trade for facilitating the outsourcing of U.S. manufacturing jobs to foreign nations so employers may take advantage of reduced costs of production by paying workers in other countries considerably lower wages than they could American employees. Dobbs began incorporating the segment "Exporting America" into his nightly television program after rejoining CNN, which contained features that highlighted Dobbs's opposition to free trade and outsourcing and exposed alleged corporate greed.

In 2003, Dobbs added a "Broken Borders" segment to his television show to draw attention to illegal immigration. More than any other single issue, Dobbs's staunch opposition to illegal immigration has made him a controversial figure, earning him praise from immigration control advocates and sparking outrage among immigrant rights advocates and Latino civil rights activists. While expressing sympathy for the plight of undocumented aliens, Dobbs has passionately asserted that the U.S. government refuses to enforce its immigration laws and that illegal aliens bring diseases, crime, terrorism, and welfare exploitation to the United States. He has expressed support for harsh civil and criminal penalties on employers who hire undocumented aliens; such sanctions were established under the 1986 Immigration Reform and Control Act but have gone largely unenforced.

Dobbs's anger over illegal immigration extends far beyond its financial ramifications, however. He regularly refers to children born in the United States to undocumented mothers as "anchor babies" because such children are U.S. citizens who then entitle their mothers to certain benefits despite the fact that these parents are not citizens themselves. In 2006 Dobbs criticized ethnic holidays, such as Cinco de Mayo and St. Patrick's Day, as ethnocentric because such celebrations entail displays of other nations' flags. Dobbs has also referred to Latino civil rights organizations, such as the Mexican American Legal Defense and Education Fund (MALDEF) and the League of United Latin American Citizens (LULAC), as ethnocentric. In addition, Dobbs's program has entertained the theory that illegal immigrants from Mexico are part of a conspiracy promoted by the Mexican government to reclaim the southwestern United States, which was annexed in 1848 at the conclusion of the Mexican-American War. Dobbs advocates using the National Guard to patrol the U.S.-Mexico border, has mocked congressional bipartisan immigration reform legislation as "the Amnesty Agenda," and heavily criticized President George W. Bush's relatively moderate views on immigration policy, which included support for a guest-worker migrant labor program.

Concern over cultural and demographic changes have occurred throughout

American history whenever a large foreign-born population has entered the nation in a relatively short period of time and has not yet been thoroughly acculturated. In the early twenty-first century, Dobbs joined other notable populists, including Patrick J. Buchanan, Congressman Tom Tancredo, and right-wing pundit Michelle Malkin in placing illegal immigration on the front burner in U.S. politics. Critics have accused Dobbs of cherry-picking data pertaining to illegal immigration and have charged him with exploiting immigration to increase viewership, while supporters maintain that Dobbs simply "tells it like it is." In either event, his ratings dramatically increased after adding the "Broken Borders" segment to his television program.

Justin D. García

See also: Palin, Sarah (1964–); Tea Party

References

Dobbs, Lou. *Exporting America: Why Corporate Greed Is Shipping American Jobs Overseas.* New York: Warner Business Books, 2004.

Dobbs, Lou. *War on the Middle Class: How the Government, Big Business, and Special Interest Groups Are Waging War on the American Dream and How to Fight Back.* New York: Penguin Books, 2006.

Eviatar, Daphne. "Nightly Nativism." *The Nation* (August 28–September 4, 2006): 18–25.

Donnelly, Ignatius (1831–1901)

Ignatius Loyola Donnelly, also known as the "The Sage of Nininger," was a congressman from Minnesota, the People's Party's vice-presidential candidate in the 1900 election, a science fiction writer, a novelist, and a fringe scientist.

He was born in Philadelphia in 1831 to Philip Donnelly, an Irish American medical doctor, and his wife, Catherine, a pawnbroker. After graduating from public high school, Ignatius passed the bar exam while working for the law office of Benjamin Harris Brewster. At 19, he published his first volume of poetry. Five years later, he was nominated for the Pennsylvania legislature.

In 1856, with his new wife, Katherine McCaffrey, in tow, he moved west, first to Iowa and shortly after to Minnesota. His populist sentiments surfaced early when he discovered the outrageous interest rates charged by moneylenders in St. Paul. He swore eternal hatred toward the so-called monied class, which he dubbed "the shameless plutocracy" (Wack). Still, he bought 640 acres of land located 30 miles southwest of Minneapolis and planned the construction of what would become the town of Nininger City, and later simply Nininger. Within a year, roughly 200 houses and businesses had sprung up. With visions of a great fortune and a utopian cooperative farm community before him, it all disappeared in the Panic of 1857, which left him near bankruptcy.

Yet despite his financial setbacks, Donnelly's political star was on the rise. In 1857, he was elected secretary of the Republican Territorial Convention. The residents of his area nominated him to the state legislature, a race he promptly lost, but he continued to make a name for himself by becoming editor and main writer for the Republican newspaper *The Minnesotan*, which put his name in front of readers across the state.

After a second failed bid for the Senate, he then became the state's lieutenant governor, under Alexander Ramsey, in 1859. When the Sioux rebelled in 1862 (also known as the Dakota War, the Sioux Outbreak, or the Dakota Uprising), Donnelly joined the troops sent to quell the uprising, further establishing him as a man of the people. From that position, he moved on four years later to become the U.S. representative for the Second District, a position he held for three terms.

Known to his fellow congressmen as highly intelligent yet erratic, Donnelly envisioned himself as a champion of the common man against the corrupt business, corporate, timber, moneylending, and railroad interests that were taking advantage of ordinary people. In his speeches, in his editorials, and on the campaign trail, he often let his rhetoric get away from him and was accused by rivals, including people in his own Republican Party, of telling bald-faced lies, including such claims as that a number of southern slaves were really white and their numbers were rising. A fervent abolitionist of the Free Labor ilk, he championed the Wade-Davis Manifesto, supported the purchase of Alaska, believed in African American suffrage, and promoted the expansion of the National Bureau of Education to educate freed blacks.

It was his support of the railroads that created a minor scandal and ultimately cost him his congressional seat. While serving on the Committee for Public Lands, which made decisions regarding railroad interests, it was discovered that he had accepted stock from at least two companies. This, coupled with his over-the-top polemics and rigid attitudes, led fellow Minnesota Republicans, representing the King-Washburn ring, to put up a rival candidate in his 1868 reelection campaign, which split the GOP vote. The King-Washburn ring included Cadwallader C. Washburn and William S. King, who dabbled in land speculation, railroads, and lumber and who were known for corruption in their pursuit of commercial and political power. Washburn also battled Charles Alfred Pillsbury in the wheat and flour industries and eventually established General Mills. Like many states, Minnesota allowed several candidates from the same party to run for the same office as long as there was major-party support. The ballot thus featured two Republican candidates and one Democrat, which basically split the Republican vote. King-Washburn decided it was worth losing the seat for two years to get rid of Donnelly. Suspecting that he had little chance of winning, Donnelly also campaigned for the open Senate seat, an opportunity that never materialized because he could not get the party's nomination.

After brief stints as a lobbyist for the Atlantic and Pacific Railroad and as the Washington, DC, reporter for the *St. Paul Dispatch*, Donnelly returned to Minnesota disillusioned by what he saw as corruption in the Republican Party. In 1870, he tried to return to Congress under the People's Party–Democrat Party coalition but was unable to gain any traction with voters. After crisscrossing the state a couple of times on the lecture circuit, he suffered another political setback when the candidate he supported, Horace Greeley, found his hopes for the presidency foundering.

From there, Donnelly went on to organize the new Grange Party in Minnesota. Joining forces with the Democrats, Donnelly spearheaded the antimonopolist movement and was elected to the state senate from 1874 to1878. While serving, he started and edited a new newspaper called the *Anti-Monopolist.* Leaving the Grange Party behind, Donnelly formed a new party called the Anti-Monopolist Party. With the Anti-Monopolists, Greenbackers, and Democrats, he formed a coalition ticket to make one more attempt to return to the House of Representatives, only to be met with defeat. Believing his failure was due to lumber company fraud, the monied interests, and Republican corruption, Donnelly decided to return to his law career and to writing.

Donnelly made his biggest impact on future generations as a writer rather than a politician. His most famous work was *Atlantis: The Antediluvian World*, published in 1882. He claimed that the story of Atlantis told in Plato's dialogues between Timaeus and Critias was a real event, tying it to the Great Flood in the Bible. Atlantis, located in the Atlantic Ocean adjacent to the Mediterranean Sea, was the place where civilization and culture first took root. It was a true antediluvian world, a place of peace and happiness, and its memory inspired the legends of Asgard, Olympos, Alcinous, the Garden of Eden, the Gardens of Hesperides, Mesophalos, and the Elysian Fields. Atlantean kings and queens were remembered as the ancient gods and goddesses. The first to manufacture iron and develop an alphabet, the entire island disappeared in a terrible calamity. The few survivors were able to make their escapes to the west and east on rafts, giving rise to the various flood and deluge myths. In a sequel a year later, *Ragnarok: The Age of Fire and Gravel*, he contended that it was a massive comet that not only destroyed Atlantis but took out the mammoths as well.

In 1888, Donnelly published *The Great Cryptogram: Francis Bacon's Cipher in the So-Called Shakespeare Plays*, in which he proposed that Bacon had written most of William Shakespeare's oeuvre, a popular theory of the time. Donnelly claimed that Bacon had left ciphers in various plays proving his authorship. The book, despite a successful promotional tour of England, met mixed reviews and sold poorly.

Meanwhile, Donnelly returned to politics, this time placing his hope in a new party called the Minnesota Farmers' Alliance, and he was actively involved in the formation of its platform. The Alliance's goals fostered ideals that Donnelly had held his entire public career—to protect farmers and the common man from monopolies, monied interests, and corrupt politicians. It also sought a more equitable tax system, an income tax, congressional regulation of interstate commerce, and the establishment of local cooperative stores.

With the backing of the Alliance, Donnelly returned to the state legislature in 1887 but failed in the next year to win the governorship under the newly formed

Farmer Labor party. When he realized he had no chance of winning the state-wide election, he dropped out. Nor did he succeed in his bid to return to the state legislature, this time as a Democrat. In 1889, he came up on the losing side again in his bid for the U.S. Senate.

Donnelly took his concerns about his political losses and his failures to correct the national policies that oppressed the common man and wrote a successful science fiction novel, *Caesar's Column: A Story of the Twentieth Century*. Set in 1988 New York, an elite few exploit underprivileged workers, resulting in an underground movement called the Brotherhood of Terror, which seeks to bring down civilization. He followed it up with a second novel, *Doctor Huguet*, which detailed his concerns about racism and its lasting effects on American culture.

In 1890, Donnelly was the keynote speaker at the Minnesota Convention of the Northwest Alliance and again ran for the state senate, this time under the Alliance Labor Union banner, and won.

Donnelly then turned his attention to the People's Party, an outgrowth of the Farmers' Alliance. He was actively involved in the formation of the platform at the St. Louis convention, at which he was a keynote speaker, and he wrote the preamble of the Omaha convention's platform, which included abolition of the national banks, a graduated income tax, direct election of senators, an eight-hour work day, civil service reform, and the abandonment of the gold standard. His concern over the gold standard was the backbone of his novel *The Golden Bottle*, which claimed that the only way the United States could be prosperous was to have money universally available. He made one last attempt at statewide office, running for governor as a Populist, and again went down to defeat.

Donnelly continued to write and publish throughout his later years. Stepping down from a leadership role in the Farmers' Alliance in 1895, he was honored by a number of Minnesota politicians with a golden cane and pen, which was to be "used unhesitatingly against enemies of your cause" (Dudek). In the next year his wife died, and a few months later he married his secretary, Marion Hanson.

In poor health, it appeared that his public life was done, but in a surprise move he accepted the nomination as the People's Party's vice-presidential candidate, under Wharton Barker, in 1900. It proved to be a pivotal mistake for both the party and himself. The once great orator was a mere shadow of himself, and he suffered a stroke in the middle of a campaign speech. Donnelly never recovered. He died just after midnight on January 1, 1901, of a heart attack.

Trevor Jason Soderstrum

See also: Abolitionism; Granger Movement

References

"Cadwallader Washburn." National Park Service. http://www.nps.gov/resources/person.htm?id=123. accessed January 3, 2013.

Carlson, W. Bernard. "Technology and America as a Consumer Society, 1870–1900." In Charles W. Calhoun (ed.), *The Gilded Age: Perspectives on the Origins of Modern America*, 2nd ed. (pp. 29–52). New York: Rowman & Littlefield, 2007.

Dudek, Lisa. "Donnelly, Ignatius Loyola." Literary and Cultural Heritage Map of Pennsylvania, Pennsylvania State University. http://www.pabook.libraries.psu.edu/palitmap/bios/Donnelly__Ignatius.html. Accessed January 3, 2013.

"King, William Smith, (1828–1900)." Biographical Dictionary of the United States Congress. http://bioguide.congress.gov/scripts/biodisplay.pl?index=K000218. Accessed January 3, 2013.

Wack, Henry Wellington. "Ignatius Donnelly: Recollections of a Great Baconian." Sir Francis Bacon's New Advancement of Learning. http://www.sirbacon.org/ignatiusdonnelly.htm. Accessed January 3, 2013.

Douglass, Frederick (1818–1895)

Frederick Augustus Washington Bailey was born into the lowest station in nineteenth-century American society; however, over the course of a lifetime, he would transcend his origins and become one of the towering figures in U.S. history. After escaping from slavery, adopting his now-famous surname, and establishing himself in the free North, Frederick Douglass embarked on a remarkable career in which he held positions in the federal government and became a passionate advocate for African Americans and women. In February 1895, after waging sustained, occasionally successful, and often frustrating fights against slavery, racism, black disfranchisement, lynching, and the oppression of women, Douglass passed away, leaving the mantle of race leadership to a new generation of African Americans.

Douglass's childhood and adolescence was indicative of the myriad experiences of African Americans enslaved throughout the antebellum South. In February 1818, he was born on Maryland's Eastern Shore, the son of an enslaved mother and a white father who, Douglass later insisted, was also his owner. Douglass's mother was absent during his childhood, and Douglass lived in his grandmother's cabin until he was separated from her and brought to the plantation of a prominent local planter. After several years of working as a field hand, Douglass lived in Baltimore, where he hired himself out as a caulker in that city's shipyards. There, primarily through his own clandestine efforts, Douglass learned to read, an accomplishment that he later credited with helping clarify his views on slavery and freedom. Douglass's growing impulse for physical liberation surfaced in a fight with an overseer, an unsuccessful attempt to run away from a farm where he was sent to work, and, finally, his successful escape from Baltimore and bondage.

At the age of 20, Douglass, along with his new bride, established himself in New Bedford, Massachusetts, where he soon invested himself in the burgeoning abolitionist movement. Douglass became a regular attendee at local antislavery meetings, sometimes speaking out from the audience to share his firsthand account of the so-called peculiar institution. On August 16, 1841, Douglass gave his first public speech at a Massachusetts Anti-Slavery Society convention held in Nantucket. Attendees, including the famed abolitionist William Lloyd Garrison, hailed the powerful speech, and

Editor, orator, and abolitionist Frederick Douglass was the foremost African American leader of the 19th century in the United States. He was also an advocate for woman suffrage. (Library of Congress)

shortly thereafter Douglass joined Garrison as an agent of the Massachusetts Anti-Slavery Society.

During the next two decades, Douglass became a devout abolitionist, unrivaled in his commitment to the cause of emancipation and African American progress. Douglass traveled the free states of the North and Midwest sharing his experiences of slavery and championing the abolitionist cause. He often did so at considerable personal risk: while Douglass officially purchased his freedom in 1846 and alleviated the prospect of a return to slavery, incensed proslavery mobs remained a potent threat throughout his career. Despite these difficulties, Douglass persevered in his activism, eventually augmenting his speaking engagements with attempts to spread abolitionism through the written word.

Like hundreds of other formerly enslaved African Americans during the nineteenth century, Douglass found particular power within the autobiographical medium. In 1845, he published the *Narrative of the Life of Frederick Douglass*, a chronicle of his journey from slavery to freedom that he would later update in *My Bondage and My Freedom* (1855) and *Life and Times of Frederick Douglass* (1881, revised 1892). Douglass's autobiographical writings, particularly the first, contain many tropes common to the slave narrative; yet amid recollections of familial separation, physical punishment, and eventual escape, they also evince an increasingly self-confident and self-reliant intellectual who rose above the simple label of fugitive slave.

Indeed, at a relatively early stage in his career, Douglass expanded his literary and reform efforts beyond the autobiographical genre and abolitionist cause. In 1847, after breaking ties with Garrison, embarking on a prolonged abolition campaign in Great Britain, and eventually moving to Rochester, New York, Douglass started *The North Star.* Later renamed *Frederick Douglass' Paper*, it not only championed emancipation but also addressed national politics and advocated for the rights of African Americans in the urban North. In 1848, Douglass sought new subscribers for his incipient paper at Elizabeth Cady Stanton's Seneca Falls convention. Along with a sympathetic audience for *The North Star*, Douglass found a cause—woman suffrage and equal rights—that he remained loyal to throughout his life.

As the sectional crisis intensified and the Civil War approached, Douglass entertained more radical ideas to help the United States fulfill its democratic promise. Although he briefly considered Haiti as a permanent refuge for African Americans, Douglass, unlike his Black Nationalist contemporaries, never fully committed himself to the idea of emigration. Instead, he excoriated white Americans for their country's hypocritical inequality—one of his most famous orations asked "What, to the Slave, Is the Fourth of July?"—and advocated for African Americans to seize their freedom and equitable inclusion in national life by any means necessary. Douglass even befriended John Brown, supported some of his ideas to emancipate enslaved blacks, and, ultimately, lamented not doing more to aid Brown's failed raid on Harper's Ferry.

In 1861, with the Confederate bombardment of Fort Sumter and the outbreak of war, Douglass saw the opportunity for the United States to realize his martyred friend's vision and eradicate slavery and racial inequality. Douglass encouraged African Americans to join the Union Army, and he became a recruiter for the Fifty-fourth Massachusetts Regiment—a unit that two of his sons would join. He urged President Abraham Lincoln to come to the aid of his sons and other black troops who faced discrimination within the Union Army and potential retribution if captured by Confederate forces.

After the defeat of the Confederacy and the adoption of the Thirteenth Amendment to the Constitution effectively ended slavery, Douglass turned his attention to the plight of the South's freedmen and women. Douglass traveled throughout the country, drumming up support for the enfranchisement of African Americans, and he subsequently served an unsuccessful stint as president of the Freedman's Savings and Trust Company. While his commitment to black progress momentarily diverted his attention from women's rights, Douglass did call for an amendment enfranchising women following the ratification of the Fifteenth Amendment to the Constitution.

African Americans' political gains were fleeting, but Douglass managed to receive some of the political posts that the Republican Party conceded to its African American constituents during Reconstruction and its aftermath. In 1877, Douglass became the U.S. marshal of the District of Columbia, and, following his removal from that position, Douglass gained an appointment as recorder of deeds for the District of Columbia. After a period of public controversy and private strife—he married a white woman after the death of his first wife—Douglass assumed the post of U.S. minister resident and consul general to the Republic of Haiti. Although his service there from 1889 to 1891 garnered the disdain of the white press, Douglass received plaudits from Haitians for his fair handling of diplomatic matters. Indeed, two years after leaving Haiti, Douglass represented that country as the commissioner of the Haitian exhibit at the World's Columbian Exposition in Chicago.

In his final years—in his final moments—Douglass maintained his passionate interest in the equal treatment of all Americans. On the evening of February 20, 1895, while telling his wife about his attendance at that day's National Council of Women meeting, Douglass's heart stopped and he collapsed to the floor of his Anacostia home. The great orator, writer, political activist, and social reformer thus passed away in a terrible yet fitting fashion.

Douglass remained a powerful presence in American society even after his death. His legacy is seen in the numerous prizes still given in his honor, the monuments erected in his memory, the public buildings named after him, and his continued representation in American popular culture. Yet Douglass's permanent imprint is perhaps best found in the civil rights activists who succeeded him. Individuals like W. E. B. Du Bois and Ida B. Wells-Barnett—whom Douglass befriended and joined in the antilynching crusade—acknowledged Douglass's influence and adapted his ideas of morality and social justice to the era of Jim Crow. While Douglass may have delivered his final, great speech on the "Lessons of the Hour," he truly provided an enduring vision of freedom and equality that transcended his time.

Brandon Ronald Byrd

See also: Abolitionism; African Americans and Populism; Wells, Ida B. (1862–1931)

References

Foner, Philip S. *Frederick Douglass: A Biography.* New York: Citadel Press, 1964.

McFeely, William S. *Frederick Douglass.* New York: W. W. Norton & Company, 1991.

Quarles, Benjamin. *Frederick Douglass.* New York: Athenaeum Press, 1968.

Drought

A drought is a period of decreased water supply in a region. Drought is most frequently the result of a shortage of rainfall caused by the persistence of high-pressure systems in the atmosphere. Droughts have been known throughout history and are commonly seen as normal variations in weather. Some areas, however, are more prone to droughts than others. Droughts can be of short or long duration. Droughts frequently have significant impacts on whole ecosystems, including plants, agricultural systems, animals, human health, and regional economies. Moreover, droughts have had political effects, evoking popular discontent and demand for redress.

Droughts can diminish crop production, lead to social unrest, create permanent habitat destruction and desertification, motivate mass migration, create situations of starvation and dehydration, and create the needed situation for dust storms and massive erosion. The misery that drought brings can also create wars over natural resources, test political stability, and encourage the formation of new political parties.

Human activity can exacerbate the impact of a drought. In the American prairie lands, decades of bad agricultural techniques such as deep plowing of fine topsoil with tractors and displacing natural grasses that kept soil in place together with a lack of crop rotation, contour plowing, or use of cover crops and fallowed fields led to massive erosion in the Dust Bowl of the 1930s.

Initially, settlers of the American Great Plains were filled with rosy predictions by the land speculators who encouraged them to homestead. Even though the Plains were known to be arid, these farmers believed that "rain followed the plow," an error that resulted in inappropriate agricultural techniques for the region and ultimately resulted in environmental devastation. Early setters enjoyed unusually wet years and bumper crops, and others were encouraged by these successes to follow in their footsteps. Yet, with less than 20 inches of rainfall per year, the fragile ecosystem of the Plains could not handle these intensive agricultural practices for long.

There were 20 straight months of drought in Texas in 1886–1887, and blizzards killed cattle during the winters. Recurrent droughts occurred during the 1890s, and the Plains suffered more droughts in the 1930s and 1950s. Also drought hit the wheat-producing areas of the Great Plains, and farmers went into debt and crisis in the late 1880s. The combined drought and debt intensified anger against grain-elevator owners, lenders, bankers, and railroads as the farmers felt long abused by these entities.

Discontented American farmers developed multiple organizations to address their grievances, which fueled the Populist movement and led to numerous new laws regarding transportation, banking, and tariffs designed to protect the environment and people's livelihood.

Climate scientists predict that as climate changes, there will be both more rain and more areas stricken by drought in the future. Increased heat and evaporation in some areas will result in more rain than normally expected while the number of droughts occurring will rise because climate change will be uneven, and currently dry places will get dryer. The areas of aridity will also grow larger.

Present-day populist movements on both the Right and Left are arguing over the proper response to global warming and related greenhouse gas emissions. Politics and global agreements will continue to influence the future of droughts.

John O'Sullivan

See also: Agricultural Issues, Regional; Environmentalism; Farmers' Mutual Benefit Association (FMBA); Homestead Act (1862); New Deal; Plains and Midwest, Populism in the; Populism; *Progressive Farmer*

References

Cooper, Michael. *Dust to Eat: Drought and Depression in the 1930's*. New York: Clarion Books, 2004.

Holmes, William. *American Populism*. Lexington, MA: D. C. Heath and Co., 1994.

Withgott, Jay, and Scott Brennan. *Environment: The Science behind the Stories*. Portland, OR: Pearson, 2005.

Woodruff, Nan. *As Rare as Rain*. Champaign: University of Illinois Press, 1985.

E

Eddy, Mary Baker (1821–1910)

Christian Science was a movement born during a time of religious experimentation and alternative understandings of how to live a proper spiritual and moral life. Nineteenth-century New England was overwhelmed with would-be prophets, social reformers, and liberal Christians. Mary Baker Eddy stood out not only for her sex but for her thoughts, her publications, and her scripture. Further, Eddy's movement prospered, primarily because of her commitment to the meticulous system of beliefs and practices she spent her life creating.

Mary Baker Eddy (née Mary Morse Baker) was born on July 16, 1821, in New Hampshire. Her parents, Mark and Abigail Baker, were devout Congregationalists. Eddy would eventually reject the tradition of her parents because of its more severe doctrines, like predestination, while retaining a solid belief in the Bible and in Jesus, as a healer, especially. A quiet and introspective child, Eddy was plagued by ill health in her youth. Disease and tragedy seemed to follow her wherever she went, taking her first husband, George Washington Glover, and her mother when she was only 22. She was left pregnant with little means to support herself until she was remarried, nearly 10 years later, to Daniel Patterson. During her marriage to Patterson, she was again struck by a series of illnesses, which left her chronically weak. Eddy consulted various healers, homeopathic doctors, and anyone with a nontraditional approach to healing—as conventional medical methods had all seemed to fail her. In 1862, she approached Phineas Parkhurst Quimby, a practitioner of magnetic healing, which was a technique that involved placement of magnets on pressure points on the body. Certain of Quimby's views may have influenced Eddy's later religious thought. While there is some controversy about this connection, he did believe that any person could channel the healing power of Christ simply by right thinking and mental clarity. Whatever Quimby's influence, Eddy left his side feeling refreshed. In 1866, Eddy suffered a near-fatal fall on ice, which left her unable to move. Convinced that death was imminent, Eddy began to read accounts of Jesus's miraculous healings from the New Testament. Three days later, Eddy stood up and proceeded to walk again. This was a turning point in Eddy's vocation: she now knew her purpose was to be a healer and evangelist.

Eddy's own experience with illness and healing had proved to her that the mind played an incredible role in the well-being of the body. After her fall and miraculous recovery, Eddy spent the next few years studying the Bible and testing a thought-based system of healing. Over time, Eddy became increasingly convinced that humans all bore divine healing power but had simply lost the ability to access it due to wrong thought or clouded understanding. By refocusing the human mind and awakening it to its awesome power, any person could conquer illness or injury. Eddy eschewed modern medicine, including drugs or doctors, believing them to be futile. Rather than rely on these human inventions, Eddy encouraged people to turn to an alternative system of healing that combined the practices she had tested through her healing experiments and belief in God, Christ, the New Testament, and the coming Kingdom. Fittingly, she called her system Christian Science.

Eddy began teaching in 1870. Soon thereafter, she began to accumulate a group of followers, comprised in part by the spiritual seekers characteristic of the age, as well as disaffected Christians who were looking for an alternative form of Christian practice. Then in 1875, Eddy produced what would become her greatest legacy both in Christian Science and in the narrative of American religious history. *Science and Health* (later called *Science and Health with Key to the Scriptures*) became a text on par with the Bible in the Christian Science canon. In the text, Eddy puts forward her belief that pain, disease, sin, and even death were illusory because they did not rise from God. By changing one's worldview to one where humanity was a mirror image of God (rather than a diseased and sinful race as portrayed by traditional Christianity), humans could overcome all threats to the body and the mind. The book offered Eddy's views on a wide array of subjects from traditionally religious topics such as creation, to the apocalypse and marriage, to more scientific questions about medicine, being, and physiology. In addition, the book explained both how to practice Christian Science and how to teach it—a feature that would ensure the perseverance of the movement after she died. Eddy spent the majority of her life editing and perfecting the text of *Science and Health.*

Besides *Science and Health*, Eddy's writing and publishing career was prolific. Her *Manual of the Mother Church* went through 88 editions during her lifetime, the last one published in the final year of her life, 1910. The *Manual* served as the central regulating doctrine of the Church of Christ, Scientist—the church's official name. It contained church by-laws on all subjects from membership, to ecclesiastical structure, to personal discipline and liturgical practices. The intention of the *Manual* was ostensibly to create a secure system of church polity so that the church would be able to thrive according to Eddy's rule far into the future. She also founded the *Christian Science Journal* and the *Christian Science Sentinel*, both of which were intended to disseminate her ideas and keep Christian Scientists connected to the goings-on of the church.

Eddy had divorced Patterson and later married Asa Gilbert Eddy in 1877, though it was a short-lived union as he died in 1882. Eddy then made a home in Boston, which became the hub of Christian Science in the United States and, later, throughout the world. In last several decades of her life, Eddy experienced a series of highs and lows. In 1894, construction of the First Church of Christ (known as the Mother Church) was completed in

Boston, where Eddy served as pastor, though she eventually named her text *Science and Health* as the church's only true pastor. In 1898, Eddy created the Christian Science Publishing Society and in 1908 another periodical, the *Christian Science Monitor*. In spite of the success of Christian Science and her many publications, Eddy was a controversial figure in the press. This was abetted by several very long and public trials involving former students, who accused her of practicing dangerous and misleading methods of healing. In spite of these accusations, her movement grew.

Eddy died on December 3, 1910. The announcement of her death was met with an outpouring of homage to the visionary woman who had overcome so many ills and illnesses in life through the power of her mind, simultaneously inspiring future generations to do the same. While her movement did outlive Eddy, the number of churches have declined in the last 30 years with somewhere between 900 and 1,100 churches still operating in the United States.

Lydia Eeva Natti Willsky

See also: Burned-over District; Gilded Age; Modernism; Progressivism

References

Bates, Ernest Sutherland. *Mary Baker Eddy: The Truth and the Tradition*. London: G. Routledge & Sons, 1933.

Eddy, Mary Baker. *Mary Baker Eddy: Speaking for Herself*. Boston: The Mary Baker Eddy Collection, 2002.

Eddy, Mary Baker. *Science and Health with Key to the Scriptures*. Boston: First Church of Christ, Scientist, 1934.

Gill, Gillian. *Mary Baker Eddy*. Reading, MA: Perseus Books, 1998.

Peel, Robert. *Mary Baker Eddy*. 3 vols. New York: Holt, Rinehart and Winston, 1966.

Zaimov, Stoyan. "Christian Scientists Looking to Grow Membership amid Shrinking Numbers." *The Christian Post*, 14 June 2012. http://www.christianpost.com/news/christian-scientists-looking-to-grow-membership-amid-shrinking-numbers-76536/#ftRMqsdXMKb8HXi2.99. Accessed January 3, 2013.

Eight-hour Day

With the worldwide Industrial Revolution (c. 1750–1850) came a drastic change to the work day. Laborers who worked in massive, complex factories faced a new work ethic and management hierarchy that was drastically different from the guilds or typical preindustrial agrarian economies. While Britain was the main industrial powerhouse at the dawn of the nineteenth century, other countries worked hard to become industrialized as well, which led to a race for output and product. As a result workers, including women and children, had to work long, hard days up to 16 hours long, with a six-day work week. The long days and the harsh conditions caught the attention of socialist writers, such as Robert Owen, who demanded the 10-hour day in 1810 and formulated the eight-hour day in 1817. He is noted for creating the slogan "eight hours labor, eight hours recreation, eight hours rest," the first to call for the eight-hour work day. As the United States moved into the most eventful stage of its industrialization

(c. 1870s–1919), it followed a similar path. In both eras, these periods of labor unrest led to unionization and to the adoption by some workers of alternative political philosophies, including anarchism, socialism, and communism. In the United States, the fear of these movements led to a movement that was simultaneously populist and compatible with laissez-faire economics. Known as Progressivism, it incorporated the demands both of disgruntled American laborers and agrarians as well as the concerns of many middle-class Americans.

Despite the fact that many in the United States connect the eight-hour day to Ford Motor Company's radical "five dollars a day for eight hours of work" movement in 1914, the idea had been part of many labor platforms since the late eighteenth century. In 1791 carpenters in Philadelphia went on strike, demanding the establishment of a 10-hour work day. In 1835 there was yet another strike in Philadelphia by Irish coal heavers, demanding that the work day should be from 6:00 to 6:00, with two hours for meals and 10 for work. The specific eight-hour day for work was sought as early as 1836, but it was not gained by particular labor groups until 1842 when Boston ship carpenters established an eight-hour work day in their industry. Other cities followed suit. The Illinois legislature passed a law that granted laborers an eight-hour work day after agitation by Chicago labor organizations. The law, however, proved to be highly ineffective, as it was littered with loopholes and contradictions that allowed employers to disobey it.

With laborers across the United States calling for the eight-hour day, President Ulysses S. Grant signed the National Eight Hour Law Proclamation on May 19, 1869, which was proposed by Congress on June 25, 1868. While this law recommended an eight-hour work day, it only affected federal employees. Riots and strikes continued. The United Mine Workers gained the eight-hour day in 1898; the Building Trades Council of San Francisco gained it in 1900; and, with the passing of the United States Adamson Act in 1916, railroad workers gained the eight-hour day along with the payment of overtime, which was the first federal law to regulate the working day of private companies. Finally the eight-hour day for all working people was granted under the Fair Labor Standards Act in 1937 as part of the New Deal, which also granted overtime and bonus salaries for individuals who worked longer than a 40-hour work week.

It is important to note that, as the world was becoming more industrialized, exploited laborers and workers outside the United States also sought the eight-hour day. Australia and New Zealand achieved great progress for the eight-hour day prior to the twentieth century. Spain was one of the first European countries to create a national law supporting the eight-hour day, and the United Kingdom was one of the first countries to regulate the work day for women and children under the age of 18. The Factory Act of 1833 limited the work day for children in factories in particular. Children from the ages of 9 to 13 worked only eight-hour days; from 14 to 18 years old they worked

12-hour days. Children under the age of 9 were required to go to school. Women and children gained the 10-hour work day in 1847. The French Revolution of 1848 gave laborers the 12-hour day. The International Workingmen's Association demanded an eight-hour day at the Geneva Convention in August of 1866, bringing international awareness of the need for an eight-hour day. The Second International Workingmen's Association meeting in Paris in 1889 supported May 1, 1890, as a day for international demonstrations calling for the eight-hour day, resulting in the international May Day labor holiday. While the United States now celebrates Labor Day on the first Monday in September, American laborers had previously commemorated the holiday on the first of May, resulting in the Haymarket Square Riot of 1886.

It did not take long for laborers to demand shorter work days after the Industrial Revolution. While the eight-hour day was not sought until the mid-nineteenth century, shorter work days spanning 10 hours or less were called for by various socialist and labor groups by the late eighteenth century. Labor groups, unions, and socialist movements added to the cries for shorter work days, and early in the twentieth century countries began to give in, regulating shorter work days on the national level. Moreover, many laborers would have to wait till the mid-twentieth century before succeeding in obtaining a regulated eight-hour work day across the globe.

Marianne E. Kupin

See also: Flint Strike (1936–1937); Haymarket Riot (1886); New Deal; Populism; Progressivism; Rochdale Plan; Waite, Davis (1825–1901)

References

The American Presidency Project. "Proclamation 182—Eight Hour Work Day for Employees of the Government of the United States," May 19, 1869. http://www.presidency.ucsb.edu/ws/index.php?pid=70245#axzz1zQhWlaWH. Accessed January 3, 2013.

Ford Motor Company. "Henry Ford's $5-a-Day Revolution." *Ford*, January 5, 1914. http://corporate.ford.com/about-ford/heritage/milestones/5dollarday/677-f-dollar-a-day. Accessed January 3, 2013.

Haverty-Stacke, Donna T. *America's Forgotten Holiday: May Day and Nationalism, 1867–1960*. New York: New York University Press, 2009.

Kimber, Julie, and Peter Love. *The Time of Their Lives: The Eight-Hour Day and Working Life*. Melbourne: Australia Society for the Study of Labor History, 2007.

McCarthy, Terry. *An Abridged History of the Trades Union and Labour Movement from the Industrial Revolution to the Present Day*. London: Saddle and Stitch, 2009.

Owen, Robert. "Foundation Axioms." Society for Promoting National Regeneration, 1833.

U.S. Department of Labor. "Fair Labor Standards Act of 1938, as Amended." http://www.dol.gov/whd/regs/statutes/FairLaborStandAct.pdf. Accessed January 3, 2013.

Electricity

Electricity is the physical phenomena associated with the existence and movement of electrical charge. Two of the most important phenomena to modern society are electromagnetic induction, which produces electric current that powers motors and electronic devices, and electromagnetic radiation such as radio, microwave, and x-ray waves. Electricity became increasingly important in the United States after the 1880s, primarily in connection with the growth of cities and the rise of factories, both of which needed new and safer sources of lighting and power. Political and social movements focused more and more on the importance of electricity to modernization, economic progress, and social equality from the 1890s through the first several decades of the twentieth century.

Though the phenomena of electrical charge was observed and studied by ancient Egyptians, Greeks, Romans, and Arabs, the first scientific study of electricity did not begin until after 1600. William Gilbert, Robert Boyle, Benjamin Franklin, Luigi Galvani, and Allessandro Volta all investigated this area of science before 1800. Hans Christian Olmsted, Andre Marie Ampere, and Michael Faraday all made significant contributions to the scientific understanding of electricity before 1850, and James Maxwell developed the theoretical formulas necessary for a deeper understanding of the connections between electricity and magnetism in the 1861 and 1862 with his work *On Physical Lines of Force.*

The importance of electricity to the United States came during the second half of the nineteenth century, coinciding with the second American industrial revolution and the subsequent advancements in railroads, communications, manufacturing, and power transmission. Thomas Edison organized his scientific laboratory at Menlo Park in the 1870s to develop and patent numerous electrical technologies and began powering lower Manhattan with the Pearl Street Station in 1881. Joseph Swan and Hiram Maxim developed viable incandescent lighting networks for city streets and factories in the 1880s and 1890s. Nikola Tesla and George Westinghouse partnered from 1888 to 1891 to work on the competing alternating current (AC) technologies, such as traction motors, long-distance power distribution, and wireless transmission of energy and radio waves. Alexander Graham Bell invented the telephone in 1875, expanding the nation's communications networks through cities and rural areas alike by 1900. That year, more than 6,000 independent phone companies had 600,000 phones in operation and Bell Telephone had another 800,000, focused primarily on long-distance service.

The debate over the feasibility of AC or direct current (DC) as the most efficient and economic means of transmitting electrical power to growing cities and manufacturing districts became known as the "battle of the currents." This conflict dominated the story of electricity in the 1880s and 1890s. Edison's DC power networks and patented technologies were already being used by cities on the East Coast. However, Edison knew his DC systems could not transmit over long distances. Westinghouse and Tesla had begun work on long-distance power transmission using AC networks in the late 1880s and were focused primarily on allowing the rural United States to benefit from the modern electrical technologies they had to offer. While both parties had economic interests in the success of their electrical systems, they also promoted their ideas and inventions as the quickest, most egalitarian methods of modernizing the United States and the population as a whole. Lighting systems allowed homes and businesses to work into the night. The cheap electrical power that Edison and Westinghouse promised, and delivered, allowed all classes of Americans to utilize new devices in their workshops, homes, and kitchens. Men and women both could benefit from the prospects of electrical technology.

As the American people increasingly accepted and adopted electrical power in their lives, the economic benefits of electrical power became important to politicians as well. They knew that they needed to support the growth of electrical power infrastructures, especially in the rural United States. The leaders of the Populist movement in the late nineteenth century were concerned with the concentration of power and wealth in the hands of a few. They sought out and promoted ideas that supported and promoted the independence of farmers, laborers, and small-scale businessmen. Electrical power networks fit this philosophy, and the leaders in electrical development and politicians could easily support both sides. Capitalists and urban elites subscribed to the mantra of modern economic opportunity and industrialization on an ever-expanding scale, an easy sell for electric industry leaders. To the farmers, laborers, and small businessmen, advocates of wide-scale expansion of electrical networks could promote modernity, electrical tools to ease workloads, and connection with the larger world through communication networks. The rural population could no longer be easily ignored or shut out of politics. With electricity and its accompanying technologies, they learned about the world as fast as city people, and their voices could be heard just as quickly—at least in theory.

Electricity became increasingly important to American society in the 1920s and 1930s. Despite the hard sell, most rural areas had gone without the benefits of electricity for popular use, including light, running water, and better phone systems. The Roosevelt administration's creation of, and its success with, the Tennessee Valley Authority led directly to the Rural Electrification Administration. In 1930, only 10 percent of rural areas had access to electricity, while 90 percent of urban areas were on the grid. Between 1930 and 1940, this percentage was raised to more than 80 percent for farmers and rural villages. The debate over public utilities in towns across the United States after 1900 involved primarily electricity and water, leading politicians into deeper involvement with scientists and investors who understood both the complexity and economic import of the developing electrical technologies. By the 1940s, electricity was seen as a necessity to modern American life and economic vitality, far surpassing the initial interest in electricity for pure scientific inquiry and small-scale application. Electricity literally became the lifeblood of the United States, powering businesses and communication and connecting citizens not only from coast to coast but from farm and village to city.

Paul Nienkamp

See also: Gilded Age; New Deal; Progressivism; Tesla, Nikola (1856–1943)

References

Brigham, Jay L. *Empowering the West: Electrical Politics before FDR*. Lawrence: University of Kansas Press, 1998.

Brown, D. Clayton. *Electricity for Rural America: The Fight for the REA*. Westport, CT: Greenwood Press, 1980.

Hughes, Thomas P. *Networks of Power: Electrification in Western Society, 1880–1930*. Baltimore, MD: Johns Hopkins University Press, 1983.

Marvin, Carolyn. *When Old Technologies Were New: Thinking about Electric Communication in the Late Nineteenth Century*. New York: Oxford University Press, 1988.

Ostler, Jeffrey. *Prairie Populism: The Fate of Agrarian Radicalism in Kansas, Nebraska, and Iowa, 1880–1892*. Lawrence: University of Kansas Press, 1993.

Tobey, Ronald C. *Technology as Freedom: The New Deal and the Electrical Modernization of the American Home*. Berkeley: University of California Press, 1996.

"The Elite"

In popular usage, *elite* is a contentious term used by admirers and detractors alike to denote the ability to use economic and political power for both positive and negative ends. A loose definition corresponds to the word *aristocracy*, a situation that entitles one to privileges and the right to exercise power based on his or her inherent traits and advantages, including wealth derived from status. In the United States, the term *elite* has often been used instead of *aristocracy* because in the rest of the world *aristocracy* is primarily based on hereditary titles and primogeniture. The positive connotation of the term *elite* is obscured by the fact that elitism as a philosophy is viewed with suspicion, if not outright contempt, especially during periods of populist unrest when there is a focus on the "the people" and the latter's perceived needs.

Characteristics universally associated with elites are privilege, power, and ownership. All varieties of pundits, from comedians to serious authors, have mocked elitism and highlighted the need for a shift of power back to the majority. In an article entitled "Preparing for Power: Twenty-Five Years Later," Peter W. Cookson Jr. and Caroline Hodges Persell note that not only have American elites positioned themselves on the upper end of the economic and social hierarchy but also "increasingly took on the role of a leadership class and increasingly saw the projection of American power as a necessary adjunct to domestic tranquility and increased economic power" (Howard 16). Thus, in essence, the American elite has created its own version of a European aristocracy, in which economic and political power is bequeathed to the next generation, through education and social connections, to become a self-perpetuating leadership class.

Scholars and philosophers have been able to identify the emergence of such elite systems and the type of education that supports them throughout history. In the United States, an entire education system had to be put in place to enable the creation of what C. Wright Mills referred to as "the power elite" (1956). In the *Republic*, Plato subscribes to the view that "Individuality is an achievement, and only the philosopher has the talent to achieve it, for only he provides each element in his make-up with what is best for it" (Ferrari xxviii). Physicist Hendrik Lorenz adds that "even in the favorable conditions of Socrates' ideal city, only a small elite of outstandingly talented individuals would be eligible for, and could appropriately benefit from, the *Republic*'s educational program" (Santas 154–155). At one level Plato's views on elites conflate ethical and intellectual superiority, making no serious distinctions between one and the other. However, Plato's elitism is more of an ethical kind rather than power for power or for profit's sake, which contrasts with the American situation. Mills observes that "there have been signs of a merger of economic, political, and military elite in a new corporate-like class. Together, as an elite of power, will they not seek, as all powerful men everywhere have always sought, to buttress their power with the mantle of authoritative status?" (Mills 76). Education, then, could be used to turn the best and the brightest into the best leaders, or the wealthy can dominate education and the power structures as an economic aristocracy.

Populists generally decry the accumulation of power for the few over the many, and in that scenario, the elites become tyrannical, a situation that is detrimental to the betterment of the majority of Americans. This critique has reemerged in the twenty-first century via the Occupy movement and found negative expression through presidential candidate Mitt Romney's gaffes about average Americans and their relationship with government. The power elites to whom Mills refers are essentially opportunists, devoid of the ethical or intellectual traits that would in the past have set them apart. Author and talk-show host Christopher Hayes has researched the more recent rise of elites and elitism as embodied in meritocracy, or the idea that some people are intrinsically better than others. He argues that Americans have embraced inequality to the point that they are complicit in the nation's economic collapse and related social failures of the early twentieth century. He states "it is those same elites who have been responsible for the cascade of institutional failure that has produced the crisis of authority . . . Major League Baseball, Enron, Iraq . . . the consistent theme that unites them all is elite malfeasance and elite corruption" (Hayes 22–23). Therefore, the elites have manufactured their power yet failed to wield it wisely or ethically, all the while maintaining their dominant social and economic positions.

Ideally, a meritocracy would give the poor a chance to move upward simply by virtue of talent. Instead, power relations reproduce themselves without giving the deprived an opportunity to enter the predetermined system of privileges. While pointing out that "unequal outcomes make equal opportunity impossible," Hayes recognizes that the so-called meritocracy is in fact a contradiction in terms in that

> the Iron Law of Meritocracy makes a different prediction, that societies ordered around the meritocratic ideal will produce inequality without the attendant mobility. Indeed, over time, a society will grow both more unequal and less mobile as those who ascend its heights create means of preserving and defending their privilege and find ways to pass it on across generations (Hayes 57–59).

Disenchanted populists have done much to define the term *elite* and set the tone of the discussion, yet scholars such as sociologists John Higley and Michael Burton have also attempted to define the term more objectively. Higley and Burton distinguish "three basic types of political elites" based on "structural integration," which relates to "the relative inclusiveness of formal and informal networks of communication and influence among elite persons, groups, and factions" and "value consensus." The *disunited* political elites occur when "structural integration and value consensus are minimal," while the *consensually united* come together when "structural integration is extensive in the sense that overlapping and interlocked communication and influence networks encompass and tie together all influential factions and sector elites, with no single faction or sector elite dominating the networks"; the last are the *ideologically united* where "structural integration is extensive in the sense that a single communication and influence network encompasses all elite members" (Higley and Burton 9, 13–14). Owing to globalization, elites seem to be moving towards the *ideologically united*, which is how Mills sees power elites. The superrich in Mumbai and Lagos—two Third World cities—have more in common with the superrich in New York and Paris than with the middle classes and the poor in their own countries. This kind of ideological unity of the wealthy classes on an international plane accentuates global class-based divisions, thereby eliminating any real competition that might challenge the existence of the few at the top by the many at the bottom.

Prakash Kona

See also: Bacon's Rebellion (1676); Bourbon Democracy; Mills, C. Wright (1916–1962); "The People"; Shays's Rebellion (1786–1787); World's Industrial and Cotton Centennial Exposition (1884–1885)

References

Ferrari, G. R. F., ed. *Plato: The Republic.* Translated by Tom Griffith. Cambridge, UK: Cambridge University Press, 2003.

Hayes, Christopher. *Twilight of the Elites: America after Meritocracy.* New York: Crown Publishers, 2012.

Higley, John, and Michael Burton. *Elite Foundations of Liberal Democracy.* Lanham, MD: Rowman and Littlefield, 2006.

Howard, Adam, and Rubén A. Gaztambide-Fernández. *Educating Elites: Class Privilege and Educational Advantage.* Lanham, MD: Rowman and Littlefield Education, 2010.

Mills, C. Wright. *The Politics of Truth: Selected Writings.* Selected and Introduced by John H. Summers. Oxford, UK: Oxford University Press, 2008.

Santas, Gerasimos, ed. *The Blackwell Guide to Plato's Republic.* Malden, MA: Blackwell Publishing, 2006.

Emancipation Proclamation (1863)

President Abraham Lincoln issued the Emancipation Proclamation on January 1, 1863. In it he declared, "All persons held as slaves within said designated [rebellious] States, and parts of States, are, and henceforward shall be free." Lincoln's rationale for issuing the proclamation avoided moral arguments. Rather, he wrote that emancipation was a "fit and necessary war measure" that would deprive the Confederacy of military and agricultural labor. Yet this measure has continued to be remembered as a moment in which the president used his war powers to instigate the beginning of civil rights for those enslaved in the United States, thus embracing the needs of the powerless over the needs of the powerful in the South.

Lincoln began his presidency in 1861 without an emancipation agenda. Even so, many southerners feared that a Republican administration threatened their property and personal security. Lincoln tried to allay those fears in his inaugural address, stating, "I have no purpose, directly or indirectly, to interfere with the institution of slavery in the States where it exists. I believe I have no lawful right to do so, and I have no inclination to do so." For Lincoln, the Constitution allowed slavery to exist in the southern states, but he had become the leader of the first party, originating in the North, that generally held animosity toward the South and slavery.

Subsequent events challenged Lincoln's ability to keep his inaugural pledge. After hostilities between North and South began at Fort Sumter in April 1861, proemancipationist U.S. Senator Charles Sumner privately urged Lincoln to free the slaves and thus define the conflict in moral terms. Lincoln resisted these overtures, knowing that public opinion would oppose it. In May, Union General Benjamin F. Butler at Fortress Monroe, Virginia, issued an order to deal with enslaved people fleeing to Union lines. Butler refused to return the runaways to their owners in compliance with the Fugitive Slave Act. Because slaves were considered property under the law rather than people, he argued that the fugitives could be used in the war effort against the government; hence they should be treated as contraband. Congress later codified the essence of Butler's order as the First Confiscation Act. Shortly after Lincoln signed that legislation, General John C. Frémont in Missouri issued an order that freed the slaves of Confederate supporters. Lincoln directed Frémont to modify the order on legal terms and cautioned the general that emancipation would turn southern Unionists, especially in the loyal border states, against the federal government.

In December 1861, Secretary of War Simon Cameron's proposal to emancipate and arm former slaves further tested Lincoln's patience. Lincoln forced Cameron to modify his report to Congress. Lincoln reiterated his opposition to these policies within the next six months to Union General David Hunter. Hunter, serving in South Carolina, first began recruiting and organizing black regiments. After abandoning this activity, Hunter issued an order in May 1862 freeing all enslaved people in Georgia, Florida, and South Carolina. Lincoln directly countermanded this order, claiming that power was the commander-in-chief's alone to exercise and only when necessary to the preservation of the government.

Lincoln was not against freeing slaves, but he wanted to do so within the bounds of the law. Personally, Lincoln believed in gradual, compensated emancipation and explained his views in a March 6, 1862, message to Congress, which that body passed as a joint resolution a month later. In practice, Lincoln and Congress succeeded in abolishing slavery in the District of Columbia in April. That legislation provided compensation to loyal slave owners residing in the capital and also offered funds to colonize freed persons to Liberia, Haiti, or South America. In mid-July, Lincoln failed in his initial efforts to persuade the Union states where slavery remained legal (Delaware, Maryland, Kentucky, and Missouri) to adopt similar measures. Some scholars point to the evolution of Lincoln's personal stance on slavery as a result of the constant pressure brought by Quakers inside and outside of government, yet Lincoln's interpretation of the law did not change. Concurrently, the president privately confided to two cabinet members that he planned to issue an emancipation proclamation.

On July 22, Lincoln read his first draft of the Emancipation Proclamation to his assembled cabinet. Cabinet members' opinions were divided: half, notably Secretary of War Edwin M. Stanton, supported it, while the other half opposed it, citing foreign policy and political reasons, especially the upcoming midterm elections. Lincoln left the meeting without a firm decision on the matter and continued privately debating the issue with advisors. On August 22, Lincoln shared his thoughts in a public letter to *New York Tribune* editor Horace Greeley. "My paramount object in this struggle *is* to save the Union," Lincoln wrote, "and is *not* either to save or to destroy slavery. If I could save the Union without freeing *any* slave I would do it, and if I could save it by freeing *all* the slaves I would do it; and if I could save it by freeing some and leaving others alone I would also do that. What I do about slavery, and the colored race, I do because I believe it helps to save the Union" (Donald 368).

By September, Lincoln concluded that emancipation was necessary to preserve the Union and win the war. He feared that issuing the proclamation might be viewed as a politically desperate act and sought a military victory to bolster its reception. General George B. McClellan had commanded the eastern Union forces for most of the war and had mostly pursued a defensive strategy. When he missed the opportunity to rout the Confederate army at Antietam on September 17, Lincoln concluded a change in command and strategy was imperative. Lincoln redefined the Civil War when he issued the Preliminary Emancipation Proclamation on September 22 and removed McClellan from command on November 7.

The Preliminary Emancipation Proclamation was a warning to Confederate states. Lincoln defined the proclamation's purpose as "restoring the constitutional relation between the United States" (Guelzo 255). He presented rebelling states with the option of returning to the Union by January 1, or else slaves residing in those states would "thence forward, and forever free." Because the action only affected disloyal states, Lincoln also recommended that the border slave states enact legislation for the "immediate or gradual abolishment of slavery."

Lincoln reiterated the plan in his second annual message to Congress on December 1, 1862. In it, he also suggested a constitutional amendment providing for gradual, compensated emancipation in loyal states. He concluded his message, "The fiery trial through which we pass, will light us down, in honor or dishonor, to the latest generation. . . . In *giving* freedom to the *slave*, we *assure* freedom to the *free*—honorable alike in what we give, and what we preserve. We shall nobly save, or meanly lose, the last best, hope of earth" (Foner 237).

One month later on January 1, 1863, Lincoln issued the Emancipation Proclamation. The proclamation declared that all enslaved people in the Confederate states were free, with the exception of those individuals in Union-controlled areas of Tennessee, Louisiana, and Virginia. The proclamation also exempted slavery in the Union border states. A final provision of the proclamation allowed for freedmen to enlist in the armed services, although it refrained from authorizing African American soldiers for combat roles.

The Emancipation Proclamation elicited various reactions. Antislavery advocates were generally thrilled, although abolitionists criticized the geographical limits of the proclamation. Similarly, many British and French officials viewed the proclamation as impotent because it affected slavery where the federal government was unable to enforce it. Most southern whites and northern antiwar Democrats outright condemned the action. While evidence is scarce regarding the response of enslaved people, many received the news gladly and sought opportunities to reach freedom at Union lines. The most troubling reception for Lincoln politically came from moderate Republicans, war Democrats, and border-state Unionists. This diverse political bloc expressed its dissatisfaction at the polls, where Democrats gained 28 seats in the U.S. House of Representatives and won gubernatorial elections in New Jersey and New York.

While Lincoln was confident in his presidential authority to issue the Emancipation Proclamation, he was not as certain about legal challenges to the document, especially if a case regarding it reached the U.S. Supreme Court, which had many of the same justices who had ruled in *Dred Scott*. To avoid such a scenario, Lincoln kept trying to convince Unionist leaders in border states and other slave states to legally abolish slavery in their jurisdictions. In March 1863, the voters in what became West Virginia approved a state constitution mandating gradual emancipation. In 1864, Unionists in Arkansas and Louisiana ratified new state constitutions abolishing slavery. Lincoln witnessed the first success of his border-state policy when Maryland voters approved a new constitution with uncompensated, immediate emancipation in October 1864. Missouri voters followed suit a few months later.

On January 31, 1865, the U.S. House of Representatives joined with the U.S. Senate in approving a constitutional amendment to abolish slavery. The next day congressmen drafted and signed a joint resolution submitting the proposed amendment to the states for ratification. Against congressional protocol, President Lincoln added his signature to the resolution in a show of support for the measure. On December 18, the states ratified this Thirteenth Amendment to the U.S.

Constitution, abolishing slavery throughout the United States and completing what the Emancipation Proclamation began two years earlier.

Lincoln donated his handwritten manuscript of the Emancipation Proclamation to raise money for the Chicago Northwestern Sanitary Fair in 1863. The purchaser of the document donated it to the Chicago Soldiers' Home, where it remained until 1871 when it burned in the Chicago Fire. Photographs and lithographs of the original manuscript survive. The official engrossed copy of the proclamation, copied by a clerk and signed by Lincoln, is at the National Archives, Washington, DC. It still represents one of the first efforts on behalf of the federal government to affect change for the downtrodden.

Chandler S. Lighty

See also: Abolitionism

References

Donald, David H. *Lincoln*. New York: Simon & Schuster, 1995.

Foner, Eric. *The Fiery Trial: Abraham Lincoln and American Slavery*. New York: W.W. Norton, 2011.

Guelzo, Allen C. *Lincoln's Emancipation Proclamation: The End of Slavery in America*. New York: Simon & Schuster, 2004.

Emery, Sarah (1838–1895)

Sarah E. V. Emery was a prominent author and lecturer for the Farmers' Alliance and held offices in the Woman's Christian Temperance Union, both nationally and in her home state of Michigan. Emery's greatest significance derived from her ability to communicate populist critiques of the American economic system in a simple, direct, and commonsense manner.

Sarah Ellen Van de Vort was born in Phelps, New York, in 1838. She began her career as an educator early, teaching in the Finger Lake region of the state when she was only 18. She studied at New York's Clinton Liberal Institute, where she established her ideals as a committed Universalist. As such, she strongly advocated for prison and asylum reform, and she was strongly against capital punishment. In 1866, she moved to Midland, Michigan, in part because Michigan did not have capital punishment. There, she continued to work as an educator. In 1870, she married Wesley Emery and moved to the state capital, Lansing, where she lived for the rest of her life.

Emery believed that the promise of American liberty had been ravaged by social and economic crimes, such as prostitution, alcoholism, anarchy, business failure, and foreclosure. Ultimately, these crimes could be laid at the feet of the United States' rich and powerful elite, who only cared to maintain their wealth and power at the expense of the rest of society. Based on this set of beliefs, she joined the Greenback Labor Party and served as a Michigan delegate to the national convention of 1884. She also worked in Michigan for the Knights of Labor.

As her activism expanded, she wrote what became her seminal work, *Seven Financial Conspiracies Which Have Enslaved the American People* (1887), in which she argued that the "heartless money power" had used the U.S. political system to control the national money supply. This situation, she asserted, would lead to despotism. She maintained that these conditions could be overcome with woman suffrage, temperance, a firm government control of the money supply, a prohibition on alien ownership of land, and government ownership of national transportation and communication networks. By 1895, more than 360,000 copies of this pamphlet had been sold.

Over the next couple of years, her state and national activism expanded. The *State Republican* (Lansing) reported in 1888 that she was considering a run for state superintendent of public instruction on both the Democratic and Union Labor tickets. In 1891, she joined the People's Party and became an associate editor of the party journal, the *New Forum* (St. Louis). That same year, she attended the supreme council of the National Farmers' Alliance and Industrial Union in Indianapolis with Annie L. Diggs and Mary Elizabeth Lease. In 1892, she published *Imperialism in America*, which expanded on her earlier arguments about the "heartless money power." In this second pamphlet, she cautioned against the control of much of the United States' land by railroads and rich foreign bankers. In 1893 and 1894, Emery edited and published *The Corner Stone*, an eight-page monthly newspaper that distilled and redistributed news from other Populist papers.

While Emery was a committed Populist and Alliance member, she was also committed to temperance and woman suffrage. She asserted that when compared to the "heartless money power," alcohol had an equal power to restrict American access to freedom. Further restricting American access to freedom was the denial of equal citizenship, which debased all of society. Emery urged that Democratic conventions to include a woman suffrage plank.

In 1892, Emery was one of the six women featured in Annie L. Diggs's article for *The Arena*, "The Women in the Alliance Movement." Emery died of cancer in Lansing in 1895, leaving future income from her books first to her husband and then to Paul Vandervoort, who was president of the National Reform Press Association.

Kirstin L. Lawson

See also: Diggs, Annie L. (1853–1916); Farmers' and Laborers' Union of America (FLUA); Flower, Benjamin Orange (1858–1918); Greenback Party; Knights of Labor; Lease, Mary (1850–1933); National Reform Press Association (NRPA); People's Party; The Press and Populism; Prohibition (1919–1933); Vandervoort, Paul (1846–1902); Woman's Christian Temperance Union (WCTU)

References

Adams, Pauline, and Emma S. Thornton. *A Populist Assault: Sarah E. Van De Vort Emery on American Democracy 1862–1895.* Bowling Green, OH: Bowling Green State University Popular Press, 1982.

Postel, Charles. *The Populist Vision.* New York: Oxford University Press, 2007.

Environmentalism

Environmentalism is an ideology, a general philosophy, a science, and a social movement with concerns for the conservation and protection of the natural environment. As an ideology, it is a system of beliefs, a set of values, and a number of ideas that organize and shape perceptions of the world. As a science it is a set of empirically based hypotheses that seek to understand the world and its interrelated systems. As a social movement it is myriad activist groups around the world, small and large, that attempt to implement policies to preserve the environment. Environmentalism can take the form of a popular political party or ideas within a political system that shape policy decisions. Environmentalists seek to influence public thought or institutional and social structures about issues related to the biosphere. People who identify themselves as environmentalists sometimes also identify themselves as "greens."

The modern environmental movement has its roots in the Industrial Revolution when urbanization, the burning of fossil fuels, and waste from manufacturing sites sensitized people to pollution. Untreated human waste in large cities made people ill, and calls for reform and infrastructure became insistent. Benjamin Franklin addressed the problems of rubbish in Philadelphia as early as the 1780s. In the 1800s John Muir and Henry David Thoreau made key aesthetic and philosophical arguments for the preservation of the natural world. Muir made powerful observations about the natural environment, lobbied Congress to form Yosemite National Park and set up the Sierra Club, which was a populist organization that lobbied for protection of the natural environment and is still one of the United States' oldest and largest environmental groups.

In the twentieth century people in the United States became aware of deforestation, the demise of several species of animals, and poor land stewardship. In the early 1960s Rachel Carson's *Silent Spring* sensitized people to chemical pollutions. In the early 1970s the U.S. Congress created the Environmental Protection Agency (EPA) and passed the Endangered Species Act, which Richard Nixon signed into law in 1973.

Environmentalists commonly see structural sources in the United States as the cause of many environmental problems, such as the seemingly cozy relationship between governments and private-sector polluters. Environmentalists also critique cultural elements such as the dominant cornucopia view of nature, a constant economic growth ethic, excessive consumer culture, materialism, faith that technology will solve all environmental problems, and a belief in individualism that makes social sensitivities difficult.

Many of the goals supported by environmentalism are also associated with liberal religious groups, social justice movements, feminism, and pacifism. Environmentalists who identify themselves as "green" politically may also advocate grassroots democracy, heavy investments in human capital, investments in mass transit instead of highways, conservation, measuring well-being in quality-of-life terms instead of gross national product or the consumer price index, strong environmental protection and labor laws, full-cost accounting, a green tax shift, moral purchasing decisions, accounting reforms that would advantage small business and environmentally friendly industries, increased consumption taxes, investments in cities instead of urban sprawl, bioregionalism, and all forms of sustainability.

Environmentalism is a powerful social movement that uses protest, lobbying, activism, and education to influence policy decisions and meet conservation goals. There is tremendous diversity within the environmental movement, but common positions include sensitivity about living and working in sustainable ways. Other common concerns include deforestation, climate change, new energy sources, peak oil, chemical pollution, nuclear proliferation, genetically engineered foods, environmental justice, sustainable fishing industries, mercury in the food chain, industrial waste, nuclear waste, and air and water pollution.

Environmentalists are frequently conservative about their beliefs in technology and commonly subscribe to the "precautionary principle." That principle generally advises that it is best to avoid taking risks in areas where one does not fully understand or is unable to cope with negative outcomes. Environmentalists would, for example, warn against something like deep-sea drilling, as the costs of a disaster outweigh the good resulting from the new source of oil.

Some strands of environmentalism lend themselves to other overt political goals. Greens want to make creating a sustainable world with renewable energy a political goal. Greens critique what they see as unsustainable practices. They demand an end to subsidies and tax credits to already profitable corporations, and they call such practices "corporate welfare." Greens are frequently against the war on drugs, which they see as a war on poor people, and they also argue that the war on drugs has negative environmental consequences and erodes civil liberties. Greens generally do not believe in voluntary approaches to a cleaner environment and want a strong EPA and strong penalties to violators.

Greens are also critical of globalization when that means corporations relocating production to countries with no labor protections or environmental laws. Many greens feel global manufacturing is detrimental to the environment because it weakens social and environmental laws, weakens labor laws, strengthens global capital, and creates further stratification. They also argue that globalization is the opposite of bioregionalism and that bioregionalism is preferred.

Bioregionalism (or bioregional democracy or watershed cooperation) is the theory that social organization should be based on the bio- or ecoregion instead of a region determined by economic or manufacturing boundaries. Bioregionalism is a reform movement designed to heighten the political process for better protecting the environment on a local level for local residents. Bioregionalism stresses that social plans should be locally prioritized and approved for ensured sustainability. There needs to be regional control over natural commons and natural resources; resources should not be controlled by multinational corporations in the name of profit, efficiency, and globalization. Greens are critical of the parts of globalization that override local labor and environmental concerns or further economic policies that enable even greater division between the world's richest and poorest.

While environmentalism and the modern environmental movement could be considered a populist-driven movement, environmentalism is also experiencing a backlash. Currently, environmentalists are struggling with the signature problem of the era, climate change. Strong forces on the political right such as the Tea Party group, which was significant in the 2010 election, employ populist climate-change denial rhetoric. The Tea Party movement and other climate-change deniers argue that environmentalists are antiprogress, un-American, antiwealth, and antimankind. Despite strong evidence and near consensus of most of the world's climate scientists, climate-change deniers argue that the science of climate change is not clear enough to act upon. Climate-change deniers argue that the common man wants to "drill oil here and drill now," (or, "drill, baby, drill," as Sarah Palin famously said), and that out-of-touch elites on The Left want to tax the working class to force a new green energy system that is not needed.

Environmentalists argue that the science of climate change is clear and they are working to mobilize their base to educate and lobby. In terms of climate-change policies, the popular U.S. environmental movement seems to be at an impasse with Congress and the intransigent energy corporations that disproportionately fund their elections and profit mightily from the current polluting energy system. Now that both the environmentalist position and the pro-carbon-fuel position have taken on a populist posture, it remains to be seen if science can assist this populist debate and resolve it with intelligent policy.

John O'Sullivan

See also: Drought; Plains and Midwest, Populism in the; Populism; Progressivism; Palin, Sarah (1964–); Tea Party

References

Adams, Ian. *Political Ideology Today.* Manchester, UK: Manchester University Press, 2002.

Brown, Lester. *Plan B 4.0: Mobilizing to Save Civilization.* New York: W. W. Norton & Company, 2009.

Gyorgy, Andrew, and George D. Blackwood. *Ideologies in World Affairs.* Hoboken, NJ: John Wiley & Sons, 1975.

Kirdar, Uner, ed. *Change: Threat or Opportunity for Human Progress?* New York: United Nations Publications, 1992.

McCarthy, Deborah, and Leslie King. *Environmental Sociology: From Analysis to Action.* New York: Rowman & Littlefield Publishers, 2005.

Weinstein, Jay. *Social and Cultural Change: Social Science for a Dynamic World.* Boston: Allyn Bacon, 1997.

Eugenics

The eugenics movement came to prominence in both Europe and the United States during the late nineteenth century, at a time of massive social change. In particular, social and political tensions and discord increased due to rapid industrialization and in the United States were compounded by massive immigration. The period from 1880 to 1910 represented the height of immigration to the United States, and these latest waves of new migrants raised questions concerning the racial impact their arrival would have on the American mainstream. Eugenics provided an analysis of this perceived reproductive

English scientist Sir Francis Galton (1822–1911). Galton is the founder of eugenics and is best known for his work in anthropology and heredity. (Bettmann/Corbis)

threat and proposed a radical solution to protect the United States' existing racial mix.

The intellectual roots of eugenics rested with Sir Francis Dalton (1822–1911), a cousin of Charles Darwin and himself a fellow of the Royal Society. In 1869, ten years after Darwin's publication of the *Origin of the Species* and two years after Karl Marx's first volume of *Das Kapital*, Dalton published *Hereditary Genius*, which examined intelligence as a product of family inheritance. Essentially, Dalton's conclusions suggested that selective breeding could produce more desirable people. In 1883 he formulated the term "eugenics" to define the general process where positive natural abilities were passed, through inheritance, from one generation to the next. By studying human communities, Dalton also believed that decaying societies could be analyzed through an examination of inherited characteristics to discover how social problems became manifest.

Dalton's ideas were given a boost in the United States when in 1877 Richard Dugdale (1841–1883) published his study of the Juke family, a name given to a mentally substandard family group, resident in Upstate New York, who had produced a number of criminals and dull-witted family members. If such negative traits could be demonstrated as the product of family inheritance, then actions could be taken to limit reproduction among such peoples. It was also argued that a more careful breeding of humans might improve the races by removing negative traits, as in the selective breeding of both dogs and horses. Such beliefs soon buttressed the emerging science of eugenics, which seemed to offer a favorable method to reform mankind while eliminating the worse aspects of human suffering and social failure.

In practice the early eugenics movement created a racial hierarchy that placed the Nordic European peoples at the top with African Americans at the bottom and other races placed somewhere in between. Using this assumed formation of quality and superiority, racial prejudices could be reinforced as scientifically valid. In addition, many came to see the so-called inferior races as obstacles to the popular idea of progress. During this era, the idea of racial inferiority was extended beyond physical or mental deficiencies to embrace whole peoples, including Native

Americans and Asians, as well as all others deemed to have regressive traits. In terms of its late-nineteenth-century application, eugenics became the rationale used to explain Anglo-Saxon supremacy, a view that was promoted by several influential writers. For example, John Fiske (1842–1901) and Josiah Strong (1847–1916) saw in the concept of scientific racism a method to validate the current supremacy of Anglo-Saxon civilization as well as to justify imperial expansion.

Increasingly the nation's social ills such as poverty, disease, and violence were also examined in light of the emerging concerns over a changing racial and national makeup. The Immigration Restriction League, created in 1894, saw the arrival of so-called inferior races as the source of many current problems. Their solution was in numerical restrictions on immigrants and the use of literacy tests to restrict citizenship. These goals would later be realized in the immigration quota systems introduced in the 1920s.

Given the nationalist components that formed key sections of the Populist platform, eugenics teaching did appeal to a number of prominent Populists such as Mary E. Lease of Kansas, Texas's Bettie Gay (1836–1921), and North Carolina's Populist Senator Marion Butler, all of whom at different times exploited racial or nativist concerns. Even African American Populists, such as John B. Rayner, on occasion employed eugenics ideas when explaining the black condition in the South. Mary Lease's book *The Problem of Civilization* (1895) was in effect little more than a racist and imperialist tract that clearly promoted the superiority of the white race.

Although eugenics ideology unfolded during the height of Populism, its concepts were more extensively adopted during the Progressive Era. The eugenics model for racial improvement became entangled with the general reform impulse, and the further influx, during these years, of what was perceived as racially inferior immigrants stimulated many to combine eugenics and reform as part of the same national battle against disorder and moral turpitude.

Prominent proponents of the cause such as the cereal magnate and nutritionist John Harvey Kellogg (1852–1943) made racial improvement a goal of the utmost importance. In 1906, he organized the Race Betterment Organization and promoted the organization's ambitions through conferences held at his Battle Creek, Michigan, home. In 1910 the Eugenics Record Office was founded to argue for not only immigration control but control over marriages and the sterilization of those deemed inferior. The popularity of the movement was reflected in its extensive and positive media coverage and in its several professional associations, such as the Galton Society, created in 1918.

The movement's intellectual foundations were strengthened by a number of important academic supporters such as Charles P. Davenport (1866–1944), a Harvard-trained biologist and member of the National Academy of Sciences who became a leading advocate during the Progressive Era. After becoming director of the Cold Spring Laboratory in 1910, he helped establish the Eugenics Record Office, and his 1911 book *Heredity in Relation to Eugenics* was extremely popular and widely used for many years as a college teaching text.

In addition, there was Lothrop Stoddard (1883–1950), a Harvard-trained historian whose racial theories were outlined in his popular book, *The Rising Tide of Color against White World Supremacy* (1920), which defined the growth of nonwhite populations as a force that challenged the very existence of Western civilization. Stoddard also served on the boards of several progressive organizations such as the Birth Control League, which later evolved into Planned Parenthood.

Perhaps the most famous eugenicist of the era was Madison Grant (1865–1937), who was educated at Yale and Columbia and was a lawyer by vocation. According to Grant's racial theories, the dominant and superior Nordic European peoples were being eroded by the presence of so many inferior peoples such as those from southern and eastern Europe and the southern hemisphere. He outlined his views in his widely known *The Passing of the Great Race* (1916). Grant's influence had a great influence upon the development of the hereditary branch of American anthropology. Eugenics remained an influential force until the 1930s, when the brutality of Nazism discredited ideas of racial superiority.

Theodore W. Eversole

See also: Boas, Franz (1858–1942); Butler, Marion (1863–1938); Grant, Madison (1865–1937); Lease, Mary (1850–1933); Rayner, John (1850–1918)

References

Bashford, Alison, and Philippa Levine, eds. *The Oxford Handbook of the History of Eugenics.* New York: Oxford University Press, 2010.

Bruinius, Harry. *Better for All the World: The Secret History of Forced Sterilization and American Quest for Racial Purity.* New York: Vintage Press, 2007.

Cantrell, Gregg. *Feeding the Wolf: John B. Rayner & The Politics of Race, 1850–1918.* Wheeling, IL: Harlan-Davidson, 2001.

Gillette, Aaron. *Eugenics and the Nature-Nurture Debate in the Twentieth Century.* New York: Palgrave-Macmillian, 2007.

Stern, Alexandra. *Eugenic Nation: Faults and Frontiers of Better Breeding in Modern America.* Berkeley: University of California Press, 2005.

Evangelicalism and Populism

Evangelicalism and populism share deep historical ties. Since its development in the mid-eighteenth century, evangelical Protestantism has maintained—in greater and lesser degrees—a populist mentality, most commonly expressed in the form of antiauthoritarianism, antielitism, egalitarianism, and personal sovereignty.

Although there is some scholarly debate regarding the origins of the category, the religious beliefs and performances most closely associated with what we have come to define as evangelicalism in the United States first emerged during a period of Protestant revivalism in the mid-eighteenth century known commonly as the First Great Awakening. What distinguished early evangelicalism from other forms of Protestantism was its adherents' strong penchant for personal religious experience that was open to all and unmediated by clerical elites. For example, many evangelicals viewed the act of converting as a highly emotional yet scripted performance whereby participants wept for their past transgressions, followed by an intense period of pleading for mercy. One achieved salvation not by the verdict of a religious leader or governing body nor by formal baptism into a particular religious community. Instead, one recognized salvation in one's personal feelings of liberation from the constraints of one's sinful past. In other words, the evangelical conversion experience in the eighteenth century was, at its core, an exercise in personal sovereignty. Furthermore, most evangelicals during this time—such as the charismatic preacher George Whitefield—acknowledged that salvation was available to all who desired the experience of being born anew. Sincere repentance and impassioned faith were the only prerequisites. For the eighteenth-century revivalist and those evangelicals that would follow in the next two centuries, all had equal access to the grace of God regardless of their station in life. Whether it was in the salvific experience or in other highly emotional and personal ritual performances, eighteenth-century evangelicalism helped amplify—or for some historians, even engender—the populist sentiments of egalitarianism and antiauthoritarianism that shaped colonial dissatisfaction in prerevolutionary New England.

Evangelicalism persisted in the late eighteenth and early nineteenth centuries with the Second Great Awakening. While the First Great Awakening took place mainly in the confines of Puritan New England, this second wave of evangelical revivalism surfaced mainly along the western frontier and in other rural regions such as Upstate New York. Traveling evangelists—known as circuit riders—held protracted camp meetings where participants often responded to strong condemnatory sermons with equally strong emotional conviction. Similar to much of the scholarship on the First Great Awakening, historians often characterize this reemergence of evangelical fervor in populist terms, emphasizing the period's widespread antielitism and democratic ambiance. In his book *The Democratization of American Christianity*, Nathan Hatch famously argued that American Christianity transformed into what he terms a "mass enterprise" in the early part of the nineteenth century (1989). He suggested that the antiauthoritarianism of the Revolutionary War, coupled with the emotional revivalism of the Second Great Awakening, produced a new brand of American Christianity that subscribed to populist ideas of egalitarianism and democratic reform. While there are some noticeable shortcomings in his logic—namely that not all evangelicals were as egalitarian as he suggested, especially when it came to issues pertaining to gender and race—Hatch did demonstrate that evangelicalism in the late eighteenth and early nineteenth centuries had populist tendencies that were, in large part, responsible for its growing popularity and gradual formation as a religion that attracted many lower-class, rural Americans.

In the early twentieth century, evangelicalism took on an even more explicit populist identity. In 1906, Pentecostalism, a branch of evangelicalism, emerged in American culture as a grassroots revival that appealed to the poor and disenfranchised. Although many first-generation

Pentecostals were at least partially apolitical—arguing that all forms of human government are finite and should be abandoned in light of the impending apocalypse—most harbored strong suspicions of those in positions of authority, often castigating politicians as well as academics for their perceived willingness to partner with the forces of the antichrist. Likewise, with the rise of the more separatist Christian fundamentalism during the 1910s and 1920s, evangelicalism became even more closely aligned with a Manichean dualism that placed it in opposition to the supposed elitism of urban, liberal intellectuals. Influenced by premillennial eschatology and commonsense realism, many fundamentalists, such as the famed William Jennings Bryan, saw in American culture a moral devolution caused by the wayward—or in some cases outright insidious—reasoning of political and academic leaders. They accused those in the seats of power of being out of touch with the moral outlook of the average working citizen. Some, such as Charles Blanchard, went so far as to say that the ethical paradigms of the elites were nothing short of insanity and did not correspond with the moral codes of the sane and fair-minded populace. Like the forms of evangelicalism that emerged in prior centuries, Pentecostalism and fundamentalism formed among the lower classes, who felt not only socially displaced but also deeply embattled against those in positions of authority.

Evangelicalism emerged yet again in the latter half of the twentieth century as a populist force in American political discourse. Looking to shirk much of their fundamentalist past, many evangelicals during this time sought to recapture the egalitarian and antiauthoritarian sentiments that defined the movement in the eighteenth and nineteenth centuries. Furthermore, many of these neo-evangelicals were not content with simply criticizing those in power from a distance, as were their fundamentalist predecessors, but desired to be intimately engaged in the political process as a voice for many—though not all—in the lower and middle classes. With the presidential inauguration of Jimmy Carter (1976), an evangelical from rural Georgia, followed by the mobilization of the Moral Majority (1979) by minister Jerry Falwell, evangelical leaders in the late twentieth century began to plant themselves firmly in the political arena as a lobby on behalf of the nonelites who comprised most of their constituency. Today, the "evangelical Right," with its particular brand of conservative populism, remains a key player in the nation's political and cultural spheres. Yet at the same time, with the publication of recent works such as Michael Lindsay's *Faith in the Halls of Power: How Evangelicals Joined the American Elite* (2007) and Jeff Sharlet's highly publicized book entitled *The Family: The Secret Fundamentalism at the Heart of American Power* (2008), many are beginning to suggest that evangelicalism is transitioning from being a populist to a politically elite religious community.

Questions over the qualities of contemporary American evangelicalism do not overshadow its strong populist past. Since its initial emergence in the First Great Awakening, evangelicalism has maintained, more or less, a penchant for antiauthoritarianism, antielitism, and egalitarianism, while flourishing among those in the lower classes by providing them not only with a sense of hope for a better tomorrow but with feelings of personal sovereignty and empowerment in their everyday lives.

Jonathan W. Olson

See also: Bryan, William Jennings (1860–1925); Carter, James Earl "Jimmy" (1924–); "The Elite"; Moody, Dwight (1837–1899); Palin, Sarah (1964–); Socialism, Christian; Sunday, Billy (1862–1935)

References

Anderson, Robert Mapes. *Vision of the Disinherited: The Making of American Pentecostalism.* Peabody, MA: Hendrickson, 1979.

Boles, John. *The Great Revival: Beginnings of the Bible Belt.* Lexington: University of Kentucky Press, 1972.

Hart, D.G. *That Old-Time Religion in Modern America: Evangelical Protestantism in the Twentieth Century.* Chicago: Ivan R. Dee, 2002.

Hatch, Nathan. *The Democratization of American Christianity.* New Haven, CT: Yale University Press, 1989.

Lindsay, Michael. *Faith in the Halls of Power: How Evangelicals Joined the American Elite.* New York: Oxford University Press, 2007.

Marsden, George. *Fundamentalism and American Culture.* 2nd Edition. New York: Oxford University Press, 2006.

Sharlet, Jeff. *The Family: The Secret Fundamentalism at the Heart of American Power.* New York: Harper, 2008.

Expositions. *See* Trans-Mississippi Exposition (1898); World's Industrial and Cotton Centennial Exposition (1884–1885)

F

Farmers' Alliance

The Farmers' Alliance movement emerged out of the experience of farmers in the Patrons of Husbandry, a popular social and financial alternative to farmers' clubs in the late nineteenth century, during a period of national focus on urbanization and industrialization. Because the Patrons, also known as Grangers, disavowed political activity officially, the Farmers' Alliance was born out of the need for farmers to act politically to achieve their goals, which included greater federal oversight of the railroads and telegraph services, a larger money supply to help them pay loans, a federal subtreasury to make loans to farmers, the direct election of U.S. senators, a graduated income tax, and direct democracy, especially access to the referendum and initiative. The Farmers' Alliance was successful on the local level but eventually morphed into the People's Party in the 1890s.

Local Granges, originally conceived by Oliver Hudson Kelley in 1864, were the roots of the Farmers' Alliance. He had lived on a farm in Minnesota and had worked for the U.S. Department of Agriculture. Kelley envisioned a national organization that could combine the education provided by agricultural societies with the camaraderie and elaborate ceremonies of the Masons.

The prospect of establishing cooperatives for the purchasing and marketing of crops and farm equipment attracted farmers to the Granges. By 1873, Grangers were acquiring materials at wholesale costs, cutting out the hated "middleman," who seemed to hike prices beyond fair value for working farmers. They even dabbled in manufacturing their own farm machinery, although these efforts failed for various reasons, hampering their efforts. Granges usually had written constitutions with specifically outlined requirements for members. The system featured a hierarchy of local, county, state, and national associations. It was supposed to be a secret society, which were in fashion in the period. There was a hierarchy of members within the Grange system, and, like the Masons, members worked to reach various levels or degrees. The Grangers were able to maintain their educational and social aspects as intended, but as time passed, too many members crept into politics.

Inevitably, Grangers were unable to stay out of local politics. Granger laws in Iowa, Illinois, Minnesota, and Wisconsin regulated railroads and grain elevators. In the South, Grangers looked to overthrow Reconstruction. Unlike many of the northern Grangers, these were not just yeoman farmers but planters, who had a stake in taking back local politics.

The Farmers' Alliance emerged in this environment in 1877. The Northern Alliance, created by farm editor Milton George, spread from western New York to Chicago by 1880. Primarily due to the fact that there were no dues, by 1881 the National Farmers' Alliance boasted 24,500 members. The majority of the members came from Kansas and Nebraska, and thus Alliance activity was centered in the northern Plains by 1886. The same broad organization was occurring across the South, especially in Texas, which had been home to 40,000 Grangers.

In Texas, the Lampasas County Farmers' Alliance surged into politics by supporting the Greenback Party in 1880. The Greenback ticket for county office that year included two Alliance members. The Alliance came under attack by those who thought it was home to anarchists and communists. In response, the Alliance professed only including people thought to be of good character, who were of the "producing class" (McMath 70). Oddly, this translated into school teachers and ministers, but not African American farmers.

Farmers' Alliances came and went across the South in the early 1880s, but by 1886, the Alliance had found strength across northern Texas and was looking to expand into the Plains. This was partially due to the growth of railroads across the region, which drew farmers into commercial cotton production. In January 1884, S. O. Dawes became a traveling lecturer and traversed the South, promoting the Alliance. Like the Granges, Alliances in Texas had formed cooperatives for buying and selling supplies for the commercialization of cotton, flour, and wheat.

Alliance men then joined with the Knights of Labor during 1885 and 1886 to strike against the network of railroads controlled by Jay Gould, including the Union Pacific, which attempted to fire workers and raise prices. In March 1885 the cooperation of the Alliance and the Knights forced Gould's corporation to rehire workers and raise wages at Sedalia, Missouri. Workers were sometimes members of their local chapters of the Knights of Labor and the Farmers' Alliance at the same time.

In 1886, Texas Alliance members joined forces with a Louisiana Alliance, forming the National Farmers' Alliance and Cooperative Union. It created an exchange by which it could forgo the middleman on crop sales. Its president, C. W. Macune, organized a cotton crop sale directly to England and New England in 1887. The exchange did not last long, as capital was in short supply. But the Alliance was making more waves by mobilizing cotton farmers across the South to fight back against low prices. By the end of 1887 the Alliance was well established across North Carolina, Mississippi, Alabama, and Georgia.

Alliance members in the South were primarily operators of mid-sized properties. Tenants and planters did not join as often as these owners who fell between the two. In addition, African Americans were not allowed in the Alliance, but they began their own organizations, including a Colored Farmers' Alliance. This group also preached economic and political cooperation. It gained its leadership from preachers and community leaders. The all-white National Farmers' Alliance and Co-operative Union encouraged its members to open their cooperatives to African American Alliances, and many answered the call because making money and saving money were the primary objectives of Alliances.

The Texas Alliance met in St. Louis on December 3, 1889, and named itself the National Farmers' Alliance and Industrial Union (NFAIU). This Alliance managed to bring two of the most powerful alliances, those of Kansas and the Dakotas, under its fold, thus creating the largest Alliance in the country. In St. Louis the NFAIU adopted a platform that included public ownership of railroads and federal subtreasuries that would provide farmers with low-cost loans based on their crops. Some even hoped to eliminate banks, the futures market, commission merchants, and private warehousemen. When the annual meeting of the NFAIU convened in Ocala, Florida, in the next year, it added the direct election of U.S. senators and a graduated income tax to its platform.

The NFAIU leadership wanted the group to be a national political force and convened in Omaha in January 1891 to make plans to form a national party, which became the People's Party, better known as the Populists. The People's Party had success in some Alliance strongholds such as Kansas but could not bring the South and the East into the fold; thus it consolidated its efforts in the presidential election of 1896 with those of the Democratic Party to back William Jennings Bryan.

Bryan lost the election, but many of the interests of the Farmers' Alliances lived on, such as the direct election of U.S. senators (the Sixteenth Amendment), the graduated income tax (the Seventeenth Amendment), and the subtreasury plans. In addition, the racism of the Alliance and the sexism of the Alliance remained long into the twentieth century. While the Alliance welcomed cooperation with African American Alliances, it never supported integration. Chinese exclusion planks existed in the bylaws of Western Alliances. Further, while at least one-fourth of Alliance members in the United States were women, woman suffrage was never an Alliance plank.

Raymond Nolan

See also: African Americans and Populism; Alliance; Bryan, William Jennings (1860–1925); Colored Farmers' Alliance (CFA); Democratic Party; George, Milton (1833–unknown); Granger Movement; Greenback Party; Illinois Woman's Alliance (IWA); Kelley, Oliver Hudson (1826–1913); Knights of Labor; Macune, Dr. C.W. (1851–1940); National Woman's Alliance; Northern Alliance; Ocala Convention of 1892; People's Party; Progressivism; Subtreasury Plan; Texas, Populism in; Union Pacific Railroad; Western Alliance; World's Industrial and Cotton Centennial Exposition (1884–1885)

References

McMath, Robert C., Jr. *American Populism: A Social History, 1877–1898*. New York: Hill and Wang, 1992.

McMath, Robert C., Jr. *Populist Vanguard: A History of the Southern Farmers' Alliance*. Chapel Hill: University of North Carolina Press, 2010.

Trachtenberg, Alan. *The Incorporation of America: Culture and Society in the Gilded*

Age. 2nd Ed. New York: Hill and Wang, 2007.

Wiebe, Robert H. *The Search for Order, 1877–1920*. New York: Hill and Wang, 1967.

Farmers' and Laborers' Union of America (FLUA)

The Farmers' and Laborers' Union of America was among the most significant and influential organizations to emerge from the agrarian movements in the United States during the nineteenth century. The union was founded in 1889 when the National Farmers' Union and Cooperative Union merged with the Agricultural Wheel to form the National Farmers' and Laborers' Union of America. Their first meetings were held in December of that year in St. Louis. The FLUA brought together farmers' and laborers' coalitions from both the North and the South. The union asserted the need for unity among farmers, yeoman laborers, and skilled tradesmen, to challenge the authority and power of the corporate monopolies and so-called "combines." They called for the end of laws that favored capital over labor. They also called for free education for all. Yet, reactively, they also demanded an end to the movement of migrant labor into the United States.

Social suffering arose from the great industrial combines and corporate conglomerates and their close associations with political representatives who manipulated legislation and laws to meet the needs of corporations. The union sought the abolition of national banks and monopolies. The basis for their movement was education and cooperation. As its leaders asserted during their founding convention, the opposition to power of economic and political elites could only be founded upon direct cooperation among direct producers:

> The advancement of civilization, the development of the natural resources of our country, the promotion and perpetuation of our free institutions, the stability, power and influence of our republican system of government, the creation and successful operation of all our gigantic enterprises, which gives strength and influence to government, depends largely, if not wholly, upon the intelligent application of the true principles of co-operation. The most, if not every failure of all the various business efforts of our order, is due to a want of a proper understanding and a strict adherence to the business principles of co-operation.
>
> It is the foundation that underlies the whole superstructure of our noble order, and a strict adherence to its principles will lead the membership to a degree of prosperity that shall gladden the hearts of all, and bring joy and contentment around the family circle.
>
> I would recommend that you spare no effort in providing the necessary facilities for the better education of the membership in these great principles (National Farmers' Alliance and Industrial Union).

Against the cooperation of free producers, the FLUA counterpoised the destructive powers of the monopolies. In particular, the union identified the monopolization of finance as the basis from which all other monopolies, trusts, and oppressive institutions emerged and consolidated their power and privilege. Monopoly control of finances was identified as the source of unemployment (as entrepreneurs lacked the capital to grow small businesses and farmers the capacity to maintain farms) as well as the reduced prices of workers' and farmers' products. It was also identified as the support for the mortgages on homes and farms under which workers and farmers were burdened. The monopoly control of finance was viewed as responsible for bankruptcy among those forced to borrow and for the resulting economic crises and depressions.

Union members believed that land must belong to those who in some way work the soil or who produce goods directly from it. This is a social vision founded on the yeoman, or free laborer, who associates with others in craft rather than mass industrial, production. In the view of FLUA members, those who own and control their own land and homes will give more care to society, and to its upkeep and safeguarding, than will those who are dispossessed or those who are absentee landlords with no direct connection to the land or homes they control. Those civilizations with concentrated land ownership were destined to decline. In some cases these perspectives drifted into nativism and called to end or prohibit foreign ownership of land in the United States.

The union was not opposed to private business or corporate ownership per se. Indeed, members affirmed what in their view were rights to ownership and what they viewed as legitimate profit. What concerned them was the concentration of ownership and power and the illegitimate profit secured in part through government regulations such as those that restricted labor organizing, as in unions and farmers' associations. Similarly they criticized government grants that allowed corporations to concentrate wealth and tax policies that rewarded larger corporations rather than small business owners, farmers, and workers. Most of all, they opposed the state-capital relationships that facilitated monopolization and the rising power of corporations, as in the railroad companies, to determine how goods and services would be distributed.

The union called for the easing of mortgages and for financial support for agricultural and industrial workers. Part of this involved calls for monetary reforms that would allow a sufficient volume of circulating medium to enable people to carry out transactions on a cash basis, freeing people from the restraints and burdens of credit. A revised monetary policy, which would include free silver, should be set according to the needs of farmers and industrial workers rather than those of speculators and financial capital. The union leaders also advocated against monopoly accumulation of land. Prosperous and vital societies, they argued, were founded upon widespread land ownership involving most of the population. Through monopolization, people lost their farms, homes, and land, leaving them vulnerable to exploitation by monopoly firms. For the FLUA, in the United States, monopolization meant that fertile and productive lands that might be used for agriculture or productive labor were controlled by railroads and corporations whose first concern is profit.

Initially the union asserted a nonpartisan character aligned with and supportive of no specific political party. The primary concern was popular education on issues of economy and the mobilization of farmers and laborers to press their specific demands directly. Indeed, one of the problems facing farmers and laborers was viewed as their capture within mechanisms of "machine politicians," or party politics, which neglected farmers' and workers' own interests and rendered them as part of a political mass to be represented.

Attempts to unite with the Knights of Labor and the Colored Farmers' Alliance in a broad unified movement proved unsuccessful. By 1889 the union had folded itself into the People's Party and fielded national candidates for the elections of 1892. While its economic successes were largely local and short-lived, the FLUA did help to develop social movement experiences and cooperative resources among people in poor rural communities.

Jeffrey Shantz

See also: African Americans and Populism; Agricultural Wheel; Colored Farmers' Alliance (CFA); Cooperative Commonwealth; Gilded Age; Gold Standard/Free Silver; Knights of Labor; People's Party; Producerism

References

Drew, Frank M. "The Present Farmers' Movement." *Political Science Quarterly* 6 (2): 282–310.

Lester, Connie. *Up from the Mudsills of Hell: The Farmers' Alliance, Populism, and Progressive Agriculture in Tennessee, 1870–1915.* Athens: University of Georgia Press, 2006.

National Farmers' Alliance and Industrial Union. *National Farmers' Alliance and Industrial Union. Proceedings of the Farmers and Laborers Union of America, at St. Louis, Mo., December 3–7, 1889.* Washington, DC: The National Economist Print, 1889.

Saloutos, Theodore. *Farmers Movements in the South 1865–1933.* Lincoln: University of Nebraska Press, 1964.

Farmers' Clubs

Farmers' Clubs developed during the mid-1800s, with later champions like Joseph B. Killebrew in Tennessee and Leonidas Lafayette Polk in North Carolina. Both men were journalists and used their publications to promote their ideas on rural collectivism and agricultural education. Farmers' Clubs laid the groundwork for agrarian reform societies such as the Grange, the Agricultural Wheel, and the Farmers' Alliance.

Early Farmers' Clubs sprang up in Illinois as evidenced by a convention of farmers in 1858 tasked with developing a collective movement that would advocate for farmers' concerns. After the Civil War, additional clubs were organized and gathered in Illinois for annual conventions. In 1873, delegates from local clubs and Granges organized into the Illinois State Farmers' Association to promote the welfare of farmers. The association's mission, however, eventually became fractured between the more passive clubs and the more active Grange groups. Also in 1873 Kansas held a farmers' convention with 250 delegates of clubs and Granges concerned with price control and taxation reform. Additional conventions of Farmers' Clubs were held in Wisconsin, Missouri, and Indiana.

Around the same time Joseph Buckner Killebrew was hired by Nashville's *Union and American* to travel through Tennessee organizing Farmers' Clubs and simultaneously selling subscriptions to the paper. Killebrew promoted education and scientific agriculture while encouraging social reform through collective organization. Killebrew grew in prominence and was appointed to be the state's first commissioner of agriculture, immigration, statistics, and mines. In 1871, Nashville hosted the first meeting of the National Agricultural Congress of delegates from 11 states and 40 agricultural and mechanical associations.

North Carolina farmer, entrepreneur, and editor Leonidas Lafayette Polk also utilized the concept of Farmers' Clubs as grassroots societies, encouraging the integration of science into agricultural education. Polk promoted the clubs in his newspaper, the *Progressive Farmer.* Polk's vision for Farmers' Clubs was to develop a collective community while educating farmers on the latest scientific and agricultural techniques. He also urged members to lobby legislators for reform so that farmers could achieve the same economic success as their counterparts in industry and manufacturing. The clubs often met in schools, and they gained popularity during through the 1880s. Polk's commitment to education was instrumental in developing Raleigh's College of Agriculture and Mechanic Arts, known today as North Carolina State University.

By the late 1880s, farmers became less interested in education and agricultural science and more concerned with realizing fundamental economic change. Farmers' Clubs fell out of favor as their members turned to more politically active organizations such as the Farmers' Alliance in the hopes of seeing real legislative social and economic reform.

Carla W. Garner

See also: Agricultural Newspapers and Farmer Unrest; Agricultural Wheel; Granger Movement; Polk, Leonidas L. (1937–1892); The Press and Populism

References

Ayers, Edward L. *The Promise of the New South: Life after Reconstruction.* New York: Oxford University Press, 1992.

Buck, Solon J. *The Granger Movement: A Study of Agricultural Organization and Its Political, Economic and Social Manifestations, 1870–1880.* Lincoln: University of Nebraska Press, 1963.

Hunt, James Logan. *Marion Butler and American Populism.* Chapel Hill: University of North Carolina Press, 2003.

Lester, Connie L. *Up from the Mudsills of Hell: The Farmers' Alliance, Populism, and Progressive Agriculture in Tennessee, 1870–1915.* Athens: University of Georgia Press, 2006.

Postel, Charles. *The Populist Vision.* New York: Oxford University Press, 2007.

Farmers' Mutual Benefit Association (FMBA)

The Farmers' Mutual Benefit Association was an organization formed in Illinois by farmers in the early 1880s. As first constituted, its goals and purposes were primarily economic in nature—to get farmers the best possible prices for their crops. Thanks to adhering strictly to its central mission, an appropriate organizational structure, and good recruiting techniques, the organization enjoyed steady and manageable growth throughout the 1880s. It began to decline in 1890 when it joined the People's Party, thus betraying its own core mission and straying into partisan politics.

The Populist movement was the product of farmers joining together for economic improvement. One of the various groups formed for such purposes was the Farmers' Mutual Benefit Association (FMBA) of Illinois. The FMBA is less well known than many of the other groups that formed the Populist coalition, but, in some important ways, it was more successful than some of its better-known peers.

The FMBA was formed in the fall of 1883 by five farmers from Vienna, Illinois (in Johnson County). These men began to suspect, correctly, that their immediate buyer, the man who would purchase their crops for resale in the St. Louis market, was cheating them. By arranging for transportation to and sale in St. Louis themselves not only could the farmers get a better price for their crops prior to shipping but they were able to make more money by cutting out the middle man. Word about the five farmers' achievement spread, and the arrangement, formalized as the Farmers' Mutual Benefit Association, spread rapidly. By winter of 1883, just a few months after its original founding, the FMBA developed a formal structure, membership badges, and highly formal initiation rituals, as its members believed the organization had to remain a secret. The reasons why are not specified by commentators but can be imagined, including the similarity of this organization to Grange cooperatives.

The FMBA's structure was highly centralized. Farmers wanting to establish new locals had to petition a central governing body, usually referred to by historians as the general assembly (whether or not that was the body's actual name, however, is not specified). The FMBA grew steadily and remained true to its central, formative mission. Recruitment was mostly by word of mouth, and by 1886 it had about 2,000 members.

However, from the spring to fall of 1887, the FMBA appears to have decided that it needed to expand more rapidly. It hired Frank G. Blood as a professional recruiter, wrote a new constitution, and devised a new structure that incorporated three levels of administration (local, county, and central). The general assembly, which was appointed by the county-level organizations, retained all decision-making power for the organization. Three officers (president, vice president, and treasurer) and a five-member board of trustees were elected by the general assembly at its meetings, which were held once per year.

The FMBA also realized that it needed a reliable, formalized funding stream. The general assembly began to collect annual charter fees from the county and local chapters. Individual members paid dues to the general assembly and to the county and local chapters and also paid initiation fees upon their induction into the FMBA.

With an appropriate administrative structure, impressive results, and Frank Blood on its side, the FMBA grew. By October 1887 it had 389 locals and about 15,000 members (this was the last year reliable membership numbers are available). By November 1888, it had 942 locals and had spread beyond Illinois.

The FMBA had an official journal, known as *The Binder*. Frank Blood and an early member named A. M. Palmer fought over who ran the organization. Frank Blood opposed the 1887 reorganization of the FMBA, even though the same impulse that led to that reorganization also led to his being hired, and he used his control over *The Binder* to voice his opposition.

The reorganization brought trustee John P. Stelle to the forefront. He had been crippled by a childhood disease and had no formal education until the age of 13. However, he took to reading and writing extremely well. Stelle became secretary of the FMBA. In April 1888, at the request of the board of trustees, he started a new FMBA journal titled *Progressive Farmer*. It was wildly successful from the outset and absorbed *The Binder* by the fall of 1888.

The middle to late 1880s were particularly hard for farmers, following a contrastingly good economic year in 1883. Historians unambiguously agree that the FMBA and similar organizations benefited mightily from hard times. By November 1889, the FMBA had 2,181 locals, and 4,947 locals by November 1890. Indiana was now rivaling Illinois in terms of numbers of locals and importance to the organization. Indiana's increasing importance to the FMBA was reflected in the 1890 election of an Indianan, William J. Stillwell, as its president. Also that year, the FMBA members added another level of organization (state) to prevent the general assembly from becoming too large. The structure now included local, county, and state chapters as well as the general assembly.

The FMBA was invited into the Farmers' Alliance (referring to the Southern Alliance) as early as 1888. In 1889 the FMBA decided it was better off on its own. Frank Blood was sent to a conference in St. Louis to represent the FMBA and tell the Alliance its overtures were being rejected. The FMBA's membership in what was envisioned as a nationwide alliance of farmers was highly sought, presumably because of its great success. The delegates to the conference were doubtless disappointed by the FMBA's decision. However, while they could not lure the FMBA, they could lure Frank Blood. Blood betrayed the FMBA and agreed to lead the Southern Alliance in Illinois (Scott). Blood, who was hired by the FMBA for his skills at organizing and recruiting members, did rather well for the Alliance.

However, the FMBA's undoing ultimately proved not to be competition, even from Frank Blood and the Southern Alliance. In 1890 it formally joined the People's Party and failed at getting the majority of its membership to go along. Thus began its decline.

The last significant actions of the FMBA occurred in 1891, when three Illinois state senators it influenced played a key role in appointing a U.S. senator, and in 1895, when the FMBA was a signatory to a political platform that incorporated putting U.S. currency on a unified silver-gold standard.

The FMBA's political platform had much in common with other, similar farmers' groups of its day. Farmers, the argument went, were central to American life and to American prosperity. Yet they were stereotyped and oppressed by the broader culture and the broader political system and did not fully benefit from the prosperity to which they contributed so much. The concentration of wealth was, as the argument went, a major source of the farmers' distress. The rich elite owned the politicians and also charged farmers excessively for materials while devaluing their crops. Thus the only way to counteract these monied elites was to organize for political, social, or economic support.

Historians have documented that the FMBA members benefited from mixing the techniques of a labor organization with those of a business organization. They engaged in cooperative buying and selling similar to a business organization (just as Grangers had tried to do before them), but they also, like labor unions, conducted educational programs and emphasized the power of unity and collective action. The FMBA was, however, considerably less of a social organization than unions or the Grange. Among other things the FMBA purposefully excluded women, central to social life on farms, from its membership, which was consistent with gendered ideas about business and economics in the period.

Participation in partisan politics muddled the social and economic purposes of groups such as the Grange and the Alliances, which often led to their decline. The FMBA had been formed originally to do solely what its name implied, to bring economic benefits to the farmers within its membership, and initially had no political ambitions. It was perhaps unsurprising that the organization dwindled, and eventually died, when it strayed from its economic focus. Attempting to hitch its wagon to a particular political party, almost by definition, proved fatal to the FMBA's very reason for existence. There was, ultimately, no party label on the price of grain.

Steven D. Koczak

See also: Gold Standard/Free Silver; Granger Movement; People's Party; *Progressive Farmer*; Rochdale Plan; Farmers' Alliances; South, Populism in the Subtreasury Plan

References

Destler, Chester. "Consummation of a Labor-Populist Alliance." *Mississippi Valley Historical Review* 27 (4): 589–602.

Drew, Frank. "The Present Farmers' Movement." *Political Science Quarterly* 6 (2): 282–310.

Durden, Robert. *The Climax of Populism: The Election of 1896*. Lexington: University of Kentucky Press, 1965.

Haynes, Fred. "The Collapse of the Farmer-Labor Bloc." *Social Forces* 4 (1): 148–156.

Hicks, John. *The Populist Revolt: History of the Farmers' Alliance and the People's Party*. Minneapolis: University of Minnesota Press, 1931.

Hicks, John. "The Sub-Treasury: A Forgotten Plan for the Relief of Agriculture." *Mississippi Valley Historical Review* 15 (3): 355–373.

Peffer, William. *Populism, Its Rise and Fall*. Lawrence: University Press of Kansas, 1992.

Scott, Roy V. "The Rise of the Farmers' Mutual Benefit Association in Illinois, 1883–1891." *Agricultural History* 32 (1): 44–56.

Farmers' Transportation Convention

Depending upon one's point of view, the Farmers' Transportation Convention was either a one-time event in Chicago in 1880 or a series of events that occurred almost annually for several years in that decade. Whichever way it is defined, the Farmers' Transportation Conventions were important in the farmers' fights against the railroads and in the formation and implementation of the Northern Alliance. Annual Farmers' Transportation Conventions were held from 1880 to 1883, were skipped in 1884 and 1885, and were held again in 1886 and 1887. The first convention was, as the name implied, concerned primarily with the issue of transportation, which mostly referred to the railroad fees paid by farmers. The other conventions had broader concerns. At the 1887 convention, the Farmers' Alliance members adopted a more radical, system-challenging posture than it had previously. After the 1887 convention, the nexus of the Farmers' Alliance's story shifted from the conventions to the activities of the Alliance, as an organization, in and of itself.

In the 1880s, the issue of transportation of goods to market was a central business concern of farming. Farmers mostly had to rely on the railroads, and the railroads' fees could, and often did, eat into farmers' profit margins. Sometimes, railroad fees could turn an acceptable year economically into a marginal one and a marginal year into a bad one. Addressing farmers' difficulties with the railroads was central to the mission of Milton George, an Illinois-based farmer turned newspaperman who, in the pages of his newspaper, the *Western Rural*, raged against the railroads. The railroads, he wrote, were literally starving farmers to death.

On April 15, 1880, George formed the Farmers' Alliance in Cook County, Illinois. George's Alliance is today often referred to as the Northern Alliance to distinguish it from other, similarly named groups, most particularly one that is referred to as the Southern Alliance.

George was aware of the existence of other Farmers' Alliances or similar groups and wished to see them coalesce in a nationwide farmers' advocacy group. Though George appears to have had broader goals in mind for this nationwide coalition, transportation was clearly one of the most important business issues of the day for farmers, and thus it was around that issue that he called a convention, called the Farmers' Transportation Convention, in Chicago on October 14, 1880.

The convention adopted a series of long resolutions. The railroads were called a "virtual monopoly" and was "defiant of all existing law," the convention attendees attested. Further, the railroads were called "oppressive" to both farmers and consumers and "corrupting to our [America's] politics." The convention called upon Congress to control railroads. At this point, these men referred to controlling through laws and regulations, not direct control in the sense of nationalization of the railroads. Nationalization would be proposed at a later convention, however. The two major political parties were called upon to nominate candidates more friendly to farmers. The convention also drew up a constitution and, to a degree, achieved George's dream of a nationwide, or at least a regional, coalition of farmers' groups. The Alliance's concerns, and hence that of the first Farmers' Transportation Convention, thus went beyond the railroads and transportation.

George was thrilled with the success of the convention, and at some point it was decided, presumably by the conventioneers themselves, that the convention would be an annual event. The next one was also to be held in Chicago. It began on October 5, 1881. The third annual convention on October 4, 1882, was held in St. Louis, Missouri.

The first convention and the formation of the Farmers' Alliance occurred in the midst of hard times for farmers. It was, perhaps, inevitable that the organization itself, and the convention series with which it was associated, would rise with the failures of farmers and fall with their successes. The year 1883 was a much better year for farmers than were the previous three, and hence the 1883 convention was sparsely attended. There was no convention held at all in 1884 and 1885, and also in 1885 George stopped putting Alliance news in his newspaper. In contrast, 1884 and 1885 were bad years for farmers, and in 1886, after the harshness of the previous two years had sunk in, the conventions started being held again. By the October 1887 convention, the Alliance and the convention itself had recovered some of their former glory.

At the 1887 convention, the Alliance drew up a new constitution and sought a greater degree of formalization. It set up state and local affiliate organizations and a dues-paying structure. Hitherto, the Alliance had been almost exclusively funded through Milton George's largesse. The convention adopted a new, more radical platform. It now advocated government ownership, as opposed to merely control, of the railroads. The Alliance's calls for government ownership and operation of the railroads would only get stronger from this point onward. It also adopted the now-infamous "free silver" rallying cry of the Populists and made overtures to the Knights of Labor, a more-or-less radical labor group that happened to holds its own convention nearby. The nexus of the story of the Farmers' Alliance appears to shift dramatically from the Farmers' Transportation Convention(s) to the Alliance itself after this final meeting.

Steven D. Koczak

See also: George, Milton; Gold Standard/Free Silver; Knights of Labor; Northern Alliance; The Press and Populism; Railroad Regulation; Railroads; *Western Rural*

References

Destler, Chester. "Consummation of a Labor-Populist Alliance." *Mississippi Valley Historical Review* 27 (4): 589–602.

Drew, Frank. "The Present Farmers' Movement." *Political Science Quarterly* 6 (2): 282–310.

Haynes, Fred. "The Collapse of the Farmer-Labor Bloc." *Social Forces* 4 (1): 148–156.

Hicks, John. *The Populist Revolt: History of the Farmers' Alliance and the People's Party*. Minneapolis: University of Minnesota Press, 1931.

Hicks, John. "The Sub-Treasury: A Forgotten Plan for the Relief of Agriculture." *Mississippi Valley Historical Review* 15 (3): 355–373.

Palmer, Bruce. *"Man over Money": The Southern Populist Critique of American Capitalism.* Chapel Hill: University of North Carolina Press, 1980.

The Farmer's Wife

The Farmer's Wife, a reformist newspaper dedicated to giving rural women activists a voice in their quest for political and governmental reform, became the official paper of the National Woman's Alliance after its organization in 1891. The brainchild of Populists I. W. and Emma Pack, *The Farmer's Wife*, with its motto, "Equal Rights to All, Special Privileges to None," came into being when the Packs merged their individual publishing efforts in 1890 at Topeka, Kansas. Intended both to promote Farmers' Alliance causes and improve the quality of life for rural women, the editors of *The Farmer's Wife* initially provided a delicate balance between the New Womanhood ideas promoted by the women's movement of the mid to late nineteenth century and the traditional values and ideals held by most rural Kansas women. To accomplish this, the paper included sections dedicated to fashion, household items, agriculture, and children, in addition to those dealing with women's responsibilities and duties, especially the problems they faced in accomplishing them, their work in the National Woman's Alliance and other organizations, and the advancement of women and women's rights. *The Farmer's Wife* encouraged its readership to become educated on the political and business issues directly affecting them and provided articles on women's successes in nontraditional pursuits, such as business ownership and medicine.

Within a short period, and certainly after the formation of the National Woman's Alliance in 1891, the number of articles dealing with woman suffrage increased and the editors allowed a more aggressive tone in the paper. Arguments in favor of suffrage became more direct, citing the vote as a woman's duty and responsibility, and, at least where the casting of that vote was concerned, as a natural right. Successes in other states concerning women's rights became more prominent, and *The Farmer's Wife* provided detailed reports when Wyoming entered the Union in 1890 with full suffrage, the first state to do so; in 1893 when the state of Colorado passed a woman suffrage amendment; and in 1892 when Populist Mary E. Lease considered announcing her candidacy for the U.S. Senate seat from Kansas. The paper paid particular attention to the ways in which woman suffrage could benefit entire communities, citing the certainty of passage of prohibition laws, election of ethical and honest candidates, and passage of the types of legislation most beneficial to children and families. Popular within Kansas and boasting out-of-state subscriptions as well, the paper's success suffered following the 1892 Populist Party National Convention and the decision to remove woman suffrage and prohibition from the platform. Following the November 1894 election, which failed to produce a woman suffrage amendment to the Kansas Constitution, and despite the concerted efforts of its editors, *The Farmer's Wife* ceased publication.

Brenda Jackson-Abernathy

See also: Gilded Age; Kansas, Populism in; Lease, Mary (1850–1933); National Woman's Alliance; Pack, Emma (1850–1910); The Press and Populism; Progressivism

References

Endres, Kathleen L., and Therese L. Lueck. *Women's Periodicals in the United States: Social and Political Issues.* Westport, CT: Greenwood Publishing Group, 1996.

Federal Farm Board (FFB)

The Federal Farm Board (FFB) was established in June 1929 and intended to provide direct government assistance for agriculture. The FFB's $500 million budget was larger than any previous program authorized for a nondefense expenditure. Many Americans were still farmers, many of whom had been hard hit economically since the end of World War I. FFB supporters sought to strengthen farmer cooperatives and develop price stabilization systems. Years of populist discontent with government currency decisions, northeastern banking dominance, and poor credit terms for farmers inspired federal leaders to take an active role in agricultural affairs.

The timing of the FFB was terrible. The Smoot-Hawley Tariff of June 1930 carried import duties to highs unseen since 1828 (known as the "Tariff of Abominations"), causing severe damage to exports. Competitive traders responded in kind and created burdensome tariffs on goods that U.S. firms planned to export or sought other trading partners. In the year after Smoot-Hawley was enacted, U.S. foreign trade decreased more than 50 percent. In response to the burgeoning crisis the FFB stepped up loans to farmers and purchases of farm supplies, hoping to protect American goods for future exports when market timing was ideal. Federal credit banks were liberal with loans to agricultural cooperatives so farmers could time their crop releases.

The Grain Stabilization Corporation was established and began purchasing wheat. Initially, U.S. prices were boosted and FFB officials calculated an upcoming world wheat shortage would cause importing nations to rely heavily on U.S. sources. Canadian and Argentinean competitors grew their export businesses significantly during this period; buyers did not wait for the United States to make the surplus available.

When Smoot-Hawley was proposed, 1,028 economists signed a petition asking President Hoover to veto the legislation. Hoover opposed the bill but yielded to influential party and business leaders. The economists were correct, and Hoover's administration was held accountable. Managing agricultural inventory amid new trade barriers was an unmitigated disaster. Because every grain dealer in the world knew the United States would eventually dump its surplus on the market, prices dropped precipitously. The year 1931 was the first since the Civil War that consumption of foreign-grown cotton exceeded that of American cotton. Instead of shielding farmers from low worldwide market prices, protectionist programs and government-managed disbursements made American farmers more vulnerable to market shifts.

Corporations set up under the Farm Board lost $345 million in futile efforts to buy up surpluses. Larger inventories caused prices to fall further. In mid-1931 they ceased buying as prices continued to slide. In 1919 wheat fetched $2.16 per bushel; in 1932 it was 38 cents. Cotton dropped from 41.75 cents per pound in 1919 to preharvest 1932 rates of 4.6 cents. FFB officials received severe criticism. After the FFB asked southern farmers to destroy every third row of cotton, some southern politicians recommended that farmers instead destroy every third member of the FFB.

In response, Hoover turned to populist rhetoric, accusing speculators of depriving farmers of income and undermining public confidence by manipulating the market. Other critics called short-sellers "hyenas" and "crocodiles." Chicago Board of Trade officials countered that high yields, market management by the FFB, and reduced consumption were all to blame for price drops. Reaction to the economic catastrophe was severe. In Nebraska, farmers burned corn to keep warm. In Iowa, the former head of the state's Farmers' Union formed the militant Farmers' Holiday Association, which in 1932 called a farmers' strike and forcibly blocked deliveries of produce. Dairy producers dumped milk in ditches. Withholding products from the market was a primary form of protest. One popular slogan read, "Lets call a Farmer's Holiday, a Holiday let's hold. We'll eat our wheat and ham and eggs, and let them eat their gold."

By 1932 gross farm income fell to $5.3 billion, a drop of nearly $12 billion since 1919. The value of U.S. farms dropped by more than $35 billion. Between 1930 and 1934 nearly 1 million farms passed from their owners to mortgage holders.

Agriculture continued to be viewed differently than other sectors of the economy—one worthy of subsidies. Congress passed the Agricultural Adjustment Act in May 1933 with the hopes of reviving farming interests. The measure paid farmers subsidies not to plant part of their land and to destroy specific livestock (hogs, for example) with the hope of managing prices by limiting quantity. Creating artificial scarcity to drive up prices was not popular with many farmers and disturbing for some participants, but the action was a direct outgrowth of a poor economy and a desperate attempt to manage output in the face of reduced demand. Within four years of inception the FFB was disbanded.

Jake Sudderth

See also: New Deal; Subtreasury Plan

References

Davis, Joseph S. "The Program of the Federal Farm Board," *American Economic Review* 21 (1): 104–113.

Ferguson, J. David, and Thomas E. Hall. *The Great Depression: An International Disaster of Perverse Economic Policies*. Ann Arbor: University of Michigan Press, 1998.

Folsom, Burton, Jr. *New Deal or Raw Deal?* New York: Simon and Schuster, 2008.

Heflebower, R. B. "Price Stabilization under the Farm Board," *Journal of Farm Economics* 12 (4): 595–610.

Macdonald, Dwight. *Henry Wallace: The Man and the Myth*. New York: Vanguard Press, 1948.

Rothbard, Murray. *America's Great Depression*. 5th ed. Auburn, AL: Ludwig Von Mises Institute, 2000.

Time Magazine, "National Affairs: Hoover on Shorts," July 20, 1931.

Federal Intermediate Credit Banks (FICBs)

Passage of the Agricultural Credits Act on March 4, 1923, installed Federal Intermediate Credit Banks (FICBs), introduced by Congress in the early twentieth century to extend credit to farmers in response to the populist impetus. Congress empowered 12 FICBs to discount short- and intermediate-term notes offered by commercial banks, livestock loan companies, and thrift institutions.

FICBs underwrote collateral trust debentures, discounted agricultural paper, and made loans to cooperative associations. Loans typically had short maturities that could not exceed three years.

Critics charged that FICBs were unnecessary because they added surplus machinery to the U.S. financial system by providing loans that could be underwritten by standard banks. Advocates countered that shifts in the American marketplace made lending money to farmers undesirable and that alternative funding methods were critical.

Years of political uprisings, retraction, cooptation, and compromise evolved into the FICB program. Beginning with the Greenback Party in the mid-1870s there was a burning desire among farmers and rural settlers for more control over the markets they served and the land they worked. Frustrated Americans—suffering from declining prices, railroad rates, and deflationary currency—sent 15 representatives to Congress. Beginning in 1891, as Greenback interests fused with the Democratic Party, the People's Party became the farmers' advocate. Silver boosters sought inflationary monetary policies benefiting debtor-farmers in the Midwest and miners in the West.

After the Panic of 1907, Congress passed the Aldrich-Vreeland Act, which empowered the National Monetary Commission to investigate the crisis. Populist leaders hoped for significant banking reform and public oversight, but Senator Nelson Aldrich, chairman of the commission, and the Populists also favored a central bank in Washington and elastic currency on a gold standard.

After the Democratic Party won the White House and Congress in 1912, a congressional subcommittee known as the Pujo Committee investigated the "money trust," a perceived community of Wall Street financiers who exerted extraordinary power. The committee's report resurrected populist fervor. The committee's report singled out bankers Paul and Felix Warburg, Jacob Schiff, Frank Peabody, William Rockefeller, and Benjamin Strong Jr., indicating too much power had settled among a few individuals. The document also identified more than $22 billion in investments controlled via 341 directorships held in 112 corporations by members of the J. P. Morgan empire.

In the face of public calls for more oversight, Aldrich and his colleagues were forced to support government control of the banking system. The 1913 Federal Reserve Act incorporated 12 regional banks reporting to a seven-member board appointed by the president and confirmed by the Senate. Backers hoped revised financial oversight would provide relief from financial panics, unemployment, and business depressions. Silver advocates watched as their core issue evaporated under the weight of the new national currency, the Federal Reserve Note.

Rural advocates sought easier credit after banking was centralized. The Federal Farm Loan Act of 1916 created a regional system like the Federal Reserve. Twelve Federal Land Banks (FLBs) were established, providing mortgage credit to farmers, ranchers, and rural homebuyers.

Declining land and commodity prices in the 1920s undermined the program, and members of Congress from the Midwest and Plains states, dubbed the "Farm Bloc," pushed for broader programs. The resulting 12 regional FICBs received infusions of $60 million from the U.S. Treasury and emerged as divisions separate from FLBs.

FICBs were authorized to provide credit for the development of crops and livestock, cooperative marketing of staple agricultural products, and cooperative purchase of farm supplies. The impact of the banks was limited. Outstanding loans and discounts at the end of 1929 totaled approximately $76 million and amounted to less than 2 percent of non–real estate agricultural loans outstanding.

FICB methods undermined success. The banks were not authorized to make loans directly to individual farmers. Cooperative marketing associations, finance corporations, and livestock loan companies acted as intermediaries. The rediscounting function of the banks was a disincentive for lenders because caps on profit margins were imposed.

The Farm Credit Act of 1933 was required to assist FICBs in reaching out to individual farmers. Twelve credit associations were created for this purpose. During the same year, bank supervision was transferred from the Federal Farm Loan Board to the Farm Credit Administration (FCA). The impact was minimal. FICBs never provided more than 2 percent of non–real estate agricultural loans outstanding through 1970.

By 1988, 11 of the 12 existing FICBs merged with regional Federal Land Banks to form Farm Credit Banks (FCBs). The last remaining FICB in Jackson, Mississippi, merged with the FCB of Columbia, South Carolina, which was renamed AgFirst FCB, on October 1, 1993.

Jake Sudderth

See also: Federal Reserve Act (1913); Greenback Party; National Monetary Commission; New Deal; Progressivism

References

American Institute of Banking. *Farm Credit Administration.* New York: American Institute of Banking, 1934.

Benedict, Murray R. *Farm Policies of the U.S., 1790–1850: A Study of Their Origin and*

Development. New York: Twentieth Century Fund, 1953.

Benner, Claude L. "Has Rural Credit Legislation Gone Far Enough and in the Right Direction?" *Journal of Farm Economics* 7 (1): 84–101.

Lee, V. P. "The Intermediate Credit Banks," *Journal of Farm Economics* 7 (4): 425–434.

O'Brien, Patrick G. "A Reexamination of the Senate Farm Bloc, 1921–1933." *Agricultural History* 47 (3): 248–263.

Sparks, Earl Sylvester. *History and Theory of Agricultural Credit in the United States.* New York: Thomas Y. Crowell, 1932.

Federal Reserve

The Federal Reserve System, often referred to as "the Fed," was founded on December 23, 1913, when President Woodrow Wilson signed the Federal Reserve Act. Its original purposes were to create an elastic money supply, to provide facilities for discounting commercial paper, and to supervise banks. These functions had long been performed by the central banks of major powers in Europe such as the Bank of England or the Bank of France.

The United States had had a central bank twice early in its history. The First Bank of the United States had been created in 1791. It was the successor of Robert Morris's private bank that had helped to finance the War for Independence. As secretary of the treasury, Alexander Hamilton championed a central bank, while Thomas Jefferson, secretary of state, opposed it. That first bank lasted until 1811 as an institution that provided financial stability for the new nation.

In 1811, the charter for the First United States Bank was not renewed and might well never have been reestablished if the War of 1812 had not revealed the financial weakness of the U.S. government. In 1816 the Second United States Bank was chartered. Its right to exist was challenged in *McCulloch v. Maryland* (1819). The case established the right of the federal government to exercise implied powers that were necessary and proper for the execution of the bank's expressly delegated powers. In this case a national bank, even though not expressly mentioned in the Constitution, was a fit institution for the U.S. government to create to aid in the performance of its financial activities.

The Second Bank survived the Panic of 1819; however, its president, Nicholas Biddle, was accused of exercising poor judgment for keeping credit tight. Biddle's tight credit policy put future President Andrew Jackson and his friends into a hard spot financially. Jackson's animus toward the bank was to be lifelong. Jackson and many in the new western states were in favor of easy credit, which was not liked by the more conservative and financially better off East. In 1832 Jackson vetoed the bill to recharter the Second Bank. Thus the bank remained chartered until 1836 as originally stipulated, Jackson having done an end run around the legally sanctioned institution by removing federal funds from the bank and putting them in state banks, often referred to as Jackson's "pet banks." By 1837 the Second Bank's demise contributed, in part, to the Panic of 1837. It finally closed in 1841.

The period between 1837 and 1862 was the free banking era in which the federal government deposited its funds in state banks, divorcing the government from the banking industry. As fighting raged between North and South, the National Banking Act of 1863 was adopted to aid in financing the Union's war effort. It provided for a system of federally chartered banks with higher standards for reserves and business practices than those for most state banks. The system was also intended to create a uniform system of national currency, known as greenbacks. The banknotes were to be printed by a central federal agency to prevent counterfeiting.

To curtail the use of state-chartered banknotes a federal tax was levied on state banks. As a result the number of federally chartered banks mushroomed. However, by the 1890s state banks had bounced back through the use of checking accounts. Still, two problems remained with the decentralized national banking system. First, the reserve requirements, much of which by law had to be held in U.S. Treasury securities, fluctuated in value, which meant that banks at times were forced to recall loans or to borrow from other banks. A second major problem included seasonal liquidity spikes. These spikes were associated with the enormous agricultural activity of the country.

The westward movement provided for an enormous growth in agriculture as well as the growth of small towns across the country, both of which presented a banking challenge. The cash reserves needed to supply planters, ranchers, stockmen, and others at planting and harvesting times were great. During the growing season, the need for cash or sound checks was significantly lower. The rapidly expanding West had greatly fluctuating currency needs while in the older East, where urban and industrial growth was strong, currency needs were more stable. As a consequence a small western bank could experience currency supply problems that could easily be met by a loan between banks (banker's loan) until harvests could be delivered and paid. The eastern banks, however, often presented the less stable western banks with expensive costs. Western farmers needed a lender of last resort. This became a problem even for the U.S. government during the Panic of 1907. It turned to J. P. Morgan for large sums of money to tide it over. Morgan organized the cooperation of other New York bankers to end the panic.

Some bankers and others, especially the populists across the South and West, were worried that Morgan and Wall Street had too much power. Others were more concerned with the financial instability that the decentralized system presented. An elastic money supply could prevent or soften financial panics.

In 1908, Congress established a National Monetary Commission to develop a nonpartisan solution to the banking system's weaknesses. Nelson Aldrich—Rhode Island's Republican senator and father-in-law of John D. Rockefeller—headed the commission. He gathered a team of economists, toured Europe to visit the central banks there, and yet by 1910 had not reported back. On the night of November 22, 1910, a delegation of seven men secretly entered a private railroad car at Hoboken, New Jersey, at separate times. The car was taken to the train station at Brunswick, Georgia, where they took a boat to Jekyl (spelling was changed to Jekyll years later) Island.

There they met at the Jekyl Island Club, which was established in 1886 and owned by a group of millionaires including J. P. Morgan, Rockefeller, the Vanderbilts, and others. The group developed the Aldrich Plan, which was principally the brainchild of Paul Warburg, a German-born American banker.

By 1912, the Aldrich Plan was made public with Woodrow Wilson enlisted as a spokesman. It called for a system of financial stability, without political meddling, through a decentralized reserve financial system. The election of 1912 gave the Democrats control of the House and the Senate and put Woodrow Wilson into the White House, thus clearing the path for the Aldrich Plan.

President Wilson made the Aldrich Plan a vital issue. The bill could have failed because William Jennings Bryan, a Populist as well as Wilson's secretary of state, was a long-time enemy of Wall Street. Bryan had delivered his "Cross of Gold" speech to the Democratic Party National Convention on July 9, 1896. He opposed the gold standard that was used internationally and favored bimetallism, which would use both gold and silver coinage. Bimetallism was opposed by bankers, industrialists, and international traders because "free silver" allowed more inflation than the gold standard. Inflation was favored by farmers and ranchers because it gave them higher prices. The speech gained Bryan the nomination; however, he lost the presidential election of 1896 to William McKinley. In 1900 the United States adopted the gold standard.

Wilson gained Bryan's support by making the liabilities of the Federal Reserve liabilities of the U.S. government rather than of the private banks. In addition, farmers would be given federal loans. He also gained support because the 12 decentralized regional banks of the Federal Reserve would weaken Wall Street's influence. Moreover, regional Federal Reserve Banks, identified by number, would be controlled by a central Federal Reserve board appointed by the president with the advice and consent of the Senate. They were to engage in a coordinated effort to manage the nation's money supply. While ostensibly private, they are really entities of the federal government.

The Federal Reserve was slow to exercise its powers. Its first major role was issuing Liberty Bonds (under Treasury Department supervision) to finance the United States' war effort in 1917. After the war it was given the authority to both create and destroy money. Its financial operations during the Roaring Twenties have been seen by later scholars as aiding the stock market bubble that ended with the Great Depression.

Between 1933 and 1951 the Federal Reserve was a subordinate part of the executive branch. Its functions since the 1970s have included managing the money supply to maximize employment in equilibrium with stable prices and moderate long-term interest rates.

The Great Recession of 2008 was global in scope; however, the Federal Reserve seems to have played the stabilizing role its founders intended. Its critics put forth complaints and charges that echo populist complaints of the financial conflicts of the eighteenth and nineteenth centuries.

Andrew J. Waskey

See also: Banking System of the Late Nineteenth Century; Bryan, Williams Jennings (1860–1925); "Cross of Gold" Speech; Gilded Age; Gold Standard/Free Silver; Jefferson, Thomas (1743–1826); McKinley, William, Jr. (1843–1901); National Monetary Commission; New Deal; Progressivism; Shays's Rebellion (1786–1787)

References

Greider, William. *Secrets of the Temple: How the Federal Reserve Runs the Country.* New York: Simon & Schuster, 1987.

Griffin, G. Edward. *The Creature from Jekyll Island: A Second Look at the Federal Reserve.* Westlake, CA: American Media, 2010.

Livingston, James. *Origins of the Federal Reserve System: Money, Class, and Corporate Capitalism, 1890–1913.* Ithaca, NY: Cornell University Press, 1989.

Meltzer, Allan H. *A History of the Federal Reserve.* 2 vols. Chicago: University of Chicago Press, 2003.

Wells, Donald R. *The Federal Reserve System: A History.* Jefferson, NC: McFarland & Company, 2004.

Federal Reserve Act (1913)

Enacted on December 23, 1913, the Federal Reserve Act reformed the U.S. banking system by creating a central bank with the ability to expand and contract the money supply. This became known as the Federal Reserve System.

The United States experienced the Panic of 1907 when the established banking system nearly failed because many bank patrons withdrew money due to a fear that the banks would become insolvent after a 50 percent freefall of the stock market. Following the Panic of 1907, the U.S. government passed the Aldrich-Vreeland Act and established the National Monetary Commission. Its main purpose was to study the banking systems of major European countries and develop ideas to improve the U.S. banking system.

The National Monetary Commission published several reports regarding the state of the U.S. banking system. In a speech by Edward B. Vreeland of New York given to the House of Representatives, Vreeland noted a lack of structure in the American banking system by stating that there was little to no federal regulation over the 25,000 to 26,000 banks throughout the United States. Without a strong federal presence, banks could operate independently of each other and make financial decisions that could be detrimental to their patrons. A two-fold solution proposed that the Federal Reserve System be established to create cohesion between the banks as well as to create a sense of confidence in the banking system for both patrons and bankers in an attempt to prevent future banking panics.

One of the overarching issues with the banking system was the lack of any elasticity in currency. Prior to the Panic of 1907 there was no regulation on the issuance of currency. In addition to inspiring the nation with confidence in its banking system, the Federal Reserve Act enabled the U.S. government to control the issuance of money based on gold, consumer demand, and the state of the economy.

Populist William Jennings Bryan was in opposition to the Federal Reserve Act because he felt it gave big business influence and control over the banking system, which would ultimately limit the economic power of farmers and laborers. Bryan felt that the new system would not distribute control across the states; rather it would keep the banking power centralized in New York. Although there was much Democratic opposition to the bill, President Woodrow Wilson (D) expressed a decision to sign the bill after a few modifications. In an attempt to please Bryan and the farmers, Wilson called for 12 regional banks, which resulted in less control by New York banks.

Although there have been modifications to the Federal Reserve Act and system, it continues to govern the U.S. banking system.

Johnathan Fluitt

See also: Bryan, William Jennings (1860–1925); National Monetary Commission; Progressivism

References

Griffin, G. Edward. *The Creature from Jekyll Island: A Second Look at the Federal Reserve.* Westlake Village, CA: American Media, 1998.

Meltzer, Allan H. *A History of the Federal Reserve, Volume 1: 1913–1951.* Chicago: University of Chicago Press, 2003.

Federal Trade Commission Act (1914)

To enforce the Sherman Antitrust Act (1890), Congress passed the Federal Trade Commission (FTC) Act in 1914. This legislation, 15 U.S.C §§ 41–58, created the agency charged with ensuring competition within nontransportation industries. Transportation would be under the purview of the Interstate Commerce Commission. The FTC was administered by five commissioners, appointed by the president. Antitrust legislation had begun with the Sherman Antitrust Act of 1890, a somewhat reactive law, in that it was invoked by the government only after a monopoly or unfair trade practice existed.

As a companion to the FTC Act, Congress also passed the Clayton Antitrust Act of 1914 (Pub.L. 63-212, 38 Stat. 730, enacted October 14, 1914). It addressed certain activities that encouraged monopoly or thwarted competition. Authored by Alabama Democrat Henry De Lamar Clayton (1857–1929), the Clayton bill sought to impose strict limitations on several business operations, criminalizing specific violations: exclusive dealing arrangements, tie-in contracts, price discrimination, and certain types of stockholding. The bill also simplified claims procedures for those damaged by violations of the Sherman Act.

Two Supreme Court cases, *Standard Oil Co. v. United States* (1911), and *United States v. American Tobacco Company* (1911), served as precursors to the FTC due to the "rule of reason." The Court ruled that the Sherman Act covered only those trade restraints that were unreasonable. The issue elevated antitrust questions during the 1914 midterm election. Some believed that FTC should be modeled after the Interstate Commerce Commission.

The FTC's original goal was to prevent "unfair methods of competition" or monopoly. Perception of the new agency differed depending upon one's perspective. Those in business thought the commission would act in an advisory capacity, while progressives expected the FTC to actively reduce anticompetitive activity.

The FTC Act was passed "with the intention of correcting the deficiencies of the Sherman Antitrust Act" (Harris 142). Initially, President Woodrow Wilson did not support an administrative FTC. In January 1914, he proposed an agency to advise industry and be a source of information. His administration then supported a bill proposed by Maryland Representative James H. Covington that created the FTC as an information agency without enforcement powers. Covington's bill supplemented Clayton's by creating the Interstate Trade Commission, which could publicize unfair practices. This agency became the Federal Trade Commission. Representative Raymond Stevens of New Hampshire later presented a bill creating an agency that consisted of experts with the ability to create policies governing unfair competition. George Rublee, a former progressive, persuaded Wilson and his economic advisor, Louis Brandeis, to support the strong administrative model for a trade commission. Theodore Roosevelt had expressed the same during the 1912 presidential campaign and again during the 1914 midterm elections. Although reluctant, Wilson, under pressure from progressives, particularly Roosevelt, transferred three sections of Stevens's bill to the FTC Act, sections that empowered the agency administratively. When Congress finished, the FTC Act was much stronger.

In *The Promise of American Life* Herbert Croly, a political philosopher, editor, and intellectual leader of the progressive movement, favored the model of a strong Hamiltonian central government to the Jeffersonian republic. He supported Theodore Roosevelt in his 1912 presidential campaign. Croly later founded the influential periodical *The New Republic*. He supported five aspects of the FTC Act. These were (1) strange wording that allowed the FTC to make decisions based on the public interest, (2) cease and desist orders for extant monopolies, (3) consent decree power as related to the cease and desist orders to simultaneously encourage experimentation and compliance, (4) punishment for distribution of misinformation, and (5) allowing the FTC to act as a governing institution. Although the FTC acted as an administrative agency, its power of consumer protection increased with the Wheeler-Lea Act (1938) (Jaenicke).

The first commissioners served terms of varied lengths so that later commissioners served staggered terms of seven years. Initially, Congress allowed for a salary of $10,000 per year for each member. The FTC began official operations on March 16, 1915. At this time five men were appointed: Joseph E. Davies (seven years), Edward N. Hurley (six years), William J. Harris (five years), Will H. Parry (four years), and George Rublee, who served only until the conclusion of the next session of the U.S. Senate. Since its inception, the Federal Trade Commission has increased competitiveness by preventing monopolies, prohibited unfair or deceptive advertising practices, regulated the promotion of tobacco products, and limited advertising directed at children.

In recent years, the FTC developed a National Do Not Call Registry to help consumers deal with telemarketers, and prohibited pharmaceutical companies from delaying entry of generic drugs into the marketplace.

Ralph M. Hartsock

See also: Clayton Antitrust Act (1914); Interstate Commerce Act (ICA) (1887); Progressivism; Roosevelt, Theodore (1858–1919)

References

Cornell University Law School. United States Code, Title 15, Chapter 2, Subchapter 1. Federal Trade Commission. http://www.law.cornell.edu/uscode/15/usc_sup_01_15_10_2_20_I.html. Accessed January 3, 2013.

Croly, Herbert. *The Promise of American Life.* New York: Macmillan, 1909.

Federal Trade Commission, 90th Anniversary Symposium, September 22–23, 2004. http://www.ftc.gov/ftc/history/docs/90thAnniv_Program.pdf. Accessed January 3, 2013.

Harris, Richard A., and Sidney M. Milkis. "The Federal Trade Commission, Consumer Protection, and Regulatory Change." In *The Politics of Regulatory Change* (pp. 140–224). New York: Oxford University Press, 1996.

Jaenicke, Douglas Walter. "Herbert Croly, Progressive Ideology, and the FTC Act." *Political Science Quarterly* 93 (3): 471–493.

James, Scott C. *Presidents, Parties, and the State: A Party System Perspective on Democratic Regulatory Choice, 1884–1936.* New York: Cambridge University Press, 2000.

Levy, David W. *Herbert Croly of the New Republic.* Princeton, NJ: Princeton University Press, 1985.

Felton, William Harrell (1823–1909)

William Harrell Felton was born in 1823. He served as a Methodist minister, farmer, Confederate army surgeon, and U.S. congressman from 1875 to 1881. While mainly remembered as the husband of Rebecca Latimer Felton, his second wife and the first woman to officially serve in the U.S. Senate, he was one of the most prominent politicians in Georgia after Reconstruction ended and was a champion of farmers in that region.

Born on the family plantation near Lexington, Georgia, to John and Mary D. Felton, William received his undergraduate degree from the University of Georgia's Franklin College in 1843 and his medical degree from the Medical College of Georgia, Augusta, the next year. Soon after, he married Ann Carlton, the daughter of a prominent Athens merchant family.

From descriptions of contemporaries, Felton appears to have suffered from some kind of palsy or neurological condition that affected his ability to practice medicine for any prolonged time or later to serve as a full-time minister in the Methodist church. His wife's obituary for him noted, "[T]he strain of the work was too much for his nervous system" (Felton 12).

His first wife's sudden death in 1852 changed the direction of his life. On the heels of her death, he was elected to the Georgia state legislature and became a supply preacher in the church, becoming ordained in 1857. Only a widower for a few months, it was while speaking at the graduation service of Madison Female College that he met the class's valedictorian,

Rebecca Ann Latimer, and a few months later married her.

The couple retired to a small plantation outside of Cartersville, Georgia, until the start of the Civil War. During the conflict, the Feltons and their children moved to Macon, where William served the Confederacy as a surgeon in the military hospitals there. After the war, the family returned to Cartersville. Dr. Felton then ran afoul of local Reconstruction officials when he violated the law in the eviction of an African American tenant, but the case was dismissed due to lack of evidence. The Feltons held extremely conservative racial views throughout their public careers.

In 1874, William Felton decided to oppose the Bourbon Democrats who controlled the area and run for the U.S. Congress. In what Rebecca later called "the fiercest political battle ever known to the state at that time," her husband won his 14-county district by a mere 82 votes (Northen). Drawing on the rhetorical lessons he learned in the pulpit, he spoke logically but attacked opponents with "satire and scathing denunciation of error and evil" (Northen).

Serving on the Ways and Means Committee, he was a strong supporter of tariffs on luxury goods, but more important, he was a proponent of bimetallism. A writer in the *Cartersville News*, a paper the Feltons owned for a year and a half, noted, "Perhaps the most distinguished feature of his career in Congress was his skillful diagnosis of the financial depression then afflicting the country. He brilliantly advocated the remonetization of the silver dollar. His speeches read like prophecy in the light of contemporary financial disasters" (*The Cartersville News*).

With Rebecca working as his campaign manager, aide, and writer of numerous commentaries and letters to the editor, theirs was a political partnership. Constituents often joked that they were blessed with having two government representatives instead of one like the rest of the nation.

Losing his bid for reelection in 1880, William Felton served in the Georgia House of Representatives from 1884 to1890. In those years, he was deeply involved in trying to end the convict lease system, which put wage laborers and small-scale farmers and businessmen at a disadvantage. At both the state and national levels, he pushed for vocational education. His wife claimed that his political legacy could be summed up as "securing proper scope and authority to the Railroad Commission of Georgia, for a reformatory for juvenile offenders, and for the second lease of the Western and Atlantic Railway" (Northen). Negotiated at the Felton's home, the Western and Atlantic Railway contract put $420,000 annually in the Georgia state coffers for nearly three decades.

William Felton spent the last 19 years of his life out of the public eye, retiring to his plantation home where he died in 1909. With the exception of woman suffrage, which she embraced after his death, Rebecca continued to be a public advocate of "their" progressive politics until her death in 1930. At the age of 87, Governor Thomas Hardwick appointed her to fill the U.S. Senate seat of Thomas E. Watson, who had recently died, a position she held for one day while the Congress was in session. Yet it made her the first female senator in U.S. history.

Trevor Jason Soderstrum

See also: Bourbon Democracy; Gold Standard/Free Silver; Railroad Regulation

References

"Dr. William H. Felton." *The Cartersville News*, September 30, 1909.

Felton, Rebecca Latimer. *My Memoirs of Georgia Politics*. Greenville, SC: The Index Printing Company, 1911.

Northen, William J. *Men of Mark in Georgia*. n.p.: A. B. Caldwell, 1906. http://www.archive.org/stream/menofmarkingeorg04nort/menofmarkingeorg04nort_djvu.txt.

Feminism

The derivations of modern feminist principles are commonly assumed to be from the Enlightenment period of the seventeenth and eighteenth centuries. Yet the Mexican nun Sor Juana Ines de la Cruz (1651–1695) was also one of the first advocates of women's education. Regardless of the point of origin, early sex-based equality supporters and contemporary feminist activists shared similar impetuses—specifically, an equitable role for men and women in the public and private sectors, an emphasis on the values of education and knowledge, and a more egalitarian understanding of innate ability regardless of sex. Feminist thinking and activism is commonly categorized into three categories: radical, liberal, and socialist. Radical feminism seeks a foundational change in gender relations, thereby evoking a cultural and political environment that emphasizes the autonomy and agency of women. Liberal feminism is focused on the removal of institutionalized social and political barriers that prevent the achievement of equality. Socialist feminism primarily points toward the relationship between the patriarchal and capitalistic structures that historically subordinated women. Mary Wollstonecraft's "A Vindication of the Rights of Woman" (1792) is often heralded as the foundational text for contemporary feminist principles and practices. But Wollstonecraft's essay never utilized the word *feminism*, thus sparking a debate on whether this text is actually feminist or humanist. To counter this concern, historians such as Eileen Hunt Botting utilize the term *protofeminist* as a means to describe early woman-based philosophical traditions (Botting 265).

Educational reform was a central area of concern for supporters of equality based on gender. In "The Subjection of Women" (1869), John Stuart Mill advocated for women's liberty and equal opportunity, specifically in terms of education. Alice Rossi writes that Mill contended, "women's thoughts are thus as useful in giving reality to those thinking men" (Rossi, 221). Mill's ideas presaged contemporary feminism, which argued that men's liberation, in addition to women's social freedom, was imperative to dismantling an oppressive patriarchal system, thus reprising this type of egalitarianism. Mill also campaigned for woman suffrage and "objected to the British common-law principle of coverture" (Freedman 53) that established a wife's personage and property as legally represented by the husband after marriage. Yet critics argue that

Wollstonecraft and Mill were gilded by privilege and that both ignored the influence of class, labor, and economic disenfranchisement.

Throughout the nineteenth century, gender-based equality was the movement's predominant concern, known as first-wave feminism. In 1848 at the Seneca Falls Convention, Elizabeth Cady Stanton read the "Declaration of Rights and Sentiments," which articulated that the history of mankind was the "history of repeated injuries and usurpations on the part of man toward woman" (Stanton 70). Voting rights were not the central component of this convention. Rather, early gender-equality supporters focused on property rights for women, changes in parenting practices, equal labor contracts, and women's rights as a direct offshoot of human rights.

In the late nineteenth and early twentieth centuries, suffragists such as Stanton, Lucy Stone, and Susan B. Anthony worked toward ensuring that the right to vote was granted to women. It was only in the 1920s that the U.S. Senate passed the Nineteenth Amendment granting this right. Individuals such as Margaret Sanger utilized the suffragist movement as a platform to advocate for a woman's right to birth control and control of her own body. In 1923, Alice Paul strove to ratify the Equal Rights Amendment (ERA) that sought to eliminate discrimination based on sex. As section 1 of the ERA states, "equality of rights under the law shall not be denied or abridged by the United States or by any State on account of sex" (Vile 177). The ERA was revised in the 1970s but again failed to be ratified by the requisite number of states by the deadline. Simone de Beauvoir's *The Second Sex* (1949) powerfully illuminated this type of continuing subordination of women, despite social and political progress.

Coinciding with political, social, and economic reform, including the availability of the birth-control pill, the 1960s ushered in "second-wave feminism." Along with liberalism's emphasis on the individual, twentieth-century feminism demanded the acknowledgement of, and freedom for, a woman to act on her own free will. Retackling issues such as reproductive rights, involvement in the political process and government, equal access to education, and equal pay, 1960s feminism worked toward creating a sex-equitable society. The emphasis on the individual's well-being as central to political and social change generated the phrase "the personal is political." Women such as Bella Abzug, Shirley Chisholm, Fannie Lou Hamer, and Gloria Steinem came forward as political strategists in this era. The second-wave feminist movement also experienced several intra-movement disputes including the roles of women of color, lesbian and trans-identified activists, and the movement's stance on pornography.

Betty Friedan's *The Feminine Mystique* (1963) debunked women's desire solely to pursue housework and childrearing but was criticized for neglecting to consider women of color or the working class. The Combahee River Collective (1974) brought forward the notion of racism within the feminist movement and the need to acknowledge the multiplicities of identity. Their work demonstrated that those who suffered from a particular discrimination were those who were most capable to write from that perspective. Global feminism echoes a similar awareness. In "The Project of Feminist Epistemology: Perspectives from a Nonwestern Feminist," Uma Narayan argues that "it may be politically counterproductive for nonwestern feminists to uncritically echo the themes that Western feminist epistemology seeks to restore the value, cognitive and otherwise, of 'women's experience' " (McCann and Kim 334). These epistemologies only represented the interests of the privileged class that were disguised as universal human interests. The assumption that a singular feminist identity could encompass global identities and differences reiterated positivism and a hegemonic form of feminism. Women in developing and postcolonial nations and women of color and various ethnicities have proposed different nuances to feminism. Gloria Jean Watkins, also known as bell hooks, suggests replacing "I am a feminist" with "I advocate feminism" (hooks 1984: McCann and Kim 55), thereby creating space for a multiplicity of political and personal identifications.

Material feminism, considered a branch of radical feminism, argues that material conditions have a direct impact on social conditions in relation to gender. First coined in 1975 by Christine Delphy, material feminists point toward the divide between the public and private spheres and a woman's home responsibility as burdensome, thereby negatively affecting the standard of living. Material feminists also call for a reconceptualization of double duty (women's paid labor outside the home and unpaid labor inside) in an attempt to include domestic work as a viable form of production. In fact, feminist writers, such as Donna Harraway, examine the interplay between materialism, capital, patriarchal oppression, and biopolitics as a means to include civil, political, and cultural reform in relation to the redistribution of wealth.

There is frequent debate within feminist discourses regarding the influence, inclusion, or even exclusion of Marxist theory. Both radical and socialist feminists take issue with Marxist theory, arguing that the understanding of the relationship between gender, patriarchy, and capitalism is incomplete. However, Marxist feminists contend that the elimination of capitalism would eradicate sexism, racism, homophobia, and other social oppressions. More so, Marxist feminists see the divide between private and public lives perpetuated by a gendered division of labor. Establishing distinct modes of material production, women's work within the home and the rearing of children are viable forms of production within capitalism. Nevertheless, capitalism has worked to separate and discount home (private) work from public work, thereby further concretizing the divide between women and men.

Third-wave feminism, from the 1990s to the present, primarily identifies and counteracts the failures of second-wave feminism, such as embracing a multiplicity of identities pertaining to ethnicities, nationalities, religions, transgenderism, sex-positivity, and individualist sexualities. Moreover, third-wave feminism attempts to deconstruct essentialist definitions of identity and social binaries to facilitate the fluidity of identity. In the introduction to *Manifesta* (2010), a text that explores the nuances of third-wave feminism, authors Jennifer Baumgardner and Amy Richards suggest that feminism can change with every generation and individual.

Historically, both first- and second-wave feminism are often cited as reflecting the values of middle-class white women, largely marginalizing black feminists, global feminists, and other women of different age, race, sexuality, ability, and culture. Stanton and Anthony are frequently accused of mobilizing based on bourgeois ideologies and privileges rather than on a more comprehensive reflection of class and racial systems. Moreover, participation in the abolition movement played a central role in either dividing or buttressing support for women's rights. Sarah and Angelina Grimké urged women's rights activists to support the abolition movement. Sojourner Truth's speech "Ain't I a Woman" (1851) testified to the inseparability of race and sex. Reaching beyond these first two waves, scholars have made room for the larger company of voices that have emerged because of the civil rights movement and its spinoffs based on sex and gender. Feminism is a critical perspective on local and global systems. The work of feminist activists in the past and the present seeks a wholesale dismantling of oppression while advancing equality regardless of sex and gender.

Elisabeth Woronzoff-Dashkoff

See also: Sanger, Margaret (1879–1966); Stanton, Elizabeth Cady (1815–1902)

References

Baumgardner, Jennifer, and Amy Richards. *Manifesta: Young Women, Feminism, and the Future.* New York: Farrar, Straus and Giroux, 2010.

Beauvoir, Simone de. *The Second Sex.* New York: Alfred A. Knopf, 1957.

Botting, Eileen H., and Sarah L. Houser. " 'Drawing the Line of Equality': Hannah Mather Crocker on Women's Rights." *American Political Science Review* 100 (2): 265–78.

Freedman, Estelle. *No Turning Back: The History of Feminism and the Future of Women.* New York: Ballantine Books, 2003.

Friedan, Betty. *The Feminine Mystique.* New York: W.W. Norton & Company, 2001.

Haraway, Donna J. *Simians, Cyborgs, and Women: The Reinvention of Nature.* New York: Routledge, 1990.

Hartmann, Heidi I. "The Unhappy Marriage of Marxism and Feminism: Towards a More Progressive Union." *Capital & Class* 3 (2): 1–33.

McCann, Carole, and Seung-kyung Kim, eds. *Feminist Theory Reader: Local and Global Perspectives.* 2nd ed. New York: Routledge, 2009.

Painter, Nell Irvin. *Sojourner Truth: A Life, a Symbol.* New York: W.W. Norton & Company, 1997.

Rossi, Alice, ed. *The Feminist Papers: From Adams to de Beauvoir.* Boston: Northeastern University Press, 1988.

Sargent, Lydia. *Women and Revolution: A Discussion of the Unhappy Marriage of Marxism and Feminism.* Cambridge, MA: South End Press, 1999.

Stanton, Elizabeth Cady. "Declaration of Rights and Sentiments." Internet History Sourcebook. http://www.fordham.edu/halsall/mod/senecafalls.asp. Accessed January 3, 2013.

Stanton, Elizabeth Cady. *A History of Woman Suffrage, Vol. 1.* New York: Fowler and Wells, 1889.

Vile, John R. *Encyclopedia of Constitutional Amendments, Proposed Amendments, and Amending Issues, 1789–2002.* Santa Barbara, CA: ABC-CLIO, 2003.

Wollstonecraft, Mary. *A Vindication of the Rights of Women.* New York: W.W. Norton & Company, 1967.

Film

The ability to capture motion on film, which could then be replayed to audiences at any time, anywhere, was an important technological development that spanned from the Gilded Age into the postmodern era. Film both represents and shapes low and high cultures. It unites and divides audiences, and since its inception it has been one of the primary ways in which Americans express their identities and anxieties. In its short life, it has become one of the cornerstones of American popular culture.

A series of optical toys that were developed in the 1830s led to what is now referred to as "film." It began in 1833 with Joseph Plateau's phenakistiscope. The device was a cardboard disc with 16 notches cut out of it and 16 sequential drawings or paintings placed between each notch. The viewer held the painted side of the disc facing a mirror and rotated it while looking through the notches at the reflection, which gave the effect of a moving image. Optical toys invented subsequently to the phenakistiscope included the Zoetrope (William Horner, 1834), kinematoscope (Philadelphian Coleman Sellers, 1861), and phasmotrope (also spelled phasmatrope by Henry Renno-Heyl, 1870). One of the last optical toys, the praxinoscope, was created by French inventor Charles Emile Reynaud in 1877. It was a projector device with a mirrored drum that created the illusion of movement with picture strips. Thomas Edison was one of the key inventors of the era, creating the efficient incandescent light bulb in 1879, which was later used for film projectors. Edison also created one of the first known motion picture cameras.

The silent era of film began in approximately 1880. In terms of content, the films of the silent era can be categorized as trick, comedy, or actuality films. The trick films were full of action, usually involving people and objects disappearing, reappearing, and the backward running of action scenes. Comedy films tended to include slapstick, also including chase sequences. Generally, the trick and comedy films were fast-paced as opposed to the actuality films. Sociologist Pierre Sorlin observes that during these years Dickson in the United States and Lumière in France were filming scenes of daily life—hence the use of the term *actualities*. Actualities recorded topical events, including the filming of strange places and exotic phenomena. American actuality films displayed scenes from the Spanish-American War, the Boer War, and biographical actualities of world leaders such as William McKinley and Theodore Roosevelt. Author Nigel Hamilton suggests moviegoers did not appear to be as interested in these actuality films (which later evolved into documentary and biographical films). Audiences preferred to watch fictional, voyeuristic films featuring elements such as boxing and other dramatized films.

Audience tastes soon changed, and the novelty of short, manic 15-minute films (the length of the reel) wore off in the 1910s. Filmic technology continued to evolve, and one-reel films became three-reel films. The length of the film increased as well as the size of the subject. However, the use of the classical narrative structure in film became common practice before technology extended film duration. The form of narration that was active during this time is deemed "classical" by scholars of silent film, a mode formulated around 1909, although it can be discerned as early as 1907. Explaining the term, film historians Lee Grieveson and Peter Krämer state that the classical feature film is characterized by the overriding objective of telling a particular kind of story, focusing on goal-oriented characters who set in motion a series of causally linked events in which they confront and overcome, or less often are overcome by, counterforces to the achievement of their goals. In either case, the ending closes the issue definitively by resolving, usually happily but sometimes tragically, all of the tensions between the characters and their surroundings that were set up at the beginning. The first short film with a developed narrative is *The Great Train Robbery* (1903), directed by Edwin S. Porter. The film duration time was 12 minutes and consisted of (as the title implies) a robbery, the formation of a posse, and a final showdown in the woods. *The Great Train Robbery*, marketed as a reenactment film, participated in the shift from actuality to fiction. The film created the illusion of authenticity by combining actuality and reenactment and led the way for future films with narratives on the recreation of true stories.

Three years after the first narrative film, the first full-length feature film, created by Charles Tait, was filmed and released in Australia: *The Story of the Kelly Gang* (1906). It ran for approximately 70 minutes. Only 9 minutes of the original film have been recovered. *The Story of the Kelly Gang* is inscribed in the UNESCO International Memory of the World Register, and nearly one-quarter of the original feature film was restored by the National Film and Sound Archive (NFSA), Canberra, Australia. The film showed reenactments of the important events of Ned Kelly's life. The first feature film with recorded musical accompaniment was *Don Juan*. It is best remembered as the film that introduced the Vitaphone synchronized sound process to the public. The first feature-length part-talkie was *The Jazz Singer*.

The studio era, which began in roughly 1930, inspired emulation in Great Britain, France, and many other countries. Hollywood studios released films under their unique trademarks and generally featured classical narrative films, a holdover from the silent era. This "studio system," as it became known, thrived until the 1960s. In the silent film era studios executives deliberately had not listed actors' names in the credits, thus keeping the audiences focused on the studio brand itself. Ivan Butler describes the studio styles and features of MGM (Metro-Goldwyn-Mayer), Paramount, Universal, and Warner Brothers as all "glitter and gloss," smart cosmopolitanism, horror cycles, and "the swift, hard-hitting social indictments or contrasting lavish musicals," respectively (Butler 49). As a result, viewers could select films from a particular studio to suit their tastes. But over time, audiences demanded to know the names of their favorite actors, and star power soon trumped studio branding.

Generally, the term "new Hollywood" applies to American cinema after World War II, when the studio system began to collapse and commercial television began to sweep the suburban landscape. In the postwar decade, motion pictures came to be produced and sold on a film-by-film basis, and watching TV rapidly replaced going to the movies. The key to Hollywood's survival and the most important aspect of its postwar transformation has been the steady rise of the movie blockbuster. In terms of budgets, production values, and market strategy, Hollywood has been increasingly hit-driven since the early 1950s. The idea of the blockbuster reached its peak in the mid-1970s, despite (and in some ways because of) the concurrent emergence of competing media technologies including cable TV and home video (VCRs). This was the first period of sustained economic vitality and industry stability for Hollywood since the classical era.

Film historian David Bordwell argues that the classical style that reached its peak in the studio era still dominates Hollywood filmmaking. Yet whether blockbuster or story-driven, film's populist appeal lies in its ability to reach enormous audiences, quickly disseminate ideas, and create a virtual community of viewers.

Penny Spirou

See also: Capra, Frank (1897–1991); Electricity; Gilded Age; Griffith, D. W. (1875–1948), and *The Birth of a Nation* (1915); Leisure; Popular Culture; Progressivism; Reagan, Ronald, Populist Rhetoric of

References

Adair, Gene. *Thomas Alva Edison: Inventing the Electric Age*. New York: Oxford University Press, 1996.

Australian Screen. "The Story of the Kelly Gang." http://australianscreen.com.au/titles/story-kelly-gang/. Accessed June 12, 2012.

Beeton, Sue. "Rural Tourism in Australia—Has the Gaze Altered? Tracking Rural Images through Film and Tourism Promotion." *International Journal of Tourism Research* 6 (3): 125–135.

Bordwell, David. *The Way Hollywood Tells It: Story and Style in Modern Movies*. Berkeley: University of California Press, 2006.

Butler, Ivan. "Into the Thirties." In Peter Cowie, ed., *A Concise History of the Cinema, Volume 1: Before 1940*. London: A. Zwemmer, 1971.

Douglas, Leo, and Graham Enticknap. *Moving Image Technology: From Zoetrope to Digital*. London: Wallflower Press, 2005.

Grieveson, Lee, and Peter Krämer. *The Silent Cinema Reader*. London: Routledge, 2004.

Hansen, Miriam. *Babel & Babylon: Spectatorship in American Silent Film*. Cambridge, MA: Harvard University Press, 1991.

McCaffrey, Donald W., and Christopher P. Jacobs. *Guide to the Silent Years of American Cinema*. Westport, CT: Greenwood Press, 1999.

Musser, Charles. "Moving towards Fictional Narratives: Story Films Become the Dominant Product, 1903–1904." In Lee Grievson and Peter Krämer, eds., *The Silent Cinema Reader*. London: Routledge, 2004.

National Film and Sound Archive. "The Story of the Kelly Gang." http://nfsa.gov.au/collection/film/story-kelly-gang/. Accessed January 3, 2013.

O'Leary, Liam. *The Silent Cinema*. London: Studio Vista, 1965.

Schatz, Thomas. "The New Hollywood." In Jim Collins, ed., *Film Theory Goes to the Movies*. London: Routledge, 1993.

Sorlin, Pierre. "How to Look at an 'Historical' Film." In Marcia Landy, ed., *The Historical Film: History and Memory in Media*. London: Althlone Press, 2001.

Strauven, Wanda. *The Cinema of Attractions Reloaded*. Amsterdam: Amsterdam University Press, 2006.

Flint Strike (1936–1937)

The 1936–1937 United Auto Workers (UAW) strike against General Motors (GM) was an important turning point in the history of organized labor in the United States. The UAW was founded in 1935 by thousands of union members and activists displeased that the American Federation of Labor (AFL) continued to oppose organizing unskilled laborers and that the auto workers' division of the AFL had not been permitted to select its own leaders. The UAW was initially a small organization with limited membership and influence. It had experienced slow growth in membership as the result of efforts to organize workers at smaller automotive plants. As a strategy for growth and survival, in 1936 UAW leadership formulated the plan of organizing workers at the largest auto manufacturer in the United States, General Motors, which employed more than one-half of the country's auto workers.

In late 1936, the UAW began initiating strikes at GM plants and Fisher body plants, which produced components for GM, in several locations including Atlanta, Georgia, in November, and Kansas City, Missouri, and Cleveland, Ohio, in December. By late December, workers at GM's Flint, Michigan, plant were considering a strike. The Flint factory contained key body-production capacity for GM's Buick, Oldsmobile, and Pontiac lines and was vital to the company. On December 30, when union leaders learned of GM's plan to relocate dies and other production components from the Flint plant to other facilities in which the presence of organized labor was weaker, they initiated a sit-down strike. Auto workers occupied the factory, denying GM management access to the facility and its equipment.

Upon taking possession of the Flint facility, approximately 1,200 workers set about adapting to their situation. They welded shut possible entry points or erected barricades, often made of unfinished vehicles. Life inside the facility was orderly, with democratically elected committees formed for education, entertainment, food, health and sanitation, information, safety, and security, and each worker was assigned specific tasks and shifts. Rules were established to maintain order, including the prohibition of alcohol and gambling. A court was also formed to meet out punishments for individuals who transgressed these rules. Careful attention was paid to maintenance and cleaning of company-owned property as well as personal cleanliness. While the living conditions inside the factory lacked

Members of the United Automobile Workers union stage a sit-down strike in the Fisher body plant factory in Flint, Michigan in 1936. (Library of Congress)

many of the creature comforts of home, it was not totally devoid of amenities. Car benches were adapted to become chairs and beds. Running water, food, cigarettes, and recreational outlets, such as concerts and games, were available, and workers could chat with their families and friends through windows and even visit with their children. While the striking workers remained inside, many of their family members, including a well-organized women's auxiliary and other supporters, maintained a picket line outside the entrance to the plant.

The Flint strike attracted public attention and became the focal point of a national movement among auto workers to unionize. The Great Depression had significantly reduced both the total number and the average wages and benefits of U.S. auto workers. Workers also voiced concerns over arbitrary firings and other aspects of job security, including prolonged layoffs, as well as strenuous and dangerous working conditions and efforts on the part of management to intimidate workers and prevent unionization. The latter helped cultivate public sympathy for the striking workers. President Franklin D. Roosevelt, Michigan Governor Frank Murphy, and many other officials voiced support for the striking workers. The strike quickly spread, and within a matter of a few weeks more than 100,000 GM workers from dozens of plants in 14 states were striking, paralyzing the company.

Sentiment supporting the auto workers was not universal, and polls at the time indicated that public opinion was divided between GM and the striking workers. Many GM shareholders and those with ties to the company, as well as numerous media outlets and elected officials in company towns such as Flint, denounced the strike and regarded the sit-in as illegal, essentially equivalent to theft of company property. A Michigan state court issued an injunction against the sit-in, which was ignored by the UAW. In Flint, local government officials, the radio station, and the newspaper, *The Flint Journal*, supported GM. On January 11, 1937, local police attempted to storm the Flint plant and lobbed teargas at workers inside. Strikers used fire hoses and hurled objects to repel attempts by local police to enter. After several hours of struggle, police efforts to forcibly take the facility ceased. In an effort to prevent further violence between strikers and local law enforcement, Michigan National Guard units were deployed to the site by the state's governor.

Following a national UAW conference in Flint, the union presented a list of formal demands to GM in January. The UAW insisted that negotiations apply to all represented GM workers, not just those of the Flint plant. It called for company recognition of the UAW as the bargaining agent of workers, wage increases, a 30-hour work week with overtime pay, rehiring of all employees previously fired for union involvement, layoffs managed by seniority with the company, and a slower and safer assembly line. Initially GM unequivocally rejected all UAW demands, and the company and its supporters denounced the ongoing strike, but by February some of the company's leaders, including Vice President William Knudsen, began to accept that negotiations and the accommodation of collective bargaining and at least some of the auto workers' demands were necessary to end the costly strike.

President Roosevelt requested that GM negotiate with the workers, and the company eventually complied. An agreement was reached on February 11 in which the UAW was recognized as the bargaining agent of employees who were union members. The company agreed to a 5 percent pay increase for workers, to end discrimination against union members, and to begin negotiations concerning other matters. Through the agreement reached with GM, the UAW became the bargaining agent for more than 100,000 of its workers. Over the next year, the UAW saw its membership expand to more than 500,000 members nationally, making it one of the largest and most powerful labor unions in U.S. history.

Barry Mowell

See also: American Federation of Labor (AFL); Automobile; Chávez, César E. (1927–1993); New Deal; Roosevelt, Franklin Delano (1882–1945); United Auto Workers (UAW)

References

Baulch, Vivian, and Patricia Zacharias. "The Historic 1936–37 Flint Auto Plant Strikes." *The Detroit News*, June 23, 1997.

Norwood, Stephen. *Strikebreaking and Intimidation: Mercenaries and Masculinity* in *Twentieth-Century America*. Chapel Hill: University of North Carolina Press, 2001.

Shogan, Robert. *Backlash: The Killing of the New Deal*. Chicago: Ivan R. Dee, 2006.

Flower, Benjamin Orange (1858–1918)

Editor and social reformer Benjamin Orange Flower passionately addressed many of the most controversial issues of his time, including economic equality, education, immigration, spiritualism, and women's rights. Flower was also one of the few eastern editors to champion Populism, especially the presidential candidacy of William Jennings Bryan.

Flower was born October 19, 1858, in Albion, Illinois, descended from social reformers going back to his great-grandfather, Richard Flower, in England. Following his education at a Kentucky Bible college, he returned to Albion briefly in 1880 to begin a career in journalism. He also worked for six years in Philadelphia before moving to Boston, where he created a new monthly magazine, *The Arena*, in December 1889.

Taking its name from Heinrich Heine's belief that people must fight for ideas like gladiators in an arena, Flower's publication was one of several popular magazines to address social problems in an outspoken, crusading style. Flower also established the Arena Publishing Company, which for six years issued the works of Hamlin Garland and other reform-minded authors.

Shortly after the Omaha Convention of 1892, Flower wholeheartedly endorsed the People's Party: "I have observed its growth and tendencies with profound interest, and I am convinced that it is not only the most purely democratic party in America to-day, but that it *possesses a moral energy not present in the spoils-seeking parties*" (July 1893, emphasis in the original). Similarly, when William Jennings Bryan was nominated for president by both Populists and Democrats in 1896, Flower enthused, "The election of Mr. Bryan will mean the rejuvenation of democracy and the salvation of republican government from a lawless plutocracy, the most dangerous of all despotisms" (November 1896).

Due to a combination of ill health and financial difficulties, Flower surrendered the editorship of *The Arena* in late 1896. However, he continued to edit several other publications, including *New Time* and *Coming Age*, both of which eventually merged with *The Arena*, thereby allowing him to resume his editorial role from 1900 until *The Arena* ceased publication in August 1909. Flower subsequently edited two additional publications, including one espousing anti-Catholic beliefs. He died in a hospital in Cambridge, Massachusetts, on December 24, 1918.

James I. Deutsch

See also: Bryan, William Jennings (1860–1925); Emery, Sarah (1838–1895); Garland, Hamlin (1860–1940); People's Party; Trans-Mississippi Exposition (1898)

References

Cline, Howard F. "Benjamin Orange Flower and *The Arena*, 1889–1909." *Journalism Quarterly* 17 (2): 139–150, 171.

Holleran, Karen. "Benjamin Orange Flower." In Hester Lee Furey, ed., *American Radical and Reform Writers*. 2nd series (pp. 134–140). Detroit: Gale, 2009.

Matusow, Allen J. "The Mind of B.O. Flower." *New England Quarterly* 34 (4): 492–509.

Force Bill (1890)

Also known as the Lodge Bill or the Election Bill of 1890, the Force Bill, as it became known in the South and West, was introduced by Republican Representative Henry Cabot Lodge and Senator George Frisbie Hoar, both of Massachusetts, and supported by President Benjamin Harrison. The bill was designed to close loopholes in the Fifteenth Amendment used by white southern Democrats to prevent blacks from voting. It also allowed the federal government greater oversight over elections and was seen by many as a further attempt to whittle away states' rights. Southern politicians used the filibuster against the bill in the Senate until western Republicans agreed to let the bill die in exchange for the South's support of the Sherman Silver Purchase Act.

The Force Bill became a wedge between factions at the National Farmers' Alliance and Industrial Union (NFAIU) annual meeting in Ocala, Florida, in December 1890. With the representatives of 25 states present to decide both on a platform and a slate of political candidates for the 1892 election, a representative from Mississippi introduced a resolution putting the Alliance on record as opposing the Lodge Bill. It put the thorny racial issue at the center of the formation of the new political movement. While it passed by a voice vote, on the last day at the convention, South Dakota's Alonzo Wardall called for the resolution to be stricken from the minutes of the Ocala meeting. With a vote along regional lines, his motion was tabled, thus jeopardizing the movement to bring the two factions together before it had even begun.

Trevor Jason Soderstrum

See also: Ocala Convention (1890); Sherman Silver Purchase Act (1890)

References

Welch, Richard E. "The Federal Elections Bill of 1890: Postscripts and Prelude." *Journal of American History* 52 (3): 511–526.

Freedom Riders

The Freedom Riders was an activist group that was formed in the midst of the civil rights movement to protest the segregation of both southern buses and terminal facilities. Throughout the summer of 1961, the group mobilized white and black activists to test a recent Supreme Court ruling (*Boynton v. Virginia*) that outlawed discrimination in interstate transit. The Freedom Riders quickly captured national attention in May 1961 when 13 members (seven black and six white) of the group filed onto two south-bound buses in Washington, DC. The riders encountered staunch opposition from local whites in both Anniston and Birmingham, Alabama, leaving the group unable to reach their intended destination: New Orleans, Louisiana. Fellow activists quickly rallied behind the riders, and the Freedom Rides (as they came to be known) continued throughout the summer.

Established in May 1961 by the Congress of Racial Equality (CORE), one of the most influential activist groups of the civil rights movement, the Freedom Riders' goal was to draw attention to the South's blatant disregard of basic constitutional rights. CORE National Director James Farmer explained that the group was created to continue the momentum of the sit-ins "by 'putting the movement on wheels' " (Anderson 51). Subsequently, CORE officials devised the Journey of Reconciliation (later renamed the Freedom Rides), a plan to send groups of integrated riders throughout the South on both the Greyhound and Trailways bus lines. Riders were to board the buses at Washington, DC, tour the South, and conclude their expedition in New Orleans, Louisiana. Black riders would sit in the front of the buses, with their white counterparts riding in the back. Likewise, white participants were instructed to use rest-stop facilities (waiting rooms, restrooms, restaurants, etc.) that were designated for blacks while black riders were directed to use white-only amenities. Initial volunteers were fully aware of the dangers that were associated with such an ambitious plan and sought to channel the anticipated racism into an emergency situation that would force the Kennedy administration to intervene on their behalf.

The Freedom Riders' first major exhibition was scheduled for early May 1961. On Thursday, May 4, 13 integrated riders assembled in Washington, DC, and

A bus carrying civil rights Freedom Riders is fire-bombed during a caravan to advocate black voting rights in 1961. The Freedom Riders were civil rights advocates, both black and white, who traveled to the South from the North on buses in 1961 as volunteers for the Congress of Racial Equality. (Library of Congress)

boarded two buses (one operated by Greyhound, the other by Trailways) bound for New Orleans, Louisiana. The riders departed the District of Columbia bus terminal amid a flurry of newspapermen and photographers, who had been summoned by Director Farmer to guarantee adequate media exposure for the group. The journey through Virginia and North Carolina was relatively uneventful. The events that occurred in Rock Hill, South Carolina, however, eerily foreshadowed the troubling circumstances that the group would soon face. John Lewis, a black activist involved in the Nashville student movement, and another Freedom Rider were knocked to the ground inside the local Rock Hill bus terminal while attempting to use the white waiting room. The two men escaped unscathed, and the group continued their journey throughout South Carolina and Georgia. The situation became increasingly perilous when the first bus entered Anniston, Alabama. There, the Freedom Riders were met by an angry mob of 200 whites that lacerated the tires of the bus and hurled stones at it. The driver of the bus successfully navigated through the angry mob, but the bus was quickly overtaken just outside of town. The bus was set ablaze, and the Freedom Riders were severely beaten with clubs and blackjacks. When the second bus arrived in Anniston, the riders were similarly victimized but decided to continue on to Birmingham, Alabama.

When the bus pulled into the Birmingham terminal, the riders were again met by an angry mob. Despite the fact that the local police headquarters was only two blocks away from the station, no officers came to aid the Freedom Riders. Local police officials claimed that (because it was Mother's Day) most of the officers had been home with their mothers during the melee. Ten minutes passed before officers arrived on the scene, leaving the mob ample time to escape in waiting automobiles. Despite the incident, the Freedom Riders wanted to continue on towards Montgomery, Jackson, and New Orleans. However, Alabama Governor John Patterson warned the riders to leave the state, and the Justice Department promptly arranged a flight. Student Non-violent Coordinating Committee (SNCC)–affiliated students from Nashville vowed to complete the original itinerary, and the Freedom Rides continued throughout the summer. By September 1961, a demoralized Kennedy administration instructed the Interstate Commerce Commission to take legal action against any form of segregation in interstate bus transit. The Freedom Riders played a significant role in the civil rights movement, and their actions underscored a continued devotion to nonviolent protest.

Christopher Lewis Leadingham

See also: Congress of Racial Equality (CORE); Interstate Commerce Act (ICA) (1887); King, Martin Luther, Jr. (1929–1968)

References

Anderson, Terry H. *The Movement and the Sixties*. New York: Oxford University Press, 1995.

Levy, Peter B. *The Civil Rights Movement*. Westport, CT: Greenwood Press, 1998.

Luders, Joseph E. *The Civil Rights Movement and the Logic of Social Change*. New York: Cambridge University Press, 2010.

Morris, Aldon D. *The Origins of the Civil Rights Movement: Black Communities Organizing for Change*. New York: The Free Press, 1984.

Packard, Jerrold M. *American Nightmare: The History of Jim Crow*. New York: St. Martin's Press, 2002.

Free Silver. *See* Gold Standard/Free Silver

Freethinkers

Freethinkers are people who reject social norms based on custom, tradition, and religious ideals while favoring a society based on reason, free inquiry, and science. Strains of freethinking exist as early as Greece and Rome; it was not until the Enlightenment, however, in the seventeenth and eighteenth centuries that freethinking became more tolerated, if it did not result in social disorder. By the twenty-first century, freethinkers are now visible throughout society even while they are not universally accepted.

In American history, freethinking is often associated with the conflict between religious and secular worldviews. This conflict is present in the debates surrounding the Constitution. The absence of a direct reference to God within the document produced a great deal of consternation for many Americans. The First Amendment clause prohibiting Congress from establishing a national church did not resolve the conflict between secular and religious ideals in the operation of the U.S. government. This conflict was inflamed by the publication of Thomas Paine's deistical tract *The Age of Reason* in 1794. According to Paine, all traditions and authority structures based on Biblical authority should be rejected as the Bible did not pass the test of reason because of its reliance on miracles and unproven testimony. Many of Paine's critics linked free thought with the excesses of the French Revolution. Although Paine pleaded for the right of every person to have the freedom to express his or her opinions openly, his open rejection of biblical authority and organized religion was not well received. In his later years Paine was ostracized by most Americans for his alleged atheism.

After the Civil War, a new wave of secularists organized to demand a constitutional amendment to ensure the complete secularization of the U.S. political system as a matter of civil rights. For many, the political system of the late nineteenth century showed signs of backsliding into a government that enforced Christian morality and dogma rather than existing as a neutral entity. Much like the experience of Thomas Paine a century earlier, fear of free thought was combined with fear of other social events such as woman suffrage, unionization in the workforce, and socialism, which created a backlash against secularist thought. Support for traditional religious structures combined with a fear of social change led many to cast any variety of freethinking as a danger to the public. Thus, after the upheavals of the late nineteenth century, many Americans embraced conservative reform during the Progressive Era.

The social upheaval of the 1960s brought the traditional structures of society into question to an unprecedented degree. In response to social issues as diverse as abortion, school prayer, and gay marriage, there is a new conservative mobilization based on supporting the traditional role of religion as the arbitrator of public morality. The culture war between secular and religious ideals in the twenty-first century United States is unresolved.

Patrick Callaway

See also: Bush, George W., Populist Rhetoric of; Ingersoll, Robert (1833–1899); Progressivism; Sanger, Margaret (1879–1966); Tea Party

References

Jacoby, Susan. *Freethinkers: A History of American Secularism.* New York: Henry Holt and Company, 2004.

Paine, Thomas. *The Age of Reason.* New York: Carol Publishing, 1995.

Schaller, Michael. *Right Turn: American Life in the Reagan-Bush Era, 1980–1992.* New York: Oxford University Press, 2007.

Warren, Sidney. *American Freethought, 1860–1914.* New York: Gordian Press, 1966.

G

Garland, Hamlin (1860–1940)

An American novelist and essayist, Hamlin Garland was the author of novels that focused on the life of midwestern farmers. He was named after Hannibal Hamlin, who became Abraham Lincoln's first vice president. Initially called Hannibal Hamlin Garland, he dropped the "Hannibal" and went on to write numerous novels about the lives and problems of ordinary rural people.

Born on September 14, 1860, on the family farm near West Salem, Wisconsin, Hamlin Garland was the second of the four children of Richard Hayes Garland and his wife Charlotte Isabella (née McClintock). His father, a carpenter, had been born in Maine in 1830, and with his own parents he had traveled along the Erie Canal into the Great Lakes. There they had met Hugh McClintock, a borderman from Ohio. Richard Hayes Garland married Hugh's daughter Charlotte, eight years his junior.

Soon after Hamlin Garland was born, his family moved to Mitchell County, Iowa, and there they ran another farm. It was a hard life, and the young Hamlin Garland learned that hard work kept the farm going. He attended an overcrowded country school, which undoubtedly led to his later championing of the concept of social reform.

The family decided to move further west and relocated to Brown County, in the Dakota Territory, in 1881. It was a bleak farm, and Hamlin Garland sought work at nearby farms to help support the family. He decided to leave agriculture and started teaching during the winter of 1882–1883, working in Illinois. He was largely self-taught and later credited much of his knowledge at that time to John Richard Green's *Short History of the English People* and Chambers's *Encyclopedia of English Literature*.

In 1884, Garland moved to Boston, where he read widely and ended up being appointed as a lecturer at the Boston School of Oratory. He had already been fascinated by the work of Hippolyte Taine, and it was not long before he moved from teaching to writing. Some of this was certainly at the urging of Joseph Kirkland, who urged Garland to use his harsh upbringing as a way of trying to encourage social change. After writing many magazine articles, especially in *Harper's Weekly* and then in *Arena*, Garland produced his first major work, *Main-Travelled Roads*, which was published in 1891. It came, however, at a time of family tragedy, coinciding with the death of his sister and his mother being crippled by a stroke.

Garland continued writing and produced three significant pieces in 1892. In *A Member of the Third House*, Garland presented a savage attack on the state of politics in the United States at the time. Garland was critical of the corrupt political practices of the Gilded Age United States. His next book, *Jason Edwards*, also published in 1892, attacked the rigging of land sales and other fraudulent practices. In a third book, *A Spoil of Office*, he tried to champion the cause of the farmers from the American West in the hope that they would come together and form a united political force that might be able to change the nature of politics.

Garland then wrote a number of books on a variety of topics, which were not as successful. He returned to great popularity, however, with his Middle Border Series, which included four autobiographical works: *A Son of the Middle Border* (1917), *A Daughter of the Middle Border* (1921), *Trail-Makers of the Middle Border* (1926), and *Back-Trailers from the Middle Border* (1928). He continued writing through the 1930s with four volumes of his memoirs: *Roadside Meetings* (1930), *Companions on the Trail* (1931), *My Friendly Contemporaries* (1932), and *Afternoon Neighbors* (1934). He died on March 4, 1940, in Los Angeles.

Justin Corfield

See also: Anderson, Sherwood (1876–1941); Cather, Willa (1873–1947); Gilded Age; West, Populism in the

References

Garland, Hamlin. *Afternoon Neighbors*. New York: The Macmillan Company, 1934.

Garland, Hamlin. *Companions on the Trail*. New York: The Macmillan Company, 1931.

Garland, Hamlin. *My Friendly Contemporaries*. New York: The Macmillan Company, 1932.

Garland, Hamlin. *Roadside Meetings*. New York: The Macmillan Company, 1930.

Higgins, John E. "A Man from the Middle Border: Hamlin Garland's Diaries." *Wisconsin Magazine of History* 46 (4): 294–302.

Newlin, Keith. *Hamlin Garland: A Life*. Lincoln: University of Nebraska Press, 2008.

Garrison, William Lloyd (1805–1879)

On July 4, 1854, William Lloyd Garrison publicly burned a copy of the U.S. Constitution. Far from honoring the document commemorated on that day of national celebration, with his act Garrison declared the Constitution to be a symbol of degradation, sin, and most relevant to his cause, slavery. "To-day, we are called to celebrate the seventy-eighth anniversary of American Independence. In what spirit? With what purpose? To what end?" he asked. Calling the Constitution "the source and parent of all the other atrocities—'a covenant with death, and an agreement with hell,' " Garrison watched as it burned, finally exclaiming, "So perish all compromises with tyranny!" (Yacavone).

This militarism and refusal to compromise would come to define William Lloyd Garrison both in his character and in his stalwart attack on the institution of slavery. Garrison was one of the most renowned, loved, and alternately loathed actors in the debate over slavery in the nineteenth century—primarily for his radical stance on emancipation and for the abolitionist newspaper he edited and produced for three decades, *The Liberator.* Born in Newburyport, Massachusetts, in 1805 to Abijah and Fanny Garrison, young William endured a productive, albeit difficult, childhood. His father abandoned the family when Garrison was only three years old. At the tender age of nine, he began his work as an apprentice shoemaker, then cabinetmaker, and finally—and fortuitously—a printer. By the time Garrison was 17, he was publishing articles in his local newspaper, and by 20 he had gained the reputation of an established printer and talented journalist. His articles began to reflect the turn in his thoughts toward politics and reform in general and toward antislavery in particular. One person who noticed this shift with interest was Benjamin Lundy. Lundy ran the Quaker newspaper, pointedly titled *The Genius of Universal Emancipation*, a periodical whose primary purpose was the gradual emancipation of slaves. Though they had met in Boston in 1828, their partnership did not begin until 1829 when Lundy walked from Baltimore to Bennington, Vermont, where Garrison was heading up a paper of which the purpose was advocating the reelection of John Quincy Adams. Lundy hoped to convince Garrison to put his reformatory energies behind antislavery. In his writing, Garrison had developed a polemical style that was vitriolic, passionate, and even violent in the pursuit of his causes. This did little to deter Lundy but rather convinced him that Garrison would be an asset to *Genius*. Garrison agreed to accept the coeditor position at *Genius*. He wrote in his final editorial in the Bennington paper, "I trust in God that I may be the humble instrument of breaking at least one chain, and restoring one captive to liberty; it will amply repay a life of severe toil" (Garrison and Garrison 121).

As one historian notes, Garrison was "hot" in a "cold age" (Chapman 34). On his way south to Baltimore, Garrison stopped in Boston and delivered the address that marked the beginning of his mission. At the Park Street Church on another July 4—this time in 1829—Garrison railed against the complacency of government, Christianity, and the American people, arguing that they were all complicit in the perpetuation of slavery. Upon his arrival in Baltimore in August and given the somewhat cool reception of his oration at Park Street, Garrison determined that a more radical platform was needed. He began to call for immediate emancipation. Though his time in Baltimore was short-lived, Garrison made a lasting impact. He managed to incur a bounty on his head by Georgia officials after his support of the Walker Appeal. David Walker, a freed Boston slave, attacked the idea of colonization as a curative to slavery, which echoed Garrison's unapologetic commitment to immediate, uncompensated emancipation. Garrison also spent seven weeks in prison for slandering a fellow Massachusetts native, Francis Todd, whom he had accused of participating in the domestic slave trade. Arthur Tappan, the famed New York antislavery reformer, eventually paid his bail.

In 1830, the partnership between Lundy and Garrison dissolved, at least in a professional sense. Lundy believed in gradual emancipation, and Garrison was not a person who tolerated caution, even when it was well-meaning. Once back in Boston, Garrison and his publishing partner, Isaac Knapp, swiftly began production of Garrison's own journalistic project. The first issue of *The Liberator* was published on January 1, 1831. In it appeared a letter "To the Public" in which Garrison made many pledges, from promising to uphold the Declaration of Independence to making amends with God for the blight of slavery. He concluded this letter stating, "I am in earnest—I will not equivocate—I will not excuse—I will not retreat a single inch—and I will be heard" (Swift 82). Heard he most certainly was.

The Liberator remained in publication from that first issue until January 1, 1866, and the newspaper stopped publication following the ratification of the Thirteenth Amendment, which abolished slavery. Though it had only 3,000 subscribers (nearly three-quarters of whom were African American), the paper gained both national renown and derision and made the name William Lloyd Garrison synonymous with the slavery debate. The primarily proslavery South reviled the publication, as did many northerners. Though the North was generally more friendly to the idea of emancipation, most people, even those with pronounced antislavery tendencies, were concerned with the fallout of what they saw as hasty Garrisonian abolitionism. Furthermore, being associated with Garrison during this time brought with it the threat of violence. Garrison was often the subject of threats and plots, all of which he welcomed for the sole reason that it meant his ideas were being heard and were generating debate.

In addition to *The Liberator*, Garrison founded the New England Anti-Slavery Society in 1832. Then in the following year, he, along with Arthur Tappan, founded the American Anti-Slavery Society. The two men would part ways in 1839, with Tappan founding the American and Foreign Anti-Slavery Society with his brother Lewis. The source of their split was the fact that Garrison desired to admit women—including Elizabeth Cady Stanton, Susan B. Anthony, and Lucretia Mott—to the American Anti-Slavery Society, whereas Tappan wished to keep the Society men-only. This is indicative of Garrison's general attitude. He believed that reform, particularly that which dealt with civil liberties and human rights, should be universal. To seek to bring about one type of reform while shunning another was the height of hypocrisy. During his lifetime, Garrison worked with the woman's rights and temperance movements, particularly after slavery was officially abolished in 1866.

Despite starting several projects, Garrison established a family and remained active in the larger movement of reform and civil rights. In 1834, Garrison married Helen Eliza Benson, the daughter of retired abolitionist George Benson. With Helen, he had five sons and two daughters, all while ensuring steady publication of *The Liberator* and tending to his many antislavery commitments. Though he had gained the reputation of being a vicious opponent of slavery, he was also becoming renowned for his policy of nonviolent resistance. This pacifistic stance did not help him when, in 1835, he was dragged through the streets by an unruly mob after delivering an address to the Anti-Slavery Society in Boston. Then, in 1849, Garrison became embroiled in the trial of Washington Goode. Goode was a black sailor who had murdered Thomas Harding, another black seaman. For his crime, Goode had been sentenced to death. Garrison argued against the verdict, claiming it had been handed down on the basis of race, not evidence. Notwithstanding Garrison's passionate plea, Goode was hanged in the spring of 1849.

After slavery was abolished, Garrison resigned his post at the American Anti-Slavery Society and dissolved *The Liberator.* He continued to work for causes that inspired him, like the civil equality of freed slaves and women. He participated in several speaking tours and continued to write for newspapers around the country. On May 24, 1879, Garrison, who had long been suffering from kidney disease, died peacefully in his home. Abolitionist Theodore Dwight Weld and the new president of the American Anti-Slavery Society, Wendell Phillips, both delivered eulogies at his memorial service. His legacy lived on in his children, who pursued reform after his death, and in the millions of freed black slaves who benefited from his refusal to compromise with tyranny.

Lydia Eeva Natti Willsky

See also: Abolitionism; Emancipation Proclamation; Prohibition (1919–1933)

References

Chapman, John Jay. *William Lloyd Garrison.* New York: Moffat, Yard and Company, 1913.

Frederickson, George M. *William Lloyd Garrison.* Englewood Cliffs, NJ: Prentice-Hall, 1968.

Garrison, Wendell Phillips, and Francis Jackson Garrison. *William Lloyd Garrison, 1805–1879: The Story of His Life Told by His Children.* 4 vols. New York: Century Co., 1889.

Mayer, Henry. *All on Fire: William Lloyd Garrison and the Abolition of Slavery.* New York: St. Martin's Press, 1998.

Merrill, Walter M. *Against Wind and Tide: A Biography of William Lloyd Garrison.* Cambridge, MA: Harvard University Press, 1963.

Swift, Lindsay. *William Lloyd Garrison.* Philadelphia: George W. Jacobs & Company, 1911.

Yacavone, David. "A Covenant with Death and an Agreement with Hell." http://www.masshist.org/objects/2005july.cfm. Accessed January 3. 2013.

George, Henry (1839–1897)

Henry George, an American economist and social reformer, promoted a tax on land values that became known as the Single Tax. George advocated abolishing existing property taxes and tariffs and, instead, imposing a single tax or rent on the unimproved value of the land. George sought to encourage investment in new buildings and industrial facilities and to discourage land speculation and the concentration of land ownership. George died in 1897 after the peak of Populist protest had waned.

George was born in Philadelphia, Pennsylvania, on September 2, 1839. His formal education ended at age 13. As a young man, he spent months at sea on a voyage to Australia. After returning to Philadelphia, he worked as an apprentice typesetter. In late 1857, he then sailed as a ship's steward on a vessel bound for California. The next year, he made a failed attempt to mine gold in British Columbia and returned to San Francisco broke. As did many failed miners, George pursued work in his previous fields and found employment as a printer and journalist. George edited several San Francisco, Oakland, and Sacramento, California, newspapers between 1866 and 1879 including his own *San Francisco Daily Evening Post* from 1871 until 1875. George's editorials advocated various reforms, including trade unionism and the eight-hour day. George opposed monopolies of all forms, and the concentration of land in the hands of a few speculators and wealthy individuals troubled him.

An 1869 conflict with the Associated Press and Western Union contributed to George's disdain for monopolies. The California Press Association and a rival publisher controlled access to the Associate Press wire and made access too expensive for George's employer and several other San Francisco newspapers. George's employer sent him to New York City to negotiate directly with the wire service. George failed to obtain favorable terms and tried to circumvent the syndicate. He made an arrangement for a Pennsylvania newspaper to send wire news to San Francisco using Western Union. The telegraph company, closely aligned with the Associated Press, a relationship of which George was unaware, quickly discovered his ploy. Western Union harassed George for months and finally made its services too expensive for his employer to bear. George assailed the monopoly for limiting freedom of the press.

In 1871, George published *Our Land and Land Policy, National and State*. In the tract, he argued that public lands should be distributed in 80-acre or 40-acre allotments rather than in the 160-acre allotments authorized by the Homestead Act of 1862. George believed the change would mean additional land for ordinary homesteaders rather than for speculators or investors. George called for the forced divesting of huge tracts of privately held land and advocated a tax to restrict the concentration of land holding.

The newly elected Democratic governor of California, William S. Irwin, appointed George to a patronage position as state inspector of gas meters in 1876. The position allowed George to continue to write.

George again articulated his call for land reform in *Progress and Poverty: An Inquiry into the Causes of Industrial Depressions, and of Increase of Want with Increase of Wealth—The Remedy*, published in 1879. In *Progress and Poverty*, George proposed the nationalization of land ownership, the redistribution of land, and the imposition of a single tax on land values. George wrote that the concentration of land ownership caused the growing economic disparity between the rich and poor in the United States. George believed that land ownership itself resulted in economic gain and wanted the government to use the revenue from his proposed tax on land to alleviate the wants of those who did not own land. True to his fear of the concentration of power, George believed local governments, rather than the federal government, should administer the single tax.

A post–Civil War depression struck the United States from 1873 to 1878 and created an audience receptive to George's proposals. *Progress and Poverty* attracted readers throughout the United States and Europe. George moved to New York City in 1880 to write and lecture. He also lectured in Europe and Australia throughout the 1880s.

In the 1890s, Single Tax advocates and other nonconformists joined the Populist coalition. Many supporters of George's ideas joined the Farmers' Alliance and voted for the People's Party. Single Taxers became an important part of the Populist movement in urban areas. George himself did not embrace Populism and preferred to concentrate exclusively on the tax issue. George, unlike many Populists, remained skeptical of government centralization.

George made several unsuccessful attempts at elected office. George campaigned for mayor of New York City in 1886 as the candidate of the United Labor Party, the political arm of the Central Labor Union. George finished second to the candidate backed by Tammany Hall's Democratic machine and ahead of the third-place Republican candidate, future President Theodore Roosevelt. George again represented the United Labor Party in the 1887 campaign for secretary of state of New York. George finished third in the election.

George ran for mayor of New York City as an independent Democrat in 1897. He died October 29, 1897, four days before the election.

Jeff Wells

See also: Crime of '73; Depression of 1873; Depression of 1893; Gilded Age; Homestead Act (1862); People's Party; The Press and Populism; Roosevelt, Theodore (1858–1919)

References

Barker, Charles Albro. *Henry George*. New York: Oxford University Press, 1955.

Cord, Steven B. *Henry George: Dreamer or Realist?* Philadelphia: University of Pennsylvania Press, 1965.

De Mille, Anna George. *Henry George: Citizen of the World.* Edited by Don C. Shoemaker. Chapel Hill: University of North Carolina Press, 1950.

George, Henry. *Henry George: Collected Journalistic Writings.* 4 vols. Edited by Kenneth C. Wenzer. Armonk, NY: M. E. Sharpe, 2003.

Hill, Malcolm. *The Man Who Said No! The Life of Henry George*. London: Othila Press, 1997.

Postel, Charles. *The Populist Revolt.* New York: Oxford University Press, 2007.

Rose, Edward J. *Henry George*. New York: Twayne Publishers, 1968.

Thomas, John L. *Alternative America: Henry George, Edward Bellamy, Henry Demarest Lloyd, and the Adversary Tradition.* Cambridge, MA: The Belknap Press, 1983.

George, Milton (1833–unknown)

Milton George was the founder of the chief organization for farmers in the northern and northwestern states during the 1880s, the National Farmers' Alliance, or Northern Alliance. Even after his direct connection with the Alliance ended, it continued to operate and have the same goals as those he had envisaged. Without George's financial support and guiding hand, the Northern Alliance could not have been as influential as it was. This organization, along with others, led directly to the creation of the People's Party, the full political manifestation of Populist angst in the late nineteenth century.

George was the eldest son of a Quaker family, born in 1833 near Hillsboro, Ohio. His father moved the family when George was six years old to pursue opportunities in Illinois. They settled on a farm near Farmington in central Illinois. George helped on the family farm before establishing himself in agriculture. He married the daughter of prosperous merchant in 1860 and achieved considerable success in farming during and after the Civil War. By 1871, George was prosperous enough to move to Cook County, near Chicago, and purchase another farm. He and a younger brother operated it until 1889, when George donated it to become a home for boys.

In 1872, George took a position as the assistant editor of the *Western Rural and Family Farm Paper*, a weekly farm publication. The paper had an established reputation among the rural population as well as a greater circulation than the *Prairie Farmer*, its main rival. The Great Chicago Fire of 1871, however, completely destroyed the paper's publishing and editorial facilities. The publisher, Horatio N. F. Lewis, received a $17,000 loan from George to continue in operation. By 1876, however, the *Western Rural* was in dire straits and George assumed control of it to protect his investment. He instituted a number of policies, including honesty in all advertisements, respect for subscribers, and editorials free from outside influence. George also hired David Ward Wood, a talented writer, to help with editorials.

George saw his paper as a way to help correct injustices suffered by farmers, whom he viewed as the foundation of American civilization. The concentration of wealth among a few people led to corruption of governments. Soon George was writing editorials calling on farmers to use their voting power to support farmer-candidates and to reject lawyers and "partisan blow-hards" who dominated the legislatures (Scott, "The Agrarian Movement," 24). He renounced the idea of a third party, however, and believed that farmers could make changes through the existing major parties. The key to this was the organization of farmers into a nonpartisan and loosely organized farmers' alliance. The alliance would educate farmers about issues that affected them. These issues included such things as the adulteration of foods and the replacement of butter by oleomargarine, the need for free school books for all children, and the high cost of insurance for crops and farms. Later, George included such issues as monopolies, the banking system, and equal taxation.

George's greatest anger was reserved for the railroads, however. Railroads were necessary for farmers to get their products to market and to bring supplies to them. However, during the 1870s, railroads were known for excessively high shipping rates, rebates to certain favored shippers, monopolies in areas in which no competition existed, and control over land granted them by the federal government. His solution was federal government regulation, comparing the railroads to public highways.

To obtain regulation of the railroads, George believed that farmers had to submit petitions with large numbers of signatures. He distributed thousands of petitions to farmers throughout the Midwest. Early efforts in 1879 were unsuccessful and caused him to realize that a national organization was needed. In November 1879, George used his editorials in the *Western Rural* to encourage farmers to create "cheap transportation clubs" to get petitions signed. He printed a model constitution for such a club as well.

No clubs organized, so George called a meeting of the local farmers at the office of the *Western Rural* on April 15, 1880. They adopted George's model constitution and elected Wood as president and George as secretary. They also accepted by-laws that George wrote and his offer to use the *Western Rural* office for semimonthly meetings. Other groups throughout the Midwest followed the Cook County club's example and received charters from them. By October 1880, George published claims that clubs existed from Ohio to the Pacific Coast.

The first national meeting of delegates from the clubs was held on October 14, 1880. George made all arrangements and paid the expenses involved. The delegates adopted a constitution for a national organization with local, state, and national alliances. The central board of officers had only limited control. The organization was named the National Farmers' Alliance. George offered to pay all the expenses of the new organization for the first year. He discouraged the idea of assessing local alliance dues for members and hoped that contributions from private individuals would support the Alliance.

During the first year, the Alliance grew rapidly in numbers and chapters, spurred by hard times faced by farmers in the Midwest. By the time the second national meeting was held in Chicago on October 5 and 6, 1881, it had 24,500 members and 940 alliances in 10 states. Although he did not hold any office, George again dominated the meeting. The delegates accepted resolutions that he drafted. These included demands for graduated income tax; reduction of salaries for public officials in accord with their job; election, not appointment, of officials; and an interstate commerce law to allow the federal government to regulate the railroads. George again offered to pay all expenses for the organization.

While the National Farmers' Alliance was quickly growing, some critics believed it was more concerned with increasing the circulation of the *Western Rural* than with helping farmers. The *Prairie Farmer* and other influential farming papers criticized the way George dominated the Alliance. Even though the Alliance claimed 100,000 members by its third national meeting, only a few delegates showed up at the St. Louis meeting. George again pledged to pay the Alliance's expenses because no other source of income was found. George also published a songbook for local alliances that included songs to make meetings more enjoyable, a model program for meetings, and an outline of officers' duties. When some state alliances seemed to be falling apart, George sent money directly to them. Few delegates showed up for the annual meeting in 1883. George was elected secretary, and the constitution was amended to allow the officers to act for the Alliance until the next meeting. The other officers did little, so George virtually controlled the Alliance until the next meeting was held in 1886. He continued to pay all the expenses for the Alliance for the next four years.

George offered an honorary membership to any farmer and organized an agency for cooperative buying. The Economy Club took orders from farmers and passed them on to wholesalers, who sent the goods directly to the farmers. George bragged that members could save 20 to 60 percent off of retail prices. Meanwhile, the honorary memberships introduced the idea of organization to thousands of other farmers and helped create a database of names of people who might be willing to participate in Alliance actions.

The next annual meeting was held on November 11, 1886, in Chicago. George reported a membership of more than 500,000 in 16 states. Although the Alliance was reviving, delegates realized that changes were needed to reach the organization's goals. The next meeting, in Minneapolis on October 5, 1887, was the most important in the National Farmers' Alliance. Changes to the constitution increased the power of state leaders and removed that of George. Assessments were made against local alliances so the national body was self-supporting and no longer dependent on George. Soon, the Alliance moved toward more direct political action. Other farm publications gave more space to National Farmers' Alliance activities as it was no longer so closely connected with the *Western Rural.*

George continued to be active in issues related to farming concerns, but after 1887 he no longer dominated the national agricultural scene. The National Farmers' Alliance continued to use the organization blueprint and ideas created by George, including such things as local groups of farmers and the same constitutions. When the Alliance was largely absorbed by the People's Party in 1892, the new party accepted many of George's ideas. The move towards political partisanship, however, went against George's beliefs. By 1896, he had moved to the Republican Party, ending his connection with the national farming organizations.

Tim J. Watts

See also: "Goodbye, My Party, Goodbye"; Long-Haul/Short-Haul Discrimination; Northern Alliance; People's Party; Railroad Regulation; *Western Rural*

References

Scott, Roy V. *The Agrarian Movement in Illinois, 1880–1896.* Urbana: University of Illinois Press, 1962. http://www.archive.org/stream/agrarianmovement00scot/agrarianmovement00scot_djvu.txt.

Scott, Roy V. "Milton George and the Farmers' Alliance Movement." *Mississippi Valley Historical Review* 45 (1): 90–109.

Gilded Age

The term "Gilded Age" refers to the late-nineteenth-century economic golden age enjoyed by the middle and upper classes after the nation recovered from the Panic of 1873 and the intense political, cultural, and economic transformations of the Industrial Revolution. Men known as robber barons—rich businessmen and other captains of industry who employed sometimes unscrupulous labor practices—flourished during this era of rapid capital accumulation. These businessmen were influenced by their upper-middle class, Anglo-Saxon, Protestant worldviews, which, with their philanthropic deeds, influenced the American social world. The nation experienced an American Renaissance, seen in the growth of public cultural institutions such as museums, libraries, opera houses, and more. Ironically, the Gilded Age is also famed for its excessive economic and political corruption and the growth of business monopolies, corrupt third-party politics, and exploitative labor conditions, making this era almost as famous for reform as for opulence. The 1873 book of the same name, *The Gilded Age*, by authors Mark Twain and Charles Dudley Warner, best describes the age from the perspective of those who did benefit from its riches as the robber barons had. Gilding means to cover a base material with a layer of gold. Twain and Warner thus insinuated that this American golden age had a worthless core. They satirized its corrupt politics and its unnecessary opulence, represented by the grand summer mansions in Newport, Rhode Island, of Cornelius Vanderbilt and William Waldorf Astor, the era's most wealthy magnates.

From roughly 1870 to 1900, the United States transformed from a rural economy of regional communities into the world's leading industrial nation. The country's ample land, natural resources, diverse climates, and navigable geography created optimal conditions for the extraction, production, and transportation of goods. New technologies in iron-making (such as the Bessemer process), printing, and other innovations produced more goods faster than had been possible prior to the Civil War. This mass production of books, steel, iron, and other commodities gave American industrialization new energy. New communication technologies, including the telegraph and telephone, and the scientific rationalization of factory work, typified by Taylorism, allowed for coordinated, nationwide management and efficiently organized labor that further increased production. Eventually, companies evolved into corporations and expanded in new legal arrangements such as trusts, pools, or monopolies to finance large-scale enterprise. These large entities, while fostering productivity and capital accumulation, also became associated with abusive business practices, using their economic and political power to exclude competition and commit corrupt labor practices. These injustices motivated the passing of the Sherman Antitrust Act in 1890—the first federal antitrust law—and the onset of the trust-busting Progressive Era ushered in by presidents William McKinley and Theodore Roosevelt in the late nineteenth and early twentieth centuries.

Scandal also plagued U.S. politics on the national and local levels, and voter participation for the eligible—propertied, white males—grew exponentially from the end of Reconstruction in 1877 to the

1890s, due both to widespread bribery and the need for political reform. During the two-term presidency of Ulysses S. Grant (1869–1877), two investors bribed the assistant treasurer of the United States in 1869 for information on the federal government's gold-selling initiatives, resulting in the collapse of gold prices on the notorious Black Friday. Just a few years later, Grant's vice president Schuyler Colfax accepted dividends from the Union Pacific Railroad (and its fraudulent company Crédit Mobilier) in exchange for minimal government interference or investigation into its business practices. Even on the municipal level, the conviction of New York City politician William "Boss" Tweed, who bribed the urban population for votes and stole millions of dollars from the New York City taxpayers, marred the reputation of the Democratic Party and party politics as a whole. The People's Party, born from farmers who organized as a third party to protest rigged foreign and domestic markets, crop overproduction, and a lack of direct political representation, embodies the Gilded Age's changing structures of commerce and politics.

Only a fraction of the public enjoyed the economic and social benefits of the Gilded Age. Large populations of immigrants, people of color, and the working classes experienced hardships. The Reconstruction era (1865–1877) and the enacting of Jim Crow laws (1876–1965) during the Gilded Age heightened race-based tensions and segregation within local communities, and many African Americans (along with other people of color) were socially and physically persecuted by vigilantes in its aftermath. The first federal immigration laws took effect during the Gilded Age, specifically targeting Asian immigrants as "undesirable." For the working classes, many corporations and other businesses took advantage of the era's unregulated labor practices to exploit their workers. The Haymarket Riot of 1886 was one of many organized working-class protests for better labor laws and an eight-hour work day. Finally, Susan B. Anthony and others introduced the Nineteenth Amendment in 1887, but Congress flatly denied its passage. Women would have to wait nearly 30 more years for suffrage.

The Gilded Age's notoriously unregulated political machines, big businesses, and urban population booms contributed to the onset of investigative journalism (muck-raking) and reforms that affect today's contemporary politics and policies. Ida Tarbell's investigative journalism on oil trusts in her 1902–1904 serialized bestseller, *The History of the Standard Oil Company*, fueled growing public awareness of the need for antitrust intervention in the U.S. economy. In 1911, the government ordered the breakup of Standard Oil. Upton Sinclair's 1904 serial, *The Jungle,* exposed the unsafe and inhumane practices of the meat-packing industry. In 1906, Congress passed the Pure Food and Drug Act, which mandated federal inspection and safety standards for food sold to the public. If the Gilded Age's unbridled opulence, rapid capital accumulation, and numerous technological innovations dazzled Americans with the hope of unlimited opportunities, the era's proliferation of corruption also unmasked the problems of consolidated power in special interests and made relevant the social need to protect consumers, minorities, working classes, and the poor.

Colleen Marie Tripp

See also: American Federation of Labor (AFL); Crédit Mobilier Scandal; Democratic Party; Depression of 1873; Depression of 1893; Drought; Electricity; Farmers' Alliance; Farmers' Clubs; Granger Movement; Haymarket Riot (1886); Homestead Strike (1892); Progressivism; Pullman Strike (1894); Robber Barons; Sinclair, Upton (1878–1968); Twain, Mark (1835–1910); Tweed, William M. (1823–1879)

References

Cherny, Robert. *American Politics in the Gilded Age, 1868–1900*. Wheeling, IL: Harlan Davidson, 1997.

Lears, Jackson. *Rebirth of a Nation: The Making of Modern America, 1877–1920*. New York: Harper Perennial, 2010.

Trachentenberg, Alan. *The Incorporation of America: Culture and Society in the Gilded Age*. New York: Hill and Wang, 2007.

Twain, Mark, and Charles Warner. *The Gilded Age: A Tale of Today*. New York: Penguin Classics, 2001.

Gilman, Charlotte Perkins (1860–1935)

Charlotte Anna Perkins Gilman was an author, lecturer, social reformer, and major theorist of the early-twentieth-century feminist movement in the United States.

Born Charlotte Anna Perkins on July 3, 1860, in Hartford, Connecticut, Perkins was the great-niece of Harriet Beecher Stowe. Perkins grew up in near poverty after her father abandoned the family when she was nine years old. The family reportedly moved 19 times in 18 years, with Perkins receiving a total of four years of formal education at various institutions, including the well-respected Rhode Island School of Design.

Perkins's somewhat reluctant first marriage to Charles Walter Stetson in 1884 brought on a deep depression, intensified by the birth of their daughter Katherine Beecher Stetson in 1885. Suffering from melancholia (possibly postpartum depression), Perkins sought a rest cure with Dr. S. Weir Mitchell in Philadelphia. Renowned for treating women with nervous disorders, Mitchell's therapy included forced rest, assisted bathing and dressing, and the banning of all arts or letters. After returning home Perkins suffered a nervous breakdown from the strain of this oppressively infantile routine, which she later dramatized in her 1892 novel, *The Yellow Wallpaper*. Perhaps her most famous work, the novel suggests that women, when forced to subsume their natural desires for work and intellectual engagement to the demands of subjugated domesticity, face insanity.

After leaving Stetson in 1888, Perkins relocated to Pasadena, California. There she began to thrive as an author and social reformer. Influenced by Edward Bellamy and Fabian socialism, Perkins promoted the inclusion of women in society through labor, politics, and education, their domestic and maternal labors to be taken over by a professional class dedicated to those tasks. Perkins subscribed to cultural feminism, a contemporary belief that feminine traits, once introduced, would lead to a more natural, humanist society, correcting the dystopian order caused by male domination. Perkins's reformist efforts as writer and lecturer provided strong sociological arguments for female autonomy through the professionalization of domestic work as a necessary factor of social progress. Throughout the 1890s Perkins engaged in lecture tours, refining her ideas while promoting persuasive sociological arguments in support of the growing women's movement in the United States. She also served as the 1895 delegate to the International Socialist and Labor Congress in London.

In 1898 Perkins published her first major contribution to the women's movement, what is now considered a classic feminist manifesto: *Women and Economics*. Perkins argued that women had to eliminate their economic dependency on men, which forced them to perform housework and sex in return for survival. Only by working outside the home could women gain personal autonomy and a more equal social position that better represented the natural order as exemplified by all other species. The book was generally well received by critics and academics. Considered quite radical for the time, it was a bestseller and translated into several languages.

In 1900, Perkins married her cousin, George H. Gilman, and resided in New York while continuing to write and tour the lecture circuit. Later works expanded or refined parts of *Women and Economics* along with Gilman's views on the vices of men, including *Concerning Children* (1900), *Human Work* (1904), *The Man-Made World* (1911), and *His Religion and Hers* (1923). She also single-handedly wrote, edited, and published *Forerunner Magazine* from 1909 to 1916. Although a leading feminist of the era, Gilman was concerned mostly with middle- and upper-class white women, aligning herself with eugenic thought based on social Darwinism in many of her works and lectures.

Initially published as a serial in *Forerunner*, Gilman's 1915 novel *Herland* described a populist, all-female utopian world based on her ideas. Her views on the benefits of feminizing society were shared by other eminent sociologists, such as Lester Ward and Jane Addams, with whom she stayed at Hull House for a short time. Gilman and Addams also cofounded the Woman's Peace Party in 1915, although Gilman was never active in the organization.

Gilman wrote her memoirs, *The Living of Charlotte Perkins Gilman: An Autobiography* in the years directly preceding her death. Living in Pasadena near her daughter, Gilman ended her own life on August 17, 1935, through an overdose of chloroform after a failed battle with inoperable breast cancer. In 1994, Gilman was introduced into the National Women's Hall of Fame in Seneca Falls, New York.

Christina D. Mune

See also: Addams, Jane (1860–1935); Bellamy, Edward (1850–1898); Feminism; Progressivism; Social Darwinism

References

Allen, Judith A. *The Feminism of Charlotte Perkins Gilman: Sexualities, Histories, Progressivism.* Women in Culture and Society. Chicago: University of Chicago Press, 2009.

Davis, Cynthia J. *Charlotte Perkins Gilman: A Biography.* Stanford, CA: Stanford University Press, 2010.

Gilman, Charlotte Perkins, and American Council of Learned Societies. *Women and Economics*. 1898. Reprint; Berkeley: University of California Press, 1998.

Gilman, Charlotte Perkins, and Catherine Golden. *Charlotte Perkins Gilman's The Yellow Wall-Paper: A Sourcebook and Critical Edition*. Routledge Guides to Literature. New York: Routledge, 2004.

Goldman, Emma (1869–1940)

Emma Goldman was a prominent anarchist, political activist, public speaker, and writer in the early twentieth century. Her widespread lecture tours and prolific publications helped shape the anarchist movement and other radical causes in both North America and Europe. She also advocated for birth control, free speech, peace, labor reform, and women's equality. After one of multiple arrests in 1917 and subsequent deportation from the United States in 1919, she spent the remaining years of her life living in Canada and Europe, where she continued to give lectures and write. She died in 1940 in Toronto, Canada.

Goldman was born on June 27, 1869, in Kovno, Russia (present-day Lithuania), to Abraham and Taube Bienowitch Goldman. Her father used violence to correct the behavior of his children, particularly Emma, who demonstrated a rebellious streak early in life. When Goldman was seven, the family moved to Königsberg, where she enrolled in school. After the family moved to Saint Petersburg, Goldman had to work in a corset shop, ending her formal education. During this time, Goldman began to educate herself on radical politics.

In 1885, Goldman and her sister, Helena, moved to Rochester, New York. Her experiences working in textile factories further fueled her political advocacy. Following a brief marriage in 1887, Goldman moved to New York City. While there, she met Alexander Berkman and Johann Most, two anarchists. Goldman impressed Most, and he adopted her as his protégé. As her star began to rise and she continued to develop her own ideas, however, she found herself at odds with Most. They parted ways, but she and Berkman became lovers and, later, lifelong friends.

Following the violence of the 1892 Homestead Strike, which killed seven Pinkerton agents and nine strikers, Goldman and Berkman decided to assassinate the factory manager, Henry Clay Frick. Goldman helped plan and fund the attack, and Berkman attempted to carry it out. He failed and was arrested. Goldman continued to defend him, even after other anarchists, like Most, decried Berkman's action. She also continued her labor advocacy and spent one year in jail for rallying downtrodden workers, suffering from the Panic of 1893, to radicalism. This period of incarceration allowed her to further her political education and also to learn a new trade in the infirmary. Following her release, she continued to lecture but began earning a living as a midwife. Her work with poor women stimulated a lifelong advocacy for birth control access.

Goldman was arrested again after Leon Czolgosz, an anarchist, assassinated President William McKinley in 1901, and the police tried to link her to the murder. Eventually released due to a lack of evidence, she returned to her activism. In 1906, she published *Mother Earth*, a magazine for radical expression. She also published her first book, *Anarchism and Other Essays*. Her support of Margaret Sanger's birth control crusade led to her arrest and a two-week sentence in 1916 for violating the Comstock Law.

World War I was a pivotal time for Goldman. She encouraged men to resist the draft, founding the No Conscription League with Berkman. In 1917, they were arrested and were deported in 1919 to Russia. Originally a supporter of the Bolshevik Revolution, Goldman quickly found herself appalled by its injustices, corruption, and complete lack of free speech. Pressured to work for Lenin's government, she took a position as a collector of information for the future Museum of the Revolution. Her experience in Russia also changed Goldman's position on political violence as a means to an end.

Convinced that Lenin had perverted the revolution, Goldman and Berkman left Russia in 1921. They spent several years in Berlin, where she began writing articles for the *New York World* about her experience in Russia and working for the communist government. She later published those essays in a book, *My Disillusionment in Russia*. This was not her title; she also protested the fact that the publisher omitted some of her later essays. The publisher relented and agreed to publish the deleted essays under the title *My Further Disillusionment in Russia*. Fellow political advocated reacted to Goldman's exposé on Leninist injustice with dismay.

In 1924, Goldman moved to London. When the English government began to indicate that it might deport Goldman, a fellow anarchist, James Colton, married her, giving her British citizenship and security. She continued to travel and lecture throughout the 1920s. In 1928, she began her autobiography, demanding Berkman's help as her editor. The two spent two years in Saint-Tropez, France, and the book, *Living My Life*, was published in 1931. Spring-boarding off the enthusiastic reviews, she received permission to lecture in the United States in 1933. Goldman had continued to consider herself an American, and she eagerly returned to New York in 1934 and tried to renew her visa after its expiration, to no avail.

Following Berkman's suicide in 1936, Goldman turned her attention to the Spanish Civil War. The Spanish anarchists invited her to Barcelona, where she threw herself into lecturing and writing in support of the anti-Franco forces. The anarchists failed, however, and after the Nationalist movement won, Goldman returned to England. She moved to Canada in 1939, where she watched with unease the march to war. As much as she despised fascism, she did not support the idea of a war.

On February 17, 1940, Goldman suffered a stroke that left her mute and paralyzed on her right side. Following a second stroke, she died on May 14, 1940. Her friends and supporters successfully petitioned the U.S government to allow her body to be buried in Chicago. Following her death, she initially faded into obscurity, but the radical movements of the 1960s and 1970s sparked a renewed interest in her life and works. She is remembered as a crusader for individual rights and freedoms.

Meredith Lee May

See also: Comstock, Anthony (1844–1915); Czolgosz, Leon (1873–1901); Depression of 1893; Homestead Strike (1892); Sanger, Margaret (1879–1966)

References

Drinnon, Richard. *Rebel in Paradise: A Biography of Emma Goldman.* Chicago: University of Chicago Press, 1961.

Falk, Candace. *Love, Anarchy, and Emma Goldman.* New York: Holt, Rinehart and Winston, 1984.

Goldman, Emma. *Living My Life.* 2 vols. 1931. Reprint, New York: Dover Publications, 1970.

Morton, Marian J. *Emma Goldman and the American Left: "Nowhere at Home."* New York: Twayne Publishers, 1992.

Gold Standard/Free Silver

The principle focus of American monetary Populism during the latter half of the nineteenth century involved the debate over whether or not to base the currency of the United States on the gold standard or to allow the free coinage of silver. The populist free silver movement in the South and the West began shortly after the Civil War with an attempt to preserve the paper currency standard adopted by the Greenback Labor Party in 1862. Post–Civil War attempts to appreciate the dollar to resume gold convertibility at the prewar rate put pressure on traders, producers, manufacturers, and farmers. The initial support for greenbacks, or paper money, came from manufacturers and railroad workers. Western farmers and miners joined with the Greenbackers in the early 1870s as farm and mineral prices began a decline. However, Populist monetary demands shifted from an emphasis on greenbacks and paper currency to free coinage of silver. In 1873, silver was removed from circulation by the treasury and the federal government as its price began to decline relative to gold. Miners and greenback supporters developed a plan to remonetize silver at the old 16-to-1 rate against gold. Populists believed that exerting pressure on the federal government to buy silver well above the market rate would subsidize silver miners and keep the country off of the gold standard and on a de facto silver standard. The declining price of silver bullion directly benefited bondholders and wealthy individuals with fixed incomes. Yet the deflation of the economy negatively affected debtors in the South and the West. For silver supporters, limited coinage of bullion meant less paper money or greenbacks in circulation. As a result, miners and farmers in the midwestern and plains states and the South were negatively affected by the lack of paper money in the economy. Populists argued that the free coinage of silver contributed to inflation. Free silver supporters claimed that greater circulation of paper currency would ultimately help farmers and miners to get out of debt.

Supporters of the gold standard were primarily concentrated in the financial and commercial centers on the East Coast with ties to European trade and among textile and machinery manufacturers predominantly oriented toward global markets. In contrast, free silver support came from western miners, farmers, and ranchers heavily invested in the mining and ore-processing industry. Political agitation for the free coinage of silver came to a head amid the agricultural depression that began in 1888. In 1890 the Sherman Silver Purchase Act was passed by the treasury under the Bland-Allison Act. This legislation drastically increased the amount of silver bullion that was purchased each month by the government and the treasury. Yet this legislation was considered too weak by western Populists in particular because it did not authorize the free and unlimited coinage of silver that supporters desired. The Sherman Act ultimately failed to appease antigold interests, but hopes rose after the 1892 elections gave the Democrats, who had ran on a prosilver platform, control of the presidency and both houses of Congress for the first time since the 1850s.

In reality, the Populist concerns about gold versus silver were superficial. The pressing issue facing the nation following the election of 1892 was what actions should be taken by the federal government to prevent the deflation of the economy. Declining prices benefited bondholders and individuals with stagnant incomes while injuring debtors. Industrial laborers directly profited from deflation except during periods of depression when unemployment rates rose. This fact explains why the Populists gained little support among this population. In contrast, southern farmers and those from Plains states who had been oppressed by the crop lien system were negatively affected by the downward spiral in the economy.

At the beginning of the 1890s, debates over federal monetary policy centered on the coinage of silver. From its inception, the U.S. currency had been based on a bimetallic standard. Gold and silver were coined, and the number of grains of each in dollar coins was continuously adjusted to reflect the commercial value of both metals. An act of Congress in 1792 established a ratio of 15:1—371.25 grains of silver and 24.75 grains of gold. Each form of specie, gold and silver, was worth one dollar at the mint. However, in 1834 the ratio was changed, reducing the overall value of gold to reflect the new finding of precious metals in California. The discovery of the Comstock Lode in Nevada and increased silver mining in Colorado steadily decreased the price of gold until, in 1874, it became profitable for miners to coin silver bullion. Yet when the Silverites attempted to coin their bullion, they discovered that the Coinage Act of 1873 had devalued the metal due to the fact that no silver had been presented to the U.S. mint in years, which had literally demonetized the metal. Therefore, the tradition of a bimetallic currency was rapidly becoming extinct.

Western silver miners quickly protested this so called "Crime of '73," and supporters of inflation, who were eager to place more money into circulation regardless of its metallic base, joined the populist Silverites in demanding a return to bimetallism. Conservative politicians, still advocating for greenback currency, vehemently resisted. The end result was a series of compromises among the various factions. Western silver miners complained because their bullion brought in only half of what it had at the beginning of the 1870s. Debtors argued that as a result of the decline in prices, the dollars they used to meet their financial obligation were worth twice as much as in 1865. Indebted farmers spent more money yet received less for what they put out. This continued deflation of the value of paper money contributed to the further devaluation of U.S. currency. Supporters of the gold standard were concerned that unrestrained silver coinage would be authorized by the government, resulting in the collapse of the dollar. A financial panic brought on by the financial collapse of the London banking house of Bearing Brothers coincided with a severe industrial depression. This global economic recession eroded the financial confidence of Silverites and gold bugs alike.

President Grover Cleveland felt that the controversy over free coinage had contributed to the depression by upsetting the confidence of the business community. He believed that the only viable solution to the nation's fiscal woes was to return to a single gold standard. Cleveland called a special session of Congress, and he successfully pushed through a repeal of the Sherman Silver Purchase Act in 1893. However, the repeal of the Sherman Act only served to split the national Democratic Party. The president's Populist supporters in the South and the West largely abandoned him. Cleveland had reneged on his campaign promise to preserve bimetallism, and his political support in the South and the West eroded because of his support of the gold standard.

As a result of Cleveland's support of the gold bugs, Populist Silverites aggressively sought a new candidate who would actively endorse the free coinage of silver. The Populist platform in the presidential campaign of 1896 demanded free coinage of silver at a ratio of 16 to 1. The two major parties found it increasingly impossible to avoid the free silver controversy. During the 1894 congressional election, the Populist vote had increased by 42 percent. Southern and western leaders of the Democratic Party feared that they would lose the support of their constituency unless they publicly repudiated the fiscal policies of the Cleveland administration. Western Republicans, led by Senator Harry M. Teller of Colorado, threatened to throw their support to the Populists unless their party fully endorsed silver coinage.

Meeting in St. Louis to select a nominee in June of 1896, the Republican Party wholeheartedly announced its support of the gold standard. The Republican platform proclaimed "We are therefore opposed to the free coinage of silver . . . the existing gold standard must be maintained" (Garraty 701). The Republicans nominated William McKinley of Ohio for president. McKinley, highly regarded for his staunch support of the protective tariff and widely supported by labor, was expected to run strongly in the Midwest and the East. However, the gold bug candidate McKinley faced fierce opposition from the Silverite Populists. In July the Democratic Party assembled for its convention in Chicago. Grover Cleveland and the pro-gold forces fought an uphill battle, but the Populist Silverites handily defeated the supporters of the gold standard. The high point of the Chicago convention came when a young Populist ideologue from Nebraska by the name of William Jennings Bryan took the podium. Bryan passionately spoke out against gold, supporting the plight of western miners and farmers against the eastern banks and trusts. Bryan's Populist rhetoric evoked riotous applause from the Silverites in the audience. The pro-silver Nebraskan ended his speech with a metaphor that would dramatically set the tone for the 1896 campaign. Bryan asserted, "You shall not press down upon labor this crown of thorns. You shall not crucify mankind upon a cross of gold" (Garraty 702). The religious metaphor of the common Populist sacrificing himself upon the cross of gold became the political rallying cry of the Silverites. At the conclusion of the convention, the Democrats unanimously adopted a platform endorsing bimetallism and endorsing the free coinage of both silver and gold at the ratio of 16:1. They went on to nominate Bryan for president.

The Democratic nomination of Bryan in 1896 placed tremendous pressure on the Populists. If they threw their support behind Bryan, they risked losing their unique party identity. However, if they nominated their own candidate, they would most likely ensure McKinley's election. The Populists were not successful at finding a candidate of enough stature to run against Bryan. In the final analysis, the Populists supported the Democratic candidate, but exercising their clout within the party, they successfully nominated Watson as vice president instead of the favored Arthur Sewell of Maine.

Economic historian Milton Friedman argues that the movement for the free and unlimited coinage of silver was doomed to failure with the passage of the Coinage Act of 1873. Populists were understandably outraged by the "Crime of '73"; however, by the early 1870s the instigation of the gold standard became inevitable. In 1896 when Bryan was nominated for president and delivered his infamous "Cross of Gold" speech, it was simply too late to reverse the trend toward the adoption of the gold standard. The elimination of the free coinage of silver had significant consequences as a result of the decline in the world price of silver in relation to gold. Friedman claims, "Had there been no decline in the silver-gold price ratio—it would have been irrelevant whether the fateful line was included in the act of 1873 or omitted" (1168). In any instance, the antebellum condition of the effective gold standard would have continued when the government resumed specie payments. The increase in the gold-silver price ratio began well before the passage of the act of 1873. The 15:1 ratio remained in place when the U.S. government resumed payments to miners in 1879. According to Friedman, the gold-silver price ratio of 15:5 was a standard decades before gold discoveries in California and Australia in the 1850s. The rising of the price of gold continued steadily after 1870 when one European country after another converted from bimetallism to the gold standard. Therefore, the support for the silver standard and a bimetallic currency was rapidly eroding by the climax of the free silver movement in 1873 and was outmoded by the nomination of

Bryan in 1896. William Jennings Bryan and the supporters of free silver were waging a hopeless struggle at the end of the century. McKinley's election to the presidency in 1896 effectively did away with any hope of maintaining the free and unlimited coinage of silver.

Global economic support for the gold standard eroded during World War I. Gold-backed currency was briefly reinstated from 1925 to 1931 as the gold exchange standard. However, this attempt to revive the gold standard broke down in 1931 after Britain's rejection of gold in the aftermath of substantial gold and capital outflows. In 1933 Franklin Delano Roosevelt attempted to nationalize gold owned by private citizens and abolished contracts where payment was specified in gold. From 1946 to 1971, many countries operated under the Bretton Woods system. This attempt to modify the gold standard resulted in most countries settling their international balances in U.S. dollars, but the U.S. government promised to redeem other central banks' holdings of dollars for gold at a rate of $35 per ounce. This method of payouts for balances rapidly depleted U.S. gold reserves. Ultimately, this method reduced confidence in the ability of the United States to redeem its currency in gold. Finally, in August 1971, President Richard Nixon publicly announced that the United States would abandon redeeming paper currency for gold. This abandoning of the Bretton Woods system represented the final step in gold-backed currency.

Christopher Allan Black

See also: Bland, Richard P. (1835–1899); Bryan, William Jennings (1860–1925); Cleveland, Grover (1837–1908); Crime of '73; Democratic Party; McKinley, William, Jr. (1843–1901); People's Party; Sherman Silver Purchase Act (1890); Silver Republicans; St. Louis Convention of 1896

References

Bardo, Michael D. "Gold Standard." *The Concise Encyclopedia of Economics*. http://www.econlib.org/library/Enc/GoldStandard.html. Accessed January 3, 2013.

Carnes, Mark C., and John A. Garraty. *American Destiny: Narrative of a Nation*. Vol. 2. New York: Penguin, 2003.

Freidman, Milton. "The Crime of 1873." *Journal of Political Economy* 98 (6): 1159–1194.

Frieden, Jeffrey A. "Monetary Populism in Nineteenth-Century America: An Open Economy Interpretation." *Journal of Economic History* 57 (2): 367–395.

Garraty, John A. *The Story of America*. New York: Holt Rinehart & Winston, 1994.

Goldwater, Barry M. (1909–1998)

Barry Goldwater was a conservative U.S. senator from Arizona, a one-time Republican presidential candidate in 1964, and a tireless promoter of his home state and the American West. He served in the Senate from 1954 to 1964 and again from 1968 until his retirement in 1986. Following his career in public service, Goldwater often was called upon by sitting presidents for advice and political consultation. As a part of his 1964 presidential bid, Goldwater promoted a form of conservative populism that advocated a reestablishment of rights and freedoms that seemed threatened by the growing liberal state under the Kennedy and Johnson administrations. While most Americans were not ready for Goldwater, they later embraced a similar rhetoric, espoused by Ronald Reagan, who had stumped for Goldwater during the campaign.

Barry Morris Goldwater was born January 1, 1909, in Phoenix to Baron and Josephine Williams Goldwater. Baron was the son of Michael "Big Mike" Goldwasser, a Jewish immigrant from Poland who arrived in the Arizona Territory after operating a saloon and brothel in gold rush–era San Francisco. Goldwasser established the family fortune through a chain of clothing stores. Josephine, an Episcopalian who descended from Rhode Island founder Roger Williams, worked as a nurse in Chicago before settling in the Arizona Territory in the hopes of ameliorating a lung condition. She met Baron Goldwater in 1906 while shopping in one of the family's stores.

Upon Goldwater's birth, the Arizona Territory was on the verge of statehood; Goldwater's earliest memory of his mother was of her sewing the 47th and 48th stars on to their U.S. flag to commemorate the new states of Arizona and New Mexico. As a boy, Goldwater lived a small-town life, ingrained with the ruggedness, self-reliance, and frontier ethos of the American West. As a teenager, he was a mediocre student, failing nearly half of his high school courses. Hoping to improve his scholastics, his parents sent their son to the Staunton Military Academy in Virginia. There he excelled in his studies, graduating in 1928 and eventually enrolling at the University of Arizona, Tucson. Yet without the rigorous structure of military school, Goldwater left the university after his freshman year.

Upon returning to Phoenix, Goldwater worked in the family business and discovered that he had a flair for merchandising. Specifically, he designed desert fashions for men inspired by his personal exploits and hobbies of river rafting on the Colorado, nature photography, hiking, and aviation. Though he proved successful in running the family business after Baron's death in 1929 and was fully in charge by 1936, Goldwater believed he was destined for a different path. As a young man, his politics were heavily influenced by his uncle Morris, a former mayor of Prescott, Arizona, and a states' right advocate who was suspicious of large government. During the Great Depression, New Deal programs directed hundreds of millions of dollars to Arizona. Goldwater expressed resentment toward federal assistance, believing private citizens and not the government were responsible for their own livelihoods. In 1934, he removed the National Recovery Administration's emblem from his stores' windows to protest its price setting. In 1938, Goldwater drafted an open letter to President Roosevelt, stating that the president's economic policies, tax regulations, and relief programs catered too much to labor and hamstrung private business owners.

When the United States entered World War II, Goldwater's age and poor eyesight prohibited him from flying combat missions. He instead served the Air Corps in logistical and training capacities at Yuma, Arizona, and also instructed pilots who served in Chiang Kai-shek's Chinese nationalist army. By 1944, he was stationed in India, flying supply missions over the Himalayas to Chinese air fields. In August, he returned to the United States to serve in a training unit in California. Three months after the Japanese surrender, Goldwater returned to Phoenix to continue his work in the family retail business.

Goldwater's trajectory from retail merchant to politician began in the late 1940s. He sharpened his public speaking skills by lecturing on the history and geography of Arizona. Delivering speeches and presentations to the Lions' Club, Rotary Club, and numerous parent-teacher associations, Goldwater spoke at length on topics such as Navajo culture and Arizona's national monuments. In 1946, he began community drives and campaigns in Phoenix to raise private funds for a new hospital and civic center. In that same year, Goldwater was appointed to the Colorado River Commission, the agency entrusted to secure the state's claims to the Colorado River water. From his position, he fought a rapidly growing California's claims to the water, claims that he believed would hamper Arizona's postwar development.

Also in 1946, Indianapolis newspaper publisher Eugene Pulliam arrived in Phoenix and purchased the *Republic* and the *Gazette*. Politically, Pulliam sought to create a Republican presence in the state. Eventually Pulliam and Goldwater joined forces. In 1949, with Pulliam's editorial backing, Goldwater won a seat on the Phoenix City Council. From his councilman's perch, he was the leading Republican office holder in the state. Guided by theories of fiscal responsibility and limited government, Goldwater sought private solutions for issues such as municipal transit, parking, and road repair. In 1949, he became president of the Phoenix Country Club, giving him added stature and prominence.

With his business connections and success on the city council, Goldwater set his sights on the U.S. Senate. In 1954, he ran against incumbent Ernest McFarland, who had authored the G.I. Bill. While many in Arizona felt Goldwater had little chance of unseating McFarland in what was then a heavily Democratic state, he believed that his long association with and dedication to Arizona would prove indispensable. With President Eisenhower's popularity as an asset, Goldwater won McFarland's senate seat by more than 7,000 votes. Following his victory, Goldwater campaigned for other Republican hopefuls around the country and joined his party members in trying to dismantle the New Deal. After Senator Joseph McCarthy's censure in 1953, Goldwater emerged as the Republican standard-bearer. In 1958, with Arizona voting on the right-to-work issue, Goldwater campaigned against the requirement that all workers needed union membership as a condition of employment. He also faced off publicly with United Auto Workers president Walter Reuther, whom he accused of sponsoring socialism and whom he labeled more dangerous than the Soviet Union.

After Lyndon Johnson's assumption of the presidency in 1963, Goldwater accused him of expanding the social welfare programs of the New Deal and being too soft on communism abroad.

Goldwater accepted the Republican presidential nomination in 1964 but lost resoundingly to the incumbent Johnson. Many Democrats accused Goldwater of being too extreme, notably for his willingness to consider nuclear weapons as a tactic for dealing with communism. After his failed presidential bid, Goldwater continued making speeches for Republican candidates, penned several opinion columns for the *Los Angeles Times*, and helped prevent the large-scale development of Camelback Mountain in Arizona.

In 1968, Goldwater reentered the Senate, where he remained until 1986. He was a firm supporter of Richard Nixon, who won the presidency in 1968. As the Watergate scandal grew in intensity through 1973, Goldwater maintained that Nixon was innocent of any wrongdoing. But as the scandal reached higher into the White House, it was Goldwater who, in 1974, convinced Nixon that his only choice was to resign. In his last years in the Senate, Goldwater was critical of other Republicans. During the 1980s, as the Republican Party advanced a new conservatism under Ronald Reagan, Goldwater expressed disdain for the religious right. Singling out figures such as Rev. Jerry Falwell and Pat Robertson, Goldwater stressed that the Republican Party had aligned more with the teachings of the Bible than with principles of democracy.

When the issue of gays in the military surfaced politically in the early 1990s, Goldwater, whose grandson had a gay friend facing discharge from the Air Force, championed the cause, stating that sexual orientation had minimal effect on one's defense of his country. When the Democrats captured the White House in 1992, Bill Clinton often consulted Goldwater on political matters. In 1996, Goldwater suffered a stroke that greatly affected his memory. Finally, on May 29, 1998, Barry Goldwater died of natural causes at his home in Paradise Valley, Arizona.

Stephen E. Nepa

See also: Great Society; McCarthy, Joseph (1908–1957); New Deal; Reagan, Ronald, Populist Rhetoric of; Tea Party

References

Clymer, Adam. "GOP's 1964 Nominee Laid Basis for 1980 Reagan Victory." *New York Times*, May 30, 1998, A1.

Goldberg, Robert Alan. *Barry Goldwater.* New Haven, CT: Yale University Press, 1995.

Goldwater, Barry M. *With No Apologies: The Personal and Political Memoirs of United States Senator Barry M. Goldwater.* New York: Morrow, 1979.

Kazin, Michael. *The Populist Persuasion: An American History.* New York: Basic Books, 1995.

Perlstein, Rick. *Before the Storm: Barry Goldwater and the Unmaking of the American Consensus.* New York: Perseus Books, 2009.

Reisner, Marc. *Cadillac Desert: The American West and Its Disappearing Water.* New York: Penguin Books, 1986.

Gompers, Samuel (1850–1924)

Samuel Gompers, a critical individual in the U.S. trade union movement, was the president of the American Federation of Labor (AFL) from 1886 to 1894 and

1895 to 1924 as well as the vice president of the Cigarmakers' International Union from 1886 to 1924.

Samuel Gompers was born on January 26, 1850, in London, England, where he was raised until 1863. As a child, Gompers's father apprenticed him to a shoemaker; however, he could not handle the noise of that craft and eventually began working as a cigarmaker. Gompers later stated that he preferred the trade of cigarmaking because there was a society among them that was not present among the shoemakers. While in London, Gompers attended the Jew's Free School from 1856 to 1860, which was, at the time, one of the largest elementary schools in Great Britain. Although he ranked third in his class, the financial situation of his family required him to leave the school. Gompers continued his education through night classes as well as in the cigar factory, where he listened to coworkers debate current events.

Due to import duties levied against Europe by the United States, Gompers and his family decided to emigrate to the United States. They were able to emigrate with the assistance of the Cigarmakers' Society of England. They left England on June 10, 1863, and arrived in New York, New York, on July 29, 1863. The Gompers family regularly changed residences throughout the Lower East Side of Manhattan, and Samuel moved from job to job due to lockouts and strikes. In addition to his work as a cigarmaker, Gompers helped form and become the president of the Arion Base Ball and Social Club as well as continuing his education with free classes at the Cooper Union. In the summer of 1866, Gompers met a London-born tobacco stripper, and they were married on January 28, 1867.

Although Gompers joined the Cigarmakers' Local Union in 1864, he stated that his interest in the labor movement began in 1873 when he started working in a cigar factory owned by a socialist immigrant named David Hirsch. While at Hirsch's factory, Gompers met Ferdinand Laurrell, who was affiliated with the Scandinavian section of the International Workingmen's Association. Laurrell translated Karl Marx's *Communist Manifesto* and inspired Gompers to learn to read the German language. A pamphlet by Carl Hillmann titled *Praktisch Emanzipationswinke* proposed the idea that trade unions functioned as the catalyst of fundamental social and political change and that they were natural, historically based instruments for advancing the working class. Hillmann's ideas inspired Gompers throughout his entire life.

During the 1870s the cigar industry was completely transformed with the introduction of the cigar mold, which reduced the skill needed to produce cigars. The cigar mold allowed unskilled workers, women, and children to produce cigars outside of the factory, often in tenement homes owned by the cigar company. The shift in cigar production to the tenement-home system was a pivotal event in Gompers's involvement in the labor movement. In addition to the tenement-home system, the craft of cigarmaking experienced industrialization and new regulations limiting conversation and smoking, both of which had been generally allowed under the old ways of traditional cigarmaking and had allowed a sense of community and artisanal autonomy as a part of the craft.

The cigar-manufacturing workplace was one that encouraged the exchange of ideas; the introduction of the cigar mold and increased regulations threatened not only the cigarmakers but also the craft of cigarmaking itself. Inspired by the railroad strikes of 1877, many of the New York City cigar-shop workers struck because of pay cuts and the newly imposed factory limitations on conversation and smoking; more than 10,000 workers, including Gompers, joined the Great Strike. The Great Strike solidified Gompers's belief that a union's financial security and stability should outweigh political party activity. While Gompers advocated a diminished role for politics, he did acknowledge there was importance to political lobbying as well as to publications. Gompers attended a hearing by a federal committee headed by Henry Blair of New Hampshire on the relations between labor and capital. In the hearing, Gompers voiced support for the creating of the Federal Bureau of Labor and Statistics, the abolition of the contract labor system, the enforcement of the federal eight-hour law, and the incorporation of trade unions. In his battle with the tenement-house cigar production system, Gompers published his findings for an antitenement campaign in the *New Yorker Volkzeitung* and the *Cigar Maker's Official Journal*. The anti-tenement-house campaigns and lobbying caused a split in the Cigarmakers' International Union Local 144 between the leadership and the union's socialist members.

Gompers's emphasis on financial stability was the platform that allowed the American Federation of Labor to be an attractive option to nonaffiliated labor unions. Due to his platform of financial stability Samuel Gompers was elected president of the AFL at its founding convention in 1886. Although he did not approve of political affiliations being the forefront of the union's priorities, Gompers did encourage union members to be politically aware and active. The difference in ideas between Gompers and the socialist members proved to be a perpetual issue as Gompers's ideologies sided with capitalism. As a result of his willingness to work with businesses and his conservative approach, Gompers and the AFL witnessed a split between some of their members, similar to the split in the Cigarmakers' International Union Local 144.

The extreme socialist members split from the AFL to form the Industrial Workers of the World (IWW), who wanted to unite workers through industry rather than craft. Through industrial unionism, the IWW could create solidarity with the working class and unite them against the capitalist business owners. In addition to his willingness to work with business owners, Gompers created tension with the Socialist Party and other unions when he refused to support Eugene Debs of the American Railway Union during the 1894 Pullman strike. Not only did this cause a lasting conflict with Debs, who later emerged as a leading member of the Socialist Party, it also was a contributing cause of Samuel Gompers's loss in the 1895 AFL election to John McBride; the only year since his election in 1886 that Gompers would not be the president of the AFL. After regaining the presidency, Gompers relocated the AFL headquarters from New York, to Indianapolis, Indiana, to Washington, DC. In 1912 the AFL members adjusted their previous political views and supported Woodrow Wilson, and through their support they saw the passage of the 1914 Clayton Act and the Adamson Act in 1916. Samuel Gompers also served as an advisor of labor for Wilson at the Treaty of Versailles.

While attending a Pan-American Federation of Labor meeting in Mexico City, Mexico, Gompers fell ill and was rushed to San Antonio, Texas. Shortly after arriving in San Antonio, Gompers died at the age of 74 on December 14, 1924. Throughout his life Gompers was able to have a significant impact on the development of the AFL while maintaining his goal of a unified group of workers that spanned across race, class, trades, and political affiliations.

Johnathan Fluitt

See also: American Federation of Labor (AFL); Baseball and Populism; Debs, Eugene (1855–1926); Gilded Age; Industrial Workers of the World (IWW); McBride, John (1854–1917); Progressivism; Pullman Strike (1894)

References

Gompers, Samuel. *The Samuel Gompers Papers.* 10 vols. Edited by Stuart B. Kaufman. Champaign: University of Illinois Press, 1986.

Gompers, Samuel. *Seventy Years of Life and Labor: An Autobiography.* 2 vols. New York: E. P. Dutton & Company, 1925.

"Goodbye, My Party, Goodbye"

"Goodbye, My Party, Goodbye," also published as "Goodbye, Old Party, Goodbye," was a political campaign song. It employed a technique common to the time, that of a pastiche, in which the new text is set to a known tune; this song was set to the tune of "Goodbye, My Lover, Goodbye," the original words and music composed by T. H. Allen (Allen 1882). "Goodbye, My Party, Goodbye," primarily used in the elections of 1890 and 1892, reflected dismay with the two major political parties, Republican and Democrat, in their treatment of railroads and monopolies. On occasion it was called "The Populist Anthem." Some contemporary commentators credited the song with influencing the Kansas vote in favor of James B. Weaver, the Populist candidate for president in 1892.

The original barbershop ballad by Allen was in 6/8 time, in G major; it began with a melody nearly identical to the English folk song "Good-bye, My Lover, Goodbye." The chorus was sung in 4/4 time. The new text for this Populist song was by Courtland Snow White, the poet of the People's Party. Little is known of White's birth, childhood and early adult life, but he was listed as a wagon-maker and blacksmith in the *Southwestern Business Directory* (1889) in Halstead, Harvey County, Kansas. White had composed poems to be sung as pastiches with other songs known to the people, such as "The Alliance Goes Marching On," to the tune of "The Battle Hymn of the Republic."

The version of "Goodbye, Old Party, Goodbye," as found in *The Alliance and Labor Songster* (1891; 1975), was transposed to F major, with the following text by White:

It was no more than a year ago,
Good-bye, old party, good-bye.
That I was in love with my party so,
Good-bye, old party, good-bye.
To hear aught else I never would go;
Good-bye, old party, good-bye.
Like all the rest I made a great blow,
Good-bye, old party, good-bye.

(Chorus:)
Bye, party, bye, lo; bye party, bye, lo;
Bye, party, bye, lo; Good-bye, old party, good-bye.

I was often scourged with the party lash,
Good-bye, old party, good-bye.
The bosses laid on with demands for cash,
Good-bye, old party, good-bye.
To do aught else I deemed it rash,
Good-bye, old party, good-bye.
So I had to take it, or lose my hash,
Good-bye, old party, good-bye.
(Chorus)

I was raised up in the kind of school,
Good-bye, old party, good-bye.
That taught to bow to money rule,
Good-bye, old party, good-bye.
And it made of me a "Kansas fool,"
Good-bye, old party, good-bye.
When they found I was a willing tool,
Good-bye, old party, good-bye.
(Chorus)

The old party is on the downward track,
Good-bye, old party, good-bye.
Picking his teeth with a tariff tack,
Good-bye, old party, good-bye.
With a placard pinned upon its back
Good-bye, old party, good-bye.
That plainly states "I'll never come back,"
Good-bye, old party, good-bye.
(Chorus)

Another version, "Good-bye, Poor Benny, Good-bye," with text by C. S. White, was published in the newspaper *Topeka Mail* in 1892, shortly after the defeat of President Benjamin Harrison by Grover Cleveland (White 1892). Three verses addressed Benjamin Harrison's reelection loss in November 1892; lyrics also negatively mention William McKinley's Tariff Act of October 1890 ("You choked to death on McKinley's bill"). The tariff was so unpopular that the Republicans lost the House of Representatives in the 1890 midterm elections. The fourth verse extols the President-elect: "Grover Cleveland is the boy":

It came to pass on election day.
Good-bye poor Benny, good-bye,
That Cleveland had a walk away,
Good-bye poor Benny, good-bye.
Once you thought that you could win it,
Good-bye poor Benny, good-bye,
But now you find that you're not in it,
Good-bye, poor Benny good bye.
(Chorus)

Bye Benny, bye-lo, bye Benny by-lo,
Bye Benny bye-lo, good-bye poor Benny, good-bye.
The voters split on the tariff trash,
Good-bye poor Benny, good-bye,
It knocks your election all to smash,
Good-bye poor Benny, good-bye;
To be sure it is a bitter pill,
Good-bye poor Benny, good-bye.
You choked to death on McKinley's bill,
Good-bye poor Benny good-bye.
(Chorus)

Boodle is on the downward track,
Good-bye poor Benny, good-bye.
The "Reps" are left to hold the sack,
Good-bye poor Benny, good-bye.

We have buried the g. o. p's. so deep,
Good-bye poor Benny, good-bye.
They will take their everlasting sleep,
Good-by poor Benny, good bye.
(Chorus)

Grover Cleveland is the boy,
Good-bye poor Benny, good-bye,
The People's Party wish him joy,
Good-bye poor Benny, good-bye.
So Benny is forced to make a "sneak,"
Good-bye poor Benny, good bye,
And take a trip up Salty Creek,
Good-bye poor Benny, good-bye.
(Chorus)

As with many political movements, poems, slogans, and songs formed a powerful means of communication. For purposes of familiarity, song texts were added to existing known tunes.

Ralph M. Hartsock

See also: Cleveland, Grover (1837–1908); McKinley, William, Jr. (1843–1901); People's Party; The Press and Populism

References

Allen, T. H. *Goodbye, My Lover, Goodbye.* New York: Harms, 1882.

Vincent, Leopold. *The Alliance and Labor Songster.* Indianapolis: Vincent Bros., 1891. Reprint, New York: Arno Press, 1975.

White, C.S. *The People's Songster for Campaign Purposes and a Jolly Time Generally.* Indianapolis, IN: Vincent Bros., 1892.

Granger Movement

The first organization for farmers that appeared in the United States was the Grange, also known as the Patrons of Husbandry. The Grange was founded in 1867 by seven men, although O. H. Kelley most often gets the credit for the organization's beginnings. For the next 10 years, the Grange served farmers through social networks and educational programs. It reached its peak in the mid-1870s, when it began to involve itself in state and national politics. It brought attention to the unfair practices of railroads and granaries and caused the passage of a series of laws known collectively as Granger laws in an attempt to curb their abuses. The Grange entered a period of decline around 1876 and soon faded from the scene. It left in its wake a number of legacies, including the knowledge that farmers could be a potent political force if they asserted their collective power. In this sense, the Grange paved the way for later similar movements, including the Farmers' Alliance and the Populist Party.

William M. Ireland, William Saunders, Francis M. McDowell, John R. Thompson, John Trimble, and Aaron B. Grosh were all involved it the Grange's origins, but it is Oliver Hudson Kelley who is most often cited as its founder. Shortly after the end of the Civil War, Kelley toured the devastated South. As a member of the Department of Agriculture, he was mostly interested in the region's farming conditions. He was appalled to observe that most southern farmers were abusing their lands with outdated and backward farming practices. The remedy, he felt, was to bring farmers together so that they could discuss their agricultural problems and discover solutions among themselves. This effort resulted in the founding of the Grange in 1867.

American society, inspired by the Granger movement of the 1860s–1870s. The title is a variation on the movement's motto, "I Pay for All." Composed primarily of midwestern farmers, the Grange was an organization dedicated to combating the monopolistic practices of the railroads and grain elevators in the decade following the Civil War. (Library of Congress)

The Grange quickly grew in popularity. It gained most of its support in the Midwest and Northwest, especially in Minnesota, Kelley's home state. At the time of the financial panic of 1873, the Grange was established in all but four states. In the wake of the panic, national membership in the organization surged to more than 800,000 members. By this time, the Grange envisioned unified farmers allied against merchants, railroads, and granaries.

From the beginning, the Grange was unique in American history. It was one of the first organizations to embrace gender equality by opening its membership to both men and women. Originally, its primary focus was to educate farmers to alleviate some of their suffering. The Grange was a self-help organization for farmers, and on the local level, it organized barbeques, picnics, and parades for its members. In its early years, it was infused with secret ceremonies and symbolic rituals, not unlike the Freemasons. On a deeper level, the Grange developed cooperatives to allow farmers more economic freedom. Eventually, the Grange acquired a substantial amount of operating money from dues and cooperatives. It soon came to own cotton gins, stores, and grain elevators. It also sought to pool members' savings together into a credit union to limit the corrupting power of banks. By the mid-1870s, the Grange was purchasing new farm machinery at bargain prices. This machinery was stored in Chicago mail-order warehouses and was for sale, to members, through catalogs with minimal markup to provide farmers with further savings. One of the first mail-order warehouses established for this purpose was Montgomery Ward. Grangers desired carry out their mail-order business efficiently, which led them to be the first group advocating a rural free delivery system for the mail.

Before long, the Grange delved into politics. The issues that provoked their political involvement were depressed farmer incomes, indebtedness, and the unfair practices of railroads and grain warehouses. Grangers supported the free coinage of silver, and, partly because of their influence, the federal government passed the Bland-Allison Act in 1878, establishing the Morgan silver dollar as a common form of U.S. currency. Granger activity in the Northwest focused on the railroads and grain warehouses, which charged high prices to ship and store agricultural crops. Because they relied so heavily on these businesses, farmers had few options other than to pay the exorbitant fees. These abuses led many Grange organizations to push for reform in their respective state legislatures. The result was a series of Granger laws that attempted to curb the oppressive power of railroads and granaries. Generally, Granger laws set or established fair rates for customers. Many states created commissioners to ensure that these regulatory laws were observed. The Supreme Court apparently agreed with the Grangers. In 1876 it ruled, in *Munn v. Illinois*, that a business of a public nature (grain warehouses in this case, but the ruling also applied to railroads) could, in fact, be regulated by the state. The ruling was a huge victory for the Grange because it affirmed the constitutional validity of the Granger laws. The Grange eventually formed an alliance among its members, pledging to support only those political candidates who espoused their cause. Failing that, the organization threatened to form an independent party.

At the time the Granger movement seemed to be most potent, it began to decline. Its demise was associated with poor fiscal management and organizational difficulties arising from its rapid growth in membership. A decade after *Munn v. Illinois*, a subsequent Supreme Court ruling in *Wabash, St. Louis & Pacific Railroad Company v. Illinois* (1886) reversed the decision, denying states the power to regulate interstate rates for railroads. By that time, however, the Granger movement was superseded by another organization called the Farmers' Alliance.

The Grange movement was significant in American history. It taught the farmers that they had considerable power. Other farmer movements of the late nineteenth century, like the Greenback Party (founded in 1874), the Farmers' Alliance in the late 1880s, and the People's Party in the 1890s, were outgrowths of the Grange. The Grange helped to spawn the mail-order catalogue industry. It also spread the demand for farmer education by disseminating knowledge and providing access to new technology.

The Grange never completely disappeared from the American scene, and it has survived through time. In 2005, it boasted 300,000 members in 3,600 communities in 37 states. Its headquarters is presently in Washington, DC.

Clay Ouzts

See also: Bland, Richard P. (1835–1899); Department Stores and Mail-Order Catalogs, Depression of 1873; Farmers' Mutual Benefit Association (FMBA); Kelley, Oliver Hudson (1826–1913); Gold Standard/Free Silver; Greenback Party; People's Party; Public Education; Railroad Regulation; Rochdale Plan

References

Nordin, D. Sven. *Rich Harvest: A History of the Grange, 1867–1900.* Jackson: University Press of Mississippi, 1974.

Woods, Thomas A. *Knights of the Plow: Oliver H. Kelley and the Origins of the Grange in Republican Ideology.* Ames: Iowa State University Press, 1991.

Grant, Madison (1865–1937)

Madison Grant was born in New York City and lived a life of privilege. He attended private schools, summered at the family estate on Long Island, and attended Yale, then Columbia University, from which he received a law degree. Grant became interested in natural science and conservation and became secretary of the New York Zoological Society. Grant wrote articles such as "The Vanishing Moose, and Their Extermination in the Adirondacks" (1894), "Condition of Wildlife in Alaska" (1910), a pamphlet on the Rocky Mountain goat (1905), and an account of the movement to save California redwoods (1919).

Grant's naturalist writings display a taste for precise description of such things as the dimensions of a breed of an animal's skull, distinctions between species, and their population ranges, as well as a concern for the survival and even the dignity of the animals. In his pamphlet on the Rocky Mountain goat, Grant wrote, "As a result of this scarcity of direct knowledge many myths have gathered around this mountain dweller, leading, as usual in our North American game animals, to an abundance of inappropriate names. The name 'goat' is objectionable [for example]." (Grant, *Rocky Mountain Goat*, 11) Grant clearly abhorred the practice of shooting the animals from the decks of steamers "by hunters who took a wanton delight in seeing the wounded animals fall down the precipitous banks" (Grant, *Rocky Mountain Goat*, 13).

Grant began his article "Saving the Redwoods" by raising the alarm about the accelerating pace of the destruction of animal and plant populations, noting that however fast conservation efforts have developed, "it has been too slow to keep pace with the forces of destruction. . . . The forests are now threatened with annihilation" (Grant, *Saving the Redwoods*, 91). Grant's conservation work was extensive: he organized the American Bison Society, was one of the founders of the Bronx Zoo and of the Save-the-Redwoods League, and helped create Glacier National Park, among many other efforts. These activities made him a favorite of conservation-minded public figures such as Theodore Roosevelt.

In 1916, after his pamphlet on the Rocky Mountain goats and before taking up the plight of the redwoods, Grant published what was to become his most widely read and notorious work, *The Passing of the Great Race; or, The Racial Basis of European History.* In this work Grant presented his view of the superiority of the "Nordic" racial type, a population he felt had originated in a migration of proto-Teutonic people to the hardier climate of Scandinavia where weaker specimens died off. He characterized the "Nordic race" as having light straight brown or blonde hair, light skin, a straight nose, and a "long skull" (Grant, *Passing of the Great Race*, 167). He contrasted this type to the "Slavic Alpines," whom he described as "peasant stock," and to the "Mediterraneans" of Spain, Italy, parts of Greece, and North Africa.

Grant's book was a success. The changing patterns of immigration in the late nineteenth and early twentieth century meant that there were fewer northern and western Europeans arriving in the United States and a great influx of people from eastern and southern Europe. A great number of Americans feared this change. This led to the rise of the eugenics movement, which professed the belief that there were superior and inferior races and that the superior races should be encouraged to lead the country while other races should be kept from entering the country and kept from intermarrying with the superior whites. The inferiors, eugenics supporters held, should at a minimum be kept out of the country, and the most inferior—which included the physically and mentally disabled, the "immoral," and even the poor—should be forcibly sterilized. Grant advocated the establishment of ghettos for "inferior races" and even considered the idea of extermination. *The Passing of the Great Race* was translated into German in 1925 and was taken up by the National Socialists (Nazis). Hitler wrote Grant that the book was his "Bible" (Spiro).

Grant's work was attacked by scientists and anthropologists, including Franz Boas. Grant was forced out of the American Anthropological Association in 1918 and formed his own organization, the Galton Society, to promote eugenicist views. He helped pass laws restricting immigration. Grant and his ideas fell out of favor in the 1930s, in part due to his association with the rise of the Nazis in Germany and because Americans began concentrating their racial struggle on black versus white, but he continued to be a force against unregulated immigration. Grant also continued his conservation efforts until his death in 1937.

William C. Bamberger

See also: Boas, Franz (1858–1942); Environmentalism; Eugenics; National Parks; Progressivism

References

Grant, Madison. *The Passing of the Great Race, or The Racial Basis of European History.* New York: Scribner's Sons, 1921.

Grant, Madison. *The Rocky Mountain Goat.* New York: New York Zoological Society, 1905.

Grant, Madison. *Saving the Redwoods.* New York: New York Zoological Society, 1919.

Spiro, Jonathan P. *Synopsis of Defending the Master Race: Conservation, Eugenics, and the Legacy of Madison Grant.* Burlington: University of Vermont Press, 2006.

Grasshopper Plagues

During the late nineteenth century, particularly between the years 1874–1877, farmers west of the Mississippi River were devastated by huge grasshopper swarms that transformed previously healthy farms and communities into wastelands. It is estimated that these plagues caused more than $200 million worth of agricultural damage, or $116 billion in contemporary value. This environmental disaster threatened the settlement of frontier places, many of which had been populated by the federal government's homestead policy designed to get agricultural lands into the hands of actual farmers rather than speculators. The agitation of these farmers led to the formation of a number of local groups to force the government to respond to the needs of so many suffering in the Midwest and Great Plains.

These plagues of locusts were the largest ever to hit North America and were the previous century's equivalent to the 1930s droughts and subsequent Dust Bowl. The Rocky Mountain locust, *Melanoplus spretus*, is a relatively small flying insect, measuring roughly 1.25 to 1.4 inches. Yet during the 1870s, they swarmed in the greatest concentration of insects ever recorded. One swarm measured 198,000 square miles, greater than the size of California, consisting of 12.5 trillion insects and weighing 27.5 million tons. The last congregation of these locusts was spotted near Manitoba, Canada, in 1902. These plagues are most famously depicted in fictional accounts such as Laura Ingalls Wilder's *On the Banks of Plum Creek* and Larry McMurtry's *Lonesome Dove*.

These giant locust plagues formed from two unique environmental conditions coming together in the 1870s. Droughts marked the late 1860s and early 1870s, with 1875 being the driest year in recorded history to that point. Not only did these droughts cause economic hardships for farmers, but they also weakened their crops' defenses and increased the nutritional value of the vegetation, causing sugar to concentrate in the leaves. The droughts suppressed fungal diseases that kept locust populations in check and accelerated their maturation. Thus, not only were more grasshoppers hatching, but they also were growing into adulthood faster, while the plants' resistance to attack was lower.

These drought conditions were coupled with a unique Great Plains low-level jet stream, which meant plenty of wind and warm air. As one meteorologist noted, it was "one of the most prominent meteorological phenomena of the central United States" (Lockwood 23). A constant southerly wind allowed these olive-green insect swarms to congregate together, uniting to form massive swarms.

Farmers during this time period referred to dry autumn days at the end of long, hot summers as "grasshopper weather." The arrivals of these swarms were compared to black, summer snowstorms or massive, slow-moving eclipses. One individual described them thus: "On the horizon they appear as a dust tornado, riding upon the wind like an ominous hail storm, eddying and whirling like the wild dead leaves in an autumn storm, and finally sweeping up to and past you, with a power that is irresistible" (Lockwood 8). Those who witnessed these "summertime blizzards" of insects commented on the eerie silence when they were spied on the horizon. As they drew closer, a sound akin to a distant threshing machine could be heard, and when they finally landed, pioneers had trouble describing the unique noise that came with the pests that bombarded the landscape and buildings around them. The most common description was that of a deafening grass fire with its crackling and rasping noises.

Moving up to 10 miles per day, the typical swarm consumed up to 50 tons of vegetation per day. The insects ate everything they could, from fabric and flesh to window blinds and paint. If remnants of human sweat were left on the wooden handles of farm implements, the bugs would eat these, too. Human beings and animals were often left bleeding with nicks on their throats and any exposed skin. Bats and small birds disappeared. Wells, ponds, and streams became undrinkable stews of dead locust bodies. The eggs and meat of chickens that ate these grasshoppers were inedible, giving off a "reddish-brown oil of a very pungent and penetrating odor" (Lockwood 3). Turkeys gorged themselves to death, while in contrast cattle and horses starved to death with little or no grains or grass left to sustain them. The smell of millions of dead locusts was almost unbearable. Farm families often faced starvation and economic ruin. In contemporary terms what would be known as a "fire sale" was called "grasshopper prices."

The grasshopper plagues created difficult situations for farmers who lost their crops and were left with nothing but dead locusts. In their aftermath, these swarms left not only total devastation but also egg pods that would hatch the next year. A single square inch of soil could contain 150 eggs. As one Minnesota farmer estimated, "940,896,000 eggs to the acre, or the nice little pile of 6,586,272,000 on seven acres of my farm" (Risjord 121). These pods ensured that the cycle reoccurred the next year. To survive, many farmers had to eat the creatures that had destroyed their livelihoods. While the Ute, southern Paiute, and Shoshokos Indians had consumed grasshoppers as a part of their diets, white settlers in the region learned to fry them with butter, salt, and pepper.

Not only were farmers and townspeople of the region affected by the swarms, railroads were brought to a standstill in places. Trains killed so many bugs that the rails became too oily for anything to run on them, especially in areas that had steep grades. In Texas it was reported, "The cars for about ten days were so much obstructed on the Texas Central line as to necessitate their stopping occasionally to clear the track of the grasshoppers" (Irwin).

While many turned to God, believing the swarms were some kind of divine punishment akin to the plagues that the Egyptians faced at the time of Moses, others tried every method they could conceive to destroy the creatures and their eggs. They burned them, beat them, drowned them, plowed their eggs under, crushed them, poisoned them, swung ropes to shake the plants, fired guns at them, built hopperdozers, burned hay to act as smokescreens, used brush whips, paid bounties, invented "deceives" to capture or destroy them, and even used dynamite or crude kerosene flamethrowers to blow up their seedbeds. In the case of both deceives and hopperdozers, farmers attempted to capture the locusts in some type of box or with a sticky substance that would allow for their death and a failure to reproduce, while some methods were just efforts in frustration.

Most farmers and public officials realized that they could not battle these creatures on their own and needed government support if they were going to continue farming in the Midwest, especially the frontier areas. With huge groups of refugees and armed mobs stealing food and supplies, something had to be done. As a committee appointed to look into the matter in Altona, Missouri, noted, "We must have aid, or many will be compelled to abandon their crops. We have not seed to plant with, or the money to buy. The condition of our country is truly alarming. People have become discouraged; many are talking of leaving their homes; some are living on bread and water. Unless we get assistance from some quarter, many are bound to suffer" (Irwin). This appeal to the government was especially important as many settlers had been lured by the appeal of free government land under the Homestead Act or other land deals that gave Americans incentive to risk moving into these areas.

Things were at a crisis point. Farm ownership in Dakota, Minnesota, Nebraska, and Kansas fell by 50 percent in the 1870s as a legion of families moved away, their farms decimated by the grasshopper plagues. As a Missouri newspaper editor noted,

> The owners having paid out all their money, sold everything they could get along without, and mortgaged their farms to get money to carry their stock through the winter and plant their crops, now are left with nothing to eat, their stock have starved to death, and they have no money, and no means of raising any by loan or mortgage, to buy food or to get away from here to more favored sections of the country. (Savage 235)

When the locust swarms first appeared and slowly rolled across the Midwest and the Great Plains states, they caused the greatest damage in Kansas and Nebraska. The states' responses at first were inadequate and inconsistent. Farmers and local townspeople formed relief committees and began to put pressure on state legislatures to act. Minnesota and Missouri were the first to pass legislation to pay bounties for locusts. The St. Paul legislature commissioned $5 per bushel of eggs and $1 per bushel for nymphs. Kansas, Minnesota, and Nebraska all passed bills authorizing townships, counties, and districts to have the right to conscript able-bodied men into forced labor to combat the pests. Various states passed relief measures to provide food allotments and seed grants for the next year. Yet the demand was greater than the funds allocated.

The states quickly realized that the scope of the crisis was too great for them to handle. The Kansas House and Senate passed concurrent resolutions requesting the federal government to provide appropriate federal funds for assistance and relief. Minnesota moved next to get the federal government involved. The governor sent a letter to the U.S. Congress that stated, "This state is entitled to two years quota of arms, estimated at $8,160. I respectfully request to turn over to me, instead of arms, a quantity of rations, equivalent in value" (Lockwood 76). The state legislature followed up by informing the federal government that if it did not issue a liberal bounty for the destruction of eggs, grasshoppers would spread across the entire country. They then extended the deadline for property taxes and asked the federal government to show the same kind of charity.

As the state governments of this region continued their appeals, Congress agreed to amend the Homestead Act to allow farmers whose crops were destroyed to leave their homestead for up to six months. General E. O. C. Ord, who sat on the Nebraska Relief and Aid Association board, passed out surplus army rations and clothing to settlers in Nebraska and Kansas. Finally, in 1875, Congress reacted by approving $150,000 in food and clothing and another $30,000 for seed distribution. It is estimated that 107,535 people received aid: 700 tons of pork, 1,000 tons of cornmeal, 150 tons of bean and sugar, 100 tons of coffee and tea, and 40 tons of salt were handed out.

The next year in October the governors of the affected states, university professors, and experts in entomology met in Omaha, Nebraska. Everyone there agreed that the federal government was the only institution large enough to address the crisis and that funds should also be approved to set up an entomological commission to outline methods for controlling locusts.

Within a few weeks, Congress approved a three-man committee, which was the first time funds had been directed at scientific research to address a national crisis. The committee urged effective pest control methods be applied, dispelled several myths such as the strange efforts to eradicate the pests, and urged the digging of ditches; that funds be released for bounties; that agricultural crops in the area be diversified; and that pesticides, particularly Criddle mixtures (developed by Norman Criddle specifically in response to the grasshopper plagues), be used to combat the swarms. While no one really knows why, the swarms of Rocky Mountain locusts quietly vanished until the species went extinct at the turn of the twentieth century.

Trevor Jason Soderstrum

See also: Agricultural Issues, Regional; Drought; Environmentalism; Homestead Act (1862); Kansas, Populism in

References

Irwin, Lyndon N. "Grasshopper Plagues and Trains." http://www.lyndonirwin.com/hoptrain.htm. Accessed January 3, 2013.

Lockwood, Jeffery A. *Locust: The Devastating Rise and Mysterious Disappearance of the Insect That Shaped the American Frontier.* New York: Basic Books, 2005.

Risjord, Norman K. *A Popular History of Minnesota.* St. Paul: Minnesota Historical Society, 2005.

Savage, Candace. *Prairie: A Natural History.* Vancouver, BC: Greystone Books, 2011.

Great Society

The Great Society was a federal initiative to improve the quality of life for all Americans, especially the poor, during the presidency of Lyndon Baines Johnson. After a period of postwar prosperity, the number of Americans living in poverty had increased to more than 20 percent of the population. This increasing income disparity had been obscured by the Cold War, McCarthyism, and fears of communist infiltration.

President Lyndon Johnson used the idea of the Great Society to enlist support for his civil rights legislation, for Medicare and Medicaid programs, for environmental protection policies, and for the "War on Poverty." While these are the best-known parts of the Great Society, Johnson envisioned a social agenda greater than the New Deal and made 252 legislative requests in total. The president first used the term in a graduation speech at the University of Michigan on May 22, 1964: "We have the opportunity to move not only toward the rich society and the powerful society, but upward to the Great Society." He envisioned "an end to poverty and racial injustice," "a place where every child can find knowledge to enrich his mind and enlarge his talents," and "a place where the city of man serves not only the needs of the body and the demands of commerce but the desire for beauty and the hunger for community" (Johnson).

The roots of Johnson's Great Society lay in the president's childhood in central Texas, an area marked by flash floods and droughts. His relationship with his father, Samuel Ealy Johnson Jr., a struggling cattle farmer, speculator, and Populist Democrat—a congressman who served five terms in the Texas House of Representatives—also influenced the future president's worldview. The desolate hill-farming, poverty-ridden community surrounding Johnson City became a hotbed of the People's Party and its ideals. Samuel Johnson adhered to these ideals even after Populism disappeared as a political movement. His son credited the influence of his father's Populism throughout his own political career. These principles were reaffirmed when Lyndon Johnson taught mostly poor Mexican children at the Welhausen School in Cotulla, Texas, following his graduation from college. After signing the 1965 Higher Education Act, he remembered this event as part of the formation of his populist ideals:

> I shall never forget the faces of the boys and the girls in that little Welhausen Mexican School, and I remember even yet the pain of realizing and knowing then that college was closed to practically every one of those children because they were too poor. And I think it was then that I made up my mind that this nation could never rest while the door to knowledge remained closed to any American. ("History")

The Great Society was, in Johnson's mind, an effort to bring "the good life" to all Americans.

Johnson did not envision the Great Society in a vacuum. When he became John F. Kennedy's vice president, he had been one of the most powerful Senate majority leaders in U.S. history. At the time, many Americans had not realized the promises of the New Deal. Michael Harrington's *The Other America* and Homer Bigart's series of articles in the *New York Times* about the poor of Appalachia stunned readers in the early 1960s. On the campaign trail, Kennedy campaigned in the coal-mining areas of West Virginia while African Americans continued the fight for civil rights in the South, focusing the nation's attention on poverty and inequality. While much of Kennedy's social legislation was blocked by southern Democrats, he was able to sign the Area Redevelopment Act (1961), an experimental food stamp program, and the Manpower Development and Training Act (1962) before his death. Johnson's political knowledge, his ability to understand and work with southern Democrats, the force of his personality, and his summoning of the image of the assassinated Kennedy all allowed him to put the Great Society in motion.

Johnson believed that the role of the federal government was to help people overcome their disadvantages. Soon after Kennedy's death, Johnson participated in a series of meetings with economist Walter Heller, a key advisor to the former president and chairman of the Council of Economic Advisors. Heller suggested a War on Poverty as a means of stimulating the national economy, which Johnson, given his populist leanings, enthusiastically embraced. The War on Poverty was envisioned as a multifaceted attack on the causes of poverty, a "hand up" rather than a "handout." Politicians and policymakers would not treat the symptoms of poverty but rather its causes, which included housing, health, employment, education, civic participation, and psychological barriers caused by years in a self-perpetuating underclass.

To open the door for his antipoverty initiative, in early 1964, Johnson pushed through a targeted massive tax cut and organized a task force, headed by Sargent Shriver, head of the Peace Corps, to formulate what would become the Economic Opportunity Act (EOA). Signed into law in August, the EOA was the backbone of Johnson's Great Society. It established the Office of Economics Opportunity, which oversaw Legal Services, Head Start, Job Corps, Volunteers in Service to America (VISTA), college work-study programs for low-income students, and the Community Action Programs. The EOA also established a host of other programs that were placed under other agencies and departments such as rural loan programs, Adult Basic Education, and the Neighborhood Youth Corps.

Congress also created programs to increase food stamps and unemployment compensation during this time. Johnson's food stamp program would come to be used by nearly 10 percent of the population and 60 percent of those in poverty, and the Women, Infants, and Children (WIC) program assisted this demographic with food in addition to other programs. In 1965, his administration also sought to address the medical needs of the elderly and welfare recipients through the Medicare and Medicaid programs. In 2000, almost 40 million Americans, or roughly a little more than one out of seven Americans, were using the program.

In addition to fighting poverty, the Great Society also included civil rights legislation to help people of color have greater opportunities to enter the political and economic mainstream of American life. Because so much of poverty seemed to stem from the discrimination that African Americans and other minorities faced, President Johnson signed two major civil rights bills into law. The Civil Rights Act of 1964 prohibited discrimination in hotels, restaurants, and public facilities and authorized the Justice Department to initiate desegregation suits. The Voting Rights Act of 1965 outlawed discriminatory practices in elections and authorized programs for voter registration. The Texas-born president established two new executive branch departments—the Department of Housing and Urban Development and the Department of Transportation. In addition, environmental protection legislation was a priority. Laws passed during these years including the Water Quality Act of 1965, the Clean Air Act of 1965, the Clean Water Restoration Act of 1966, and the Air Quality Act of 1967. Finally, several pieces of legislation designed to protect all Americans—such as the Highway Safety Act of 1966, the Fair Packaging and Labeling Act of 1966, and the Wholesome Meat Act of 1967—also became law.

Even though Johnson would have to cut back Great Society programs in the face of the Vietnam conflict, his social agenda transformed the nation. In 1961, only 45 domestic social programs existed; when Johnson left office, 435 programs helped the American people. Spending on social programs increased from $9.9 billion at the beginning of the decade to $25.6 billion by 1968. During his term the poverty rate fell from 22 percent to 13 percent of the population. The Great Society expanded the federal government's role in social welfare, giving economic opportunities to a wide variety of Americans, and increased the standard of living of many stuck in poverty.

While 226 of President Johnson's 252 legislative requests had been passed, the 1966 midterm elections brought more conservatives into Congress. Moreover, growing public frustration over the Vietnam War caused a shift in legislative priorities. Many programs were cut back or reenvisioned to pay for the war. Reverend Martin Luther King Jr. stated, "One of the greatest casualties of the war in Vietnam is the Great Society . . . shot down on the battlefield of Vietnam" (Bush). Johnson echoed this thought, telling his biographer, Doris Kearns Goodwin, "I knew from the start if I left a woman I really loved—the Great Society—in order to fight that bitch of a war in Vietnam then I would lose everything at home" (Daniels 28). While many of the Great Society's poverty programs continued under future administrations, the Office of Economic Opportunity, which had oversight over the majority of the poverty programs, was dismantled under the Nixon and Ford administrations. Moreover, President Ronald Reagan's first budget in 1981 cut funding for many of these programs.

The Great Society's lasting impact on society is still debated. Some liberals came to view the Great Society as a lost opportunity. Others, such as Joseph A. Califano Jr., an aide to President Johnson, cited the decline in the percentage of the poor to demonstrate the programs' successes. Conservatives criticize Johnson's

War on Poverty as an example of the failures of government engineering, pointing to the disintegration of the African American family and the lack of economic progress compared to the money spent.

Trevor Jason Soderstrum

See also: Democratic Party; Environmentalism; New Deal; Poverty Campaigns; Progressivism; War on Poverty

References

Bush, Lawrence. "May 22: The Great Society," *Jewish Currents*, May 21, 2012. http://jewishcurrents.org/may-22-the-great-society-10263. Accessed January 3, 2013.

Daniels, Robert Vincent. *Year of the Heroic Guerrilla: World Revolution and Counterrevolution in 1968.* Cambridge, MA: Harvard University Press, 1996.

"History." College of Education, Texas State University, San Marcos. http://www.education.txstate.edu/about/History-Facts.html. Accessed January 3, 2013.

Johnson, Lyndon Baines. "The Great Society," speech delivered May 22, 1964, Ann Arbor, MI. http://www.americanrhetoric.com/speeches/lbjthegreatsociety.htm. Accessed January 3, 2013.

Stossel, Scott. *Sarge: The Life and Times of Sargent Shriver.* Washington, DC: Smithsonian Books, 2004.

Greenback Party

The Greenback party was a nineteenth-century U.S. political party. A product of agrarian discontent in the decades following the Civil War, Greenbackism embodied the idea that the federal government should maintain or increase the currency supply in the country to meet the demands of the expanding U.S. economy. Greenbackers, who took their name from the wartime treasury notes issued by the federal government, argued that an inflated currency would help wipe out farm debt incurred during periods when prices on agricultural commodities were high and thus offer financial relief to farmers during tough times. Greenbackers were wary of big banks, railroads, and eastern business monopolies, all of which they felt were conspiring against famers' interests. Influenced in part by the writings of Alexander Campbell of Illinois, who was a protégé of antebellum currency reformer Edward Kellogg, the greenback movement gained prominence among farmers and laborers following the Panic of 1873.

Government policy during the Civil War helped drive the guiding principles of Geenbackism. During the conflict, the federal government issued around $400 million in paper currency, or "greenbacks," to help fund the Union war effort. These notes were not backed by government specie. Once the war ended, conflict arose as to whether or not these notes should be recalled, shifting the national economy back to a bullion-based system. After the economic downturn in 1873, many argued that the U.S. government should seize control of the economy and ease the burden on farmers and laborers by placing more paper currency into circulation and through the unlimited coinage of silver. Greenbackers believed that it would be easier to pay off their debts with more money in circulation and that more money circulating would also create inflation that would in turn raise the prices of farm commodities.

Agitation over the United States' economic policies came to a head in 1875 when Congress passed the Specie Resumption Act, which called for a reduction in the number of greenbacks in circulation. President Ulysses S. Grant and many members of the Republican Party, which generally represented the wealthier creditor classes, promoted this legislation that tied government currency to the price of gold. Conversely, while the Specie Resumption Act satisfied the big banks and other creditors, it made it more difficult for farmers to repay their obligations because the gold-based money supply could not be easily expanded.

After failing to convince the Democratic Party to adopt their views, members of the Greenback movement met in November of 1874 in Indianapolis, Indiana, to form an independent political party called the Greenback Party (sometimes referred to as the Independent Party or the National Party). At their organizational meeting the Greenbackers clarified whom they perceived as their enemies and protested against a host of government economic policies that they believed favored the wealthy. Hard times had driven many farmers and workers to believe that some type of conspiracy was at work involving wealthy creditors and other monied interests who controlled the foundation of the nation's economy. The Greenback Party held its first major political convention in Indianapolis in May 1876 with almost 250 delegates representing 17 states. The convention nominated Peter Cooper of New York as its first presidential candidate. A successful businessman and philanthropist, Cooper had a history of supporting reform movements including abolition and programs designed to give better treatment to Native Americans. Following the Civil War, Cooper gave speeches around the country on monetary reform and was a staunch opponent of the gold standard. He won his party's nomination by a wide margin despite the fact that at the time he was 85 years old, making him the oldest person to ever run for president. Cooper's running mate was 62-year-old Samuel F. Cary of Ohio, an attorney who had briefly served in the U.S. Congress as a Republican following the Civil War. Like Cooper, Cary supported antislavery causes before the conflict and was also involved in the prohibition movement. Republican Rutherford B. Hayes won the 1876 election over Democrat Samuel Tilden, with the Cooper-Cary ticket running a very distant third, garnering 75,973 popular votes, which amounted to almost 1 percent of the total votes cast, and no electoral votes. While the Greenback Party was not really a factor in the presidential election's outcome, the party did manage to have 15 candidates elected to Congress.

Despite the defeat in the presidential election, the Greenback Party continued to agitate for more money in circulation and in 1878 began expanding its platform in hopes of attracting into the fold more farmers as well as urban industrial workers. After partnering with several labor organizations, the Greenback Party changed its name to the Greenback-Labor Party. The party continued to condemn the big banks and railroads and also pressed for an eight-hour work day, which had become one of the central demands of labor union organizers of the period. In return for labor's support, the Greenbackers also endorsed the establishment of a labor bureau within the federal government and a reduction in Chinese immigration. Moreover, the party tried to attract members of the National Grange of the Patrons of Husbandry, the nation's leading farmers' organization, which had been founded in 1867 and by 1880 included almost 1 million members. Like the Grangers, the Greenback-Labor Party promoted a graduated income tax and proposed that government land should be given to farmers rather than sold to land speculators.

In June 1880, the Greenback-Labor Party held its national convention in Chicago, where members nominated James Baird Weaver as the party's standard-bearer in the upcoming presidential election. The 47-year-old Weaver was a lawyer and politician from Iowa who had at one time been a loyal Republican. Convinced that the Republican Party had become corrupted by wealthy special interest groups, he won a seat in Congress in 1878 as a Greenbacker. Rather than run for reelection in 1880, he accepted the Greenback-Labor Party's presidential nomination, with Texas lawyer Benjamin J. Chambers being chosen as his running mate. Weaver was a tireless campaigner who toured much of the country giving speeches criticizing the national Republican and Democratic parties and promoting farmers and industrial laborers as the backbone of American society. As was the case four years earlier in the presidential election of 1880, the Greenback-Labor Party ran a distant third behind Republican James A. Garfield, who won the contest, and Democrat Winfield Scott Hancock. The Greenback-Labor Party received 305,997 votes out of more than 9 million total votes cast and was unable to attract even a single electoral vote.

Interest in the Greenback-Labor Party peaked in 1880, but the party survived through one more presidential election cycle. In 1884 the party met again in Indianapolis and nominated Benjamin Franklin Butler for president. A lawyer and politician from Massachusetts, Butler served as a general in the Union army during the Civil War, becoming one of the war's more controversial figures as a result of policies that he dictated during the Union occupation of New Orleans. Butler began his political career before the war as a Democrat, but he eventually switched to the Republican Party. After the conflict he served in the U.S. House of Representatives as a Republican and as governor of the state of Massachusetts as a Democrat. Butler's running mate was Absolom M. West of Mississippi, a railroad executive who served as a general of Mississippi militia during the Civil War and was active in prewar Democratic politics. The Greenback ticket polled 175,096 popular votes, just under 2 percent of the total votes cast, and no electoral votes. This placed the party once again a distant third behind the Democratic victor Grover Cleveland and Republican nominee James G. Blaine. After the election the Greenback-Labor Party began to decline. In many states the party merged with the Democrats, while some Greenbackers found temporary political homes in other small, independent parties.

While the short-lived Greenback-Labor Party never backed competitive presidential candidates, Greenbackism left an important political legacy in the United States in that it helped make U.S. monetary policy a viable subject for political debate at the national level. The movement also pushed for a number of government reforms, such as a graduated income tax and shorter hours for industrial workers, that would eventually be adopted. It also helped lay the groundwork for future agrarian movements, most prominently the Populist movement and the People's Party of the late nineteenth century. In 1892 the People's Party nominated James B. Weaver, the former Greenbacker, as their first presidential candidate.

Ben Ray Wynne

See also: Democratic Party; Depression of 1873; Gold Standard/Free Silver; Gilded Age; Granger Movement; People's Party; Populism

References

Goodwyn, Lawrence. *The Populist Movement: A Short History of the Agrarian Revolt in America*. New York: Oxford University Press, 1978.

McMath, Robert C., Jr. *American Populism: A Social History, 1877–1898*. New York: Hill and Wang, 1990.

Ritter, Gretchen. *Goldbugs and Greenbacks: The Antimonopoly Tradition and the Politics of Finance, 1865–1896*. New York: Cambridge University Press, 2001.

Griffith, D. W. (1875–1948) and *The Birth of a Nation* (1915)

Despite inauspicious beginnings, D. W. Griffith, who died in 1948, made nearly five hundred films and gained the respect of such artists and directors as Charlie Chaplin, Orson Welles, Alfred Hitchcock, and John Ford. Griffith became the single most important figure in revolutionizing the film industry in the early twentieth century. His silent film *The Birth of a Nation* is considered the first major work of modern American cinema but is just as recognized for its overt racism as for its pioneering filmmaking.

Griffith, whose full name was David Llewelyn Wark Griffith, was born on January 22, 1875, in Crestwood, Kentucky. After his father, who had served as an officer in the Confederate army and as a

D. W. Griffith was the single most important and influential figure in the development of the American narrative film, and his 1915 film *Birth of a Nation* revolutionized the motion picture industry. (Library of Congress)

Kentucky state legislator, died when Griffith was only 10, his mother moved the family to Louisville, Kentucky, where she opened a boarding house that failed. To help with finances, Griffith left high school and worked at various jobs. After failing as a playwright, he decided to become a movie actor. In 1908, he joined the Biograph Company in New York City as a writer and actor but soon assumed the main director's position.

While with Biograph, Griffith turned previously experimental filmmaking techniques, such as camera movement, lighting, close-ups, long shots, flashbacks, fade-ins and fade-outs, and cross-cutting editing, into established techniques for making films. Though not the inventor of these techniques, Griffith employed them so effectively that he pioneered filmmaking as an art form. Working with a select group of Biograph's stock talent, including Mary Pickford, Lionel Barrymore, and Lillian Gish, Griffith was also able to develop a more fitting film-acting style. He became fundamental in laying the foundations of the movie industry in Hollywood through seasonal filming in California. In 1913, Griffith directed and produced *Judith of Bethulia*, one of the earliest feature films produced in the United States and the first Biograph feature film. When Biograph proved resistant to longer features, Griffith left the company, taking his cameraman and the stock actors with him. He formed his own production company, buying rights to Thomas Dixon Jr.'s novel *The Clansman* (1905).

Griffith began filming *The Clansman* in 1914 and released it in 1915. He spent a record-breaking budget on the movie, which was over three hours long. Griffith retitled the film in its initial release because he did not believe the original title did justice to the scope of the movie. *The Birth of a Nation* became the first real blockbuster and the highest-grossing film ever until surpassed by *Gone with the Wind* (1939). Griffith directed every scene himself, using all of the tools and techniques that he had developed during his time with Biograph. He even had a musical score composed for the movie and hired the Los Angeles Philharmonic Orchestra to play it for the premiere, something that had never been done before. *The Birth of a Nation* became the first film screened in the White House, supposedly causing Woodrow Wilson to proclaim, "It is like writing history with Lightning. And my only regret is that it is all so terribly true." Though debatable as to whether Wilson ever actually uttered this phrase, the anecdote is now recounted at the beginning of most prints of the film. *The Birth of a Nation* was so trailblazing that film historians almost universally consider it the foundation of the modern American film industry as a narrative art.

Despite its groundbreaking artistic and financial success, *The Birth of a Nation* was a tremendously polarizing movie upon its release and has remained so to this day. The film depicts the friendship between two families divided by the Civil War, the northern Stonemans and the southern Camerons, from the antebellum period to Reconstruction. Despite the film's strengths in marrying human scenes with an epic backdrop, Griffith shot it from a southern perspective. He depicted Reconstruction as a period in which the conquered Confederacy was subjected to northern carpetbaggers who wanted to destroy the South's old values while looting the region with the help of unruly and sexually aggressive freedmen. In this context, the Ku Klux Klan (KKK) was dramatized as a group formed in defense of the South and its white women as the object of desire for the newly freed blacks. Many of the actors playing the former slaves were white actors in obvious blackface.

The KKK was such a part of the film that when it premiered klansmen in full dress publicized its opening. Though seriously debated, critics argue the "second-era" KKK owed its birth to the film, as the KKK formed again at Stone Mountain, Georgia, later that year. The National Association for the Advancement of Colored People (NAACP), founded just a few years before *The Birth of a Nation* premiered, wanted the film banned, protested its premiere, and directed a public education campaign against it. Screenings led to riots in some cities where it did show, including Boston and Philadelphia, and anger prevented it from opening in several midwestern cities, including Chicago, Minneapolis, and St. Louis. In some places where the film opened there were reports of whites attacking blacks, and there was even a case of a white man murdering a black teenager.

Griffith was shocked by the backlash over the film, believing it to be an antiwar film that was accurate about the Civil War and Reconstruction. Despite (and even because of) its blatant racism, the film is important as a mirror of its own time. For instance, when many Americans opposed World War I, it served as a reminder of the horrors of war and the negative impact war had on people. Even in its racism, *The Birth of a Nation* was in step with the Dunning School, which depicted Reconstruction as a time when the South fell prey to northern carpetbaggers and southern scalawags while suffering from the enfranchisement of freed blacks. In his defense of the film, Griffith expressed paternalistic attitudes towards blacks, and during its second run, he added two opening title cards to defend the film with his "A PLEA FOR THE ART OF THE MOTION PICTURE." Despite its polarizing effect, the importance of *The Birth of a Nation* could not be ignored, and it was regularly considered the greatest American film until the 1960s.

Griffith released his next film, *Intolerance: Love's Struggle throughout the Ages* (1916), largely in response to his critics. In sweep and scope, *Intolerance* was even more ambitious than *The Birth of a Nation*. At three and a half hours, and costing more to make than any film to that time, Griffith used monumental sets and thousands of extras to show the negative impact of intolerance with four different historically set stories. His parallel editing between these stories and his use of music for narrative structure were revolutionary. Though *Intolerance* was a critical success and did solid box office business, it was not a success financially.

Griffith would never again match the heights of success he reached with *The Birth of a Nation* and *Intolerance*, but he remained an important filmmaker. He directed several films for the Allied war effort and, in an effort to help maintain artistic control of his films, he joined others who believed in film as art and became a cofounder of United Artists with Charlie Chaplin, Mary Pickford, and Douglas Fairbanks. While with United Artists, he had some commercial and critical success, particularly with his films *Broken Blossoms* (1919), notable for its soft-focus photography and early interracial love story; *Way Down East* (1920), his greatest commercial success since *The Birth of a Nation*; and *Orphans of the Storm* (1921), in which he returned to an epic backdrop, this time the French Revolution. Though both were financially unsuccessful, Griffith also forayed into full-sound features with his last two films, *Abraham Lincoln* (1930) and *The Struggle* (1931).

Griffith died in Hollywood on July 23, 1948, of a cerebral hemorrhage. But his legacy had been established before his death, and Americans honored him posthumously as well. In 1936 he was honored with a special Academy Award for his contributions to film art, and in 1940 the Museum of Modern Art did a retrospective of his work. His image was put on a postage stamp in 1975 for the 100th anniversary of his birth. Two decades earlier, in 1953, the Director's Guild of America instituted the D. W. Griffith Award as its highest honor; nevertheless, true to the controversy surrounding his best-known work, the Guild renamed the award the DGA Lifetime Achievement Award in 1999 because of the racial stereotypes fostered by *The Birth of a Nation*.

Christopher Strangeman

See also: Film; Ku Klux Klan (KKK); Leisure; Progressivism

References

Barry, Iris. *D.W. Griffith: American Film Master*. New York: Museum of Modern Art Press, 2002.

Henderson, Robert M. *D.W. Griffith: His Life and Work*. New York: Oxford University Press, 1972.

Schickel, Richard. *D.W. Griffith: An American Life*. New York: Simon and Schuster, 1984.

Stokes, Melvyn. *D.W. Griffith's The Birth of a Nation: A History of "The Most Controversial Motion Picture of All Time."* New York: Oxford University Press, 2007.

Williams, Martin. *Griffith: First Artist of the Movies*. Oxford, UK: Oxford University Press, 1980.

Gronlund, Laurence (1846–1899)

Laurence Gronlund was a Danish American socialist whose ideas and writings influenced various constituencies of the Populist ranks along with other American radicals, reformers, and theorists. Gronlund's socialist treatise *The Co-operative Commonwealth* (1884) is his most influential and best-known work. Other important books include *Our Destiny* (1890) and *The New Economy* (1898). As a result of these works, Gronlund ranks among the most influential socialist theorists of the nineteenth-century United States.

A native of Denmark, Gronlund migrated to the United States in the years immediately following the U.S. Civil War. While working as an attorney, educator, and lecturer, Gronlund realized that the United States and other English-speaking nations lacked an approachable

English-language explanation of scientific socialism. Thus, in 1884, Gronlund published *The Co-operative Commonwealth* with the intention of addressing this deficiency. In this influential work, Gronlund laid out an American socialism that stressed change through the evolutionary progression of ideas rather than through violent, class-based revolution. This evolutionary process culminated with the emergence of a final-stage commonwealth defined by cooperation rather than conflict and competition. Well received, *The Co-operative Commonwealth* sold approximately 60,000 volumes in the United States.

Gronlund's ideas, as expressed in the *Co-operative Commonwealth*, influenced American reformers and radicals. Among those whose philosophies were self-admittedly shaped by Gronlund one can find American socialist leader Eugene Debs and such Populists as Henry Demarest Lloyd and Julius Wayland. Edward Bellamy also drew heavily upon the ideas of *Co-operative Commonwealth* when writing his utopian novel *Looking Backward* in 1888.

Like Bellamy, many of the most radical Populists embraced the utopian aspects of Gronlund's socialism and set up utopian cooperative communities across the nation. The most famous of these include the Kaweah Co-operative Community in California and the Ruskin Community in Tennessee. Cooperative communities could also be found in Colorado, Mississippi, Oregon, and Texas.

Many mainstream Populists embraced his ideas of large-scale cooperative enterprises and the centrality of trade unionism to future societies. The slogan "cooperative commonwealth" subsequently became a common phrase among American Populists in the 1890s. For his part, Gronlund openly associated with the People's Party in 1892, promoting it as the only moral and truly American reform party.

Gronlund has also been credited with bringing Fabian socialism to the United States and supporting a number of political and social reforms that would ultimately shape American society. Among these, he advocated the establishment of a national department of labor and agriculture, eight-hour work days, state income taxes, government subsidies for farmers, government protection for labor unions, and public works programs for the unemployed.

Jonathan Lavon Foster

See also: Bellamy, Edward (1850–1898); Cooperative Commonwealth; Debs, Eugene (1855–1926); Gilded Age; Haskell, Anna Fader (1858–1942); Haskell, Burnette G. (1857–1907); Kaweah Colony; People's Party; Progressivism; Socialism, Christian

References

Brundage, David. *The Making of Western Labor Radicalism: Denver's Organized Workers, 1878–1905*. Urbana: University of Chicago Press, 1994.

Gemorah, Solomon. "Laurence Gronlund: Utopian or Reformer?" *Science and Society* 33 (4): 446–458.

Jenkin, Thomas P. "The American Fabian Movement." *Western Political Quarterly* 1 (2): 113–123.

Maher, P. E. "Laurence Gronlund: Contributions to American Socialism." *Western Political Quarterly* 15 (4): 618–624.

Postel, Charles. *The Populist Vision*. Oxford, UK: Oxford University Press, 2007.

Guthrie, Woodrow Wilson "Woody" (1912–1967)

Woody Guthrie was a socially conscious hillbilly singer. He was slender, with wild hair and a beard, and had a folksy writing style. Born on July 14, 1912, shortly after Woodrow Wilson got the Democratic nomination for president, Guthrie died in 1967 of Huntington's disease. He was a controversial embarrassment in his hometown of Okemah, Oklahoma, but a national treasure to the millions who listened to the more than 1,200 songs he wrote and performed.

Oklahoma in Guthrie's youth was in the waning years of its prairie radicalism and Christian socialism, but not in the Guthrie household. Guthrie's father, a real estate agent and Okemah city clerk, was a model Democrat, opposed to Eugene Debs and socialism. Woody grew up as a Democrat, working on his father's unsuccessful campaign for corporation commissioner. He moved further left when the Democrats failed to act on race relations and redistribution of income.

With the onset of the Great Depression, Guthrie hoboed to California, where he stayed from1936 to 1940. From 1940 until his death he lived and worked mostly in the East. He may or may not have joined the California Communist Party, but in 1939 he wrote a column, "Woody Sez," for the *People's Daily World* in San Francisco. Despite the portrayal of him in the movie *Bound for Glory*, Guthrie was more than a populist by 1940.

Guthrie shared the left-wing populism of Oklahoma's Will Rogers as well as Walt Whitman's belief in the common man, and his music and writings incorporate the old populist rejection of concentrated wealth. His belief in democracy's future and the pursuit of happiness was as old as Daniel Shays and Thomas Jefferson. Guthrie's targets included bankers, lawyers, utilities, and gouging businesspeople.

Guthrie's work included "Pastures of Plenty," "Hard Travelin," "So Long It's Been Good to Know You," and other songs of Dust Bowl migrants as well as outlaws such as "Pretty Boy" Floyd and Jesse James. Guthrie portrayed Jesus as a socialist outlaw in "They Laid Poor Jesus Christ in His Grave" and as a working-class carpenter supporting the rights of the common people before being betrayed by the selfish rich. "This Land Is Your Land" answered Irving Berlin's "God Bless America," which offended Guthrie because it glibly told people not to worry because God was taking care of them.

In Okemah, many in the 1950s and early 1960s regarded Guthrie as a communist. The local American Legion successfully pressured the city to cancel Woody Guthrie Day after his death because of his supposed communism. When his wife and son donated papers and recordings to the library, they did so secretly because the locals feared an influx of "hippies." An earlier attempt to donate was blocked by the right-wing American Security Council, and Oklahomans refused to accept that a "communist" wrote the state song, "Oklahoma Hills," preferring to credit his cousin, Jack Guthrie.

Slowly the people of Oklahoma came to accept Guthrie as one of their own.

In 1972 one of the city's three water towers read "Home of Woody Guthrie," while the other two read, "hot" and "cold." The first Woody Guthrie Festival took place in 1998 after Guthrie was in the Oklahoma Hall of Fame. Guthrie was inducted into the Rock and Roll Hall of Fame and got a lifetime achievement Grammy in 2000. In 2004 his portrait was finally approved for the state capitol; artist Charles Banks said that he had wanted to do the portrait for 20 years but could not get any cooperation. His portrait of Guthrie was dedicated at the Woody Guthrie Folk Festival in Okemah in July 2004. Belatedly, Guthrie joined Will Rogers, Sequoyah, Robert S. Kerr, and Jim Thorpe as famous Oklahomans honored in the capitol rotunda.

John H. Barnhill

See also: Democratic Party; New Deal; Pop Culture; Progressivism; Rogers, Will (1879–1935); Socialism, Christian

References

Briley, Ron. " 'Woody Sez': Woody Guthrie, the People's Daily World, and Indigenous Radicalism." *California History* 84 (1): 30–43, 69–70.

Collins, Rob. "Portrait of a Populist." *Oklahoma Gazette*, June 2, 2004. http://www.woodyguthrie.org/merchandise/oklahomagazette.htm. Accessed January 3, 2013.

Cray, Ed. *Ramblin' Man: The Life and Times of Woody Guthrie*. New York: W.W. Norton & Company, 2004.

Dunbar-Ortiz, Roxanne. "One or Two Things I Know about Us: Rethinking the Image and Role of the 'Okies.' " *Monthly Review* 53 (3). http://www.monthlyreview.org/0702dunbar.htm.

Jackson, Mark Allan. "Prophet Singer: The Voice and Vision of Woody Guthrie." PhD dissertation, Louisiana State University, 2002. http://etd.lsu.edu/docs/available/etd-1112102-151209/unrestricted/Jackson_dis.pdf. Accessed January 3, 2013.

H

Hanna, Mark (1837–1904)

Marcus Alonzo Hanna is one of the engineers of modern political campaigning. His connection with industrialization, big business, and the Republican Party made him one of the most influential political kingmakers of the late nineteenth century. He was essential to the presidential campaign of William McKinley in 1896. That election embodied the tactics and philosophy future political strategists would use throughout the twentieth century to attract the American populace to vote based on campaigns more akin to advertising than to political substance.

On September 24, 1837, Hanna was born into a family that was part of the rising American business class. His father, a long-time Whig (later a Republican), instilled in him hardworking ethics and Republican values. As a young adult, Hanna worked in his father's grocery store and eventually became partner and owner after his father's death in 1862. Hanna continued to gain business experience and clout when he also became a partner in his father-in-law's business in 1867. Hanna used both businesses to propel him even deeper into the world of big business.

Hanna believed that the government should do everything in its power to help businesses succeed. Even before he began working with Republican politicians, one of Hanna's most fundamental beliefs was that the future success of the United States was tied up in big business. Hanna's first experience in national politics came when he helped to organize and fund his friend John Sherman's campaign for the Republican nomination for president in 1884 and later in 1888. While Hanna's candidate lost both bids, Hanna gained the much-needed experience of running and managing a national campaign. It was during the late 1880s that William McKinley, an Ohio senator, first caught his attention, beginning a relationship that would carry them both to the White House.

By 1896, Hanna was a long-time friend and associate of William McKinley and was one of his right-hand men for the presidential election in 1896. First, Hanna worked to ensure that McKinley would receive the Republican nomination. Then Hanna increased McKinley's appeal to both northern and southern Republicans. He rented a home in Georgia to establish a southern headquarters for McKinley. His work paid off. After McKinley was named as the Republican nominee, Hanna himself was selected to chair the Republican National Committee.

Hanna understood that defeating the Populist and Democrat candidate William Jennings Bryan was going to take a lot of work. He not only campaigned heavily in the North and South but also established centers in the western portions of the

United States to try to cut into Bryan's popularity. Hanna poured himself into McKinley's presidential campaign, on which he spent more than $100,000 of his own money. He also raised and directed more than $3.5 million in campaign finances. Hanna even paid more than 1,000 workers to help in the campaign and helped to devise the "front-porch" campaign—the most famous aspect of the McKinley's presidential election campaign. The front-porch campaign encouraged different delegations to visit McKinley on his front porch and bring their problems and concerns to him personally. McKinley also gave speeches from his home. This method contrasted perfectly with Bryan's whistle-stop campaign. McKinley and Hanna believed that the campaign stood no chance if attempted to beat Bryan at his own game of stump speeches, and thus they settled on the front-porch strategy.

Hanna also used mass amounts of political propaganda to outshine Bryan's campaign. Hanna established two major headquarters—one in Chicago and one in New York. He sent out speakers, created posters, handed out campaign buttons, and printed political pamphlets in multiple languages to reach out to immigrants. Hanna portrayed Bryan as a wild man from the countryside. His propaganda claimed that Bryan would destroy the United States with his unsafe economic policies. In the end Hanna's campaign strategies and fundraising were successful. McKinley beat Bryan in a landslide. He carried the South and the West by more than 6 million voters. He swept the Northeast and Midwest regions by more than 7 million votes. Moreover, McKinley beat Bryan by 95 electoral votes. The 1896 election saw one of the biggest spikes in voter participation in U.S. history. Hanna's message convinced Americans that the fate of the nation depended on their individual votes and on the election of William McKinley. Hanna is credited for orchestrating one of the most efficient and organized campaigns of the nineteenth century.

After the election, President McKinley offered Hanna a position on his cabinet but Hanna refused, believing it would appear to be patronage for his work on the campaign. Instead, McKinley appointed Hanna's long-time friend, John Sherman, as secretary of state. Hanna was then able to run for and fill Sherman's vacancy in the U.S. Senate. Hanna continued his friendship with McKinley while serving as a senator and helping to run McKinley's reelection campaign in 1900. Hanna served as an Ohio senator from 1897 until his death on February 15, 1904.

Mark Hanna's legacy was born in the state and national media. He had a longtime rough relationship with the media even before he became one of William Randolph Hearst's targets. In 1880, Hanna purchased the *Cleveland Herald*, an act that pitted him against Edwin Cowles, a fellow Republican and owner of the *Cleveland Leader*. Seeing Hanna as a threat, Cowles used his paper to launch a number of critical attacks on his rival. It is the *Leader* that first described Hanna as a ruthless politician who was willing to do anything to win. Hearst and Homer Davenport used these same themes to discredit Hanna in political cartoons during the 1896 presidential election. The media created an image of Hanna single-handedly running McKinley's campaign and answering to big business. This perception gave birth to Hanna's mythology.

While it is true that Hanna was influential during McKinley's campaign, Hanna was not the sole decision maker. William McKinley, along with a fellow strategist, Charles Dawes, helped to devise McKinley's political strategies. Nevertheless, Hanna's ability to raise a significant amount of money and run an efficient campaign set an example that the national Republican Party followed throughout the twentieth century.

Autumn C. Lass

See also: Bryan, William Jennings (1860–1925); Gilded Age; McKinley, William, Jr. (1843–1901)

References

Horner, William. *Ohio's Kingmaker: Mark Hanna, Man and Myth.* Columbus: Ohio University Press, 2010.

Josephson, Matthew. *The Presidential Makers: The Culture of Politics and Leadership in an Age of Enlightenment, 1896–1919.* New York: Frederick Ungar, 1966.

Williams, R. Hal. *Realigning America: McKinley, Bryan, and the Remarkable Election of 1896.* Lawrence: University Press of Kansas, 2010.

Haskell, Anna Fader (1858–1942)

Anna Fader Haskell worked as a labor activist, socialist reformer, suffragist, and educator throughout central and northern California during the late nineteenth and early twentieth centuries. Haskell was associated with the radical, labor-oriented *Truth* newspaper, the Nationalist Club of San Francisco, the Kaweah Co-Operative Commonwealth colony, the Woman's Rights Club of San Francisco, and the Woman's Congress of 1894. She also amassed 30 years of teaching experience in California schools before her death in 1942.

Born in Trinity County, California, in 1858 to gold rush–era pioneers, Anna Fader completed high school in Salinas. She then resided with her family in Sonoma County until 1881. In the fall of that year, the independent-minded Anna struck out for San Francisco without accompaniment in hope of securing employment. After finding work as a waitress in a local diner, she moved in with the family of a recent acquaintance, Helen Haskell. Anna soon fell in love with Helen's brother Burnette, whom she wed on July 21, 1882.

After marrying, Anna found her life significantly influenced by her husband's activism. Fiercely independent, nonconformist, and reform-minded, Anna proved well suited for such activities. By the mid-1880s, she had devoted substantial effort to his newspaper, *Truth*, serving as a typesetter and editor and performing secretarial duties. Likewise, she took a particular interest in the Bellamyist National Club of San Francisco (Nationalist Club), founded by Burnette and headquartered at the couple's house. After having been nominated for the position of club president, Anna deferred in favor of the secretary position. This role, she felt, kept her closer to the action. As secretary, she organized meetings, developed programs, and even spoke before the membership.

Beyond headquartering the Nationalist Club at her home, financial needs required Anna to open her home to boarders. Labor Unionists, anarchists, Farmers' Alliance lecturers, and a variety of activists from around the country made use of the Haskell boarding house. From time to time, Anna was also known to stage boxing matches at the house and, on occasion, to participate in the matches. By this time, she had also developed a reputation as a skilled and energetic labor organizer for her work among the unemployed in San Francisco's Golden Gate Park.

While Anna found purpose in the causes of labor and social reform, Burnette's obsessive devotion to the same strained their marriage. Increasingly, his activities as head of the International Workingman's Association and, after 1886, as founder of the Kaweah Co-Operative Commonwealth colony resulted in him assuming the role of absentee husband. As an avowed atheist, Anna also found Burnette's interest in spirituality troubling.

In 1890, Anna moved with Burnette and their young son Aseroth—whom Burnette had named after an ancient Phoenician god—to the Kaweah colony. She remained at Kaweah until 1892, all the while prone to episodes of depression and experiencing the deprivations and hardships that accompanied pioneer life. As a means of employment, she taught school while at the colony. She despised this task, finding the children undisciplined and the facilities lacking. More than anything, however, she detested the drudgery of household chores associated with life at Kaweah.

Upon returning to San Francisco, Anna became active in the suffragist movement for a brief period. Between 1892 and 1894, she participated in the city's Woman's Rights Club and attended the Woman's Congress of 1894. Yet her and her husband's peak days of social activism had come to an end. Disillusioned by the failure of the Kaweah colony and his other ventures, an emotionally distant Burnette turned increasingly to alcohol. Anna subsequently left him in April 1896 and obtained a divorce the following year.

Free from Burnette, Anna found contentment in her son, the religion she had previously eschewed, and the occupation she had despised while at Kaweah. Beginning in 1898, she taught school at various locations across northern California. After retiring in 1928, she survived on her teacher's pension until her death in 1942.

Jonathan Lavon Foster

See also: Bellamy, Edward (1850–1898); Haskell, Burnette G. (1857–1907); Gilded Age; Kaweah Colony

References

Kozakavich, Stacy Colleen. "The Center of Civilization: Archaeology and History of the Kaweah Co-operative Commonwealth." Ph.D. Dissertation, University of California, Berkeley, 2007.

O'Connell, Jay. *Co-operative Dreams: A History of the Kaweah Colony.* Van Nuys, CA: Raven River Press, 1999.

Ogden, Annegret S. *The Great American Housewife: From Helpmate to Wage Earner, 1776–1986.* Westport, CT: Greenwood Press, 1986.

Postel, Charles. *The Populist Vision.* Oxford, UK: Oxford University Press, 2007.

Haskell, Burnette G. (1857–1907)

Burnette G. Haskell served a significant role in the labor and utopian community movements of California in the late nineteenth century. Haskell is best known as the founder of San Francisco's International Workingman's Association and for his leadership role in the utopian Kaweah Co-operative Commonwealth near Visalia, California. At various times before in death in 1907, Haskell was a self-avowed socialist, communist-anarchist, cooperatist, and Bellamy Nationalist.

A first-generation native Californian, Burnette G. Haskell was born in Sierra County in June 1857 to pioneer parents. After attending, but failing to graduate from, the University of California, University of Illinois, and Oberlin College, Haskell took and passed the California bar in 1879. He soon eschewed a career in law in favor of journalism. This opportunity presented itself as his uncle offered the young man a position as editor of his newly created weekly newspaper *Truth*.

As editor of *Truth*, Haskell stumbled upon the issue that ignited his passion and defined the course that his life was to take. While covering the meetings of San Francisco's Trades and Labor Assembly, the young reporter began to identify with laborers. He subsequently immersed himself in the study of labor and labor organization, quickly becoming known as the most well-read man in the California labor movement. Haskell's studies led him to the conclusion that San Francisco's existing labor organizations were too restrictive and conservative. By then a self-confirmed socialist, he founded the International Workingman's Association (IWA).

Haskell's IWA prospered early on. Drawing inspiration from Marx's and Engel's First Socialist International and Bakunin's International Working People's Associations, the group attracted between 5,000 and 10,000 members by the early 1880s. The IWA's strongest areas proved to be the Pacific Coast and Rocky Mountain states. *Truth* served as its official mouthpiece, with articles often noted for their violent tone in regard to the working-class struggle.

By the mid-1880s, Haskell's interest in the IWA waned as he found the prospects of successful class revolution less likely and the allure of utopian separatism increasingly attractive. After reading Laurence Gronlund's *Cooperative Commonwealth* in 1884, Haskell joined with James J. Martin to found the Kaweah Co-operative Commonwealth colony in the area that became, six years later, the Sequoia National Park. The colony aimed to show that practical socialism could succeed in a self-supportive cooperative settlement. As the Kaweah colony consumed Haskell's interest, the IWA suffered. Without Haskell's leadership, the organization fell into decline and dissolved by the late 1880s.

His experiment with cooperative living faced a similar destiny. Discrepancies with land-claim titles, internal factionalization, poor relations with the Southern Pacific Railroad, establishment of Kaweah land as a national park by the federal government, and prosecution for cutting timber on federal land ended Haskell's dreams for the Kaweah colony by 1891.

As Haskell attempted to keep the Kaweah colony afloat, he also became deeply involved with Bellamy Nationalism. This movement took its inspiration from Edward Bellamy's 1888 utopian novel *Looking Backward*. Bellamyites across the country formed Nationalist Clubs in the years following the book's publication. These clubs stressed the development of a classless society defined by cooperation rather than competition. All means of production, including land, industry, and retail establishments, would be owned by the government and operated for the benefit of the people. Haskell founded an influential Bellamyite Nationalist Club in San Francisco in the spring of 1889. While he hoped to employ the popularity of such clubs to recruit new colonists to Kaweah, he also promoted the transformation of San Francisco into a Nationalist city. While this failed to occur, California Nationalist clubs proved popular, accounting for more than half of all such clubs nationwide in 1890. Many of these Nationalists ultimately joined with Farmers' Alliance members to form California's Populist People's Party in 1891.

Following his flirtation with Bellamy Nationalism and the ultimate failure of the Kaweah colony, Haskell spent the remaining years of his life in obscurity, attempting to gain compensation from the federal government for losses incurred as the result of the Kaweah colony's failure. Specifically, he sought compensation for the $50,000 road the Kaweans constructed leading into the Giant Forest. This road served for decades as the only entrance into Sequoia National Park. Disgruntled, alone, and rumored to be addicted to alcohol and opium, the socialist, communist-anarchist, and cooperative utopian died in a shack overlooking the Pacific Ocean near San Francisco in June 1907. His funeral was conducted by the Sailors Union of the Pacific.

Jonathan Lavon Foster

See also: Bellamy, Edward (1850–1898); Gilded Age; Gronlund, Laurence (1846–1899); Haskell, Anna Fader (1858–1942); Kaweah Colony; People's Party

References

Bean, Walter. "Ideas of Reform in California." *California Historical Quarterly* 51 (3): 213–226.

Cross, Ira B. *A History of the Labor Movement in California*. Berkeley: University of California Press, 1935.

DeFord, Miriam Allen. *They Were San Franciscans*. Caldwell, ID: Caxton Printers, 1941. Reprint, Freeport, NY: Books for Libraries Press, 1970.

Hine, Robert V. *California's Utopian Colonies*. Berkeley: University of California Press, 1983.

Hine, Robert V. "A California Utopia: 1885–1890." *Huntington Library Quarterly* 11 (4): 387–405.

Hine, Robert V. *California Utopianism: Contemplations of an Era*. San Francisco: Boyd & Fraser Publishing Company, 1981.

Lewinnek, Elaine. "The Kaweah Co-operative Commonwealth and the Contested Nature of Sequoia National Park." *Southern California Quarterly* 89 (2): 141–167.

Lewis, Ruth R. "Kaweah: An Experiment in Coöperative Colonization." *Pacific Historical Review* 17 (4): 429–441.

McGreevy, John T. "Farmers, Nationalists, and the Origins of California Populism." *Pacific Historical Review* 58 (4): 471–495.

Postel, Charles. *The Populist Vision.* Oxford: Oxford University Press, 2007.

Hayes, "Lemonade" Lucy (1831–1889)

Lucille "Lucy" Ware Webb Hayes, popularly known as "Lemonade Lucy," was President Rutherford Hayes's wife, a staunch abolitionist, feminist, and supporter of the temperance movement. She is considered one of the most popular first ladies in the history of the United States and a representative of the era of the "New Woman."

Born in Chillicothe, Ohio, on August 28, 1831, the youngest of three children, to Dr. James Webb and Maria Cook, Lucy Webb enjoyed a comfortable childhood despite her father's death from cholera when she was two. The attitudes of her grandfather Isaac Cook, a local judge and member of the state legislature, had a lasting effect on her, including his ideas about public education, temperance, and antislavery.

Lucy Webb Hayes (1831–1889), wife of President Rutherford B. Hayes. (Library of Congress)

In 1844, the Webb family moved to Delaware, Ohio, where the teenaged Lucy attended school, took college courses at Ohio Wesleyan, and met a 24-year-old lawyer named Rutherford B. Hayes. She then enrolled at Cincinnati Wesleyan Female College. It was during this time that she embraced many of the feminist ideas of the time, believing that women were just as smart as men and should be seen as men's equals in most things and their superiors in others, and she internalized Methodism's emphasis on personal morality. Upon graduating from school in 1850, she renewed her friendship with Rutherford Hayes, and they were married two-and-a-half years later on December 30, 1852.

The two purportedly enjoyed a happy partnership, with the future president admitting that his wife often helped him with his wavering Christian faith. Starting in November 1853, the couple had the first of their eight children, five of whom survived infancy: Birchard Austin, Webb Cook, Rutherford Platt, Fanny, and Scott Russell. Until the Civil War, Rutherford built up his law practice and made political connections. It was Lucy's constant pushing and moral compass that caused him to leave the Whigs and join the newly formed Republican Party over the issues of temperance and abolition. It was at the same time that Lucy Hayes came under the sway of feminist and abolitionist Lucy Stone and attended many of her lectures.

When the war started, Rutherford Hayes became a major in the 23rd Ohio Volunteer Infantry. The couple saw the war as a "holy and just cause," although Lucy was critical of what she considered President Abraham Lincoln's foot-dragging on the slavery issue (Schneider and Schneider 126). Often joining her husband at various posts (he was quickly promoted to the rank of colonel and then brigadier general), Mrs. Hayes became popular among his troops for her "mothering." In one famous incident, after tending to her husband's wounded arm for two weeks, she returned to Ohio by rail and noticed a group of wounded soldiers who were not given any room on the train. Commandeering a Pullman car, she made several wealthy patrons move so that the soldiers could have space. She mended soldiers' uniforms, traveled rough roads, and was extremely vocal about Confederate mistreatment of Union soldiers. Despite battling her own rheumatism and the recent death of an infant, she proved to be Hayes's most valuable asset with his soldiers.

After the war, Rutherford Hayes used his military service as a springboard to a political career. In 1864, he was elected to the U.S. House of Representatives. Lucy, with her "Radical Republican" views, constantly had her husband's ear and was his main political advisor. One of her major concerns was the Freedman's Bureau's efforts to help former slaves, and she was concerned about Andrew Johnson's pragmatic attitude towards the former Confederacy.

In 1857, Lucy encouraged her husband to run for the office of governor of Ohio, which he won. While influencing legislation behind the scenes, she was extremely careful to act publicly in the traditional female role. Yet her influence could be seen in her husband's efforts to reform the welfare and prison institutions in the state. She raised private funds to establish the Home for Soldiers' Orphans at Xenia, Ohio, and then lobbied to get the state to take over the expense of running it.

Even though Mrs. Hayes had rigid opinions on the issues of the day, the people of Ohio fell in love with her. As her husband wrote, "Lucy employs herself about the soldiers' orphans . . . about the decoration of soldiers' graves and about the deaf and dumb pupils at the Reform Farm for boys" (Schneider and Schneider 127). She was also very careful to not publicly contradict her husband's stance on woman suffrage, education, or other areas of equality. When individuals tried to get her on the record about such things, she avoided the questions by acting busy with something else, often using her children as props. She also publicly refused to participate in any temperance crusades, knowing such activity would hurt her husband's political career.

In 1872, Hayes lost his bid to become a U.S. senator, and the couple retired from public life for the next four years. Feeling slighted by President Ulysses Grant, they moved to Fremont, Ohio, until Rutherford could run for a third term as governor in 1875. Yet the Hayeses made plans for Rutherford to go beyond just being a governor, and in 1876 he accepted the Republican nomination for president.

The presidential election of 1876 was one of the closest in U.S. history. In fact, it was so close that the outcome remained unknown for months. While Samuel J. Tilden won the popular vote, there was some dispute regarding the electoral votes. In what became known as the Compromise of 1877, certain Democrats in Congress, mostly southerners, agreed to award 20 disputed electoral votes to Hayes in exchange for an end to military occupation of the South, thus effectively ending Reconstruction, leading to the social and economic abuses of African Americans there.

President Hayes had a difficult time in office while Lucy fulfilled her role as first lady with greater success than did her husband in his position. Many saw the first lady as a representative of the "New Woman." She was modest and careful to maintain a middle-class appearance by accepting the limits of her "sphere," yet she also had a public persona. While her husband was constantly under political attack, Lucy was beloved throughout the United States. Journalist Mary Clemmer Ames coined the term *first lady* to describe her. Yet she was not above some criticism, mostly relating to her refusal to serve liquor at events in the White House. While she did not advocate or publicly comment on prohibition, the Woman's Christian Temperance Union applauded her actions and commissioned a full-length painting of her, which still hangs in the president's residence. She felt that the president and his family should be moral examples for the rest of the nation. In other words, she lived her Methodist faith. For this stance, she earned the nickname "Lemonade Lucy." In accordance with her religious beliefs, she also banned dancing, billiards, and card-playing on the premises. Despite any criticism she received she tried to maintain a serene appearance, which many felt at times she paid for in the form of almost crippling headaches.

Similar to women of her class, Lucy entered the social reform arena of the Gilded Age New Woman. Lucy was extremely involved in various charities and good works, such as supporting and helping out at nearby Hampton College, the national Deaf Mute College, decorating Civil War soldier's graves, and pushing for the completion of the Washington Monument. Keeping in touch with the soldiers in her husband's former regiment, she became known as "Mother Lucy." Surprisingly, her longest lasting and most famous legacy during her time at Pennsylvania Avenue was the annual Easter-egg-rolling party.

While Lucy continued to have her husband's ear and remained active in reform, their four years in the White House were a bit of a disappointment. With Congress equally divided, Rutherford Hayes made himself a lame duck by announcing before he arrived in Washington that he would not seek a second term. He struggled to restore the power lost during the Grant administration's years of corruption and decline. With federal troops removed from the South, the Hayeses hoped that through conciliation they could achieve harmony with the former Confederacy. Lucy became his main ambassador. The *Richmond Dispatch* noted, "Mrs. Hayes has won the admiration of people wherever she has been" (Schneider and Schneider 130).

Instead the South became a one-party region and rolled back the newly granted rights of African Americans.

One of the few accomplishments that Rutherford Hayes could take pride in was his attempt to break up the spoils system and end much of the corruption that had marked the previous administration. The president also tried to address the nation's monetary policy. Farmers wanted soft money or a silver standard. Trying to lessen the economic difficulties, Hayes used what little political capital he had to push through the Bland-Allison Act, which called for the government to purchase at least $2 million of silver every month.

Upon leaving the White House in 1881, Lucy received numerous tributes and requests for public appearances, particularly by temperance organizations, all of which she rejected. She continued to serve as president of the Methodist Episcopal Woman's Home Missionary Society and remained active in other local activities.

On June 25, 1889, she died of a stroke. The entire nation grieved the loss of the first lady. While she tried to walk the tightrope of feminine domesticity, she often referred to her husband's political career as "ours," and many commented that the wrong Hayes had been elected. With her public appearances and college education, she changed the role and expectations of the president's wife forever. It is little wonder that President Benjamin Harrison claimed upon her death that she was "most idolized woman in America" (Holloway 34).

Trevor Jason Soderstrum

See also: Abolitionism; Bland, Richard P. (1835–1899); New Woman; Prohibition (1919–1933); Woman's Christian Temperance Union (WCTU)

References

Holloway, Laura Carter. *The Ladies of the White House, or, In the Home of the Presidents: Being a Complete History of the Social and Domestic Lives of the Presidents from Washington to the Present Time.* New York: Bradley, 1882.

"Lucy Ware Webb Hayes." White House website. http://www.whitehouse.gov/about/first-ladies/lucyhayes. Accessed January 4, 2013.

Schneider, Dorothy, and Carl J. Schneider. *First Ladies: A Biographical Dictionary.* 3rd ed. New York: Facts on File, January 2010.

Haymarket Riot (1886)

The Haymarket Riot, the very name of which tends to mischaracterize what it was about, was one of the most significant events in American labor and Populist history in the nineteenth century. A peaceful meeting of anarchist activists that ended in violence and the execution of several anarchist activists, the Haymarket Riot marked a significant setback for the American labor movement. It also severely marginalized the anarchist movements of this period and set back the movement for an eight-hour work day by decades.

The movements and events that led up the Haymarket Riot originated in the post–Civil War labor movements. The rise of the Knights of Labor (KOL) began as a secret society in the 1870s but had "gone public" by the 1880s under the leadership

The police charge rioters in old Haymarket Square in Chicago, Illinois, on May 4, 1886. The riot occurred when a bomb exploded among a group of policemen as they attempted to disperse a giant labor rally in the city's Haymarket Square. Eleven people died in the incident. (Library of Congress)

of Terrence V. Powderly. The KOL had a membership growing into the tens of thousands and was notable for its inclusive mode of unionization that welcomed unskilled and skilled workers, as well as, unprecedentedly, women and African Americans. The riot also grew out of the immigrant-dominated radical movements, whose activists, along with the KOL, pushed for an eight-hour work day at a time when the average work day was as long as 12 hours. The event that precipitated the meeting at Haymarket Square in Chicago's Near North Side was a massive strike at the McCormick Reaper Works on May 1, 1886. Violence there between the strikers and the strikebreakers brought in by the company resulted in police involvement and brutal treatment of the strikers by the Chicago police.

The meeting on May 4, 1886, convened by Albert Parsons, an Anglo-American anarchist and former Confederate Army veteran, along with several immigrant colleagues, was intended as a peaceful protest against the antistriker police brutality and as such was immediately targeted as a threat by Chicago police Captain John Bonfield. Although Chicago Mayor Carter H. Harrison had visited the Haymarket meeting and declared it nonthreatening, Bonfield nonetheless sent police reinforcements to break it up. Arriving just as the meeting was near its conclusion, the police captain ordered the last speaker, Samuel Fielden, to stop speaking and the crowd to disperse peacefully. Fielden attempted to explain that the meeting was peaceful and that they would be dispersing shortly, but the police captain persisted in ordering the group to disperse. Then, without warning, a bomb was thrown into the crowd and exploded, resulting in several deaths. The police immediately began shooting, killing several people, including fellow officers. In the days that followed, the Chicago police implemented a dragnet that resulted in the arrest and detaining of hundreds of people, most of whom were immigrants, anarchist activists, or both. Albert Parsons himself fled to Wisconsin but later turned himself in, becoming one of the eight activists who were brought to trial, all of whom, except Parsons, were immigrants.

Observers later recognized the trial of the Haymarket activists as one of the worst miscarriages of justice in American history. It was very much influenced by the antianarchist hysteria stirred up and fanned among the public by the Chicago newspapers. By choosing to try the men as a group rather than as individuals, skewing the selection of the jury towards jurors with known prejudice against anarchism, and conducting the trial in a manner that gave the prosecution far more latitude than the defense, the court guaranteed that there would be no fair trial. Although the men on trial managed to assemble a highly competent defense team, headed by Captain William P. Black, the decision to try the men on conspiracy charges, essentially trying them for their anarchist views, further guaranteed the outcome. When Judge Joseph Gary ordered the jury to convict the men, the jury did not take long to oblige, sentencing seven of the men to hang, and one to 15 years in prison with hard labor.

In the weeks and months following the verdict, as antianarchist hysteria died down, there were concerted efforts to appeal the case, but to little avail. In March 1887, the Illinois State Supreme Court upheld the convictions, and the U.S. Supreme Court subsequently declined to hear the case. With efforts at appeal exhausted, a proclemency movement was mounted that eventually went international and included many staunch opponents of anarchism who nonetheless opposed the death penalty or were outraged by the way the trial had been conducted. Efforts to stay the execution included a last-minute appeal by American Federation of Labor President Samuel Gompers to then Illinois Governor John Ogelsby, who commuted two of the sentences to life imprisonment. Otherwise these efforts, which included a last-minute effort by defense lawyer Moses Salamon to get Parsons's execution stayed on a technicality, came to naught. Although one of the condemned activists, Louis Lingg, managed to commit suicide with an exploding cigar on the morning of the execution, the remaining five went to the gallows. In 1893, the new Illinois governor, John P. Altgeld, pardoned the surviving Haymarket activists at cost to his own political career.

The Haymarket Riot and its aftermath would have chilling effects on radical labor and anarchist movements in the United States for years after, even as the conviction of the activists grew increasingly controversial. Although it did not kill off the American labor movement, it did force it in a different direction, contributing to the demise of the Knights of Labor and the rise of the narrowly focused "pure and simple trade-unionism" of the American Federation of Labor. It contributed to an antipopulist "law and order" sentiment among the American public and severely stalled the progress of the movement toward an eight-hour day, something that would not finally be implemented until the New Deal. Even recounting the history of the Haymarket Riot has been affected by the politics that surrounded the event, which until recently has been largely treated as an anarchist riot against law and order rather than as a peaceful populist protest that was violently put down by the police. Lingering controversy over the Haymarket Riot has been reflected in the repeated vandalism of the police memorial, which was finally relocated to the Chicago Police Training Academy, and the recent efforts to place a workers' memorial at the site, an effort that finally succeeded in 2004.

Susan Roth Breitzer

See also: Altgeld, John P. (1847–1902); American Federation of Labor (AFL); Anarchism; Charles H. Kerr Publishing Company; Eight-hour Day; Gompers, Samuel (1850–1924); Knights of Labor; New Deal; Populism; Powderly, Terence V. (1849–1924); Progressivism.

References

Avrich, Paul. *The Haymarket Tragedy.* Princeton, NJ: Princeton University Press, 1984.

Green, James. *Death in the Haymarket: A Story of Chicago: The First Labor Movement and the Bombing That Divided Gilded Age America.* New York: Pantheon Books, 2006.

Nelson, Bruce C. *Beyond the Martyrs: A Social History of Chicago's Anarchists, 1870–1900.* New Brunswick, NJ: Rutgers University Press, 1988.

Hepburn Act (1906)

The Hepburn Act, officially known as *An Act to Amend an Act Entitled "An Act to Regulate Commerce," Approved February Fourth, Eighteen Hundred and Eighty Seven, and All Acts Amendatory Thereof, and to Enlarge the Powers of the Interstate Commerce Commission*, is a U.S. federal law that increased the authority of the Interstate Commerce Commission over railroads and certain other types of carriers. In 1906, Congress gave the commission the power to set maximum rail rates and review railroad finances. The act also put an end to the practice of providing free railroad passes to loyal shippers.

The Hepburn Act, which was the brainchild of Republican Congressman William Peters Hepburn, was enacted to stop corporate giants such as Standard Oil Company from receiving discounted transportation rates, which gave them an unfair advantage over their competition. To ensure compliance, the act made Interstate Commerce Commission orders legally binding; railroads had to either obey or contest the Interstate Commerce Commission orders in federal court. To speed the process, appeals from the district courts went directly to the U.S. Supreme Court.

While the Hepburn Act is considered one of the most important pieces of railroad legislation in the first half of the twentieth century, economists and historians both suggest that it led to the demise of railroads as the prominent means of commercial transportation in the United States. According to such scholars, the Hepburn Act, with its many restrictions, prevented railroads from effectively competing with the giant, unregulated trucking industry. Despite this, the act represented a regulatory victory for farmers who had been protesting unfair rate practices since the late nineteenth century.

Robert Van Trombley

See also: Farmers' Transportation Convention; Interstate Commerce Act (ICA) (1887); Long-Haul/Short-Haul Discrimination; Progressivism; Railroad Regulation; Roosevelt, Theodore (1858–1919)

References

An Act to Amend an Act Entitled "An Act to Regulate Commerce," Approved February Fourth, Eighteen Hundred and Eighty Seven, and All Acts Amendatory Thereof, and to Enlarge the Powers of the Interstate Commerce Commission. Public Law 337. U.S. Statutes at Large 34 (1907): 584.

Edwards, Adolph. *The Roosevelt Panic of 1907.* New York: Anitrock, 1907.

The Interstate Commerce Act, Full Text of the Act to Regulate Commerce as Amended to Date, Including the Elkins Hepburn Acts, and of the Supplementary Act Relating to the Testimony of Witnesses before the Interstate Commerce Commission. Together with the Texts of the Expedition Act, the Anti-Trust Act of 1890, the Employers' Liability Act. Chicago: The Railway Age, 1906.

Martin, Albro. *Enterprise Denied: Origins of the Decline of American Railroads, 1897–1917.* New York: Columbia University Press, 1972.

Morris, Edmund. *Theodore Rex.* New York: Modern Library, 2002.

The Safety Equipment Laws. Chicago, 1906.

Stone, Richard D. *The Interstate Commerce Commission and the Railroad Industry: A History of Regulatory Policy.* New York: Praeger, 1991.

Herron, George Davis (1862–1925)

George Davis Herron was born January 21, 1862, in Montezuma, Indiana, to Isabella Davis and William Herron. The couple was able to afford only a limited elementary education for their son. At age 10 he was apprenticed to a printer where he learned to support himself as a printer and an editor. He then entered Ripon College in 1879 where he gained his only formal education. Poverty and poor health forced him to leave school.

In 1883, Herron became a Congregational minister in Zanesville, Ohio. In that same year he married Mary V. Everhard, the daughter of the mayor of Ripon. She eventually bore him five children. Between 1883 and 1889 he served a number of small congregations in several states. Painfully aware of his limited education, he studied intensely on his own. His studies of theology, philosophy, and contemporary theologically liberal socioeconomic criticism affected him deeply, which led him to join the new Society of Christian Socialists in 1889. In 1890 he moved to the Congregational church in Lake City, Minnesota.

His reputation spread soon after 1890 when delivered a provocative sermon, "The Message of Jesus to Men of Wealth," at the Minnesota Congregationalist Club in Minneapolis. In December 1891 Herron accepted a call to be associate pastor at the Congregationalist church of Burlington, Iowa. His sermons and speeches were published in book format. In 1892 he was given an honorary Doctor of Divinity degree. Herron's sermons soon enchanted Mrs. Elizabeth D. Rand, a wealthy widow, and her daughter Carrie. In 1893 Mrs. Rand endowed a chair of Applied Christianity at Iowa College (later Grinnell College) in Grinnell, Iowa. He was given the chair, and Mrs. Rand and Carrie moved to Grinnell, where Herron taught for seven years.

As a professor Herron wrote a number of works including *The Christian Society* (1894), *Social Meanings of Religious Experiences* (1896), and *Between Caesar and Jesus* (1899). He taught that the day would soon arrive in which a true Christian social order on the earth would fulfill the promise of the Kingdom of God as a present reality. Then all things would be organized into a society in accord with the divine will. He constantly denounced the rich as he preached a gospel of social redemption. Because he was a leader of the Kingdom movement, his lectures and sermons gained a wide hearing during the droughts, labor strikes, and financial panics of the 1890s.

Herron's views during this time became increasingly radical both theologically and economically. By 1900 he was preaching a hard-line socialism that was deterministic. Instead of followers, he found he was gathering critics and opponents who viewed him as an opponent of social and religious order. Consequently, Herron left college teaching to help with the organizing of the American Socialist Party. In May 1901 he married Carrie Rand at Rochester, New York, in a service conducted by a Christian socialist minister, William Thurston Brown, author of *Socialism and Primitive Christianity* (n.d.). They then moved to a villa in Fiesole, Italy.

On June 4, 1901, Herron was defrocked by the Congregational church of Grinnell for having deserted his wife Mary in favor of Carrie Rand. The alimony Mary received was likely provided by Carrie Rand. His personal problems and removal to Italy did not forestall Herron's political activities, and in 1904, Herron nominated Eugene Debs at the 1904 Socialist Convention. When Elizabeth D. Rand died in 1905, she left a bequest to establish the Rand School of Social Science. The Herrons now lived abroad among socialists, especially in Germany, where Herron was a movement leader. In 1914 Carrie Rand died.

Herron was deeply disturbed both by the outbreak of World War I and by the failure of socialists to remain unified. Instead of maintaining a pacifist unity, the socialist movement fractured into nationalist supporters of the war effort and those opposed to the war. He began assisting President Woodrow Wilson with reports on German morale prior to American entry into the war. During the war he acted as an American interpreter of Wilson's war aims.

After the war Herron turned to interpreting Wilson's peace aims. He wrote *The Defeat in the Victory* (1921). He was disappointed both by the 1919 Paris Peace Conference and the Treaty of Versailles, which he saw as a betrayal. He died in Munich, Germany, on October 9, 1925.

Andrew J. Waskey

See also: Charles H. Kerr Publishing Company; Debs, Eugene (1855–1926); Socialism, Christian

References

Briggs, Mitchell P. *George D. Herron and the European Settlement.* Stanford, CA: Stanford University Press, 1932.

Brown, William Thurston. *Socialism and Primitive Christianity.* Chicago: Charles H. Kerry and Co., n.d. http://www.scribd.com/doc/48277590/Socialism-Primitive-Cristianity-William-Thurston-Brown. Accessed January 4, 2013.

Cort, John C. *Christian Socialism.* Maryknoll, NY: Maryknoll, 1988.

Handy, Robert T. "George D. Herron and the Kingdom Movement." *Church History* 19 (1950): 7–115.

Highlander Folk School

Currently known as the Highlander Research and Education Center, the Highlander Folk School is located in New Market, Tennessee. It is an institution that acts as a cultural center and specializes in leadership training for social justice, community organizing, and educating individuals on initiatives to better their lives. Its mission is to "to provide an educational center in the South for the training of rural and industrial leaders, and for the conservation and enrichment of the indigenous cultural values of the mountains" (Williams and Beard 139). It emerged during the late 1920s when the southern rural poor were forgotten and excluded from the prosperity of the urban United States and thus the purview of American lawmakers and other leaders. With its populist roots, it has grown to encompass a growing list of modern issues but has maintained its base as an educational institution that focuses on the needs of ordinary Americans, which are not generally addressed by state or national elites.

Founded by Methodist minister James A. Dombrowski, educator Don West, and activist Myles Horton, the center was the brainchild of Horton, who was involved in a Presbyterian summer Bible school in Ozone, Tennessee, an area in the throes of economic collapse in the late 1920s. He saw almost no connection between the Bible school and the "daily problems faced either by the children or their hard-pressed parents. . . . I couldn't put this into words, but such education failed to connect with their lives" (Adams and Horton 2). He decided to invite the parents to church in the evenings to talk about their problems. During these "community meetings," Horton tried to address their issues as best as he could or to connect the parents with someone who could help them. He then asked these mountain people to share their newfound knowledge with their neighbors. Over time he received reports on what advice was received well and what was not.

Upon graduating from Cumberland College, Horton attended Union Theological

Seminary in New York City where he was exposed to the "social gospel" that had come into vogue during the Great Depression. Throughout his time there he kept the Ozone project in the back of his mind and wondered if an institute based on the Danish folk schools, which he had had a chance to witness first-hand, would work for the mountain people of Tennessee. Central to the educational philosophy and operations of the school, he believed, was that poor people must be educated to act and speak for themselves, allowing them to gain influence over the public decisions that affected their lives.

On November 1, 1932, Horton and his friends founded what would eventually become the Highlander Folk School in the town of Summerfield, located in Grundy County, Tennessee. Barely established, the school faced its first major challenge during the coal miners' strike in the town of Wilder-Davidson in Fentress County. When he discovered that the Red Cross was only supplying food to the strikebreakers, Norton organized food drives in Nashville to feed the striking miners and their families. The National Guard promptly arrested him. Out of that experience he learned that "the tie-in with the conflict situations and participation in community life keeps our school from being a detached colony or utopian venture. . . . [O]ur efforts to live out our ideals makes possible the development of a bit of proletarian culture as an essential part of our program of workers' education" (Jones). The Highlander Folk School's focus would be to teach, not to lead.

During the 1930s and 1940s, the Highlander Folk School led community and union organizing drives and provided information about the government to unregistered and ill-informed voters. Spreading the populist message, after several victories, reversals, and defeats Horton and his colleagues decided to increase their efforts toward connecting education with unionization throughout the South. According to the Works Progress Administration (WPA) history of Tennessee (1939), the school was "one of the few training schools for labor leaders in the South. In two small buildings, whose size helps to limit the student body to about 20, the school offers informal, discussion type lectures on cultural and economic subjects. . . . A year-around community and county program is carried on and members of the school attempt to preserve the culture of the mountain people" (Tennessee Writer's Project 512).

Throughout the 1940s, alumni from Highlander were involved in almost every major union effort in the South. Yet, in 1952, Horton believed that the school should change its focus toward the betterment of race relations, as racism seemed to be the major stumbling blocked to unionization in the region. With the addition of Rev. John Beauchamp Thompson, Highlander developed literacy programs to help blacks register to vote. The civil rights anthem "We Shall Overcome" was adapted from a gospel song by Myles's wife, Zilphia Horton.

With its efforts to empower African Americans, the school came under increased attacks. In 1957, the Georgia Commission on Education released a pamphlet entitled, "Highlander Folk School: Communist Training School, Monteagle,

Tennessee." The Federal Bureau of Investigation began an investigation of its purported communist ties. Finally, in 1961, the state of Tennessee planted moonshine on the school's property to revoke its charter and seize its land.

One year later, the school reincorporated as the Highlander Research and Education Center and moved to Knoxville, where it stayed until 1971. Currently located in New Market, the center is focused on environmental justice movements, ethnic diversity, workers' health and safety, and lesbian, gay, bisexual, and transgender issues.

Trevor Jason Soderstrum

See also: Copland, Aaron (1900–1990); Pop Music; Social Gospel; Workingman's School

References

Adams, Frank, and Myles Horton. *Unearthing Seeds of Fire: The Idea of Highlander.* Winston-Salem, NC: John F. Blair, 1975.

Jones, James B., Jr. "Myles F. Horton, Tennessee's 'Radical Hillbilly': The Highlander Folk School and Education for Social Change in America, the South, and the Volunteer State." http://www.southernhistory.net/index.php?name=News&file=article&sid=10263. Accessed January 4, 2013.

Tennessee Writers' Project. *Tennessee: A Guide to the State*. Chattanooga, TN: Hastings House, 1949.

Williams, Horace Randall, and Ben Beard. *This Day in Civil Rights History.* Montgomery, AL: New South Books, 2009.

Hightower, Jim (1943–)

James Allen "Jim" Hightower, a well-known radio personality, speaker, and writer, also stands out as the rare contemporary example of a populist commentator whose political orientation is liberal rather than conservative. Notably, Hightower, who has often been regarded as "America's number one populist," views politics less in terms of left against right than in terms of the top versus the bottom. Nonetheless, Hightower has in recent decades become increasingly regarded as a progressive spokesman for ordinary Americans against the elites of both Wall Street and Washington.

Jim Hightower was born on January 11, 1943, and grew up in Denison, Texas. He was raised in a family whose occupational backgrounds range from small-business owners to tenant farmers. Hightower worked his way through college, attending the University of North Texas, and after graduation he began his long career in progressive politics, first working as a legislative aide to Texas Senator Ralph Yarborough. His subsequent career has included work as a political activist with the Agribusiness Accountability Project, as editor of the *Texas Observer*, and as director of the Texas Consumer Association. He has also successfully run for, and served, two terms as the Texas agricultural commissioner between 1982 and 1991.

Amid this varied career, by the 1990s, Hightower was increasingly focusing on political commentary, in writing, on the radio, and eventually on the Internet. He had previously managed the 1976 "Fred Harris for President" campaign and endorsed Jesse Jackson's presidential campaign in 1988. He is the author of seven bestselling books and currently publishes the populist newsletter *The*

Hightower Lowdown, which has received awards from both the Alternative Press Association and the Independent Press Association.

During the last couple of decades, Hightower has also become a popular radio commentator, with his daily "Common Sense Commentaries" syndicated on more than 150 radio stations nationwide. He is also a public speaker who has given more than 100 speeches per year. He has remained a popular political figure and media personality into the early twenty-first century, even as populist media commentary has increasingly been associated with conservative pundits such as Rush Limbaugh and Glenn Beck.

Susan Roth Breitzer

See also: Bush, George W., Populist Rhetoric of; Neo-Populism; Obama, Barack, Populist Rhetoric of; The Press and Populism; Tea Party

References

Hertzke, Allen D. *Echoes of Discontent: Jesse Jackson, Pat Robertson, and the Echoes of Discontent*. Washington, DC: CQ Press, 1993.

Hightower, Jim. http://www.jimhightower.com. Accessed January 4, 2013.

Hill, James J. (1838–1916)

A railroad baron, philanthropist, and gentleman farmer, James J. Hill founded the Great Northern Railway, the first transcontinental line built with no public money or land grants. Known as the "Empire Builder," Hill's self-made wealth facilitated the construction of the rail lines that linked St. Paul, Minnesota, with Seattle, Washington. Born in Rockwood, Ontario, Canada, in 1838, Hill migrated to the United States before the age of 20. He settled in St. Paul, Minnesota, where he soon found employment in the dynamic and ever-evolving transportation industry of the mid-nineteenth century. He initially found work as a bookkeeper for a steamboat company in St. Paul. In 1878, after 20 years of employment related to river shipping on the Red and Mississippi Rivers, Hill switched his entrepreneurial interests from water to land. Along with several partners, Hill invested in the nearly bankrupt St. Paul and Pacific Railroad. Rechristened the Great Northern Railway in 1890, the line eventually extended north to Canada, across the Rocky Mountains, and onward to the Pacific Ocean. Hill's story of pluck, ambition, and luck shares multiple parallels with other Gilded Age captains of industry and transportation tycoons from Andrew Carnegie to E.H. Harriman.

Politically categorized as a Bourbon Democrat, Hill frequently clashed with Populist leader and Minnesota native Ignatius Donnelly. Although Donnelly served multiple terms in the state legislature, Hill and other power brokers of Minnesota's Democratic Party thwarted his aspirations for statewide and national office. Hill also sought to prevent agrarian and labor reforms championed by Donnelly. Nonetheless, Hill participated in a White House conference on October 2, 1902, at the behest of President Theodore Roosevelt that included the prominent Populist leader William Jennings Bryan, steel baron Andrew Carnegie, and prominent labor reformer John Mitchell. A vigorous advocate for agricultural improvement, Hill promoted such practices as crop diversification and scientific breeding. His vast network of business interests were in fact tightly wedded to the agricultural prosperity of the upper Midwest, despite his opposition to agrarian labor reforms. In 1910, Hill synthesized his views on agrarian issues in the book *Highways of Progress*. At his death in 1916, Hill's fortune was estimated at $63 million.

Anna Thompson Hajdik

See also: Bourbon Democracy; Donnelly, Ignatius (1831–1901); Gilded Age; Plains and Midwest, Populism in the; Railroads

References

The Agribusiness Council. "William Jennings Bryan Recognition Project." http://www.agribusinesscouncil.org/bryan.htm. Accessed January 4, 2013.

Roberts, Kate. "James J. Hill: Building a Fortune While Connecting the Nation." In *Minnesota 150: The People, Places, and Things That Shape Our State* (pp. 74–74). St. Paul: Minnesota Historical Society Press, 2007.

Strom, Claire. "James J. Hill: Empire Builder as Farmer." *Minnesota History* 54 (6): 242–253.

Wingerd, Mary Lethert. *Claiming the City: Politics, Faith, and the Power of Place in St. Paul.* Ithaca, NY: Cornell University Press, 2001.

Hill, Joe (1879–1915)

Joe Hill is an American legend to the thousands of individuals who continue to believe in him and the cause for which he fought. For members of the labor and civil rights movement, union organizers and activists, and socialists and leftists, he is a mythic hero. John Pietaro, writing for the magazine *Political Affairs*, sees Joel Emmanuel Hagglund, commonly known as Joe Hill, as the guiding light behind the Industrial Workers of the World (IWW), standing as a beacon of revolutionary arts for the entire labor movement.

Joel Emmanuel Hagglund was born in Gavle, Sweden, on October 7, 1879. He was the youngest of Olof Hagglund and his wife Margareta's eight children. Olof died soon after Joel's eighth birthday. Two of his siblings had died earlier from childhood illnesses. After his father's death, Joel Hagglund and his five brothers and sisters went to work to support the family. His first job was in a rope factory; when he was older he shoveled coal on a steam engine for a construction company. When Hagglund was 12 he contracted a form of tuberculosis and underwent massive doses of radiation from x rays, followed by painful operations that left his neck and nose scarred.

In January 1902, Hagglund's mother died. In October of the same year Hagglund and his brother Paul booked passage to New York City. On arrival at Ellis Island they were virtually penniless and desperate to find jobs. They had high hopes because of the stories they had heard about the United States being the land of wealth. Yet the only job that Hagglund could find was cleaning spittoons for pennies a day.

Unable to make a living, the Hagglund brothers decided to leave New York City. What happened to Joel Hagglund for the next eight years is sketchy, but investigative

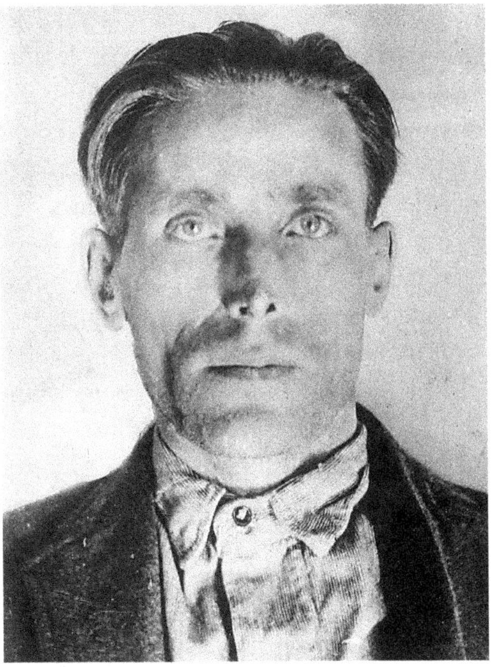

Joe Hill (aka Hillstrom), labor activist and Wobbly songwriter (1879–1915). (Library of Congress)

authors at the Public Broadcasting Service (PBS) and KUED Channel 7 at the University of Utah, as well as scholars at the Joe Hill Project, have tried to fill in the gaps of his life story.

Between 1906 and 1910, Joel Emmanuel Hagglund changed his name to Joseph Hillstrom while laboring in the fields picking fruit and on the docks. Friends in the labor movement maintain that he was forced to live underground by powerful companies because of his ceaseless advocacy of workers' rights. A less favorable point of view maintains that he turned to petty crime to support himself. As a result, he was a shadowy figure during this time.

In 1910, while working on the docks in San Pedro, California, Joseph Hillstrom came into contact with members of the Industrial Workers of the World. The IWW, pejoratively known as "Wobblies," was a radical union founded in Chicago, Illinois, in June 1905. In late 1910, he wrote a letter to the IWW newspaper, *Industrial Worker*, stating that he had become a member of the union; then he denounced the police for their hostility toward the Wobblies and to workers generally. This letter is distinctive because he signed his name as "Joe Hill," the first documented use of this name. Joe Hill became a singer-songwriter, supporting the IWW's efforts to become "One Big Union" by writing songs that were meant to inspire confidence and a sense of solidarity among workers. His songs both celebrated the virtues of labor and denounced large corporations and the "bosses" who exploited working men and women for profit. In "Workers of the World, Awaken," he reminded working men and women that "If the workers take a notion/They can stop all speeding trains/Every ship upon the ocean/They can tie with mighty chains" (IWW). By 1923, when the IWW published its *Little Red Songbook*, Hillstrom was listed simply as Joe Hill.

His work on behalf of labor and with the IWW brought him trouble. In 1911, Hill was reportedly beaten by police in Fresno, California. He spent 30 days in jail on a charge of vagrancy. He claimed that this was nothing more than a trumped-up attempt by power interests to silence him during a longshoreman's strike. The police, on the other hand, claimed that Hill was a prime suspect in the armed robbery of a streetcar, but he was not prosecuted for lack of evidence.

Hill then reportedly left California for Chicago in 1913, making a fateful stop in Utah. While the actual events are undocumented, the IWW claims that on January 10, 1914, two men entered a grocery store owned by former police officer John Morrison. One of the masked assailants killed Morrison and his oldest son, Arling, who was thought to have wounded one of the men before dying. Soon after, Hill reportedly arrived at the home of Dr. Fred McHugh. McHugh witnessed a gun that Hill later dumped during a car trip with a friend of the doctor. Hill gave no explanations for the gun, and McHugh notified the police in the morning. Police shot Hill while trying to arrest him, wounding him in the hand.

Joe Hill was held without bail. The prosecutor argued that the crime had been a robbery gone wrong despite witness testimony that it was an act of revenge. Hill was informed that the state would seek the death penalty. Without money or a government-provided public defender, Hill represented himself. Later he accepted the help of two Salt Lake City attorneys. Halfway through the trial Hill fired both men, claiming they had joined in a conspiracy to convict him of a crime he did not commit. Hill was nevertheless convicted of murder and sentenced to death.

Because of his work in the labor movement and his apparent martyrdom to the cause, Joe Hill has been featured in songs by Joan Baez, Pete Seeger, and Paul Robeson, testifying to Hill's undying influence as a champion of the downtrodden. This sense of immortality resonates in a biography by William M. Adler, *The Man Who Never Died: Times and Legacy of Joe Hill, American Labor Icon* (2011). To demonstrate the power his memory holds for many people, authors Stephen and Tabitha King named their son Joe Hill in honor of this fallen hero of the working man.

On November 15, 1915, Joseph Emmanuel Hagglund was executed by firing squad. Prior to his death sentence, Hill sent a telegram to "Big Bill" Haywood, president of the Industrial Workers of the World. According to Steven Greenhouse in "Examining a Labor Hero's Death," the five-word message read: "Don't waste time mourning. Organize!" This became a rallying call for the IWW: "Don't Mourn! Organize!" For many years these were considered Joe Hill's last words. However, according to Tad Tuleja, writing for *The New York Public Library Book of Popular Americana*, Hill's final words were the defiant "Let her Go! Fire!" (Tuleja 169).

John G. Hall

See also: Industrial Workers of the World (IWW); Pop Music

References

Adler, William M. *The Man Who Never Died: The Life, Times, and Legacy of Joe Hill, American Labor Icon*. New York, Bloomsbury, 2011.

AFL-CIO. "Joe Hill (1879–1915)." http://www.aflcio.org/About/Our-History/Key-People-in-Labor-History/Joe-Hill-1879-1915. Accessed January 4, 2013.

Greenhouse, Steven. "Examining a Labor Hero's Death." *New York Times*, August 26, 2011.

IWW. *Little Red Songbook*. http://www.angelfire.com/nj3/RonMBaseman/songbk.htm. Accessed January 4, 2013.

"Joe Hill: The Man Behind the Martyr." PBS/KUED7, University of Utah. http://www.kued.org/productions/joehill. Accessed January 4, 2013.

"The Joe Hill Project." http://www.joehill.org/index.html. Accessed January 4, 2013.

Mims, Robert. "Martyr of Murderer? Labor Marks Anniversary of Joe Hill's Execution." *Albany Times Union* (Albany, NY), July 16, 1990.

Pietaro, John. "The Brief, Revolutionary Life of Joe Hill." *Political Affairs*, November 3, 2009.

Stegner, Wallace. *Joe Hill: A Biographical Novel*. New York: Bloomsbury, 2011.

Tuleja, Tad. *The New York Public Library Book of Popular Americana*. New York: Macmillan, 1994.

Hiss, Alger (1904–1996)

Alger Hiss was a former State Department official accused in 1948 by *Time* editor (and former underground communist) Whittaker Chambers of being part of an underground communist cell in Washington, DC, in the 1930s. In response to a lawsuit by Hiss, Chambers later accused Hiss of spying for the Soviet Union and turned over evidence to support his charges. Subsequently, Hiss was indicted by a grand jury and convicted of perjury (the statute of limitations for espionage had expired) in 1950. Until the day he died in 1996, Hiss insisted that he was innocent. Evidence from the Russian archives, however, and the top-secret Venona project has led many scholars to believe that Hiss did spy for the Soviet Union.

Alger Hiss was born in 1904 in Baltimore, Maryland. Despite tragedy in his youth (a sister committed suicide, and his brother died of Bright's disease), Hiss excelled academically and became a skillful networker. Hiss attended Johns Hopkins University where he was inducted into Phi Beta Kappa. Later, he transferred to Harvard Law School where he came to the attention of Professor (and future Supreme Court justice) Felix Frankfurter. After graduation, Hiss served as a law clerk to the prominent Supreme Court Justice Oliver Wendell Holmes for one year. After his clerkship, Hiss accepted a position with a law firm in Boston.

Hiss left the law firm in 1933, however, to work for the federal government at the beginning of Franklin D. Roosevelt's administration. During the decade, he held a number of positions in the federal government including as a lawyer in the Justice Department, as legal counsel for the Nye Committee (investigating the reasons for U.S. entry into World War I), and as a lawyer in the Department of Agriculture.

In 1936, Hiss accepted a position in the State Department working for Assistant Secretary of State Francis Sayre. By 1944, he was the head of the Office of Special Political Affairs. In this position, Hiss organized the Yalta Conference (later attending the conference in February 1945) and helped in the creation of the United Nations. At the founding of the United Nations in San Francisco in 1945, Hiss was chosen as the temporary secretary general of the organization. In 1946, Hiss left the State Department to accept the position of president of the Carnegie Endowment for International Peace.

In August 1948, Whittaker Chambers testified before the House Committee on

Un-American Activities (HUAC) that during the 1930s he recruited federal government officials into the Communist Party, including Alger Hiss. Hiss immediately responded by vehemently denying being a communist or knowing Chambers. The members of HUAC and the audience responded favorably to Hiss's testimony. Initially, the members of the committee wanted to drop the investigation of Hiss. However, California Congressman (and HUAC member) Richard Nixon and HUAC chief investigator Robert Stripling persuaded the rest of the committee to pursue the investigation. Both men detected evasiveness in Hiss's testimony. They also were aware of rumors over the years that Hiss was affiliated with the Communist Party. Nixon and Stripling convinced the committee that all they needed to do was prove that Chambers and Hiss knew each other.

In the course of their investigation, HUAC found Chambers to be a persuasive witness. In great detail, he described Hiss's homes, family members, and hobbies. Confronted with Chambers's account, Hiss modified his testimony to claim that he knew Chambers as a journalist, George Crosley. According to Hiss, Crosley had lived with the Hiss family for a brief period of time before the relationship was terminated due to Chambers's mooching. However, Hiss could not find anyone else who knew Chambers as George Crosley.

The cases shifted to espionage after Hiss sued Chambers for repeating his allegations outside of HUAC on *Meet the Press*. In response to Hiss's lawsuit, Chambers turned over 64 pages of typewritten documents that he insisted were summaries of State Department reports given to him by Hiss. He turned over additional information to HUAC investigators in December 1948. Chambers led investigators to a hollowed-out pumpkin on his Maryland farm and pulled out microfilm canisters. He told investigators that the microfilm contained State Department reports that were acquired from Alger Hiss.

The new evidence led to the calling of a grand jury in New York City. The grand jury indicted Hiss on December 15, 1948, on charges of perjury. In 1949, Hiss was tried on charges of perjury. The jury, however, deadlocked, leading to a second trial. In 1950, another jury found Hiss guilty of perjury and sentenced him to five years in prison. Despite this, he was released early in 1954 for good behavior.

Until the day he died, Hiss insisted that he was innocent of the charges against him. Various explanations were given in Hiss's defense. It was claimed that Whittaker Chambers sneaked into Hiss's home and typed the State Department summaries, that the Federal Bureau of Investigations (FBI) forged the Woodstock typewriter identified as belonging to Alger Hiss, or that Hiss obtained the microfilmed State Department documents from another source. Then in the early 1970s, Hiss benefited from distrust of Richard Nixon due to the Watergate scandal. If Nixon lied about Watergate, then some believed he could have framed Hiss.

Hiss's defense was undermined by the publication of the book *Perjury* by historian Allen Weinstein in 1978. Weinstein initially researched the Hiss case believing that Hiss was innocent. However, after examining State Department documents and FBI files, Weinstein concluded that Hiss knew Chambers and had spied for the Soviet Union.

In the aftermath of the Cold War, further evidence reinforced Hiss's guilt. Evidence was found in Hungarian archives that Hiss's friend Noel Field confessed to Hungarian authorities that Hiss was a Soviet spy. In 1996, a decrypted cable from the top-secret Venona project (created during World War II to break encrypted Soviet codes) described a Soviet agent codenamed ALES who appeared to be Alger Hiss. In 1999, Allen Weinstein's book *The Haunted Wood* revealed that Alger Hiss was mentioned in KGB files. Likewise, former KGB officer Oleg Vasilliev published the book *Spies* in 2009 (based on thousands of pages of notes from the KGB files), which identified Hiss in the KGB files.

Alger Hiss died in 1996 still maintaining his innocence, while most scholars today believe that Hiss did spy for the Soviet Union, questioning the extent of the espionage.

Jason Roberts

See also: Hollywood Ten; McCarthy, Joseph (1908–1957); New Deal; Roosevelt, Franklin Delano (1882–1945); Rosenberg, Julius (1918–1953), and Rosenberg, Ethel (1915–1953)

References

Haynes, John, and Harvey Klehr. *Venona: Decoding Soviet Espionage*. New Haven, CT: Yale University Press, 1999.

Hiss, Alger. *In the Court of Public Opinion*. New York: Alfred A. Knopf, 1957.

Hiss, Alger. *Recollections of a Life*. New York: H. Holt & Company, 1988.

Jacoby, Susan. *Alger Hiss and the Battle for History*. New Haven, CT: Yale University Press, 2009.

Shelton, Christina. *Alger Hiss: Why He Chose Treason*. New York: Threshold Editions, 2012.

Swan, Patrick. *Alger Hiss, Whittaker Chambers, and the Schism in the American Soul*. Wilmington, DE: ISI Books, 2003.

Tanenhaus, Sam. *Whittaker Chambers: A Biography*. New York: Random House, 1997.

Weinstein, Allen. *Perjury: The Hiss-Chambers Case*. New York: Alfred A. Knopf, 1978.

White, G. Edward. *Alger Hiss's Looking Glass Wars*. Oxford, UK: Oxford University Press, 2004.

Historians of Populism

The movement that led to the formation of the National Farmers' Alliance and the People's Party of the 1890s endured in the twentieth century as a popular topic for historians and other scholars. The trend continues in the twenty-first century as new books build upon or challenge the existing historiography. The historians of Populism, from both the previous and the current century, hail from a variety of backgrounds and utilize many forms of historical analysis.

Participants and publicists for the Farmers' Alliance assembled the first histories of the agrarian movement. W. Scott Morgan published several editions of his *History of the Wheel and Alliance* between 1889 and 1891. Nelson A. Dunning also edited *The Farmers' Alliance History and Agricultural Digest* (1891).

Frank L. McVey wrote the first scholarly work on Populism, *The Populist Movement* (1896), when the future of the People's Party was still in doubt. McVey opposed the Populist platform of free silver, monetary reform, and cooperative agrarian power and argued that the movement was rooted in the past. McVey portrayed Populism as a "socialistic" reaction to industrialization.

Frederick Jackson Turner, the author of the famous frontier thesis, saw the Populists as representatives of a primitive society, unable to appreciate a developed society. Unlike McVey, Turner viewed the Populists with sympathy because of their close association with the frontier, which he viewed as the wellspring of American democracy.

John D. Hicks and other progressive historians saw the Populists as forward looking and the predecessors of Progressives and New Dealers. Solon J. Buck declared that the Populists were the direct precursors of Progressivism in his work *The Agrarian Crusade* (1920). Vernon L. Parrington, a former Populist, linked Populism to previous reform movements such as the Locofocos, the early Republican Party, and Greenbackers in *Main Currents in American Thought* (1930). Hicks, a student of Turner, studied the wheat farmers of the upper Midwest and used economics rather than ideology to explain the appeal of Populism to certain regions. Hicks's *The Populist Revolt* (1931) established the parameters for the studies that followed.

Beginning in the 1930s, Marxist writers used class analysis to explain agrarian activism. Anna Rochester, in *The Populist Movement in the United States* (1943), saw Populism as an early attempt to organize by farmers, producers, and the industrial working class. Chester McArthur Destler traced Populism's origins to the Age of Jackson in *American Radicalism, 1865–1901* (1946). Other Marxist scholars of Populism included Norman Pollack, the author of *The Populist Response to Industrial America* (1962), one of the mid twentieth century's most influential titles in this genre.

The rise of fascism and militarism abroad, World War II, and the Cold War caused some scholars to question popular movements and to seek consensus rather than conflict in American history. The Populists, as outspoken dissidents, did not easily conform to the consensus explanation. Richard Hofstadter, in his influential *Age of Reform: From Bryan to F.D.R.* (1955), viewed Populism as dangerous and radical. Hofstadter believed that the Populists were antiurban and existed outside of the American mainstream.

Allan Bogue joined Hofstadter's criticism of the Populists. Bogue's *Money at Interest: The Farm Mortgage on the Middle Border* (1955) studied mortgages in several states and found not only that interest rates were reasonable but that mortgage companies had tried to avoid foreclosure. Bogue concluded that, despite Populist claims, the eastern money interests did not reap windfall profits at the farmers' expense and that the agrarian revolt lacked an economic trigger. He attributed the Populist furor at the financial industry to the Jacksonian antibank tradition.

Often reacting directly to Hofstadter's *Age of Reform*, scholars of the late 1950s and 1960s restored the Populists' reputation as protectors of democracy and progress. Paul W. Glad argued in *McKinley, Bryan, and the People* (1964) that both 1896 presidential candidates were essentially conservative. Walter T. K. Nugent, the author of *The Tolerant Populists: Kansas Populism and Nativism* (1963), concluded that Kansas Populists were neither bigoted nor irrational. Robert Durden defended the 1896 Populist nomination of William Jennings Bryan as essential to the future of the People's Party in *The Climax of Populism: The Election of 1896* (1966).

The mid-1960s found scholarly opinions of Populism divided between the defenders of Hofstadter and his critics. Pollack had offered a sympathetic defense of the Populists, arguing that the People's Party was forward-looking, accepted industrialization, and presented a socialist alternative vision for the United States' future. Pollack attributed consensus historians' attacks on the Populists to a contemporary fear of popular revolt. O. Gene Clanton continued the defense of the Populists as constructive and progressive in *Kansas Populism* (1969).

Inspired by the tumultuous 1960s, the "new" social historians of the 1970s and 1980s questioned the consensus historians' link between democracy and progress and sought to learn more about the average supporter of the Populist movement. Samuel P. Hays, in *American Political History as Social Analysis* (1980), encouraged historians to look beyond the rhetoric of Populist leaders to examine the lives of the masses. Lawrence Goodwyn, in *Democratic Promise* (1978), studied Texas Populism and argued the movement grew out of the Farmers' Alliance's cooperative efforts and its subtreasury plan. Goodwyn asserted that the Populists resisted the era's prevailing commercial order and development.

Another group of historians used an ethnocultural interpretation inspired by the works of Paul Kleppner's *The Cross of Culture: A Social Analysis of Midwestern Politics, 1850–1900* (1970) and Richard Jensen's *The Winning of the Midwest: Social and Political Conflict, 1888–1896*, which attributed Gilded Age political affiliation to religious practices. The ethnocultural interpretation acknowledged a conflict, albeit not one based on economics. Peter H. Argersinger studied Kansas and rejected ethnocultural interpretation in favor of economics in *Populism and Politics: William Alfred Peffer and the People's Party* (1974). James Edward Wright studied Colorado and argued that ethic motivations trailed economic considerations in *The Politics of Populism: Dissent in Colorado* (1974).

The next two decades saw more scholars portray the Populists as Democrats revolting against progress and commercial change. Robert McMath, in *Populist Vanguard* (1975), sees the farmers who opposed corporate interests in the Cross Timbers fence war as precapitalists fighting to defend a traditional culture of mutuality, limited property rights in land, and self-sufficiency. Steven Hahn, the author of *Roots of Southern Populism: Yeoman Farmers and the Transformation of the Georgia Upcountry, 1850–1890* (1983), linked Populism to changes in the rural economic system. John L. Thomas attributed Populist ideology to republican civic virtue and Protestant morality in *Alternative America* (1983).

In the twenty-first century, Charles Postel challenged the argument that the Populists fought progress. In *The Populist Vision* (2007), Postel argues the Populists embraced modernity and sought to promote innovation. Matthew Hild's *Greenbackers, Knights of Labor, and Populists, Farmer-Labor Insurgency in the Late-Nineteenth-Century South* (2007) returned attention to state- and regional-level studies. Hild studied Alabama, Texas, and Arkansas and found that laborers, rather than farmers, proved more important to Populist political strength than the organizational framework created by the Farmers' Alliance. Connie L. Lester, the author of *Up from the Mudsills of Hell: The Farmers' Alliance, Populism, and Progressive Agriculture in Tennessee, 1870–1915* (2006), made the rise of the People's Party in Tennessee part of a long struggle for economic security by that state's farmers.

Historians of Populism often use biographies to explore the movement's leaders. C. Vann Woodward's *Tom Watson: Agrarian Rebel* (1938) was among the earliest. Stuart Noblin wrote *Leonidas LaFayette Polk: Agrarian Crusader* (1949). More biographies appeared in the 1960s including Destler's *Henry Demarest Lloyd and the Empire of Reform* (1963), Martin Ridge's *Ignatius Donnelly: The Portrait of a Politician* (1962), and Michael J. Brodhead's *Preserving Populist: The Life of Frank Doster* (1969).

State and local studies provide another common framework for historians of Populism. A. M. Arnett inaugurated this approach with *The Populist Movement in Georgia* (1922). Roscoe Martin, a political scientist, published *The People's Party in Texas* (1933). The 1960s and 1970s brought a surge of state and regional studies including William Ivy Hair, *Bourbonism and Agrarian Protest: Louisiana Politics, 1877–1900* (1969); Mary Ellen Glass, *Silver and Politics in Nevada: 1892–1902* (1969); and William Warren Rogers, *One-Gallused Rebellion: Agrarianism in Alabama, 1865–1896* (1970). Argersinger measured the influence of Kansas Populists on the national movement in *Populism and Politics: William Alfred Peffer and the People's Party* (1974). Worth Robert Miller, in *Oklahoma Populism* (1987), found that settlers from Kansas imported Populism into the new Oklahoma territory. Jeffrey Ostler used a comparative approach in *Prairie Populism* (1993). Ostler argued that a competitive two-party system hampered the development of the People's Party in Iowa and the lack of such a system fostered its growth in Kansas and Nebraska.

The significance of the influence of the silver issue on the movement in the mining states of the mountains interested Thomas A. Clinch, in *Urban Populism and Free Silver in Montana* (1970); Wright, in *The Politics of Populism: Dissent in Colorado* (1974); Robert W. Larson, in *New Mexico Populism* (1974); and Joseph Gaboury, in *Dissension in the Rockies: A History of Idaho Populism* (1988).

Populist attitudes toward race and the relationship between whites and blacks within the movement provide challenging topics for historians. C. Vann Woodward, the first scholar to examine southern Populism, defended the Populists' views on race in his biography of Tom Watson. William F. Holmes, in a 1975 article published in the *Journal of Southern History*, found that black farm laborers did not rush to join the movement because their economic interests diverged from those of white farm owners. Gerald H. Gaither, in *Blacks and the Populist Revolt: Ballots and Bigotry in the "New South"* (1977) found that white Populists stopped trying to cooperate with blacks when they realized the party would not receive their full support. Goodwyn discovered an interracial coalition among Texas Populists. Gregg Cantrell, in *Kenneth and John B. Rayner and the Limits of Southern Dissent* (1993), explored the life of a black Populist organizer who sought votes from white Democrats and black Republicans.

Analysis based on race, class, and sex emerged as an interpretative force in the late twentieth century. Michael Lewis Goldberg, in *An Army of Women* (1997), considered the gendered history of politics in Gilded Age Kansas.

Other scholars examine the prevalence of populist movements throughout American history or of populist movements other than the agrarian Populism of the 1890s. Political scientist Margaret Canovan included American politicians such as Huey Long and Jimmy Carter in her international study *Populism* (1981). Michael Kazin unearthed a pervasive American populist impulse in *The Populist Persuasion: An American History* (1995). American populism exists on both the political Left and Right. Leon Fink explores a leftist populist movement in *Workingmen's Democracy: The Knights of Labor and American Politics* (1983). Chip Berlet and Matthew N. Lyons examine the other end of the spectrum in *Right-Wing Populism in America: Too Close for Comfort* (2000).

Future historians interested in populism will find that the terms *populism* and *populist* remained common in the twenty-first century. Scholarly works are starting to appear that study the first decade of the new millennium. John Lukacs, in *Democracy and Populism* (2005), condemned populism and the politicians that embraced the label. Lukacs accused President George W. Bush of provoking the war in Iraq in an effort to gain popularity.

Historians' perceptions of populism, especially the agrarian Populist movement of the 1890s, changed throughout the twentieth century and the early years of the twenty-first century as scholars developed new interpretative frameworks. Progressive, Marxist, consensus, revisionist, ethnocultural, race, and gender historians all debated the subject. Populism promises to remain a favored subject regardless of whatever historiographical trends emerge.

Jeff Wells

See also: Agricultural Wheel; Bush, George W., Populist Rhetoric of; Gilded Age; Gold Standard/Free Silver; Greenback Party; Knights of Labor; New Deal; Populism; Progressivism; Railroad Regulation; Subtreasury Plan

References

Argersinger, Peter H. *Populism and Politics: William Alfred Peffer and the People's*

Party. Lexington: University of Kentucky Press, 1974.

Arnett, A. M. *The Populist Movement in Georgia: A View of the "Agrarian Crusade" in the Light of Solid-South Politics*. New York: Columbia University Press, 1922.

Berlet, Chip, and Matthew Nemiroff Lyons. *Right Wing Populism in America: Too Close for Comfort*. New York: Guilford Press, 2000.

Bogue, Allan G. *Money at Interest: The Farm Mortgage on the Middle Border.* Ithaca, NY: Cornell University Press, 1955.

Brodhead, Michael J. *Preserving Populist: The Life of Frank Doster.* Reno: University of Nevada Press, 1969.

Buck, Solon J. *The Agrarian Crusade*. New Haven, CT: Yale University Press, 1920.

Canovan, Margaret. *Populism*. New York: Harcourt Brace Jovanovich, 1981.

Cantrell, Gregg. *Kenneth and John B. Rayner and the Limits of Southern Dissent*. Urbana: University of Illinois, 1993.

Clanton, O. Gene. *Kansas Populism, Ideas and Men*. Lawrence: University Press of Kansas, 1969.

Clinch, Thomas A. *Urban Populism and Free Silver in Montana, A Narrative of Ideology in Political Action*. Helena: University of Montana Press, 1970.

Destler, Chester McArthur. *American Radicalism, 1865–1901*. New London: Connecticut College Press, 1946.

Destler, Chester McArthur. *Henry Demarest Lloyd and the Empire of Reform*. Philadelphia: University of Pennsylvania Press, 1963.

Dunning, Nelson A. *The Farmers' Alliance History and Agricultural Digest*. Washington, DC: The Alliance Publishing Company, 1891.

Durden, Robert. *The Climax of Populism: The Election of 1896*. Lexington: University of Kentucky Press, 1966.

Fink, Leon. *Workingmen's Democracy: The Knights of Labor and American Politics* Urbana: University of Illinois Press, 1983.

Gaboury, William Joseph. *Dissension in the Rockies: A History of Idaho Populism*. New York: Garland, 1988.

Gaither, Gerald H. *Blacks and the Populist Revolt: Ballots and Bigotry in the "New South*." Tuscaloosa: University of Alabama Press, 1977.

Glad, Paul W. *McKinley, Bryan and the People*. Philadelphia: J.B. Lippincott Co., 1964.

Glass, Mary Ellen. *Silver and Politics in Nevada: 1892–1902*. Reno: University of Nevada Press, 1969.

Goldberg, Michael Lewis. *An Army of Women: Gender and Politics in Gilded Age Kansas*. Baltimore, MD: Johns Hopkins University Press, 1997.

Goodwyn, Lawrence. *Democratic Promise: The Populist Moment in America*. New York: Oxford University Press, 1976.

Hahn, Steven. *The Roots of Southern Populism, Yeoman Farmers and the Transformation of the Georgia Upcountry, 1850–1890*. New York: Oxford University Press, 1983.

Hair, William Ivy. *Bourbonism and Agrarian Protest: Louisiana Politics, 1877–1900*. Baton Rouge: Louisiana State University Press, 1969.

Hays, Samuel P. "New Possibilities for American Political History: The Social Analysis of Political Life." In Samuel P. Hays, *American Political History as Social Analysis*. Knoxville: University of Tennessee Press, 1980.

Hicks, John D. *The Populist Revolt: A History of the Farmers' Alliance and the People's Party*. Minneapolis: University of Minnesota Press, 1931.

Hild, Matthew. *Greenbackers, Knights of Labor, and Populists, Farmer-Labor Insurgency in the Late-Nineteenth-Century*

South. Athens: University of Georgia Press, 2007.

Hofstadter, Richard. *The Age of Reform: From Bryan to F.D.R.* New York: Alfred A. Knopf, 1955.

Holmes, William F. "The Demise of the Colored Farmers' Alliance." *Journal of Southern History* 41 (2): 187–200.

Jensen, Richard. *The Winning of the Midwest: Social and Political Conflict, 1888–1896.* Chicago: University of Chicago Press, 1971.

Kazin, Michael. *The Populist Persuasion: An American History.* New York: Basic, 1995.

Kleppner, Paul. *The Cross of Culture: A Social Analysis of Midwestern Politics, 1850–1900.* New York: The Free Press, 1970.

Larson, Robert W. *New Mexico Populism: A Study in Radical Protest in a Western Territory.* Boulder: Colorado Associated University Press, 1974.

Lester, Connie L. *Up from the Mudsills of Hell: The Farmers' Alliance, Populism, and Progressive Agriculture in Tennessee, 1870–1915.* Athens: University of Georgia Press, 2006.

Lukacs, John. *Democracy and Populism: Fear and Hatred.* New Haven, CT: Yale University Press, 2005.

Martin, Roscoe. *The People's Party in Texas: A Case Study in Third-Party Politics.* Austin: University of Texas Press, 1933.

McMath, Robert, Jr. *Populist Vanguard: A History of the Southern Farmers' Alliance.* Chapel Hill: University of North Carolina Press, 1975.

McVey, Frank L. "The Populist Movement." *Economic Studies* 1 (3): 131–209.

Miller, Worth Robert. "A Centennial Historiography of American Populism." *Kansas History* 16 (1): 54–69.

Miller, Worth Robert. *Oklahoma Populism: A History of the People's Party in the Oklahoma Territory.* Norman: University of Oklahoma Press, 1987.

Morgan, W. Scott. *History of the Wheel and Alliance.* St. Louis: C.B. Woodward, 1891.

Noblin, Stuart. *Leonidas LaFayette Polk: Agrarian Crusader.* Chapel Hill: University of North Carolina Press, 1949.

Nugent, Walter T.K. *The Tolerant Populists: Kansas Populism and Nativism.* Chicago: University of Chicago Press, 1963.

Ostler, Jeffrey. *Prairie Populism: The Fate of Agrarian Radicalism in Kansas, Nebraska, and Iowa, 1880–1892.* Lawrence: University Press of Kansas, 1993.

Parrington, Vernon L. *Main Currents in American Thought.* New York: Harcourt, Brace, 1927.

Pollack, Norman. *The Populist Response to Industrial America.* New York: W.W. Norton, 1962.

Postel, Charles. *The Populist Revolt.* New York: Oxford University Press, 2007.

Ridge, Martin. *Ignatius Donnelly: The Portrait of a Politician.* Chicago: University of Chicago Press, 1962.

Rochester, Anna. *The Populist Movement in the United States: The Growth and Decline of the People's Party—A Social and Economic Interpretation.* New York: International Publishers, 1943.

Rogers, William Warren. *One-Gallused Rebellion: Agrarianism in Alabama, 1865–1896.* Baton Rouge: Louisiana State University Press, 1970.

Thomas, John L. *Alternative America: Henry George, Edward Bellamy, Henry Demarest Lloyd, and the Adversary Tradition.* Cambridge, MA: The Belknap Press, 1983.

Turner, Frederick Jackson. "The Problem of the West." *Atlantic Monthly* 78 (467): 289–297.

Woodward, C. Vann. *Tom Watson: Agrarian Rebel.* New York: Macmillan and Co., 1938.

Wright, James Edward. *The Politics of Populism: Dissent in Colorado.* New Haven, CT: Yale University Press, 1974.

Holcomb, Silas Alexander (1858–1920)

A politician from Nebraska, Silas Alexander Holcomb ran in the 1895 state gubernatorial elections on a fusion ticket between the People's Party and the Democratic Party, becoming the state's ninth governor.

Born on August 25, 1858, in Gibson County, Indiana, Silas Alexander Holcomb was the son of John Cook Holcomb and his second wife, Lucinda Reavis (née Skelton). His father, born in 1825 at Fort Branch, Gibson County, was the son of Elihu Holcomb from Anderson County, South Carolina; his mother had also been born in Gibson County.

Growing up on the family farm, Silas Holcomb worked hard with his three older half-brothers. It was a difficult childhood, which saw him trudging to the local village schools. The family resources were stretched by an increasingly large family. After Silas, his parents had seven more children, although three died in infancy. When Silas Holcomb was 19, his father died.

Silas Holcomb had already been teaching at local schools for four years and was heavily involved in self-education. He was now the main breadwinner for the family and unable to continue working on the family farm. He, his mother, and his younger brothers and sisters, in 1879, moved to a farm in Hamilton County, Nebraska.

In an attempt to establish a career, Silas Holcomb had started teaching himself law. He then joined a law firm in Grand Island, Nebraska, and in 1883 was successful enough to establish his own legal practice in the town of Broken Bow, Nebraska. On April 13, 1882, at Mills, Iowa, he married Alison Bronson, and they eventually had three children.

As a country lawyer, Silas Holcomb established a successful practice in pleading the cause of many poor and often indebted farming families. Trying to provide social support for them became the bedrock of his political program, which unapologetically sought to give these poor farmers a greater say in the running of the county as well as the state. In 1891 he was nominated to stand for the elections as a district judge on a third-party ticket. It was a bit of a surprise when he won.

The People's Party was emerging as an important political force in Nebraska, and it was obvious to most observers that Silas Holcomb would end up supporting it. He was named as their candidate for election to the state supreme court. Again it was a three-way contest against a Democrat and a Republican. Holcomb lost the election, but he had proved himself as a redoubtable campaigner and also as a possible candidate for higher office.

The agrarian upheavals of the 1890s saw the emergence of widespread debt among the farming families in Nebraska and other states as the farmers had to borrow to try to keep their farms going. Many of the farms had been established on poor soil, and farmers had pursued unsustainable farming practices that led to further indebtedness as the crop yields started to decline.

Holcomb did not advocate full-scale debt repudiation, but many of his supporters urged him to support this. Holcomb was elected governor of Nebraska in 1894, having been chosen as a fusion candidate by the People's Party and the

Democratic Party. He had the support of William Jennings Bryan, and his success could be credited to his personal appeal because it coincided with a resurgence of the Republican Party in the state.

In 1896, as the Democrats continued to work closely with the Populists, he was reelected as governor. Again he refused to repudiate debt, but he did advocate, and indeed introduce, many moves to ensure that there was no need for the farmers to go into further debt. Retiring as governor in 1899, Holcomb was appointed a justice of the Nebraska Supreme Court in the following year and was the chief justice of the state from 1904 until 1906. He then went back to practicing law and was a member of the Nebraska Board of Commissioners of State Institutions from 1913 until 1919.

In ill health by 1919, he retired from public office and moved to Bellingham, Washington, and lived there with his daughter until he died on April 25, 1920. He was buried at Broken Bow, Nebraska.

Justin Corfield

See also: Bryan, Williams Jennings (1860–1925); People's Party; Plains and Midwest, Populism in the; Third Parties

References

Morton, Julius Sterling. *History of Nebraska from the Earliest Explorations of the Trans-Mississippi Region.* Lincoln: Western Publishing and Engraving Company, 1918.

Hollywood Ten

The Hollywood Ten were a group of film industry employees who, in October 1947, were called to testify in front of the House Committee on Un-American Activities (HUAC) about their alleged involvement with the Communist Party. The Hollywood Ten consisted of director Edward Dmytryk, director and screenwriter Herbert J. Biberman, and screenwriters Lester Cole, Alvah Bessie, Ring Lardner Jr., John Howard Lawson, Albert Maltz, Samuel Ornitz, Dalton Trumbo, and Adrian Scott. These men became victims of the virtual witch hunt for suspected communists in the United States during the Cold War.

The 10 men were called as unfriendly witnesses and refused to testify; for their refusal to cooperate they received prison sentences and were blacklisted from the Hollywood film industry. The group invoked the Fifth Amendment, their right to decline to testify, and on November 24, 1947, Congress voted to cite them for contempt. Once convicted, their prison terms ranged from six months to one year. Soon after the men refused to testify, 50 members of the Association of Motion Picture Producers, the Motion Picture Association of America, and the Society of Independent Motion Picture Producers met in New York City to compose a strongly worded response to both the HUAC allegations and the contempt charges brought against the Hollywood Ten. Because the executives had convened at the Waldorf-Astoria Hotel, the document they produced became known as the Waldorf Statement. This document disavowed the actions of the Hollywood Ten and exiled them from the Hollywood film industry until they denied under oath any affiliation with the Communist Party. The statement also declared that executives would not knowingly employ any person who was a

Ten Hollywood personalities, the "Hollywood 10," stand with their attorneys outside district court in Washington, D.C., before arraignment on contempt of Congress charges, January 9, 1948. The ten were charged for refusing to cooperate with the House Un-American Activities Committee. From left, front: Herbert Biberman, Attorney Martin Popper, Attorney Robert W. Kenny, Albert Maltz, and Lester Cole. Second row, from left: Dalton Trumbo, John Howard Lawson, Alvah Bessie, and Samuel Ornitz. Top row, from left: Ring Lardner Jr., Edward Dmytryk, and Adrian Scott. (AP Photo)

communist, thereby beginning the practice of blacklisting, which would ultimately lead to the firing of more than 300 writers, actors, directors, and producers. The HUAC allegations that communist agents had inserted subversive messages into films lacked any concrete evidence, but films that portrayed socialist ideas, revealed anticapitalist sentiments, attacked anti-Semitism, or praised Russia attracted the attention of the committee. *We Who Are Young* (1940), *Tender Comrade* (1943), and *Crossfire* (1947) were just some of the films that may have implicated those involved with their production, including screenwriter Dalton Trumbo and director Edward Dmytryk. However, despite the lack of evidence, studios were disinclined to make films that dealt with social issues and instead, over the next seven years, produced numerous anticommunist propaganda films including *I Married a Communist* (1949), *Atomic City* (1952), and *My Son John* (1953).

Most of the Hollywood Ten never worked in Hollywood again, although some submitted scripts either pseudonymously or anonymously. For instance, before the HUAC investigations Dalton Trumbo had been a top screenwriter with an MGM contract, commanding $75,000 per screenplay. He had been nominated for an Academy Award for Best Writing, Screenplay, for the Ginger Rogers film *Kitty Foyle* (1940). Trumbo also wrote the screenplays for the decidedly patriotic Spencer Tracy films *A Guy Named Joe* (1943) and *Thirty Seconds over Tokyo* (1944). Once he was subpoenaed, however, to appear before HUAC, Trumbo found he was suspended without pay by his employers under regulations established by the Waldorf pact. It has been reported that the day Trumbo returned from the HUAC hearings he was signed by independent producers the King Brothers—Frank, Maurice, and Herman King—to write the screenplay for *Gun Crazy* (1950). The contract was for just $3,750, but realizing that he was now considered unemployable by the major studios, Trumbo agreed to the King Brothers's terms. Moreover, as Trumbo was still under contract to MGM, he penned the screenplay for *Gun Crazy* using the screenwriter and novelist Millard Kaufman as a front to avoid being sued by MGM for breach of contract. Thus, during the 1950s, Trumbo came to write a number of screenplays either anonymously, using the name of a nonblacklisted screenwriter as a front or pseudonymously. Submitting original screenplays using the name of an established screenwriter meant paying the screenwriter for the use of his or her name, but it also meant that Trumbo could earn a living in Hollywood, albeit under the radar. Trumbo's films of the 1950s include *The Prowler* (1951, originally uncredited), *Carnival Story* (1954, uncredited), *The Green-Eyed Blonde* (1957, writing as Sally Stubblefield) and *Terror in a Texas Town* (1959, writing as Ben Perry); two of his screenplays written using a front won Academy Awards—*Roman Holiday* (1953) and *The Brave One* (1956). Trumbo's screenplay for *The Brave One* was credited to Robert Rich, nephew of the King Brothers, and Trumbo only belatedly received the Oscar for his work on the film shortly before his death in 1975. Similarly, in a poignant footnote to the history of the Hollywood Ten, December 1992 saw the Academy of Motion Picture Arts and Sciences amend its records to credit Trumbo with the Oscar for *Roman Holiday*, presenting Trumbo's widow with a statuette the following year. The Academy Award had originally been credited to Ian McLellan Hunter, the front Trumbo had used. It was not until 1960, with the release of *Spartacus*, that Trumbo would again receive an onscreen credit. Executive producer and star of the film Kirk Douglas decided to defy the blacklist. *Spartacus* is a story of rebellion, and it is highly likely that the film's ending, where a group of men retain their ideals and dignity in the face of persecution and suffering, held great personal resonance for Trumbo.

One of the Hollywood Ten did manage to forge a Hollywood career under his own name not long after the HUAC investigation. Edward Dmytryk, who had directed the critically acclaimed *Crossfire* (1947), one of the first films to deal with anti-Semitism, fled to England before serving his jail term. There he directed several British thrillers, including *Obsession* (1949). Fearing that he might never work again in either Hollywood or Britain, Dmytryk chose to go before HUAC again, this time to reveal that several other members of the Hollywood Ten had pressured him into making clear his procommunist sentiments in his films. Dmytryk's testimony damaged the cases of several members of the Hollywood Ten who were at that time involved in court cases with their previous employers, but by publicly renouncing communism, Dmytryk was allowed back into the Hollywood firmament and went on to direct films including *The Caine Mutiny* (1954), *Raintree County* (1957), *The Young Lions* (1958), *The Carpetbaggers* (1964), and *Bluebeard* (1972).

Victoria Williams

See also: Capra, Frank (1897–1991); Film; Hiss, Alger (1904–1996); McCarthy, Joseph (1908–1957); Popular Culture; Rosenberg, Julius (1918–1953), and Rosenberg, Ethel (1915–1953)

References

"Awards for Dalton Trumbo." IMDb. http://www.imdb.com/name/nm0874308/awards. Accessed January 4, 2013.

Bernstein, Matthew, ed. *Controlling Hollywood: Censorship and Regulation in the Studio Era*. London: The Athlone Press, 2000.

Ceplair, Larry, and Steve Englund. *The Inquisition in Hollywood: Politics in the Film Community: 1930–1960*. Berkeley: University of California Press, 1979.

Chapman, Roger. *Culture Wars: An Encyclopedia of Issues, Viewpoints, and Voices*. Vol. 1. New York: M.E. Sharpe, 2010.

Dmytryk, Edward. *Odd Man Out: A Memoir of the Hollywood Ten*. Carbondale: Southern Illinois University Press, 1996.

"Hollywood Ten." Spartacus Educational. http://www.spartacus.schoolnet.co.uk/USAhollywood10.htm. Accessed January 4, 2013.

Pearson, Glenda. "The Red Scare: A Filmography." http://www.lib.washington.edu/exhibits/AllPowers/film.html. Accessed January 4, 2013.

Schwartz, Richard. "How the Film and Television Blacklists Worked." http://comptalk.fiu.edu/blacklist.htm. Accessed January 4, 2013.

Homestead Act (1862)

Passed by a Union-controlled Congress and signed into law on May 20, 1862, by President Abraham Lincoln, the Homestead Act represented two decades of effort to organize and settle western lands. Including the additions made to the original legislation in 1909 and 1916, approximately 270 million acres of land were distributed and more than 1.5 million new homesteads granted. The Homestead Act provided a means for landless Americans and immigrants to claim farms at a reduced cost, which helped settle the interior of the country, encouraged Indian removal, and closed the frontier. Homesteaders became some of the most active western Populists during the 1890s.

Prior to the Civil War, legislative proposals for free land distribution in the West met with strong resistance from Southerners in Congress who disliked the idea of increasing the number of yeoman farmers. They believed this would further weaken the influence of slaveholders on the national level. Once the South seceded, northern Republicans who controlled Congress implemented a land policy that sought to strengthen the idea of "Free Soil, Free Labor." Free-soil ideology proposed that free western lands be made available for Americans and new immigrants. Republicans believed that agriculture was a key component of strong economic growth. This opportunity would help increase wages for other workers because laborers would have the option of going west to farm. It also helped alleviate the land shortage in areas of the East and Midwest. Farming represented the simplest way to use the natural resources of the country for the benefit of many. According to historian Richard White (1993), some believed that the opportunity for free land would eliminate poverty. The Homestead Act, as passed in 1862, sought to encourage private ownership of the public domain in accordance with long-held ideas about republicanism and farm ownership made popular by Thomas Jefferson. Historian Heather Cox-Richardson (2007) claimed it served as proof that the federal government worked for the good of citizens.

The requirements to claim a 160-acre homestead included paying a small filing fee, improving the land, and residing on the claim for a minimum of five years. No restriction on sex, race, ethnicity, or age was placed on the act, although claimants had to be the head of household and immigrants had five years to apply for citizenship. If homesteaders wanted to gain title to their land quickly, they could pay $1.25 per acre after six months of residence. To further encourage settlement of public lands, the federal government gave land grants to railroad companies and to the states (the Pacific Railway Act and the Morrill Land-Grant College Act, respectively), which meant that settlers looking for western land had alternative options.

Conditions for homesteaders varied by location. On the Great Plains, a lack of trees forced settlers to build homes into hillsides, called dugouts, or construct homes from large pieces of sod, which were dried and laid on top of one another like bricks. The natural insulation of these materials helped with the extreme weather conditions of the region, but problems of cleanliness and natural disasters plagued many homesteaders. As an alternative to the sod or dugout homes, some settlers built log homes or small shacks from lumber and tar paper. Problems with drought, flooding, locusts, hail, blizzards, and fierce thunderstorms plagued many homesteaders' attempts to farm. The isolated and dirty conditions along with the hard work made homesteading difficult. Living apart from major cities and far from rail lines made it difficult for some homesteaders to profit in the cash-poor economy of the Plains. Some took on debt to purchase supplies, seed, and equipment for their farms. At relatively high interest rates, inability to pay back these loans forced some farmers off their land. Farmers who homesteaded were forced to depend on the railroads to move their products to market, which later resulted in conflicts between western farmers and railroad corporations.

One of the benefits of homestead agriculture was the relative ease of preparing the land for crops. Without trees or brush to clear, farmers could expect high yields once the prairie sod was broken.

Producing crops such as corn and wheat on the Plains was cheaper than producing them in the East. With good weather some farmers paid for their claims and equipment within two seasons. One of the long-term effects of the Homestead Act was the increased production of grain crops. These were used for both export markets and domestic markets, which increased in the late 1800s because of growing immigration to urban areas. Additionally, the livestock industry benefited from the availability of grassland for cattle and sheep.

Despite high hopes for the success of the Homestead Act, problems existed with the plan. Approximately 400,000 new farms were formed and millions of acres were distributed, but it did not remove poverty-stricken people from cities. The original allotment of 160 acres did not provide enough land for successful small farms in some areas of the arid West, particularly without irrigation. One popular theory of the late 1800s claimed that rain followed the plow. Settlers in dry regions believed that if they plowed up the rich prairie land it would generate moisture and regular rainfall. The failure of this theory caused many farms to be started on land that did not receive enough precipitation for small-scale grain farms. Speculators continued to participate in the distribution and sale of cheap land that could be purchased by settlers. States and railroad companies also received large land grants during this time period, which they sold for profits to settlers. Some states did not participate in the Homestead Act. For example, Texas possessed its own public-land dispersion policy formulated before its statehood. None of the original 13 states, Vermont, Maine, Kentucky, Tennessee, or West Virginia had public land for sale under the Homestead Act because they had no large tracts of federal land left for distribution. Native American lands were opened later to settlers under additional legislation.

Some terms of the Homestead Act allowed large claims to be filed. For example, a family could have older children make individual homestead claims of their own, eventually resulting in members of one family owning hundreds of acres of land. Ranchers, timber companies, and mining companies also had employees file claims, which the company ultimately bought to consolidate large holdings of land. "Improving the land" was left to interpretation. Some settlers built simple, small, windowless claim shacks on their lands. This allowed them to claim the homestead but did not necessarily fulfill the intent of the act, which was to fill the Plains with small, operational family farms.

By giving almost 200 million acres of land to railroad companies to encourage the building of new rail lines, Congress eliminated this land from being claimed for under the Homestead Act. Between 1862 and 1873 settlers purchased more western land than they claimed under the Homestead Act. Almost half of all settlers who tried to claim homestead land failed before earning ownership to their claims. Some of this failure had to do with the fact that not all western land eligible for homesteading proved to be good for small farms. Many of the challenges for farmers who claimed land under the

Homestead Act later emerged as elements of the populist uprising, namely the regulation of railroad and interest rates, increased circulation of currency, and cooperative ventures, which became hallmarks of the People's Party of the 1890s. Homesteaders experienced a shift in power in the decades following the passage of the act; farmers no longer featured as the central element in economic stability. Industrial interests overshadowed the role of farmers, and no places felt that more keenly than the areas recently settled by the Homestead Act. Federal land policy also changed to account for the problems with the original act. Irrigation, forest planting, and large-scale land use for ranching, mining, and timbering forced adjustments in the amount of acreage available to settlers.

In 1976, the Federal Land Policy and Management Act stopped use of the Homestead Act for the lower 48 states. However, Alaska received an exemption from this act, and the last homestead claimed under the Homestead Act was claimed in 1988 near the Stony River in Alaska. A total of close to 1.6 million homesteads were granted, which accounted for approximately 270 million acres of land, or about 10 percent of all the land in the United States.

Megan Birk

See also: Long-Haul/Short-Haul Discrimination; Plains and Midwest, Populism in the; Railroads; Union Pacific Railroad

References

Cox-Richardson, Heather. *West from Appomattox: The Reconstruction of the United States after the Civil War*. New Haven, CT: Yale University Press, 2007.

Gates, Paul W. *History of Public Land Law Development*. Washington, DC: U.S. Government Printing Office, 1968.

Gates, Paul W. *The Jeffersonian Dream: Studies in the History of American Land Policy and Development*. Albuquerque: University of New Mexico Press, 1996.

Phillips, Sarah T. "Antebellum Agricultural Reform, Republican Ideology, and Sectional Tension." *Agricultural History* 74 (4): 799–822.

White, Richard. *"It's Your Misfortune and None of My Own": A New History of the American West*. Norman: University of Oklahoma Press, 1993.

Homestead Strike (1892)

The Homestead Strike occurred from June 30, 1892, to November 20, 1892, at the Homestead Steel Works in Homestead, Pennsylvania, between the Amalgamated Association of Iron & Steel Workers and the Carnegie Steel Company. The strike was a result of a series of unsuccessful collective bargaining attempts between the Amalgamated Association of Iron & Steel Workers and the Carnegie Steel Company. The dispute resulted in a lockout followed by a lengthy strike, which culminated in a violent fight between the strikers and the Pinkerton National Detective Agency. This altercation represents one of several major events that led leaders of the industrial working classes and angry farmers to consider melding their movements for social and economic justice.

In the early 1890s, the price of steel fell, which prompted Henry Clay Frick, general manager of the Homestead Steel Works, to reduce operating costs. Frick felt that the Amalgamated Association of Iron & Steel Workers was a hindrance to the mill's operation and sought to break the union. Andrew Carnegie, owner of the Homestead Steel Works, had been a public supporter of organized labor; however, he discreetly supported Frick in his effort to break the union. Prior to the end of the collective bargaining agreement between the union and the mill, Carnegie and Frick agreed to increase production of steel in case they had to close the mill to break the union.

In February 1892, negotiations between Frick and the Amalgamated Association of Iron & Steel Workers began. The union asked for increased wages, and Frick countered with a wage decrease. With no agreement in sight, Frick locked some of the employees out of certain sections of the mill. On June 29, 1892 a full lockout was in effect, and the mill was barricaded with a 12-foot-high barbed-wire fence. Carnegie and Frick felt that the workers' desire for employment would outweigh their loyalty to the union. Only 750 of the 3,800 workers were members of the union; however, when workers met to vote on the strike, 3,000 voted in favor of a strike. On June 30, 1892, in conjunction with the Knights of Labor, the Amalgamated Association of Iron & Steel Workers initiated a strike.

During the strike the union workers attempted to keep the plant closed by driving off strikebreakers solicited by the mill. In response to the striking union workers and failed attempts to disperse the group by local sheriffs, Frick enlisted the help of the Pinkerton National Detective Agency. When the Pinkertons attempted to enter the mill by barge, a dispute erupted and gunshots were fired; it is unknown who fired first. The violence continued as the union workers tossed dynamite into the river; they even poured oil in the river in an attempt to ignite the water around the barges. Due to the violent outburst, Pennsylvania Governor Robert E. Pattison ordered the state militia to the Homestead Mill to restore order.

After a strike lasting four months, on November 20, 1982, the workers voted to return to work. In response to the violent outbreak, authorities attempted to charge strike leaders and strikers with crimes; however, the attempts were unsuccessful. The physical victory over the Pinkertons was met by a larger defeat as Carnegie managed to force the unions out of the Homestead Mill as well as other mills in the Pittsburgh region.

Johnathan Fluitt

See also: Cleveland, Grover (1837–1908); Knights of Labor; Pullman Strike (1894)

Resources

Foner, Philip Sheldon. *History of the Labor Movement in the United States.* New York: International Publishers, 1975.

Krause, Paul. *The Battle for Homestead, 1880–1892: Politics, Culture, and Steel.* Pittsburgh, PA: University of Pittsburgh Press, 1992.

Warren, Kenneth. *Triumphant Capitalism: Henry Clay Frick and the Industrial Transformation of America.* Pittsburgh, PA: University of Pittsburgh Press, 1996.

I

Illinois Woman's Alliance (IWA)

The Illinois Woman's Alliance (IWA) was founded on August 18, 1888, by a coalition of members from 26 women's and civic organizations in Chicago. Guided by the principles of "justice to children and loyalty to women," the IWA's formation was a result of public outrage generated by a series of undercover exposé articles written by Nell Nelson and published on the front page of the *Chicago Times*. The articles offered a first-hand view of the working conditions present throughout most of Chicago's garment and packingtown districts, including Philip Danforth Armour's meat-packing facility later featured in Upton Sinclair's book *The Jungle*. Newspaper editor Charles Chapin noted Nelson's articles were in such demand that the paper's presses were overtaxed. Nelson successfully infiltrated nearly 50 firms, documenting and exposing a social norm of abuse (physical, emotional, and financial) towards women and children in the workplace. Nelson's series of exposé articles began a major movement toward social and political reform, beginning with the formation of the IWA.

The focused reform efforts of the IWA were categorized by author Meredith Tax (1980) into four main areas: (1) a campaign against sweatshops, (2) a campaign to protect children (focused on both legislation against child labor and passing a compulsory education bill), (3) the placement of public baths in Chicago's working-class districts; and (4) a drive for inspections of state institutions (asylums, police courts) because members felt women were being abused. The IWA lobbied extensively to effect change. Its primary and most successful campaign was a lobbying effort for compulsory education legislation to combat the excessive use of child labor. In December 1888 the IWA successfully petitioned the Chicago Common Council to pass compulsory education legislation. Then, in early 1889 the IWA sponsored a compulsory education bill before the state legislature providing for a 12- to 24-week school year. The bill was passed in May 1889. The IWA then began petitioning for external inspections of factory working conditions, public bathing facilities, and enforcement of labor practices, securing success in each of these endeavors.

In addition to these local legislative changes, the IWA also fuelled a national movement towards labor reform; they modeled a successful mode of social organizing that had broad-reaching effects. Historian Bessie Louise Pierce (1957) noted that the establishment of the IWA illustrated a social realization that unified action was important if the poor working conditions of women and children were to be improved. Specifically, the impact of Nelson and the IWA influenced other civic organizations including the National Consumers League, Hull House, and the Trade & Labor Assembly of Chicago. Likewise, Nelson and the IWA's geographic impact spanned multiple states, including New York, Massachusetts, Pennsylvania, Nebraska, Iowa, and Illinois. Positive social and legislative changes, both small and large, then followed through the actions of other organizations following the IWA model of social organizing.

In reflecting back on her exposé series and the success of the IWA, Nelson stated the articles were written with both "a feeling of interest and a sense of responsibility greater than ordinarily follows obedience to a newspaper assignment." Sadly, however, the IWA was a relatively short-lived organization, lasting only six years and dissolving in 1894 due to internal political and turmoil. Nevertheless Tax (1980) noted, "During the six years of its existence, the Illinois Women's Alliance accomplished more in the way of practical reform and political education than many organizations that have lasted five times as long."

Eric W. Liguori

See also: Addams, Jane (1860–1935); Eight-hour Day; Gilded Age; Plains and Midwest, Populism in the; The Press and Populism; Public Education

References

Chapin, Charles. *Charles Chapin's Story: Written in Sing Sing Prison*. New York: G.P. Putnam's Sons, 1920.

Nelson, Nell. *The White Slave Girls of Chicago*. Chicago: Barkley Publishing Company, 1888.

Pierce, Bessie Louise. *A History of Chicago*. Vol. 3. New York: Alfred A. Knopf, 1957.

Scharnau, Ralph. "Elizabeth Morgan, Crusader for Labor Reform." *Labor History* 14 (3): 340–351.

Tax, Meredith. *The Rising of Women: Feminist Solidarity and Class Conflict, 1880–1917*. New York: Monthly Review Press, 1980.

Industrial Workers of the World (IWW)

The Industrial Workers of the World (IWW), popularly nicknamed the "Wobblies," has stood out as one of the best-known yet most misunderstood labor organizations in American history. It has also stood out, historically, as one of the originators of modern industrial unionism—characterized by organizing workers by industry rather than by craft, a mode of organization that made it possible for the many unskilled workers left out of the craft-based model of organizing to have the protections of unionization. As such, it became one of the most inclusive labor organizations in history, organizing women, immigrant, and African American workers when other unions would not, and striving toward the goal of "one big union" that would include all workers. The IWW was (and remains) unabashedly militant and uncompromising in its dedication to workers' rights.

Although at its peak the "one big union" never numbered more than 10,000 members at a time, its influence in American labor history has been significant, and the "Wobblies" have inspired fear and loathing out of proportion to their numbers.

The union's radical stances made it a common target of antiradical efforts, creating many negative associations with unionization. Yet the IWW has also played an energizing role in the larger working-class movement, providing great labor songs (most famously "Solidarity Forever") and romanticized labor heroes, including the populist martyr Joe Hill. Public knowledge of the IWW, however, has been traditionally characterized by a lot of misinformation, chiefly that the organization died out in the 1920s, despite the current presence of the organization on the Internet at www.iww.org. Nonetheless, the post-1920s history of the IWW, as well as its international history, has remained underreported and sketchy until recent times.

The Industrial Workers of the World was founded on June 27, 1905, in Chicago, and its first and only president was William B. "Big Bill" Haywood. Although there had been some efforts at industrially based organizing following the demise of the Knights of Labor, mainly through the efforts of Eugene V. Debs's American Railway Union, the IWW stood out as the most assertive rejection of the increasingly narrow, craft-based, "pure and simple" trade unionism of the American Federation of Labor. The founding of the IWW was assisted by activists from the Socialist Trades and Labor Alliance of the Socialist Labor Party, the Western Federation of Miners, the Socialist Party of America, and the remnants of the International Working Peoples' Association. During its second convention in 1906, the IWW became divided between conservatives and radicals, resulting in the departure of one of the IWW's largest constituent union, the Western Federation of Miners, and at the 1908 convention the union was further divided between political activists and those who favored direct action, costing the IWW its supporters in the Socialist Labor Party.

Despite these early divisions within the organization, the IWW was noted for its strong presence among native-born miners in the West as well as among immigrant industrial workers in the Northeast. One of the union's most famous and successful labor actions was the 1912 textile strike in Lawrence, Massachusetts, that featured the call for "Bread and Roses"; other notable IWW strikes during this decade include those mounted by the textile workers in Lowell, Massachusetts, and the silk workers in Paterson, New Jersey. During World War I, the IWW took a lead in organizing unemployed workers, and in 1915 it became a leader in the antiwar movement. During this period, the IWW acquired its first and most famous martyr in activist Joe Hill, who was executed on a dubious murder charge in Utah at the instigation of the "copper bosses" and subsequently became celebrated in song and legend. Other IWW labor actions during this period included a number of miners' strikes, most notably at the Mesabi Iron Range in Minnesota.

The United States' entry into World War I, and accompanying stateside efforts to "sell the war" and quell dissent, led to stepped-up persecution of the IWW and its activists. One of the most famous incidents was the Bisbee deportation, in which 1,200 striking copper miners were deported from Bisbee, Arizona, across the border and left to die in the Mexican desert. In addition, 100 IWW activists in Chicago were tried for espionage in 1918. Following the war's conclusion, labor unrest contributed to the postwar Red Scare that incited new violence against the IWW, with the most notorious incident being the lynching and maiming of IWW activist Wesley Everett in Centralia, Washington, in 1919. Then the 1920 "Palmer Raids," ordered by U.S. Attorney General A. Mitchell Palmer to ferret out "subversives," resulted in the trial and deportation of many IWW activists, notably Haywood, who jumped bail and fled to Russia.

The Red Scare failed to crush the IWW. Rather, the IWW's organizing efforts continued and increased into the 1930s, supporting the miners in the famous Harlan County Coal Strike and, with the onset of the Depression, again taking a lead in organizing the unemployed. During the first Roosevelt administration, the IWW attempted to organize autoworkers and Works Progress Administration (WPA) construction workers, and in the mid-1930s the Wobblies joined in the Popular Front's antifascist activism. Although the IWW enjoyed some organizing successes during the 1930s and 1940s, the advent of the Cold War led to a serious decline in the organization's fortunes. In 1949, the IWW was placed on the government's list of "subversive organizations," and the Wobblies' refusal to sign onto the Taft-Hartley anti-Communist affidavits contributed to the organizations' decline to the point that, by 1955, the IWW came closer than it ever had in its history to dying out on its 50th anniversary.

Yet the IWW rebounded during the 1960s and played an important role in the radical activism of that decade. In the 1970s and 1980s, the Wobblies replaced a national administration with regional organizing committees and diversified their organizing field. In the 1980s, the IWW also attempted to build a labor-environmentalist alliance, and the IWW formed IWW-Earth First!, which attempted to bring support for both workers in the environmental movement and broach issues of the environment. The dual mission strained the alliance, yet the IWW's environmental efforts continued into the 1990s with the "Redwood Summer," a campaign that made alliances with the timber workers and was only partially disrupted by an attack on the IWW activists and subsequent attempt to frame the leaders of the campaign in the highly contested pipe bombing of Judi Bari's car. In 1995, the IWW entered the Internet age as only the second union, and the first international union, to have its own website. And as the twentieth century has given way to the twenty-first, the IWW organizing efforts in the United States and abroad have continued to increase; currently the IWW has branches in the United States, Canada, western Europe, and Africa. In recent years, the IWW has attempted to organize workers at many well-known consumer chains, most famously Starbucks. The IWW also has, most recently, become an active and vocal supporter of the Occupy Wall Street movement.

In its long history, the Industrial Workers of the World has stood out as a militant, populist radical union that has remained utterly beholden to neither employers nor mainstream political parties. It has played a major role in promoting the idea of industrial unionism, even when its inclusiveness and its militancy placed it at the margins of the labor movement. In recent times, the IWW has been a leader in promoting the idea of "open-source unionism"—organizing workers rather than workplaces and not waiting for certification to act on behalf of the workers it organizes. The IWW's endurance into the twenty-first century, especially amid an otherwise declining American labor movement, is evidence of its durability as an essentially populist organization. It has also remained an important contributor to labor and working-class arts and culture.

Susan Roth Breitzer

See also: American Federation of Labor; Environmentalism; Gompers, Samuel; Knights of Labor; Populism; Progressivism; Producerism; Red Scare of 1919

References

Buhle, Paul, and Nicole Schulman. *Wobblies!: A Graphic History of the Industrial Workers of World*. London: Verso, 2005.

Dubofsky, Melvyn, and Joseph A. McCartin. *We Shall All Be: A History of the Industrial Workers of the World*. Urbana: University of Illinois Press, 2000.

The Judi Bari Website. http://www.judibari.org/. Accessed January 7,2013.

Thompson, Fred, John Bekken, and Utah Phillips. *The Industrial Workers' of the World: Its First 100 Years: 1905 through 2005*. Chicago: Industrial Workers of the World, 2005.

Ingersoll, Robert (1833–1899)

Robert Green Ingersoll, the late-nineteenth-century Populist and activist in the Freethought movement, has in recent times become a darling of atheists and secular humanists. Yet Ingersoll, a Republican politician as well as a Populist orator and writer who was both admired and reviled in his time, was actually a far more complex figure than popularly portrayed. Ingersoll was born in 1833 in Dresden, New York, and was the son of a Presbyterian minister who was himself controversial for his support of the abolitionist movement. Early in his own career, Ingersoll was fired from a teaching job for making a joke about baptism, an event that demonstrated the differences between his beliefs and those of more mainstream, conservative Americans. It also showed the risks of making light of Christian beliefs during this period in American history. Ingersoll practiced law and eventually rose to become attorney general of Illinois. A talented orator in a time when public speaking was a major form of entertainment, Ingersoll also became a prominent figure in the post–Civil War Republican Party. Although Ingersoll was not initially known for supporting Progressive causes, he eventually became a champion of African American civil rights and women's rights. Notably, although Ingersoll took these radical stances, he also praised the virtues of home family and had a happy marriage and stable family life.

But Ingersoll was best known during his lifetime for his willingness to oppose the religious establishment, especially its more conservative wing and what he saw as its oppressive role in American life. In numerous writings, speeches, and interviews, he attacked the commonly accepted foundations of the Judeo-Christian religious tradition (though speaking well of the Jews as a people). One of his most famous works, *Some Mistakes of Moses*, provided a harsh and detailed critique of the Old Testament. Between 1866 and 1899, Ingersoll devoted himself to lecturing and won a variety of admirers who included the prominent minister Henry Ward Beecher. He made friends with nineteenth-century notables as diverse as Walt Whitman, Mark Twain, Elizabeth Cady Stanton, and Andrew Carnegie. Ingersoll died on July 21, 1899, in Dobbs Ferry-on-Hudson, New York. Thanks to the publication of his collected speeches following his death, Ingersoll has remained an influential figure among American atheists, agnostics, and secular humanists.

Susan Roth Breitzer

See also: Abolitionism; Freethinkers; Stanton, Elizabeth Cady (1815–1902); Twain, Mark (1835–1910); Whitman, Walt (1819–1892)

References

Ingersoll, Robert Green. *Sixty-Five Press Interviews with Robert G. Ingersoll: What the Great Agnostic Told Reporters during a Quarter-Century as a Freethinker and Enemy of Superstition*. Austin, TX; American Atheist Press, 1983.

Ingersoll, Robert Green. *Some Mistakes of Moses*. New York: Prometheus Books, 1986.

"People & Ideas: Robert Ingersoll." *God in America*. http://www.pbs.org/godinamerica/people/robert-ingersoll.html. Accessed January 7, 2013.

"Who Was Robert Ingersoll?" Humanist Society of Santa Barbara. http://www.santabarbarahumanists.org/ingersoll/index.htm. Accessed January 7, 2013.

International Monetary Conferences

A series of International Monetary Conferences were held in Paris in 1867, 1878, and 1881 and in Brussels in 1892 to discuss international monetary coordination. Emperor Louis Napoleon of France invited 20 nations to the first conference in 1867, where he hoped to build on the momentum of the recently inaugurated Latin Monetary Union (LMU) between France, Italy, Belgium, and Switzerland. At the 1867 conference, France invited all other major powers (including the United States) to join the LMU and adopt a franc-based monetary union. The conferees concluded that they would petition their governments to form a union founded on a gold standard. This effort failed because the Bank of France refused to participate and because the governments of several of the conferees were not interested in the proposal. The strongest resistance from other governments emerged in Prussia (which had no desire to give up its silver standard), Britain (which was on a gold standard but did not want to be a member of a franc-based union), and the United States (which had substantial silver interests).

A series of events in the early 1870s destabilized the international monetary system, leading the United States to call for another three international monetary conferences. In 1871, the newly unified Germany abandoned its silver standard for a gold standard. This switch dumped silver on the market, lowering its price and disturbing the long-stable international silver-to-gold ratio of roughly 15.5 to 1. The German adjustment, combined with new silver discoveries in the late 1860s in the United States, pushed Scandinavia onto a gold standard in 1872; the Netherlands and the United States followed suit in 1873. In the United States, this abandonment of silver (and commitment to redemption of the inflationary greenback currency) became known as the "Crime of 1873."

A coalition of indebted farmers and western silver miners pushed for the remonetization of silver after 1873, succeeding with the Bland-Allison Act of 1878, which required Congress to purchase and mint between $2 and $4 million of silver per month. In 1878, the United States also called the second international monetary conference, this time to establish a stable bimetallic international monetary system. This conference was not successful in garnering international support for bimetallism. Britain remained defensive of its gold standard, while many other European powers were suspicious that the United States had inflationary intentions. The two subsequent conferences in 1881 and 1892 also failed. After the progold Cleveland administration took office in 1893, the earlier prosilver acts were repealed and the United States returned to a gold standard. Cleveland's abandonment of silver set the stage for the unsuccessful Populist attempt at the presidency in 1896 and marked the end of the international monetary conferences.

Daniel Kuehn

See also: Bland, Richard P. (1835–1899); Cleveland, Grover (1837–1908); Crime of '73; Gilded Age; Gold Standard/Free Silver; People's Party

References

Einaudi, Luca L. "From the Franc to the 'Europe': The Attempted Transformation of the Latin Monetary Union into a European Monetary Union, 1865–1873." *Economic History Review* 53 (2): 284–308.

Reti, Steven P. *Silver and Gold: The Political Economy of International Monetary Conferences, 1867–1892*. Westport, CT: Greenwood Press, 1998.

Velde, Francois R. "Following the Yellow Brick Road: How the United States Adopted the Gold Standard." *Economic Perspectives* 26 (2): 42–58.

Interstate Commerce Act (ICA) (1887)

The Interstate Commerce Act (ICA) of 1887 (24 Stat. 379), passed during the first term of the Grover Cleveland administration, imposed an extensive regulatory regime on the railroad industry and created the Interstate Commerce Commission (ICC). Major provisions of the act targeted unreasonable shipping rates of railroad companies, secret rebates discriminating against small rail carriers, and the monopolistic practices of railroad trusts. The ICA mandated that rates charged by railroad companies be "reasonable and just." The act required that freight standards be free of preferences in routes and markets. The ICA represented a challenge to laissez-faire proponents and the marked insertion of the federal government into the economic affairs of private industry. The act also realigned regulatory control from the states into the federal orbit.

The ICA grew out of the economic unrest of the 1870s, chiefly among midwestern and southern farmers, over corporate influence and wealth more generally, and the untrammeled power of the railroad industry particularly. During this period, society relied on railroads as the primary mode of individual and freight transport. Railroads wielded extensive control over freight and passenger rates, the determination of routes and branch service, and the formation and conduct of trusts. Passengers were disadvantaged due to exorbitant fares and limited routes; freight carriers and shippers operated in a landscape of tiered pricing schemes and disadvantageous freight ranking; and private railroad concerns were hobbled due to price fixing and the manipulation of markets by larger firms. Predatory practices led to the bankrupting of independent railroads and the consolidation of firms into trusts unchecked by competitive pressures. The power exercised by railroads therefore was more than a matter of getting from point A to point B but the ability of individuals and competing businesses to exercise individual and commercial freedom.

Even as piecemeal action on the state government level attempted to bring some measure of reform, railroads operated across state lines, making comprehensive change impractical and incomplete. Southern and midwestern states, for example, created independent regulatory commissions and enacted economic and safety legislation aimed at railroads. The U.S. Supreme Court further denuded state regulatory control in the 1886 case of *Wabash v. Illinois* (118 U.S. 557). The Court ruled decidedly against the State of Illinois, holding that the Commerce Clause restricted the ability of states to regulate activities impacting interstate commercial affairs such as those carried on by railroads. The situation was compounded by the long-standing laissez-faire policy of postbellum politicians, thus equaling inaction at the federal level. With the campaign of Grover Cleveland promising reform both within and outside the federal government, prospects for substantive change seemed promising. Upon taking office Cleveland's reform agenda led to a partial rejection of the spoils system, cutting government waste and exalting merit above party affiliation. The passage of the ICA constituted the most extensive component of his reform agenda and the beginnings of federal regulation.

As the primary vehicle of ICA power, the Interstate Commerce Commission represented a turning point in the regulatory power of the federal government over private industry. The ICC continued to evolve through various administrative edicts and congressional legislation throughout the twentieth century. The administration of Theodore Roosevelt is noteworthy for championing updates to the ICA in an effort to close various regulatory loopholes. The Elkins Act of 1903 and Hepburn Act of 1906 gave the ICC additional teeth, eliminating railroad rebates and putting firm rate limits in place. With the evolution of the transportation sector in the United States, judicial interpretation of Commerce Clause power, expanded congressional legislation, and executive action, the ICC regulated overland transportation and pipelines as well. The Motor Carrier Act of 1935 gave the ICC the power to regulate truck transport. In the 1990s, and with the relegation of the railroad industry into a sea of transport options, lawmakers began to reexamine the role of the ICC in the economic and transportation future of the United States. Bureaucratic efficiency and cost savings were also a factor in the reassessment of the ICC's role. As a result, in 1995, the ICC was abolished and its responsibilities transferred to the Department of Transportation (DOT). DOT is responsible for the preexisting duties of the ICC, along with an enhanced regulatory structure overseeing transportation and commerce.

The ICA signified the beginnings of federal regulatory legislation, serving as a critical first step in a proactive government committed to modern commercial reform.

Jonathan C. Bergman

See also: Cleveland, Grover (1837–1908); Federal Trade Commission Act (1914); Granger Movement; Hepburn Act (1906); Long-Haul/Short-Haul Discrimination; Railroad Regulation; Railroads; Roosevelt, Theodore (1858–1919); Transportation Act of 1920

References

Bryant, Keith L., and Henry C. Dethloff. *A History of American Business*. Englewood Cliffs, NJ: Prentice-Hall, 1983.

Dos Passos, John R. *The Inter-State Commerce Act: An Analysis of Its Provisions.* 1887. Reprint, Ithaca, NY: Cornell University Library, 2009.

Hoogenboom, Ari, and Olive Hoogenboom. *A History of the ICC: From Panacea to Palliative*. New York: W.W. Norton and Company, 1976.

McNulty, Timothy J. "ICC Faces Extinction in Budgetary Cuts; Regulatory Agency Considered a Relic." *Chicago Tribune*, February 7, 1995.

Nevins, Allan. *Grover Cleveland: A Study in Courage*. 1932. Reprint, Norwalk, CT: Easton Press, 1989.

Phillips, Don. "On the Track to Extinction? ICC Approves Giant Rail Merger, Now Awaits Elimination." *Washington Post*, July 21, 1995.

Posner, Richard A. *Antitrust Law*. Chicago: University of Chicago Press, 2001.

Pusateri, Joseph C. *A History of American Business*. Arlington Heights, IL: Harlan Davidson, 1984.

Stone, Richard D. *The Interstate Commerce Commission and the Railroad Industry: A History of Regulatory Policy*. New York: Praeger Publishers, 1991.

Irons, Martin (1827–1911)

Martin Irons was an activist with the Knights of Labor and is best known as the leader of the Great Southwestern Railroad Strike. His role in the strike that led to his blacklisting in the railroad industry and eventual marginalization in the late-nineteenth-century labor movement has been long misunderstood and misportrayed, giving rise to an image of a hotheaded labor leader whose impulsiveness led to a disastrous strike. More recent scholarship has demonstrated, however, that Irons and his role as a labor leader were in fact more complex than traditionally understood. Irons was born in Scotland in 1827 and immigrated to the United States in 1841 at the age of 14. Little is known of his early life except that as a young man he trained as a machinist and for several years drifted throughout the southwestern United States, pursuing work with the railroads. During those years, Irons joined the local machinists' union and became involved in socialist and populist political movements, including the Grange.

In 1885, Irons joined the Knights of Labor and shortly thereafter founded District Assembly 101, the local that represented the railroad workers who worked for financier Jay Gould's Southwestern Railroad Lines. As a leader of District Assembly 101, Irons played a controversial role in the Great Southwestern Railroad Strike of 1886, a strike that stands out as one of the largest strikes in railroad history during this period and that was noted for the unprecedented unity between black and white workers that it created. An earlier strike in 1885 broke out in response to management efforts to cut wages and benefits as cost-saving measures and was settled with the assistance of the Knights of Labor, which subsequently organized the railroad workers into District Assembly 101. The 1885 strike led to a settlement that included rehiring of the strikers and payment of back wages. However, when the Gould railroad management continued to cut wages and refused to hire members of the Knights of Labor, the workers went on strike again. The resulting strike, which was called on March 1, 1886, included 200,000 workers but was hampered by the lack of support from the skilled trainmen and by the use of sometimes violent direct action. As the strike, which initially enjoyed significant public support, went down to defeat in the wake of procompany court injunctions, Irons received blame for the continuation of strike violence, although there is less proof than was once commonly believed that he had encouraged the violence. Following the strike's defeat, Irons was blacklisted from railroad work and forced to take an assumed name to find any work at all. From 1894 onward, he was supported by G. B. Harris, the secretary of the Social Democratic Party, and enjoyed some success as a Populist orator. As a speaker and activist, Irons promoted the cause of organized labor and of land ownership as the key to independence, and his activism highlighted the close relationship between labor and Populist activists of this period. Irons died in Bruceville, Texas, in 1911.

Susan Roth Breitzer

See also: Granger Movement; Knights of Labor; Powderly, Terence V. (1849–1924); Texas, Populism in

References

Allen, Ruth Alice. *The Great Southwest Strike.* Austin: University of Texas Press, 1942.

Allen, Ruth A. "Irons, Martin." *Handbook of Texas Online*. http://www.tshaonline.org/handbook/online/articles/fir07. Accessed January 7, 2013.

Case, Theresa Ann. *The Great Southwest Railroad Strike and Free Labor.* College Station: Texas A&M University Press, 2010.

Hild, Matthew. *Greenbackers, Knights of Labor, and Populists: Farmer-Labor*

Insurgency in the Late Nineteenth-Century South. Athens: University of Georgia Press, 2007.

Ivins, Mary Tyler "Molly" (1944–2007)

Mary Tyler "Molly" Ivins was a reporter, columnist, and self-described populist mainly located in Austin, Texas. Her humorous insights on politics in the Lone Star State and the West have been printed in 10 books, and during the course of her life she won numerous journalism awards and recognitions, including the Eugene Debs Award, the Ivan Allen Jr. Prize, and the David Brower Award. Ivins often claimed that she took the greatest pleasure from having the distinction of being banned from the Texas A&M campus, having the Minneapolis police department's mascot pig named after her, and publicly mooning the Ku Klux Klan. She is most famous for her profiles on the Bush political family and is credited with giving George W. Bush the nickname "Shrub." She had no fears about confronting the establishment on the local or national level.

Born in Monterey, California, on August 30, 1944, she was raised in Houston, Texas, in the home of her father Jim Ivins, an oil executive. Ivins received a bachelor's degree in history from Smith College and her master's degree from the Columbia School of Journalism in 1967. She also studied at Scripps College, Claremont, California, and at the Institute of Political Science in Paris, Sciences Po.

After three summers of interning for the *Houston Chronicle*, Ivins got her first job at the *Minneapolis Tribune*, where for three years she was a beat reporter until she got a job back in her home state as the coeditor and political reporter with the *Texas Observer* in Austin. Her colorful style caught the attention of the *New York Times*, which offered her the western political beat in 1976. She eventually became the Rocky Mountain bureau chief, with oversight of nine states in that region. Her antiauthority temperament and her folksy style led to clashes with the senior editors of the paper. The most famous of these was a 1980 column in which she described a New Mexico small-town chicken-slaughtering festival as a "gang-pluck."

In 1981, Ivins returned to Texas as a columnist for the *Dallas Times Herald*. After a few years, senior management decided to transfer her to their Austin bureau because her humorous barbs had caused a great deal of animosity with city leaders and prominent citizens. During this time, she became popular on the speaking circuit due to her down-home style and lively stories.

As George H. W. Bush rose to national prominence, so did Ivins. She quickly became a voice for those trying to understand Texas politics and the Bush family's place there. In 1991, she gained national attention with the release of her book *Molly Ivins Can't Say That, Can She?*, which spent 29 weeks on the bestseller list. When in the same year the *Dallas Morning News* bought the *Times Herald* and closed it down, Ivins went to work for the *Fort Worth Star-Telegram* because the editors allowed her to stay in Austin. With a Texan in the White House, her column, syndicated by Creators Syndicate, was printed in more than 400 newspapers across the United States.

In 2001, Ivins was diagnosed with stage III inflammatory breast cancer. Two years later, with her cancer in remission, she left the *Star-Telegram* to become an independent journalist. When George W. Bush became president of the United States, she enjoyed a new surge of popularity and national attention, especially after the releases of two books with fellow reporter Lou Dobbs, *Shrub: The Short but Happy Political Life of George W. Bush* in 2000 and *Bushwhacked: Life in George W. Bush's America* three years later.

Molly Ivins's cancer returned in 2003. After undergoing another course of chemotherapy, the cancer appeared to have gone into remission until 2005. Taking leave from her column, she fought the disease over the next few months. She wrote her final two columns just weeks before dying in an Austin hospice on January 31, 2007, at the age of 62.

Ivins described her style of journalism as populist, stating, "A populist is someone who is for the people and against the powerful, and so a populist is generally the same as a liberal—except we tend to have more fun" (Crowther). For her, any institution, organization, or politician that stood in the way of democracy was fair game for lampooning and exposure. She would bristle at claims by people on the Right that she was a socialist, retorting, "I guess I'm a left-libertarian and a populist, and I believe in the Bill of Rights the way some folks believe in the Bible" (Crowther). Through her years of reporting on Texas politics she believed in holding the powerful accountable and took pleasure in pointing out financial connections between corporations and politicians. Just before she died Ivins summed up the thrust of her career: "Either we figure out how to keep corporate cash out of the political system or we lose the democracy" (Crowther). In terms of the continuing public conversation about transparency, she thus summed up the problems that have continued to plague the nation and sparked the Occupy Wall Street movement.

Trevor Jason Soderstrum

See also: Bush, George W., Populist Rhetoric of; Dobbs, Louis Carl (1945–); The Press and Populism; Texas, Populism in

References

Crowther, Hal. "Reflecting on the Late Molly Ivins, Her New Bio and Her Crusade against Corporatized America: She Told You So." IndyWeek.com, February 10, 2010. http://www.indyweek.com/indyweek/reflecting-on-the-late-molly-ivins-her-new-bio-and-her-crusade-against-corporatized-america/Content?oid=1300158.

Eugene V. Debs Foundation. http://debsfoundation.org/foundation.html. Accessed January 7, 2013.

Ivan Allen Jr. Prize for Social Courage. http://ivanallenprize.gatech.edu/home/. Accessed January 7, 2013.

J

Jefferson, Thomas (1743–1826)

Thomas Jefferson was a key advocate of enlightened liberal democracy who served in a range of public offices including president of the United States (1801–1809), vice president of the United States (1797–1801), governor of Virginia (1779–1781), minister plenipotentiary to France (1784–1789), and secretary of state (1790–1793). He made his most lasting contributions, however, with his pen, drafting the Declaration of Independence and writing "A Summary View of the Rights of British America," *Notes on the State of Virginia*, and such notable proposed legislation for his native Virginia as "A Bill for the More General Diffusion of Knowledge" and the Virginia Statute for Religious Freedom. Though he was a leading member of the slaveholding Virginia gentry, Jefferson based his vision of the American republic on civil equality and the citizen's political and economic independence, which he sought to achieve primarily through land reform, disestablishment, and public education. Fundamentally, he advocated an agrarian vision of a nation made up primarily of small- to mid-scale farmers in which power was decentralized to the states, in contrast to the strong federal government advocated by the Federalists, especially his political nemesis, Alexander Hamilton. Many of Jefferson's quotations and ideas have been used by later populists, particularly right-wing populists, who view strong central government as the source of the nation's ills.

Thomas Jefferson was born on April 13, 1743. Though his mother came from one of Virginia's first families, the Randolphs, his father, Peter Jefferson, was a rugged, self-made man, who died in 1757 when Jefferson was 14. In 1762, he graduated from the College of William and Mary at Williamsburg. Five years later, he was admitted to the provincial bar after studying law with the colony's foremost lawyer, George Wythe. In 1769, Jefferson was elected to the Virginia House of Burgesses. During his early years as lawyer and legislator, Jefferson took part in several reform-minded cases and legislative projects.

In 1774, responding to growing tensions with Britain, Jefferson wrote the widely read pamphlet "A Summary View of the Rights of British America," denying Parliamentary sovereignty over the colonies. Jefferson was chosen to represent Virginia in the Second Continental Congress in Philadelphia in 1775. In June 1776, he was appointed to a committee with John Adams, Benjamin Franklin, Roger Sherman, and Robert R. Livingston to draft the Declaration of Independence. Jefferson's draft was edited initially by Adams and Franklin and then by the Congress, largely to curb its more radical passages.

The Declaration's assertions that "all men are created equal" and that government's just powers come from "the consent of the governed" put Jefferson's commitments to equality and popular sovereignty at the heart of the American political creed (Jefferson 19).

Jefferson left Philadelphia for Virginia in September 1776, seeking to achieve his goals both of civil equality and weakening the aristocracy through legal reform. Because land ownership was central to his conception of an independent republican citizen, he started with land reform. He signaled this commitment in his draft constitution for Virginia, which included a provision that would have entitled adult citizens to acquire 50 acres of land from the state, thereby ensuring their independence. His first targets were the common-law doctrines of primogeniture, which required that the eldest son inherit all of the father's land, and entail, which allowed persons to require their heirs to keep the land within the family. Both doctrines were designed to keep large estates intact from generation to generation, thereby perpetuating the aristocracy and limiting land availability to yeomen, or small-scale farmers (Jefferson 32). Jefferson's bill abolishing entail became law in 1776, but his bill abolishing primogeniture was not enacted until 1785. Jefferson expected both reforms to "prevent the accumulation and perpetuation of wealth in select families" and "make an opening for the aristocracy of virtue and talent," both of which were, for Jefferson, "essential to a well ordered republic" (44, 32). As president, Jefferson continued his land-reform campaign by negotiating the Louisiana Purchase in 1803, one reason for which was that it would provide land and independence for the young nation's growing population of republican citizens; additionally, it secured the lucrative port of New Orleans, thus expanding access to eastern U.S. and overseas markets for farmers and planters in the Old Southwest.

Jefferson also targeted the inequality caused by established religion, which in Virginia was the Anglican Church (after 1776 known in the United States as the Episcopal Church). As part of his campaign for legal reform, he drafted the Virginia Bill for Religious Freedom, which became law in 1786. Jefferson urged strict separation of church and state to protect the secular realm of politics and the freedom of the individual human mind from the corrupting alliance of church and state, as well as the inequality that resulted from official preference of a particular denomination.

Public education was as essential to Jefferson's political ideology as land ownership and the separation of church and state. Traditionally, liberal education had been limited largely to the elites. If the republic was to survive, Jefferson insisted, all its citizens would need to be educated enough to be "able to guard the sacred deposit of the rights and liberties of their fellow citizens" (Matthews 365). For Virginia, Jefferson proposed "A Bill for the More General Diffusion of Knowledge," which outlined an elaborate public school system that would enable the most talented students to rise "without regard to wealth, birth, or other accidental condition or circumstance" (ibid.). As president, he sought funding from Congress for public education and a national university.

In the 1790s, Jefferson became the spearhead of the Republican faction and the articulator of its popular, agrarian-based ideology. He opposed the fiscal policies of Alexander Hamilton and the Federalists, which were designed to produce an economy based on manufacturing and commerce and a government grounded on support from the nation's creditors and monied interests. Instead, Jefferson promoted his vision of an agrarian republic, in which all men were educated and owned enough land to be self-sufficient and, therefore, politically independent.

Jefferson was elected president in 1800 and reelected in 1804. His first term was very successful. His second term, however, was marred by increasing hostilities with Britain and a hugely unpopular and failed embargo instituted to address them. He spent his retirement years conducting a memorable correspondence with his old friend and colleague John Adams and playing the central role in founding the University of Virginia, the most enduring act of his campaign for public education. Jefferson died on July 4, 1826, exactly 50 years after the Declaration of Independence was adopted.

Michael D. Hattem

See also: "The Elites"; Shays's Rebellion (1786–1787)

References

Bernstein, R. B. *Thomas Jefferson.* New York: Oxford University Press, 2003.

Cogliano, Francis D., ed. *A Companion to Thomas Jefferson.* Malden: Blackwell, 2012.

Jefferson, Thomas. *Thomas Jefferson: Writings.* Edited by Merrill D. Peterson. New York: Library of America, 1984.

Matthews, Richard K. *The Radical Politics of Thomas Jefferson: A Revisionist View.* Lawrence: University Press of Kansas, 1984.

Oberg, Barbara B., and J. Jefferson Looney, eds. *The Papers of Thomas Jefferson Digital Edition.* Charlottesville: University of Virginia Press, Rotunda, 2008.

Staloff, Darren. "The Politics of Pedagogy: Thomas Jefferson and the Education of a Democratic Citizenry." In Frank Shuffleton, ed., *The Cambridge Companion to Thomas Jefferson* (pp. 127–142). New York: Cambridge University Press, 2009.

Jones, Mary Harris/Mother Jones (1837–1930)

Mary Harris Jones, better known as Mother Jones, was a prominent labor leader and organizer during the late 1800s and the early 1900s. She gained national notoriety by traveling to areas of labor strife to organize and assist the striking workers. Mother Jones aided the coal miners of West Virginia and Colorado, the steel workers of Pennsylvania, and the streetcar workers in Chicago. She argued for class solidarity and equality through her version of class warfare, which emphasized collective action. She believed that all workers, regardless of skin color or nationality, were one and the same and needed to band together to defeat the capitalists who were keeping

The "grandmother of all agitators" Mother Jones, labor leader and community activist, in 1902. (Library of Congress)

them from what was rightfully theirs. After years of fighting for "her boys," she died in 1930.

Mary Harris was born on August 1, 1837, in Cork, Ireland, into a family of farmers. Her father and oldest brother left in 1847 during the potato famine and traveled to Canada, where the rest of the family joined them in Toronto in the early 1850s. Jones attended public school in Toronto through high school and then went to Monroe, Michigan, where she taught at a Catholic school for a year. She continued south to Chicago and sewed dresses for the wealthy women of the city. She then moved to Memphis, Tennessee, where she married George Jones, an ironworker and member of the National Union of Iron Molders. The yellow fever epidemic of 1867 killed George and their four children; Jones returned to Chicago and opened a dressmaking shop where she again sewed for the wealthy. The Great Chicago Fire of 1871 destroyed her store and left Jones homeless.

Mary Jones's name appeared in print for the first time when she participated in Coxey's Industrial Army. This protest march of unemployed workers was begun by Ohio businessmen Jacob Coxey. Jones volunteered to help organize the Kansas City section of the group; in the end her group was only able to reach St. Louis. After the failure of Coxey's Army to achieve its stated goals, she traveled to Birmingham, Alabama, to help the United Mine Workers with its strike; while the strike was not successful, this was the beginning of the relationship between the union and Jones. During her travels Jones also traveled in the South and saw the use of child labor in the mills; Jones claimed that it was the children in these mills who gave her the nickname "Mother Jones."

Jones was hired by the United Mine Workers Association (UMWA) to travel around the country to bring miners into the union and organize strikes. She led several marches during the 1900 Pennsylvania anthracite coal strike. In 1902 she traveled to southern West Virginia to aid in the strike that was starting there. A statewide injunction was issued outlawing union meetings, and Jones was arrested on June 20 for speaking at a rally outside of Parkersburg, West Virginia. While she was not sentenced to jail, it was during this trial that the prosecuting attorney labeled her "the most dangerous woman in America."

In the summer of 1903 Jones focused on ending child labor. She went to Philadelphia during the silk weavers' strike and tried to gain recognition for the strike by taking the child workers to city hall. When this failed she organized almost 400 textile workers in Kensington, Pennsylvania, and began a march to New York City. Six days into the march Jones decided to change the objective of the march and traveled to Oyster Bay, New York, to speak with President Theodore Roosevelt. She arrived at the president's home on July 29 but was turned away because Roosevelt had known Jones was coming and had gone on a camping trip with some of his family to a nearby bay. The strike ended a few days later.

Jones traveled to Colorado to help in the coal strike that was beginning there in late 1903. She was arrested on March 26, 1904, after martial law was declared, and she was deported from the state; she attempted to return to the strike zone but was deported again. She attempted to reenter the state through Utah but was quarantined there under the belief she had contracted smallpox; she escaped the quarantine and traveled the East Coast to raise funds until the strike ended in June.

She became disillusioned with the infighting of the UMWA and resigned her position in January 1905 to become a lecturer for the Socialist Party. She attended the first few meetings of the Industrial Workers of the World (IWW), and while she did not participate actively in the group she did raise funds for three of its leaders who were arrested for the murder of the Idaho governor in 1905. Jones then became a leader in the campaign to free the leader of the liberal party in Mexico, Manual Sarabia, who was arrested in Arizona for conspiring to cross into Mexico and incite rebellion. She severed her ties with the Socialist Party in 1911 when the party's national secretary refused to repay a loan she gave to him.

Rejoining the UMWA in 1912, Jones traveled once again to southern West Virginia during the Paint and Cabin Creek strikes that lasted until 1913. She led more than 200 miners to Charleston on August 15, 1912, to present their grievances to the governor. She then organized a group of women to harass strikebreakers and help set up tent colonies for the striking miners; she also traveled to Washington, DC, to testify before a congressional investigative committee. She was arrested on February 13, 1913, for conspiracy to commit murder in connection with the shooting of a mine guard. The ruling of the court martial was never known, but she was imprisoned until May 7, after the strike had ended.

She returned to Colorado in late summer of 1913 and helped to start the miners' strike that started there on September 16. To help the strikers achieve their goals, Jones negotiated with the Mexican government to limit the flow of replacement workers. On her return from the Mexico trip, she was arrested by the National Guard after she crossed the border on January 4, 1914. She attempted to return to the strike zone two more times but was caught each time. After being released for the third time she went to Washington, DC, and testified before the

House Subcommittee on Mines, which was investigating the Colorado mining industry. She attempted to meet with John Rockefeller Jr. on multiple occasions in 1914, as he was the owner of Standard Oil, which controlled some of the mines in Colorado, but was turned away each time. Rockefeller invited Jones to his home in January 1915, and she finally met him on January 28.

Jones participated in the streetcar strikes in 1916 and was blamed for inciting a group of women who overturned a streetcar in New York City. She then went to Pittsburgh in February 1919 to assist the steel workers who were striking. She was again arrested in August for speaking without a permit. After her release she traveled from steel center to steel center across the United States to raise funds and assist strikers.

She again traveled to West Virginia and went to the southern counties of Mingo, Logan, and McDowell to aid in the strike. In January 1921 she attended the Pan-American Federation of Labor in Mexico City as an AFL delegate. She returned to West Virginia and in August gave a speech after the death of Sid Hatfield; she urged the striking miners not to kill the pro-operator sheriff in Logan County. She attended the UMWA national convention and asked for the union to come back together so it could better aid its members.

Her final appearance at the UMWA convention was in February 1922, while her final act of union organizing came in the summer of 1926 when she spoke to striking dressmakers in Chicago. She returned to Washington, DC, and stayed in the home of the Powderlys. After making occasional visits to Maryland to visit her friends, the Burgesses, their home turned into her permanent residence.

Mother Jones died on November 30, 1930, at the age of 93. Her involvement in the labor strikes and activities brought national attention to the plight of the common worker and helped to bring positive changes to the lives of "her boys." She despised suffragists because she believed they were taking the focus away from an equitable society based on class and believed they were neglecting their duty of raising the children of the nation. She also hated anyone who she believed was not doing enough to create proper social change; one of these enemies included the head of the UMWA, John L. Lewis. Her personal opinions applied to the dead as well as the living. She called Jesus "the greatest agitator of them all" and believed that Washington, Lincoln, and Jefferson were all "Reds." Jones was able to use her notoriety to focus the nation's eyes on the suffering of the workers she loved dearly.

Kristopher Allen

See also: American Federation of Labor (AFL); Coxey, Jacob (1854–1951); Coxey's Army; Cripple Creek War (1894); Industrial Workers of the World (IWW); Powderly, Terence V. (1849–1924); Roosevelt, Theodore (1858–1919)

References

Cordery, Simon. *Mother Jones: Raising Cain and Consciousness.* Albuquerque: University of New Mexico Press, 2012.

Gorn, Elliott J. *Mother Jones: The Most Dangerous Woman in America.* New York: Hill and Wang, 2001.

Jute-bagging Trust

Jute, synonymous with the coarse textile burlap, was widely used during the late nineteenth century to wrap cotton bales for domestic and international transport and sale. In 1888, a business cartel known as the jute-bagging trust (also known as the jute trust or jute cartel) formed in the United States to control the production, distribution, and price of this packaging material. The trust colluded to limit production and sharply increase jute-bagging prices, drawing the wrath of the Populist movement, particularly in the South, where farmers relied upon jute to prepare their cotton for market. The Southern Farmers' Alliance and the Georgia Alliance were at the forefront of efforts to boycott jute and to substitute cotton baling as an alternative. By the spring of 1891 Populists had forced prices to below 1888 levels, and the outcome of the conflict is generally interpreted as a victory, if a somewhat hollow one, for the Populist cause.

Jute was an essential component of the transatlantic cotton economy. Every cotton bale that was packaged and shipped to the various exchange markets required roughly seven yards of jute baling. Although there were high protective tariffs in place against the importation of manufactured jute textile, most of the jute used to package southern cotton was produced—either in St. Louis, Missouri, or Brooklyn, New York—from raw jute imported from India. On the eve of the jute conflict, the annual American cotton crop required more than 50 million yards of jute bagging.

In the post–Civil War period, the price of jute bagging remained flat, but prices crashed dramatically when Congressman Roger Mills introduced a bill to end the protective tariff against jute textile imports in early 1888. Mills's efforts triggered a panic among jute producers and distributors, who, fearing their reserves would become worthless, began to cut prices and liquidate stocks. As a response to this sudden crisis, industry leaders began efforts not only to lobby against the proposed bill but to organize the collaboration of the production and distribution of jute bagging. The large St. Louis firm of Warren, Jones, and Gratz urged other companies to join the cartel. The plan involved the further coordination and centralization of jute distribution and—perhaps more importantly—to restrict production by offering smaller firms money to remain idle.

The immediate outcome of the formation of the trust was a sharp increase in the price of jute. In late July and early August 1888, the price of jute nearly doubled. southern cotton producers were already reeling under the weight of the one-crop system and declining cotton prices of the 1880s. Cotton farmers allied with southern Populists had the organizational capacity to mobilize against the trust and immediately began two related efforts to break the power of the new cartel.

First, Populists began a far-reaching boycott of jute, not only as baling but for twine and packaging for other farming supplies such as fertilizer. Populist farmers also boycotted merchants who continued to be involved with the jute trust and who sold or purchased jute products. Second, the Populists began to use a variety of substitutes for jute bagging. After initially experimenting with pine straw, they turned to cotton. Populists argued that the use of cotton baling would not only break the trust but would increase overall demand for cotton, thus raising prices and benefiting southern farmers.

But the widespread adoption of cotton baling remained problematic. Not only were there insufficient amounts of cotton baling, it was significantly more expensive than jute. But there was a possible solution to this dilemma involving the tare, or the deduction by the various exchange markets to account for the weight of the baling. The international exchanges used the "Liverpool system": for each 500-pound bale, buyers deducted 24 pounds to account for the jute packaging. The Populists urged a revision of the Liverpool system and a deduction in the tare, which would more than offset the higher price of cotton. The major cotton exchanges ultimately balked at revising the tare, and cotton baling was unable to supplant jute. Southern farmers eventually returned to jute bagging.

The legacy of the jute conflict remains ambiguous. On one hand, jute remained the standard packaging material for southern cotton and was increasingly controlled by a small number of firms. Thus, southern Populists failed in their efforts to break the trust and to find a viable substitute. On the other hand, the Populists forced these firms to sharply lower prices to pre-1888 levels. In this light, the jute conflict remains one of the great displays of collective strength by southern Populism and can be interpreted as a triumph for the Populist movement.

Jeffrey D. Howison

See also: Gilded Age; Robber Barons; Tenant Farming

References

Holmes, William F. "The Southern Farmers' Alliance and the Jute Cartel." *Journal of Southern History* 60 (1): 59–80.

Schwartz, Michael. *Radical Protest and Social Structure: The Southern Farmers' Alliance and Cotton Tenancy, 1880–1890.* Chicago: University of Chicago Press, 1976.

Woodward, C. Vann. *Tom Watson: Agrarian Rebel.* London: Oxford University Press, 1938.

K

Kansas, Populism in

While the Populist movement was initially a southern phenomenon directly connected to the abuses of the crop lien system, during the 1880s the movement spread to other parts of the country, particularly to the Great Plains. No Plains state played a more prominent role in the Populist movement than Kansas. The principal motivation for Kansas farmers was not the same as for tenant farmers in the South, however. During the late 1870s, Kansas experienced an agricultural boom. Prices for such commodities as wheat and corn rose, land prices increased, and railroad tracks expanded. For the many farmers who migrated to Kansas in the 1870s, getting a piece of the economic pie meant getting land, and getting land meant going into debt. As long as prices remained strong, however, all was well.

In the early 1880s, however, the expansion bubble burst. Commodity prices fell rapidly. Wheat, for instance, dropped from $1.19 per bushel in 1881 to $0.49 per bushel by 1894. By the early 1890s, the typical Kansas farmer was paying more to produce a crop of wheat or corn then that crop would pay at harvest time. As commodity prices dropped, land values fell. By the early 1890s most farmers owed more on their mortgages than their property was worth. By 1890, Kansas had a per capita debt that was four times the national average, while the assessed value of its property was only approximately 50 percent of its mortgaged value.

The state of Kansas entered the Union as a fiercely Republican state. In the 1880s, Kansas was still solidly Republican. To economically distressed farmers, however, the Republican leaders of Kansas appeared tone deaf to their plight. For this reason, many Kansas farmers became attracted to the monetary theories of the Greenback Party and the cooperative ideas of the Farmers' Alliance. The latter organization had attempted to mitigate agrarian distress by uniting farmers into cooperatives, the primary purpose of which was to unite farmers as sellers and purchasers, getting them fair value for crops and cheaper credit from lenders. The first real Alliance activism in Kansas occurred in Cowley County (southeastern Kansas) and was largely brought about by the efforts of Henry Vincent, who with his brothers edited *The American Nonconformist and Kansas Industrial Liberator.* By December 1888, the larger Southern Alliance moved into Kansas, establishing the Kansas State Alliance and electing former Greenback Party member Benjamin Clover as president. The Kansas State Alliance absorbed many of the other Alliance organizations and, by 1890, could boast a membership of 100,000 members and 2,000 suballiances.

As staunchly Republican as most of the farmers of Kansas were, by 1890 there was also considerable enthusiasm for independent political action. Career politicians, such as Republican U.S. Senator John J. Ingalls, seemed indifferent to the suffering of the agrarian economy. Farmers wanted relief from usurious banking practices, protection from steep railroad rates, and an expanded money supply, preferably paper based, to counteract the deflation caused by the return to the gold standard. A March 25, 1890, convention in Topeka led to the formation of the People's Party State Central Committee. When the state central committee gathered again in Topeka in the summer of 1890 to contemplate a course of action, delegates decided to call for a separate convention to meet in in the same town on August 13, 1890, with the task of nominating Alliance candidates for state and congressional offices.

The Topeka convention endorsed the public ownership of transportation and communication, the unlimited coinage of silver, an equitable taxation system, the use of paper (fiat currency), and a prohibition against alien ownership of railroads. In an eventful campaign that featured charismatic speakers such as Mary Elizabeth Lease, a lawyer and wife of a Wichita druggist, and "Sockless" Jerry Simpson, a colorful farmer who resided in Medicine Lodge, Kansas, and was the Alliance candidate for the 7th congressional district, Alliance candidates shocked Republicans. While gubernatorial candidate John Willits was defeated, Alliance supporters captured five of eight congressional seats as well as taking 96 of 125 seats in the lower house of the state legislature. The latter victory would allow Alliance candidate William A. Pfeffer, the editor of the *Kansas Farmer*, to succeed incumbent John J. Ingalls in the U.S. Senate.

The Kansas success created momentum for national independent political action that helped create the National People's Party in 1892 and led to the drafting of the Omaha platform and the nomination of former Greenbacker and Union General James B. Weaver as a presidential candidate. Weaver carried five states, including Kansas. The Populist groundswell also led to the election of a Populist governor in Kansas, Lorenzo Lewelling, as well as several state executive offices. While continuing to send five of eight Populist congressmen to Washington, the Populists lost their majority in the state house to the Republican Party, largely as the result of electoral fraud.

While Populists controlled the state government from 1893 to 1895, divisions over such issues as prohibition and woman suffrage divided the movement. Also a contributing factor to party divisions was poor appointments made by Governor Lewelling. Finally, purists within the People's Party resisted the fusionist arrangement with the Democratic Party in the 1894 elections. In the elections of 1890 and 1892, Democrats and People's Party candidates had often collaborated, agreeing on supporting a single candidate for congressional or state house seats. When this cooperation ended, the People's Party was supplanted by the Republican Party in the fall 1894 elections.

Although the People's Party had made an impressive showing in the early 1890s, there were a number of forces working against its continuation as a viable independent political organization. Traditional party loyalties reinforced by sectionalism continued to challenge the autonomy of the People's Party. Even more threatening was the increasing popularity of the silver issue. In many western states where the mining of silver was a cornerstone of the local economy, mine owners and mine workers feigned agreement with the People's Party, as did many members of the Democratic Party. In reality, many of these groups had little real interest in farm issues but used the free silver issue to coopt the People's Party. In a fateful decision, the People's Party decided to forgo nominating its own candidate for president in 1896 and instead endorsed Democratic nominee William Jennings Bryan, whose principal issue was the unlimited coinage of silver. In Kansas, People's Party officials once again endorsed fusion with Democratic candidates in an effort to turn back Republicans. Although Populist candidates carried Kansas in the 1896 elections, electing George Leedy as governor, the decline in the effectiveness of the People's Party in the nation was also reflected in Kansas. Fusion with the Democratic Party narrowly focused the once broad Populist agenda on a single issue: silver. Additionally, the economy improved in the late 1890s. New gold finds allowed the expansion of currency and the rise of agricultural prices. The latter, combined with a boom harvest, allowed the Republicans to dominate Kansas politics after 1898 and for years into the future.

Bruce Tap

See also: *American Non-Conformist*; Gold Standard/Free Silver; Greenback Party; Lease, Mary (1850–1933); Lewelling, Lorenzo D. (1846–1900); Peffer, William A. (1831–1912); People's Party; Plains and Midwest, Populism in the; Populism

References

Argersinger, Peter H. *The Limits of Agrarian Radicalism: Western Populism and American Politics.* Lawrence: University Press of Kansas, 1995.

Clanton, O. Gene. *Populism: The Humane Preference in America, 1890–1900.* Boston: Twayne Publishers, 1991.

Davis, Kenneth S. *Kansas: A Bicentennial History.* New York: W.W. Norton & Company, 1976.

Goodwyn, Lawrence. *Democratic Promise: The Populist Moment in America.* New York: Oxford University Press, 1976.

Goodwyn, Lawrence. *The Populist Moment: A Short History of Agrarian Revolt in America.* New York: Oxford University Press, 1978.

Postel, Charles. *The Populist Vision.* New York: Oxford University Press, 2007.

Kansas City Conference (1901)

The Kansas City Conference was held on June 19, 1901, as an attempt to inaugurate a third-party movement in Missouri. It resulted in the creation of the Allied Third Party, to be used as a way to increase the role of the public in the legislative process and to promote Populist issues on the state level.

After the 1900 presidential election, which saw the Populist Democratic candidate William Jennings Bryan lose for the second time, conservative Democrats were successful at gaining control of the party mechanisms at the national level and in many states. In response, many Bryan supporters and others with Populist leanings became dissatisfied with the Democratic Party. The Kansas City Conference resulted from dissatisfaction with the state Democratic Party in Missouri and was attended by a number of representatives from Populists of different persuasions including Free Silver Republicans, Socialists, Bryan Democrats, and public ownership advocates. The conference was an attempt to unite several smaller parties in Missouri to try to contest political control of the Democrats and Republicans in the state.

The members of the executive committee approved a platform that endorsed direct legislation of the people by ballot initiative and referendum, along with the direct election of president, vice president, federal judges, and senators. The conference also supported the creation of a department of labor and equitable arbitration, the public ownership of all public utilities such as railroads and telegraphs, a progressive income tax, and more local control for cities in the state.

While William Jennings Bryan did not officially endorse the new party, party leaders did travel to his home in Lincoln, Nebraska, to discuss the new party, and their platform endorsed many of the same measures he supported in his previous campaigns. The party originally hoped to expand to other states with the goal of nominating a candidate in the 1904 presidential election, but it did not move beyond some unsuccessful congressional and local contests in Missouri.

Michael A. Ridge Jr.

See also: Bryan, William Jennings (1860–1925); People's Party; Silver Republicans; Third Parties

References

Coletta, Paolo E. *William Jennings Bryan: I: Political Evangelist, 1860–1908*. Lincoln: University of Nebraska Press, 1964.

Langland, James. *The Chicago Daily News Almanac for 1902*. Chicago: The Chicago Daily News Company, 1902.

Townsend, Malcolm. *Handbook of United States Political History for Readers and Students*. Boston: Lothrop, Lee & Shepherd Co., 1905.

Kaweah Colony

Kaweah Colony was a utopian settlement by established in 1885 by a group of residents wanting to own land in the Sierras of eastern Tulare County, California. The Kaweah Co-Operative Commonwealth colony residents claimed land under the Timber and Stone Act of 1878, which attracted the attention of Land Patent Office agents who suspected fraud and refused to approve the 12,000 acres of land for what they considered to be a large number of claims. Fifty-three claims were made by colonists, many of whom used the same address for their claims. While awaiting the adjudication of the timber claims, residents continued the process of establishing their utopian society near the Kaweah River.

Founded on the socialist principals of Laurence Gronlund, author of *The Co-operative Commonwealth*, and led by San Francisco labor activists Burnette G. Haskell and James J. Martin, the colony employed a labor-check method of payment that was dependent on work performed in exchange for cash. The colony had decided to use timber as the main source of income and built a road to the timber claims. By the end of four years, 18 miles of camp roads were built with simple tools while the government had opted for the creation of Sequoia National Park. This resulted in the denial of land patents to the residents of the Kaweah Colony and their future removal from the land.

Though membership never exceeded more than 300, by 1892 the colony had disbanded, yet vestiges of its brief existence still remain. Its newspaper, the *Kaweah Commonwealth*, which was printed on a weekly basis and had a running time of two years from 1890 to 1892, is extant. Also, the Kaweah Post Office and the road leading to California's first, and the United States' second largest, national park are both contributions for which the colonists were responsible. The road built by the colonists represented part of the only entrance to Sequoia National Park until 1926.

Gustavo Adolfo Aybar

See also: Cooperative Commonwealth; Gilded Age; Gronlund, Laurence (1849–1899); Haskell, Anna Fader (1858–1942); Haskell, Burnette G. (1831–1889); Homestead Act (1862)

References

Elliott, John, and Sarah Barton Elliott, eds. "The History of Kaweah Colony," Kaweah Commonwealth. http://www.kaweahcommonwealth.com/kaweahcolonyhistory.html. Accessed January 7, 2013.

Hine, Robert V. *California's Utopian Colonies*. San Marino, CA: Huntington Library, 1953.

O'Connell, Jay. *Co-Operative Dreams: A History of the Kaweah Colony*. Van Nuys, CA: Raven River Press, 1999.

Kelley, Oliver Hudson (1826–1913)

O. H. Kelley was a founding member of the Patrons of Husbandry, the farmer's organization better known by the name he borrowed from a popular nineteenth-century novel, "the Grange." Due to his central role in spreading the "Gospel of the Grange," he is remembered as "Father Kelley" by many Grangers.

Oliver Hudson Kelley was born the fifth son of a Boston tailor in 1826. As a young man, he held several white-collar jobs, including newspaper reporter, telegrapher, and as support staff for the legislature of the Minnesota territory. Thwarted dreams of becoming rich from land speculation resulted in Kelley occupying a claim and taking up farming despite a lack of agricultural experience. In 1852, at Itasca, Minnesota, Kelley founded the Benton County Agricultural Society, which sought to bring commercial farming to the frontier under more favorable conditions for the farmer. He also tried to develop a town site but suffered severe financial losses in the panic of 1857.

Kelley then focused on commercial farming, which made him aware of several structural barriers to success emanating from big business syndicates, including railroads that exploited their monopolies by overcharging farmers for transporting their grain to market. During the winter of 1864–1865, Kelley drew on political connections to gain a clerkship in the new U.S. Department of Agriculture's central office. In 1866, Kelley was given the responsibility for touring and collecting data on the state of southern agriculture. Despite his status as a New England Yankee in the post–Civil War milieu, Kelley took advantage of his membership in the Masons to bridge the North-South cultural divide. This experience convinced Kelley of the potential for a secret society to create bonds among farmers across the United States' different regional cultures.

With this background, Kelley became the visionary behind the Grange. After struggling to develop rituals and a constitution for an agricultural organization, he recruited the other six founding members. Kelley's correspondence with these men from 1867 suggested a secret society where people would be admitted to degrees within a framework of Grange ritualism. In contrast to the Masons, the Grange was a family organization open to both sexes. Passage through the degrees was related to practical and moral lessons, invoking the symbolism of the common tools of rural life.

This basic structure was accepted by the founders, and the first Grange was established at Washington, DC, in January 1868. That spring, Kelly undertook a journey from the capital back to his homestead in Minnesota to organize Granges. The trip was something of a failure. He was only successful in establishing one permanent Grange at Fredonia, New York. Kelley even had to borrow his train fare home from the Masons Lodge in Madison, Wisconsin. It is unclear whether the Grange would have continued had it not been for Temperance Lane Kelley giving her husband's cause a $500 cash injection from a secret inheritance.

While the group in the District of Columbia had been more concerned with individualistic self-improvement, his wife's support allowed Kelley to refocus the Grange as organization for uniting farmers in the face of mutual challenges. His experience with the agricultural society in Benton County proved to be valuable in changing the organization's focus. Kelley also shifted his campaigning strategy, promoting the Grange through newspaper articles and holding large promotional events, including a free "Strawberry Pic-Nic" at his own farm. Soon newspapers began endorsing Kelley's populist vision for the Grange, which sought to both insulate farmers against exploitive business interests and provide a forum for education and socialization among rural people. This strategy produced a strong base in Minnesota from which the movement was able to expand rapidly. By December 1873, there were about 9,000 Granges established in the United States and eastern Canada with a total estimated membership of 700,000. As a result, Kelley was in a strong position to push for legislative change, and he also began establishing alternative structures, including cooperatives, for both the purchasing of supplies and the selling of agricultural production, challenging the hold that big business had on North American farmers.

However, by the mid-1870s some of these initiatives failed and Grange membership began to decline. Kelley's reputation was also tarnished when his brother-in-law, the master of the New York City Grange, was found to have been dishonest in business dealings with other Granges. The charter of that Grange was revoked in 1875 amid public uproar. Following this incident and a failed attempt to organize an order for more radical members within the organization, Kelley's enthusiasm for the Grange waned. He resigned from his position as secretary in 1878, and although he occasionally spoke at Grange events, he never held another national office within the organization.

Many Grangers who shared his activist agenda left the movement around the same time. Often, their energies were transferred to the Greenback Party and the Farmers' Alliance. The latter's success in endorsing candidates for Congress, state legislatures, and governorships in the 1890 elections was a major influence on the founding of the People's Party. The 1892 Populist platform was written by one of Kelley's early Grange organizers from Minnesota. As such, it is not surprising that the People's Party platform showed preferences for Kelley's Populist policies, which had helped to drive the Grange's early success.

During his later life, Kelley focused much of his time developing the town of Carrabelle, Florida, which he founded in 1877. He died in Washington, DC, in 1913. His northwestern legacy is represented by the Kelley Farm National Historical Landmark, originally purchased by the National Grange in 1935, now run as a living museum by the Minnesota Historical Society. Kelley was inducted into the National Agricultural Center's Hall of Fame in October 2006.

Christopher William Hrynkow

See also: Granger Movement, Greenback Party, People's Party

References

Barns, William D. "Oliver Hudson Kelley and the Genesis of the Grange: A Reappraisal." *Agricultural History* 41 (3): 229–224.

Gilman, Rhoda R., and Patricia Smith. "Oliver Hudson Kelley: Minnesota Pioneer, 1849–1868." *Minnesota History* 40 (7): 330–338.

Howard, David H. *People, Pride and Progress: 125 Years of the Grange in America*. Washington, DC: National Grange, 1992.

Kelly, Oliver H. *Origins and Progress of the Patrons of Husbandry in the United States: A History from 1866 to 1873*. Philadelphia: A.J. Wagenseller, 1875.

Kramer, Dale. *The Wild Jackasses: The American Farmer in Revolt*. New York: Hastings House Publishers, 1956.

Martin, Edward Wilson. *History of the Grange Movement: Or the Farmer's War against Monopolies*. Philadelphia: National Publishing Company, 1873.

New York Times Archives

Nordin, Sven D. *Rich Harvest: A History of the Grange, 1867–1900*. Jackson: University of Mississippi Press, 1974.

Robinson, William L. *The Grange, 1867–1967: First Century of Service and Evolution*. Washington, DC: National Grange, 1966.

Woods, Thomas A. *Knights of the Plow: Oliver H. Kelley and the Origins of the Grange in Republican Ideology*. Ames: Iowa State University Press, 1991.

Kellie, Luna (1857–1940)

Luna Elizabeth Sanford Kellie represented many of the rural men and women who were drawn to the Farmers' Alliance of the 1880s, the forerunner of the People's Party of the 1890s, as they struggled with the harsh conditions associated with farming throughout the South and Midwest. Kellie rose to prominence in the Nebraska Farmers' Alliance for her stirring speech, "Stand Up for Nebraska," at the January 1894 meeting of the Nebraska Farmers' Alliance. The speech expressed her "mid-road" politics as she and a minority of other Nebraska Populists rejected fusion with the Democratic Party. She served as state secretary for the Alliance and published a weekly newspaper until 1901. Although Kellie lived until 1940, she had left Populist politics by the early 1900s, a disillusioned woman.

Luna Elizabeth Sanford Kellie was born on June 9, 1857, in Pipestone, Minnesota, one of five children born to James and Martha Sanford. The Sanfords moved around, with stays in Minnesota, Wisconsin, Illinois, and eventually St. Louis, Missouri. Kellie attended a girls' seminary when the family lived in Rockford, Illinois. In St. Louis, Kellie's mother died in a malarial typhoid outbreak. There, Kellie also met her father's foreman on the Northern Pacific railroad bridge, James Thomas Kellie, a Canadian immigrant. They were married in 1874 and followed her father and his new wife to homestead in Nebraska in 1875. It was as farmers living first in Adams County and eventually in Kearney County, Nebraska, that the Kellies became staunch Farmers' Alliance members as they struggled to support themselves and their family of 11 living children.

The Kellies lost their first farm in 1883 and moved to a timber claim in Kearney County in 1884. This marked their entry into Alliance politics. Ten years later, Kellie wrote and gave a speech, "Stand Up for Nebraska," that drew local and regional attention. In her speech, Kellie cautioned that the People's Party could not fully replace the Alliance and that important educational work remained to be done. This work emphasized the political education of the farmer. The majority of Nebraska Populists favored merging with the Democratic Party, a result of their frustration with their ability to influence national politics on issues of concern to the farmer: credit and railroad prices. In contrast, the Kellies represented a small but active minority considered to be middle-of-the-road, members of the Farmers' Alliance who wanted to create an independent People's Party separate from both the Republicans and Democrats. It was at the 1894 Farmers' Alliance convention that Kellie delivered her speech and was elected as the Alliance party secretary, a position she appeared to hold until at least 1899 when the Farmers' Alliance party in Nebraska formally dissolved. Kellie's role in the state party was similar to those of other women as the Farmers' Alliance provided for women's participation in Alliance politics, primarily in supportive positions, but recognized women as valued members. Kellie received no money for her position, despite significant duties that included scheduling speakers for the state, as well as coordinating and promoting lecturer John H. Powers's speaking schedule.

Along with her duties as secretary, Kellie played a major role in regional Populism with the publication of her weekly newspaper, *Prairie Home*, from 1896 to 1901. Kellie wrote, edited, and published the *Prairie Home* from her farm located near Minden, Nebraska, with the help of her entire family, most particularly her daughter Jessie. The paper reprinted articles from other Populist presses and contained articles written by notables of the day, including Eugene Debs, Elizabeth Cady Stanton, and socialist Edward Bellamy. As the state's Populist politics began to fail, so too did interest in Kellie's weekly. With the sale of the press, Kellie retired from politics, refusing even to vote once women gained that right in 1920.

The Kellies' experiences represented the typical participation of midwesterners in the Farmers' Alliance, even if the family was a part of the minority of Nebraskans who did not support fusion with the Democratic Party. Kellie's involvement in the state party, both as a speaker and later as the state secretary, demonstrated the inclusive nature of the Farmers' Alliance with respect to women's political participation. Although Kellie changed her stance on woman suffrage, eventually supporting the National Farmers' Alliance position opposing female enfranchisement, the Alliance recognized her political activities, even nominating her as the Populist candidate for public instruction on the state ticket. Her nomination had been forwarded by Omaha labor unions as a respected party member who would attract voters. In her speech, "Stand Up for Nebraska," Kellie reminded her fellow Populists that all were working for industrial freedom. Along with her activities in the Farmers' Alliance, Kellie supported temperance and the Methodist Church. She died on March 4, 1940, in Phoenix, Arizona. She is buried in Heartwell, Nebraska.

Amy M. Hay

See also: Middle-of-the-Road Populists; People's Party; Plains and Midwest, Populism in the; The Press and Populism; Powers, John H. (1831–1918); Timber Culture Act (1873)

References

Kellie, Luna. *A Prairie Populist: The Memoirs of Luna Kellie.* Edited by Jane Nelsen Taylor. Iowa City: University of Iowa Press, 1992.

Ostler, Jeffrey. *Prairie Populism: The Fate of Agrarian Radicalism in Kansas, Nebraska, and Iowa, 1880–1892.* Lawrence: University of Kansas Press, 1993.

King, Martin Luther, Jr. (1929–1968)

Martin Luther King, Jr., was a minister, theologian, and central leader in the civil rights movement. He grew to prominence as an organizer for black civil rights in the American South and quickly became a national figure fighting for racial justice during the 1950s and 1960s.

On January 15, 1929, Martin Luther King Jr. was born into an upper-class black family in Atlanta, Georgia. Although he was originally named Michael, King's father changed his name in 1934 in honor of the founder of the protestant reformation.

Dr. Martin Luther King Jr. (Library of Congress)

King also had one brother and one sister. At the early age of 15, he completed grade school and enrolled at the elite all-black Morehouse College in Atlanta where he graduated in 1948 with a bachelor of arts degree in sociology. In 1951, King continued his education by completing a bachelor of divinity degree at Crozer Theological Seminary in Chester, Pennsylvania, and a doctoral degree in theology from Boston University in 1955. His dissertation was entitled "A Comparison of the Conceptions of God in the Thinking of Paul Tillich and Henry Nelson Wieman." While studying in Boston, King met his future wife, Coretta Scott, who was a music student at the same university. They were married on June 18, 1953, at her family's home in rural Alabama. The couple went on to have four children. In 1954, King began his ministerial career as pastor of the prominent Dexter Avenue Baptist Church in Montgomery, Alabama. While serving in this first post, King was catapulted into the national civil rights spotlight during the Montgomery bus boycott of 1955.

Following the arrest of Rosa Parks for refusing to give up her seat to a white passenger on a Montgomery bus, local ministers and activists formed the Montgomery Improvement Association, a group focused on organizing protests of the city's bus system to end segregated service. King was elected president of this activist organization at its inception, due mostly to the fact that he was a relatively new resident of Montgomery and had few political enemies in local black or white circles. This elected position was also the first time that King was able to utilize the nonviolent activist strategies he had learned from Indian activist Mahatma Gandhi.

In 1957, King joined other southern civil rights leaders in Atlanta to form the Southern Christian Leadership Conference (SCLC). Again, King agreed to serve as president of the SCLC, an organization that became one of the central civil rights activist groups in the United States for the next decade. Three years after the SCLC was established, he returned to Atlanta to pastor the Ebenezer Baptist Church.

King's national and international notoriety as a civil rights leader continued to grow during the first half of the 1960s. At the March on Washington for Jobs and Freedom in 1964, he delivered his famous "I Have a Dream" speech to thousands of civil rights supporters gathered in the nation's capital. Later that year, King and other civil rights activists reached a milestone when President Lyndon Johnson signed the Civil Rights Act of 1964. Also the same year, King became the first black American to be awarded the Nobel Peace Prize for his civil rights leadership. King and his colleagues had another major victory the following year with the signing of the Voting Rights Act of 1965, ensuring that all black Americans had the right to vote.

In the final years of his life, King broadened the scope of his activism by initiating the Poor People's Campaign. This new crusade focused on broader economic inequalities that affected diverse racial groups throughout the United States. In April 1968, King traveled to Memphis, Tennessee, to support city garbage workers who were striking for better working conditions as part of this campaign. While in his hotel room on April 4, King was fatally shot by a repeat criminal, James Earl Ray, and was buried the following week in Atlanta. After his death, Coretta Scott King established the Martin Luther King, Jr. Center for Nonviolent Social Change to raise awareness of many of the social justice issues that King had championed during his lifetime. In 1983, President Ronald Reagan established an annual celebration of King's life on the third Monday of January.

Lance Edward Poston

See also: African Americans and Populism; Congress of Racial Equality (CORE); Freedom Riders; Great Society; Poverty Campaigns

References

Bass, Jonathan. *Blessed Are the Peacemakers: Martin Luther King, Jr., Eight White Religious Leaders, and the "Letter from Birmingham Jail."* Baton Rouge: Louisiana State University Press, 2007.

Carson, Clayborne. *The Autobiography of Martin Luther King, Jr.* New York: Warner Books, 1998.

Garrow, David. *Bearing the Cross: Martin Luther King, Jr., and the Southern Christian Leadership Conference*. New York: HarperCollins Publishers, 1999.

Knights of Labor

The Knights of Labor was the largest and most successful attempt at an all-inclusive labor union in American history. When most labor organizations were based upon skill, trade, and white male exclusivity, the Knights of Labor was unique in the collective organization of skilled and unskilled labor, along with African Americans and women. Uriah Smith Stephens, James L. Wright, and a small group of Philadelphia tailors founded a secret organization known as the Noble and Holy Order of the Knights of Labor in 1869. The Knights of Labor reached its zenith in the early to mid-1880s with several prominent and highly visible victories against the railroad industry. By most estimates, the union counted close to 700,000 members at its height in early 1886. The organization was characterized by a rapid rise in membership and a meteoric decline following the tumult of the Haymarket Square Riot of May 4, 1886. Remnants of the union continued to operate until 1949, when the last 50-member local terminated affiliation with the order.

Although the Knights of Labor is typically categorized as a labor union, it only acted as such on occasion. Uriah Stephens and his fellow Philadelphia tailors founded the organization to promote the producer's ethic of republicanism and for the social and cultural uplift of American laborers. The guiding vision of the Knights of Labor emphasized cooperation with management over division and always rejected any hint of socialism and radicalism. According to the order's constitution, the Knights existed to challenge "the recent alarming development and aggression of aggregated wealth" by industrialists, bankers, and stock speculators, as the Knights feared that these conditions would give way "to the pauperization and hopeless degradation of the toiling masses (Powderly 128)." The Knights of Labor called for an end to convict and child labor, for equal pay for men and women, and agitated for the eight-hour work day at the same wage as a longer shift. To promote greater prosperity for working people, the Knights of Labor lobbied for state bureaus of labor to oversee workplace conditions on a state-by-state level and worked toward the formation of labor cooperatives to promote greater fairness within the capitalist system.

The Knights of Labor attempted to create an all-inclusive labor union that crossed the boundaries of skill, race, and gender. Only bankers, stockholders, liquor manufacturers, and lawyers were denied membership because the founding members believed that these professions failed to contribute to society in any meaningful way. The organization achieved success coinciding with the collapse of the National Labor Union (NLU) in 1873. The NLU existed as a national coalition of trade unions, with an estimated 700,000 members at its height. The NLU relied on a policy of electoral politics as a means of advancing its agenda. But repeated losses at the ballot box, combined with a disastrous downturn of the national economy, proved to be the union's undoing. The demise of the NLU left behind a void that the Knights of

Labor filled. The Knights gained early popularity among Pennsylvania mine workers during the depression of the 1870s and counted 28,000 members in 1880, with that number jumping to 100,000 by 1885.

Both the highest level of membership, power, and prestige and the precipitous decline of the order were overseen by Terence Powderly, the son of Irish Catholic immigrants of Carbondale, Pennsylvania. Powderly joined the Knights of Labor in 1876, rose to the position of secretary of a district assembly the following year, and led the Knights as grand master workman between the years 1879 and 1893. Powderly was a strict advocate of moderation and cooperation between labor and management. The grand master workman condemned striking as a "relic of barbarism," much to the chagrin of the more radical elements of the growing organization. Powderly's dual commitment to moderation and Roman Catholicism paid off in 1882. In that year, Powderly secured a concordat with Cardinal James Gibbons of Baltimore. Powderly dropped the prefix "Noble and Holy Order" and any vestige of freemasonry from the Knights, and Gibbons agreed to remove the sanctions against Catholics joining the Knights, officially providing the organization with a valuable new demographic.

While Powderly emphasized lawful cooperation, the rank and file of the organization called for more direct action in the early 1880s. Authority within the Knights of Labor was decentralized, leaving the grand master workman with very little practical authority on regional and local levels. A desire for more immediate action and tangible gains caused the Knights to take a more radical turn in the 1880s and to more closely resemble a labor union. The Knights waged a successful and highly visible strike against the Union Pacific Railroad in 1884 and followed up with a victory against Jay Gould's own Wabash Railroad the following year. Success against the railroads caused membership to skyrocket in the mid-1880s, and enthusiasm for striking among the members (despite Powderly's ambivalence) continued to rise. By 1886, membership numbers stood at around 700,000. The organization included an estimated 10,000 women and, despite segregated locals in the American South, 50,000 African Americans. The rapid growth of local organizations forced Powderly to place a moratorium on the issuing of new charters. While the organization was open to the skilled and unskilled, women, and African Americans, Chinese workers were uniformly excluded. Terence Powderly was an avid supporter of the Chinese Exclusion Act and encouraged West Coast branches to campaign for passage of the legislation.

The year 1886 marked both the high point and the beginning of the rapid decline of the Knights of Labor. Frequent internal disputes between skilled and unskilled labor weakened the organization in the midst of a large and flourishing membership. A failure of the organization in a well-publicized strike against the Missouri Pacific Railroad caused a loss of credibility and prestige. But it was the turmoil surrounding the eight-hour movement that led to the Knights' decline. The call for an eight-hour work day took a decidedly radical turn on May 1, when 340,000 workers across the United States staged a one-day work stoppage to draw attention to the campaign for the eight-hour day. Chicago's radical labor leaders called for a May 4 mass meeting in the city's Haymarket Square. In the midst of radical rhetoric and an inflamed crowd in the square, a contingent of Chicago police officers arrived on the scene to violently disperse the gathering. Amid the chaos, a dynamite bomb exploded among the police, causing them to open fire. In the ensuing struggle, seven police officers were killed (mostly from friendly fire) in addition to numerous civilians. The sensationalist press blamed anarchists and radicals for the bloodshed. One of the anarchists was allegedly a member of the Knights of Labor.

Allegations of radicalism, anarchism, and terrorism caused membership of the Knights of Labor to plunge. The decline of the Knights of Labor correlated with the rise of Samuel Gompers's new American Federation of Labor, which focused exclusively on trade unionism rather than on the all-inclusive labor concept and thereby drew skilled workers away from the Knights of Labor. By 1890, membership in the Knights of Labor had dropped to 100,000. James Sovereign replaced Terence Powderly as grand master workman in 1893. In 1895, the union took another blow when members of the Socialist Labor Party bolted from the Knights to found a more socialist-based rival organization known as the Socialist Trade and Labor Alliance. By the turn of the twentieth century, membership of the Knights of Labor stood at a paltry 17,000 workers.

Jason Hostutler

See also: American Federation of Labor (AFL); Depression of 1873; Eight-hour Day; Gilded Age; Gompers, Samuel (1850–1924); Haymarket Riot (1886); Powderly, Terence V. (1849–1924); Robber Barons; Union Pacific Railroad

References

Phelan, Craig. *Grand Master Workman: Terence Powderly and the Knights of Labor.* Westport, CT: Greenwood, 2000.

Powderly, Terrence. *Thirty Years of Labor: 1859–1889.* Columbus, OH: Excelsior Publishing House, 1889.

Weir, Robert E. *Beyond Labor's Veil: The Culture of the Knights of Labor.* State College: Pennsylvania State University Press, 1996.

Weir, Robert E. *Knights Unhorsed: Internal Conflict in Gilded Age Social Movement.* Detroit, MI: Wayne State University Press, 2000.

Wright, Carroll D. "An Historical Sketch of the Knights of Labor," *Quarterly Journal of Economics* 1 (2): 137–168.

Know Nothings

The Know Nothings were members of a short-lived nativist organization that experienced great political success in the mid-1850s. The name was most likely a self-moniker, possibly hinting at their fraternal secret society origins, and not a derisive nickname coined by detractors. They are best remembered for their anti-immigrant, specifically anti-Catholic, stances. Branches of the organization existed in the northern and southern United States and were most active in urban areas. The Know Nothings gained strength after the Kansas-Nebraska Act, as disgruntled voters expressed their frustration with the two-party system. The emergence of the Republican Party as an antislavery party siphoned off Know Nothing support and led to their demise.

The explosive growth of nearly 3 million mostly unskilled and Catholic immigrants in the late 1840s and early 1850s, who failed to easily or readily assimilate into the dominant Protestant American culture, led to tensions between the natives and the newcomers. Some native-born Americans viewed Catholicism as antithetical to the American values of democracy, egalitarianism, and freedom. Like-minded Americans sought to curtail immigrant political influence with residency restrictions on voting, strict naturalization requirements, and promotion of native-born candidates and patronage recipients. Nativists also organized fraternal societies to plan strategies, exert influence, and create fellowship with other anti-Catholics. In 1850, Charles B. Allen founded one such organization, the Order of the Star Spangled Banner (OSSB), in New York City. There was little distinguishable about this organization from any other such group that existed throughout the nation. In 1852, however, another nativist group, the Order of United Americans, seized control of the OSSB and actively worked to establish lodges and councils throughout the country. Members of the OSSB became known as the Know Nothings sometime in 1853. By October 1854, the OSSB, an organization that two years previously had 43 members, now had a membership of 1 million.

The Know Nothings' phenomenal growth can be attributed to several factors. First, American nativism historically flourished when there were controversies. In 1852, the First Plenary Council of American Bishops met in Baltimore and pushed for more parochial education, which in turn increased requests from Catholics to state legislatures for funds for private schools. Recurrent friction over Catholic or Protestant bible reading in public schools, which had caused riots in 1844 Philadelphia, ignited again in 1853 in Maine with a few protesting Catholics burning Protestant bibles and the resident Catholic priest being tarred, feathered, and carried out of town on a rail. Disputes over Catholic Church property laws, a Vatican representative's American tour, and President Franklin Pierce's appointment of James Campbell, a Catholic, as postmaster general also contributed to nativists' ire.

Another factor that influenced the Know Nothings' growth had little to do with anti-Catholicism. In 1854, Congress passed the Kansas-Nebraska Act, which lifted restrictions on slavery's expansion into U.S. territories. Many northern voters, upset with the actions of their elected representatives, expressed their antiparty displeasure by joining the Know Nothings. In the midterm elections of 1854, Know Nothing–endorsed candidates swept into power. The organization won majorities for state offices in Indiana, Pennsylvania, Massachusetts, and Maine; these last three states also elected governors who carried

Know Nothing endorsements. The Know Nothings had strong showings in New York and Ohio.

Once in office Know Nothing politicians succeeded in enacting some nativist-inspired legislation regarding church property and naturalization, as well as temperance legislation that appealed to some of their membership. Ultimately their political successes were mixed because the Know Nothings were not centralized and were often divided internally along partisan lines and subissues, which prevented them from effectively unifying both statewide and nationally.

No issue was more divisive to the party than slavery. The Know Nothings attempted to create a strong central organization at a Philadelphia convention in June 1855; instead the party was irrevocably fractured with the passage of a platform plank known as Section 12 that promised to "abide by and maintain the existing laws upon the subject of Slavery." Section 12 passed the convention while most northern, antislavery Know Nothings, led by Massachusetts's Henry Wilson, boycotted the debate. Wilson's strategy at the convention sought to unify all antislavery forces into a single party.

While Wilson failed to accomplish his mission at the convention, Salmon P. Chase and his gubernatorial boosters in Ohio found success in fusing the state's Know Nothing electorate with the emerging Republican Party. Chase's campaign platform avoided nativist issues and stressed antislavery, thereby deprecating Know Nothings' primary political precept. Chase went on to win the election. Elsewhere in the North, Know Nothing popularity either declined, as in Pennsylvania, or became more identified as an antislavery party, as in Massachusetts. They still maintained influence in the Upper South, especially in Maryland, where half of the congressmen were party members, and in Kentucky, where Charles S. Morehead became governor.

Recognizing that the party had a sectional identity crisis, moderates tried to reunify the party in Cincinnati in November 1855. That convention pledged to restore the Missouri Compromise, thereby alleviating the slavery issue. This attempt at reconciliation was quickly undone when voting for speaker began in the U.S. House of Representatives. Americans (the political party name appropriated by Know Nothings) and opposition party legislators dominated the membership of the Thirty-fourth Congress. Despite this, the prolonged and divisive votes for speaker revealed once again the deep sectional loyalties dividing the Know Nothings.

In 1856, the American Party nominated former president Millard Fillmore as their presidential candidate. This nomination convinced any of the antislavery faction left in the party to abandon it. In 1850, President Fillmore supported the Fugitive Slave Law, and as presidential candidate in 1856 he favored conciliation with the South. During the campaign, Know Nothings resurrected nativist prejudices in suggesting that Republican presidential candidate John C. Frémont was a Catholic. The Know Nothings' performance in the election of 1856 was underwhelming. Fillmore received about a fifth of the popular vote and won only Maryland's electoral votes. In Congress, Know Nothings picked up four seats in the Senate but lost more than 35 seats in the House.

Fillmore's defeat effectively spelled the end of the Know Nothings as a political organization, although some holdouts helped form the Constitutional Union Party and ran Know Nothing Senator John Bell of Tennessee for president in 1860. Most Know Nothings transferred their membership to the Republican Party, which presented a delicate balancing act for leading party politicians, such as Abraham Lincoln. Lincoln had always been privately critical of Know Nothings, once commenting, "When the Know-Nothings get control," it [the Declaration of Independence] will read "all men are created equal, except negroes, and foreigners, and catholics" (Anbinder 266). Publicly, Lincoln knew he could not alienate this important faction in the party. He regularly corresponded with former Know Nothings during the campaign of 1860 and appointed Edward Bates, a former Know Nothing, as attorney general. Nativism did not die with the Know Nothings, but a history of the organization shows that religious and ethnic controversies were necessary to keep the public's attention, and in the 1850s slavery controversies, including the Kansas-Nebraska Act, the Dred Scott case, and John Brown's raid, overshadowed nativist issues.

Chandler S. Lighty

See also: Shays's Rebellion (1786–1787)

References

Anbinder, Tyler. *Nativism and Slavery: The Northern Know Nothings and the Politics of the 1850s*. New York: Oxford University Press, 1992.

Levine, Bruce. "Conservatism, Nativism, and Slavery: Thomas R. Whitney and the Origins of the Know Nothing Party." *Journal of American History* 88 (2): 455–488.

Voss-Hubbard, Mark. *Beyond Party: Cultures of Antipartisanship in Northern Politics before the Civil War*. Baltimore, MD: Johns Hopkins University Press, 2002.

Ku Klux Klan (KKK)

Although the Ku Klux Klan (KKK) is perhaps best known as a small fringe group advocating racism and violence, in the 1920s the group galvanized millions of men and women across the nation through populist appeals that pitted white, native-born, Protestant Americans against a dizzying array of "others" including Catholics, Jews, blacks, immigrants, foreigners, bootleggers, and alleged immoralists of every kind.

The original KKK was founded in 1865 in an attempt to preserve the power of white southerners during the instability of the Reconstruction era and persisted until 1872. In 1915, William Simmons began rebuilding the Klan from a headquarters in Atlanta, Georgia. Simmons's Klan combined the white supremacist views of the original KKK with the structure and practices of the fraternal orders that were a social mainstay of the times. It was not until 1920 that the organization began to spread rapidly nationwide through strategies developed by the KKK's public relations duo, Elizabeth Tyler and Edward Clarke. In 1923, Robbie Gill Comer founded the Women of the Ku Klux Klan, which was headquartered in Little Rock, Arkansas, and was officially allied with the men's Klan in Atlanta. The majority of Klan membership, which is generally estimated to have included 4 to 5 million men and 1 million women, was organized through these two entities. A great variety of smaller unaffiliated Klan and Klanlike groups were also active during this period. Although the KKK of the 1920s grew rapidly, its decline in the 1930s was similarly dramatic. The disintegration of the organization has been attributed to a series of scandals involving Klan leaders and may also reflect a decline in leisure time due to the economic hardships brought on by the Great Depression.

Klan membership requirements, for both men and women, included three key demographic features—members had to be white, Protestant, and born as citizens in the United States. Applicants were also evaluated to determine if they were morally upright members of their communities. Accepted members then had to pay a fee between $10 and $25, or approximately $115 to $287 adjusted for inflation, which made some degree of affluence a de facto membership requirement. Once initiated, Klanspeople were officially citizens of what they termed the "Invisible Empire" that operated inside the United States. All people who were not citizens were "Aliens" who inhabited an "Alien World." This imagined empire spawned a host of related organizational terms, and so, for example, the Klan's leader had the title *imperial commander* or *emperor*, and this person could issue instructions called *imperial proclamations* and call for conventions called *Imperial Klonvokations*. This rhetorical concept of the Invisible Empire is the core term for arranging the Klan's populist appeals: members of the Invisible Empire were true and pure, while Aliens endangered American heritage, liberties, and rights.

The Alien threats to the Invisible Empire were constructed in a variety of ways. Klan literature taught that the United States was threatened by groups with foreign allegiances including Catholics, immigrants, and Jews. The Klan argued that these groups would subvert American interests to those of their home cultures. Klan materials from this time, including sermons, essays, and cartoons, detailed in particular the dangers of Catholicism, which required its adherents to recognize the authority of the Pope over the authority of the U.S. government. The Klan also aimed to preserve what they believed to be the purity of the white race. Anxieties about miscegenation and the obligation of both men and women to protect American womanhood were woven throughout Klan texts. Education, religiosity, and domestic life were also promoted by the KKK as ways to maintain the integrity of the white race and culture. It is worth noting that Klan materials from this period spend precious little time expounding upon the racism that is its hallmark. Instead, bias provided an implicit conceptual underpinning for nearly all of its arguments but infrequently became explicit. Most generally, Klan teachings promoted the authority of the U.S. government and therefore derided those who broke the law—even if they were white, native-born, and Protestant. This component of Klan populism targeted individuals such as bootleggers, corrupt officials, and philanderers and labeled them as undesirable outsiders of the Invisible Empire.

This constellation of threats was adaptable. In fact, scholars have suggested that the KKK's success in the 1920s was due in part to its ability to adapt its ideological emphases to match the concerns of local communities. Klan newspapers from the Chicago, Illinois, area, for example, show heightened concerns about bootlegging, the Klans in Texas were interested primarily with the enforcement of law and order, while Indiana Klans emphasized the dangers of Catholicism. Klan populism also reflected changes in the political landscape. Thus, Klan materials in the 1930s reflect issues absent from earlier texts such as communism and membership in the World Court.

The KKK's influence on political and social society occurred on several levels. The Klan's populist efforts to organize racism and discrimination had materially negative outcomes. For example, Klans organized boycotts against businesses owned by "Aliens," and an uncountable number of violent crimes were committed in the name of the Klan, particularly in the South and Southwest. The Klans also exerted symbolic influence on society through the promotion of virulent and divisive discourses as well as public spectacles such as cross-burnings and parades.

Abigail Selzer King

See also: Dixon, Thomas, Jr. (1864–1946); Griffith, D. W. (1875–1948), and *The Birth of a Nation* (1915); New Woman; Prohibition (1919–1933); Scopes Trial (1925)

References

Alexander, C. C. *The Ku Klux Klan in the Southwest*. Norman: University of Oklahoma Press, 1995.

Blee, K. M. *Women of the Klan: Racism and Gender in the 1920s*. Berkeley: University of California Press, 2009.

Jenkins, W. D. *Steel Valley Klan: The Ku Klux Klan in Ohio's Mahoning Valley*. Kent, OH: Kent State University Press, 1990.

Newton, M. *The Ku Klux Klan: History, Organization, Language, Influence and Activities of America's Most Notorious Secret Society*. Jefferson, NC: McFarland & Co, 2007.

Pegram, T. R. *One Hundred Percent American: The Rebirth and Decline of the Ku Klux Klan in the 1920s*. Lanham, MD: Rowman & Littlefield, 2011.

Schrems, S. *Who's Rocking the Cradle?: Women Pioneers of Oklahoma Politics from Socialism to the KKK, 1900–1930*. Norman, OK: Horse Creek Publications, 2004.

Tucker, T. *Notre Dame vs. the Klan: How the Fighting Irish Defeated the Ku Klux Klan*. Chicago: Loyola Press, 2004.

L

Lease, Mary (1850–1933)

Mary Elizabeth Lease, or Mary Ellen, was active in the woman suffrage movement and the People's Party and also as an orator, writer, and activist, particularly in the Great Plains. She is perhaps best remembered for allegedly shouting, "Kansas had better stop raising corn and begin raising hell," a statement she denied ever making, and she is credited with giving the People's Party its name (Peck 453). She was famously fictionalized in Hamlin Garland's *A Spoil of Office* in 1893.

While Lease liked to claim that she was born in 1853, she was really born Mary Clyens in Ridgeway, Pennsylvania, in 1850 to Irish immigrants. She blamed the Democratic Party for the deaths of her father and brothers during the Civil War. At the age of 20, she moved to Kansas to teach school at the Osage Mission. It was there that she met her husband, Charles L. Lease, a local pharmacist, in 1873. The couple tried their hand at farming in Kingman County, Kansas, and later Denison, Texas, but failed both times. During this time they had six children, four of whom lived to adulthood.

Moving to Wichita, Kansas, in 1883, Charles returned to his previous occupation, while Mary became actively involved in several community organizations. Her public speaking career began when she started raising money for a group called the Irish National League, an Irish political organization that sought to help poor tenant farmers. She later became involved with the Farmers' Alliance and the Knights of Labor, which led to her involvement with the People's Party. She was also passionately involved in the temperance movement and the woman suffrage movement. She studied law in her free time and was the first woman to pass the Kansas bar. In 1888, she left the Republican Party to go to work for the Union Labor Party, and she spoke at its state convention.

Roughly six feet tall, she had a passionate speaking style that could capture an audience's attention, and she was not above stretching the truth. Not one to mince words, she relied on passion and emotion to move her listeners. *Emporia Gazette* editor William Allen White, who was extremely critical of her, claimed that she had a "golden voice—a deep, rich contralto, a singing voice that had hypnotic qualities" and that "she could recite the multiplication table and set a crowd hooting and harrahing at her will" (Risjord 80, Norton 541). She had a presence that her supporters and detractors could admire or admonish.

Critics found her extremely unattractive and claimed that she was foul-mouthed, vulgar, and often illogical. Those enraptured by her called her "Queen Mary" or "Mother Lease," and those disgusted by

Mary Elizabeth Lease won fame and notoriety with her fiery speeches for the People's Party in the 1890s. (Library of Congress)

her antics called her "the Kansas Pythoness" or "Mary Yellin." Another reporter summed her up, "As one of those radical, strong, warm natures which feels and has impulses rather than thoughts. She can see a wrong and feel an injury quickly, but would be slow and far from sure in her remedies. Her mind is untrained, and while displaying plenty of a certain power, is illogical, lacks sequence and scatters like a 10-gauge gun" (Clanton 392). Lease embodied the emotion of Populism, leaving others to present the logical remedies of regulation, subtreasury plans, and banking reform.

By 1890, Kansas farmers were under severe financial pressure because of high interest mortgages, a financial recession, and unreasonable railroad rates, leading to the creation of the People's Party, which Mary quickly joined. She believed there were "two great enemies of thought and progress, the aristocracy of royalty and the aristocracy of gold" (Lease, Cooper Union Hall Speech), believing that the common man was a "wage slave" to big business. She stated in one speech, "Wall Street owns the country. It is no longer a government of the people, by the people, and for the people, but a government of Wall Street, by Wall Street, and for Wall Street. The great common people of this country are slaves, and monopoly is the master" (Lease, "In Defense of Home and Hearth"). That year she delivered 160 speeches. She even left the state and began speaking across the West and South for the Populist cause.

Lease also pushed feminist ideals and claimed that it was men's inability to do the right thing that was forcing women to enter politics. She stated, "Thank God we women are blameless for this political muddle you men have dragged us into. . . . Ours is a grand and holy mission . . . to place the mothers of this nation on an equality with the fathers." She echoed the ideas of "social housekeeping" espoused by Progressive reformers without the commitment to the feminine ideals of submissiveness and domesticity.

By 1892, Lease was actively involved in trying to transform the People's Party into a national movement. At the newly formed party's first national convention in Omaha, Nebraska, in July, Mary was asked to give the speech that seconded the nomination of James Baird Weaver of Iowa for the party's candidate for president of the United States. While by no means a practical politician, she campaigned with Weaver across the heartland and former South, passionately expressing the People's Party's platform of free silver, a graduated income tax, and the nationalization of railroads, telegraphs, and telephones.

While the Populists did not win the presidency, they received more than 1 million votes, roughly 8.5 percent of the popular vote; carried the states of Idaho, Nevada, Colorado, and Kansas; and held 22 electoral votes. Lease returned to Kansas to help her party win control of the state government and rescue the state's farmers from the "vested interests." She was a forceful proponent behind the election of Lorenzo D. Lewelling as the new governor and was held in such high regard that she was nominated for the U.S. Senate but could not garner enough legislative votes to put her in office. At a time when women still could not vote in national elections, Mary Lease nearly became the first female senator in U.S. history. Instead she was the first woman to be appointed as the state superintendent of charities.

Yet Lease struggled when the Democrats and Populists joined forces to achieve electoral victory, particularly with Lewelling's efforts to stay clear of the issues of prohibition and woman suffrage and his distribution of political appointments to Democratic allies in an attempt to keep this coalition together. Finding themselves bogged down in a war with Republicans, which became known as the Kansas Legislative War of 1893, coupled with the need to keep the fusion together along with claims of corruption and the realities of governing, caused the Populists to abandon many of their reforms.

Even the leading Populist newspapers in Kansas began to take potshots at the new administration. Lease added fuel to the fire with a November 10, 1893, interview in the *Topeka Daily Capital*. She stated that Lewelling had no "backbone" and was a "weak man." She threw several other verbal jabs regarding corruption in the administration and its moderate positions. Mary backtracked a few days later in the *Wichita Beacon*, claiming that she never said anything negative of Governor Lewelling, a "brave, noble man" (Lease, "In Defense of Home and Hearth").

Things between the administration and Lease were moving toward a breaking point as Lewelling had repeatedly approached her regarding appointing Democrats to jobs under her control, which she bristled at each and every time. Tired of her insubordination, on December 28, 1893, Lewelling notified Lease that he would remove her from her position on the Board of Charities.

A few days later, she disputed this, claiming in the *Kansas City Star* that it was not her refusal to do the administration's bidding but rather that she intended to introduce a woman suffrage plank at the next Populist state convention and that the governor was going to stand in the way of women's rights to keep their partnership with the Democrats. She stated, "Let me say now that the woman suffrage plank will go in and that there will be three tickets in the field. As to fusion the people won't stand it" (Clanton 393).

While Lewelling tried to take the high road, Lease continued her attack on her fellow Populists. A few weeks later, she claimed that the governor and his cohort had taken bribes from railroad interests, that they were attempting to peddle phony affidavits regarding a sexual relationship between General James Weaver and herself, and that the statehouse was in the pockets of Kansas City gamblers. An insider in the governor's office simply noted, "I am no longer surprised at anything she says. The woman is crazy" (Clanton 144).

In February, the state Supreme Court ruled that the administration could not remove her from office. Yet she made a clean break with the People's Party and wrote a book, *The Problem of Civilization Solved*, that advocated colonizing Latin America, annexing Canada and the West Indies, and establishing a free trade zone across the entire western hemisphere. Moving to New York, she announced that she was now a socialist while pursuing more practical activities, including teaching, practicing law, and writing for the *New York World*.

In 1902, Mary Lease divorced her husband and continued to work for the political causes in which she so fervently believed. She found of peace with the rise of Theodore Roosevelt and the Progressive movement, seeing his presidency as the natural outgrowth of almost everything the Populists wanted, stating, "The Progressive party has adopted our platform, clause for clause, plank by plank" (Hicks 421).

Mary Lease left public life in 1921 to spend the remaining years moving between her surviving children's homes. Twelve years later, she quietly passed away on the family farm in Sullivan County, New York, on October 29, 1933.

Trevor Jason Soderstrum

See also: Garland, Hamlin (1860–1940); Gilded Age; Kansas, Populism in; Knights of Labor; Lewelling, Lorenzo D. (1846–1900); Plains and Midwest, Populism in the; Progressivism; Prohibition (1919–1933)

References

Buhle, Mari Jo. *Women and American Socialism, 1870–1920.* Champaign: University of Illinois Press, 1983.

Clanton, O. Gene. *Kansas Populism: Ideas and Men*. Lawrence: University Press of Kansas, 1969.

Hicks, John D. *The Populist Revolt: A History of the Farmers' Alliance and the People's Party.* Minneapolis: University of Minnesota Press, 1931.

Lease, Mary. "In Defense of Home and Hearth: Mary Lease Raises Hell among the Farmers," n.d. http://historymatters.gmu.edu/d/5304/. Accessed January 7, 2013.

Lease, Mary. Cooper Union Hall Speech, August 12, 1896. http://www.spartacus.schoolnet.co.uk/USAleaseM.htm. Accessed January 7, 2013.

Norton, Mary Beth. *A People and a Nation: Since 1865*. Farmington Hills, MI: Cengage Learning, 2005.

Peck, Harry Thurston. *Twenty Years of the Republic, 1885–1905*. New York: Dodd, Mead & Company, 1906.

Risjord, Norman K. *Populists and Progressives*. Lanham, MD: Rowman & Littlefield, 2005.

Leisure

Leisure is an element of American culture that influences social, economic, and political experiences. Types of leisure include tourism, hobbies such as reading or sports, or even participation in a culture of beauty and celebrity. Americans understand leisure as free time, and this concept has followed a historical trajectory toward commercialized leisure, which since the nineteenth century has become increasingly a commodity. Because of its relationship to work and its identity as the antithesis of work, the development of leisure has had a profound influence on American life. Leisure, thence, can be defined as the free-time moments that influence culture.

Because humans can imbue political aspects into many of their activities, public events have combine leisure with the political needs of the organizers and supporters. In the case of national expositions and other fairs, local and state boosters used these events to portray their regions in a positive manner to attract settlers and business. Moreover, other events have caused reactions intentionally or unintentionally. In the case of the Ku Klux Klan of the 1920s, the social nature of the meetings of the organization led to Klan picnics and vacations while at the same time engendering criticism for the Klan's racist, Anglocentric values and aims.

Leisure is part of the American populist impulse. The leisure industries of the nineteenth century sought to provide entertainment to Americans of all classes. Workers who had spent long days in factories and other arduous labors looked forward to Sundays, when they could attend sporting events, parks, and amusement parks and indulge in games or rest. At the same time, many of the middle and upper classes were using their leisure time for the benefit of improvement, especially during the Progressive Era. In the twentieth century, leisure time became known as private time. This rhetorical shift did not so much remove leisure from the public sphere as change the emphasis of leisure toward being an individual right, such as the pursuit of happiness. The original nineteenth-century concept of leisure as a populist, public good thus reflected the shift of populism from a left-wing, communal ideal to a right-wing, individualized right.

Patrice Natalie Delevante

See also: Baseball and Populism; Farmers' Clubs; Film; Granger Movement; Ku Klux Klan (KKK); National Parks; Pop Music; Popular Culture; Progressivism; Punk Music; Sutro, Adolph (1830–1898); Trans-Mississippi Exposition (1898); Urbanization; Vaudeville; World's Industrial and Cotton Centennial Exposition (1884–1885); Zoot Suit Riots (1943)

References

Kasson, John F. *Amusing the Million: Coney Island at the Turn of the Century.* American Century. New York: Hill and Wang, 1978.

"The Making of Modern America: Commercialized Leisure, 1880–1920." http://www.digitalhistory.uh.edu/disp_textbook_print.cfm?smtid=2&psid=3316. Accessed January 7, 2013.

Lewelling, Lorenzo D. (1846–1900)

Lorenzo Dow Lewelling was elected the governor of Kansas at the head of a Populist sweep of the state in 1892. Virtually unknown and a political novice when elected, Lewelling's troublesome tenure as governor may have made the federal election of a fusion candidate in 1896 more difficult.

Lewelling was born in Salem, Iowa, on December 21, 1846, to a Quaker family. Orphaned early in his life, he was raised by an older sister. Despite his Quaker upbringing, Lewelling enlisted in an Iowa regiment when the Civil War broke out; his family, however, was able to obtain his discharge because he was not yet of legal age. After the war, he attended Whittier College in Salem and graduated in 1868, after which he taught and served as a school superintendent at the Iowa State Reform School. In 1887, he and his family moved to Wichita, Kansas, where he worked as a produce dealer and merchant.

Although he had been a Republican in Iowa, he did not work for that party in Kansas. Instead, he was named chairman of the People's Party of Sedgwick County. In that capacity and because he was one of the founding members of the Farmers' Alliance in the Wichita area, Lewelling was invited to welcome delegates to the 1892 Populist State Convention, which was held in that city. His passionate speech exhorting the party to "go forth to victory" excited and impressed the delegates so strongly that they nominated him for governor. With Democratic support, especially from Lewelling's home city of Wichita, the Populist ticket won with a margin of less than 5,000 votes out of 320,000. Once elected, Lewelling arranged patronage positions for his Democratic supporters, an action that would lead to a loss of support among Populists in 1894.

In January 1893, the newly elected Populists and Republicans entered into a month-long dispute over the control of the Kansas legislature. Republican candidates asserted that they had been certified by local elections clerks, while Populists argued that those certifications had been fraudulent. Each side in this "Legislative War" swore in its own leadership and membership, and each side held competing legislative sessions. The Kansas state constitution gave the governor and the state Senate the power to decide the legality of the Kansas House; Lewelling and the Senate recognized the Populist House rather than the Republican House. When the Republican House members refused to dissolve, Lewelling attempted to negotiate a compromise. On February 14, however, the situation suddenly escalated when Republicans attempted to arrest the chief clerk of the Populist House for being in contempt. Populists responded by locking the doors to the Representative Hall and asked the sheriff to protect them. The sheriff, who was a Republican, refused. Lewelling commanded the adjutant general to guard the House and maintain order. On the following morning, Republicans used a sledgehammer to break down the door to the legislative chamber, and the Populists withdrew. Lewelling ordered the state militia to remove the Republicans, but the commanding officer instead stationed his troops around the capitol in support of the local armed populace who had come to the support of the Republican House. In the face of potential bloodshed, Lewelling conceded the House temporarily, and the state Supreme Court, itself dominated by Republicans, reaffirmed the election certifications less than two weeks later. This episode led to the perception that Lewelling was politically weak, further leading to a loss of support in 1894.

In response to the rapidly disintegrating economic conditions of the Panic of 1893, Lewelling issued an executive proclamation in December of that year. Known as The Tramp Circular, the proclamation asserted that the growing unemployment in Kansas and the nation was, in part, a result of industrialization and the development of machines that did the work that used to be done by people. These now "superfluous" people, only guilty of being poor and unemployed, were regularly harassed by police and arrested for being idle. Lewelling declared that "simple poverty" should "cease to be a crime."

Despite his clear support in "The Tramp Circular" for the working classes who were deeply affected by the Panic of 1893, Lewelling did not enjoy the level of support in the 1894 election that he had enjoyed in 1892. Populists had been disappointed by his performance during the Legislative War, and they were upset by the political patronage he had dispensed after his election. Further, his administration opposed woman suffrage and prohibition, both issues that were held dear by many Populists. As a fusionist, Lewelling generally supported the effort to simplify the party's platform down into the lowest common denominator—in this case, financial reform in the demand for free silver.

In an attempt to regain Populist support, Lewelling appointed Mary Elizabeth Lease to the Board of Charities. In particular, he had hoped that this appointment would quell her very vocal attacks against him. Instead, Lease ramped up her rhetoric; in response, he attempted to fire her. Lease filed suit against him, arguing that he was not firing her because of her job performance but because of her political opposition to fusion. The state Supreme Court ruled in Lease's favor in February 1894, thus supporting and reinforcing Populist discontent with the governor.

Lewelling lost reelection in 1894 in a surge of GOP support. The loss for Kansas Populists in that election and for national Populists in 1896 should not be attributed solely to his failure of leadership. However, his failure in leadership contributed to middle-of-the-road Populist dissatisfaction with fusion. In 1896, he was elected to the state Senate and served there until his death in Arkansas City, Kansas, from heart disease on September 3, 1900.

Kirstin L. Lawson

See also: Kansas, Populism in; Kellie, Luna (1857–1940); Lease, Mary (1850–1933); People's Party; Plains and Midwest, Populism in the

References

Argersinger, Peter H. *Populism and Politics: William Alfred Peffer and the People's Party.* Lexington: University Press of Kentucky, 1974.

Goldberg, Michael Lewis. *An Army of Women: Gender and Politics in Gilded Age Kansas.* Baltimore, MD: Johns Hopkins University Press, 1997.

Goodwyn, Lawrence. *Democratic Promise: The Populist Moment in America.* New York: Oxford University Press, 1976.

Lewis, John L. (1880–1969)

John Llewellyn Lewis served as president of the United Mine Workers of America (UMWA) from 1920 to 1960. From 1933 to 1946, Lewis worked closely with Franklin Delano Roosevelt's administration to create legislation that greatly benefited the union movement, most notably the 1933 National Industrial Recovery Act (NIRA) and the National Labor Relations Act (NLRA) of 1935. During World War II, Lewis and the UMWA attempted to use the war for leverage in increasing wages and benefits. Their actions resulted in the U.S. Congress passing the Smith-Connally Act in June 1943, which was designed to put restrictions on labor unions. The remainder of Lewis's career in the labor movement was marked by constant conflict with both the federal government and other union leaders.

Lewis was born on February 12, 1880, in Lucas County, Iowa, to Thomas Lewis and Ann Louisa Watkins. His father was a coal miner who lived in poorly constructed company housing from the time of Lewis's birth to the early 1890s. By the late 1890s, John Lewis was working in a local coal mine alongside other family members. In 1901, Lewis became a charter member of the new UMWA local that organized in the area where he worked and was elected its secretary. He eventually began working at a coal mine in Panama, Illinois, where he was elected president of UMWA Local 1475 in 1910. Within a year, he received an appointment as field representative for the American Federation of Labor (AFL), where he worked for six years for Samuel Gompers. In 1917, he became the UMWA's vice president and then president in 1920. At the time he became president, the UMWA had approximately 400,000 members. By the early 1930s, the union had lost roughly 80 percent of its membership.

With the ascent of Roosevelt to the presidency, Lewis seized the opportunity to reverse the UMWA's flagging fortunes. He worked with the administration in creating prolabor New Deal legislation, particularly the NIRA, which encouraged workers to unionize. The union subsequently sent large numbers of union organizers into the coalfields to rebuild the UMWA's membership. Lewis's efforts on the NLRA in 1935 allowed for the expansion of the union movement to mass-production industries, such as the automobile and steel industries. Although Lewis helped create opportunities for the expansion of unions, the AFL proved reticent to move aggressively to organize new unions. In response, Lewis helped create the Committee for Industrial Organization (CIO) in 1935. Although the CIO was initially associated with the AFL, Lewis determined that it should become a separate entity. In 1938, the organization changed its name to the Congress of Industrial Organizations and became independent, with Lewis serving as its president. During this period, when he became the most powerful labor leader in the county, he consolidated his influence in the Roosevelt administration through the creation of labor's Nonpartisan League, which was used to funnel money to politicians who supported organized labor's political agenda. Although labor's Nonpartisan League was short-lived due to Lewis's political activities during World War II, it did mark the entry of the labor movement's money and votes into the nation's political arenas, an area where they have been very influential even to this day.

The onset of World War II changed the relationship between Lewis and the Roosevelt administration. Lewis justifiably feared that the militarization of the nation's economy would compromise the growth that the union movement had experienced during the New Deal. He began criticizing Roosevelt publicly, which resulted in Lewis's polarization from both the Roosevelt administration and other labor leaders who remained steadfast in their support of the president. This led Lewis to disassociate the UMWA from the CIO in 1942.

In 1942, Roosevelt's administration created the National War Labor Board to address the needs of organized labor in the war effort. All of the major labor unions in the country, including the UMWA, had pledged to the Roosevelt administration that in exchange for his attention to their respective issues and challenges that they would not strike during the war. The UMWA broke the pledge in 1943 on three different occasions. Congress responded with the passage of the Smith-Connally Act, which marked the first time in the twentieth century that the U.S. Congress had passed legislation that harmed the labor movement. The UMWA continued to pursue its independent agenda, which led in 1947 to the passage of amendments to the NLRA that made it easier for employers to combat efforts by their employees to unionize.

Despite the obvious harm that Lewis had personally done to the organized labor movement nationally, he remained the president of the UMWA until 1960. After World War II, the coal industry began aggressively mechanizing, and it needed fewer workers. The UMWA, which had become very corrupt, began negotiating contracts that provided improved benefits and pay for workers in exchange for allowing coal companies to significantly reduce the labor force. These contracts proved very profitable for UMWA officials at the expense of the coal miners. Lewis died in Washington, DC, on June 11, 1969.

John Russell Burch Jr.

See also: American Federation of Labor (AFL); New Deal; Nonpartisan League (NPL); Roosevelt, Franklin Delano (1882–1945)

References

Dubofsky, Melvyn, and Warren Van Tine. *John L. Lewis: A Biography.* New York: Quadrangle, 1977.

Zieger, Robert H. *The CIO, 1935–1955.* Chapel Hill: University of North Carolina Press, 1995.

Zieger, Robert H. *John L. Lewis: Labor Leader.* Boston: Twayne, 1988.

Lewis, Sinclair (1885–1951)

Henry Sinclair Lewis was born in Sauk Center, Minnesota, the son and grandson of physicians. He was the youngest of three brothers. Lewis was a solitary boy who spent most of his time reading and writing in his diary. He attended Oberlin Academy and then, in 1903, entered Yale. His earliest published works appeared in Yale's literary magazine, and Lewis became one of its editors. After graduation Lewis moved around the country, settling for a time in California, where he wrote for newspapers and began turning out stories for popular magazines. He also sold plotlines to Jack London.

After publishing one pulp novel, *Hike and the Aeroplane* (1912), under the pseudonym Tom Graham, Lewis published his first serious novel, *Our Mr. Wrenn* (1914). Over the next six years Lewis wrote several novels that were largely ignored. Then, in 1920, Lewis published his first great novel, *Main Street.* The novel is set in Gopher Prairie, an ugly small town in Minnesota. It is generally recognized as being a stand-in for Lewis's own home town, Sauk Center. A newly married woman, Carol Kennicott, relocates from Saint Paul to Gopher Prairie and is appalled at the small-mindedness, hypocrisy, and intellectual lethargy she finds there. She does her best to invigorate the town by introducing progressive ideas, but the conservative powers that be defend the status quo and Carol makes no headway. She eventually leaves her husband and Gopher Prairie but later returns and becomes a quiet, stubborn presence.

Main Street was an enormous success, selling hundreds of thousands of copies and making Lewis a rich man. The novel was slated to receive the Pulitzer Prize for 1921, but a board of trustees overturned the decision at the last minute. Five years later when the Pulitzer Committee tried to award the prize to Lewis for *Arrowsmith*, he refused it. Lewis's follow-up to *Main Street* was *Babbitt* (1922), a less realistic, more satirical novel. George Babbitt is a real estate agent, narrow-minded and conservative even as he decries these traits in others, including his parents.

In the context of the new, more consumer-oriented culture of the 1920s, Lewis focuses in on idealism in conflict with the selfish motivations of most of the American population. *Arrowsmith*, for example, is the story of the struggles of an idealistic doctor with a gift for research who comes into conflict with greedy elements within the medical establishment. *Elmer Gantry* (1927) is the story of a football player who cynically follows a path of least resistance through the gullibility of others to become a charismatic and unscrupulous evangelist. Its depiction of religious hypocrisy is so convincing that it was banned in some U.S. cities for a time. *Dodsworth* (1929) is a novel about the shallowness of the lives of the affluent Americans. Samuel Dodsworth is the former head of a successful automobile company. When he is bought out, he becomes wealthy enough that he never has to work again. At loose ends, he and his wife travel to Europe, where they are only condescendingly accepted by the aristocrats there. When they return home, Dodsworth finds his old friends to be provincial and dull. He is left suspended unhappily between worlds.

By the 1930s, Lewis's alcoholism had come to dominate his life. His second marriage failed, and his literary powers began to fail him as well. The only one of Lewis's later novels to achieve the brilliance of his early works was *It Can't Happen Here* (1935), about a charismatic president, Berzelius "Buzz" Windrip. He is beholden to big business but is elected on a platform that promises reform, thus appealing to the voters' patriotism. When Windrip is elected he begins to strip American citizens of their individual rights. A newspaperman, Doremus Jessup, realizes what is happening and fights to raise Americans' awareness before it is too late. This depiction of a fascist takeover in the name of patriotism and security preceded the official Nazi takeover of Germany and the rise of fascism in Italy, but Lewis surely saw the signs of its coming. The title became a catchphrase that still persists today, employed by everyone from Frank Zappa to Ron Paul.

In his later years Lewis moved restlessly around Europe, never wanting for money as several of his early novels were made into films and the books continued to sell. When Lewis suffered a heart attack he was told to stop drinking. He refused and died in Rome at age 65.

William C. Bamberger

See also: Cather, Willa (1873–1947); Evangelicalism and Populism; Garland, Hamlin (1860–1940); Progressivism; Scopes Trial (1925)

References

Hutchinson, James M. *The Rise of Sinclair Lewis, 1920–1930*. University Park: Pennsylvania State University Press, 2001.

Lingeman, Richard. *Sinclair Lewis: Rebel from Main Street*. Nepean, ON: Borealis, 2005.

Lindsay, Vachel (1879–1931)

Nicholas Vachel Lindsay, 1879–1931. (Library of Congress)

Poet, essayist, and novelist Vachel Lindsay was born Nicholas Vachel Lindsay in Springfield, Illinois, on November 10, 1879, to Vachel Thomas Lindsay and his wife Catherine Frazee Lindsay. Vachel Thomas Lindsay earned his living as a physician, and his wife Catherine was a Kentucky-born, European-trained landscape and portrait artist. In one of two defining experiences of his life, Lindsay's three younger sisters, Isabel, Ester, and Eudora, died of scarlet fever in March and April 1888. Perhaps in part because of this loss, Lindsay and his family were intensely religious, claiming affiliation with both the Swedenborgians and the Church of Christ. Consequently, religion colored Lindsay's poetry and prose throughout his life. In addition to the loss he felt from the death of his sisters, Lindsay also suffered from epilepsy, which caused personal pain as well as the fear of social stigma. Lindsay, who not only wrote but performed his poetry, lived in constant, lifelong fear of suffering an epileptic seizure during his performances.

Springfield, Illinois, was the capital of the state, and Lindsay was born and raised within a few hundred yards of the governor's mansion. By 1880 Springfield was no longer a small town except when compared to Chicago, which dominated the state economically and politically. Part of Lindsay's populist mystique can be derived from his embrace and celebration of Illinois, excluding Chicago; the new localism, the city beautiful campaign, and the temperance movement were implicit criticisms of large metropolitan areas and their residents.

In his own day, Lindsay was a Populist poet. He wrote a poem for Populist Illinois Governor John Altgeld, "The Eagle That Is Forgotten"; a poem for Democratic and Populist presidential candidate William Jennings Bryan, "Bryan, Bryan, Bryan, Bryan"; and a series of poems praising the beauty and virtue of agrarian life, especially in contrast to the shame of the cities, including poems such as "The Broncho Who Would Not Be Broken from Dancing" and "Factory Windows Are Always Broken." However, many who "accused" Lindsay of Populism cast aspersions on his poetic ability, ridiculing his talent by linking his readership and audience with the poor and uneducated without necessarily addressing his politics. Lindsay believed in the egalitarian rights of the common people and the moral superiority of agrarian culture. Embedded in his philosophy was the assumption that agrarian culture always, and correctly, chose middle-class leadership, if only after protracted debate. And it was this moral leadership Lindsay emphasized, particularly in opposition to economic aggrandizement that Lindsay referred to as the rule of Mammon.

One of Lindsay's primary themes was an attempt to broaden the definition of community in light of the millions of new immigrants sweeping into the country at the turn of the twentieth century. Lindsay argued for a broadening of the categories of race to allow for the inclusion of the new immigrants in American culture. His philosophy, as seen in his pioneering text on film criticism, *The Art of the Moving Picture* (1915), emphasized educating the new immigrants to the vicissitudes of both American culture and Protestant morality. He always spoke and wrote of accepting the Catholic Christianity of the new immigrants, but Lindsay's understanding of Catholicism always emphasized an Americanized Catholicism with Protestant assumptions.

Lindsay looked for ways to mass produce the moralizing and Americanizing efforts of the settlement house movement, and his solution to the problem of uplift was film, which would inculcate the masses to the proper moral order, teaching American values. Lindsay's focus on race, ethnicity, and community parallels both Jane Addams's (1860–1935) work at Hull House and his artistic training in the Ash Can School of Art, which emphasized racial and class distinctions that could be seen, depicted, and understood at a glance. In the twenty-first century, we might think of these techniques as caricatures or racial profiling. But the proponents of the Ash Can School would not have made these distinctions. They focused on the lives of the new immigrants in Boston, New York, and Philadelphia, trying to depict the reality of their lives, the poverty, the struggle, and the joy, visually. Symbols and symbolism were the key to their art.

Lindsay's only novel, *The Golden Book of Springfield*, demonstrates his assumption of the necessity for the Americanization of the new immigrants as well as the normative nature of a midwestern, agrarian, Populist base. "The Higher Vaudeville" was Lindsay's rubric for his poetic theory, and the idea was to take an artifact of popular culture and turn it to a moral or ethical purpose. Lindsay's novel *The Golden Book of Springfield* bears a striking resemblance to Ignatius Donnelly's *The Golden Bottle* (1892) in terms of both structure, action, and theme, just as Lindsay's poem "The Congo" (1914) resembled Paul Dunbar's and Marion Cooks's *In Dahomey* (1904), and Lindsay's short story "The Golden Faced People" drew from Cal Stewart's "Uncle Josh in a Chinese Laundry" (1901).

Lindsay's technique, as he explained in great depth in *The Art of the Moving Picture* (1915), relied upon borrowing the theme, structure, or storyline from a work of popular theatre or fiction and then improving on that work. Cal Stewart (1856–1919) was a popular vaudevillian who wrote and performed at the end of the 1890s and was a friend of Mark Twain. Cal Stewart's skit and short story, "Uncle Josh in the Chinese Laundry," is pointedly racist, depicting the stereotype of an irritable, bumbling Chinaman who spoke little or no English, had virtually no understanding of American social conventions, and as a result was disparaged, abused, and relegated to the status of an immigrant outsider.

Lindsay took the caricature of the outsider Chinaman and turned it around. He argued that if white Americans found themselves as a minority population dominated by the Chinese, then Americans would discover themselves to be just as dependent, subservient, and abused as any Chinese immigrant in the United States. The white race could be enslaved just as any other, given the right conditions. Lindsay used popular culture to address the themes of race and status in the United States, turning the borrowed material to examine those themes in a new light.

The major characters, icons, and heroes that Lindsay focused on in his poetry and prose all addressed the issues of race, status, and morality. These same heroes were almost always from the Midwest: John P. Altgeld, William Jennings Bryan, Abraham Lincoln, and Jane Addams, among others.

John Altgeld embodied virtually all of the themes Lindsay would embrace: prohibition, Populism, morality, opposition to inordinate wealth (Altgeld supported the free silver issue), and the Americanization of the new immigrants. Governor Altgeld was most famous for freeing the surviving Haymarket prisoners, which was one of the reasons Theodore Roosevelt lambasted Altgeld as a communist. Lindsay's poem "The Eagle That Is Forgotten," (1913) emphasized the issues of wealth, entitlement, and poverty: "The others that mourned you in silence and terror and truth, / the widow bereft of her crust, and the boy without youth, / the mocked and the scorned and the wounded, the lame and the poor / That should have remembered forever, ...

remember no more." The fact that Altgeld himself was an Americanized German immigrant who had fought for the Union during the Civil War allowed Lindsay to hold Governor Altgeld up as almost the perfect model for a new and expanded sense of American community. The poem influenced Harry Barnard to title his definitive biography of John Altgeld: *Eagle Forgotten: The Life of John Peter Altgeld* (1938).

Altgeld embraced temperance, but prohibition was more than a simple moral issue for Lindsay. It was also a statement on race and religion that reflected the complexities of Populism specifically and American culture generally. Populism is most often seen as a Protestant political statement, and Protestants generally disapproved of the use of alcohol. However, the use of alcohol was not condemned within Catholicism. Part of Lindsay's life-long perspective, seen in *Art of the Moving Picture* and *The Golden Book of Springfield*, was to equate race, religion, and moral standing with a person's position on prohibition. In *The Golden Book of Springfield*, Lindsay went to great pains to demonstrate that the truly Americanized immigrant embraced prohibition.

Another of Lindsay's heroes, William Jennings Bryan, also embraced prohibition. Bryan was the Illinois native who ran for president on the Democratic ticket in 1896, supported by the Populists. He ran on the silver platform and was endorsed by Governor Altgeld. Lindsay's poem "Bryan, Bryan, Bryan, Bryan" (1919) depicts the East/West, rich/poor, entitled/dispossessed dichotomies of the Populist movement: "And all these ['prairie schooner children'] in their helpless days / By the dour East oppressed, / Mean paternalism / Making their mistakes for them, / Crucifying half the West, / Till the whole Atlantic coast / Seemed a giant spiders' nest ['the towns of Tubal Cain']. . . ." And "Where is that boy, that heaven-born Bryan, / That Homer Bryan, who sang from the West? / Gone to join the shadows with Altgeld the Eagle, / Where the kings and the slaves and the troubadours rest." Here we see Lindsay's lament of the failed Populist movement and how Lindsay's oratorical style mimicked that of William Jennings Bryan. The social effect of Populism is thus passed from generation to generation in the person of Lindsay and his artistic style.

Lindsay wrote of the president who hailed from Springfield, Illinois, Abraham Lincoln (1809–1865), who also spoke in favor of prohibition: "Abraham Lincoln Walks at Midnight" (1914). He wrote of Jane Addams, who founded Hull House in Chicago, Illinois, and a supporter of prohibition: "To Jane Addams at the Hague" (1917). And he wrote a whole series of poems depicting the evils inherent in the industrial East: "Factory Windows Are Always Broken," "The Drunkards in the Street," "The Drunkard's Funeral," "The Leaden-Eyed," "The Gamblers," "The Trap," "Why I Voted the Socialist Ticket," and perhaps one of his best and most important poems, "The Broncho That Would Not Be Broken from Dancing." In "The Broncho That Would Not Be Broken," Lindsay lamented the mechanization and regimentation, driven by capitalism, that was destroying the West. Here he demonstrated an awareness that the agrarian, Populist movements he so often praised were not so pure and economically unmotivated as he might have us believe.

David W. Bates

See also: Addams, Jane (1860–1935); Altgeld, John P. (1847–1923); Bryan, William Jennings (1860–1925); Charles H. Kerr Publishing Company; Cooperative Commonwealth; Donnelly, Ignatius (1831–1901); Film; Gilded Age; Gold Standard/Free Silver; Prohibition (1919–1933)

References

Barnard, Harry. *Eagle Forgotten: The Life of John Peter Altgeld.* Secaucus, NJ: Lyle Stuart, 1938

Donnelly, Ignatius. *The Golden Bottle: Or the Story of Ephraim Benezet of Kansas.* Whitefish, MT: Kessinger Publishing, 2003.

Lindsay, Vachel. *The Art of the Moving Picture.* Edited by Martin Scorsese. Introduction by Stanley Kauffmann. New York: The Modern Library, 2000.

Lindsay, Vachel. *Collected Poems.* New York: The Macmillian Company, 1923.

Lindsay, Vachel. *The Golden Book of Springfield.* Introduction by Ron Sakolsky. Chicago: Charles H. Kerr Publishing Company, 1999.

Lindsay, Vachel. "The Golden-Faced People: A Story of the Chinese Conquest of America." *The Crisis: A Record of the Darker Races* (November 1914): 36–42.

Riis, Thomas L., ed. *The Music and Scripts of "In Dahomey."* Madison, WI: A-R Editions, 1996.

Stewart, Cal. "Uncle Josh in a Chinese Laundry." *Uncle Josh's Punkin Centre Stories.* Chicago: Stanton and Van Vliet Company, 1905.

Lodge Bill. *See* Force Bill (1890)

Long, Huey (1893–1935)

Huey Long rose from modest origins to serve the state of Louisiana as a railroad commissioner, governor, and U.S. senator. Known for his flamboyant dress, fiery oratory, political genius, and profound corruption, Long rekindled the nineteenth-century Populist tradition and carried it well into the twentieth century. He was assassinated in 1935.

Huey Pierce Long was born on August 30, 1893, in Winn Parish, Louisiana. As a young man Long worked as a traveling salesman before enrolling in Tulane University's law school. He absorbed law so rapidly that within eight months he had passed the bar exam. He entered politics in 1918 and captured the devotion of common people so completely that he was governor by 1928. As governor, Long popularized a vision of government that would work to lift up the poor, improve the state, and keep corporations from running roughshod over the people. Despite his election to the U.S. Senate in 1930, Long was reluctant to give up the powerful governorship and delayed taking his Senate seat until 1932. Senator Long continued to tighten his grip on Louisiana politics as he prepared for a presidential bid. His "Share Our Wealth" program, launched in 1934, proposed confiscating much of the richest Americans' wealth to finance guaranteed minimum incomes for all Americans and served as the core of his campaign. Although Long's plan was vague, it resonated with many Americans.

Long battled fierce critics during his lifetime, and historians agree that he and his political machine took corruption to extremes and helped institutionalize it in Louisiana's political culture. He was, however, enormously popular with Louisianans and was quickly gaining a national following when he was killed. Louisianans could point to significant improvements in the state's infrastructure and public works —new bridges and paved roads, hospitals and schools, and money lavished upon Louisiana State University to help make it one of the finest schools in the South. The people of Louisiana were grateful to Long for their state's physical transformation and for the jobs he created. All these he presented as his free gifts to the people. In reality, they were purchased at an enormous cost.

Long accomplished so much in part because his political machine's wheels were greased by forced campaign contributions from state employees and by kickbacks from those who wished to do business with the state government. Patronage was distributed to supporters, and enemies found themselves unemployed. Huey Long largely financed public works with taxes on corporations and through the sale of bonds. Taxpayers' immediate financial contribution thus remained minimal as the public works saddled future generations with enormous debt and as voters accepted corruption and infrastructure improvements without substantive reforms that genuinely raised the standard of living for the poor and the working class. Long produced results but damaged and almost destroyed the democratic process in Louisiana. He died on September 10, 1935, after being shot two days earlier in the Louisiana capitol by Carl Weiss.

Alicia Rodriquez

See also: New Deal; Rogers, Will (1879–1935); Roosevelt, Franklin Delano (1882–1945)

References

Brinkley, Alan. *Voices of Protest: Huey Long, Father Coughlin, and the Great Depression*. New York: Alfred A. Knopf, 1982.

Hair, William Ivy. *The Kingfish and His Realm*. Baton Rouge: Louisiana State University Press, 1991.

Williams, T. Harry. *Huey Long*. New York: Alfred A. Knopf, 1969.

Long-Haul/Short-Haul Discrimination

The concept of long-haul/short-haul discrimination deals with the discriminatory practices of railroad operators toward farmers, merchants, and travelers after the Civil War and before the passage of the Interstate Commerce Act of 1887. Midwest and Plains-region farmers in particular encountered practices where railroad operators and owners charged less to transport goods and people along the entire length of a line or even longer distances, for example between New York and Chicago, than for goods to be shipped between intermediate points on a line or regionally to Minneapolis, Minnesota; Omaha, Nebraska; or even between local depots. The Grange, and especially the Farmers' Alliance, made this one of their primary platform issues, citing it as a clear predatory and discriminatory practice that required state and federal government intervention, which farmers and merchants could rally behind. However, even after the passage of the Interstate Commerce Act and the creation of the Interstate Commerce Commission, discriminatory practices continued, and legal action was rarely enforced before 1900.

As railroad operators and companies moved past the Great Lakes and midwestern states in the 1860s and 1870s, numerous small operators were bought out by larger, better-financed "captains of industry," such as Cornelius Vanderbilt and Jay Gould, or were overshadowed by the great trunk lines, such as the Union, Central, Northern and Southern Pacific lines and the Great Northern line, which connected the West Coast with the rest of the nation.

As operators expanded their lines and citizens pushed further and further into the Great Plains to grow corn and wheat, the owners realized that advanced systemization and standardization would be required to achieve greater efficiency and improve profits. Owners agreed upon the standard-gauge track width of 4 feet 8.5 inches in the 1880s, and in 1883 railroad companies introduced standard time zones to the United States. But most important to the operators was the cost of shipping goods and the rates charged for commodities and passengers, which they could coordinate and monopolize because they controlled huge shares of the primary and secondary railroad lines.

Farmers encountered the greatest discrimination. In Minnesota, local farmers paid 25 cents per hundred pounds of grain going to St. Paul. But elevator operators shipped grain at 12.5 cents per hundred pounds between the Twin Cities and Chicago. Farmers in Illinois could send a tub of butter to New York for 30 cents, while local farmers in Upstate New York, with little competition, paid 70 cents to ship butter only 170 miles.

Western farmers became increasingly concerned about the long-haul/short-haul discrimination they encountered through the 1870s and 1880s. Farmers were almost entirely dependent on the railroads to ship their commodities to cities and to bring in manufactured goods necessary for survival in the more remote areas of the country. The Grange, Farmers' Alliance, and Populist movement all quickly recognized this fundamental philosophy of their constituents. These groups harnessed the anger they encountered into a policy of direct action behind which they could rally the farmers and merchants.

The Grange began supporting railroad legislation in the 1870s at the local level. Illinois legislators passed a law in 1871 setting reasonable maximum freight rates. Minnesota passed similar legislation in 1874. Railroad executives, however, continually informed governors that they intended to ignore the laws, and most laws were modified so that the railroad owners were not inconvenienced. By the early 1880s, Missouri, Nebraska, Kansas, and several southern states had passed similar rate-scheduling laws.

After the Supreme Court heard the *Wabash v. Illinois* case in 1886 and state commissions were prohibited from interfering with trade beyond their own borders, several presidents—first Chester

Arthur and then Grover Cleveland—urged Congress to enact a law that guaranteed "reasonable and just" interstate freight rates. The grassroots support of various populist movements had achieved national recognition over the long-haul/short-haul conflict.

Politicians, farmers, and railroad operators continued to debate the economic importance of rates and production into the twentieth century. People tended to agree that national transportation networks were undeniably connected with national economic growth and American vitality. Farmers produced all of the foodstuffs required by cities, which continued to expand manufacturing output. Railroads were the only way to efficiently and economically move goods east and west, and north and south—from the small-scale producer to the collection points and from the factories to the consumers who purchased the finished goods. The collective will and organization of the small-scale producer affected a dramatic shift in politics at the state and national level in the 1870s and 1880s to benefit the people rather than the more powerful captains of industry or robber barons. Populists saw success in tangible ways, even though the 1887 Interstate Commerce Act would need further support to be effective, primarily with railway rate laws in 1903 and 1906, the creation of the Bureau of Commerce and Labor, and enforcement of antitrust legislation after 1903. Despite some victories in terms of populist demands, businessmen and academics still defend the economic necessities of long-haul/short-haul rate differences into the late twentieth and early twenty-first centuries.

Paul Nienkamp

See also: Electricity; Gilded Age; Granger Movement; Interstate Commerce Act (ICA) (1887); Railroad Regulation; Railroads; Robber Barons

References

Friedman, David D. "In Defense of Long-haul/Short-haul Discrimination." *Bell Journal of Economics* 10 (2). http://www.daviddfriedman.com/Academic/Long_haul_Short_Haul/Long_haul_Sht_Hl.html. Accessed January 7, 2013.

Gordon, Sarah. H. *Passage to Union: How Railroads Transformed American Life, 1829–1929*. Chicago: Ivan R. Dee, 1996.

Hoogenboom, Ari, and Olive Hoogenboom. *A History of the ICC: From Panacea to Palliative*. New York: W.W. Norton and Company, 1976.

Martin, Albro. *Railroads Triumphant: The Growth, Rejection, and Rebirth of a Vital American Force*. New York: Oxford University Press, 1992.

McMath, Robert C., Jr. *American Populism: A Social History, 1877–1898*. New York: The Noonday Press, 1993.

Ostler, Jeffrey. *Prairie Populism: The Fate of Agrarian Radicalism in Kansas, Nebraska, and Iowa, 1880–1892*. Lawrence: University of Kansas Press, 1993.

Stover, John F. *The Life and Decline of the American Railroad*. New York: Oxford University Press, 1970.

Loucks, Henry Langford (1846–1928)

Henry Langford Loucks was an important leader of the Dakota Farmers' Alliance during the 1880s and the Southern Alliance during the 1890s. Loucks helped develop a system of elevators, insurance programs, and buying cooperatives that provided services to farmers at prices lower than other vendors could. He also helped move the rural groups into the People's Party, where they could exercise political power on a national scale. Although Loucks's political efforts were ultimately unsuccessful, they helped to popularize the idea that government should be responsive to the needs of the people and that direct government involvement in economic affairs was appropriate.

Loucks was born on May 24, 1846, in Hull, Ontario, Canada. His father was a merchant, and Loucks attended the Canadian common schools. When he was 19 years old, Loucks went to work as a merchant in the iron-producing areas of northern Michigan for two years. He returned to Canada for 12 years before moving to Missouri in 1879, where he was a lumber contractor and a steamboat man. In 1884, Loucks and his family bought a two-section farm in Deuel County in the Dakota Territory.

Unfortunately, Loucks took up farming in Dakota at the end of an era of financial expansion. Prices for agricultural products were falling, and loans to purchase land, equipment, and seed were hard to obtain. Interest rates rose, and railroads, required to get grain and other products to market, charged high shipping rates. Loucks formed a farmers' club among his neighbors to work to improve the situation. In 1885, this club and similar ones in the surrounding states gathered together to create the Northern Alliance, also known as the National Farmers' Alliance. The following year, Loucks was elected president of the Dakota Farmers' Alliance. He was regarded by all who met him as a good-humored man who wanted to work with others for improvements. Loucks also became the editor of the *Dakota Ruralist*, the newspaper of the Dakota Alliance. At the time, it was the only daily newspaper in the United States advocating socialism.

Loucks was an energetic leader who had a vision for improving the financial and political situation of the farmers. One of his first acts as president was to issue a resolution calling on the territorial railroad commissioners to force railroads to reduce their shipping rates by a third. Legislators who would not support such a move were threatened with Alliance opposition. Although some Alliance members were elected to the territorial legislature in 1886, they were often outmaneuvered by opposing political leaders.

Economically, Loucks quickly got two companies chartered to help farmers. One was the Dakota Farmers' Alliance Company, which was a buying cooperative. Using the combined buying power of the members, the company could purchase machinery and farming supplies from manufacturers at very low prices. It then sold the goods to members for 20 to 30 percent less than the retail cost. The other company formed by the Alliance was the Alliance Hail Association. The Association provided low-cost hail insurance to farmers to protect their crops. In 1887, the first year of operation for the association, more than 8,000 farmers bought the insurance.

By 1890, the Dakota Farmers' Alliance had 500 chapters and 40,000 members. It had created elevators for grain, warehouses for other products, and cooperatives where members could buy household items and farming supplies for low costs. These efforts often were in competition with railroads and established interests but helped force down the prices they charged. Unfortunately, the depression resulting from the Panic of 1893 caused many of the Alliance businesses to fail.

In June 1889, Loucks helped organize a merger of the Dakota Farmers' Alliance and the Southern Alliance, leaving the more conservative Northern Alliance behind. He was elected vice president of the new Southern Alliance. Loucks supported a more radical political program that called for more government control over railroads and elevators, regulation of monopolies, fair taxation that included an income tax, prohibition of alcohol, and woman suffrage. Other political initiatives included government ownership and operation of public utilities, popular election of senators, secret ballots, and elimination of child labor. At the local level in South Dakota, the Dakota Farmers' Alliance and the Knights of Labor joined together in 1890 to form the Independent Party and nominate Loucks for governor. The dominant Republican Party adopted many of the most popular issues of the Independent Party and campaigned hard to attract Alliance voters. Although Loucks lost the election, one-third of the voters cast ballots for the Independents.

In the spring of 1892, the Southern Alliance president, Leonidas L. Polk, died unexpectedly, and Loucks succeeded him as leader of the Alliance. He also became a supporter of the new People's Party that formed that the same year. Loucks served as chairman for the Populist convention that met in Omaha that summer. He encouraged members of the Southern Alliance to join the People's Party because he believed it offered the best opportunity to achieve the group's political goals. In some areas, Democrats and Populists joined forces (a process known as fusion) to support candidates. Loucks did not support fusion in South Dakota, which resulted in separate Populist, Democrat, and Republican tickets. The Republicans were able to win an overwhelming victory in the state. Likewise, the Populist candidate for president, James B. Weaver, was soundly defeated in the November general election in 1892.

After the 1892 election, thousands of members left both the Northern and Southern Alliances. The People's Party absorbed the remainder of the Southern Alliance. While Loucks supported this process, he was still reelected president of the Southern Alliance. In November 1893, he also became president of the new National Farmers' Alliance and Industrial Union. By 1896, Loucks had reversed his position on fusion. Populists and Republicans who supported the free coinage of silver joined Democrats to support William Jennings Bryan for president. The coalition successfully swept the South Dakota elections in 1896, even when Bryan went down to defeat nationally.

By 1898, Loucks had once again turned against fusion. He believed that the Democrats did not really support the goals of the

Populists. When the state Populist convention voted to continue fusion with the Democrats, Loucks left the party. He joined the Republican Party and offered to sway the Populist vote toward them if the party supported an initiative and referendum amendment. In 1898, the legislature passed the measure to amend the state's constitution. It was approved by voters in the general election of 1898, making South Dakota the first state to have a formal process for voters to approve laws.

After 1900, Loucks continued to write on reformist issues and occasionally to run for office. He was an unsuccessful candidate for the U.S. Senate in 1914 and 1924. He also published a number of books, including *The Great Conspiracy of the House of Morgan Exposed and How to Defeat It* (1916). He died in Clear Lake, South Dakota, on December 29, 1928.

Tim J. Watts

See also: Depression of 1893; Farmers' Clubs; Knights of Labor; Northern Alliance; Omaha Convention of 1892; People's Party; Plains and Midwest, Populism in the; Polk, Leonidas L. (1837–1892); Railroad Regulation

References

Hendrickson, Kenneth E., Jr. "Some Political Aspects of the Populist Movement in South Dakota." *North Dakota History* 34 (1): 77–92.

Remele, Larry. " 'God Helps Those Who Help Themselves': The Farmers' Alliance and Dakota Statehood." *Montana: The Magazine of Western History* 37 (4): 22–33.

Schell, Herbert S. *History of South Dakota*. Lincoln: University of Nebraska Press, 1975.

Luhan, Mabel Dodge (1879–1962)

Mabel Dodge Luhan was a patron of American literature and modern art through influential salons she hosted at her apartment in Greenwich Village (1912–1917) and at her home in Taos, New Mexico (1917–1962). The cultural vanguard that congregated around her included avant-garde artists Alfred Stieglitz, Georgia O'Keeffe, John Marin, and Marsden Hartley, writers D. H Lawrence and Gertrude Stein, writer and photographer Carl van Vechten, dancer Isadora Duncan, and radical journalists John Reed, Hutchins Hapgood, and Lincoln Steffens. Luhan's gatherings served as a focal point for culturally transformative artistic and literary communities in downtown Manhattan and in the Southwest.

Luhan was born in Buffalo, New York, on February 26, 1879, to a wealthy family. She was raised according the ideals of Victorian womanhood, against which she ultimately rebelled. She attended St. Margaret's Episcopal School for Girls in Buffalo, Miss Graham's School in New York City, and the Chevy Chase School in Washington, DC. Luhan went on her first tour of Europe in 1896. After the death of her first husband in a hunting accident, she moved to Paris in July 1904, where she met Edwin Dodge while staying at Hotel Meurice. She and Dodge married in October and moved to Florence, Italy, the following year. They purchased Villa Curonia, a fifteenth-century estate built by the Medicis in the Tuscan hillside overlooking the city.

At Villa Curonia, Luhan developed her first salon, entertaining actors, writers, musicians, expatriate socialites, and royalty. Guests included Italian actress Eleanor Duse, English actor and director Gordon Craig, American sculptors Janet Scudder and Jo Davidson, French writer André Gide, and Gertrude and Leo Stein. Luhan first met the Steins in 1911 when she visited them in Paris, where she was introduced to modern art through their collection of postimpressionist and Cubist paintings, including groundbreaking works by Cézanne, Matisse, and Picasso.

In 1912, as her marriage to Dodge disintegrated, she returned to New York and settled into an apartment at 23 Fifth Avenue near Washington Square in Greenwich Village. The Village was a bohemian center of artistic experimentation, radical politics, and cultural experimentation. The following year, Luhan resumed her salon, attracting a rebellious group of activists and writers. She hosted political discussions between anarchist Emma Goldman and socialists Max Eastman and Bill Haywood, who was a founding member of the Industrial Workers of the World (IWW). She supported Eastman and John Reed's leftist magazine *The Masses*, contributing writing and serving on the advisory board. Luhan also hosted Margaret Sanger and the Women's Birth Control League and helped to popularize Sigmund Freud's theories.

Luhan was equally important to the development of modern art. She contributed writing to Stieglitz's pioneering photographic journal *Camera Work*, which, by 1912, also featured artworks by Rodin and Picasso. Influenced by Stieglitz and Stein, she became a key promoter of the 1913 Armory Show, an exhibition famous for introducing European and American modern art to New York audiences. In addition, Luhan supported the careers of sculptor and painter Maurice Sterne, whom she married in 1917, and Isadora Duncan. Her fundraising efforts enabled Duncan to found her influential dance school.

In 1917, as the United States entered World War I, Luhan left Greenwich Village for Taos, New Mexico. The following year, she purchased 12 acres of land and a modest adobe house, which by the late 1920s she expanded into her Los Gallos estate with multiple guesthouses. After her divorce from Sterne in 1922, she married Antonio Luhan, a Native American from Taos. Throughout the 1920s much of the New York avant garde visited Los Gallos. Artists including Andrew Dashburg, Marsden Harley, Anges Pelton, Rebecca and Paul Strand, Georgia O'Keeffe, John Marin, and set designer Robert Edmund Jones were drawn to Taos as an escape from urban life. Their presence, along with poet Robinson Jeffers; writers Willa Cather, D. H. Lawrence, and Mary Austin; and social activist John Collier, helped to establish vibrant artist colonies in Taos and Santa Fe. Other visitors included Edward Weston, Ansel Adams, Martha Graham, and photographers John Candelario and Laura Gilpin.

Luhan penned numerous memoirs chronicling her cultural milieu. She portrayed her formative years and her salons in Florence and Greenwich Village in *Intimate Memories: Background* (1933), *European Experiences* (1935), and *Movers and Shakers* (1936). Her writings on Taos include *Lorenzo in Taos* (1933), an account of her relationship with D. H Lawrence; *Edge of Taos Desert: An Escape to Reality* (1937); and *Taos and Its Artists* (1947).

Luhan died in Taos on August 13, 1962. In 1970, filmmaker Dennis Hopper, who had first visited Los Gallos while editing *Easy Rider* (1969), purchased the estate. Hopper brought his own circle of luminaries including Jack Nicholson, Bob Dylan, and John Wayne to Taos. The Mabel Dodge Luhan house became a landmark in 1991 and now serves as a conference center and historic inn.

Jillian E. Russo

See also: Cather, Willa (1873–1947); Goldman, Emma (1869–1940); Industrial Workers of the World (IWW); New Woman; Sanger, Margaret (1879–1966)

References

Burke, Flannery. *From Greenwich Village to Taos: Primitivism and Place at Mabel Dodge Luhan's*. Wichita: University of Kansas Press, 2008.

Luhan, Mabel Dodge. *Movers and Shakers*. Albuquerque: University of New Mexico Press, 1936.

Rudnick, Lois Palken, ed. *Intimate Memories: The Autobiography of Mabel Dodge Luhan*. Albuquerque: University of New Mexico Press, 1999.

Rudnick, Lois Palken. *Utopian Vistas: The Mabel Dodge Luhan House and the American Counterculture*. Albuquerque: University of New Mexico Press, 1996.

M

Macune, Dr. C. W. (1851–1940)

Dr. Charles Macune was a physician and journalist from Texas who also became a charter member of the Texas Farmers' Alliance. In the late 1880s, he called for a national organization to unite all of the Alliances in the West and across the Cotton Belt. His efforts resulted in the creation of the National Farmers' Alliance and Cooperative Union, which became the National Farmers' Alliance and Industrial Union in 1889. He was the editor and publisher of the *National Economist*, a weekly newspaper and organ for the organization, until 1893, when the paper folded and publication ceased. He constantly campaigned for an expanded money supply, a more active role of the federal government in the lives of hard-pressed farmers, and an end to the crop lien system that impoverished southern farmers and drove them into tenancy. He is most known for the subtreasury plan, which he developed and advocated, as an answer to the country's financial crisis in respect to farmers.

Born in Kenosha, Wisconsin, as the third child and only son of William and Almira S. (McAfee) Macune, young Charles' early life was unsettled. His father, a blacksmith and minister, caught gold rush fever and decided to move his family to California. Along the way, he contracted cholera and died at Fort Laramie, Wyoming, leaving his children orphaned. His mother moved the family to Freeport, Illinois, where Macune received his education, but for financial reasons he was forced to drop out of school.

As a young man, Macune struggled to find a suitable profession, and during the 1870s he pursued a variety of careers. He worked as a farm laborer for a while until he became a doctor's apprentice. Still unsettled, he painted houses and even worked for a circus in Kansas. He moved to Texas after that, where he gained experience as a hotel manager and a journalist. At this time, he continued his medical studies under a local physician in San Saba. In 1879, after his certification to practice medicine in Texas, he settled in Cameron with his wife, Sallie Vickery, and established his practice.

Macune's interest in money theories and greenback politics led him to become involved in the newly emerging Alliance movement in Texas. In 1886, he became a charter member of the local Alliance in Milan County. Within the year, he was elected as a delegate to the state Alliance convention, and he soon became the chairman of the Executive Committee of the Texas State Alliance. At the time, Texas Alliances were expressing antimonopolist sentiments, and they demanded some form of help for starving, cash-strapped, drought-stricken farmers across the state.

Macune was an organizer and a visionary. By 1887, he was trying to expand the cooperative activities of the Texas Alliance to include other states in the Cotton Belt and in the West. He was the driving force behind the creation of the National Farmers' Alliance and Cooperative Union, which unified the various alliances into a single entity. During that same year, he founded the Farmers' Alliance Exchange of Texas in Dallas. The Exchange, it was hoped, would give farmers easier access to credit and loans, but it failed after only two years due to a lack of operating capital and poor business management.

By 1889, Macune gave the movement cohesion and direction. He was already lobbying Congress and mailing out Alliance literature in an effort to bring about reform and change. As the movement grew (it boasted more than 1,000,000 members in 1890), it became necessary to create a formal publication for the organization. To this end, Macune established a weekly newspaper called the *National Economist*, which became the Alliance's official voice. He remained editor of the *National Economist* until 1893, when he left his position and the newspaper folded.

Meanwhile, the situation for farmers across the South seemed to worsen. Trapped in a crop lien system, they found themselves in perpetual debt to merchants, banks, and landlords, and the ranks of farm tenants swelled. At the same time, prices for agricultural products, which steadily decreased during the late 1800s, hit new lows. The answer to these economic woes, Macune believed, should come from the federal government. It was time, he thought, for the government to abandon its laissez-faire attitudes and adopt a more proactive approach to helping its suffering citizens. One response, argued Macune, was to adjust the currency supply and increase the money in circulation. A more flexible money system would bring great relief to farmers.

Even more important, though, was Macune's advocacy for something he called the subtreasury plan. His idea was officially proposed and adopted at the five-day National Alliance convention in St. Louis in 1889. The plan was unique, calling for the federal government to establish and operate storage warehouses in every county where nonperishable agricultural produce exceeded more than $500,000 annually. Farmers would be able to store their crops in the warehouses until prices increased and they could reap a better profit on their goods. Additionally, crops acted as collateral. Loans, with an interest rate of only 1 percent, could be made by the government based on 80 percent of the crops' value. Warehouses would issue receipts to farmers that could then be used to pay debts. Under the plan, the middlemen, like bankers and merchants, who raked profits away from farmers would be removed and the crop lien system could be replaced. Instead, the government became the bank. A further benefit was that the money supply could be expanded at harvest time, when the farmers most needed it.

Alliance members across the board supported the subtreasury plan. However, there were many critics. Merchants and landlords complained about losing profits they garnished from the crop liens, bankers railed about losing their monopoly over borrowed capital, and agricultural speculators worried about the plan's impact on their wallets. Democrats, too, concerned about a third-party political movement, denounced the idea as radical. Unfortunately for the Democrats, their denunciation of the subtreasury plan, according to historian Lawrence Goodwyn (1976), actually fueled the formation of an independent People's Party.

Macune, himself a Democrat, did not advocate a third party. Nevertheless, he continued to agitate for an expansion of currency and the national adoption of the subtreasury. In 1890, he went to Congress with other Alliance leaders and testified to the Senate Agriculture Committee on the merits of his plan. At the Alliance's Ocala Convention in 1890, Macune created, and became the president of, the National Reform Press Association. Its goals were to coordinate all of the Alliance newspapers and to emphasize a grassroots understanding of the Alliance, its issues, and its goals.

After 1890, momentum built in the Alliance to form a third party. Macune expressed caution and preferred to work for reform within the two-party system. This stance brought him into open conflict with Leonidas Polk, a past Alliance president and the most vocal proponent for the independence movement. Indeed, it was Polk who presided over the meeting that created the People's Party in 1892.

By 1893, Macune's influence in the movement he helped to orchestrate waned. The conflict with Polk, the collapse of the *National Economist*, and the new direction of the party caused him constant frustration. Consequently, he distanced himself from the Populists, even though the party adopted his subtreasury plan as part of its 1896 platform.

By the end of the decade, Macune was again in search of a career. He dabbled in law for a few years until he settled on the ministry as a Methodist preacher. In 1902, he pastored his first church. He continued to preach for the rest of his life, and after World War I he became involved in foreign missions. He believed, until the day that he died, that the Alliance had left a significant mark on American history. In 1920, he wrote a history of the Alliance and deposited the manuscript in the library at the University of Texas. He died on November 3, 1940, in Fort Worth, Texas.

Clay Ouzts

See also: Peonage; Polk, Leonidas L. (1837–1892); The Press and Populism; Subtreasury Plan; Tenant Farming; Texas, Populism in

References

Goodwyn, Lawrence. *Democratic Promise: The Populist Moment in America.* New York: Oxford University Press, 1976.

McMath, Robert C., Jr. *Populist Vanguard: A History of the Southern Farmers' Alliance.* Chapel Hill: University of North Carolina Press, 1975.

Piott, Steven. *American Reformers, 1870–1920: Progressives in Word and Deed.* Lanham, MD: Rowman & Littlefield, 2006.

Maxwell, Samuel (1825–1891)

Samuel Maxwell was born on May 20, 1825, and died on February 11, 1891. He is known best for his role as an active member of the People's Party and as a

U.S. congressman who represented the third congressional district of Nebraska.

Maxwell was born in New York State just outside the town of Syracuse. Although not much is known about his childhood, when he was 19 years old he moved with his family to Michigan and became involved in a variety of pursuits. He worked in the areas of agriculture and education while beginning his studies in the field of law. After a brief hiatus in Nebraska—where he worked for a brief period as a farmer—Maxwell returned to Michigan and finished his law degree. He became a member of the bar in 1859 and quickly returned to Nebraska, where he began practicing law in the small town of Plattsmouth.

In the 1850s, Maxwell became increasingly interested in Nebraska politics and was eventually chosen as a delegate for the territory's first Republican Territorial Convention. He also went on to participate in the Territorial House of Representatives, the Territorial Constitutional Conventions, and the State Constitutional Convention. Maxwell was elected to the first Nebraska State House of Representatives in 1866 and a year later was appointed by the first state governor of Nebraska, David Butler, to the board of commissioners to assist in the development of capitol building plans and the selection of university lands. He was first elected to the Nebraska Supreme Court in 1872 but failed to win the Republican nomination for governor that same year. Maxwell later held the office of chief justice on three separate occasions and also published several books on the topics of law and politics. In the early 1890s Maxwell joined the nascent People's Party and, at the age of 72, was elected to the U.S. House of Representatives. While in Congress he lobbied for monetary reform such as the establishment of postal savings banks, which afforded those of lower socioeconomic status the opportunity to save their money in safe locations. Samuel Maxwell served one term before his death in 1891 at the age of 76.

Jonathan W. Olson

See also: Plains and Midwest, Populism in the

References

"Maxwell, Samuel." *Biographical Directory of the United States Congress, 1774–Present*. Washington, DC: Congress, 1998. http://bioguide.congress.gov/scripts/biodisplay.pl?index=M000270. Accessed January 7, 2013.

"Samuel Maxwell, 1825–1901 (Guide to Microfilm)," Nebraska State Historical Society. http://www.nebraskahistory.org/lib-arch/research/manuscripts/family/sammaxwell-microfilm.htm. Accessed January 7, 2013.

McBride, John (1854–1917)

Labor leader John McBride sought alliances with political organizations, particularly the People's Party, as a means toward achieving greater economic equality in the United States. As president of both the United Mine Workers and the American Federation of Labor, McBride envisioned Populist solidarity among farmers, artisans, small businesses, social reformers, and wage laborers.

McBride was born July 25, 1854, in Wayne County, near the coal fields of eastern Ohio. At the age of eight, he started working in coal mines like his father, Thomas McBride, an immigrant from Ireland. John McBride rose quickly through the ranks, becoming active in local mining associations before helping to organize the Ohio Miners' Union and serving as its first president from 1883 to 1889.

McBride became active in the Knights of Labor and also represented Stark County as a Democratic member of the Ohio House of Representatives in the mid-1880s. Believing that political action was the most direct path toward improving the conditions of workers, McBride ran as the Democratic candidate for Ohio secretary of state in 1886 but lost the race when several leading Ohio Democrats refused to endorse him.

Recognizing that labor unions needed a national platform, McBride worked in the late 1880s to create the organization that became the United Mine Workers of America and served as its second president (1892–1894). McBride also formed an independent labor party, which he successfully merged with the Ohio People's Party in August 1894.

From these positions in December 1894, McBride became the only person ever to defeat Samuel Gompers in an American Federation of Labor presidential election. After Gompers narrowly won back the presidency in December 1895, McBride owned and edited a weekly newspaper in Columbus, Ohio. He moved to Phoenix, Arizona, for reasons of health in 1911.

Throughout his life, McBride favored mediation and consensus—rather than antagonism and conflict—between labor and capital. He was helping to mediate a mine labor dispute in Globe, Arizona, on October 9, 1917, when he was struck by a runaway horse, knocked through a plate-glass window, and killed.

James I. Deutsch

See also: American Federation of Labor (AFL); Gilded Age; Gompers, Samuel (1850–1924); Knights of Labor; Northeast and Industrial Midwest, Populism in the; People's Party; Populism

References

Kaufman, Stuart B., Peter J. Albert, and Grace Palladino, eds. *The Samuel Gompers Papers*. Vol. 4, *A National Labor Movement Takes Shape, 1895–98.* Champaign: University of Illinois Press, 1991.

Pierce, Michael. "The Populist President of the American Federation of Labor: The Career of John McBride, 1880–1895." *Labor History* 41 (1): 5–24.

Postel, Charles. *The Populist Vision*. New York: Oxford University Press, 2007.

McCarthy, Joseph (1908–1957)

Senator Joseph "Joe" McCarthy from Wisconsin is best known for his role in launching the most famous Red Scare in U.S. history. During his time in office from 1947 to 1957, Joseph McCarthy led the most extreme anticommunist movement within the United States during the twentieth century, a passion that made him one of the most controversial and hated politicians of all time.

On November 14, 1908, Joseph Raymond McCarthy was born into the poor Irish immigrant family of Timothy and Bridget McCarthy from Wisconsin. Joe's family life revolved around farming.

At 14 years old, he dropped out of junior high school to help support his family. McCarthy quickly reenrolled, however, in school and entered Little Wolf High School at the age of 20. In June 1930, McCarthy graduated high school at the age of 22 and became the first in the McCarthy family to earn a high school diploma, an act that opened new doors.

After high school, McCarthy was admitted into Marquette University in the fall of 1930. McCarthy eventually decided to pursue a career in the law. While in law school at Marquette, McCarthy worked full time, was a member of the boxing team, and participated in many different extracurricular activities. All of these distractions prevented him from being a serious student. Nevertheless, in 1935 McCarthy earned his law degree and turned his attention toward politics.

McCarthy first attempted to gain access to the world of politics in 1936 when he ran for district attorney in Shawano County. McCarthy became a successful campaigner and organizer for the Democratic Party. It was during this campaign that McCarthy first learned that to gain political relevancy and power he had to be at the center of a sensational issue. McCarthy then launched unfounded accusations against his opponent. Although unsuccessful in his first attempt, he was successfully elected to a nonpartisan district circuit judge position in 1939. As a district court judge, McCarthy was generally considered to be hard-working, clever, and fair.

While a district court judge, McCarthy gave many speeches that urged the people of Wisconsin not to give in to calls for intervention in Europe in 1939. Like many Americans, however, he changed his attitudes after the bombing of Pearl Harbor. In July 1942 McCarthy resigned from his judgeship and joined the marines. McCarthy believed that the marines offered him the best possibility of becoming a war hero, which would further his political career once he returned to the United States. McCarthy served as an intelligence officer for dive bombers. He left the marines as a captain in 1945 and returned to Shawano County covered in glory.

McCarthy used his service to gain political prestige. For example, he broke his leg during an initiation ceremony but sent a press release back home stating that he was wounded in battle. McCarthy exaggerated his participation in missions and flyovers, and he played up his nickname of "Tail-Gunner Joe." It was during World War II that McCarthy switched his political affiliations from Democrat to Republican. After resigning his commission in 1945, McCarthy regained his district circuit judgeship. Using his judgeship, military service, and his newfound conservatism, McCarthy ran again for Wisconsin's Senate seat in 1946.

In what has become a legendary campaign, McCarthy challenged the three-time incumbent Robert La Follette for the Republican primary nomination. Using the lessons learned from his previous campaigns, McCarthy attacked his opponent's weaknesses (authentic and artificial) while claiming his own superiority. For the first time, McCarthy used accusations of communism as one of the primary methods to discredit La Follette. In the end, McCarthy mustered approximately 5,000 more votes than La Follette.

Following his surprising victory, the general election of 1946 seemed anticlimactic. McCarthy ran against the Democratic nominee, Howard McMurray, and beat him in a landslide. McCarthy thus became the youngest member of the U.S. Senate in 1947.

His first three years in the Senate were lackluster. While popular in Wisconsin, McCarthy was unable to gain power and access to committees in Washington, DC, due to his explosive and aggressive personality. However, on February 9, 1950, McCarthy gave a speech to the Ohio County Republican Women's Club in Wheeling, West Virginia, that completely remade his political career. Building upon growing fears of communism, the heightening of the Cold War, and the Alger Hiss case, Joseph McCarthy claimed to have access to a list of 205 known communists working in the State Department. McCarthy instantly became a sensation. When pressed for more information, McCarthy changed the number from 205 to 57 but continued to claim that the U.S. government was being infiltrated by communist spies. McCarthy used his newfound popularity to gain more power in the Senate and the Republican Party.

In response to McCarthy's numerous charges, Congress created the Tydings Committee to investigate his accusations. Democrats supported the committee in hopes it would silence his embarrassing allegations while Republicans hoped that it would help them gain control of Congress and the White House in the upcoming elections. While the committee concluded that McCarthy's claims were fraudulent, the damage had been done. Congress never voted to accept the Tydings Committee's findings, voting strictly along party lines. It represented the widening gap between Republicans and Democrats during the Cold War.

Following the Tydings Committee, McCarthy became the face of anticommunism. To his supporters and to many Republicans, McCarthy was a national hero. His enemies denounced his ideas as "McCarthyism" and as an unjustified persecution of liberal Americans. McCarthy even used the Korean War to make accusations against President Harry Truman, Secretary of Defense George Marshall, and Secretary of State Dean Acheson.

From 1950 to 1952, McCarthy not only won his own reelection but also became one of the most successful campaigners for the Republican Party—especially for Dwight D. Eisenhower. After his reelection, McCarthy was named as the chairman of the Senate Committee on Government Operations, which allowed him to launch his own series of investigations against his supposed communist spies. From 1952 to 1954, McCarthy investigated a number of high-profile politicians and departments for their suspected involvement in communism. Many Americans began to follow McCarthy's example, accusing neighbors, friends, and enemies of being communists. McCarthyism created mass fear and hysteria within the U.S. public.

Eventually McCarthy took his charges too far and accused the U.S. military of harboring communist spies in 1954. His accusations pitted him directly against President Eisenhower. Using his newfound power, McCarthy called hearings to investigate the U.S. Army. These hearings became known as the Army-McCarthy hearings. They were nationally televised and drew more than 20 million viewers. McCarthy was never able to produce any real evidence that the U.S. Army was treacherously harboring communist spies. McCarthy then used personal attacks against the army attorney, which lost him what little credibility he had left. Following the affair Republicans lost control of the Senate and McCarthy was publicly censured, ending his reign of terror.

Following his censure, Joseph McCarthy became a broken man both physically and emotionally. He was a pariah in the U.S. Senate. He eventually was hospitalized for severe alcoholism. During his final years, McCarthy continued to publicly accuse individuals and entities of being communist spies or sympathizers. No one, however, was listening. Joseph McCarthy died on May 2, 1957, from alcoholism. While he remained in the Senate until his death in 1957, he was never again was able to regain his power, status, or popularity. McCarthy became the face of everything that was wrong with the domestic Cold War—hysteria, fear, and false accusations.

Recently, some scholars have called for a reevaluation of McCarthy's legacy. The decryption of the Venona Soviet files, as well as newly released Senate hearing transcripts, indicate that McCarthy's accusations might not have been completely off base. This new evidence suggests that many of McCarthy's accused communists were in fact communists or involved in Soviet espionage. Nevertheless, Joseph McCarthy continues to represent how fear can lead Americans and its politicians to willingly and knowingly wage war on civil liberties within its own borders.

Autumn C. Lass

See also: Democratic Party; Hiss, Alger (1904–1996); Hollywood Ten; Rosenberg, Julius (1918–1953), and Rosenberg, Ethel (1915–1953)

References

Herman, Arthur. *Joseph McCarthy: Reexamining the Life and Legacy of America's Most Hated Senator.* New York: Free Press, 2000.

Johnson, Haynes. *The Age of Anxiety: McCarthyism to Terrorism.* New York: Harcourt, 2005.

Powers, Richard Gid. *Not without Honor: The History of American Anticommunism.* New Haven, CT: Yale University Press, 1995.

Reeves, Thomas. *The Life and Times of Joe McCarthy: A Biography.* New York: Madison Books, 1997.

McKinley, William, Jr. (1843–1901)

The apogee of William McKinley's career was his election as the 25th president of the United States in the hotly contested election of 1896. As the Republican standard-bearer he represented the antithesis of the Populist drive for change. McKinley symbolized both the gold standard and the high tariff policies that had been often blamed for the impoverishment of American agriculture and the American farmer. His victory in 1896 helped forge a Republican hegemony in national politics that lasted until 1932, with only the Woodrow Wilson presidency breaking this domination.

William McKinley Jr., June 7, 1898. (Library of Congress)

Born in Niles, Ohio, of mixed Scottish and English heritage, McKinley's American roots stretched back to eighteenth-century Pennsylvania. The McKinley family became early settlers in Ohio in the 1790s, and William McKinley Jr. was one of nine children born to William and Nancy McKinley. He attended local schools in Poland, Ohio, and later Mount Union College in Alliance, Ohio, and for a term at Allegheny College in Meadville, Pennsylvania.

The coming of the Civil War saw McKinley enlist as a private in the 23rd Ohio Infantry in June 1861. Stationed largely in West Virginia, McKinley served under Rutherford B. Hayes, a future president. Hayes promoted McKinley to sergeant in recognition of his bravery in battle against Confederate units. Other promotions followed during the course of the war with McKinley becoming a second lieutenant after the battle of Antietam in 1862. By the time his enlistment ended in September 1865, he had achieved the rank of brevet major.

Following the war McKinley continued his education at Albany Law School in New York and was admitted to the bar in 1867. He established a law practice in Canton, Ohio, and served as a prosecuting attorney for Stark County. He also entered the political ring, giving his support to his former Civil War commander in Rutherford Hayes's campaign for the Ohio governorship. It was also in this period that he met and married Ida Saxton.

McKinley's own emergent political ambitions were particularly aided by Rutherford Hayes. Hayes introduced him to the influential base of Ohio Republican politics. McKinley was elected to the House of Representatives in 1877 and served until 1882 but was defeated for reelection. He successfully returned to the House in 1885, where he served until 1891. In Washington, McKinley rose to prominence as chairman of the important Ways and Means Committee and was instrumental in passing the McKinley Tariff of 1890, which raised duties to what was then the highest level on record. McKinley lost his seat by a narrow margin of 300 votes in the face of the 1890 Democratic election revival. In 1891 McKinley won the Ohio governorship, defeating Democrat James E. Campbell, and was reelected in 1893, defeating

Lawrence T. Neal. As governor, McKinley increased corporate excise taxes, curtailed antiunion practices, and attempted to address the plight of Ohio's poor through a variety of private charity schemes. Now a national figure in the Republican Party, McKinley also started to test the waters for the presidency but was unsuccessful in 1892. However, by vigorously campaigning for Benjamin Harrison's reelection, McKinley endeared himself to the party establishment.

In 1896, after leaving the governorship and with the support of his rich friend, the Cleveland industrialist Mark Hanna, McKinley began to campaign earnestly for the Republican presidential nomination. Republican prospects seemed particularly good following major sweeps in the 1894 congressional elections. With the lingering effects of the 1893 panic associated with Democratic incumbent Grover Cleveland, and with the many divisions within the Democratic Party over the silver issue and Populist challenges to its base, McKinley's prospects were flourishing. In addition, Mark Hanna emerged as a master manipulator and the first of a breed of campaign managers who would have such an impact on U.S. politics in the future. McKinley won the nomination handily and, with the advice of Mark Hanna, designed his "Front Porch" campaign strategy that saw him remain at home and address the nation from his Ohio base.

As a candidate McKinley took on the Democrat nominee and Populist favorite William Jennings Bryan in a transformative election that introduced twentieth-century politics to the American public. Backed by a huge campaign fund of more than $3.5 million, Hanna made use of the new advertising media to persuade the public. McKinley linked the gold standard to prosperity, deflected the bimetallist challenges of "free silver" as economically destructive, and offered a place for all the United States' new immigrants in the political process. His strategy worked well, for McKinley won the election handily with more than 51 percent of the popular vote and with an unassailable 271 Electoral College votes.

A return to prosperity and industrial growth also aided McKinley during the election. Industrial trusts continued to expand and consolidate and were not yet confined by the 1890 Sherman Antitrust Act, which gave evidence to this growth. It was not until the Progressive Era that these constraints of trade issues, posed by the growing monopolies, were partially addressed. The monetary system was also temporarily stabilized by the Gold Standard Act of 1890, which established set values, ending many of the deflationary issues that had plagued the economy since the 1870s and contributed much to the agricultural unrest of the Populist era.

McKinley's presidency also witnessed the United States' emergence on the world stage through the acquisition of overseas territories. The United States was joining the ranks of the major powers. As a first step in this drive, the Hawaii annexation issue reappeared with the necessary support for acceptance. The annexation treaty was finally signed in June 1897, backed by a joint resolution in July 1898, followed by the creation of a territorial government in 1900.

The Spanish-American War further contributed both to the expansionistic atmosphere and the emergent economy. Stemming from long-term Spanish abuses in Cuba and sparked by the sinking of the USS *Maine* in Havana Harbor, a war fury was stoked by "yellow journalism," leaving McKinley little option but to take the United States to war in April 1898. After a swift and highly successful 90-day campaign, Spain was utterly defeated. As a result of the Treaty of Paris that ended the war, Puerto Rico, Guam, and the Philippines became U.S. territories, and as an immediate aftermath Cuba became an occupied territory, although permanent withdrawal and independence were guaranteed. Although the war and the acquisition of overseas territory received massive public support, those in the anti-imperialist camp saw these events as real challenges to the United States' republican ideals.

For McKinley and the Republicans the war strengthened an expanding economy that characterized domestic growth until the Panic of 1907. In particular, the politics of the protective tariff continued in McKinley's first term, most clearly seen in the passage of the 1897 Dingley Tariff. This tariff's effect was to obliterate the modest reductions seen in the 1894 Wilson-Gorman Tariff Act. McKinley signed the new tariff bill in July 1897. The Dingley Tariff increased duties from 40 to 50 percent and also restored some aspects of reciprocity treaties. In addition, McKinley's presidency was, at times, subject to criticism over the standard cronyism of the period. A particular example was the promotion of aged Ohio Senator John Sherman to head the State Department, which led to accusations that this was payback for Mark Hanna's elevation to the Senate.

The McKinley presidency witnessed the further rise of Jim Crow restrictions on African Americans and the steady reversal of Reconstruction-era civil rights gains. This direction was most notably reflected in the 1896 *Plessy v. Ferguson* case that institutionalized segregation through its separate-but-equal provisions. McKinley did little, other than a few African American governmental appointments, to take a stand against the period's increasingly racist atmosphere, which was accompanied by a rise in intimidation and lynching. As a committed Christian and abolitionist, McKinley was sympathetic to the plight of African Americans, but he failed to fully employ or enforce existing civil rights legislation through fear of further alienating the South.

The election of 1900 saw President McKinley emerge as the Republican standard-bearer with a young Theodore Roosevelt, whose popularity arose from his Spanish-American War celebrity, as his vice-presidential nominee. The 1900 election again saw the Democrats nominate William Jennings Bryan with Adlai E. Stevenson of Illinois as his vice-presidential running mate. The Democratic Party chose to drop free silver as a campaign issue and adopt imperialism as its key campaign plank. This decision marked an essential end to the Populist ethos that had gained entrance to the party platform in the 1896 election.

While McKinley stayed at home, Roosevelt out-traveled William Jennings

Bryan and brought a new enthusiasm to Republican electioneering. Supported by a rich campaign coffer, the Republicans "called for four more years with a full dinner pail," and in the face of a lower voter turnout, McKinley won reelection by a higher margin than in 1896, taking 52 percent of the popular vote and 292 electoral votes. McKinley's second term in office would prove to be short lived, for he was assassinated by anarchist Leon Czolgosz on September 14, 1901, allowing maverick Republican Theodore Roosevelt to assume the presidency.

Theodore W. Eversole

See also: African Americans and Populism; Bryan, William Jennings (1860–1925); Cleveland, Grover (1837–1908); Czolgosz, Leon (1873–1901); Gilded Age; Gold Standard/Free Silver; Hanna, Mark (1837–1904); Progressivism; Roosevelt, Theodore (1858–1919); Wilson-Gorman Tariff (1894)

References

Glad, Paul W. *McKinley, Bryan, and the People*. Philadelphia: J. P. Lippincott Company, 1964.

Gould, Lewis L. *The Presidency of William McKinley*. Lawrence: Regents Press of Kansas, 1980.

Jones, Stanley L. *The Presidential Election of 1896*. Madison: University of Wisconsin Press, 1964.

Kent, Noel J. *America in 1900*. Armonk, NY: M.E. Sharpe, 2000.

Knoles, George H. *The Presidential Campaign and Election of 1892*. New York: AMS Press, 1971.

Morgan, H. Wayne. *William McKinley and His America*. Syracuse, NY: Syracuse University Press, 1963.

Phillips, Kevin. *William McKinley*. New York: Times Books, 2003.

Mencken, H. L. (1880–1956)

Henry Louis Mencken, better known as H. L. Mencken, was an American journalist, literary and social critic, essayist, and editor of two influential magazines, *The Smart Set* and *The American Mercury*. He edited both of these magazines in collaboration with drama critic George Jean Nathan. Mencken also wrote over 30 books, including *A Book of Prefaces*, but *The American Language* is perhaps his greatest literary achievement. In this book, Mencken clarified the differences between American and British English, defining in print the outlines of common American speech. While not a populist in political outlook, Mencken's broad appeal, fame, and influence made him a household word throughout the United States and influenced the public thinking of his era.

Mencken was born on September 12, 1880. He was the eldest of four children. His parents were August Mencken and Anna Margaret Abhua Mencken. August and his brother owned the Mencken Cigar Company. About his childhood Mencken once wrote that he was born in the center of a comfortable and complacent bourgeoisie and was embraced with an affection that kept him fat, saucy, and contented. As a result he grew up with a sense of self-confidence that played an important role in his life.

Mencken attended private schools in Baltimore, Maryland, and graduated from the Polytechnic Institute there in 1896. He began his career as a reporter for the *Baltimore Morning Herald* in 1899 when he was 19 years old. He started as a cub reporter but soon became city editor and then editor. In 1906, he left the *Herald* to work for the *Baltimore Sun*. From 1914 to 1923, Mencken was also the coeditor with drama critic George Jean Nathan of the literary magazine *The Smart Set*. In 1924, Mencken and Nathan founded *The American Mercury*, a monthly. The magazine published the works of Theodore Dressier, Edna St. Vincent Millay, Joseph Conrad, Sherwood Anderson, Carl Sandburg, and a host of other up-and-coming American writers and poets. Though busy with his periodicals, he continued his relationship with the *Baltimore Sun* until 1948, when he suffered a stroke and was no longer able to write. Mencken became known as the "Sage of Baltimore" for his idiosyncratic but adept social criticism and prolific output, and was often compared to Mark Twain. Even though he never went to college, Mencken became one the most influential American writers of the twentieth century.

Mencken was an inspiration to other writers such as Richard Wright, the author of *Native Son* and his autobiography *Black Boy*. After reading an editorial in a southern newspaper criticizing Mencken, he became curious and wanted to read Mencken's books, but African Americans were not allowed to check books out of the library. He came up with an ingenious plan and conspired with a white coworker to forge a note to be able to get the books he wanted. The first book he got was *A Book of Prefaces*. Years later he wrote in *Black Boy* that he was jarred and shocked by Mencken's style. According to him *A Book of Prefaces* was his gateway to world literature.

While many writers found Mencken inspirational, to his many detractors he was a scourge. His critics characterized him as a bigot, racist, anti-Semite, misogynist, and misanthrope, and according to Richard O'Mara in the *Christian Science Monitor*, Mencken was an incredible egotist. However, William H. A. Williams, in *H. L. Mencken Revisited*, writes that these were only "snippets" of Mencken's personality and his "colorful" writing. Williams asserts that during his career Mencken helped many black authors, including Richard Wright. He also supported the antilynching bill and repeatedly denounced the KKK, and he criticized the Roosevelt administration for refusing admittance of Jews seeking refuge from Nazi Germany.

Mencken was undoubtedly one of the most controversial and prolific authors of his generation, and possibly the most quoted. Mencken's legacy is archived in the Mencken Room of the Enoch Pratt Free Library in Baltimore, which holds myriad artifacts left by the Sage of Baltimore: his Corona typewriter, his desk, his books, and nearly every word of the estimated 15 million (some say 50 million) he wrote during his lifetime.

Finally, he was a libertarian of the most extreme variety, and his literary theory, like his politics, was based chiefly on the freedom to speak the truth. Mencken died on January 29, 1956, in Baltimore, Maryland.

John G. Hall

See also: Anderson, Sherwood; Ku Klux Klan; Roosevelt, Franklin Delano; Twain, Mark

References

Kramer, Hilton. "Who Reads Mencken Now?" *New Criterion*, January 1, 2003.

McCarthy, Daniel. "The Irrepressible Mencken." *The American Conservative*, January 30, 2006.

Mencken, H.L. *The American Language*. New York: Bartleby.com, 2000. http://www.bartleby.com/185/. Accessed January 7, 2013.

Mencken, H.L. *A Book of Prefaces*. New York: BiblioBazaar, 2009. Kindle Ebook: http://www.gutenberg.org/ebooks/19355. Accessed January 7, 2013.

Nolte, William H., ed. *H.L. Mencken's Smart Set Criticism*. Washington, DC: Regnery Publishing, 1987.

Spivak, Lawrence, and Charles Angoff. *America Mercury Reader.* Baltimore, MD: American Mercury, 2001.

Merritt, Ada Chase (1852–1933)

Ada Chase Merritt, like many Americans, moved westward in the mid-1800s, leaving Michigan with her family to raise stock in Austin, Nevada, in 1864, and later to Salmon, Idaho, with her husband Henry Merritt and two children. Chase spent much of her adult life running a small-town newspaper and raising her children, and she was involved in local and state politics. She was a Democrat in a mostly Republican area and eventually supported the People's Party.

Although she was born in Clinton, Louisiana, on February 24, 1852, Merritt grew up in Michigan. Little is known about her education in Michigan or later in Nevada. She met and married her husband, Henry Clay Merritt, in 1870 while living in Austin, Nevada, and their two children were born in Austin and nearby Elko. The couple followed the Chase and Merritt families north to Salmon, Idaho, in 1883, where Henry Merritt took a job as a mine superintendent. He was killed in a river accident a year later, leaving his widow to teach school for a short time until she became part owner in the *Idaho Recorder.*

Started in June 1886, the *Recorder* came under the ownership of Merritt and O. W. Mintzer in July 1888. The partnership of a Republican and Democrat was meant to make the paper independent, at least until the Republican ran and won a slot in the state assembly. Merritt bought out Mintzer in October and was the sole owner and editor of the paper until she sold it in 1906. As a weekly, the *Recorder* focused primarily on local and county news. Merritt even added a "People's Column" open to anyone who wished to publish something. While the paper appeared to be sufficiently profitable, Merritt, as many westerners and small-business owners did, bartered subscriptions for necessities such as her winter fuel supply.

By the late 1880s, Merritt became more politically involved. She criticized the Republican majority more visibly, including her former partner Mintzer. While she urged county voters to ratify the state constitution, she herself did not support woman suffrage. She was not, however, above family nepotism, endorsing her brother Hal H. Chase for county assessor in 1890, a position he won as one of only two Democrats elected in the county. Merritt endorsed a Populist platform in 1894 but was now facing a rival Republican-sponsored paper, the *Lemhi Republic*. During the five-year period of the *Republic*'s existence, Merritt and the *Recorder* mounted a major, decidedly political, battle. In 1893 she attended the state's silver convention as a delegate. Even though only a few Populists won state offices in the 1894 elections, the *Recorder* remained true to its cause, running the subtitle "Free and Unlimited Coinage of Silver at a Ratio of 16 to 1" until 1902.

Merritt and her son became embroiled in a major scandal in that same year. In 1900, Merritt had been elected county treasurer. In 1901, Merritt and her new assistant, George W. Walsen, traveled to Omaha, Nebraska, and Chicago to buy new printing equipment. These capital investments led to a biweekly publication of the paper, now competing with the *Lemhi Herald*. In the May 20, 1902, edition of the paper, Merritt reprinted an article that had appeared in the *Pocatello Advance* under the headline "The Arrest of Walsen." The reprinted story revealed that Walsen and Merritt had been secretly married in Omaha in December. Promoting a new mining route, Walsen left Salmon at the end of March. Shortly thereafter, Merritt discovered that $6,000 of county funds was gone. Merritt, as county treasurer, and her son Allen, the deputy treasurer, were the only ones who knew the combination to the safe. Walsen had gained knowledge of the combination and stolen the money. The story continued, telling of Merritt's efforts to locate Walsen and entice him to Denver, Colorado, so he could be arrested. Although this attempt failed, Walsen agreed to meet Merritt in Salt Lake City, Utah, where he was eventually arrested. It turned out that Walsen had a criminal record, having served three terms in prison for forgery in Colorado and one more in Utah. The reprinted article ended with an expression of sympathy and endorsement for Merritt, applauding her determination in finding and bringing Walsen to justice. During the next several months the scandal played out with numerous, bitter, and public exchanges between the editors of the *Recorder* and the *Lemhi Herald*. By May 1903, the court case against Walsen had been dismissed, Merritt had pled guilty to aiding in the escape of a prisoner and been fined $50, the stolen funds had been reimbursed, and Walsen and Merritt were divorced.

Merritt sold the *Recorder* in 1906, when she was 54 years old. Both her age and the loss of the county printing contract might have been factors in her decision. Aside from her public life as a small-business owner and opinion maker, Merritt had been active in Salmon's community life for over two decades. She attended the local Methodist Episcopal church, participated in the City Chautauqua Literary and Scientific Circle, belonged to numerous clubs and groups, and had been elected county treasurer in 1900. Her life after the *Recorder* was nomadic, with stays in Caldwell, Idaho, and Salt Lake City, where she was married to Joseph Crain in 1912 until his death seven years later, with extensive travels between 1920 and 1928 as a wealthy woman's companion. She eventually moved to California where her daughter lived, and died in Santa Monica in November 1933. The November 22 obituary in the *Salmon*

Recorder-Herald noted Ada Merritt's death.

Amy M. Hay

See also: Democratic Party; Gilded Age; Gold Standard/Free Silver

References

Bennion, Sherilyn Cox. "Ada Chase Merritt and *The Recorder*: A Pioneer Idaho Editor and Her Newspaper." *Idaho Yesterdays* 25 (4): 22–30.

Bennion, Sherilyn Cox. *Equal to the Occasion: Women Editors of the Nineteenth-Century West.* Las Vegas: University of Nevada Press, 1990.

Middle-of-the-Road Populists

Also called "mid-roaders," these Populists, led by famed orator Thomas E. Watson, avoided joining with major parties of the time and preferred to independently pursue the People's Party's goals. The term *middle of the roaders* is not reference to a moderate political platform but rather a reflection of the group's desire to remain separate from both the Democratic and Republican parties. In fact, they were considered more radical than their partisan counterparts. Generally, westerners were fusionists as they shared the prosilver stance of Democrats. Fusionists were Populists who wished to join with the Democratic Party to benefit from their greater following and their mutual interest in the free silver policy issue. Conversely, the mid-roaders, comprised primarily of southerners, advocated pressing forward with a hard Populist stance to build on the growing strength of the party rather than diluting their principals by joining another party. These issues were significant as they could divide an already small third-party movement.

The middle-of-the-road Populists became most well known during 1896 after internal turmoil within the People's Party. However, the term appeared as early as 1892 in a campaign song published by Denver's *Rocky Mountain News*, which went as follows:

> Side tracks are rough, and they're hard to walk
> Keep in the middle of the road;
> Though we haven't got time to stop and talk
> We keep in the middle of the road.
> Turn your backs on the goldbug men,
> And yell for silver now and then;
> If you want to beat Grover, also Ben,
> Just stick to the middle of the road.
>
> Don't answer the call of goldbug tools,
> But keep in the middle of the road;
> Prove that the West wasn't settled by fools,
> And keep in the middle of the road.
> They've woven their plots, and woven them ill,
> We want a Weaver who's got more skill,
> And mostly we want a Silver Bill,
> So we'll stay in the middle of the road.
> (Haynes 469)

Silverites, those who supported the policy, pushed for both gold and silver to be used as currency. This was universally acknowledged to cause inflation, but there was disagreement on the impact that this inflationary monetary policy would have. This policy was favored by some Populists because it was believed that it would help raise prices, and thus incomes, because it would raise the amount of total money available. Some thought that it would allow farmers the ability to pay off debts and earn a greater amount of money for their crops, for example.

There was a shared concern by fusionists and mid-roaders that the existence of the People's Party ticket during the 1896 presidential election would only cut into the Democratic votes and ensure the victory of Republican candidate, William McKinley, the "gold bug." However, middle-of-the-road Populists also feared that joining with the Democratic Party would diminish the Populist platform and would lead to followers being absorbed into the Democratic Party by default.

The conflict between the mid-roaders and fusionists came to a boil leading up to the national convention as even the date of the People's Party national convention became a point of contention. The fusionists had a strong voice within the organization and scheduled the convention to occur after the Democratic and Republicans national conventions to capitalize on the popularity of William Jennings Bryan, the Democratic nominee. The Populists' convention occurred in St. Louis during July 24–26, 1896. Middle-of-the-road Populists struggled but lost as the majority of Populists also endorsed William Jennings Bryan as the People's Party candidate. One of the most vocal supporters was Herman Taubeneck, who served as the national chair of the party from 1892 to 1896 and was also an ardent Silverite. Mid-roaders argued against selecting Bryan as the nominee for numerous reasons, but among them was that Arthur Sewall, the Democratic vice-presidential choice, was a wealthy Maine banker who took a hard antilabor stance. Tom Watson, editor of the *People's Party Paper*, was likely the candidate the mid-roaders would have chosen. While he did not receive the presidential nomination, he was selected as the vice-presidential choice by Populists to replace Sewall.

As was protocol at the time, presidential candidates did not attend the convention and instead awaited news of their nomination. As Watson was not there, he could not discuss this melding of parties. He accepted the nomination under the false notion that Bryan would accept Watson's nomination and run on a dual Populist-Democratic ticket. However, this was not the case, leaving Watson and other mid-roaders in a difficult situation as Watson would not campaign for Bryan because of the deceit, but he also refused to step down. Some mid-roaders such as famed lecturer Mary Lease of Kansas, fearing a loss to Republicans, came to terms with this disappointment and begrudgingly campaigned for Bryan while using the election as a platform to spread awareness to the larger Populist movement.

Despite their support, Bryan was defeated by William McKinley. Following the defeat, infighting continued as mid-roaders and fusionists blamed each other for the loss of the election. On July 4, 1897, the People's Party staged a national conference in Nashville, Tennessee, to regroup. This was not successful, however, and resulted in the middle-of-the-road Populists meeting at a separate convention in Cincinnati, Ohio, on September 5, 1898. This caused a splitting of the People's Party between the middle-of-the-road Populists and the fusionist and general Populists. During the campaign of 1900, two Populist conventions were held. The main, or fusionist, branch held theirs in Sioux Falls, South Dakota, while mid-roaders held theirs on May 9, 1900, as well, again in Cincinnati.

The Democratic Party, however, took a conservative turn shortly after, allowing both branches of Populists to consider rejoining. The fusionist wing of the party offered an olive branch, which led to a united call for both groups to meet in St. Louis, Missouri, on February 22, 1903. During this meeting, it was agreed that the alliance with the Democratic Party would be dissolved in favor of pursuing an independent ticket.

The discovery of gold in the Yukon, coupled with increased imports of agricultural products from Europe, simultaneously helped improve the position of the farmer and diluted interest in the People's Party. By the 1904 election, only 200 delegates attended the Populists' convention. In 1908, an even smaller delegation appeared to renominate Thomas E. Watson for the presidency and to select Samuel W. Williams of Indiana as the vice president. The biggest shared sentiment, however, among the attendants was that this was the end of the party. The Populists were able to poll for their candidates and found only 28,131 votes, nearly 17,000 of which came from Georgia. Ultimately, the concerns of the middle-of-the-road Populists proved correct. It was the willingness to band with the Democratic Party that led to the quick downfall of the Populists, as their party platform and membership was largely absorbed by the Democratic Party.

Rahima Schwenkbeck

See also: Agricultural Newspapers and Farmer Unrest; Bryan, Williams Jennings (1860–1925); Gold Standard/Free Silver; Lease, Mary (1850–1933); McKinley, William, Jr. (1843–1901); Sewall, Arthur M. (1835–1900); Silver Republicans; St. Louis Convention of 1896; Taubeneck, Herman E. (c. 1855–unknown); Williams, Samuel W. (1851–1913)

References

Goodwyn, Lawrence. *The Populist Moment: A Short History of the Agrarian Revolt in America*. New York: Oxford University Press, 1978.

Haynes, Frederick Emory. *James Baird Weaver.* Iowa City: State Historical Society of Iowa, 1919.

Hicks, John D. *Populist Revolt: A History of the Farmers' Alliance and the People's Party.* Minneapolis: University of Minnesota Press, 1931.

Kazin, Michael. *The Populist Persuasion: An American History.* Ithaca, NY: Cornell University Press, 1998.

McMath, Robert C., Jr. *American Populism: A Social History: 1877–1898*. New York: Hill & Wang, 1992.

Midwest, Populism in the.

See Plains and Midwest, Populism in the

Mills, C. Wright (1916–1962)

C. Wright Mills is widely considered the most significant public intellectual of the twentieth-century United States. A professor of sociology at Columbia University, Mills was an interdisciplinary thinker working across the traditional fields of economics, philosophy, and sociology who launched a radical critique of power relations in American society following

World War II. His scholarly work attempted to educate everyday citizens about how a ruling oligarchy—the so-called power elite—came to manufacture and manipulate public consent in the postwar era. Advocating for a truly participatory democracy with his acerbic sociological analyses and rhetorical wit, Mills soon became an icon for the modern progressive tradition in American life.

Charles Wright Mills was born on August 28, 1916, in Waco, Texas. He attended the University of Texas in Austin, where he received a B.A. in sociology and an M.A. in philosophy, both in 1939. Mills continued his studies at the University of Wisconsin in Madison, where he earned a Ph.D. in sociology with a dissertation on pragmatism in 1941. Because of chronic hypertension, he was exempted from military service in World War II. After a short appointment at the University of Maryland, he moved to Columbia University in 1945, which housed one of the leading academic programs in sociology. Mills first worked as a research associate in the Bureau of Applied Social Research and then joined the department of sociology as an assistant professor. Over the next 15 years, he led an extremely productive scholarly life—making major contributions to the study of social stratification, publishing a variety of critical works in academic and popular venues, and lecturing throughout the United States, Latin America, and Europe. Despite disagreements with colleagues over sociological methodology and professional demeanor, Mills was promoted to full professor and remained at Columbia until his untimely death from a heart attack on March 20, 1962.

Many scholarly profiles on Mills's contributions to American sociology and public life have strong hagiographic impulses that continue to dwell on his powerful personal aura. Described variously as a "native radical" (Tilman) or a "postmodern cowboy" (Kerr), Mills was a complex and enigmatic individual, who intentionally cultivated the image of an intellectual rebel. With his Texas drawl, BMW motorcycle, and blue-collar attire, he not only attacked the pretentiousness of life in the ivory tower but also—in keeping with his motto to "take it big!"—unleashed a no-holds-barred critique of misplaced American triumphalism during the Cold War.

During his university studies, Mills's intellectual horizon was expanded by thinkers working in both the classical tradition of sociology and a number of codisciplinary subjects: the American pragmatists John Dewey, G. H. Mead, and C. S. Pierce; the institutional economist Thorstein Veblen; and the great European masters such as Sigmund Freud, Karl Marx, and Max Weber. Through his relationship with Hans Gerth, an émigré professor from Nazi Germany at Wisconsin, Mills was greatly influenced by Weber's methodological orientation in the social sciences. He was particularly struck by Weber's call to explore how larger historical changes shaped human ideas, behaviors, and institutions and to link social phenomena to the daily meanings of ordinary people.

Taking Weber's call to investigate large-scale social trends as a catalyst, Mills articulated—while still acknowledging his debt to mainstream traditions—a distinctly native radical theory to uncover the repressive effects of class divisions and concentrated political power in the United States. In developing this new orientation, Mills challenged the dominant theoretical presuppositions of institutional sociology. He was a staunch critic of both general theorizing ("grand theory") and quantitative research ("abstract empiricism") because these techniques failed to critically examine their own methodologies and aims, while simultaneously divorcing themselves from the everyday concerns of public life. Mills firmly believed that intellectuals should not be engaged in disinterested observation but rather in active social critique: to fearlessly question authority and promote core democratic ideals. As an oppositional figure, he criticized his colleagues for not using their academic freedom to responsibly work for a free and just society. Mills outlined this need for intellectuals to make important connections between their personal biography and historical-political processes in his magnum opus, *The Sociological Imagination* (1959).

While still remaining a patriot citizen-scholar, Mills undertook—from the late 1940s to the late 1950s—his intensely critical assessment of American society by combining pragmatic approaches, scientific methodologies, and radical social theories. This project resulted in a powerful trilogy of books that addressed the alienation of the masses and the dangerous concentration of political power in contemporary life. The first book, *The New Men of Power* (1948), explored the working class; the second, *White Collar* (1951), the new middle class; and the third, *The Power Elite* (1956), the ruling class. The second book established Mills's national reputation as a social critic, and the third gained him worldwide attention and acclaim. All of these books were contrary to the largely uncritical stance of mainstream sociology with respect to American liberalism.

Mills forwarded two complementary arguments in his trilogy of American social stratification. First, the continued bureaucratic organization of postwar life—prompted by the modern division of labor and accelerated by capitalist consumption and mass medial saturation—caused citizens to become increasingly alienated from themselves. People became resigned to their status as mere cogs in the state-corporate machine, forfeiting the need for autonomous and independent thought or individual and collective responsibility. Second, this increase in mass bureaucratization resulted in a society dominated by the deliberate concentration of power in the hands of the "power elite," a small group of political, business, and military leaders. This process involved the centralization of political power not only in the executive branch but also in close partnerships between the federal government, large national corporations, and the military industry. Mills believed that these relationships were a serious threat to democracy by undermining the active participation of the U.S. citizenry in everyday public life. This critique foreshadowed President Dwight Eisenhower's own ominous warning of the "military-industrial-congressional complex" in his farewell address of 1961.

Throughout his life and academic career, C. Wright Mills worked tirelessly and passionately in support of democratic reforms and in strong opposition to political authoritarianism, capitalist exploitation, and military-industrial domination. His publications, which were also printed in the popular press, always returned to questions around social inequality. In this regard, he shared many similarities with both Marx's concept of alienation and Veblen's critique of American capitalism. Mills did not, however, adequately address those inequalities arising from race, sex, or sexuality, and he was vague about how radical mechanisms of social transformation might eventually abolish the specter of alienation. Nevertheless, he had a profound effect on the New Left by providing the movement with a critical voice and an arsenal of oppositional vocabulary. Although the world has considerably changed since his time, Mills's ideas continue to resonate today. The new millennium has sparked a renewed interest in his call to "take it big!" and to courageously critique our era of global financial crises and intense political polarization.

Mirko M. Hall

See also: "The Elite"; Veblen, Thorstein (1857–1929)

References

Geary, Daniel. *Radical Ambition: C. Wright Mills, The Left, and American Social Thought*. Berkeley: University of California Press, 2009.

Hayden, Tom. *Radical Nomad: C. Wright Mills and His Times*. Boulder, CO: Paradigm Publishers, 2006.

Horowitz, Irving Louis. *C. Wright Mills: An American Utopian*. New York: Free Press, 1982.

Kerr, Keith. *Postmodern Cowboy: C. Wright Mills and a New 21st-Century Sociology*. Boulder, CO: Paradigm Publishers, 2009.

Tilman, Rick. *C. Wright Mills: A Native Radical and His American Intellectual Roots*. University Park: Pennsylvania State University Press, 1984.

Treviño, A. Javier. *The Social Thought of C. Wright Mills*. Thousand Oaks, CA: Fine Forge Press, 2012.

Modernism

Modernism emerged as a cultural response to the technological, societal, and scientific developments of the late nineteenth century. Its very name reflects the value placed by modernists on the present and the future. Conversely, modernists rebelled against the past. Modernism attempted to make distinctive cultural forms for the present. Modernism was an international movement with most of its major figures clustered in Europe. Despite this, the United States contributed a vital element of the movement's development, especially in music, architecture, and literature. Every area of culture was affected by modernism, and as such, modernism touched the common man. Even in religion, the term *modernism* was applied to progressive Protestant leaders who sought to reintroduce Christianity to the modern man.

In literature, characteristics for modernism included the independence of the protagonist, differing points of view in the narrative including stream of consciousness, and the relaxing of traditional cultural mores. The greatest work was done by expatriates living in Europe. Among these were the poets Ezra Pound (1885–1972), T. S. Eliot (1888–1965), and Gertrude Stein (1874–1946). The major writers and poets of this period are generally referred to as the "Lost Generation," those born between 1891 and 1905. In the United States, the major writers were Ernest Hemingway (1899–1961) of *The Sun Also Rises* (1926), F. Scott Fitzgerald (1896–1940) of *The Great Gatsby* (1925), William Faulkner (1897–1962) of *The Sound and the Fury* (1929), and John Steinbeck (1902–1968) of *The Grapes of Wrath* (1939). A closely associated stream of artistic development during this period was the Harlem Renaissance. Writers such as Langston Hughes (1902–1967) and Jean Toomer (1894–1967) embodied modernist ideas and wrote works that exemplified the movement.

In visual art, no single modernist movement emerged. Instead, a number of varying artistic movements developed under the broad label of modern art. Major international styles of modern art included cubism, futurism, Dada, and surrealism. Each of these styles contributed to American modernism in art. Cubism, exemplified by Pablo Picasso's *Les Demoiselles d'Avignon* (1907), redefined how to portray reality on canvas. Futurism focused on portraying the urban setting. Dada reacted to society and its tastes in an extreme way. Marcel Duchamp (1887–1968) presented a urinal as *Fountain* (1917) and was rejected by art critics. Surrealism sought to explore the unconscious as represented by Salvador Dali (1904–1989). Although the major figures of these styles were European, their influence was felt in the United States. American styles included precisionism and regionalism. Precisionism's leading exponent was Charles Sheelet (1883–1965). Grant Wood (1891–1942) and his *American Gothic* (1930) illustrated regionalism. Aspiring writers and artists congregated in central locations throughout the country such as Greenwich Village in New York City.

In modern architecture, the United States made valuable contributions to the international movement through the Chicago school. The Chicago school developed shortly after the Chicago fire of 1871. Its formation coincided with a time when technological advances began to allow larger structures than had been possible in the past. The Chicago school, or Commercial style, often designed buildings for businesses. This modern style was built by first constructing an iron or steel skeleton that allowed the architects to build taller skyscrapers, such as the Empire State Building (1931). In addition to commercial buildings, modern architects, such as Frank Lloyd Wright (1867–1959), excelled at designing residential homes, as seen in Wright's now iconic home, Falling Water (1936). Influential figures included William Le Baron Jenney (1832–1907), Louis Henry Sullivan (1856–1924), and, most famous of all, Wright. Other major schools of thought in modern architecture included art nouveau, which was popular in Europe, and the craft movement, which reacted against the Industrial Revolution by emphasizing human craftsmanship. The craft movement was represented in the United States by Charles Sumner Greene (1868–1957) and his brothers.

Modernism popularized new styles of music, such as jazz. Jazz itself is inextricably linked to this period through F. Scott Fitzgerald's titling the 1920s as the "Jazz Age." Jazz artists, such as Louis Armstrong (1901–1971), Duke Ellington (1899–1974), and Benny Goodman (1909–1986), embraced an African American tradition that valued improvisation. In classical music, Arthur Schoenberg (1874–1951) and Igor Stravinsky (1882–1971), both of whom immigrated to the United States, sought to modernize an old genre. As in every other area that modernism touched, Schoenberg and Stravinsky broke from the past to develop new rules for classical music. Schoenberg developed serialism, a 12-tone system of writing music. Stravinsky wrote many ballets, including *The Rite of Spring* (1913).

In religion, modernism expressed itself as an attempt to synthesize modern scientific thought and traditional Christian theology into a theology that reflected the current age. In Catholicism, modernism developed as a movement in Europe and was condemned by Pius X in 1907. At the same time that modernism was emerging in Europe, Protestant theologians in the United States sought to have a scientific faith. Rooted in the Unitarianism of New England and the influx of the German theological tradition of Friedrich Schleiermacher (1768–1834) and Albrecht Ritschl (1822–1889), theological modernists embraced critical methods of dating the Bible, arguing that the Bible was the product of the culture of the Hebrews and early church. Acceptance of the work of Charles Darwin challenged the traditional understanding of Genesis. Finally, a shift in theological emphases caused modernists to embrace the Social Gospel and deemphasize the need for personal conversion in favor of societal conversion to the principles of Christianity. Major leaders included Walter Rauschenbusch (1861–1918) of Rochester Theological Seminary and Charles Briggs (1841–1913) and Henry Sloane Coffin (1877–1954) of Union Theological Seminary, as well as such leading pastors as Harry Emerson Fosdick (1878–1969), Washington Gladden (1836–1918), and Josiah Strong (1847–1916). Conservative Protestants reacted to this liberalization of theology by actively seeking to remove modernists from their denominations and seminaries during the fundamentalist-modernist controversies of the 1920s. The fundamentalists lost these battles, and the modernists secured control of the mainline denominations.

At its root, modernism sought to gain independence from the past and embrace the present and future. Although the American experience of modernism was only a part of the international movement, artists and writers from the United States contributed notably to the field. In religion, modernism became associated with progressive views on scripture and theology in Christianity. Modernism developed as a way for the common man to express his view of being in a changing world.

Nathan V. Lentfer

See also: Eddy, Mary Baker (1821–1910); Evangelicalism and Populism; Rauschenbusch, Walter (1861–1918); Social Christianity; Social Gospel; Steinbeck, John (1902–1968); Sullivan, Louis Henry (1856–1924); Wright, Frank Lloyd (1867–1959)

References

Butler, Christopher. *Early Modernism: Literature, Music and Painting in Europe*

1900–1916. Oxford, UK: Clarendon Press, 1994.
Dorrien, Gary. *The Making of American Liberal Theology: Idealism, Realism, & Modernity 1900–1950*. Vol. 2. Louisville, KY: Westminster John Knox Press, 2003.
Gay, Peter. *Modernism: The Lure of Heresy from Baudelaire to Beckett and Beyond*. New York: W.W. Norton & Company, 2008.

Moody, Dwight (1837–1899)

Dwight Moody was the leading Christian evangelist of the late nineteenth century. Although a Congregationalist, he advocated a nondenominational approach to ministry. He first came to fame through evangelical campaigns held in the British Isles between 1873 and 1875. Moody advocated theological education for the masses and founded what became Moody Bible Institute.

Dwight Moody was a very popular and effective late 19th-century evangelist. The creator of modern mass evangelism, he preached to audiences of thousands in the United States, Canada, and Great Britain. (Library of Congress)

Dwight Lyman (D. L.) Moody was born in 1837 in Northfield, Massachusetts. He was the fifth son in a family of nine children. His father died when he was four years old, and his mother raised the family. Moody's family joined a Unitarian church when he was five, and he continued in that denomination until he was a teenager. He never attained a high level of education, and in 1854 he went to Boston to make his way as a businessman. He worked for his uncle in a shoe store and became involved in the Boston Young Men's Christian Association (YMCA). While he was in Boston, Moody joined the Congregational denomination, where he would remain for the rest of his life, and he converted to evangelical Christianity.

In 1856, Moody left Boston for Chicago. Continuing in the shoe business, Moody was known as a hard worker and had a very successful career as a shoe salesman. While in Chicago, Moody became even more involved with the YMCA and made many business connections that would help him when he embarked on his evangelism. His chief Christian work in Chicago was a Sunday school that he began for the poor at North Market Hall. Moody's ministry was characterized by evangelization regardless of class or ethnicity. The Sunday school grew, and the Illinois Street Church was founded in 1864 as a way to minister to his converts when they were too old for Sunday school. Persistence and unconventional methods characterized his religious endeavors. By June 1860, Moody decided to commit himself full-time to Christian ministry.

On August 28, 1862, Moody married Emma Charlotte Revell. They had three children, named Emma, William, and Paul. During the Civil War, Moody worked with the Christian Commission, traveled for the organization, and expanded his work near Chicago at Camp Douglas, a prison camp. He also continued his Sunday school and increased his efforts at the Chicago YMCA. He was elected president of the Chicago YMCA in 1866 and served for four years. As Moody became prominent in his work with the YMCA and the Illinois Sabbath School Union, a Sunday school organization, he began speaking at locations throughout the United States.

Moody's rise to international prominence began with his campaigns in the British Isles between 1873 and 1875. Moody had visited England in 1867 and 1872 and used the contacts that he had made then to launch his evangelical mission. He traveled with Ira Sankey (1840–1908), who sought to evangelize through music. The trip began poorly, but when he arrived in Edinburgh in late 1873, his message was warmly received, and the campaign flourished. Moody traveled throughout the British Isles, culminating with four months in London between March and June 1875.

During his time in England, Moody developed his method for mass evangelism. In planning and conducting these meetings, Moody's business background gave him an advantage. He valued unity among the churches in the cities where he held meetings and avoided cities that could not give this agreement. Theologically, Moody avoided doctrinal debates and pointed to God's love as his theme. He utilized local men to manage the major aspects of preparation, including adequate facilities, and insisted on firm financial backing so he would not need to take a monetary offering during the meetings. Moody and Sankey designed every aspect of the meetings to influence the unconverted. Moody presented himself as a common man with whom many among the masses could identify. After the sermon, Moody invited those concerned for their souls to come to inquiry rooms in the facilities to talk with faithful Christians. Moody started conducting mass evangelism by meeting in a central location in a city, but by the late 1870s, he changed his model to holding multiple meetings in different areas of a city during the course of a campaign.

When Moody returned to the United States, he came back as one of the most prominent evangelicals in the world, with a robust strategy for reaching the common man. The requests for him to conduct similar campaigns to the ones he had undertaken in England multiplied. The 1870s stand out as the greatest decade for Moody's evangelical work. He conducted evangelical campaigns in Brooklyn, Philadelphia, New York City, Chicago, Boston, and other towns and cities. While in the South, he opposed segregated meetings but relented to white leaders to maintain opportunities to preach. Between 1881 and 1884, Moody returned to the British Isles for another tour, though the results were not as great as his first campaign.

Moody continued to conduct evangelize for the rest of his life.

Despite Moody's efforts to reach the unchurched poor, his campaigns typically appealed to middle- and upper-class churchgoers. After attempting many different ways of reaching the poor, Moody shifted his efforts into training laymen to evangelize. He founded schools in his hometown of Northfield and Chicago. In Northfield, he opened the Northfield School for Girls on November 3, 1879, and the Mount Hermon School for Boys on May 4, 1881. In Chicago, Moody founded a Bible institute to train laymen for urban evangelization in 1886. In October 1890, he established the Northfield Bible Training School for women, with a similar aim as his Chicago school. These schools were one aspect of his mission to equip the faithful. He also established his Northfield Conference in 1880, an annual gathering where invited speakers taught the Bible to those who came. A result of that conference was the formation of the Student Volunteer Movement for foreign Protestant missions in 1886. In 1894, he began the Bible Institute Colportage Association, which distributed religious literature.

As a rule, Moody avoided discussing politics in the pulpit, but privately he supported Republican endeavors. Despite his concern for the conversion for the poor, he was silent on social injustice. Moody died on December 22, 1899. His efforts in developing mass evangelism provided a model for successors, such as William "Billy" Sunday and more recently Billy Graham. His later efforts in Northfield and Chicago heavily influenced the nascent Bible conference and Bible institute movements of evangelicalism.

Nathan V. Lentfer

See also: Evangelicalism and Populism; Gilded Age; Poverty Campaigns; Rauschenbusch, Walter (1861–1918); Social Gospel; Sunday, Billy (1862–1935); YMCA/YWCA

References

Dorsett, Lyle W. *A Passion for Souls: The Life of D. L. Moody.* Chicago: Moody Press, 1997.

Evensen, Bruce J. *God's Man for the Gilded Age: D. L. Moody and the Rise of Modern Mass Evangelism.* New York: Oxford University Press, 2003.

Findlay, James F., Jr. *Dwight L. Moody: American Evangelist 1837–1899.* Chicago: University of Chicago Press, 1969.